S0-AXQ-694

BIBLICAL INTERPRETATION
Past and Present

BIBLICAL INTERPRETATION

—*Past & Present*—

GERALD BRAY

InterVarsity Press
Downers Grove, Illinois
Leicester, England

Published in the United States of America by InterVarsity Press, Downers Grove, Illinois, with permission from Universities and Colleges Christian Fellowship, Leicester, England.

InterVarsity Press® is the book-publishing division of InterVarsity Christian Fellowship®, a student movement active on campus at hundreds of universities, colleges and schools of nursing in the United States of America, and a member movement of the International Fellowship of Evangelical Students. For information about local and regional activities, write Public Relations Dept., InterVarsity Christian Fellowship, 6400 Schroeder Rd., P.O. Box 7895, Madison, WI 53707-7895.

Cover photograph: Scala/Art Resource, NY. Botticelli. St. Augustine.

ISBN 0-8308-1880-4

Set in New Baskerville
Typeset in Great Britain by Parker Typesetting Service, Leicester
Printed in Great Britain by Clays Ltd, Bungay, Suffolk

Library of Congress Cataloging-in-Publication Data has been requested.

17 16 15 14 13 12 11 10 9 8 7 6 5 4 3 2 1
10 09 08 07 06 05 04 03 02 01 00 99 98 97 96

Contents

Part 3: The contemporary scene 461

Introduction: The purpose and method of this book

The last years of the twentieth century are witnessing an explosion of books about the Bible and how it should be interpreted. The study of hermeneutics, as biblical interpretation is called, has become a major growth industry, quite apart from the endless stream of commentaries and learned studies which continue to appear. But although there is now a large amount of material available, much of it is inaccessible to non-specialists and confusing to students. A high percentage of the academic work currently being produced has little bearing on the life of the church, and is remote from the concerns of the average Christian. At a time when churchgoers want to hear a clear word from God, scholars appear to be confusing issues and muddying the waters of biblical study to the point where even professional theologians find it difficult to follow what they are saying.

Recent publications also indicate that more and more scholars are bringing their own fairly well-defined agendas to the biblical text, seeking to read out of it the ideas which in fact they are importing into it. Centuries of Christian tradition are ignored, unless they can be made to provide support for some otherwise radically new opinion, and there is little concern to find an overall hermeneutical framework in which to place the latest findings of critical scholarship. New methods of reading the text are constantly being explored, but with little interest being shown in their long-term viability as principles to guide interpretation. Meanwhile, the preaching and teaching work of the church goes on with less and less input from the world of biblical scholarship. Too often the result is a weak, emotionally based Christianity which has little intellectual content and no staying power.

In the midst of such confusion, the church needs to reflect again on the whole process of biblical interpretation, and particularly on the way it has shaped Christian doctrine and spiritual life over the centuries. In a subject area which is as central to Christian faith as this one is, it is impossible to be completely objective. The sheer vastness of the material demands selectivity, which in turn demands some rational principle by which particular choices can be justified. The main guideline for this book has been the conviction that the Christian Bible belongs to the church, which is the primary place where it is read and used. Of course it can be read outside that sphere, and Christians must be ready to listen to interpreters who do not share their presuppositions. But at the end of the day, the Bible would not occupy the place which it does in western culture if it were not the sacred text of Christianity, and no secular historian or literary critic can ignore that fact. The Bible has shaped the life of the church in a way that nothing else has done, and Christians today are the product of the history of its interpretation. Outside the community of faith, the Bible loses its essential character and therefore also much of its meaning. For this reason, if for no other, it is within that context that we have chosen to place the present study.

The contents of the book

The layout of this book is straightforward and can easily be explained. The opening chapter deals with those basic concepts in biblical interpretation which remain constant through all ages and in every hermeneutical situation. These include such matters as divine revelation, the nature of the canon, the relationship of the written text to the life of the Christian church(es), and the permanent tensions which occur whenever biblical exposition is attempted.

The rest of the book is divided into three Parts. The first of these covers the period from ancient times to the beginning of critical biblical study. It is subdivided into four chapters, of which the first (ch. 2) deals with the hermeneutical methods which were practised in biblical times. This is an important subject on which a great deal has been written in recent years, and it helps us to understand how the New Testament writers understood themselves and their task. However, it is also a difficult subject, because it is easy to rely on modern theories about what ancient writers thought and to ignore their own statements. When dealing with this period, the chief requirement for the modern student is to learn how to distinguish historical fact from modern hypothesis, and to give each of these its proper weight.

Chapter 3 deals with the patristic period, which for our purposes extends from the end of the New Testament (*c.* AD 100) to the time of Gregory the Great (d. 604). This was the great age of theological definition, which depended heavily on biblical exegesis. It was in the controversies of this era that the definitive Christian doctrines of the Trinity and the incarnation of Christ were hammered out in detail. Given that modern scholars have frequently challenged the church's claim that these doctrines are based on the Bible, it is essential for us to understand how Scripture was interpreted in support of these central teachings.

Chapter 4 covers the Middle Ages from the time of Gregory the Great to that of Erasmus. This period is often neglected, especially by Protestant historians, who tend to see it as an age of ever-increasing corruption, which was not relieved until the Reformation. Yet many of the most important institutions of our society grew up during this time – the rule of law, Parliament, and the universities, for example – and the structure of the church has been permanently shaped by the parochial system, the diocesan structure, and the monastic spirit which pervaded medieval ecclesiastical life. The Reformers did not simply reject the biblical interpretation which they inherited; their aim was to purify and systematize it. As modern research is increasingly demonstrating, Luther and Calvin followed certain trends in medieval thought, and in many ways it is better to understand them as inheritors rather than as opponents of that earlier tradition.

Chapter 5 examines the impact of Renaissance humanism and the Reformation on biblical exegesis. For the first time, a serious attempt was made to systematize Christian doctrine on an exclusively biblical foundation. The Bible came to occupy a place in the life of the average Christian far more central than it had previously enjoyed, and its interpretation became a matter of great social and political importance. The principles established by the Reformers shaped traditions of exposition which continue to guide the main Protestant churches, and which have had more impact on Roman Catholicism than is generally acknowledged. Furthermore, it was from Reformation exegesis, and often in express continuity with it, that modern critical study emerged, so that this period is of basic importance for later developments.

Part 2 covers the rise of modern critical interpretation of the Bible, beginning in the late seventeenth century. Chapter 6 discusses why and how historical criticism emerged from late Reformation debates, and looks at the main lines which the first modern critics explored in their quest for a truer understanding of Scripture. Not only did they set the agenda for later scholars; they also provoked a reaction to their theories which has defined the terms on which the subsequent debate between 'liberals' and 'conservatives' has been conducted.

Chapters 7 and 8 deal with the nineteenth century. For the first time in Christian history, specialization reached the point where the study of the Testaments became separated, which led many scholars to question whether the Old Testament could properly be studied as Christian Scripture. Rapid and widespread progress in philology and later in archaeology served to temper the wilder fantasies of some earlier critics, but it was clear that a new type of biblical interpretation which purported to be purely 'scientific' had emerged, and that the groundwork was laid for what have become the major critical hypotheses today.

Chapters 9 and 10 continue the story for each Testament in twentieth-century research, which has been characterized mainly by an information explosion which threatens to submerge the discipline altogether. The result of this has been a fragmentation in which scholarly attention to detail is making it increasingly difficult to reach any kind of consensus or construct a generally accepted synthesis of the data. Modern scholarship has found itself in the awkward position of having to maintain that the Bible is sufficiently united in itself to justify the discipline of 'biblical studies', yet at the same time so diverse that there is always room for another doctoral thesis to upset currently held opinions! Whether this tension is viable in the longer term is being increasingly questioned, and many now believe that the historical-critical method of the eighteenth and nineteenth centuries has run its course, and can no longer offer creative solutions to hermeneutical problems.

Part 3 discusses current trends in biblical interpretation which try to offer alternatives to the dominant school of historical criticism. The first of these (discussed in ch. 11) comes from within the scholarly world itself, and suggests that a new hermeneutic is needed to understand the biblical text. This new hermeneutic is grounded in literary and philosophical categories, many of which are opaque to the uninitiated. Yet there can be no doubt that 'hermeneutics' is now largely identified with this type of thinking, and the church is finding itself increasingly challenged to examine to what extent it can absorb insights from the methods which this school of thought has adopted.

The second of these alternatives (the subject of ch. 12) arises from the pastoral and evangelistic ministry of the church to those on the fringes of affluent western society. Because of this, the 'oppression' felt by the poor, by women, by minority groups and by indigenous peoples around the world has come to play a prominent role in biblical interpretation. Some have claimed that this requires a radically new approach to Scripture, which is nevertheless more closely attuned to its original context and purpose than the scholasticized exposition of the western university world.

The third alternative (ch. 13) is that proposed by conservative groups within the church, led by Protestant evangelicals, whose interest in the Bible is governed by the Reformation belief in its authority and sufficiency as a source of Christian teaching. Evangelicals continue to believe that Scripture must be its own interpreter, and that it should be allowed to set the agenda for the church. They may accept that useful insights can be derived from other methods and disciplines, and they may be sensitive to the complaints of groups which feel that their concerns have been marginalized in the past, but ultimately they refuse to allow these considerations to become the dominant motive in biblical study.

Whether the outcome of current debates is likely to result in the predominance of any one of these three, or whether it will produce an 'open market' in biblical studies, in which a genuine pluralism is permitted, is the theme of the concluding chapter, which sums up the present state of affairs and tries to suggest ways in which the interpretation of Scripture may develop in the foreseeable future.

As can be seen from the above, the approach to the subject is basically chronological. Generally speaking, exegetes and interpreters are listed in order of their date of death (when known), though there are some exceptions to this in cases where a very early (or very late) death makes a different order more desirable. Persons living at the time the book went to press are normally listed in order of date of birth.

There are also one or two major exceptions to this rule which require some explanation. Philo of Alexandria, for example, is included with the church fathers of the Origenistic period (*c.* AD 200–325), because although he was a Jew who lived at the time of Jesus, his writings have always been on the fringes of Judaism, but were very influential among Christians from the late second century AD onwards. Similar considerations have led to the displacement of John Cassian, a fourth-century monk whose main influence was felt during the Middle Ages.

The format of each Part and chapter

Each Part contains a brief introduction which gives a summary of what it contains and why it is important for the subject as a whole.

Each chapter within the three Parts contains a number of subsections which are arranged in such a way as to provide maximum assistance to the student who needs to grasp the issues as quickly and as clearly as possible. The first is devoted to an outline of the period or subject, giving the major facts which need to be borne in mind when examining the aspect of biblical interpretation in question. Next there is a brief résumé of the major writers and their most important works, followed by a section dealing with the main critical, doctrinal and hermeneutical issues which have to be understood in relation to the chapter. After that, the main hermeneutical methods relevant to the period are discussed, with examples taken from the biblical texts, and competing interpretations are illustrated.

Finally, at the end of each chapter there is an examination of individual biblical books or passages which played a crucial role in biblical study in the period under discussion. At different times in history, and in different schools of interpretation, particular parts of Scripture have enjoyed a special prominence, and this has coloured the way in which the Bible has been read. In some cases, 'classical' interpretations of these texts were produced which have stood the test of time, even if nowadays they often provide target practice for scholars. Nevertheless, it is often by examining such key texts that we can come to a deeper understanding of the trends which have shaped the church's use of the Bible, and which continue to inform and challenge us today.

Note on bibliography

Because of the vast amount of material available, it is impossible to list more than a representative selection of works. Books dealing with the subject of interpretation as a whole are given in the General Bibliography at the end; those of more specialist interest are placed at the end of the relevant subsection or chapter.

Quotations in the main text are taken from books listed in the chapter bibliographies. As they are mainly intended to give a flavour of the author's ideas and approach to the subject, they have not been precisely footnoted, but most of them can be found in the introduction or conclusion to the relevant work. Comments on particular verses of Scripture will normally be found in the corresponding part of the commentary being quoted.

Acknowledgments

Writing a book of this kind requires an enormous amount of resource material, much of which is fortunately available in the library of Tyndale House, Cambridge, where the bulk of the manuscript was completed in the autumn of 1992. Special thanks are due to the Warden of Tyndale House, Rev. Dr Bruce Winter, and to the then Librarian, Dr Andrew Clarke, who offered me every assistance in writing. I am also deeply indebted to a host of readers who have supplied valuable additional information and corrections. Foremost among them, I must mention Dr Graham Davies of Cambridge, who has taken an interest in the project from the start and encouraged me during the years when I taught the subject at Oak Hill College in London, and Dr Hugh Williamson, Regius Professor of Hebrew in the University of Oxford, who was particularly helpful with the Old Testament material. For the New Testament, I owe a similar debt of gratitude to Professor I. Howard Marshall of Aberdeen. I am also grateful to Mr David Wright of New College, Edinburgh, and to Mr Mark Elliott of the Whitefield Institute, Oxford, for their assistance at many points. Both Dr Martin Selman of Spurgeon's College, London, and Dr Bruce Winter of Tyndale House, Cambridge, read chapter 13 on evangelical interpretation, and offered many helpful suggestions for improving it.

For the final stages of the work, I am indebted to the librarians of Samford University, Birmingham, Alabama, who have diligently searched out a vast amount of biographical and other information, and also to my colleagues at Beeson Divinity School, Dr Frank Thielman and Dr Kenneth Mathews, who read parts of the manuscript with great care and suggested a number of alterations which I have been glad to incorporate into the text. Finally, I owe a special debt of gratitude to another colleague and friend, Dr Christopher Metress, whose rare combination of literary genius and Job-like patience in reading the final draft has enabled me to offer a presentable book to readers on both sides of the Atlantic. *Pax tibi, Christum ferens amice.*

1

The Bible and its interpretation: Principles and definitions

The concept of revelation

The Judaeo-Christian religious tradition, which to some extent embraces Islam as well, is distinguished from the great religions of humankind by two fundamental characteristics. First, it is monotheistic, believing that there is one God who is the creator of the universe and sovereign over everything in the created order. Second, it is scriptural, believing that this God has revealed himself and his purposes in a written text which can be read, studied and applied by those who believe in him. Christians are so used to having the Bible that they do not always realize that in ancient times the claim to possess divine revelation in written form was unique to Israel, and even today it is found only in those religions which depend in some way on the Israelite experience.

The Christian doctrine of God maintains that believers have a living personal relationship with him. This relationship is made possible by Jesus Christ, the Son of God who became a man in order to die on the cross for our sins. By his resurrection he overcame the power of sin and death, and gave his followers an inheritance of eternal life. This is experienced by the indwelling presence of the Holy Spirit, the third person of the holy Trinity, who comes to dwell in our hearts, bearing witness that we have been adopted as children of God and giving us the strength to pray 'Abba, Father', in the words of Jesus himself (*cf.* Gal. 4:6). Christian faith is therefore not primarily an intellectual or academic doctrine, but a living experience of God which is indispensable and which can be had by anyone, regardless of intellectual ability or academic achievement.

In this sense, it is correct to say that the Christian faith is essentially a mystical communion of the individual heart with God, who speaks to our spirit by his Spirit. This inner witness of the Holy Spirit is fundamental to all true Christianity, but it is not exclusive. We must recognize that mysticism has sometimes acquired a bad name because it tends to emphasize individual experience, even to the point of creating a spiritual élite within the church, at the expense of objective and collective (or 'corporate') factors which are equally important. These factors are present in the written text of Scripture and in the common life of the church, which seeks to integrate the individual into a wider whole which transcends even the limits imposed by time and space. As Christians we must never deny that God speaks to individuals, but what he says is consistent with what he has already said to the church as a whole. The individuals through whom this revelation was given were specially chosen, and had an authority which no Christian today can claim. Moreover, they functioned within a tradition which had its own collegiality, so that what they said was part of a wider and more objective message.

Individual believers must therefore test their experience in the light of the common witness, and submit to its authority. We have been warned that there are spiritual forces at work which will seek to pervert the truth, and so it is only as we reform our own opinions according to the collective witness that we will be preserved from error. The existence of such a witness thus becomes a matter of supreme practical importance for the spiritual health of believers and of the community to which they belong. In ancient Israel this witness was provided by a succession of prophets, priests and kings to whom God gave his revelation. This process reached its climax in the life, death and resurrection of Jesus Christ, the great and final prophet, priest and king. Its legacy is a collection of documents which we call the Bible (meaning 'book') or Scripture (meaning 'writing').

Writing as the chief means of divine revelation was accepted at least from the time of Moses, when we are told that he received the Ten Commandments on tablets of stone, engraved by the finger of God himself (Ex. 31:18). There is evidence to suggest that much of the material in Genesis was based on earlier written sources, but writing did not then enjoy the sacred character which it was to acquire at Mount Sinai. This sacred character is especially evident in the New Testament, where Jesus frequently refers to Scripture ('it is written') as the authoritative Word of God, and even uses it in conflict with the devil (Mt. 4:3ff.). That a written text can function this way in spiritual warfare is surely evidence enough of the special character which was attributed to it.

The logic and the limitations of a written revelation are best understood if we take a personal relationship with God as our point of departure. Personal relationships have the unique character of being both fully comprehensible and deeply mysterious at the same time. We meet other people, get to know what they are like, and may even come to be able to predict their reactions to given situations, but at the same time we can always be surprised by them, and we would never claim to know them (or ourselves) exhaustively. Furthermore, we quickly learn to submit our judgments of others to what they themselves tell us – not uncritically, of course, but sufficiently to enable them to speak for themselves and let us share something of their own mental processes and outlook. If we fail to do this, the relationship will quickly break down, because there will be no communication between us. Self-revelation, in other words, plays a vital role in personal relationships, and its reliability can ultimately be known only as it is put to the test in everyday experience.

What is true of personal relationships between human beings is also true of our relationship with God, with the difference that God understands both us and himself in a way which is impossible for his creatures. What he tells us of himself is not exhaustive, and there is a great deal about him which remains hidden from our eyes, but it is accurate, and therefore 'true' within the context of the relationship. This last qualification has to be added, because many things which a believer can say about God may not be true for someone else. For example, God may be 'merciful' to us, because he has promised to look after us as his children, but he may not be merciful in the same way to those who have rejected him. This distinction is important, because without the relational context, it may be concluded that God is merciful by nature and will therefore show this mercy to everyone whether they have believed in him or not.

Central to any personal relationship is communication, and the most basic form of communication is speech. Non-verbal communication is certainly possible, and often very important, but it is remarkable how frequently it is described as a form of 'language' – 'body language' being the most familiar example. Speech is also common to all types of relationship – with parents, spouse, children, friends and other people generally. It is therefore only to be expected that it should play the major role in our relationship with God. According to the Bible, God created the world by speaking, and the same verb is used to describe the sending of his Son (Heb. 1:1). It is no accident that his revelation should be called his Word, or that this Word should be identified with God himself (Jn. 1:1).

But relationship is also a two-way communication, which implies that God's speech forms part of an intelligible discourse with human beings. For this to be feasible, human beings must be able to understand what God is saying clearly enough to make a coherent reply. This in turn means that God must speak to us in a way which makes such intelligibility possible in the first place. If God and human beings could not communicate, revelation would be impossible and the Christian faith would be meaningless. Many of the objections to Christianity are based on the idea that language about God is meaningless, because God is not a concept which the human mind can grasp. Of course it is true that God's nature is very different from ours, but it is not on that basis that we claim a relationship with him. Our relationship with God is based on shared personhood, which is a spiritual and not a material category. The Bible tells us that human beings, alone of the material creation, are made in the image and likeness of God (Gn. 1:26), which means that we actually do have something in common with him. Persons communicate with each other most effectively in speech, and that is how God has chosen to reveal himself to us.

Writing is a particular form of speech, which both extends and restricts God's primary means of communication with us. It extends it because it is a progression from one mode of communication to another, which remains unchanged in time and space. At the same time, it also restricts it, because once something is written down it acquires a permanence which makes it hard to change or deny. It is true that writing is subject to many of the same problems as oral speech: it can be corrupted; it can be ambiguous; it can be misunderstood. The absence of voice inflexion and body language may reduce or seriously distort comprehension. But these problems, except perhaps the last one, are in principle corrigible, given the right interpretative skills, and the many advantages of written communication heavily outweigh such problems.

Writing remains the same wherever it is sent and however long it lasts. There may be misunderstandings due to language or culture differences, but these can usually be overcome. Writing is also less open to distortion by interpreters who may hear things in a way that was not originally intended. An oral report cannot easily be checked, but a written document can be verified by a number of witnesses, and disagreements over interpretation can be aired publicly and debated. Writing further ensures that the same message is communicated to everyone equally. It will not necessarily be equally well understood by everyone who receives it, but that is a different question. Writing maintains the principle of equality more effectively than oral communication, and with that goes the principle of fairness. Everyone has a chance to read and understand what is being said, and if an élite group (like some medieval clerics or some modern scholars) tries to privatize the meaning of a text in its own interests, protests from the wider community are possible. This is emphatically *not* true with purely spoken or 'oracular' revelation, which is highly subject to manipulation by those in charge of it.

The public character of a written revelation also means that it can be used to form the basis for a community of believers which is both open to individual expression and bound to a common witness. It is always possible for individuals to read and interpret a written revelation in their own fashion, and this is what actually happens in the life of the churches. No two people see things in exactly the same way, and at different times those gifted with special insights have contributed to the development of a tradition of interpretation which is then made available as a resource for the church as a whole. At the same time, there is a central reference point which sets limits to the kinds of spiritual reflection and experience which are possible. For example, any suggestion that Christians might derive spiritual benefit from the worship of idols is clearly excluded by Scripture, and this serves to counteract syncretistic tendencies which might otherwise develop. It also serves as a reminder to each generation of interpreters that after their theories have come and gone, the text itself will remain inviolate, ready to speak to the next generation with the same freshness it has always spoken with in the past.

A written revelation thus serves the double function of giving those who belong to the community of believers a common focus, and of excluding elements which do not belong within the community. By establishing norms which must be accepted, a written revelation defines the character of the God whom we worship and closes the door to anything which is incompatible with it. This double function is one of the chief distinguishing marks of any scriptural religion, and Christianity is no exception to this rule. It is the teaching of the church that its written revelation strikes that balance between individual experience and common confession which is the special hallmark of the Christian's relationship with God.

BIBLIOGRAPHY

J. Baillie, *The Idea of Revelation in Recent Thought* (Oxford: Oxford University Press, 1956).
E. Brunner, *Revelation and Reason: The Christian Doctrine of Faith and Knowledge* (London: SCM, 1947).
C. F. H. Henry (ed.), *Revelation and the Bible: Contemporary Evangelical Thought* (London: Tyndale, 1959).
H. D. McDonald, *Ideas of Revelation: An Historical Study 1700–1860* (London: Macmillan, 1959).
———*Theories of Revelation: An Historical Study 1860–1960* (London: George, Allen and Unwin, 1963).
L. Morris, *I Believe in Revelation* (London: Hodder and Stoughton; Grand Rapids: Eerdmans, 1976).
R. H. Nash, *The Word of God in the Mind of Man: The Crisis of Revealed Truth in Contemporary Theology* (Grand Rapids: Zondervan, 1982).
C. H. Pinnock, *The Scripture Principle* (San Francisco: Harper and Row, 1984).
R. Swinburne, *Revelation* (Oxford: Oxford University Press, 1991).
R. F. Thiemann, *Revelation and Theology: The Gospel as Narrated Promise* (Notre Dame: University Press of Notre Dame, 1985).

The nature of Scripture

Christian faith maintains that the Bible is the normative, common witness of the spiritual truth which has been revealed to the church. There is no other source comparable to this one, and no human authority which can supersede or contradict it. Even the Roman Catholic Church, which allows to the Bishop of Rome the authority to pronounce infallibly on matters of faith and morals, does not deny this fundamental point. In Catholic theology, the pope is never more than the authoritative interpreter of Scripture; he has no power to deny it (even if many who are not Roman Catholics believe that he has already denied it by claiming even this much).

It is when we come to decide what the nature of this 'normative, collective witness' is, that we discover that there are deep divisions of principle within the Christian community. Broadly speaking, there are three main positions, which can be summed up as follows.

1. *The Bible is a collection of documents written by people at different times to describe their experience of God.* This experience gave them the inspiration to write, but it naturally varied from person to person,

and it also developed to a considerable degree over the centuries. We can therefore recognize that there is a common tradition of faith contained within the covers of the Bible, but its internal consistency is subject to the realities of spiritual development. This produces 'contradictions' if we seek to harmonize one part of the text with another without taking historical and cultural factors into account. The most notorious of these 'contradictions' are the contrast between the God of justice (Old Testament) and the God of mercy (New Testament), and the contrast between salvation by faith (Paul) and salvation by works (James).

2. *The Bible is a record made by people who heard God speaking to them and who recorded what they understood.* God's self-disclosure was perfect and infallible in itself, but human understanding is faulty. The Bible speaks of an inspired knowledge of a perfect God, but because it remains a human document, it is not a flawless witness. More conservative exponents of this thesis might argue that God himself realized this, and therefore 'accommodated' himself to the limitations of human understanding. The result is a text which, despite the errors and inaccuracies which it contains, remains a basically faithful record of a real experience which we are still called to enjoy today. In practical terms, this means that discrepancies in the passion narratives in the gospels, for example, should not force us to deny the reality of Christ's death and resurrection, which may even be more believable when we realize that the gospel writers were not simply copying one another but composing independent works which bear witness to a common event.

3. *The Bible is a Word from God given through human agents.* God spoke to human beings in words which they could understand, but in directing them to write he often gave them messages which were mysterious. This is particularly true in the case of predictive prophecy and of apocalyptic, but in a general way it applies to the entire text. The Old Testament foretells the coming of Christ, even though none of its original writers fully understood that, just as the New Testament speaks of a glorious future when Christ will return, which we do not fully understand either. In practical terms, this means that there are no discrepancies or contradictions in the written text of Scripture, except perhaps some which crept in because of the errors of later copyists. In principle, it is possible to detect these errors and remove them, so that a perfect text can be recovered. This original (or 'autograph') text is verbally inspired – the very speech of God himself – and is therefore infallible and inerrant, at least within the context of what it is trying to affirm.

When confronted with the examples of contradiction and discrepancy given above, holders of this position will insist that what appear to be contradictions are really just paradoxes which can be resolved. In their view, it is too simplistic to divide the Testaments into 'justice' and 'mercy', since each of these is found in both. Likewise, the divide between faith in Paul and works in James is based on a misunderstanding, since both Paul and James believed that faith is the essential basis of works, which in turn must follow in the life of a believer if his faith is genuine.

The first of these positions is characteristic of what is often called 'liberal' theology. 'Liberalism' is a vague and amorphous term, which may not be acceptable to those who are accused of it. Originally it referred to a particular school of radical sceptical thought, which reached its peak in the nineteenth century and is now all but dead. However, in the sense that there is a broad agreement among scholars of this type and the classical liberals of the nineteenth century that the study of Scripture is the study of a human document, not of a divine revelation (which might restrict their freedom of enquiry), there is a continuity of approach which is easily recognized by those who do not share its presuppositions, and so we may assert that this kind of theology exists, albeit in many varieties and with frequent inconsistencies and disagreements.

The strength of this approach is its openness to new ideas, and its willingness (at least in principle) to discard theories which can be shown to be untenable. Being free of the restrictions imposed by church authority or by popular devotion, it can look for truth without worrying about secondary factors which might distort the conclusions of 'scientific' research. By the same token, the great weakness of this approach is its instability. It is impossible to say for certain whether a particular theory is true or not, and given the nature of scholarly research, there will almost always be disagreements about most things. There is no target more appealing to a PhD student than an 'assured result' of modern criticism! Believers in the churches not unreasonably complain that their faith cannot be put at the mercy of scholarly in-fighting, and they often find scholarship of this type repellent – or else totally incomprehensible.

The second of these positions was held (in its conservative form) by many of the great interpreters of the early church, especially Origen and his followers. It was abandoned by the Protestant Reformers, who believed that the literal, grammatical sense of the text was God's inspired Word, without any need to make excuses for 'unacceptable' statements in it; but it has reappeared (usually in its less conservative form) among many otherwise traditional Roman Catholics and Protestants today. In the modern context, it represents a desire to merge critical biblical study (position 1) with classical Christian orthodox theology. It is probably not too much of an exaggeration to say that most people holding this position were brought up in a spiritual atmosphere in which position 3 was dominant, and they may still be emotionally committed to that at some level, but their intellectual formation has taken place under the influence of position 1. They therefore create a halfway house in which this tension within themselves can be resolved. Whether this is a creative synthesis which can produce a robust Christian apologetic in the modern world (as its defenders naturally claim) or whether it is an unsatisfactory mishmash which will eventually collapse because of its own inconsistencies (as its detractors on both sides argue) is a matter of debate which only the future will resolve for certain.

The great strength of this position is that it can move in the world of scholarship as well as in the world of piety without undue disruption to either. It can therefore exert a moderating influence on both, restraining the wilder exaggerations of some scholars while at the same time helping the church to avoid an unthinking conservatism. The main weakness is that it is prone to compartmentalization, meaning that a person holding this view may act like a radical critic in the company of those holding position 1, but at the same time behave like the most traditional of believers when associating with those who hold position 3. Those who are aware of this tension will inevitably question the integrity of the people who hold this position, but although this may be unfair, it does point to a basic inconsistency which may discourage people who hold position 2 from trying to apply their studies to their faith and life. It is perhaps not surprising that it is often within this group that the strongest resistance to systematic theology can be found.

The third of these positions is the orthodox Protestant (and to a large extent pan-Christian) view, which its detractors are liable to call 'fundamentalist'. This term is even less helpful than 'liberal', because its use tends to imply that those accused of it are uneducated and merely prejudiced in their objections to critical scholarship, which is by no means always the case. Nevertheless, there is certainly a spectrum of continuity between scholars and theologians who hold this position and less educated conservative believers, which is sometimes justified by those who hold it on the ground that the faith of the simple should not be seen as inferior to, or as essentially different from, that of the learned. The so-called 'tyranny of the experts', which is often just a form of intellectual snobbery, cannot be allowed to dominate church life, even when the contribution which scholars have to make must be honoured and accepted. For the defenders of position 3, the inner witness of the Holy Spirit is all-important, because it is he who speaks through the text to their hearts, and who applies the text to their lives. This option can really be defended only in the context of worship, because those who hold this position will do so only as part of their deeper commitment to a living relationship with God. It is for this reason that outsiders see it as 'biased' or 'predetermined' in a way which to them makes it appear 'unscholarly'. But defenders of this position argue that it is possible for them to use as much scholarly and intellectual rigour as anyone else, and that the views of their opponents are just as biased, albeit in a different direction.

The great strength of this position is that it is closest to the spiritual perception of the church through the ages. The communion of saints is more significant than the criticism of scholars, which is one reason this position maintains itself with little real change from one generation to the next. Critical theories come and go with bewildering rapidity, but holders of this view continue to stick to their guns whatever comes. Their apologetic is often virtually the same as that found in the great Reformers, and frequently it goes back to very early times. For example, there is no doubt that many early Christians held what today would be called 'dictation' theories of inspiration; they regarded the biblical writers as wind instruments, played by the breath of the Holy Spirit. Even if few modern defenders of this position go that far (and most want to insist that the natural abilities and character of the individual writers of Scripture were used by God, not suppressed by him), yet they remind us that the New Testament itself says that Scripture was written by holy people who were moved by the Holy Spirit (2 Pet. 1:21), and that all Scripture is inspired by God (2 Tim. 3:16), making it clear that not just the authors but also the text bears the stamp of God's authority.

The main weakness of this position is its tendency towards a blind and dogmatic conservatism, which clings to the thought patterns of a bygone era and does not speak to the concerns of the present age. Often, those who hold this position have a credibility problem in trying to communicate their views to a wider world. This is not necessarily because their position is untenable (as their critics would argue) but because they are unwilling to adapt their language and presentation to a new situation. It is admittedly very difficult to update doctrine without distorting it one way or another, but at the same time, Christian truth can never be allowed to appear stale and irrelevant. The great challenge for adherents of this position is to make their classical orthodoxy seem compelling when dealing with the problems of the present age, and demonstrate that its staying power is due to its intrinsic worth, not simply to historical inertia.

In the current climate of theological debate, everyone embarking on the study of the Bible will feel drawn to one of those three positions, however reluctantly (or subconsciously) they may do so. At the risk of some oversimplification, we can say that positions 1 and 2 are widely represented in the world of academic scholarship, where holders of position 2 are generally regarded as 'conservatives'. Within the church, on the other hand, it is positions 2 and 3 which tend to be most widely represented, and in this context holders of position 2 are more easily regarded as 'liberals'. It is in this way that we can best appreciate how position 2 acts as a bridge between 1 and 3, which often appear to be polemical opposites, as the over-use of prejudicial terms like 'liberal' and 'fundamentalist' indicates.

BIBLIOGRAPHY

R. Abba, *The Nature and Authority of the Bible* (London: James Clarke, 1958).

W. J. Abraham, *The Divine Inspiration of Holy Scripture* (Oxford: Oxford University Press, 1981).

P. J. Achtemeier, *The Inspiration of Scripture: Problems and Proposals* (Philadelphia: Fortress, 1980).

J. Barr, *The Semantics of Biblical Language* (Oxford: Oxford University Press, 1961).

D. M. Beegle, *Scripture, Tradition and Infallibility* (Grand Rapids: Eerdmans, 1973).

L. Boettner, *The Inspiration of the Scriptures* (Grand Rapids: Eerdmans, 1940).

D. A. Carson (ed.), *Scripture and Truth* (Grand Rapids: Zondervan, 1983).

H. M. Conn (ed.), *Inerrancy and Hermeneutic: A Tradition, a Challenge, a Debate* (Grand Rapids: Baker, 1988).

S. T. Davis, *The Debate about the Bible* (Philadelphia: Westminster, 1977).

R. W. Funk, *Language, Hermeneutic and Word of God: The Problem of Language in the New Testament and Contemporary Theology* (New York: Harper and Row, 1966).

N. Geisler (ed.), *Inerrancy* (Grand Rapids: Zondervan, 1979).
R. Gruse, *The Authority of the Bible: Theories of Inspiration, Revelation and the Canon of Scripture* (New York: Paulist Press, 1985).
H. Lindsell, *The Battle for the Bible* (Grand Rapids: Zondervan, 1976).
J. W. Montgomery (ed.), *God's Inerrant Word* (Minneapolis: Bethany, 1974).
I. H. Marshall, *Biblical Inspiration* (London: Hodder and Stoughton, 1972).
J. I. Packer, *'Fundamentalism' and the Word of God* (London: IVF, 1958).
K. R. Trembath, *Evangelical Theories of Biblical Inspiration* (Oxford: Oxford University Press, 1987).
B. Vawter, *Biblical Inspiration* (London: Hutchinson; Philadelphia: Westminster, 1972).
B. B. Warfield, *The Inspiration and Authority of the Bible* (Philadelphia: Presbyterian and Reformed, 1948).
E. J. Young, *Thy Word is Truth* (London: Banner of Truth, 1963).

The canon of Scripture

The term 'canon', which means 'rule', or standard of measurement, is applied to the list of books to be included in the Scriptures, both of the Old and of the New Testaments. It is one thing to say that the Bible is the normative, common witness to God's revelation, but quite another to decide what belongs in the Bible and what does not. This question exercised both Jewish and Christian writers in ancient times, though probably not as much as is sometimes assumed today. There is no evidence that Christians ever made a formal decision about the limits of the canon; they appear to have taken over the Old Testament from Judaism with little argument, and to have added the New Testament almost as a matter of course. There were disputes about some of the books, and even debates about the appropriateness of continuing to recognize the Old Testament, but the principle of a biblical canon was never called into question as far as we know. Because the canon of the Old Testament was established independently from that of the New, we shall look at the development of each in turn.

Old Testament

Authority to establish the canon apparently resided in the Old Testament priesthood, at least to the extent that one of the main tests of inclusion seems to have been whether a particular book had been laid up in the Jerusalem temple as part of the sacred deposit of Judaism. To qualify for this, it appears that a book had to come from either a prophet, a priest or a king, each of whom occupied a special position within the Israelite covenant. In many cases, Old Testament books may not have been the work of a single author, but the product of many hands which carefully collected and edited the material. From what we know, this activity was centred either on the royal court at Jerusalem, which was particularly active under David, Solomon, Hezekiah and Josiah, or on the temple priests, who continued their activity after the fall of the monarchy and the return from exile. It also seems that by the time of Judas Maccabaeus (164–160 BC), a priest who made himself king, there was a general feeling that no new canonical books would be forthcoming. It is from that time that we find secondary works, such as Ecclesiasticus, which consciously hark back to the authoritative Scriptures of an earlier time.

The exact extent of the Old Testament canon is still controversial. The Hebrew canon, as accepted by Jews today, consists of twenty-four books (sometimes regrouped into only twenty-two, to match the number of letters in the Hebrew alphabet), which are divided into the Law (Torah), the Prophets and the Writings (Hagiographa). Protestant Christianity has adopted this canon, though it follows the order and divisions of the Greek translation known as the Sepruagint (so called from the seventy scholars who supposedly translated it, and thus abbreviated as LXX). The effect of this is to produce thirty-nine books and an order which does not clearly distinguish the Prophets from the Writings.

The Roman Catholic and Eastern Orthodox canon of the Old Testament follows the Septuagint, which was produced at Alexandria in about 200 BC. Apart from the different order in which the books are placed, the Septuagint contains a number of books which are not in the Hebrew canon and may never have existed in Hebrew. At the time of the Reformation, these books were removed from the Protestant canon and placed at the end, where they are usually referred to as *apocrypha* ('hidden') or more correctly, as *deutero-canonical* ('of secondary status'). An even longer list can be found in Coptic sources, and is preserved today in the Ethiopian church, though as the concept of 'canonicity' is weaker there than in other parts of Christendom, it is hard to know what to make of this.

The authority of the so-called Apocrypha used to be a major source of difference between Protestants and Roman Catholics, though the ecumenical spirit of recent years has narrowed the gap considerably. Protestants are now generally more aware of the importance of intertestamental Jewish literature for our understanding of the New Testament, while Roman Catholics are now more prepared to concede that the deuterocanonical books should not be used to establish points of doctrine. This has enabled scholars from the two traditions to publish common translations of the Old Testament, in which the Hebrew canon (following the Septuagint order) is put first, followed by the Apocrypha, which is often omitted from Protestant Bibles.

The process by which the canon came into being has been carefully studied for over two centuries, and has provided much fuel for controversy. The classical view is that the Hebrew Bible was canonized in three successive stages, corresponding to the three classical divisions of the Law (Torah), the Prophets and the Writings (Hagiographa). The dating of this process varied enormously from scholar to scholar, though it was generally agreed that the canonization of the Writings was still incomplete in New Testament times. More controversially, some have argued that the discovery of Deuteronomy in the temple in 621 BC was the beginning of a process which led to its canonization. Nowadays, however, most scholars recognize that Deuteronomy and most of the Mosaic law must have been authoritative long before this date, though they also accept that there is an important distinction between a book's authority and its canonization. The argument runs that a book, or at least a collection of writings, may exert an authority within a given community before reaching its final literary form. Canonization occurs when the literary form is fixed. In the case of the Torah there is widespread disagreement about when that was, ranging from the traditional view that it took place in Moses' own time (fifteenth to thirteenth centuries BC), to the theory that it was only during and shortly after the exile (sixth century BC) that the process was completed.

The Hebrew canon as we now know it was said to represent the Pharisaical tradition, which was not universally shared within Judaism. The Samaritans had only the five books of the Torah (Pentateuch). At Alexandria, the accepted canon is supposed to have included what we now have in the Septuagint, while the Qumran community (authors of the famous Dead Sea Scrolls) may have added other works which the mainstream traditions have all rejected as pseudepigrapha.

Within this canonical scheme, the content of the Torah and of the Prophets was generally undisputed, the only exception being that some rabbinical schools (of Pharisaic tendencies) had doubts about Ezekiel, on the ground that the book contained inner contradictions too great to be resolved. This objection was never widespread, though, and we may assume that virtually everyone agreed on the canonicity of these books. The order of the Torah is constant, because of the obvious historical development contained within it, and the same is true of Joshua, Judges, Samuel and Kings, which almost invariably follow the Torah in that order. The later prophets present a more confused picture as far as their order is concerned, though the content is generally agreed. Jeremiah often comes first, followed by Ezekiel and Isaiah, though these three are frequently interchanged. More consistently, the twelve minor prophets are put at the end, and regarded as a single book.

It is when we come to the Writings that the real difficulties begin. The traditional approach to the canon maintains that this part of the Old Testament remained 'open' until very late, the final decision to close it being taken at the Council of Jamnia (Jabneh) in AD 90, when the present number of books was agreed. Furthermore, most scholars accept that there were several disputes among the Jews about what should be included, involving especially Ecclesiastes, the Song of Songs, Esther and Proverbs. These books were held to contain grave exegetical difficulties and were sometimes regarded as too 'secular' in tone, but these objections appear to have been confined to the Pharisees. There is some evidence that the Qumran community did not accept Esther, since they made no use of it, but the reasons for this are somewhat obscure and do not affect the canonical status of the book in Judaism as a whole.

More serious are the additions to Daniel and Esther, and the numerous other books which are now classified together as apocrypha. Roman Catholic historians sometimes argue that these books were originally part of the (Palestinian) Hebrew canon, but nowadays most people accept that they entered the Old Testament by being included in the Septuagint, thereby forming a separate Alexandrian canon which became standard in the Graeco-Roman world, for which the Septuagint was the main Old Testament text. Support for this can be found in the New Testament, which draws most of its Old Testament quotations from the Septuagint translation, though it must be remembered that what we now class as apocrypha is not directly quoted in the New Testament. However, apostolic use of the Septuagint was enough to enable Augustine (354–430) to argue that it ought to be accepted as fully canonical, in opposition to Jerome (340–420), who contended that only the Hebrew canon (*hebraica veritas*) was to be accepted. The Reformers sided with Jerome, and thus broke with the medieval Catholic tradition.

In recent years, this almost classical picture of canon formation has come under persistent and devastating attack. The Jamnia theory, which was first advanced by Heinrich Graetz in 1871, has been completely overturned by the researches of J. P. Lewis (1964) and S. Z. Leiman (1976), who have shown that to call the meeting of the elders there a 'council' is to give it exaggerated importance. The date is also uncertain, and may have been at any time between AD 75 and AD 117. In any case, they claim, the elders of Jamnia merely discussed the canonicity of Ecclesiastes (and probably the Song of Songs as well) without reaching a binding decision, since the same discussion continued elsewhere at a later date.

The concept of a distinctive Alexandrian canon has been effectively demolished by A. C. Sundberg (1964), who has argued that there was no appreciable difference between Alexandria and Palestine on this issue. Sundberg believed that the extent of the canon remained extremely vague in both places, but this has been convincingly challenged by R. T. Beckwith (1985), who, following the lead given by Leiman, dates the closing of the Hebrew canon at about 164 BC (in the time of Judas Maccabaeus), at which point the Prophets and the Writings, which had thitherto been jumbled together, were separated into two distinct groups. The order of the books within these groups remained fluid until the invention of printing, when standardization became important, but this order has little significance and in some quarters it has not been finally settled even now.

From the above, we may conclude that the content of the Old Testament canon was largely agreed by the time of Jesus, though there continued to be disputes among the Pharisees. The text was fairly stable (though the discoveries of Qumran have shown that there was more variety than had been suspected), but the order of books was not – a situation which continued until quite recent times, and which is still reflected in the different orders found among Jews and Christians.

New Testament

The New Testament canon is standard in all Christian churches except the Ethiopian one. It consists of the twenty-seven books normally found in English Bibles, and the order is generally the same, though occasionally Lutheran Bibles will print the catholic epistles in a different order from the one accepted as standard elsewhere. The Ethiopian church has a longer canon including seven extra books, in addition to a shorter canon identical with ours, though the tradition of that church, which was for so long isolated from the main body of Christians worldwide, must be regarded as aberrant in this respect.

The history of the New Testament canon is therefore simpler than that of the Old Testament, and we can also follow its development more closely. The apostles evidently were conscious of possessing a teaching authority in the church, which was given to them by Jesus himself (Eph. 2:20; Gal. 1:8–9; 2 Cor. 11–12). Later generations accepted this to the extent of restricting entry into the canon to those books which could be shown to have been received in the church as authentically apostolic, either because they had been written by an apostle or because they had been composed under the direction of one.

As far as the Old Testament was concerned, it appears that the New Testament writers assumed both that it was complete and that it was uniquely authoritative for them as well as for the Jews. The writers of the New Testament occasionally felt free to quote from apocryphal works, as can be seen in Jude. However, there is no indication that they regarded them as canonical. They speak of the Scriptures having been fulfilled, but not abandoned! There is some indication that the writings of the apostles were also recognized as Scripture (*cf.* 2 Pet. 3:15–16), though how early this was the case is a matter of dispute, as 2 Peter is frequently regarded as a pseudonymous work from the mid-second century. By that time, there was a clear recognition that certain books possessed a canonical authority in the church. Evidence for this comes from Papias of Hierapolis (*c.* AD 70–*c.* 140) who describes how written texts were gradually supplanting oral tradition (which he himself preferred), and who tells us something about the composition of the gospels of Matthew and Mark. Another important source is Polycarp of Symrna (*c.* AD 70–156), who alludes to about half the books of the New Testament, though he does not say anything about their canonical authority in the church.

The main spur towards developing a written New Testament canon seems to have come from the rise of competing groups which either disputed the authority of certain books or offered additional literature as authoritative Scripture. Irenaeus of Lyons (d. *c.* AD 200), writing towards the end of the second century, advocated a canon as a weapon to be used against heretics. The first and most notorious of these was Marcion of Sinope (d. *c.* 160), who was condemned at Rome in AD 144 for denying the Old Testament, and for expurgating Jewish influences from the New. Marcion accepted only Luke-Acts and the Pauline epistles as canonical, and his condemnation shows that this went against the prevailing practice of the church as a whole. About the same time, a Syrian by the name of Tatian (*c.* 160), writing in Rome, composed a harmony of the four gospels (called the *Diatessaron*), which indicates that these four enjoyed a special authority in the church at that time. Somewhat later (after AD 170), the challenge of the Montanists, who produced what they called 'new prophecy', forced the church to conclude that the New Testament canon had also been closed in principle, although there continued to be disputes about certain books.

When canonical lists begin to appear is a matter of dispute. It has traditionally been thought that the so-called Muratorian Fragment, which includes books not in the present canon (such as the Wisdom of Solomon) and omits others which are (such as Hebrews), comes from Rome in the late second century, but this has recently been challenged by G. M. Hahneman (1992), who regards it as a fourth-century document of eastern origin. Hahneman gives details of fifteen other lists from the same period, but the earliest which corresponds exactly to our canon is that given by Athanasius (*c.* 297–373) in his thirty-ninth Festal Epistle of AD 367.

Writing early in the fourth century AD, Eusebius of Caesarea (*c.* 265–*c.* 339) tells us that there were disputes concerning some of the books, especially James, 2 Peter, 2 and 3 John, Jude and Revelation. The first of these he called *antilegomena* ('disputed') as opposed to the others which were *homologoumena* ('agreed')' It seems that they were questioned largely because of uncertainty about their authorship. Revelation was in a class of its own; it should have been among the antilegomena, but for some unknown reason Eusebius relegated it to a third class of 'rejected' (*notha*) books, which included various other writings, such as the *Shepherd* of Hermas, the *Epistle of Barnabas* and so on.

In spite of Eusebius' hesitations and the rather late date of the principal canonical lists, it is certain that the main core of the New Testament canon was already accepted as such by the end of the first century, and that the disputes which continued thereafter were fairly localized. The Marcion affair, if nothing else, awakened the church to the importance of the problem, and it cannot have been left unanswered for long. Certainly by the time the Montanists appeared with their 'new prophecy', the church was conscious of the fact that the canon was closed and that any new 'revelation' had to be rejected.

Once this happened, non-canonical books were deprived of any authority, and many were regarded as heretical. Even so, however, a good many of them managed to survive and are still in existence today. In addition to the Old Testament Apocrypha, there are a number of so-called pseudepigrapha ('false writings'), which include apocalypses attributed to Adam, Abraham, Elijah, Zephaniah, Ezra and Daniel. There are also 'Testaments' supposedly written by Job, Abraham, Isaac, Jacob and each of his twelve sons. To these may be added the New Testament apocrypha or pseudepigrapha (the distinction is irrelevant, since there is no secondary canon of New Testament books). These include a number of gospels, Acts and apocalypses, though relatively few epistles. For a complete listing of these and other related works, see Evans (1992).

It is sometimes asked whether it is now possible to add to the canon. The point is made that a letter of the apostle Paul (for example) might one day be discovered in the sands of Egypt, and if it were, ought it to be added to the canonical Scriptures? Quite apart from the fact that it would be almost impossible to authenticate such a discovery, it must be remembered that not all the Pauline epistles were regarded as canonical in the ancient church. We know that he wrote letters to different places, such as Laodicea, which have not been preserved, presumably because they were not intended to be used for general teaching purposes. Canonicity is not merely a matter of authorship but of reception and use in the life of the church as well. A book discovered now would not fulfil this important condition, even if it were authentically apostolic. In this connection we need to remember that heretics in the early church often claimed to possess books of this kind, which they sometimes accused the main body of Christians of having suppressed. But the idea that there is a 'secret' gospel, concealed from the vast majority of Christians, cannot be accepted now any more than it was then. The New Testament canon is public property by definition, and it has belonged to the whole church from the first generation until now.

Another possibility which is frequently mentioned is that the canon might be reduced. The Reformers managed to get rid of the Old Testament Apocrypha, though there was ample precedent for that, and so the disappearance of other books is not to be ruled out completely. Martin Luther thought that James was 'a right strawy epistle' because it did not appear to him to preach the gospel of justification by faith alone, and he probably would not have regretted its disappearance from the canon. More recently, assertions that books such as Colossians or the pastoral epistles are not of Pauline origin are sometimes taken to imply that they should not be in the canon either. Some scholars maintain that there is a 'canon within the canon', by which they mean that there is a core of books which possess undoubted authority, whereas the others are effectively deuterocanonical. The difficulty with this is that the boundaries of this smaller canon can be decided only by the individual scholar, and are certain to be contested by others. The truth is that just as the New Testament canon grew without any formal decision-making, so there is no body generally recognized as competent to make the kind of alterations to it mentioned here. The canon is fixed in its present shape whether we like it or not, and any theory of biblical interpretation must begin with that assumption.

Perhaps the most serious problem, and one which is common to the church as a whole, is the danger of neglecting parts of the canon to the point where they become effectively non-canonical, even if they are still printed in our Bibles. Many would say that this has happened to the Song of Songs and to Leviticus, and individual churches and Christians have a way of adding to the list, if only by concentrating on their 'favourite' books and ignoring the rest. Maintaining the living authority of the entire canon is one of the church's hardest duties, and it has far more practical implications than the rather theoretical issue of whether books can be formally added or dropped. It is one of the main tasks of biblical interpretation to show the inner consistency and spiritual relevance of the entire text – a matter to which we must now turn our attention.

BIBLIOGRAPHY

R. T. Beckwith, *The Old Testament Canon of the New Testament Church* (London: SPCK, 1985).

H. Freiherr von Campenhausen, *The Formation of the Christian Bible* (London: A. and C. Black, 1972).

R. W. Cowley, 'The Biblical Canon of the Ethiopian Orthodox Church Today', *Ostkirchliche Studien* 23 (1974), pp. 318–323.

————*Ethiopian Biblical Interpretation: A Study in Exegetical Tradition and Hermeneutics* (Cambridge: Cambridge University Press, 1988).

E. E. Ellis, *The Old Testament in Early Christianity* (Tübingen: Mohr, 1991).

C. A. Evans, *Non-Canonical Writings and New Testament Interpretation* (Peabody, MA: Hendrickson, 1992).

G. M. Hahneman, *The Muratorian Fragment and the Development of the Canon* (Oxford: Oxford University Press, 1992).
H. H. Howorth, 'The Origin and Authority of the Biblical Canon according to the Continental Reformers', *Journal of Theological Studies* 8 (1906–7), pp. 321–365.
————'The Origin and Authority of the Canon among the Later Reformers', *ibid.* 10 (1908–09), pp. 183–232.
————'The Influence of St Jerome on the Canon of the Western Church', *ibid.* 11 (1909–10), pp. 321–347.
S. Z. Leiman, *The Canonization of Hebrew Scripture: the Talmudic and Midrashic Evidence* (Hamden, CT: Archon, 1976).
J. P. Lewis, 'What Do we Mean by Jabneh?' *The Journal of Bible and Religion* 32 (1964), pp. 125–132.
D. G. Meade, *Pseudonymity and Canon* (Grand Rapids: Eerdmans, 1987).
B. M. Metzger, *The Canon of the New Testament* (Oxford: Oxford University Press, 1987).
A. C. Sundberg, *The Old Testament of the Early Church* (Cambridge, MA: Harvard University Press, 1964).

The canon and biblical interpretation

In recent years there has been a great renewal of interest in the process of canonization, especially in connection with Old Testament studies. For a long time it was simply assumed that the canon was merely a collection of books made in the course of Israelite history, with little conscious forethought being given to it. However, the discovery of a sizeable body of non-canonical Jewish literature, as well as the realization that individual books of the Old Testament probably went through a process of redaction which may have lasted for several generations, have opened an entirely new perspective. It is now better understood than it once was that the selection of material for canonization must have involved some kind of theological judgment. The formation of the canon is therefore to be regarded as an act of biblical interpretation, since what was included (or excluded) was decided by the use of hermeneutical principles which remain to be rediscovered.

In working out the implications of this, most scholars now accept the traditional view that the Torah plays a fundamental role in the Old Testament canon. It is the theological foundation on which the whole edifice of Israelite religion rests. There is general agreement that Israel's identity was shaped in the first instance by its calling to be a special people, worshipping the one God Yahweh, to whom it was bound in covenant relationship. The principle of the covenant is therefore basic to the Old Testament, and it is in the Torah that this covenant is revealed and explained to the people. On a conservative interpretation, this revelation occurred in the time of Moses and the exodus from Egypt, and was handed down with only very slight modifications to subsequent generations. Others believe that the original covenant concept was subjected to a continuing process of hermeneutical re-evaluation, as Israel groped for its identity in the shifting sands of its historical experience. Not until after the great crisis of the exile was it able to reach some form of consensus, and by then much of what was contained in the Torah was no longer historically relevant.

It seems in fact that canonization as a theological principle takes on life at the point when a text can be shown to have survived as an authoritative document beyond the historical situation in which it was composed. The fact that it was preserved and 'recycled' for later use indicates that it was held to possess a normative authority which went beyond the immediate circumstances of its composition. For reasons which are not entirely clear, and which may have varied from case to case, particular writings were recognized as having a lasting spiritual authority, and these were canonized – preserved for the use and instruction of future generations. The question then arises as to whether individual books were simply added to an existing collection, centred around the Torah, or whether they were redacted with the specific aim of canonization in view. The first of these positions is the more conservative one, since it recognizes that what we now have is a series of basically original texts; the second assumes that there has been a measure of editing, possibly quite considerable in certain cases, which has produced books which 'fit' an overall hermeneutical pattern.

The main exponent of this second view is Brevard Childs, whose *Introduction to the Old Testament as Scripture* (1979), *The New Testament as Canon: An Introduction* (1984) and most recently *Biblical Theology of the Old and New Testaments* (1992) are classical statements of the theory. Childs's work has the great merit of trying to achieve a synthesis between modern critical scholarship and classical theological affirmations which will do justice to both, though his critics naturally complain that he falls between the two stools and produces a theory which is unsatisfactory from either side. Its greatest weakness is probably his belief that the history of the canon falls into two sharply distinct phases. In the first phase, called 'pre-stabilization' by Childs, the text was in the hands of the religious community, which continued to shape it according to its own theological understanding. In the second phase, that of 'post-stabilization', the community submitted itself to the authority of the text, thereby reversing the ancient relationship between them. Such a dramatic change seems to be improbable, to say the least, and it runs counter to the notion of the text's 'authority' in the pre-stabilization phase. But in spite of these reservations, there is no doubt that Childs has opened up an important area of discussion for biblical interpretation, and that in future the role of canon formation will have to be taken more seriously than has been the case in the past.

BIBLIOGRAPHY

J. Barr, *Holy Scripture: Canon, Authority, Criticism* (Oxford: Oxford University Press, 1983).

M. G. Brett, *Biblical Criticism in Crisis? The Impact of the Canonical Approach on Old Testament Studies* (Cambridge: Cambridge University Press, 1991).

B. S. Childs, *Biblical Theology of the Old and New Testaments* (London: SCM, 1992).

———*The New Testament as Canon: An Introduction* (London: SCM, 1984).

———*Introduction to the Old Testament as Scripture* (London: SCM, 1979).

———*Old Testament Theology in a Canonical Context* (Philadelphia: Fortress, 1985).

M. G. Kline, *The Structure of Biblical Authority* (Grand Rapids: Eerdmans, 1972).

J. A. Sanders, *Canon and Community: A Guide to Canonical Criticism* (Philadelphia: Fortress, 1984).

———*Torah and Canon* (Philadelphia: Fortress, 1972).

G. Sheppard, 'Canon Criticism: The Proposal of Brevard Childs and an Assessment for Evangelical Hermeneutics', *Studia Biblica et Theologica* 4 (1974), pp. 3–17.

Normative authority and biblical interpretation

The re-emergence of the canon as a factor in biblical interpretation inevitably raises the wider question of normative authority in understanding the meaning of the text. If we accept the thesis of Childs and others, it becomes apparent that we are dependent on the theology of the redactors of the canonical Scriptures for our knowledge of the original documents. Even in those cases where it might be possible to reconstruct an earlier text, there is little chance that it will ever displace the official canon. Quite apart from anything else, the sheer difficulty in obtaining a scholarly consensus wide enough to allow for the existing canon to be modified would prove to be insuperable, not to mention the widespread objections which there would be from church and other theological sources.

This fact makes us aware that there are forces at work which will ensure the preservation of the canon in its present form. These forces, by their very nature, inevitably claim to exercise authority over the recognition, and therefore over the interpretation, of the text. Foremost among them is the authority claimed by the church to exercise control over the way in which its Scriptures are understood. Every church has something to say on this subject, though the way in which its control is exercised varies considerably from one denomination to another.

The clearest statement of interpretative authority comes from the Roman Catholic Church. According to the definition of the first Vatican Council (1870), the Bishop of Rome, when speaking in his official capacity (*ex cathedra*), has the authority to make infallible pronouncements on matters of faith and morals. It must be emphasized that this authority is not regarded as the personal prerogative of the pope; rather, he is seen as the mouthpiece of what is called the church's *magisterium*, or teaching authority. This consists of the recognized tradition of the church, of the statements of official synods and councils, and of the collective opinions of the bishops, all of which are supposed to reflect what is called the *consensus fidelium* ('agreement of the faithful'). Working for the *magisterium* is a whole army of biblical scholars and theologians, whose duty it is to inform the pope and guide his decision-making. This advice need not be followed, of course, but on the whole it serves to check and to limit the exercise of papal authority in practice. Biblical scholarship in the Roman Catholic Church is now considerably freer than it once was, thanks to the permission given in the papal encyclical *Divino afflante Spiritu* (*By the Breath of the Divine Spirit*) (1943) to investigate Holy Scripture using modern critical methods where appropriate.

The Eastern Orthodox churches cling to the decisions taken at the first seven ecumenical councils (of which the last was held in 787), and have no effective mechanism, apart from the weight of tradition, for controlling subsequent developments. The general effect of this has been to discourage innovation of any kind and to make modern biblical study highly suspect. Orthodox lay people are relatively free to study the Bible using whatever critical methods they may choose, but the results of their research have little or no impact on the life of the church.

The Protestant scene is much more complicated. In theory, the mainline Protestant churches maintain a confessional position which in most cases was laid down in the wake of the Reformation. These confessions usually define Holy Scripture and declare it to be the inspired Word of God, with all that that implies. The interpretation of Scripture is the work of the Holy Spirit, who speaks to the heart of the believer in what is called his 'inner witness' (*testimonium internum Spiritus Sancti*). This is a spiritual experience known to true believers, but it is notoriously difficult to translate it into confessional or other legally binding statements. In practice, most of these churches no longer impose any confessional discipline on their members, and certainly not on biblical scholars in their midst. The last trials for heresy on these grounds took place in the USA in the 1920s, by which time most European churches had already abandoned such attempts. The struggles of the 1920s and earlier occasionally led to church divisions, when the more conservative members of a denomination left to form a new church which would maintain the confessional standards intact. Some of these have succeeded better than others, but it is among them that the struggles over biblical infallibility are most likely to be found nowadays.

Older church bodies contain a wide spectrum, ranging from the most conservative to the most liberal, and as long as a particular issue does not affect church order (such as the ordination of women, for example), there is usually a spirit of mutual tolerance, if not acceptance. One result of this is that denominational coherence has largely broken down. Conservatives band together across denominational lines, and liberals co-operate happily on an ecumenical basis, without worrying too much about traditional divisions. In this situation, conservatives are liable to forge new statements of doctrinal correctness, which are meant to supplement the Reformation confessions and carry weight across the denominational spectrum. The most prominent of these are the Chicago Statements on Biblical Inerrancy (1979) and on Hermeneutics (1982).

Liberals, by definition, shy away from making confessional statements of any kind, and prefer a scholarly consensus which is more of a reality in terms of method than it is of results. Thus it is generally accepted that the principles of historical criticism, developed since the middle of the eighteenth century, remain valid as the basis of biblical study today. This does not preclude a wide variety of conclusions which may be drawn from using these methods, and it must be admitted that 'the agreed results of modern criticism' are few. In recent years, the dominance of the historical-critical method has been challenged by new approaches, some of which have made considerable progress in academic circles. Whether any of them will succeed in dethroning the now classical historical method, though, remains to be seen.

BIBLIOGRAPHY

D. Bartlett, *The Shape of Scriptural Authority* (Philadelphia: Fortress, 1983).

J. Barton, *People of the Book? The Authority of the Bible in Christianity* (London: SPCK, 1988).

J. Boice (ed.), *The Foundations of Biblical Authority* (Grand Rapids: Zondervan, 1978).

R. E. Brown, *Biblical Exegesis and Church Doctrine* (London: Geoffrey Chapman, 1986).

D. A. Carson, *Biblical Interpretation and the Church* (Exeter: Paternoster, 1984).

W. Countryman, *Biblical Authority or Biblical Tyranny?* (Philadelphia: Fortress, 1982).

D. A. Garrett and R. R. Melick Jr (eds.), *Authority and Interpretation: A Baptist Perspective* (Grand Rapids: Baker, 1987).

D. Jodock, *The Church's Bible: Its Contemporary Authority* (Philadelphia: Fortress, 1989).

D. K. McKim, *The Authoritative Word: Essays on the Nature of Scripture* (Grand Rapids: Eerdmans, 1983).

D. G. Miller, *The Authority of the Bible* (Grand Rapids: Eerdmans, 1972).

R. J. Neuhaus, *Biblical Interpretation in Crisis: The Ratzinger Conference on Bible and Church* (Grand Rapids: Eerdmans, 1989).

M. A. Noll, *Between Faith and Criticism: Evangelicals, Scholarship and the Bible in America* (San Francisco: Harper and Row, 1987).

A. Nygren, *The Significance of the Bible for the Church* (Philadelphia: Fortress, 1963).

J. I. Packer, *Freedom, Authority and Scripture* (Leicester: IVP, 1982).

R. B. Robinson, *Roman Catholic Exegesis since* Divino Afflante Spiritu: *Hermeneutical Implications* (Atlanta: Scholars Press, 1988).

J. Rogers (ed.), *Biblical Authority* (Waco: Word, 1977).
G. H. Tavard, *Holy Writ or Holy Church?* (London: Burns and Oates, 1959).

Permanent tensions in biblical interpretation

When studying biblical interpretation, it is important to bear in mind that there are certain factors which reappear in every generation, regardless of the methods being used. These may be described as permanent tensions, which must be recognized by anyone who intends to embark on the interpretation of Scripture.

First among them is the tension between systematic, learned interpretation and unsystematic, often popular, use of the biblical text. The first of these is the business of scholars and theologians, and is what they assume biblical interpretation to be all about. It involves a careful comparison of texts and traditions, in an attempt to piece them together in a way which is coherent and meaningful. Unsystematic use of the text, on the other hand, is what many ordinary Christians practise all the time, often to the annoyance of the specialists. At the most basic level, it may consist in taking verses out of context and using them for purposes for which they were never intended. For example, the frequent use of Revelation 3:20 ('Behold, I stand at the door and knock . . .') as an evangelistic appeal is a misuse of the text, but one which has been so effective that to dismiss it out of hand runs the risk of undermining people's faith.

At a more sophisticated level, artists, writers and musicians through the ages have borrowed themes from the Bible without always submitting their imaginative powers to the control of the text. Sometimes this has had a great impact on the collective consciousness of the church, as for example, in the portrayal of hell by Dante, or of the fall of man and Satan by Milton. Many people implicitly accept the Old Testament Christology of Handel's *Messiah* without ever bothering to consider the context of the verses being used in that way, and allegorical interpretation, which has been rejected by the scholarly world since the early nineteenth century, is alive and well in hymnody, especially in negro spirituals. However much it may go against the grain, scholars must accept that the Bible speaks to people in ways which escape the control of systematic exegesis, and that this unsophisticated approach may do far more to shape the collective consciousness of subsequent generations than a mountain of PhD theses.

Another tension, closely related to the former, is that between exegesis (reading out of the text) and eisegesis (reading into the text). Even the most careful scholars are liable to draw conclusions which are not warranted by the evidence, usually because they have an agenda which led them to study a particular aspect of the Bible in the first place. A classic instance of this has been the modern rejection of the concept of 'wrath' in Romans. The word is clearly used in the text, and before theologians who rejected the notion of divine wrath appeared, it caused little difficulty. However, once it became desirable on theological grounds to reject wrath as a concept, it disappeared from the Bible, being explained away by various devices, some of which are more convincing than others. Much the same can be said for other awkward passages, such as the reference to baptism for the dead in 1 Corinthians 15:29, where the obvious meaning causes embarrassment to theologians today, or the various texts dealing with the submission of women to the authority of men (1 Cor. 11:3; 1 Tim. 2:11–15).

It requires enormous self-discipline to avoid this danger, as those who listen to (or prepare) weekly sermons know only too well. One has only to look at church pronouncements on various issues, in which the Bible is quoted, to realize how frequently exegesis can be sacrificed to the demands of the moment. This tendency, which amounts to decorating our own opinions with biblical texts in order to buttress our authority, is one of the greatest dangers of preaching, and one of the most obvious causes of its decline into disrepute.

Another tension which must be recognized is that between the unity and the diversity of Scripture. Scholarship, by its nature, tends to be analytical, and therefore prone to diversity. It looks for sources, for constructions, for clues to the prehistory of the text we now have. In doing this, it is liable to place undue emphasis on anything which can be made to appear distinctive or contradictory within the biblical narrative. The repetition of the creation story in Genesis 2, for example, will automatically be assumed to come from a different source, and be scanned carefully for evidence of a different theology as well. The idea that this may not be so, and that what appear to be two accounts may be just a literary device for describing a highly complex phenomenon, will not be entertained. Yet before the rise of critical scholarship, nobody noticed that there were two creation stories in Genesis; the 'difficulty' simply never occurred to anyone. This was not because of an exaggerated deference to the text, as there were many other problems of which the ancients were aware. It stems rather from the method of enquiry being used, a method which looks for diversity over unity.

Theologians, in sharp contrast to this, require unity for their discipline to function at all. We cannot write a book about the biblical doctrine of God if the Bible contains only impressions of the divine, gleaned from different sources, which reveal vastly different levels of conceptual development. If the Bible does not have a common theme, there can be no organized religion based on it. For centuries, it was taken for granted that Scripture spoke with a single theological voice; where there were problems of harmonization, devices such as allegory were employed to get over the difficulty. More recently, theology has become increasingly dissociated from the Bible and has looked for its systematic principle within a philosophical framework. One need only compare Calvin's *Institutes of the Christian Religion* with Barth's *Church Dogmatics* to realize how true this is. Barth, who claimed to be a biblical theologian, quotes or uses Scripture only very sparingly in his great work, whereas Calvin saw his systematics as intimately connected with his whole practice of biblical exegesis.

The loss of unity, the failure to find an adequate synthesis of its results, is one of the great weaknesses of modern critical study of the Bible. It is this factor, as much as any other, which has led some scholars to claim that the historical criticism of Scripture has reached an *impasse* from which there is no escape, and that it must be abandoned for other principles, such as that of a literary unity based on a common tradition of 'myth', as advocated by Northrop Frye in *Words with Power* (San Diego: Harcourt Brace Jovanovich, 1990).

Finally, we must mention the tension which exists between the text and its context. The historical study of the biblical text is indispensable for our understanding of its original setting, and use. Whether it is possible to recover the original intention of the writer must remain doubtful, since unless he tells us what it is, we have little to go on. Likewise, there is not much point in trying to work out what the response of the first hearers would have been, even on the doubtful assumption that there would have been only one such response. Careful study of the context in which a book was written can help us to understand it better, but it can never be the final criterion for interpretation. We must remember that part of the reality of canonization is that the text in question has survived the disappearance of its original context, and that its meaning must therefore be deeper than that.

At the same time, we have to be careful not to submerge the text in our own context, to use it for ends which would have been quite foreign to the original writers, and would probably have been rejected by them. This is a special danger in relation to certain books of the Old Testament, notably Exodus and Amos, which have recently been used to justify revolutionary movements among oppressed peoples in different parts of the world. Regardless of what our sympathies may be for these peoples, we must insist that the integrity of the biblical text be preserved. It can never be contextualized to the point of losing its transcendent authority. The challenge of the biblical message will always come from outside our situation, and speak to us with a voice which is not bound by time and space – with the voice of God himself. Lose this, and all is lost. The church today must remember that the text of Scripture stands in creative tension over against the context of the world in which it was produced, and to which it now speaks. In this way alone is its message likely to be heard in our time, as it was heard in the past.

Part 1

Before historical criticism

The four chapters in this section cover the history of biblical exegesis from before the beginnings of Christianity until the latter part of the seventeenth century. This enormous period of time is largely ignored today because the methods and assumptions of biblical interpretation during that period have usually been regarded as obsolete since the rise of historical criticism.

In some ways this is understandable, because until the eighteenth century little attempt was made to recover that knowledge of ancient societies and cultures which has done so much to enhance our understanding of the Bible. Even in ancient times, the study of Hebrew was generally neglected in the church, and contact with the Jewish roots of Christianity was soon lost. Later on, Greek also became an unknown language in western Europe, so that for nearly a thousand years it was virtually impossible for western scholars to read the original sources, even if they had had them to hand. The recovery of this material was bound to make a considerable impact on biblical studies, and it is not surprising that when this happened, many of the beliefs of an earlier age were questioned and abandoned.

Nevertheless, the first seventeen centuries of biblical exegesis cannot be dismissed as readily as some modern scholars think. It was in this period that the canonial texts came into being and acquired the authority which they now possess. It was also during this time that the doctrinal framework which Christians still regard as normative for their faith was worked out. As this was done against a particular background of biblical interpretation, knowing what that was is extremely important. Modern critics have sometimes attacked ancient exegesis of Scripture as a way of discrediting orthodox doctrinal formulations, and it is essential that we understand the former if we wish to maintain the authority of the latter.

Finally, the achievements of this period have continued to exercise their fascination on succeeding generations. The spirituality of the modern church would be very different without the devotional works and the hymnody based on the interpretation of the Bible current before the rise of historical criticism. Folk religion continues to draw heavily on mythical and poetic themes which were absorbed and developed by the collective consciousness of the church over many generations, and if we do not understand what originally lay behind this we shall be ignorant of something which is of basic importance to us. Even exponents of the latest critical theories cannot totally ignore the past, and in recent years scholars have become more aware of the extent to which their own ideas have been shaped by interacting with, and reacting to, established tradition. Perhaps most astonishing of all is the way in which elements of that tradition are now being recovered and used as weapons in the current attack on historical criticism.

It may be too early to say whether the wheel has come full circle, but interpretations of the Bible which were common in the centuries preceding the rise of historical criticism are now playing a role in our understanding of the text which would have been inconceivable a generation ago. For all these reasons, therefore, it is essential for us to get a firm grasp of this period and of the world to which it testifies.

2

The beginning of biblical interpretation

The period and the subject

Biblical interpretation as we understand it began in the period between the Testaments. It is true that there were attempts in some of the later Old Testament writings to interpret earlier canonical material. This is particularly evident in post-exilic literature, which was faced with the daunting task of explaining what had gone wrong with the promises which God had made to Israel. But even earlier than this, there is a sense in which Deuteronomy can be said to be the first example of biblical interpretation, and its appearance in the Torah enshrines the principle of hermeneutics in the most basic of all scriptural documents. At the same time we must remember that the writers of the Old Testament were working within a tradition which was still in the process of formation, and that later generations, including the writers of the New Testament, accorded their interpretations an authority equal to that of the earlier texts.

It is from about 400 BC that writings start to appear in which it is assumed that an authoritative body of Scriptures already exists. These writings are not intended to be contributions to that sacred literature, but are commentaries on it. They reflect a milieu in which regular, scholarly study of what had become sacred texts was an accepted feature of religious life. Even if not all the books now in the Old Testament canon had been written or finally redacted by that time, the transition from the earlier, creative period of literary activity to a more reflective phase was clearly well under way.

This transition was greatly assisted by the conquests of Alexander the Great (d. 323 BC) and the subsequent establishment of Hellenistic kingdoms throughout the Middle East. Although the Jews managed to win their freedom about 165 BC, and retained their kingdom as a Roman vassal state until the beginning of New Testament times, the cultural milieu in which they lived was deeply marked by the Greek spirit. This can be seen in the use of the Greek language, which in Jesus' day was widespread even in Palestine. Hebrew continued to be used to some extent, although the everyday language was Aramaic, which is closely related to it. But whereas writing in Hebrew or Aramaic was restricted to a local audience, Greek literature spread across the Mediterranean world. By 200 BC a Greek translation of the Old Testament was needed for Jews who had forgotten their mother tongue, and after that there was no looking back. By the time Christianity emerged, the use of Greek was fully accepted by most Jews, and it seemed perfectly natural that the New Testament should be written in that language.

It was during the centuries of Hellenistic domination that Judaism emerged as a religion in something like its modern form. This is the period when the synagogue and the rabbi became dominant, although the Jerusalem temple retained its importance until it was destroyed in AD 70. It was characterized by a number of schools of thought, which varied in their approaches to the Old Testament and in their attitudes to the Greek world and its culture. It used to be thought that the use of Greek was a good indicator of positive attitudes to this wider world, but research has shown that this view is untenable. No doubt supporters of Hellenization would be more likely to use Greek, but there is no sign that opponents of it preferred to use Hebrew or Aramaic. Furthermore, the surviving Hebrew and Aramaic literature reveals many traces of Hellenistic cultural penetration, so that those who wrote in the local languages were not trying to cut themselves off from the Greek-speaking world.

The Christian church, as we meet it in the pages of the New Testament, was still a largely Jewish body. Accusations that it was unduly influenced by Hellenism do not stand up to serious investigation; had Greek influence been decisive in the separation of the church from the synagogue, we might have expected an even greater schism to have occurred among the followers of Philo (*c.* 20 BC–*c.* AD 50), who was far more Hellenized than any New Testament writer. The apostles were Jews, and the religious issues with which they had to deal largely concerned the relationship between the new messianic movement and the rest of the Jewish world. It was the dispersal of the Jews after the destruction of Jerusalem and the subsequent (or consequent?) separation of the church from the main body of Judaism which brought this period of biblical interpretation to an end. After AD 70, Christian and Jewish hermeneutics would go their separate ways with only occasional and sporadic contact until the twentieth century.

In sum, biblical interpretation in its initial phase was almost exclusively a Jewish enterprise, and the variations which it contained, including those put forward by Christian writers, must be understood in the context of contemporary Judaism. It was only when the church took leave of its Jewish roots that a different pattern of interpretation came into being.

The interpreters and their work

In this initial phase of biblical interpretation, it is generally more appropriate to speak of 'schools' of thought linked to different movements within Judaism, than of individuals, although there were certainly prominent rabbis who left their mark on later hermeneutics. Of the many groups within Palestinian Judaism, the most important were the Pharisees, who were the main upholders of what is now known as the 'scribal' tradition, and their arch-rivals, the Sadducees. Somewhat on the fringes were the Essenes, with whom the Dead Sea Scrolls, discovered at Qumran in 1947, are usually associated. They too belong within the general framwork of the 'scribal' tradition, though the Qumran documents represent a highly original and somewhat primitive variant of this. Further removed were the Samaritans, who were not accepted by the other groups as Jews at all. Finally there were the Jews of the Diaspora, or Dispersion, who were mainly Greek-speaking, and whose great intellectual centre was Alexandria. They were not a readily identifiable group in the same sense as the others were, and among them were elements close to the Pharisees – Saul of Tarsus being but the best-known example. To these groups must be added the first generation of Christians, whose links were mainly with the Pharisees, but who from the beginning formed a distinct, and ultimately incompatible, element within the Jewish commonwealth.

The Pharisees. Best known of all the Jewish groups because of the strong accusation of hypocrisy levelled against them by Jesus, the Pharisees are usually thought to have been both numerous and influential among the lower classes of the population. It is probable that this has been exaggerated in the past, and recent scholarship has tended to down-play their power, without dislodging them from their important position at the heart of Palestinian Judaism.

Pharisaic biblical interpretation focused around an attitude to the Torah which distinguished between two kinds of law. The first was that written in the Torah itself; the second was a body of interpretive tradition, which had been handed down by former generations. Whether these traditions were entirely oral or partly written is a matter of dispute. In any case, all the witnesses agree that the Pharisees interpreted the Torah in the light of their own distinctive traditions, which often had the effect of negating the plain meaning of the written text.

The Pharisaic reputation for legalism appears to have been based on a concern for ritual purity, much of which was connected with the dietary laws. In pursuit of their ideal, the Pharisees drew apart from the main body of the Jewish people, who could not live up to their high standards. It seems probable that much of their influence was due to guilt feelings induced by this failure to attain the desired level of 'obedience' to the Law.

It is with the Pharisees that the rabbinic traditions of biblical exegesis are mainly associated, though they were just the most prominent of the many groups which practised broadly similar 'scribal' exegesis. The history of rabbinic exegesis has traditionally been divided into two phases, that of the Tannaim and that of the Amoraim. The first of these becomes identifiable shortly before the birth of Jesus, when there were two rival schools of thought among the rabbis. The more conservative of these was led by **Shammai** (*fl. c.* 20 BC–*c.* AD 15) and the more liberal by **Hillel** (also *fl. c.* 20 BC–*c.* AD 15). It was Hillel's school which eventually triumphed and left its mark on later Jewish exegesis. Also from this period are the Targumim, or Aramaic translations of Hebrew Scriptures, which were read alongside the sacred text and used to interpret it to the people. The dating of these Targumim is extremely controversial, but most scholars agree that they contain very early material, so it is not impossible to regard them as typical of exegesis in the Tannaitic period. Recent research has shown that there were a number of developments in exegetical techniques after AD 70, and the absence of these in many of the Targumim may help in dating them more accurately.

In the Amoraic period, which began about AD 200, the large body of oral (and partly written) traditions of earlier times was codified, to form the basis of modern Judaism. This material is divided into *halakah*, which covers matters of behaviour and conduct, and *haggadah*, which is meant to illustrate scriptural texts and edify the reader, though this distinction is not always maintained in practice.

Halakah was first codified by Rabbi Judah Ha-Nasi ('the Prince'), who is supposed to have been born in AD 135. This was the **Mishnah**, which contains both exegetical and non-exegetical material. To the Mishnah was later added the **Tosephta** ('addition'), which is ascribed to Rabbi Hiyya, a disciple of Judah Ha-Nasi. Later on there appeared the **Gemaras** ('teachings'), which seek to relate the pronouncements of the Mishnah to Scripture.

Also dating mainly from the Amoraic period, but often incorporating Tannaitic material, are the **Midrashim**, which are concerned mainly with scriptural exegesis. They are largely, but not entirely, halakic in content. Eventually this material was gathered together and supplemented by still later commentaries into the **Talmudim**, which were produced independently at Jerusalem and at Babylon towards the end of the Amoraic period (*c.* AD 500). Dating is a major problem with all of this material. The codifications were relatively late, but in a highly traditionalist society there is no doubt that much of the content goes back to New Testament times or earlier.

The difficulty is in distinguishing what can be dated early and what cannot. In some cases, material is attached to the names of particular rabbis, which helps to some extent, but even then certainty is usually unattainable, since many rabbis merely repeated what others before them had said, and some material may be wrongly attributed. On the other hand, it is safer to err on the side of an early rather than a late dating, because of the traditionalist tendency already mentioned. Michael Fishbane (1985) has demonstrated that many of the hermeneutical techniques familiar in rabbinical exegesis can be found within the Hebrew canon itself, and suggests that the rabbis may be the inheritors of traditions going back a thousand years, to the time of the Davidic monarchy. He recognizes that lack of evidence makes it impossible to trace continuity or dependence over such a long period, but the similarities are there, and they point to an underlying unity of approach which survived the passage of time relatively unscathed.

The Sadducees. The Sadducees are frequently thought to have been more aristocratic than the Pharisees, closer to the temple priesthood, and generally more deeply influenced by Hellenism than their rivals. This may have been true to some extent, but we cannot say that these things were important enough to distinguish the Sadducees as a group from other elements in contemporary Judaism. It does, however, seem that they were relatively élitist and that they did not enjoy the support of the mass of the population. After the fall of Jerusalem in AD 70 they may have faded out, although many people think that late references to a group called 'Boethusians' indicate a Sadducean element which survived the catastrophe in a slightly different guise.

The Sadducees denied the concept of resurrection, and of life after death, for which they were castigated by Jesus (Mk. 12:18–23). It seems probable that this was part of a wider rejection of oral tradition, to which was joined an insistence on the most literal interpretation of the Old Testament. Our sources also tell us that they differed from the Pharisees over many points of detail, notably in their understanding of ritual purity, but as we have virtually no firsthand knowledge of the group, it is impossible to be sure about what their true position was.

The Essenes and Qumran. The Essenes were a somewhat schismatic group who lived on the fringes of Jewish society. They are usually thought to have been the ones who established the Qumran community, but if so, it is likely that the community represented a fairly extremist wing of the Essene movement. The Qumran scrolls contain a large number of opinions which were previously unknown, and they have greatly expanded our knowledge of the range of Jewish thought in New Testament times. What is more difficult to decide is how representative these ideas were. If it is true, as many researchers have concluded, that it was members of the priestly class who first established the Qumran community, it may be that the views expressed in the scrolls were more widely held among mainstream Jews than is often thought.

One feature of the documents is that they contain vast amounts of written tradition, which has led to increased questioning of the assumption that Pharisaic traditions, for example, were mainly oral. Links with the Jerusalem temple seem to have varied according to circumstances, though there was a certain 'spiritualizing' tendency which regarded the temple as somehow corrupt and the Qumran community as 'pure' by contrast. The scrolls also contain a great deal of information about contemporary Jewish eschatology, with its strong apocalyptic and messianic elements. The consensus of the documents is that the community believed that there would be a period of war and suffering, followed by the victory of righteousness and the establishment of God's kingdom on earth. They were convinced that they were living in the end-time, and that the prophetic eschatology of the Old Testament related directly to them. These beliefs gave their biblical interpretation a unique flavour, as we shall see.

The Samaritans. The origin of this group remains somewhat obscure, and it is impossible to say exactly when it broke away from mainstream Judaism. The Samaritans regarded temple Judaism as a corruption of the ancient Israelite religion, which they alone preserved in its pure form. The Jews generally believed that the Samaritans were descendants of the Assyrian colonists who were planted in the northern kingdom after the fall of Samaria in 722 BC, and who adopted Jewish customs in a syncretistic fashion. Modern scholars are inclined to think of a schism within Judaism which may have taken place under Persian rule, in the time of Alexander the Great, or later – possibly even as late as the early Maccabean period. The key factor, all are agreed, was the establishment of a religious centre, rivalling the Jerusalem temple, on Mount Gerizim. Significantly, this is the issue which was raised by the Samaritan woman who spoke with Jesus (Jn. 4:20).

It appears that Samaritanism was a local variety of Judaism, rather than a schism, since there is no evidence that the priesthood on Mount Gerizim derived in any way from that of Jerusalem. By the end of the second century BC they had produced their own Pentateuch, edited in such a way as to justify their claims in opposition to the Jerusalem establishment. The tensions which this caused were too great for the group to be recognized as properly Jewish, in spite of its own claims. In this respect, the early Christians, though more sympathetic to Samaritans as individuals, followed the standard Jewish rejection of the group.

There is some evidence, going back to ancient times, that the Samaritans had their own Greek version of the Pentateuch, but this has now been lost and attempts to recover fragments of it have not been very successful.

The Jewish Diaspora. From at least the time of the fall of Jerusalem (586 BC), and possibly even earlier, there were large Jewish communities living outside Palestine. The most prominent and settled of these were in Mesopotamia and in Egypt. The former (usually called 'Babylonian') became increasingly prominent after AD 70, perhaps because they lived outside the Roman Empire and were therefore immune from persecution. In later centuries Babylonia would be an unrivalled centre of Jewish culture, where first the Mishnah and then the Talmud would receive their classical shape. In New Testament times, however, the main centre of Diasporan intellectual activity was Alexandria, where the Old Testament had been translated into Greek and where Jews were deeply immersed in Hellenistic civilization.

The great hermeneutical monument of this Diaspora is found in the works of **Philo** (*c.* 20 BC–*c.* AD 50), a Jew who lived and worked in Alexandria in the time of Jesus. Philo's massive output was for many centuries all that most Christians knew of Jewish biblical exegesis, and his influence on Christians was enormous, though among Jews he remained something of an outsider. For this reason, we shall consider his work and its influence in the next chapter.

In a category of his own is the great Jewish historian, **Flavius Josephus** (*c.* AD 37–*c.* 100), whose *Antiquities of the Jews* is a major source for our knowledge of Jewish attitudes to the Old Testament tradition in New Testament times.

This leaves the Christians, who in this period were still essentially Jewish. For them, the leading interpreter of the Scriptures was **Jesus** (*c.* 4 BC–AD 30) himself, a fact which is not always appreciated by Christians today. Jesus was accepted by the Pharisees as a rabbi, though he was very critical of the group in other ways. He also distanced himself from the Sadducees and from the Samaritans, though he showed an unusual degree of sympathy for the latter. We know less about his links with the Essenes, though there are similarities between his eschatology and that of the Qumran scrolls. As far as we can tell, his contacts with Diaspora Judaism were minimal. Jesus stands out from all of these, however, by the radical nature of his teaching. He claimed that he was himself the interpretation of Scripture, that everything in the Old Testament pointed to him and to his work. During his lifetime very few people seem to have believed this, or even understood what he meant by it, but his resurrection from the dead changed everything. It was that event which ultimately justified his hermeneutical claims, and which led to the formation of a distinct body of Christians, whose gospel was to prove unacceptable to mainstream rabbinical Judaism.

Jesus' most prominent follower, the apostle **Paul** (*c.* AD 5–*c.* 67), was of Diaspora origin, though at the same time he was one of the strictest of the Pharisees, and had been educated at Jerusalem. Paul's interpretation of the Old Testament is noted for its concentration on the covenant made with Abraham, which he states was fulfilled in Jesus Christ. Other important interpreters of the Old Testament were the apostles **John** (*c.* AD 5–*c.* 98) and **Matthew** (*fl. c.* AD 30–70), the evangelists **Mark** (*fl. c.* AD 30–70) and **Luke** (*fl. c.* AD 40–70) and the unknown writer to the **Hebrews** (*c.* AD 60), whose famous epistle is the earliest comprehensive essay on biblical interpretation to come from a Christian hand.

The issues

In spite of the great variety of schools of interpretation, there were some basic matters on which all Jews in New Testament times were agreed. Nobody disputed the divine inspiration of Scripture, which extended to the very words themselves, which were dictated, written and edited by the Spirit of God. The texts were said to make the hands unclean, a sign that they were holy in themselves. The human agents of this revelation were prophets; when prophecy ceased (about 400 BC), so did the writing of Scripture. Furthermore, it was universally believed that the Torah contained all the revelation needed to establish and explain the relationship between God and humankind. Because of this belief, it was also agreed that the Torah implied certain things which it did not openly state; it was the business of interpreters to explain what these things were. Lastly, it was agreed that the Old Testament had to be applied to the contemporary situation – a matter which was not always easy or straightforward. Bearing these points of agreement in mind, the main issues with which biblical interpretation had to deal in its earliest phase can be stated fairly concisely, as follows:

1. *It was necessary to demonstrate how an ancient text could continue to act as the supreme law for the Jewish people,* when in some places it was no longer fully comprehensible and in many others it was no longer readily applicable to the contemporary situation. This aim was the fundamental impulse behind the composition of most of the rabbinic exegetical literature.

2. *It was necessary to determine what the limits of Judaism were.* Pressure from heretical groups such as the Samaritans, and even more from the Hellenistic world, made it essential for Jews to work out why they could not accept these influences and how they could most effectively resist them. At the same time, the question was raised whether the Old Testament had a message for Gentiles, as well as Jews. People such as Philo clearly believed that it did, whereas Christians eventually went the whole way and incorporated believing Gentiles into a spiritual 'Israel' which was no longer subject to the law of Moses. However, this evolution was not achieved without pain, as Galatians and Acts 15 both testify, and we must not underestimate the importance of this issue for Jews in New Testament times.

3. *It was necessary to defend the claims of Judaism against rivals,* especially against Hellenistic religion (represented by Homer) and philosophy (represented by Plato and his successors). One of the main tasks confronting Philo was to demonstrate that Judaism was

superior to Hellenism both as a religion and as a philosophy, a task which he accomplished by saying that Plato stole all his best ideas from Moses. Interestingly enough, this issue surfaces only sporadically in the New Testament, and is never dealt with systematically. On the other hand, the early Christians were preoccupied with the need to demonstrate the superiority of their beliefs over against traditional Judaism, a sure sign that they would not long remain within its confines.

4. *It was necessary to determine the place of (mainly oral) tradition in relation to Scripture.* Here attitudes ranged from extreme Pharisaism, in which tradition virtually cancelled out the written text, to Sadduceeism (and Christianity), in which the traditions of the elders were rejected in favour of the sufficiency of the written text. To a large extent it was this issue, more than any other, which marked out the alignment of the different forces in Judaism at the time of Jesus. It is significant that post-biblical Judaism moved increasingly towards a codification of tradition which virtually supplanted the Torah, whereas Christians produced new Scripture which had much the same effect. In both cases, however much the Torah might be honoured, its practical inadequacy was recognized and steps were taken to deal with that problem.

5. *It was necessary to decide what the Old Testament promises to Israel meant in terms of their future fulfilment.* This was a matter of the most intense interest in New Testament times, and it forms a major theme of Jesus' own teaching. Many Jews believed that they were living in the end-times, and apocalyptic fervour seems to have been at fever pitch in the years leading up to the destruction of Jerusalem in AD 70. There was a widespread feeling that the Messiah would come to redress the wrongs done to Israel, to restore the throne of David and to establish universal peace and justice on earth. These hopes were transformed by Jesus into a spiritual creed, whose material fulfilment awaited a second coming at some unknown future date. Christians thus absorbed contemporary eshatology and at the same time removed it from the realm of everyday politics.

The methods of interpretation

Scribal (mainly Pharisaic)

Biblical interpretation in this period was dominated by the scribal concept of **Midrash** ('interpretation'), which involved the study of a text, including its content and purpose. The rabbis who practised Midrash believed that Scripture must be totally consistent with itself and inerrant. One part of the text could therefore be interpreted in the light of any other part and harmonized with it, and any contradictions were apparent, not real. As time went on, they came to believe that Scripture contained different levels of meaning, so that a single passage could mean several different things at once. But in the Tannaitic period, and especially before AD 70, this idea was resisted on the ground that Scripture, being essentially a legal document, was unambiguous. Of course, what the scribes took to be the 'obvious' meaning of any given text could sometimes be very different from what a modern scholar would accept as the original intention of the biblical writer.

In the Amoraic period, a distinction grew up between *peshat*, which was the literal sense of Scripture, and *derash*, which was the interpretation derived from it. This distinction was not recognized in the Tannaitic period, when the rabbis claimed that their Midrashim merely explained the true meaning of the literal sense of the text. In reality, of course, much of what they said was closer to *derash* than it was to *peshat*, and there was always a spectrum of interpretations which are hard to classify as one or the other. Rabbinical Midrash, in its concern to draw out the 'deeper meaning' of the text, to explain its obscurities and difficulties, and to apply it to the contemporary situation, was quite prepared to adopt methods of interpretation which went far beyond what the text actually said, but which they still believed were doing no more than bringing out its 'plain meaning'.

They achieved this result partly by reading Scripture as a legal document, in which examples of behaviour could be taken out of context and made to apply in ways which went well beyond anything the text actually said. An example of this can be found in 2 Samuel 1:1, where it is recorded that David stayed in Ziklag for two days, without besieging the city, before going up to Hebron to be crowned. This historical detail was turned into a law by Shammai, who regarded David's behaviour as a legal precedent for the view that one should sue for peace for two days before starting any siege. This so-called 'nomological' approach leads to an 'ultra-literal' interpretation, in which words are taken completely out of context and made to mean something which goes against the plain meaning of the text. For example, proof for the existence of an oral as well as a written Torah was derived from Exodus 24:12, by artificially separating the words 'written' and 'for their instruction' (an oral activity) in the phrase, 'the commandment which I have written for their instruction'.

The nomological approach to Scripture was the most common form of rabbinical exegesis in the time of Jesus, and it is within that context that the disputes between the school of Hillel (Beth Hillel) and the school of Shammai (Beth Shammai) have to be understood. It is also against that background that we must read the criticisms of Pharisaic legalism which we find in the pages of the New Testament. The only group to dissent from it was the Sadducees, who adhered to what would later be called a strictly *peshat* form of exegesis, and who may have used Hellenistic techniques of logical argument to back up their interpretation.

Because the rabbis could not accept that there was more than one valid text form of Scripture, they did a great deal to stabilize the written text and provide rules by which it was to be read. Eventually they also developed a system of vocalization (*Massorah*) which remains in use today. Usually there is no difficulty with this, but occasionally there are words which might be vocalized in a different way and produce a variant reading; hence the importance of the Massoretic vocalization for interpretation. The rabbis also 'corrected' the text by introducing the so-called *Qere* ('read') in the margin when a word in the text (*Ketiv*, 'written') did not make sense. Again there is usually no problem with this, but there are occasional instances where the *Ketiv* might be interpreted differently. The rabbis also discussed the meaning of unusual words in the text – a major problem because of the lack of extrabiblical Hebrew texts. In modern times discussions of this kind have been supplemented by the techniques of comparative philology, but they still continue.

In rabbinic literature, there are numerous examples of a literal interpretation of the Old Testament, most of which are connected with matters of practical application. The rabbis were especially concerned to draw a distinction between fulfilled and unfulfilled prophecies, an important task in view of the (often) political nature of the question.

The most characteristic feature of rabbinic interpretation, however, is its devotion to Midrash. The main aim behind Midrash was the desire to produce new religious laws (*halakot*) and broaden the application of those already in existence. To this end, there grew up a number of principles of interpretation, known as *middot* ('canons'). These went through their own process of evolution, from the seven rules of Hillel (which were almost certainly not originally derived from him) to the thirteen rules of Rabbi **Ishmael ben Elisha** (*fl.*

c. AD 110–130) and finally to the thirty-two rules of Rabbi **Eliezer ben Jose ha-Galili** (*fl. c.* AD 130–160). However, the seven basic rules of Hillel are enough to give us the flavour of rabbinical exegesis in general.

1. *Qal wa-homer:* what applies in less important cases will apply in more important ones as well.
2. *Gezerah shawah:* the use of the same word in different contexts means that the same considerations apply to each context.
3. *Binyan ab mikathub 'ehad:* repetition of a phrase means that ideas associated with it are applicable in all contexts.
4. *Binyan ab mishene kethubim:* a principle can be established by relating two texts to each other; that principle can then be applied to other texts.
5. *Kelal upherat:* in certain cases, a general principle may be restricted in its application by certain qualifications placed upon it, and conversely, particular rules may be generalized for similar reasons.
6. *Kayoze bo bemaqom 'aher:* a difficulty in one text may be resolved by comparing it with another similar passage, though verbal correspondences are not required.
7. *Dabar halamed me 'inyano:* a meaning may be established by the context.

To the modern reader, these rules make more sense as they go along. We would agree with the last two without serious reservations, but would find much greater difficulty with the first three, especially in the generalization implied in the formulation of these rules. The fourth and fifth *middot* are somewhere in the middle, and might be acceptable today with certain important qualifications.

The rabbis applied these principles by starting with a meditation on the Bible, and moving from there to a consideration of the homiletical and liturgical contexts in which the text was used. They made a detailed analysis of each text, in order to try to clear up uncertainties in the meaning. After that, they tried to discover either the basic legal principles lying behind the texts with the intention of applying them to their own situation (*halakah*), or the true meaning of events described in the texts (*haggadah*). In either case, the underlying motive was to make the Word of God relevant to their contemporary situation.

Another method common in Midrashic exegesis was the *mashal* ('comparison' or 'parable'). The purpose of the *mashal* was to convey a message by using a fictional situation to illustrate a real-life one. The *mashal* originated in an oral context, to which it owes its rather stereotyped structure. It was a particularly common device in the teaching of Jesus, which is how we are most familiar with it.

Qumranic

The exegesis of the Qumran community was marginal within contemporary Judaism but it has acquired great importance since the discovery of the Dead Sea Scrolls in 1947. An examination of these scrolls reveals that the exegetes of Qumran knew and used many scribal techniques, though they had their own approach to interpretation which at times was quite different. In particular, they believed that Scripture could be interpreted without regard to its context, that it had secondary meanings which were independent of its plain meaning, and that variant texts were nevertheless valid forms of Scripture. These beliefs, many of which were shared by Philo, constitute what has been called an 'inspirational' approach to Scripture, in contrast to the nomological approach described above. In New Testament times it seems that the two types of exegesis developed alongside each other as self-sufficient, and therefore mutually exclusive, systems of thought. Only after AD 70, when the Qumran community was no more, did the two types of exegesis meet and merge in the rabbinical academies.

Like the Scribes, the Qumran exegetes had a great concern for the establishment of the correct biblical text, and it is thanks to their library that we have some idea of just how great a task this was. They also made considerable use of the literal sense of the text, though they were especially eager to uncover its 'hidden' meaning, in which the special ideology of the Qumran community was revealed. In their eyes, the correct interpretation of Scripture provided a way of salvation and an understanding of God's purposes in history. This concept was not unknown elsewhere (*cf.* Jn. 5:39–40), but it was developed in a special way at Qumran, where the way of salvation was entrusted to the Teacher of Righteousness, who exercised a kind of papal authority over the community. In particular, Qumran had a concept of ongoing divine revelation which supplemented the Torah with additional prophecies. True to the general tendency of the time, the Torah itself gave way to this prophetic form of interpretation, which is the true hallmark of Qumran.

Today this form of interpretation is known as *pesher* ('solution'), because it purported to explain the eschatological significance of the biblical text. It was rooted mainly in the Prophets, and always had a charismatic, revelatory character. This was because it was assumed that the biblical text was a mystery (*raz*) which required interpretation (*pesher*) by the Teacher of Righteousness. The archetypal pattern of this kind of exegesis was found in the book of Daniel, where the word *pesher* occurs no less than thirty times. Daniel 9:24–27, where the prophecy of Jeremiah is reinterpreted by the archangel Gabriel, may be regarded as typical of the method. Although it was the *raz* which was God-given, it could not be understood or applied without the *pesher*, which was entrusted to the Teacher. For the Qumran community, therefore, *pesher* exegesis was not just one method among others, but the hermeneutical key which was supposed to unlock the text as a whole.

Samaritan

In general, Samaritan exegesis resembled that of the scribal tradition, though it was always more conservative. Samaritans believed that the Torah was perfect in every detail, and therefore that it could and should be interpreted literally. However, Samaritans were known to use allegorical methods in order to avoid the embarrassment caused by divine anthropomorphisms and the like. Their extreme conservatism and tendency towards literalism hindered the growth of an exegetical tradition along the lines of the Mishnah.

Jesus

It was in this mental and spiritual climate that Jesus and his followers made their appearance. The gospels reflect a situation in which the Pharisees were dominant, and it is well known that Jesus was severely critical of them. What is perhaps less fully appreciated is that his criticisms centred on questions of biblical interpretation, to which he provided a unique and most unsettling answer.

Most of the issues surrounding Jesus are controversial to some degree, and it is impossible to describe his life and work without adopting one of many possible stances towards it. What follows here is based on the assumption that the gospels are not the (historically falsified) propaganda of the early church, but a reliable record of what Jesus actually said and taught. It is intrinsically unlikely that his followers would have attributed such radical innovations to him as they did, had he not been the source of them, In fact, it is almost inconceivable that the disciples would have come to such conclusions on their own, since they were so different from anything current in contemporary Judaism.

Jesus agreed with his contemporaries that the Torah was the Word of God in the fullest sense of that term, and its authority was foundational for his own teaching. But at the same time he relativized the scriptural text in a number of different ways. First of all, he exalted Abraham and his faith as archetypal for the true religion of Israel. Moses, important and divinely inspired though he undoubtedly was, was nevertheless dependent on this older, unwritten tradition. The Torah comes across as a divine concession to human weakness, a sign that God would not let his people forget the covenant, rather than an all-perfect guide to realities in heaven and on earth. Second, Jesus declared that he was superior even to Abraham, who had actually known him and awaited his future coming. Thus the whole of Israelite religion was a looking forward to the revelation of God in Jesus himself, and if the Pharisees failed to see that, it was because they had got bogged down in the legalistic details of the Torah. Finally, Jesus claimed the authority to interpret the Torah in such a way as to make many of its provisions redundant, because in him they had been fulfilled. In other cases Jesus extended the provisions of the Torah in a way which made them radically different, as in his famous recasting of the Ten Commandments in the Sermon on the Mount (Mt. 5:21–30).

In arguing with his contemporaries, Jesus is sometimes shown to be using their own exegetical methods. This can be seen, for example, in his dealings with the Sadducees, whose literalistic interpretation of the Torah led them to deny life after death. By being equally literalistic, Jesus could quote Exodus 3:6 ('I am . . . the God of Abraham, and the God of Isaac, and the God of Jacob') as evidence that our personal relationship with God carries on after death (Mk. 12:26). Similarly, in dealing with the Pharisees, Jesus frequently used Hillel's principle of *qal wa-homer*, arguing from a lesser to a greater principle. An obvious example is his defence of healing on the Sabbath, which he justified on the ground that Moses allowed the Sabbath to be broken for the lesser purpose of circumcision (Jn. 7:23). An even more striking example of the same thing is his treatment of Psalm 82:6 in John 10:34–36, when he argues that if Scripture calls ordinary men 'gods' because they had received the Word of God, why should anyone object if he called himself the Son of God?

In trying to evaluate the significance of this, it is essential to remember that instances of this type of exegesis occur only in the context of *ad hominem* arguments made in the course of debate with Jews. Jesus was evidently prepared to defeat them on their own ground, but that does not mean that he advocated their exegetical principles as such. His own exegesis seems to reflect much more the *pesher* type, focusing very strongly on the fulfilment of prophecy. This, for example, is the theme of his first public address in the synagogue at Nazareth (Lk. 4:16–21), where he reads from Isaiah 61 and then announces that the Scripture has been fulfilled in his own person. A similar emphasis marks his exegesis on many different occasions (*cf. e.g.* Mt. 11:10; 13:14; 15:8f.; Mk. 12:10ff.; 14:27; Lk. 22:37; Jn. 6:45; 13:18). Furthermore, his use of apocalyptic terms such as 'Son of Man', 'Servant of the Lord' and 'Day of the Lord' to refer to himself and his ministry, all point to a basically *pesher* type of interpretation. Its uniqueness lies in the fact that Jesus offers himself as the comprehensive, and indeed only, key to understanding the Scriptures.

Christian (early church)

One of the curious features of Jesus' interpretation of Scripture is that he expressly states that his is not the last word on the subject (Jn. 16:12). This is not because he believed that there was something which the disciples had to understand beyond himself, but because he was aware that until his mission on earth was accomplished and until the Holy Spirit had come, the disciples would not be able to grasp the full implications of his teaching. It is for this reason that he says that after his departure the Holy Spirit will continue to guide his followers 'into all truth'.

The full significance of this can be seen in the pages of the New Testament, where the implications of Jesus' interpretation of Scripture are continually being worked out. As with the earthly ministry of Jesus, virtually all the details are to some extent controversial, compelling us to adopt one particular approach to the texts and to their value as sources. As already indicated above, the approach taken here is that the documents we have are reliable witnesses to what actually occurred, and they are used accordingly.

According to the New Testament, it was Jesus himself, after his resurrection, who directed his disciples to those passages of the Old Testament which spoke about him. This is stated in the account of the meeting on the road to Emmaus (Lk. 24:27) and again later in the same chapter (verse 45). Other indications of the importance of the forty-day post-resurrection ministry for the disciples' understanding of Scripture are Acts 1:3 and John 21:15–17. This has been hotly disputed, of course, but the New Testament uses the Old in such a creative and original way that it seems highly probable that only Jesus himself could have initiated this approach.

The New Testament writers shared the conceptual framework of contemporary Judaism, as can be seen from their writings. They all believed in corporate solidarity, expressed through a single individual. This was an ancient Semitic idea, as can be seen from the use of the term 'Israel', which was both a personal name given to Jacob and the name of a group of tribes (each of which also bore the personal name of one of the sons of Jacob). In the New Testament, the figure of Jesus Christ is also treated in this way, so that Christians are said to be 'in him', or members of his body.

The early Christians also believed that there was a pattern in Israelite history, which recurred in the life of Christ, who summed up that history in his person and work. They therefore felt free to look for correspondences in the Old Testament, which could be used typologically, as illustrations intended to foretell events in the life of Jesus. Linked to this was the concept of eschatological fulfilment. It was an axiom of the New Testament writers that they were living in the end-time, and that the death and resurrection of Jesus constituted the final act in redemptive history. Finally, they all believed that Christ was still present in the community, dwelling in their hearts by his Spirit. This became a determining factor in their exegesis, and meant that the Old Testament was to be interpreted Christologically. Everything in it somehow pointed to him, and was fulfilled in him.

From the evidence of Acts, it appears that biblical quotations were used mostly in dialogue with the Jews. This was natural, in the sense that the Jews would have known and respected the sacred text, whereas it would not have had the same impact among Gentiles. There is a heavy emphasis on literal interpretation, as can be seen in the history of Israel as recounted by Stephen (Acts 7). Stephen's version of this history is certainly different from what most Jews would have said – no Jew would have referred to Aaron as an idolater (Acts 7:40–41) – but it is still a straightforward literalist account. Midrashic elements can also be found, as for example when Peter (Acts 2:25, 34) brings together Psalms 16:8–11 and 110:1 to support the resurrection of Jesus on the basis that both passages contain the phrase 'at my right hand'. This is a clear instance of analogy (*gezerah shawah*) at work. Likewise, Paul (Acts 13:34–35) links Isaiah 55:3 and Psalm 16:10 on the basis that both contain the adjective *hosios*, which can mean either 'divine decrees' (*ta hosia*) as in Isaiah 55:3, or 'holy one' (*ho hosios*) as in Psalm 16:10.

Given the Christian attitude towards Jesus as the fulfilment of Old Testament prophecy, it is only natural that *pesher* exegesis should find a place in early Christian preaching. This is how, for example, the death of Christ 'for our sins' and his resurrection 'on the third day' came to be regarded as being 'according to the Scriptures' (1 Cor. 15:3–5); they are *pesher* interpretations of Isaiah 53:5–12 and Hosea 6:2 respectively. Peter's preaching and teaching are especially full of *pesher* exegesis, as can be seen from the use of Job 2:28–32 in Acts 2:17–21, of Psalm 118:22 in both Acts 4:11 and 1 Peter 2:7, the quotation of Isaiah 40:6–8 in 1 Peter 1:24f., and so on.

When we come to consider whether the early Christians had any system in their exegesis, it becomes clear that they cannot be tied to one school of contemporary Jewish thought. Their use of *pesher*, while extensive, is subordinate to their aim, which was to demonstrate that Christ is the fulfilment of the Scriptures. Richard Longenecker's evaluation of this phenomenon sums it up very well. In *Biblical Exegesis in the Apostolic Period*, p. 103, he writes:

> In the preaching of the early Christians . . . one looks almost in vain for any clear consciousness of employing various methods of interpretation in quoting the Old Testament. For purposes of analysis we may (rightly, I believe) catalogue their methods and trace out their respective patterns. But the first Christian preachers seem to have made no sharp distinction between literalist treatments of the text, Midrash exegesis, Pesher interpretation, and the application of accepted predictive prophecies. All of these were employed, and at times there appears a blending and interweaving of methods. What they were conscious of, however, was interpreting the Scriptures from a Christocentric perspective, in conformity with the exegetical teaching and example of Jesus, and along Christological lines. In their exegesis there is the interplay of Jewish presuppositions and practices, on the one hand, and Christian commitments and perspectives on the other, which produced a distinctive interpretation of the Old Testament.

When we turn to the individual writers of the New Testament, we are not surprised to discover that the full range of interpretive possibilities recurs. This is especially true of the apostle Paul, whose biblical interpretation and theology are often asumed to be normative for the New Testament as a whole. Longenecker lists eighty-three direct quotations from the Old Testament in the Pauline corpus, to which must be added a number of allusions as well. More than half of these quotations (forty-five) are in the epistle to the Romans, where Paul outlines his theology of the covenant of grace and the relationship of the church to Israel. There are also ten quotations in Galatians, which is a shorter treatment of the same theme. A curious feature of the quotations is their eclectic nature; just over half are from the Septuagint (LXX), and there are four which agree with the Massoretic Hebrew text over against the LXX, but the rest differ from both traditions to a greater or lesser extent. Evidently Paul felt free to use variant readings when that suited his purposes, a feature which distances him from contemporary Pharisaism and links him to the inspirational method of Qumran and of Philo.

Literalistic exegesis plays a major role in Paul, and requires little comment. Examples of it can be found in Romans 7:7 (Ex. 20:12–17), 1 Corinthians 6:16 (Gn. 2:24) and 2 Corinthians 13:1 (Dt. 19:15). The same is true of his treatment of Abraham, whom he regards as the prototype of salvation history (Rom. 4:17f.; 9:7–9; Gal. 3:8, 16). Midrashic exegesis is present, often in the form of 'pearl-stringing', *i.e.* collecting passages from different portions of Scripture in support of a particular argument, and thereby demonstrating the essential unity of the biblical text. This is especially prominent in Romans, where it can be found in 3:10–18; 9:12–19 and 10:18–21. Galatians 3:10–13 provides another well-known example.

Hillel's *middot* (see p. 59) are frequently represented, as can be seen from the following list:

Rule 1 Romans 5:15–21; 11:12 and 2 Corinthians 3:7–18
Rule 2 Romans 4:1–12
Rule 5 Romans 13:8–10
Rule 6 Galatians 3:8ff. (joining Gn. 12:3 and Gn. 22:18)
Rule 7 Romans 4:10; Galatians 3:17

Paul's interpretation of the Red Sea crossing as a baptism (1 Cor. 10:1–4) reflects the rabbinic tradition that the exodus was a baptism, and his allusion to the 'rock' which followed the Israelites in the wilderness may reflect a rabbinic conflation of Numbers 21:17 and Deuteronomy 32:1ff. There are even three passages (Rom. 10:6–8; Gal. 3:16 and Eph. 4:8) where Paul quotes Scripture out of context, a rabbinic habit which he normally avoids. Commentators have demonstrated that in the first of these instances, Paul is probably alluding to an Old Testament text, in this case Deuteronomy 30:12–

14, rather than quoting it directly. In the second instance, his restriction of the 'seed' of Abraham to Christ is a clear example of the Christocentric interpretation common to Christians generally, and is meant to indicate that only Christ fulfilled all the requirements needed to be a worthy heir and successor to Abraham. In the third instance, where the verb 'gave' replaces the 'received' of Psalm 68:18, the probability is that he was employing a variant reading, attested in the Targumim, rather than actually twisting the passage to suit his own theological ends.

Allegorical interpretation occurs twice in Paul, once in 1 Corinthians 9:9f., where it is additional to the literal sense, and again in Galatians 4:21–31, where Hagar and Sarah are used to reveal a hidden symbolism not apparent in the literal sense of the original text. However, it must be borne in mind that Paul's use of allegory is subordinate to his main argument, and illustrative of it; the argument does not depend on this particular exegetical device.

One might expect *pesher* interpretation to play a major role in Paul, but it does not. There are only a few instances of it, mostly connected with the term *raz* (which the Greek renders as *mysterion*). Examples are Romans 16:25–27; Colossians 1:26f. and Ephesians 3:1–11. It is difficult to say why this should be so; perhaps Paul's rabbinical training at the feet of Gamaliel (Acts 22:3), whose interpretation was more along nomological lines, disinclined him to this type of exegesis.

The role played by Old Testament quotations in the gospels can be summed up fairly briefly. They mostly occur in editorial comments, and buttress the belief that in Christ the Scriptures have been fulfilled. Examples from Matthew may be found in 1:23; 2:15; 2:18; 2:23; 3:3; 4:15; 8:17; 12:18–21; 13:35; 21:5 and 27:9. From John: 2:17; 12:25; 12:38; 12:40; 19:24; 19:36; 19:37. Mark has only one of this type (1:2) and Luke only three, all in the birth narrative (2:23; 2:24; 3:4–6).

Mark's use of the Old Testament is difficult to pin down, and it has even been questioned whether the fulfilment theme, so characteristic of the New Testament in general, can be found in his gospel. It seems that this idea is present, judging from the opening lines, but is not made very explicit. Luke is also sparing in his use of the fulfilment theme, though the birth narrative is certainly to be read in that light. It is in Matthew and in John that we find the most extensive use of Old Testament material, and it is to them that we now turn.

Matthew in particular uses the Old Testament to demonstrate the fulfilment theme, and he goes far beyond anything which could readily be derived from the literal sense of the text. He even manages to link the exodus to the promise of the coming Messiah (Mt. 2:15) and claims that the slaughter of the innocents by Herod is a fulfilment of Jeremiah's reference to Rachel weeping for her children (Mt. 2:18). Probably the only satisfactory way to understand Matthew's hermeneutic is to recognize that he virtually assimilates the historical experience of Israel as a nation to the life of Jesus – the ultimate in typological fulfilment. Like Israel, Jesus goes into the wilderness to be tested, and his twelve disciples represent the twelve tribes (*cf.* Mt. 4:18ff.) who are sent out to conquer the land (Mt. 10:1ff.).

Naturally, such an interpretation is immeasurably enhanced by a liberal use of *pesher* exegesis, and there is a striking similarity between his handling of the Old Testament text and that found in the Habbakuk commentary from Qumran. Matthew is generally more restrained in his interpretations then the Qumran exegete, but the general theme of eschatological fulfilment, which strains the literal meaning of the text and often relies on non-standard forms of it, is sufficiently striking to remind us of Qumranic *pesher* techniques. Matthew is certainly closer to them than to the nomological scribal tradition, for example. As with Luke, the birth narrative is especially prone to this kind of treatment; witness, for example, the application of Isaiah 7:14 to the virgin birth of Jesus (1:22–23).

Turning finally to John, we find that the life of Jesus is tied more to the cylindrical calendar of Jewish festivals than it is to the historical development of Israel, though the typological identification of Jesus with the Old Testament tradition is just as strong. The link with the Passover is especially prominent, and it is in that context that Jesus describes himself as the 'bread of heaven' (Jn. 6), the New Testament antitype of the manna in the desert. Typology is very prominent in John; Jesus is the true temple (2:18–22), the antitype of the brazen serpent (3:14), the true water-giving rock (7:37–39), the true fiery pillar (8:12), the eschatological Moses and the new Torah (5:39–47) and the true Passover sacrifice (1:29). Otherwise, John's use of the Old Testament is very similar to Matthew's, though John is generally more restrained in his use of the biblical text. Even so, the *pesher* emphasis on eschatological fulfilment is never far from the evangelist's mind, as can be seen from the actual quotations themselves: 2:17 (Ps. 69:9); 12:15 (Zc. 9:9); 12:38 (Is. 53:1); 12:40 (Is. 6:9); 19:24 (Ps. 22:18); 19:36 (Ps. 34:20) and 19:37 (Zc. 12:10).

The dominance of *pesher* exegesis in Matthew and John, in contrast to its relative absence from Mark and Luke, raises the interesting question of the author's relationship to Jesus. Both Matthew and John were his disciples, while Mark and Luke were not, which may be further evidence of the historical likelihood that Jesus' own method of biblical interpretation was dominated by the *pesher* mode, as applied directly to himself.

As far as the remaining books of the New Testament are concerned, the pattern seen above is repeated quite faithfully. Leaving aside the epistle to the Hebrews, which is reserved for special treatment below, we may say that *pesher* exegesis is prominent in 1 Peter, and both 2 Peter and Jude show remarkable similarities to the thought world of Qumran, a fact which may influence a revision of the rather late date usually assigned to those writings. On the other hand, James and the Johannine epistles avoid *pesher* exegesis, and prefer the literalist approach on the whole.

The Apocalypse (Revelation) is in a class by itself, at least within the New Testament. It belongs to a genre of literature which has recently received a great deal of attention, but which was virtually unknown until the modern manuscript discoveries of extrabiblical literature were made. Certainly, no New Testament book has ever been interpreted in so many different ways as this one, and (as we now know) with so little reason. As for its use of Scripture, the Apocalypse never quotes it directly, but this hardly matters, as 278 of its 404 verses contain allusions to the sacred text which can hardly be ignored. In the Apocalypse, *pesher* exegesis reaches its ultimate stage of development, in that the whole of the Old Testament becomes a type of the future life in heaven. The Christological interpretation of the Old Testament is taken out of history and placed firmly in eternity; the Lamb who was slain from before the foundation of the world (Rev. 13:8) is now firmly seated on the throne of the Almighty, and in him heaven and earth are for ever reconciled.

BIBLIOGRAPHY

R. Bloch, 'Midrash', in W. S. Green (ed.), *Approaches to Ancient Judaism: Theory and Practice* (Missoula: Scholars Press, 1978).

J. Bowker, *The Targums and Rabbinic Literature* (Cambridge: Cambridge University Press, 1969).

D. I. Brewer, *Techniques and Assumptions in Jewish Exegesis before 70* CE (Tübingen: Mohr, 1992).

G. S. Brook, *Exegesis at Qumran* (Sheffield: JSOT Press, 1983).

W. H. Brownlee, *The Midrash Pesher of Habbakuk* (Missoula: Scholars Press, 1979).

G. W. Buchanan, 'The Use of Rabbinic Literature for New Testament Research', *Biblical Theology Bulletin* 7 (1977), pp. 110–122.
D. A. Carson and H. G. M. Williamson (eds.), *It is Written: Scripture Citing Scripture. Essays in Honour of Barnabas Lindars, SSF* (Cambridge: Cambridge University Press, 1988).
W. D. Davies, *Paul and Rabbinic Judaism* (London: SPCK, 1948).
J. W. Doeve, *Jewish Hermeneutics in the Synoptic Gospels and Acts* (Assen: Van Gorcum, 1954).
E. E. Ellis, *Paul's Use of the Old Testament* (Edinburgh: Oliver and Boyd, 1957).
C. A. Evans, *Non-Canonical Writings and New Testament Interpretation* (Peabody, MA: Hendrickson, 1992).
C. A. Evans and W. F. Stinespring (eds.), *Early Jewish and Christian Exegesis* (Atlanta: Scholars Press, 1987).
M. Fishbane, *Biblical Interpretation in Ancient Israel* (Oxford: Oxford University Press, 1985).
R. T. France, *Jesus and the Old Testament* (London: Tyndale, 1971).
M. A. Knibb, *The Qumran Community* (Cambridge: Cambridge University Press, 1987).
R. A. Kraft and G. W. E. Nickelsburg (eds.), *Early Judaism and its Modern Interpreters* (Philadelphia: Fortress, 1986).
R. Longenecker, *Biblical Exegesis in the Apostolic Period* (Grand Rapids: Eerdmans, 1975).
S. Lowy, *The Principles of Samaritan Bible Exegesis* (Leiden: Brill, 1977).
M. J. Mulder (ed.), *Mikra: Text, Translation, Reading and Interpretation of the Hebrew Bible in Ancient Judaism and Early Christianity* (Assen: Van Gorcum, 1988).
D. Patte, *Early Jewish Hermeneutics in Palestine* (Missoula: Scholars Press, 1975).
G. Vermes, *Jesus and the World of Judaism* (London: SCM, 1983).
———*Scripture and Tradition in Judaism* (Leiden: Brill, 1961).

A case study: the epistle to the Hebrews

By any standard of measurement, the epistle to the Hebrews holds a unique place in the New Testament canon. It is not merely that it is the only book without a named author; its whole approach to Scripture and the message of Jesus is quite different from anything else in the canonical text. To say that it is different does not mean, of course, that it is incompatible with what is found elsewhere. Its theology is distinctly Pauline, and its use of both Jewish exegetical methods and Christian presuppositions finds parallels in most of the rest of the New Testament. Yet in spite of these things, it is in a category all its own, being in, but somehow not quite of, the milieu in which the rest of the New Testament was written.

This uniqueness is reflected in the vast range of opinions which have been put forward as to its origin and purpose. The excellent Greek in which it is written, and the fact that only the Septuagint is used in the biblical references, gives the impression that it comes from a Hellenized Jewish source, but the intense interest in angelology, the description of the temple as a tabernacle, and the exaltation of Melchizedek, all suggest a sectarian Jewish background not unlike that of the Qumran community. Following Yigael Yadin (1958), many scholars have adopted the view that Qumran, or something very much like it, lies behind the writing of Hebrews, but William Lane (1991) has shown that this is too simple an analysis. Other suggestions of sectarian or Gnostic influences are equally open to objection. Hebrews, it seems, has affinities with all these things, but it is not dependent on any of them.

The form and purpose of the epistle are equally controversial. It is not a 'letter' in the standard sense of that term, and the suggestion has been made that it is basically a sermon, addressed to a group of wavering Jewish Christians. The homiletic style is clearly visible in the exhortations, which recur at frequent intervals, and the precise nature of the author's warnings leaves no doubt that he has particular people in mind. At the same time, the epistle does something which no other New Testament writing attempts. It gives us a systematic and comprehensive study of biblical interpretation, and must be regarded as the first essay on hermeneutics to have been written within a Judaeo-Christian framework. This is not necessarily incompatible with a homiletic purpose; the two should be seen as belonging together. The recipients of the letter clearly needed a justification for persevering in their Christian faith, despite the problems which that was causing, and only a clearly expounded hermeneutic of Scripture could provide this.

The writer to the Hebrews bases his exposition mainly on material from the Pentateuch and the Psalms. It is remarkable how important the latter were for his Christology, and for the development of his argument as the book proceeds. Psalms 2:7; 8:4–6; 95:7–11 and 110:4 serve to establish fundamental themes of the book as a whole, and, of the rest of the Old Testament, only Jeremiah 31:31–34 is accorded similar importance. This may reflect the widespread use of the

Psalms as the hymnbook of the synagogue, but the Christ-centred, eschatological interpretation which they receive in Hebrews is altogether unique.

Hebrews differs from other New Testament books in the way in which the writer introduces his Old Testament references. Many of these are simply alluded to, but in such a way as to presuppose a deep familiarity with the text. Others are quoted at repeated intervals, as if to reinforce the point being made. These factors make it extremely difficult to decide just how many Old Testament quotes there are in the epistle; estimates range from twenty-nine to thirty-eight. Lane claims that, in addition to thirty-one clear quotations, there are four indirect quotations, thirty-seven allusions, nineteen summaries of Old Testament material, and thirteen further citations without a specific context, making a total of 104 references, crammed into only 302 verses! When quoting the Old Testament directly, the writer avoids referring to it as 'written'; instead, he prefers to say that God has 'spoken' his Word – an emphasis on the oral nature of the communication, which may reflect conservative Pharisaic tradition as well as the homiletic setting of the book. The supreme and final manifestation of divine speech is the Son (1:1–3), a statement which provides a clear link with the opening lines of John's gospel.

The exegetical techniques found in the book reflect a wide acquaintance with contemporary Jewish practice, though the traditional view that the writer was heavily indebted to Philo has now had to be abandoned. Philo was a Platonist who allegorized the Old Testament, whereas the writer to the Hebrews eschewed (non-historical) allegory, and quite possibly avoided (historical) typology as well. As with other New Testament writings, the main thrust of Hebrews is towards the eschatological fulfilment of Old Testament prophecy in the coming of Christ, an idea quite foreign to Philo. Evidence culled from rabbinic practices, especially in Diaspora Judaism, suggests that the greatest affinities of the writer to the Hebrews lie with them.

This can be seen by comparing the principles given by D. Cohn-Sherbock (1982) with the text of Hebrews. Cohn-Sherbock states that it was the usual practice of rabbis to clarify verses of Scripture which might cause confusion. An example of this can be found in Hebrews 2:8–9, where the writer is commenting on Psalm 8:4–6. It may not be clear from the Old Testament text how God has subjected all things, as the psalmist says, but as Christians we see Jesus, crowned with glory and honour, and thus know that the ultimate subjugation of all things is in his hands.

Cohn-Sherbock also mentions the rabbinical practice of 'reinforcement', by which they strengthened their exhortations by backing them up with a biblical reference. Hebrews does this in 10:19–39, by exhorting the people to remain true to their baptismal confession, and using Isaiah 26:20 and Habbakuk 2:3–4 to support this. It was also customary for rabbis to draw out the implications of biblical texts in their preaching, and Hebrews does this (8:8–13) in its treatment of Jeremiah 31:31–34. The rabbinic appeal to the literal sense of a particular word or phrase in the Bible is well attested in Hebrews, as for example in the extended appeal to the word 'today' (3:7 – 4:13).

The *middot* of Hillel are also in evidence at different points. *Qal wahomer* is found in several places, as, for example, when the writer argues that if God punished those who disregarded the Mosaic law, how much more will he punish those who disregard the gospel (2:2–4). A similar appeal from the lesser to the greater can be seen in 9:13–14; 10:28–29 and 12:25. *Gezerah shawah* (analogy) can be found in Hebrews 4:1–11 and 5:5–6. In the first of these instances, Psalm 95 is developed by referring to Genesis 2:2 and the 'Sabbath rest' of God. In the second case, Psalms 2:7 and 110:4 are linked in a way which ties the discussion of Jesus as Son to that of Jesus as priest, a crucial linkage in the epistle as a whole.

Hebrews also contains examples of 'pearl-stringing', as for instance in Hebrews 1:5–13, where three Old Testament references are placed one after the other, with minimal comment. The link words are 'Son' and 'angels', as well as the personal pronoun 'your (thy)'. The rabbinic habit of presenting listeners with lists of examples, which may originally have been borrowed from a Hellenistic practice, is amply represented in Hebrews 11, where much of the Old Testament is rehearsed.

Whether Hebrews uses typology or not is debatable, and depends to some extent on what is meant by this term. The traditional definition of typology as the recognition of divinely intended prefigurations has now often given way to the idea that typology is really the identification of historical correspondences recognized from hindsight as consistent with God's redemptive activity. It is in this second sense that typology may be discerned in Hebrews, where it plays an important role. This comes out most clearly in the central part of the book (8:1 – 10:18), where the contrast between the earthly and the heavenly sanctuaries is used as a way of presenting the typological relationship between the old and new covenants. The ritual of the tabernacle is used as a vehicle for the writer to disclose the theology of salvation which has been revealed in Christ. In doing this, the writer states that the Levitical type was inadequate, and needed to be replaced by the new and eschatologically significant sacrifice of Christ.

The overall structure of the book represents a particular approach to the biblical text. The writer begins with God, and his ways of speaking to humankind. The opening verses present us with an understanding of revelation, according to which the Old Testament is a varied and partial manifestation of God's purposes, which have now been clearly revealed to us in the Son. This Son is a being who is higher than any creature, spiritual or material, and everything in heaven and on earth is subject to him. No being can claim such authority except God himself; therefore, we are left to conclude, the Son is God. The opening chapters are a clear ontological argument for the divinity of Christ; before we consider what the Son has done, it is essential to recognize who the Son is. Modern biblical scholarship has generally fought shy of recognizing the ontological underpinnings of the Christian proclamation, and some theologians have even asserted that Jesus was a man who somehow became the Messiah and was adopted as 'Son of God' in the course of his life, death and resurrection. But the epistle to the Hebrews will have none of that; the Son is God from all eternity, co-creator with the Father and Lord of both angels and human beings (*cf.* Jn. 1:1–3).

Once this is established, the writer goes on to the sacrificial system established under the Mosaic law. This was the heart of both the Old Testament and the cultic practices centred in the Jerusalem temple and its priesthood. This system was not good enough to take away human sin, because even the high priest was himself a sinner in need of the atoning sacrifice. Only the Son, by making himself lower than the angels and becoming human, could perform a sacrifice which would be eternally valid. This he did by his death on the cross, an event which made the Levitical priesthood and its sacrifices redundant.

The true correspondence is not between Jesus and Aaron, but between Jesus and Melchizedek, the priest who had no forebears and no successors. Abraham, the father of Israel, sacrificed to Melchizedek as a sign that he recognized the symbolism of his priesthood, which was not tied to human tradition. And of course, Levi, the ancestor of Aaron, also made this sacrifice, because he was present in the loins of Abraham his father. In other words, the entire nation of Israel and its priesthood did homage to Melchizedek, the divinely appointed priest. It is this model which Jesus has appropriated, not that of Aaron, and so the Christian sacrifice has an eternal and divinely appointed character which is lacking in traditional Judaism.

What appears on the surface to be a rather curious digression into an obscure event in the life of Abraham is in fact central to the whole argument of the epistle, because on it depend both the nature of Christ's priesthood and the consequent abolition of the Levitical tradition.

The last part of the epistle (from 10:19 to the end) draws out the consequences of Christ's priestly sacrifice for us. It is because we have a sacrifice which is able to make permanent atonement for sin that we are now called to live in a new and better way. Christians are expected to form a community even more closely knit than that of ancient Israel, because it is bound together by the common experience of faith. All the examples of the patriarchs and prophets point to this one thing. The Christian, who in Christ has access to the throne of God, is in a better position than even the greatest of the Old Testament saints, who had to wait for the revelation of the Son before they could enter into the enjoyment of the promises which were made to them. The discipline and endurance now being exacted from Christians have always been the lot of men and women of faith, and were the personal experience of Jesus himself during his life on earth. The whole of the Old Testament therefore points us to the spiritual warfare which is the life of faith, and it is in that light that we should now read it.

In the context of its time, the epistle to the Hebrews set out for the church a way in which the ministry of Christ was to be understood on the basis of the Old Testament. It taught Christians where to place Jesus in the world of angels and spiritual powers which formed so much of contemporary apocalyptic literature, and showed them how only he could accomplish the task which was necessary for their salvation. In order to do this, it had to develop a hermeneutic which recognized the authority of the Old Testament canon as Scripture, but at the same time demonstrated that its central teachings had been superseded by a new revelation.

With the epistle to the Hebrews it became clear that the church could no longer regard itself as Jewish in the same sense as other Jewish groups saw themselves. For Christians, the Torah no longer possessed absolute authority, even if it was fully inspired. God who had previously spoken by the prophets had now spoken in his Son, and that changed everything. A hermeneutic which was not Christ-centred had no validity, whatever exegetical methods might be used. The writer to the Hebrews formulated a comprehensive rejection of contemporary Judaism, even as he borrowed from it. His epistle survived the demise of Jewish Christianity, to become one of the major supports for the patristic controversialists in their efforts to demonstrate and define the divinity of Christ.

BIBLIOGRAPHY

For the most recent complete bibliography of this subject, see P. Ellingworth, *The Epistle to the Hebrews* (Grand Rapids: Eerdmans; Carlisle: Paternoster, 1994).

C. K. Barrett, 'The Eschatology of the Epistle to the Hebrews', in W. D. Davies and D. Daube (eds.), *The Background of the New Testament and its Eschatology* (Cambridge: Cambridge University Press, 1954).

M. Barth, 'The Old Testament in Hebrews', in W. Klassen and G. F. Snyder (eds.), *Current Issues in New Testament Interpretation* (New York: Harper and Row, 1962).

G. Caird, 'The Exegetical Method of the Epistle to the Hebrews', *Canadian Journal of Theology* 5 (1959), pp. 44–51.

D. Cohn-Sherbock, 'Paul and Rabbinic Exegesis', *Scottish Journal of Theology* 35 (1982), pp. 117–132.

D. M. Hay, *Glory at the Right Hand: Psalm 110 in Early Christianity* (Nashville and New York: Abingdon, 1973).

G. Howard, 'Hebrews and the Old Testament Quotations', *Novum Testamentum* 10 (1968), pp. 208–216.

G. Hughes, *Hebrews and Hermeneutics: The Epistle to the Hebrews as a New Testament Example of Biblical Interpretation* (Cambridge: Cambridge University Press, 1979).

S. Kistemaker, *The Psalm Citations in the Epistle to the Hebrews* (Amsterdam: Van Soest, 1961).

W. L. Lane, *Hebrews*, 2 vols. (Waco: Word, 1991).

S. G. Sowers, *The Hermeneutics of Philo and Hebrews* (Richmond: John Knox, 1965).

R. Williamson, *Philo and the Epistle to the Hebrews* (Leiden: Brill, 1970).

Y. Yadin, 'The Dead Sea Scrolls and the Epistle to the Hebrews', in C. Rabin and Y. Yadin (eds.), *Aspects of the Dead Sea Scrolls* (Jerusalem: Hebrew University, 1958), pp. 36–55.

3

Patristic interpretation

The period and the subject

The patristic period is that of the fathers of the church, who are so called because it was they who established the basic doctrinal framework of Christianity. It may be dated from about AD 100 until at least the Council of Chalcedon (451), after which there was a long period of transition to the Middle Ages, which was not finally complete until the coronation of Charlemagne as Emperor of the West (800). This chapter takes the story of biblical exegesis up to the time of Pope Gregory the Great (d. 604), who is often regarded as both the last ancient, and the first medieval, theologian.

The patristic period was characterized by debates about the Trinity and the person of Christ. It was during these centuries that the technical vocabulary of Christian theological discourse was worked out, and two great traditions of Christian thought made their appearance. The first of these was the so-called 'eastern' or 'Greek' tradition, strongly influenced by Neoplatonic philosophical concepts and a mystical approach to the spiritual life. The second was the 'western' or 'Latin' tradition, which was shaped by Roman legal concepts, though it also felt the influence of Neoplatonism. Greek and Latin were the main languages of theological writing, though there was also a significant body of literature in Syriac (Aramaic). Writing in other languages such as Coptic or Armenian was more marginal, though in some cases these languages preserve translations of works which have now been lost in the original Greek. (This is also true of some translations into Syriac and Latin.)

The history of patristic biblical interpretation can be subdivided into periods as follows.

1. *An initial stage, beginning in New Testament times and extending to about 200.* In this period, living contact with the apostles was still felt in the church. Christian writers often continued to follow the apostolic practice of writing letters to individual congregations, which were then circulated more widely. There are few direct quotations from the New Testament in these letters, though there are several allusions to it, and there is little indication that it was regarded as canonical Scripture. Many writings of this period reveal that the church generally regarded the Jewish Scriptures as prophetic of Christ, who appeared in them under the guise of various 'types'. This is the kind of interpretation found, for example, in the *Epistle of Barnabas* (second century AD) and in Melito of Sardis (*fl. c.* 150).

At the same time, the evidence of contemporary heresies shows that the church was battling for its canon in a profound way. Marcion (d. *c.* 144) tried to dispose of the Old Testament and of a large section of the New, which he regarded as being too Jewish. Tatian (*fl. c.* 150) attempted to merge the four canonical gospels into a single text. And a number of heretics proposed a type of hermeneutic which viewed Scripture as a riddle, pointing to a higher reality which could be discerned only by those who had some kind of special enlightenment. This super-spiritual approach is now categorized as 'Gnosticism', a term developed in the nineteenth century to describe a series of different movements which had little connection with each other, apart from a similar approach to hermeneutical issues.

2. *The Origenistic stage, beginning about 200 and extending until the First Council of Nicaea in 325.* In this period, biblical exegesis was dominated by the towering genius of Origen (*c.* 185–*c.* 254), who first attempted to put Christian biblical interpretation on a systematic foundation, with commentaries devoted to particular biblical books. Origen borrowed heavily from the writings of the Jewish Platonist, Philo of Alexandria (d. *c.* 50), whose ideas came into their own in this period. We now know that Philo was a very aberrant Jewish exegete, but this would not have been so apparent to Origen and his contemporaries, who could find in his writings parallels and foreshadowings of later Christian teachings – on the Trinity, for instance. Origen's influence continued to be felt throughout antiquity, but the weaknesses of some of his positions were gradually exposed. These came to a head in the Arian crisis, which formed the main topic of the First Council of Nicaea, at which an attempt was made to define the person and natures of Christ.

3. *The great conciliar stage, beginning from the First Council of Nicaea and*

extending to the Council of Chalcedon (451). This was the golden age of patristic exegesis, in which two main schools of thought vied for influence. One of these was closely associated with the church of Alexandria, and generally followed the Platonic type of exegesis associated with Philo and Origen. The other was rooted in the theological school of Antioch which offered a contrasting type of exegesis, more literal and more in tune with what would nowadays be regarded as 'scientific'. In the battles which developed between these schools, it was the former which emerged victorious. Many Antiochene writings were suppressed, though some still exist in fragments or in translations preserved outside the Roman Empire. The main exception to this was the exegetical and homiletical work of John Chrysostom (d. 407), which, in spite of its Antiochene leanings, was always regarded as fully orthodox, and was highly prized in the eastern church.

4. *The final, or late conciliar stage, from after the Council of Chalcedon to the time of Gregory the Great (d. 604) or even to that of Charlemagne (c. 800).* There are very few biblical commentaries from this period, which was an age of intense theological controversy in the East and of social and political disruption in the West. During this time a patristic canon gradually took shape, in which certain standard interpretations of Scripture became the accepted norm. By the end of the period it was considered just as important to quote the interpretative authority of the fathers as it was to quote the biblical canon itself. At the Fifth Ecumenical Council, the Second Council of Constantinople (553), a number of ancient biblical scholars were condemned, among them the very greatest representatives of the Alexandrian church (Origen, Didymus the Blind) as well as of the Antiochene school (Diodore of Tarsus, Theodore of Mopsuestia). As a result most of their work perished, though some of it has recently been recovered in Syriac and other versions. It was also during this time that East and West gradually distanced themselves from each other, though the Roman church remained a kind of bridge between them, tilting only slowly away from the East.

The interpreters and their work

Following the periodization adopted in the previous section, the main interpreters and their work were as follows.

Before AD *200*

Marcion (d. *c.* 144). He believed that the God of the Old Testament was a deity inferior to the Father of Jesus Christ, because he was the creator ('Demiurge') of matter, which was intrinsically evil. The Christian revelation therefore had to be purified of its Jewish elements, which were primitive and unworthy of true religion. Adolf von Harnack (1851–1930) thought that Marcion was a restorer of Pauline theology in the face of Judaizing tendencies, but this idea has never been widely accepted. Marcion's radical rejection of the creator God had its philosophical basis in Platonism, which thought of matter as evil and of salvation as the separation of the soul from it. His programme of radical 'cleansing' of the New Testament reduced the canonical text to Luke-Acts and the Pauline epistles, but even these could not be understood apart from their Jewish background, and had to be purged. Marcion's hermeneutical project virtually destroyed the New Testament along with the Old, and the church has never been tempted to follow his lead, however much it may have allegorized or even ignored the Jewish Scriptures.

The Gnostics. These were a disparate band of pseudophilosophical teachers, who shared a worldview but did not constitute a single sect. Their names (Valentinus, Basilides, Hermogenes, *etc.*) are known from their followers and opponents, but it is difficult to distinguish who they were, where or when they lived, or even what they taught. Gnostic phenomena may have been present in Jewish circles even before the rise of Christianity, but the main evidence for them comes from New Testament times and afterwards. Their basic belief was that God was totally different from his creation, and that to know him involved a mental and spiritual transformation which could be accomplished only by the elect, who possessed superior knowledge (*gnōsis*). Gnostic texts, many of which functioned as 'Scripture' in Gnostic circles, have been recovered in large numbers in recent decades, most notably at Nag Hammadi in Egypt (1946). Attempts have been made to show that they represented an alternative (and even a more authentic) form of Christianity which was eventually suppressed by the mainline church, but this analysis does not stand up to serious investigation. Their teachings were secretive and bizarre, but in spite of the considerable attraction which they evidently exerted in some places, they presented no long-term threat to the public and accessible texts of mainstream Christian revelation.

Justin Martyr (d. 156). He wrote three treatises which survive, one against the Jewish rabbi Trypho (possibly to be identified with a certain Tarphon, who is mentioned in the Mishnah), and two apologies. In writing against pagan misconceptions of Christianity, Justin pleaded the antiquity of the Old Testament revelation, which prophesied the coming of Christ. He also claimed that Plato and the Greek philosophers had read Moses and got their best ideas from him. Writing against the Jews, he took a somewhat different line. The prophets were his main line of defence, but he argued that Jewish interpretation, with which he seems to have been quite familiar, was wooden and 'carnal'. Christians, by contrast, practised a 'spiritual' interpretation of Scripture, which was Christ-centred. This attitude led him to use a certain amount of typology, though he never abandoned the historical meaning of the biblical text. He invented a distinction between *typoi* (types), which applied to events in which the Holy Spirit enacted a picture of the future, and *logoi*, which were verbal prophecies of future events.

Melito of Sardis (*fl. c.* 170). Bishop of Sardis, he was highly regarded in his own time as a defender of Christian orthodoxy against various heretical movements. Of his many writings, only one, his paschal homily, is now extant. However, he is known to have written six books on the Old Testament law and prophets. A fragment of this work contains the oldest known list of Old Testament books.

Irenaeus (d. *c.* 200). His famous polemic against heretics (*Adversus Omnes Haereses*) gives us a clear idea of the way in which he thought the Bible should be read. Irenaeus borrowed and extended Justin's distinction between *typoi* and *logoi*, both of which he integrated into his main principle of interpretation, the doctrine of recapitulation, which governed his view of history. From the fall of Adam and Eve to the coming of Christ, the world sank deeper and deeper into sin. Finally, God sent his Son (the new Adam) to be born of a woman (the new Eve), and through them started the human race on the pathway of salvation and eternal life. What had gone wrong under the Old Testament was now being put right under the New. At the end of time the universe would return to its original perfection, and the saving work of Christ would be fully accomplished. Within this context, Irenaeus was prepared to accept that God revealed himself in stages, according to human capacity to absorb spiritual truth, and that some parts of Scripture had therefore become obsolete with the passage of time. His basically cyclical view of history ruled out the idea that humankind progressed from a lower to a higher stage of religious awareness, and instead claimed that revelation was meant to take people back to the knowledge of God which Adam enjoyed before his fall.

Tertullian (*fl. c.* 196–*c.* 212). He attacked different Gnostic-type heretics, as well as Marcion, and in his great apologetic work on the prescription of heretics (*De Praescriptione Haereticorum*) he defended the view that only Christians could understand the true meaning of Scripture, because they alone were in tune with God, its author. In contrast to Irenaeus, his hermeneutic was based on a linear view of history, according to which the Old Testament, or the revelation of God the Father, had been revealed by the prophets, and the New Testament, or the revelation of God the Son, by the apostles. The revelation of the Holy Spirit was contained in the so-called 'new prophecy', given to a certain Montanus and his followers (*c.* 171). Tertullian was more cautious than he is usually given credit for about attributing canonical status to the Montanist prophecies, but the logic of his thought is clear enough. Tertullian was deeply opposed to Platonism, and therefore found it hard to accept the allegorical exegesis of Scripture. His own method of interpretation was usually literalistic, though he had to admit that not everything could be read that way. He regarded the New Testament as a new law (*nova lex*), to be fulfilled by Christians with a spiritual rigour unknown to the lax and hypocritical scribes and Pharisees.

The exegesis of this period culminated in the Old Testament commentaries usually ascribed to **Hippolytus** (*fl. c.* 200) on Daniel, Song of Songs and parts of the Pentateuch. These works represent the transition to commentary writing, which at that time was a new kind of biblical interpretation. In his hermeneutical technique, Hippolytus generally followed Irenaeus, though his theological emphasis was more Christological than eschatological.

From 200 to 325

Philo Judaeus of Alexandria (d. *c.* 50). Although he lived and wrote long before the third century, and was a Jew, not a Christian, Philo exerted his main influence from this period onwards, and so is most appropriately treated here. He was a Platonist who believed that Plato got his best ideas from Moses, and that therefore Judaism could present itself as the true philosophy. He also had links with the Stoics. Following Platonic methods of interpretation employed in the analysis of the Homeric poems, Philo adapted allegorical techniques to his commentaries on the Pentateuch. The essence of allegory is the belief that above and beyond the literal meaning of a text there stands a higher (or perhaps several higher) senses. By using allegory, Philo was able to explain away difficult or unpalatable statements in the Old Testament by saying that they contained a hidden meaning of spiritual value, even if the literal sense was unacceptable to most people.

We do not know whether Philo could read Hebrew or not, nor can we say to what extent he was in touch with contemporary hermeneutical developments among the rabbis in Palestine. There are affinities between his type of exegesis and that of Qumran, though it does not seem that Philo was in direct contact with them. Recent research has tended to emphasize his Jewishness more than was the custom previously, but this cannot conceal the fact that he was a highly Hellenized Jew who wrote mainly for others like himself. He was a natural model for Christian exegetes who, like him, had been trained in Platonic theories of literary analysis. The rediscovery of Philo, and the acceptance of his hermeneutical methods among Christians, led to a development of allegorical exegesis which far outstripped anything which had been practised in the church before AD 200.

Clement of Alexandria (*fl. c.* 200). More than any other Christian teacher, Clement was responsible for having introduced Philonic exegesis into the church. He did this as part of an overall plan to base the Christian faith on a secure scientific foundation. His reasons for doing this were evangelistic; Clement wanted to show the Hellenistic world that Christianity was the fulfilment of Greek philosophy as well as of the Old Testament. Like Philo and Justin before him, he argued that Plato got his best ideas from Moses, so that Platonism had a biblical origin. In his *Stromata* (or *Stromateis*) he outlined the role of true Christian *gnōsis*, which, in sharp contrast to that of the heretics, contained a demand for moral as well as intellectual perfection.

Origen (*c.* 185–*c.* 254). By any standard of measurement, Origen was the greatest biblical scholar of antiquity. He composed a Hexapla (six versions) of the Old Testament, in which he ranged in parallel columns the Hebrew text, its transliteration into Greek letters, the Septuagint and three other Greek translations (those of Aquila, Symmachus and Theodotion, all from the second century AD). He was one of the church's rare students of Hebrew, and was extremely concerned to establish the literal sense of the scriptural text as the basis from which to develop his allegorical exegesis. However, Origen regarded the text of Scripture as an outward and perishable form which both concealed and revealed eternal spiritual truths. A fundamental separation between word and spirit was characteristic of his interpretation, and distinguished it sharply from both the rabbinical and the New Testament tradition.

Following Philo, Origen wrote commentaries on biblical books, the first Christian to do so. Most of his work was destroyed in the fifth century, when he fell out of favour and was condemned for heresy, but fragments of his commentaries on the Song of Songs, Matthew, John and Romans still survive. In addition to these, he wrote a number of short exegetical notes (*Scholia*) on Exodus, Leviticus, Isaiah, Psalms 1–15, Ecclesiastes and John's gospel, a few of which are partially preserved in other works. There were also 574 sermons (homilies) of which 186 survive, mostly in Latin translations done by Rufinus or Jerome in the late fourth century. They are of great value, because they show us how Origen was guided in his interpretation of Scripture by a deep pastoral concern which is not immediately apparent in his more theoretical writings. His most important work of biblical interpretation is his book on first principles (*De Principiis* or *Peri Archōn*), in which he develops his allegorical theories.

Dionysius of Alexandria (*fl.* *c.* 230–265). A disciple of Origen, Dionysius is in many ways the odd man out in the history of ancient exegesis. He did not reject allegorical exegesis, but it played a relatively minor role in his work. He was far more concerned with historical and literary questions, and is chiefly remembered today for denying that John the Evangelist was the author of the book of Revelation. The last book of the Bible was still widely disputed in the eastern church (though fairly generally accepted in the West), and Dionysius helped keep the issue alive for another century or more.

From 325 to 451

The writers of this period are most conveniently subdivided according to whether they were Alexandrian or Antiochene (both Greek-speaking), western (Latin) or oriental (Syriac and Armenian).

Alexandrian

Arius (*c.* 256–*c.* 336). Though often thought of as an Antiochene because of his denial of the divinity of Christ, Arius was a priest of the Alexandrian church who came to be regarded as its 'arch-heretic'. Arius claimed that Jesus was a divine creature who originated in time, though not in the same time and space framework as the rest of creation. He based this view on a number of scriptural passages, notably Proverbs 22:8ff., which he regarded as prophetic of Christ. The plausibility of his very literalistic interpretation of Scripture made him extremely dangerous to the 'orthodox' party within the church, and he proved extremely hard to defeat. However, his belief that Christ was a temporal being who originated outside the normal time and space framework was thought to be self-contradictory, and was rejected by the mainline church. He also used what has come to be known as the 'proof-text' method of biblical interpretation, which was unsatisfactory because it expounded verses out of their context and distorted their true meaning. What Arius failed to grasp was the underlying sense of Scripture, which could not be reduced to the verbal utterances of certain texts taken in isolation.

Athanasius of Alexandria (*c.* 296–373). The star theologian of the Alexandrian church, and the great defender of orthodoxy against the Arians, Athanasius developed a sophisticated hermeneutic in answer to the threat posed by Arius. He wanted the church to appreciate the whole sweep of redemptive history, which he regarded more historically than either Philo or Origen had done. At the same time, he was convinced that there were elements of God's revelation in Christ which could not be taken literally: for example, Jesus' statement that he was thirsty on the cross, or his admission of ignorance about the date of the second coming. Athanasius believed that because Jesus was God he could not have been limited in these all too human ways, and said that the Son accommodated himself to human understanding. This rather unsatisfactory view of Christ's humanity was challenged by the Antiochenes, and the issue was never fully resolved in the ancient church. Only fragments of his exegetical works remain, but a good idea of his approach can be gained from the three discourses against the Arians (*Orationes contra Arianos*), which contain his main arguments against the proof-texting method of Arius.

Didymus the Blind (319–398) was the most prolific commentator of the Alexandrian school. Like Athanasius, he was more reserved in his use of allegory than Origen, but he did not reject the method altogether. His commentary on Genesis survives in its entirety, as do fragments of commentaries on Job, Psalms, Proverbs, Ecclesiastes, Isaiah, Hosea, Zechariah, John and Acts, while many others are lost. He was a strong defender of Origen at a time when the latter's ideas were coming under attack, and was himself condemned by the Fifth Ecumenical Council (Constantinople, 553). For this reason most of his works were not preserved.

Cyril of Alexandria (d. 444) was a prolific commentator upon Scripture, as well as a theological controversialist in the Athanasian mould. He generally followed the Alexandrian tradition in his Old Testament commentaries, though he was less determined than

Origen to find a Christological meaning in every text. His New Testament commentaries are more literalistic, but still weak in terms of historical and philological analysis. Surviving commentaries by him include those on Isaiah, the minor prophets, Luke and John. In addition there are extensive fragments of commentaries on Kings, Psalms, Proverbs, Song of Songs, Jeremiah, Ezekiel and Daniel. Also very important is his book on the worship of God in spirit and in truth (*De Adoratione et Cultu in Spiritu et Veritate*), in which he gives an allegorical and typological exegesis of random Old Testament passages, in order to demonstrate that the law was abolished in letter but not in spirit.

Evagrius Ponticus (345–399). A monk whose spiritual writings have been of enormous influence on eastern Christian mysticism, he wrote commentaries on Job, Psalms and Proverbs, which survive in fragments. There are also bits of a lost commentary on Luke, and he seems to have written on Numbers, Kings and the Song of Songs as well. His exegetical methods were highly Origenistic, and he was condemned along with Didymus and Origen in 553.

Gregory of Nyssa (330–*c.* 395). Brother of Basil of Caesarea (see below under 'Antiochene' exegetes) and one of the great Cappadocian fathers, Gregory was not really an Alexandrian, though his biblical interpretation owed more to that school of exegesis than to any other. The two exceptions to this are his works on creation, written at the request of another brother, Peter of Sebaste. The first of these (*De Opificio Hominis, On the Creation of Man*) is meant to be the continuation of his brother Basil's work on the six days of creation (see below), and the second (*Explicatio Apologetica in Hexaemeron, Commentary on the Six Days of Creation*) was likewise intended to illuminate Basil's work. In both of these he follows his brother's literalistic exegesis, and avoids the allegorizing which he freely indulges in elsewhere.

Antiochene

Eusebius of Caesarea (*c.* 263–*c.* 340). A leading biblical scholar, he was responsible, along with his friend Pamphilus, for preparing a critical edition of Origen's Septuagint, as well as one of the New Testament. Many of the extant biblical manuscripts go back to codices made by them. Eusebius was also a pioneer of gospel studies. Though not the first to attempt a harmony of the gospels, he was by far the most systematic scholar which the ancient world produced. Starting with the presupposition that Matthew was the earliest gospel, he divided them according to passages common to all four, passages common to the synoptics, passages common to two of the synoptics and John, passages common to only two gospels, and passages unique to each gospel. His system, the so-called Eusebian Canons or Eusebian Sections, was translated into both Syriac and Latin, and was adopted by Jerome. In addition to this, Eusebius wrote on the prophets and the Psalms, and he also composed two books dealing with apparent discrepancies in the gospel records of the birth and of the resurrection of Jesus. Only fragments of these remain, but it is clear that these books were an important contribution to biblical criticism.

Eusebius also prepared an *Onomasticon*, or gazetteer of biblical sites, in which every place named in the Bible is described. It was translated into Latin and corrected by Jerome, and is still the most important source for our knowledge of Palestinian topography. It was originally part of a larger work, dealing with other aspects of biblical geography, but this is no longer extant. There are two very long commentaries, one on the Psalms and the other on Isaiah. The first of these can be reconstructed to a large extent from the fragments which remain, though there is no complete manuscript. The second was known only in fragments until 1934, when a complete copy was discovered and published. It is evident that Eusebius followed Origen quite closely, which is somewhat surprising, given that he was much more interested in historical and critical details than Origen was.

Diodore of Tarsus (d. *c.* 394). By any standard of measurement, Diodore was one of the greatest scholars and teachers of the Antiochene school of exegesis. He was highly regarded in his own lifetime, but was condemned at Constantinople in 499 as the originator of Nestorianism. He seems to have written commentaries on the whole of the Old Testament and most if not all of the New as well. Apart from fragments, they are now all lost. As an exegete, Diodore rejected the allegorization practised at Alexandria and stuck to the historical and grammatical method. His main concern was to expound the sense intended by the original writer, not to find hidden meanings in the text.

Theodore of Mopsuestia (d. 428). A disciple of Diodore, he was likewise condemned for Nestorianism (which taught that the two natures of Christ were autonomous, and only superficially conjoined in the person of Christ), though this was not until 553. His writings were for long lost in the western world, though several have recently been discovered in oriental manuscripts. The Nestorian church has always venerated him as its leading exponent of the Scriptures. He wrote commentaries on almost every book of the Bible, and these are distinguished by their bold critical investigations of authorship and date. His approach to linguistic and historical matters is highly scientific, and can stand comparison with modern commentaries. In addition, he was the first biblical scholar to use the techniques of literary criticism in his biblical exegesis. His overall approach was literalistic and anti-allegorical, though he showed some appreciation of typology.

The only Old Testament commentary by Theodore which is extant in Greek is the one on the minor prophets, probably because it contains nothing controversial. However, we now also have a substantial section of his commentary on Genesis in a Syriac translation, and an almost complete Syriac version of his commentary on the Psalms. For the New Testament we have substantial fragments of his commentary on the four major Pauline epistles (Romans, 1 and 2 Corinthians, and Hebrews) and a complete Latin version of his commentary on the rest of the Pauline corpus. We also now have a complete Syriac version of his commentary on John.

John Chrysostom (*c.* 347–407). Of all the members of the Antiochene school, John was the only one whose reputation survived the Nestorian crisis. More than that, he has always been the most popular of the Greek fathers, constantly read and praised from his own time until the present day. His major exegetical work can be found in the large number of homilies which have been preserved. They are distinguished for the remarkable way in which he discerns the spiritual sense of the biblical text in its literal, rather than in any allegorical meaning, and can apply it to the immediate pastoral needs of his flock. The depth of his understanding and the soundness of his exposition are unique, and have survived the passage of time, so that he is still read today with profit. The sermon series which survive cover Genesis, Psalms and Isaiah in the Old Testament, and Matthew, John, Acts and the Pauline epistles (including Hebrews) in the New.

Theodoret of Cyrrhus, or Cyrus (*c.* 393–*c.* 466). The last of the great Antiochene exegetes, Theodoret lived to witness the condemnation of Nestorius at Chalcedon in 451, an event in which he was an unwilling participant. He continued to be recognized as orthodox during his lifetime, though some of his writings were condemned in 553. In relation to his predecessors, Theodoret adopts something of a mediating position between Antioch and Alexandria. His main thrust is literalistic, but he is prepared to allow typological or allegorical explanations where these seem to be preferable. His exegetical writings are largely extant, and consist of a 'question and answer' style of commentary on the Octateuch (the Pentateuch, plus Joshua, Judges and Ruth) as well as a further commentary in the same style on Kings (including Samuel) and Chronicles. There are further commentaries on Psalms, Song of Songs, Isaiah, Jeremiah, Ezekiel, Daniel, the minor prophets and the fourteen Pauline epistles (including Hebrews). His commentary on Isaiah is particularly fine, and reveals a moderate use of allegorical exegesis in his interpretation of the messianic passages. He is at his most allegorical in his commentary on the Song of Songs, which he interprets in terms of Christ and his church.

Basil of Caesarea (329–379). Though not strictly an Antiochene, Basil's exegetical work is most closely linked to this school of thought. He never wrote biblical commentaries, and his exegesis is known to us mainly through his homilies, of which the nine on the six days of creation (*In Hexaemeron*) are his masterpiece. Also extant are eighteen homilies on the Psalms. A commentary on Isaiah which was once attributed to him is now not regarded as authentic. Basil eschewed any kind of allegorical exegesis, and paid close attention to contemporary scientific thought in his exposition of Genesis. Though now outdated in scientific terms, his homilies provide a model of exposition which is still accessible to modern students of Scripture.

Other Antiochene exegetes, whose works survive only in fragments, are **Acacius of Caesarea**, **Eusebius of Emesa** and **Apollinaris of Laodicea**, all of whom were writing *c.* 340–*c.* 360. They seem to have concentrated mainly on the Pentateuch.

Western (Latin)

The western church presented a rather different picture from the eastern during the golden age of the Councils. There were far fewer centres of theological activity, and fewer theologians or biblical scholars. Not until the First Council of Ephesus (431) was the West involved in the church's decision-making on a par with the East, and the experience was not particularly happy. Two centuries later, the Greek-speaking Maximus the Confessor was still bemoaning the fact that Latin was not a language well adapted to theological argument.

What it lacked in quantity, however, the West did its best to make up for in quality. It was fortunate that its first theologian was a man of the stature of Tertullian. In spite of his difficult relations with the church, Tertullian and his writings continued to inspire subsequent generations, and although he was eventually condemned for heresy, nobody took much notice. His work and his theological method continued to set a standard which few in the western church wished to disown. Latin exegesis really begins with **Victorinus of Pettau** (d. 304) who wrote on both Genesis and Revelation, and **Reticius of Autun** (*fl. c.* 400), who wrote on the Songs of Songs. Both men tended towards literalism, and were little influenced by Origen.

Eastern influences were, however, prominent, especially on Latin writers who had close contact with Greeks. This was true, for example, of **Hilary of Poitiers** (*fl. c.* 350–367), whose surviving commentary on the Psalms betrays the allegorizing influence of Origen. It was also true of **Ambrose of Milan** (*c.* 337–397), who followed the allegorical trend of the Origenists, though with a strong emphasis on the typological and moral aspects of allegory. Of his twenty or so exegetical works, fully half deal with different episodes in Genesis. Most of them seem to have been homiletical in origin, and they concentrate on denouncing various heretics and immoral people. Most of the rest deal with other Old Testament themes, and also have a strong moral bias. Only one is on the New Testament: a commentary on Luke, which sticks more closely to the text than is usual with Ambrose. However, the allegorical interpretation is given great prominence even in this work.

Quite different from these was **Marius Victorinus** (*fl. c.* 350–360), who wrote strictly literal commentaries on the Pauline epistles. These display a markedly anti-Jewish bias, and show that Marius's knowledge of the Old Testament was rudimentary. However, he was largely responsible for the revival of Pauline studies in the Latin-speaking world.

Ambrosiaster (*fl. c.* 370). Since the time of Erasmus, this name has been assigned to the anonymous writer of a commentary on the Pauline epistles which had been preserved under the name of Ambrose of Milan. It is a first-class piece of exegesis, which avoids allegory in favour of the literal and historical sense of the text, though it allows for a certain amount of typology. Also attributed to Ambrosiaster is a work dealing with difficult passages in both the Old and New Testaments, which has been preserved among the works of Augustine.

Tyconius (*fl. c.* 370–400). Somewhat of an oddball was Tyconius, an adherent of the Donatist sect in North Africa who fell out with them without joining the mainline church. He composed a very popular commentary on Revelation, fragments of which have been preserved. His approach is thoroughly allegorical, relating the book's imagery to the relationship between Christ and the church. In this way, he broke with the millenarian interpretation common before his time, and established what was to become the standard medieval interpretation. His main claim to fame is his *Book of Seven Rules* (*Liber Regularum* or *Liber de Septem Regulis*) which survives intact and is apparently the first handbook of biblical hermeneutics to have been written in the West. Even Augustine, who had no love for Donatists and must have found Tyconius's ecclesiology hard to swallow, appreciated this book and spoke highly of it. The book offers seven rules by which Scripture is to be read, and, while not primarily allegorical, it allows allegory to be used in cases where it helps to edify the reader who might otherwise be confronted with a difficult or ambiguous passage of Scripture.

Jerome (*c.* 347–419). Jerome (Hieronymus) was undoubtedly the greatest biblical scholar that the Latin church ever produced. Together with his friend Rufinus, he translated an enormous number of theological works from Greek into Latin, beginning with the Bible itself. Latin versions of the Bible (generally known collectively as the *Vetus Latina*, or Old Latin Bible) had been circulating for some time, but they were unsatisfactory. At the request of Damasus, Bishop of Rome, Jerome undertook a fresh translation, which he based on the Hebrew text of the Old Testament and on the Hexapla of Origen. The result was a magisterial translation which, together with the deuterocanonical books which were added by later hands, became known subsequently as the Popular, or 'Vulgate', Bible (*Biblia Vulgata*). The Vulgate quickly established itself as the main Latin version of the Scriptures, and for over a thousand years it was the standard text of the western church. Not until the time of Erasmus was its authority seriously questioned. In addition to this, Jerome also prepared a translation of the Psalms, which adhered more closely to the Septuagint than to the Hebrew. This version was adopted in Carolingian Gaul for liturgical use, and hence became known as the 'Gallican' Psalter. It continued to be used in the Roman Catholic Church until about 1950, when permission was obtained to use a newer Latin version.

Under the influence of Gregory of Nazianzus, Jerome began to translate a number of Origen's homilies on the prophets and two on the Song of Songs. But as Jerome's knowledge of Hebrew and of Jewish exegesis increased, so his attraction to Origen diminished. When controversy began over the works of Origen (about 393), Jerome sided with the anti-Origenists and broke with the allegorical tradition, at least in theory. This also led to a break in relations with Rufinus, who then began to translate Origen's works into Latin.

Jerome's exegetical work reflects the development of his thought away from Origen and back to the Hebrew. His commentaries on Ecclesiastes and Psalms belong to his Origenistic phase, while that on Genesis marks the transition. His later work on the minor prophets belongs to his anti-Origenist phase, but it is noticeable how much he was prepared to adapt Origenistic material to fit his own spiritual exposition of the text. His New Testament commentaries also reflect anti-Origenism, especially on doctrinal questions, though once again, his rejection of allegory was more apparent than real. In spite of what he says, Jerome remained tied to Origen's methods to a very large degree. There is a commentary on Matthew, on the Pauline epistles, and on Revelation. This last is really little more than a rewrite of an earlier commentary by Victorinus of Pettau, though he updated the earlier commentary by reference to Tyconius.

Pelagius (*fl. c.* 384–*c.* 420). Now known as one of the greatest heretics of the early church, Pelagius was a British monk who taught at Rome from 384 to 410. His views on grace and salvation attracted the notice of Augustine of Hippo, who began to attack them about 412. His commentary on the Pauline epistles, which is greatly indebted to Ambrosiaster, has been preserved under the names of Jerome and Primasius of Hadrumetum.

Augustine of Hippo (354–430). The greatest of the Latin fathers, Augustine's reputation rests on his theological rather than on his exegetical works. He was opposed to Jerome's use of the Hebrew text instead of the Septuagint, because he regarded this as a form of Judaizing. The apostles frequently used the Septuagint in their New Testament quotations, which led Augustine to assert that the Greek translation was inspired Scripture, on a par with the Hebrew. His view triumphed in the western church, and it was not until the Reformation that Jerome's position was vindicated. Among his vast literary output there are fourteen exegetical works of different kinds.

Augustine wrote a treatise on Christian doctrine (*De Doctrina Christiana*), which contains his theory of biblical interpretation. Basically, this was an amplification of Tyconius, whom he regarded as too simplistic. It also gives us his theory of the canon, which was that the authority of the biblical books derives from their acceptance by apostolic sees. The wider the acceptance, the greater was the authority of any particular book.

Augustine wrote commentaries on the Old Testament, in particular on the book of Genesis, which he interpreted first allegorically and then 'literally'. He also wrote about the difficult passages in the first seven books of the Old Testament, and later on eight selected passages from the text as a whole. There is also a book of notes on Job, which was put together by some of his disciples, and a very long work on Psalms (*Ennarationes in Psalmos*), which consists mainly of allegorical homilies. Like Jerome, Augustine rejected the allegorical method in theory, but continued to use it in practice.

Augustine's New Testament commentaries include two books on the Sermon on the Mount, two works on Romans, and one on Galatians. The commentaries on Paul follow a literalistic exegesis, but (perhaps surprisingly) they have never been widely read. There was also a commentary on James, which is now lost. Of greater importance are his writings on the gospels, which extend to a total of seven books. Four of these deal specifically with the problem of discrepancies in the gospel narratives, and are usually tied together as a single work, *De Consensu Evangelistarum*. Augustine generally tackled problems from a literalistic point of view, though he also frequently lapsed into allegory, especially when dealing with miracles and parables.

Oriental (Syriac and Armenian)

The fourth century witnessed a remarkable flowering of literature in Syriac, a dialect of Aramaic, which was the spoken language of Jesus. Unfortunately, the Syriac translations of the New Testament (*Peshitta*) reflect the Greek text more than they do the original Aramaic of Jesus. The same is partly true of the Old Testament, much of which seems to be a rendering of the Septuagint, though it has been demonstrated that the Pentateuch at least, as possibly also the Psalter, are dependent on a Targumic tradition, and are therefore directly linked to rabbinic exegesis. Syriac exegetical literature is mostly associated with the name of **Ephrem the Syrian** (306–373), who wrote commentaries in the literalistic style of Antioch. In Syriac there are commentaries on Genesis and Exodus, while his other works, on Tatian's *Diatessaron*, on Acts and on the Pauline epistles, are preserved in Armenian translations.

In Armenia the great native biblical expositor was **Mesrob (Mesrop)** (d. 440), under whose direction large numbers of works were translated from Greek and Syriac. He also sponsored, though probably did not write, commentaries on Joshua and Judges.

During the Christological controversies of the fifth century, the churches of Syria and Armenia were alienated from the churches of Rome and Constantinople, and eventually became what we now call 'monophysite', because of their belief that the incarnate Christ had only one (divine) nature, and not two natures, as the Council of

Chalcedon (451) had affirmed. Their biblical interpretation has remained frozen in the classical texts since that time.

From 451 to 604

The final phase of patristic exegesis is characterized mainly by its relative poverty. There are only nine Greek commentaries extant for the centuries from the Council of Chalcedon (451) to the Second Council of Nicaea (787), in spite of the intense theological activity which characterized this period, and none of them is of any real value. All but one (on Acts) concentrate on one of the three favourite areas of biblical exegesis: the wisdom literature, the gospels, and Revelation, which during this period was fully accepted in the Greek-speaking churches for the first time. For example, **Gregory of Agrigentum** (*fl. c.* 575) wrote a literalistic commentary on Ecclesiastes, which was nevertheless laced with Christological typology. On Revelation, there are commentaries by **Oecumenius** (*fl. c.* 580) and by **Andrew of Caesarea** (*fl. c.* 620). Both are highly allegorical, but the former is more Christological and amillenarian, whereas the latter sticks to a more eschatological approach. There is also an *Introduction to the Sacred Scriptures* by an otherwise unknown **Hadrianus** (*fl. c.* 525). This short work tries to explain the peculiar features of biblical language, most of which are attributed to Hebraic principles of style and composition. The most fruitful development in this period was the emergence of so-called *Catenae* ('chains'), which are compilations of extracts taken from earlier writers and related to particular books of the Bible – a kind of commentary digest. The first of these is supposed to have been produced by **Procopius of Gaza** (d. *c.* 526). The *Catenae* are of particular value because they preserve large portions of commentaries which are otherwise lost.

In the Latin West, **Prosper of Aquitaine** (*fl. c.* 400) rewrote Augustine on the Psalms; **Justus of Urgel** (*fl. c.* 550) produced a Christological commentary on the Song of Songs; **Apringius of Beja** (*fl. c.* 550) and **Primasius** (*fl. c.* 650) followed Tyconius on Revelation and **Verecundius Iuncensis** (*fl. c.* 520) wrote on nine canticles of the Old Testament, applying their message to the troubles of his own time. The commentaries of **Cassiodorus** (*fl. c.* 550) and **Gregory the Great** (*c.* 540–604) deserve special mention. Cassiodorus demonstrated a sure grasp of classical Greek patristic exegesis, and his commentary on the Psalms became a classic. Gregory specialized in a moralizing form of allegory, though he was aware of the excesses to which this was prone and warned against them. For him, personal moral edification was the chief purpose of Bible reading, and it was to this end that he dedicated his exegetical work. Most of what we now have consists of commentaries on Kings, Job and Ezekiel, as well as forty selections from the gospels. His *Moralia in Iob* (*Moral Lessons from Job*) quickly became, and still remains, the most widely admired of these.

Exegetical helps were popular in the Latin West, as can be seen from the treatises of **Eucherius of Lyon** (*fl. c.* 434–455), who established precise rules for the practice of allegory. Somewhat more ambitious was the work of **Quodvultdeus** (*fl. c.* 440), who examined the prophetical passages of Scripture with a view to explaining their obscurer features.

The issues

Patristic biblical exegesis grew up at a time when the church was faced with a number of crucial problems which it needed to solve, and interpretation of the Bible played a key role in this. The main issues confronting the fathers of the church can be set out as follows.

1. *It was necessary for them to distinguish Christianity from Judaism.* The early church had to explain why it rejected Judaism, without abandoning the Jewish Scriptures. At one extreme were people such as Marcion, who wanted to reject the Jewish heritage altogether, but found that this was practically impossible. At the other were people such as Tertullian, for whom Christianity was a more thorough-going legalism than anything the Jews had attempted. The mainline Christian church could accept neither of these positions, but it had to find a viable interpretation of the Old Testament as Christian Scripture. This task was such a top priority throughout this period that the history of exegesis can very largely be written in terms of it alone.

2. *It was necessary for them to distinguish Christianity from pagan mystery cults and from Hellenistic philosophy.* The danger of syncretism was always very real, as the recent rediscovery of New Testament apocrypha has shown. There was never any shortage of preachers and charlatans who were prepared to seize on the supernatural elements of the Christian message, such as the virgin birth of Christ or his resurrection, and create a new religion out of them. The tendency to restrict this new knowledge to an inner circle of initiates was also extremely powerful, particularly during the centuries when

Christianity was itself a proscribed sect. After the end of persecution, the main danger came from contemporary philosophy, especially Neoplatonism, whose similarity to many aspects of Christianity was frequently a trap for the unwary. Christianity could never be one philosophy among others, nor could it comfortably blend with Platonism, however appealing the latter might seem. In spite of all the allegorizing of Scripture, Christian Platonism remained an impossibility, because of biblical teaching about the essential goodness of matter. Two doctrines expressed this most clearly: divine creation out of nothing, and the resurrection of the flesh, which underlined the Christian belief that matter would be redeemed as well as spirit.

3. *It was necessary for them to define the Christian God and the nature of Christ.* We now know that the answer to this problem was to be that God is three persons in one nature, and that Christ is one (divine) person manifested in two natures (one divine and one human). But it took several centuries to reach this conclusion, and even then, the doctrine of Christ proclaimed at Chalcedon was not accepted by a large section of the eastern church. Arguments taken from Scripture played a major role in all of this, and it was no accident that different Christologies were associated with different schools of biblical exegesis.

4. *It was necessary for them to demonstrate how the Bible could and should be applied to the Christian life.* This was perhaps the most important single purpose which lay behind the production of commentaries on Scripture, and it became more important as time went on. The strangeness of the Old Testament and of much of the New had to be overcome, and this led to the development of allegorical exegesis. Though despised and rejected today, allegory performed an important task in the early church because it provided a means whereby an ancient and essentially foreign text could be applied to the practical concerns of everyday life. This in turn made ordinary Christians more conscious of the relevance of the Bible to their spiritual experience, and gave them a greater desire to hear and learn from the text.

5. *It was necessary for them to maintain the unity of the church, as a living witness of the unity of the truth manifested in Christ.* This meant that they had to provide a single, authoritative text of Scripture which would be accepted by everyone, as the prelude to formulating a single (and in practice, equally authoritative) doctrinal interpretation of it. All the great biblical scholars of the time were preoccupied with this problem, from Tatian through Origen to Eusebius, Jerome and even

Mesrob. The establishment of a fixed doctrine in the great creeds was paralleled by the establishment of a fixed canonical text, which supported that doctrine.

The methods of interpretation

When considering the methods of biblical interpretation most commonly used in patristic times, we may conveniently follow the periodization adopted above.

Before AD *200*

The period up to about AD 200 is characterized by what might be called pre-systematic biblical exegesis. Before the time of Origen there were no Christian commentaries on Scripture, and little attempt was made to offer a methodical exposition of its contents. Those who came closest to this were people such as Marcion, who was unable to do more than reject the greater part of the sacred text because it did not fit his hermeneutic. The most frequent type of exegetical literature during this period was the homily, or sermon, a mode of discourse which has continued to the present, and which was popular throughout patristic times.

Among those who took the text at face value, a basically literalistic interpretation was dominant, though the sermon style lent itself to allegory, particularly of a moralizing kind. The literalistic approach reflects the influence of the New Testament, which interpreted the Old in terms of the fulfilment of prophecy in and by Jesus Christ. This theme rapidly became the universal distinguishing mark of all Christian exegesis. Apart from Christ, the Scriptures were incomprehensible, and so it was permissible to find reference to him in any way possible. The Christocentric bias of this early period produced tendencies towards typological and allegorical exegesis, but in an unsystematic way. Many writers were probably unaware of what they were doing, as they sought to relate every Scripture passage somehow or other to Christ. It is therefore wrong to say that typology or allegory formed the basis of their hermeneutic. The factor which gave unity to their exegesis was the person and work of Christ.

The fact that Judaism had its own interpretation of Scripture, but that Jews rejected Christ, was explained by saying that Judaism read the text according to the letter, not according to the Spirit. Paul's warning in 2 Corinthians 3:6 ('the letter kills, but the Spirit gives life') became axiomatic for the fathers of the early church. To them, what Paul meant was that the literalistic exegesis of Scripture, as practised by the rabbis, was deadly. Only the spiritual interpretation, which they understood as radically Christological, was true. Defining this became the main task of patristic exegesis, and different schools of thought produced their own versions of what it was. But all were agreed that a spiritual interpretation was essential, and that to interpret Scripture in a merely literal way was to fall back into Judaism and spiritual bondage.

It was quite clear, however, that Gnostic-type interpretations could not be regarded as compatible with Christian exegesis. First of all, they were not Christocentric. To the Gnostics, Christ was at best the means to an end, and at worst irrelevant; he was not the end in himself. Second, they forged a radical divide between creation and redemption, which the Christian gospel held together in Christ. This is the importance of John 1:1–3 and Colossians 1:15–17, which speak of Christ as co-creator with the Father. The Christian emphasis on creation (and also on the incarnation of Christ, which was the entry of God into creation) was at least partly due to Gnostic and Platonic attempts to deny the goodness of matter and the absolute sovereignty of the Christian God.

We have already seen that one characteristic of this period is its interest in salvation history. This could be worked out in linear fashion, as in Tertullian, or in a recapitulatory manner, as in Irenaeus. Either way, it lent itself readily to typology. In the linear scheme, each of the three ages of human history had its own inner logic, which was reproduced on a higher level in the succeeding age. In the first age, which corresponded to the Old Testament, God made himself known imperfectly in the law and in the sacrifices. When Christ appeared, this pattern of revelation was swept away by a new law (Christ's moral demands) and a new sacrifice (Christ's death on the cross). In the third age, the post-Pentecostal reign of the Holy Spirit, Christians were called to advance towards full perfection.

Tertullian believed that many New Testament provisions, such as the permission given to widows to remarry, or the freedom not to fast when the bridegroom was present, were actually concessions to the weakness of the flesh. Jesus allowed such things because the fullness of perfection had not yet come, but they were not part of his ideal plan. He himself recognized the limitations of what was possible in his lifetime, because he promised that when the Spirit came he would do greater things, and lead God's people into all truth. Furthermore, as time went on, the second coming of Christ inevitably drew nearer, and Christians had no time to lose. It is a great mistake to imagine that this parousia hope, as waiting for the second coming is often called, diminished in late New Testament times. All the evidence is that it increased, as the gospel spread to the ends of the earth and persecution became more serious – two characteristic signs that the end was approaching. The result of this was that the New Testament principle of a sinless life of Christlike perfection cancelled out many New Testament practices which fell short of this ideal.

The recapitulatory view of history was significantly different from the linear view, because the new dispensation was not intended to replace the old one, but rather to heal its deficiencies. It is this aspect of healing and restoration which gives the cyclical view a universalistic thrust, because at the end of time all things, good and evil, will be reconciled in Christ. The linear view, by contrast, discarded the old altogether, and looked forward to something new which would replace, not reconcile, what had gone before. Many of the later differences between West and East can be explained by the fact that the former adopted the linear view of history and the latter the cyclical, and each read the Bible accordingly.

From 200 to 325

From about 200, the commentary style of exegesis introduced a note of greater systematization into Christian biblical interpretation. The commentary form originated in the intertestamental period, among the Hellenistic literary critics of Alexandria, and it was originally applied to the classics of Greek literature, which they interpreted allegorically. Soon there were many Jews who adapted this tradition to the interpretation of the Scriptures. Thus Philo inherited his ideas from disparate sources, and much of what he wrote was basically a collection of earlier material. Because of him, commentary writing was initially associated with allegorical exegesis, and the fathers never fully liberated themselves from that tradition.

Philo inherited most of his theories from Stoic and Platonic sources. From the Stoics he got the idea that philosophy was divided into three parts: logic, physics and ethics, in ascending order of importance. For him, theology was closely tied to ethics, including knowledge of the Creator as well as the right behaviour to which such knowledge would inevitably lead. From the Platonists, Philo inherited the belief that there was a fundamental contrast between the external world of passing sensation and disorder, and the internal world of unchanging reason and harmony. His was a basic distinction which characterized not only his exegesis, but also that of the entire allegorical tradition.

Philo regarded Scripture as a code book which provided a symbolic language to guide those skilled in interpreting it into eternal, spiritual truth. He completely rejected the literal sense of those biblical passages which portrayed God in human terms. He also rejected anything which might appear to diminish the glory of God. That meant that any biblical text which seemed to be nonsensical, immoral or just trivial was automatically reinterpreted in an allegorical way. Philo believed that the whole of Scripture, including the Torah, was prophecy, which God had inspired by taking possession of his chosen prophets and messengers. It was for this reason that it often appeared to be irrational, making allegorical exegesis necessary. Of course, to his way of thinking, the spiritual interpretation of Scripture was also inspired, and in this field he regarded himself as a channel through whom God was speaking.

Philo's sense of inspiration extended to the Septuagint, which he believed had been given by God, and his own freedom in quoting the text may be due to the sense that he too was inspired. Some idea of his method can be gleaned from a look at his exposition of Genesis 14 (in *De Abrahamo* 232–244):

> He collected his servants . . . made a roll-call . . . and distributed them into centuries and advanced with three battalions . . . His nephew he brought back . . . with all the horses of the cavalry . . .
>
> This is what we find in the Scriptures read literally, but those who can contemplate facts stripped of the body and naked in reality, those who live with the soul rather than the body, will say that of these nine kings, four are the power exercised within us by the four passions – pleasure, desire, fear and grief; and that the five are the five senses – sight, hearing, taste, smell and touch. For these nine are in a sense invested with sovereignty and are our kings and rulers, though not all in the same way. For the five are subject to the four . . . Griefs and pleasures and fears and desires arise out of what we see or hear or smell or taste or touch . . .
>
> There is much philosophic truth in saying that of the five kings, two fell into the wells and three took to flight (v. 10). For touch and taste descend to the lowest recesses of the body and transmit to its inward parts what may properly be dealt with by

them; but eyes and ears and smell for the most part pass outside and escape enslavement by the body . . .

This fascinating passage gives us the essence of Philonic allegory. The literal sense of the text is mentioned, only to be ignored. Whether the event described actually happened or not is completely irrelevant; history has no role to play in allegory, in sharp contrast to its function in typology. The 'facts' are what can be gleaned when the outward covering of words and events is stripped away to reveal the naked 'truth'. What we are really doing here is dealing with the passions and senses of the individual human being, and the commentary quickly slides into moral exhortation.

Note that what Philo is saying is not especially false in itself. The difficulty with allegory is not that it is morally or spiritually misleading, but that it bases moral and spiritual reflections on a false reading of the text. The Genesis passage is not saying what Philo wants it to say, and so even if what he says is true in itself, it is not related to the text he is supposed to be expounding. Allegory can be compared to astrology, where a science (astronomy) is linked to intuitive psychology without any logical connection between them.

Christians first resorted to allegory on a large scale in defence of the Old Testament against Marcion. When Marcion accused the Jews of worshipping an immoral God who demanded sacrifices, and who ordered his people to slay their enemies without mercy, his Christian opponents took refuge in an interpretation which attached a secret, spiritual meaning to something which was equally unpalatable to them. The aim of Christian commentators was to achieve a harmony between the two Testaments, and it was in this endeavour that allegory was most useful. Clement of Alexandria made some attempt to systematize this on the basis of a basic distinction between the outward and the inward sense of Scripture, but it was left to Origen to develop a comprehensive theory (*De Prin.* 4:1–23).

Origen argued that the authority of the Old Testament is confirmed by Christ, so that all interpretation of it must ultimately be Christocentric. He added that the Scriptures have a threefold sense, corresponding to body, soul and spirit. This tripartite division is based on an anthropology different from that of Philo, who identified the soul with the spirit – an option not available to the Christian, for whom soul and spirit were divided by the two-edged sword of the Word of God (Heb. 4:12). The first sense is the literal one, designed for the non-intellectual mind, but necessary as the basis from which the other senses were to be discerned. The second is the moral one, corresponding to the life of the soul. The third is the spiritual sense, the highest and most important of all. Origen gave it the special name *theoria* (vision), because it could only be grasped by revelation. For him, it was necessary for the Christian reader of the Bible to proceed from the literal to the higher senses, which he termed 'anagogical' (leading), because they led the believer closer to Christ.

Origen regarded the Bible as a divine revelation concealed in human form. God's commands are eternal and absolute, in accordance with his nature, but our circumstances are relative. This is why Scripture, which conceals God's law in human events, is often ambiguous and unclear to us. Only the inner witness of the Holy Spirit, using the gifts of biblical scholarship, can unlock the key to the Scriptures and make them intelligible to the church. The first rule of interpretation is that the clearer parts of Scripture are the basis for understanding the harder parts. It is interesting to note that this principle has survived the test of time, and is widely applied today, even though allegorical exegesis has long been rejected.

In his interpretation of Scripture, Origen usually took the literal sense at face value. He did not want to reduce the miracles of Jesus and other supernatural events to allegory, because he genuinely believed that God had intervened in human history. In these instances, he regarded the spiritual sense as an addition to the literal, not as a substitute for it. On other occasions though, he rejected the literal sense; for example, he did not accept that the trees in the Garden of Eden were real objects, nor did he believe that Jesus was literally taken into a high mountain by the devil. Sometimes it is not clear whether he accepted the literal sense or not, as in the opening chapters of Genesis, or the story of Jesus' cleansing of the temple (which he saw as an allegory of the purification of the soul). In these cases, the allegorical sense was certainly the one that mattered, whatever value might be attached to the literal one.

Origen was not comfortable with history as an interlocking series of cause and effect, and in fact he scarcely knew what to make of it. He explicitly stated that historical events are not to be regarded as types of other historical events, but as types of spiritual realities (*Comm. on John* 10, 18). It is this which distances him from earlier typologists, and which is characteristic of allegory. Particularly susceptible to allegorical interpretation were proper names, which were known to have a deeper meaning. Plants, animals and geographical place names also lent themselves to this type of treatment, as did numbers, which were often clearly symbolic in any case.

On occasion, Origen used all three senses in the same passage, as for example in his exposition of the story of Lot (Gn. 19). He accepted the historical facts, and then went on to say that spiritually it illustrates Israel's relationship to the law. Finally he brought out its moral dimension, according to which the characters in the narrative stand for virtues and vices. Often, however, the spiritual sense prevailed over the moral, or the two were mixed together. Sometimes more than one spiritual sense was possible, as in the Song of Songs, where the bridegroom and the bride might refer either to Christ and the church or to the Word of God and the individual soul.

Origen's authority as a biblical expositor was such that his methods were largely unchallenged for 150 years. By the time his theology came under suspicion, and he faced condemnation, the influence of his exegetical methods was too great to be ignored. Even Jerome, who opposed him bitterly, was compelled to borrow large chunks of his hermeneutic and adapt them to his own requirements.

Allegory may be summed up, both positively and negatively, as follows. On the positive side, it emphasized that Scripture must be approached spiritually, and be applied practically to the life of the believer. The Bible had to be a living book in the experience of the church, not a dead historical record. Allegory also made it possible for the church to appropriate very obscure passages of the Bible, which would not otherwise have been usable. We must not forget that the ancients did not have the same understanding of the historical context of the Old Testament as we have, and thus many things which are intelligible to us were mysteries to them. We should also remember that much Christian art, and some Christian literature, relies heavily on allegory for its themes. Without allegory, iconography would not have been possible, nor would we now have the great literary monuments of Dante, Milton or Bunyan.

On the negative side, allegory removed the text of Scripture from history, which went against the main thrust of the Christian religion. It encouraged an irresponsible use of the biblical text by permitting interpretations which were fanciful, even if spiritually they were more helpful than harmful. In modern times, an essentially allegorical hermeneutic has made it possible for the Roman church to proclaim dogmas such as the immaculate conception of Mary, her bodily assumption into heaven, and the infallibility of the pope, with little scriptural basis other than an allegorical interpretation of texts which have no literal bearing on any of these things.

From 325 to 451

The golden age of patristic exegesis is marked by a fundamental divide between Alexandrian and Antiochene types of interpretation. The western church felt the influence of both, in different degrees, and the Cappadocians were virtually forced to choose between them. The oriental churches of Syria and Armenia were geographical extensions of Antioch, but they underwent profound Alexandrian influence at a later stage.

Alexandrian exegesis

This was characterized by its faithfulness to the Origenistic tradition of allegorical exegesis, though this was increasingly carefully nuanced as time went on. In particular, it was believed that the church's official doctrine should be based only on the literal sense, where that could be clearly discerned. Nobody should be required to accept an interpretation of Scripture which was not plain to everyone. As a result, the great doctrinal debates of the fourth and fifth centuries were conducted mainly at the level of literal exegesis, nuanced by a Christological interpretation of the Old Testament. Thus, for example, Proverbs 8:22ff. was regarded as a foreshadowing of Christ by all sides in the Arian controversy, since once it was agreed that all Scripture referred to him, the Christological interpretation seemed 'literal' enough!

In the third century, Dionysius of Alexandria asserted that the human experiences of Christ should be taken literally, because of the historical reality of the incarnation and the genuineness of his humanity. This idea was taken up and developed by Athanasius, who regarded the incarnation as the key to understanding Scripture, in spite of the difficulties which he had in accepting the limitations of Jesus' humanity. For him the Bible was not merely a linguistic shell, behind which ineffable theological truths could be discerned, but the very Word of God in its literal ('incarnate') sense. Athanasius therefore rejected the Platonic (and Origenistic) division between the material and the spiritual, and believed that they were in harmony with one another. For Athanasius, the inspiration of Scripture was directly parallel to the incarnation of Christ, and the relationship between Word and Spirit was the same for both. Like Jesus, the Bible was fully human (though without error) and fully divine. By stating this doctrine in the way he did, Athanasius was able to link the ancient Christocentric interpretation of Scripture with the most up-to-date dogmatic affirmation of Christ's two natures.

In the course of his arguments against the atomistic 'proof-texting' interpretation of the Arians, Athanasius said that it was not enough to base one's interpretation of a biblical text on exegesis alone. All interpretation must take place in a context, and for the Christian, that context was the life and spiritual experience of the church. It was the church, as much as the Bible, which bore witness to the divinity of Christ, and therefore the Scriptures must be interpreted in a way which is consistent with this testimony. This principle led him to adopt a Christological allegorization of the Psalms. They were not merely ancient poems, but the living hymnal of the church, which uses them to praise and worship the triune God. Athanasius was the first Christian exegete to place the church so firmly in the centre of his hermeneutic, and his approach remains characteristic of both Roman Catholic and Eastern Orthodox interpretation to this day.

Once the church's doctrine was established in the creeds, they could be used as rules to govern allegorical interpretation. The harder parts of Scripture were regarded as presenting known Christian truth in an allegorical way, and it was the duty of the exegete to point this out. This development did little to curb the excesses of allegory, but it did at least make the conclusions more predictable, and more acceptable to the church at large. Once again, we are faced with the perennial dilemma of allegory: the conclusions may be fine, but the means by which they are obtained are totally unacceptable.

Didymus the Blind followed the lines laid down by Athanasius, and developed them further. He reaffirmed the value of the literal sense of the Old Testament, by saying that although it had been abolished in Christ, it had previously been fully operational as the Word of God. It was therefore perfectly natural that the Jews should reject allegorical interpretation of their Scriptures, which became necessary only after the coming of Christ. Didymus insisted that the Old Testament was not to be understood as a veiling of eternal truths which were just as valid as those of the New Testament, but rather as a preparatory teaching, pointing the ancient Israelites towards the future coming of Christ. In other words, even an allegorical reading of the Old Testament could never reveal the fullness of the gospel, which was made plain only at the time of the incarnation of the Word of God.

Antiochene exegesis

Competing with the Alexandrian approach, and in many ways profoundly opposed to it, was the exegesis of the theological school of Antioch. For the representatives of this school, the spiritual sense (*theoria*) of Scripture was not allegorical, but was to be sought in the literal sense itself. This type of exegesis corresponded with their Christology, which stressed that the humanity of Christ was not modified in any way by his divinity. The greatest exponent of the Antiochene exegetical method was Theodore of Mopsuestia, who rebuked the allegorizers for their tendency to lapse into fables far removed from historical fact. It was this question of history which most disturbed Theodore, because he recognized that an allegorical treatment of Adam, for example, would undermine the claim of Christ to be the new Adam. If the fall of humankind were merely a fable, how could redemption have any real meaning? When challenged to explain Paul's use of 'allegory' (Gal. 4:24), Theodore simply stated that Paul was using the word in a different sense, that of historical correspondence, or typology – an explanation which is still widely accepted today.

Even more striking was Theodore's literalistic use of the Psalms. Only very occasionally would he allow a Christological interpretation, as in Psalm 16:10. Most of the time, he insisted that the Psalms refer either to David or to Israelite history before the coming of Christ. Theodore did not question the Davidic authorship of the Psalter, but it is clear from his treatment of it that he was prepared to accept that it was composed over many centuries after David's time. As for Christ's use of the Psalms in reference to himself, Theodore explained this by saying that Jesus found himself in circumstances analogous to those of David, and so it was appropriate for him to 'borrow' David's sentiments.

Other Antiochene writers continued in this vein, and even rejected the notion that the entire Old Testament referred directly to Christ. Forcing texts into a Christological pattern which did not suit them merely alienated pagans, and blinded them to those passages which did prophesy the coming of the Messiah. This was the view of **Isidore of Pelusium** (*c.* 360–435), as can be seen from his correspondence on the subject (2, 195). Another Antiochene writer, **Severian of Gabala** (*fl. c.* 400–410), who practised an extreme form of literalistic exegesis, insisted that it is one thing to preserve the historical sense and add the spiritual to it, and quite another to confuse the historical sense by allegory. Like Christ himself, Scripture had two natures which could not be confused, mingled or distorted in any way.

From the modern point of view there is no doubt that Antiochene exegesis is the more attractive of the two great schools of antiquity, and it therefore comes as something of a disappointment to discover that many of its great exponents were later condemned by the church. This was because they were unable to develop a satisfactory Christology, one which would unite the two natures of Christ in a real, personal union. The close connection between Christology and biblical exegesis meant that condemnation of the one inevitably led to rejection of the other. In fairness, however, it should be said that those Antiochenes whose Christology was not suspect did not suffer, and their works became the most popular commentaries of all. This was certainly the case with John Chrysostom, and to a large extent with Theodoret of Cyrrhus as well. We must also not forget that Origen was condemned, and that his philosophical allegorizing was rejected by the church along with the literalism of Antioch.

Western (Latin) exegesis

The exegesis of the western church not unnaturally shows the strong influence of eastern tendencies. Many exegetes were attracted by Alexandrian methods, which can be seen in Hilary of Poitiers, Ambrose of Milan and the young Jerome. Antiochene exegesis made less headway, but the Latin world had its own literalist tradition which went back to Tertullian. In the fourth century, this was systematized by Tyconius in his famous seven rules, which provided Augustine with his basic exegetical framework. The seven rules are as follows.

1. *De Domino et corpore eius* (on the Lord and his body). This says that Scripture does not distinguish between the person of Christ and his body, which is the church. Thus for example, when Daniel 2:34 speaks of the stone which destroys the kingdoms of the world, he is prophesying about the coming of Christ, but when this stone subsequently becomes a mountain filling the whole earth, it is no longer Christ who is meant but the church. Scripture passes from one to the other without hesitation or distinction.

2. *De Domini corpore bipartito* (on the twofold body of Christ). Christ's body has two parts, both good and bad. There is no pure church, but the wheat and tares grow together until the harvest. It is for this reason that the bride in Song of Songs 1:5 can say, 'I am black and beautiful.'

3. *De promissis et lege* (on the promises and the Law). This rule is intended to clarify those passages in Romans and Galatians where it seems that the Law is presented sometimes positively and sometimes negatively. This is explained by referring to the preparatory nature of

the Law; it was good in its day, but inadequate as a means of eternal salvation.

4. *De specie et genere* (on the particular and the universal). This explains that Scripture sometimes moves from the particular to the general, and *vice versa.* Thus the Old Testament prophets mention cities which are figures of the church, sometimes of the whole body of Christ, and sometimes of only a part of it. A good example of this is Jonah's treatment of Nineveh, which is saved (the whole church) in spite of its wickedness (part of the church). This rule is somewhat similar to Hillel's fifth rule, *Kelal upherat,* though there is no indication that Tyconius knew of it.

5. *De temporibus (*on times). This rule seeks to resolve chronological problems in Scripture by saying that sometimes a part of the time is used for the whole and *vice versa.* Thus 'the 400 years oppression' which Israel endured in Egypt, predicted in Genesis 15:13 and mentioned again in Exodus 12:40, does not mean that Israel was oppressed for each of those years, but that the people sojourned in Egypt for that length of time, and that in the end they were oppressed.

6. *De recapitulatione* (on abbreviation). This explains why Scripture sometimes reduces to a single moment a concept which is much broader in reality. Thus the eschatological warnings of Matthew 24:15–18 and Luke 17:30ff. are valid not just for the second coming of Christ, but at all times.

7. *De diabolo et corpore eius* (on the devil and his body). This corresponds exactly to the first rule. When Scripture refers to the devil, it also includes those who belong to him, *i.e.* the wicked on this earth. Thus when Isaiah describes the fall of Lucifer (19:12), the mention of kings and peoples may be construed as a reference to the devil's body.

In practice, Tyconius's exegesis was governed by the fact that he was a renegade Donatist. It was a basic Donatist belief that the church was spotlessly pure, and Tyconius spent much of his time demonstrating that this was not so. According to him, the presence of corruption in the church did not mean that it was not the body of Christ, but rather underlined the fact that Christ was truly human. As the remains of his commentary on Revelation show, he was prepared to use allegory extensively, though it is probably unfair to judge him from this one example, since Revelation clearly lends itself to that kind of treatment.

Augustine adopted Tyconius's rules and made great use of them, especially of the first, but he was also aware of their deficiencies. In an effort to make up for these, he added the following important points.

1. The authority of Scripture rests on the authority of the church. It is as the church receives the sacred text that it acquires its authority, so that books which are less universally recognized are correspondingly less authoritative. As he originally stated this, Augustine almost certainly intended to strengthen the authority of Scripture, not weaken it. Only much later was his doctrine turned on its head, to be used by the Roman church as justification for its own claims to control the reading and interpretation of the Bible.

2. The obscurities in Scripture have been put there by God, and may be interpreted on the basis of the many plain passages. This doctrine, which repeats the view of Origen in a non-allegorical context, has continued to function as a main principle of biblical exegesis up to the present time.

3. When Scripture is ambiguous, the rule of faith can be used to interpret it. Augustine mentioned the difficult punctuation of John 1:1–2 as an example of this. It could be construed to read: '. . . and there was God. This Word was in the beginning with God', giving an Arian interpretation of Christ. But it must not be read in this way, because the church's faith says otherwise. The true reading is '. . . and the Word was God. This was in the beginning with God.'

4. Figurative passages must not be taken literally. In the debate over literalism, attention must be paid to the literary form of each text. Of course, Augustine had his own way of deciding what was figurative, which causes problems for modern readers. In his opinion, anything which did not seem to lead to good behaviour or true faith was 'figurative'. This was also true of anything wicked or unworthy ascribed to God, or to the saints; though in some cases customs have changed, so that Old Testament polygamy is not necessarily to be seen in this light.

5. A figure need not always have only one meaning. Meaning may vary with the context, as when the word 'shield' signifies both God's good pleasure (Ps. 5:13) and faith (Eph. 6:16). Augustine goes on to say that because a figure may have several meanings, it may be interpreted in a way which the author did not intend, but which accords with what can be found in other parts of Scripture. Augustine believed that the Holy Spirit had already provided for this possibility, and legitimized such a handling of the text.

6. Any possible meaning which a text can have is legitimate, whether the author realized it or not. Augustine argued that truth could be apprehended at many different levels, and it was wrong to limit a

biblical text to only one meaning. This was the argument he used to justify his widespread use of figurative (allegorical) interpretation.

His treatment of the feeding of the five thousand is a good example of this. Augustine starts off by saying that miracles are intended to remind us that the whole universe is miraculous, and that God's providential ordering of the created order is a far greater miracle than merely feeding 5,000 people with five loaves and two small fishes. The story itself contains a wealth of detail which is meant to point us to Christ. The fact that he is on the mountain reminds us that the Word is on high. The five loaves are the Pentateuch, and they are of barley because barley is hard to extract from its covering of chaff, just as the spiritual message of the Old Testament is hard to discern under the layer of outward symbolism. The little boy represents Israel, which possessed the divine nourishment but did not feed on it. The 5,000 stand for Israel under the law; they recline on the grass because their thoughts are carnal, and all flesh is grass. The twelve baskets of leftovers were the many teachings which the people could not receive. They were entrusted to the apostles, whose duty it would be to nourish the people with them at a later date.

From 451 to 604

By the end of the patristic period, exegetical methods had been fairly securely established. Allegorical interpretation, shorn of the philosophical extremes of Origen, was the norm in almost every case. The influence of Augustine in the West was all-pervasive, and his authority was accepted without question. Subsequent exegetes did little more than repeat the classics, often abbreviating them in the process, and confined originality to their own speculations about the meaning of obscure words and phrases, or the peculiarities of biblical style. The one truly creative writer was Gregory the Great, who insisted that the historical or literal sense must be preserved as the foundation on which typological and moral allegory could be built. With these principles in mind, he sifted through the vast store of patristic exegesis, and retained only those elements which he believed were of permanent value. In a sense, Gregory made a canonical selection of patristic exegesis for the benefit of future generations. His own contribution to the development of exegesis lay mainly in his belief that Scripture is a mirror of the soul. In reading the Bible, the Christian learns, from the way in which God dealt with the saints, how God also deals with us. The examples set before us in Scripture are there to teach us what our own strengths and weaknesses are, so that we may grow in faith and love, in humility and in spiritual assurance. This personal note was to be one of the chief distinguishing marks of medieval spirituality. With Gregory we have reached the end of the ancient world and the beginning of a new era, in which the shape of the modern world started to emerge.

BIBLIOGRAPHY

General works

B. Altaner and A. Stuiber, *Patrologie* (Freiburg, Basel and Wien: Herder, 9th edn, 1978).

G. W. H. Lampe (ed.), *The Cambridge History of the Bible* 2 (Cambridge: Cambridge University Press, 1969).

T. Oden (ed.), *Ancient Christian Commentary on Scripture* (Downers Grove, IL: IVP, 1996–).

J. Quasten, *Patrology*, vols. 1–3 (Utrecht and Antwerp: Spectrum, 1950–60); vol. 4, ed. A. di Bernardino (Westminster, MD: Christian Classics, 1986).

Philo

Y. Amir, 'Authority and Interpretation of Scripture in the Writings of Philo', in M. J. Mulder (ed.), *Mikra: Text, Translation, Reading and Interpretation of the Hebrew Bible in Ancient Judaism and Early Christianity* (Assen: Van Gorcum, 1988).

P. Borgen, 'Philo of Alexandria: A Critical and Synthetical Survey of Research since World War II', *Aufstieg und Niedergang der römischen Welt* II, 21–1 (1984), pp. 98–154.

D. Brown, *Vir Trilinguis: A Study in the Biblical Exegesis of Saint Jerome* (Kampen: Kok Pharos, 1992).

H. Chadwick, 'Philo and the Beginnings of Christian Thought', in A. H. Armstrong (ed.), *The Cambridge History of Later Greek and Early Medieval Philosophy* (Cambridge: Cambridge University Press, 1967).

E. R. Goodenough, *An Introduction to Philo Judaeus* (New Haven: Yale University Press, 1940; Oxford: Oxford University Press, 1962).

R. D. Hecht, 'Patterns of Exegesis in Philo's Interpretation of Leviticus', *Studia Philonica* 6 (1979–80), pp. 77–155.

P. Katz, *The Aberrant Text of Bible Quotations in Some Philonic Writings and its Place in the Textual History of the Greek Bible* (Cambridge: Cambridge University Press, 1950).

B. L. Mack, 'Exegetical Traditions in Alexandrian Judaism: A Program for the Analysis of the Philonic Corpus', *Studia Philonica* 3 (1974–75), pp. 71–112.

S. Sandmel, 'Philo's Environment and Philo's Exegesis', *Journal of Bible and Religion* 22 (1954), pp. 248–253.

T. H. Tobin, *The Creation of Man: Philo and the History of Interpretation* (Washington: *Catholic Biblical Quarterly* Monograph 14, 1983).

H. A. Wolfson, *Philo* (Cambridge, MA: Harvard University Press, 1947).

Church fathers

J. N. S. Alexander, 'The Interpretation of Scripture in the Ante-Nicene Period', *Interpretation* 12 (1958), pp. 272–280.

D. Attwater, *St John Chrysostom: Pastor and Preacher* (London: Harvill, 1959).

D. E. Aune, 'Early Christian Biblical Interpretation', *Evangelical Quarterly* 41 (1969), pp. 89–96.

W. Babcock, 'Augustine's Interpretation of Romans', *Augustinian Studies* 10 (1979), pp. 55–74.

———*Tyconius' Book of Rules* (Atlanta: Scholars Press, 1989).

J. Breck, 'Theoria and Orthodox Hermeneutics', *St Vladimir's Theological Quarterly* 20 (1976), pp. 195–219.

G. W. Bromiley, 'The Church Fathers and Holy Scripture', in D. A. Carson and J. Woodbridge (eds.), *Scripture and Truth* (Grand Rapids: Zondervan, 1983), pp. 199–224.

W. J. Burghardt, 'On Early Christian Exegesis', *Theological Studies* 11 (1950), pp. 647–658.

R. J. Daly, 'The Hermeneutics of Origen', in *The Word in the World: Essays in Honor of F. L. Moriarty* (Cambridge, MA: Weston College Press, 1973).

N. De Lange, *Origen and the Jews* (Cambridge: Cambridge University Press, 1977).

D. S. Dockery, *Biblical Interpretation Then and Now: Contemporary Hermeneutics in the Light of the Early Church* (Grand Rapids: Baker, 1992).

——— 'Typological Exegesis: Beyond Abuse and Neglect', in G. L. Klein (ed.), *Reclaiming the Prophetic Mantle* (Nashville: Broadman, 1992).

D. Dunbar, 'Hippolytus of Rome and the Eschatological Exegesis of the Early Church', *Westminster Theological Journal* 45 (1983), pp. 322–339.

M. A. Fahey, *Cyprian and the Bible: A Study in Third-Century Exegesis* (Tübingen: Mohr, 1971).

D. Farkasfalvy, 'Theology of Scripture in Irenaeus', *Revue Bénédictine* 78 (1968), pp. 313–319.

F. W. Farrar, *History of Interpretation,* Bampton Lectures, 1885 (London: Macmillan, 1886).

G. Florovsky, 'The Patterns of Historical Interpretation', *Anglican Theological Review* 50 (1968), pp. 144–155.

K. Froehlich (ed.), *Biblical Interpretation in the Early Church* (Philadelphia: Fortress, 1984).

P. Gorday, *Principles of Patristic Exegesis: Romans 9 – 11 in Origen, John Chrysostom and Augustine* (New York: Edwin Mellen, 1983).

R. Greer, *Theodore of Mopsuestia: Exegete and Theologian* (London: Faith, 1961).

M. B. Handspicker, 'Athanasius on Tradition and Scripture', *Andover Newton Quarterly* 55 (1962), pp. 13–29.

R. P. C. Hanson, *Allegory and Event: A Study of the Sources and Significance of Origen's Interpretation of Scripture* (London: SCM, 1959).

———'Biblical Exegesis in the Early Church', in P. R. Ackroyd and C. F. Evans (eds.), *The Cambridge History of the Bible* 1 (Cambridge: Cambridge University Press, 1970), pp. 412–453.

———'Notes on Tertullian's Interpretation of Scripture', *Journal of Theological Studies* new series 12 (1961), pp. 273–279.

R. E. Heine, 'Gregory of Nyssa's Apology for Allegory', *Vigiliae Christianae* 38 (1984), pp. 360–370.

R. Hill, 'John Chrysostom's Teaching on Inspiration in "Six Homilies in Isaiah"', *Vigiliae Christianae* 22 (1968), pp. 21–37.

M. W. Holmes, 'Origen and the Inerrancy of Scripture', *Journal of the Evangelical Theological Society* 24 (1981), pp. 221–232.

W. Horbury, 'Old Testament Interpretation in the Writings of the Church Fathers' in M. J. Mulder (ed.), *Mikra,* pp. 727–789.

D. W. Johnson, 'The Myth of the Augustinian Synthesis', in M. S. Burrows and P. Rorem (eds.), *Biblical Hermeneutics in Historical Perspective* (Grand Rapids: Eerdmans, 1991), pp. 100–114.

M. D. Jordan, 'Words and Word: Incarnation and Signification in Augustine's *De Doctrina Christiana',* in *Augustinian Studies* 11 (1980), pp. 177–196.

J. N. D. Kelly, *Jerome: His Life, Writings and Controversies* (London: Duckworth, 1975).

A. Kerrigan, *St Cyril of Alexandria, Interpreter of the Old Testament* (Rome: Pontificio Instituto Biblico, 1952).

G. W. H. Lampe, 'The Reasonableness of Typology', in G. W. H. Lampe and K. J. Woolcombe (eds.), *Essays on Typology* (London: SCM, 1957), pp. 9–38.

J. Lawson, *The Biblical Theology of St Irenaeus* (London: Epworth, 1948).

E. M. Lynch, *The Controversy over Patristic Exegesis 1875–1965* (Lauderhill, FL: Atlantic, 1976).

D. G. McCartney, 'Literal and Allegorical Interpretation in Origen's *Contra Celsum*', *Westminster Theological Journal* 48 (1986), pp. 281–301.

J. L. McKenzie, 'The Commentary of Theodore of Mopsuestia on John 1:46–51', *Theological Studies* 14.1 (1953), pp. 73–84.

C. W. Macleod, 'Allegory and Mysticism in Origen and Gregory of Nyssa', *Journal of Theological Studies* new series 22 (1971), pp. 362–379.

J. McRay, 'Scripture and Tradition in Irenaeus', *Restoration Quarterly* 10 (1967), pp. 1–11.

B. de Margerie, *Introduction à l'histoire de l'exégèse* (Paris: Cerf): I: *Les Pères grecs et orientaux* (1980); II: *Les premiers grands exégètes latins* (1983); III: *Saint Augustin* (1983); IV: *L'occident latin* (1990).

H. T. Mayer, 'Clement of Rome and his Use of Scripture', *Concordia Theological Monthly* 42 (1971), pp. 536–540.

R. E. Murphy, 'Patristic and Medieval Exegesis, Help or Hindrance?', *Catholic Biblical Quarterly* 43 (1981), pp. 505–516.

J. P. O'Malley, *Tertullian and the Bible* (Nijmegen: Dekker en van de Vegt, 1967).

L. Patterson, *Theodore of Mopsuestia and Modern Thought* (London: SPCK, 1926).

G. A. Press, 'The Content and Argument of Augustine's *De Doctrina Christiana*', *Augustiniana* 31 (1981), pp. 165–182.

———'The Subject and Structure of Augustine's *De Doctrina Christiana*', *Augustinian Studies* 11 (1980), pp. 99–124.

J. D. Quinn, 'St John Chrysostom on History in the Synoptics', *Catholic Biblical Quarterly* 24 (1962), pp. 140–147.

C. J. Scalise, 'Allegorical Flights of Fancy: The Problem of Origen's Exegesis', *Greek Orthodox Theological Review* 32 (1987), pp. 69–88.

M. A. Schatkin, 'The Influence of Origen upon St Jerome's Commentary on Galatians', *Vigiliae Christianae* 24 (1970), pp. 49–58.

W. A. Shotwell, *The Biblical Exegesis of Justin Martyr* (London: SPCK, 1965).

M. Simonetti, *Biblical Interpretation in the Early Church* (Edinburgh: T. and T. Clark, 1994).

G. C. Stead, 'The Scriptures and the Soul of Christ in Athanasius', *Vigiliae Christianae* 36 (1982), pp. 233–250.

M. J. Suggs, 'The Eusebian Text of Matthew', *Novum Testamentum* 1, (1956), pp. 233–245.

———'Eusebius and the Gospel Text', *Harvard Theological Review* 50 (1957), pp. 307–310.

W. Telfer, 'The Fourth Century Greek Fathers as Exegetes', *Harvard Theological Review* 50 (1957), pp. 91–105.

K. J. Torjesen, *Hermeneutical Procedure and Theological Method in Origen's Exegesis* (Berlin and New York: De Gruyter, 1986).

T. F. Torrance, *Divine Meaning: Studies in Patristic Hermeneutics* (Edinburgh: T. and T. Clark, 1995).

J. W. Trigg, *Origen: The Bible and Philosophy in the Third-Century Church* (Atlanta: John Knox; London: SCM, 1986).

C. H. Turner, 'Patristic Commentaries on the Gospel of St Matthew', *Journal of Theological Studies* 12 (1910–11), pp. 99–112.

——— 'Patristic Commentaries on the Pauline Epistles', in J. Hastings (ed.), *Dictionary of the Bible,* extra volume (Edinburgh: T. and T. Clark, 1904), pp. 484–531.

D. S. Wallace-Hadrill, 'Eusebius and the Gospel Text of Caesarea', *Harvard Theological Review* 49 (1956), pp. 105–114.

J. H. Waszink, 'Tertullian's Principles and Methods of Exegesis', in W. R. Schoedel and R. L. Wilken (eds.), *Early Christian Literature and the Classical Intellectual Tradition* (Paris : Beauchesne, 1979), pp. 17–31.

M. F. Wiles, 'Origen as Biblical Scholar', in P. R. Ackroyd and C. F. Evans (eds.), *The Cambridge History of the Bible* 1 (Cambridge: Cambridge University Press, 1970), pp. 454–488.

R. L. Wilken, 'Exegesis and the History of Theology: Reflections on the Adam-Christ Typology in Cyril of Alexandria', *Church History* 25 (1966), pp. 139–156.

D. F. Winslow, 'Christology and Exegesis in the Cappadocians', *Church History* 40 (1971), pp. 389–396.

D. Z. Zaharopoulos, *Theodore of Mopsuestia on the Bible: A Study of his Old Testament Exegesis* (New York: Paulist Press, 1989).

A case study: Genesis 1

Of great importance in the patristic period was the need to establish a Christian (or more correctly, Judaeo-Christian) worldview, over against the many different religions and philosophies with which the church had to contend. The key issue in this struggle was the doctrine of creation, which for various reasons was incompatible with pagan conceptions of the universe. Jews and Christians faced an intellectual climate in which most people believed that the material world was eternal, and that it was both chaotic and evil. They could see no link between matter and spirit, only a radical opposition which set them at odds with one another. The Judaeo-Christian view, on the other hand, was that matter was created good, by a good God, who ordered it according to his purposes. Whatever other concessions might be made to Hellenism, there could be no compromise on this point. The issue was even more serious for Christians than it was for Jews, because on it depended the credibility of the incarnation of the Son of God.

Here we shall examine three different approaches to this question. First comes the allegorical interpretation of Philo, which was adopted by the Alexandrian tradition. This is followed by the literalistic interpretation of Basil of Caesarea, supplemented and completed by Gregory of Nyssa, which may stand for the Antiochene approach to the problem, though it must always be remembered that neither man was a typical Antiochene, and Gregory in particular is generally Alexandrian in his other works. Finally we shall look at Augustine, who combined these two approaches in a synthesis which was to leave its mark on medieval thought in the West.

Philo

Philo's teaching on the subject is contained in his famous *De Opificio Mundi* (*On the Creation of the World*), a treatise in sixty-one sections. At first, it is surprising how little it ventures into the extremes of allegory; on the whole, it seems that Philo is content to develop a reasonably literalistic account of the matter. The most curious feature is his predilection for numerology, by which he explains the meaning of the six days. But the reader soon discovers that Philo reserves his allegorical treatment for the second part of the treatise, where he develops it quite clearly. Furthermore, this second part later gave rise to a further work, the *Legum Allegoria* (*Allegory of the Laws*), in which he expounds Genesis 2 and 3 in a fully allegorical manner.

Philo began by praising the beauty of Moses' account (section 1), and then went on to outline his originality as a thinker. Unlike pagans, who imagined that the material universe was eternal, Moses recognized that only the higher, spiritual realities could claim this distinction (2). The material world was in a constant state of flux, and therefore could not be eternal. But what was not eternal had to come from somewhere, and Moses revealed that the world had been created by God, whom he also calls its Father.

This creation was said to have taken place in six days, but Philo warns us not to take these literally. The six days are a framework in which the work of creation is set. Philo defends this particular scheme by saying that six is the ideal number to represent the perfection of creation. This is because three is the number of masculinity and two the number of femininity, and when these two are multiplied they give six. Six therefore is the number produced when male and female are coupled, so that human procreative activity is seen as paradigmatic of God's creative work. Philo then points out that the first day is distinguished from the others, in that nothing was created on it, and he also notes that it is not called the first day, but simply 'one'.

Philo then goes on to expound the significance of this first day (4). He claims that this was when God created the mental and spiritual worlds, before matter came into being. In this way, Philo was able to say both that the spiritual universe was a part of the created order, and that it was superior to the material part of creation. When we consider that most Greeks of the time thought that the spiritual world was an eternal part of the divine, and that matter was also eternal (though evil), we can see how significant Philo's rearranging of these things was. On the other hand, he follows the Platonic notion that the universe began as an idea in the mind of God, which was then brought into being according to this preconceived plan (5).

The creation which God made was good (6), which was another blow to Greek philosophical ideas. Its goodness was not the absolute goodness of God, of course, but a relative goodness, appropriate to its own nature. The highest manifestation of this was man, created in the image of God, and therefore a partaker of the divine goodness. Unlike the Platonists, Philo relativizes the notion of the good, making it dependent on the thing being observed. In this way he was able to praise the goodness of finite things – a logical contradiction to the Platonic mind.

In 7 Philo states that God made heaven and earth in the beginning, and defines 'beginning' as relating to the order of creation, rather than to a time sequence. He says that time was created along with the world, because it could not exist without space and the possibility of motion. Even if the entire creation was made simultaneously, argues Philo, it still does not preclude the fact that it contains an inner order, and that is what he is concerned to bring out.

In 8–9 he goes on to describe the separation of light from darkness, which he understands as the banishment of chaos by divine reason. Once this is accomplished, the way is prepared for the creation of the material world, beginning with 'heaven'. This is the part of matter most like the spiritual world, which is why it is used in the Bible to symbolize it (10). The next few sections (11–13) are devoted to the third day, and Philo uses this to explain how God ordered the cyclical patterns of reproduction as part of his creative work.

In his discussion of the fourth day (14–19), Philo returns to his numerology in order to explain why the ordering of heaven comes after the ordering of earth. The fourth day, he says, is the most appropriate for this, because the number four contains a promise of perfection, which is represented by ten. Ten is produced by adding the first four numbers together; hence the fourth day was the one reserved for the furnishing of heaven. The sun and the moon are lights for the intellect, as much as for the eyes, and they represent the presence of reason in the material world as well as in the spiritual realm of day one.

The creation of the creatures begins on the fifth day (20–22), leading up to the creation of the highest creature, man (23–29). Philo is very insistent that man is created in the image and likeness of God, which is his most important characteristic. Unlike later Christian exegetes, he treats the image and the likeness as a single thing, and identifies it with the human mind, which is an image of the mind of God. The most curious aspect of the account of the creation of man in Philo's understanding is the plural form of exhortation: 'Let us make man in our image . . .' Philo states that in principle God is the unique creator, but of course, everything he makes is good. The trouble is that man is partly good and partly evil. For this reason, says Philo, Moses had to point out that God associated other heavenly beings with himself when man was created, so that he could take credit for the good part of man, and blame the evil part on his associates.

Philo was also preoccupied with trying to explain why man was created last, although he was the highest of the creatures, but this was not too difficult to understand. God obviously wanted man to be able to enjoy the best that the creation had to offer, and so he made everything else first, in readiness for man's appearing. In 30–43 he reaches the seventh day, which he associates with perfection because of the number seven. His discussion of the meaning of this number is extremely long and detailed, and seems quite peculiar to anyone not acquainted with numerology. The contrast with the rest of the exposition is particularly striking, and the modern reader is apt to think that these sections could be omitted without any great loss. But, of course, for Philo everything in the six-day account is but a preparation for the seventh day, on which we may contemplate the wonderful perfection of God's plan. His mathematical analysis is designed to bear witness to this rational perfection, and it is for that reason that Philo spends so much time elaborating it.

Most of the remainder of the treatise (44–60) is taken up with Philo's analysis of Genesis 2:5–25, which he regards as a recapitulation of what has gone before. It is at this point that we are introduced to the allegorical significance of what we have already read. Philo regards Genesis 2 as an allegorical summary of Genesis 1, which was never meant to be taken literally. For example, he interprets the mention of 'grass' in Genesis 2:5 as a reference to a spiritual reality which was in existence before the material image was created. As he says, 'Before the earth put forth its young green shoots, young verdure was present, he tells us, in the nature of things without material shape, and before grass sprang up in the field, there was in existence an invisible grass' (44).

Most shocking of all, to our minds, is his statement (46) that the man formed from the clay of the earth in Genesis 2:7 is not at all the same as the man formed in the image of God in Gn. 1:26. The man of earth is the Adam who fell, but the man in God's image is a heavenly being who remains in his unfallen state. Unlike many of his contemporaries, for whom the idea of a heavenly man was particularly attractive, Philo does not dwell on him. Instead he concentrates his attention on the earthly man, whom he describes as a most excellent creature, made of the union of body and soul, in which the divine reason is implanted. This Adam was superior to us, his descendants, not because of his sinlessness, but because he was created first; in the course of time, the model has grown stale and worn.

Like so many exegetes after him, Philo regarded the creation of woman as the beginning of trouble for Adam (53). Woman represents all that is sensual, and it is this which has dragged the more rational male down. However, it is important to remember that he does not blame woman for the fall. That was the result of a deliberate choice on the part of the man, and he is the one who must bear the blame for it. There is none of the deep-seated misogyny which we meet with in Tertullian, for example, for whom woman was the great temptress and source of all evil. Philo's attitude to woman must be placed in its context; in comparison with others of his time, he was almost a feminist.

Philo sums up his account of creation with five theological points. We learn from Genesis 1 that God is eternal; God is One; the world was created; the world is a single universe, just as God its creator is one – there is no dualism in creation; and God rules the world by a providential ordering. Here we are on more familiar ground. Whatever we may think of Philo's allegorical tendencies, or of his numerology, we can agree that doctrinally he is one with the church in all ages. His methods of explaining these things may be out of date, but his conclusions are as valid today as they were when they were first drawn.

Basil of Caesarea and Gregory of Nyssa

Basil's great work on the creation of the world is his *Hexaemeron* (*Six Days*), which consists of a course of nine sermons, covering Genesis 1:1–26. Basil only briefly mentions the creation of man, a defect which was later corrected by his brother Gregory of Nyssa, who maintained Basil's literalistic exegesis of the text.

The *Hexaemeron* is written in a homiletic style, which accounts for much of its freshness and the directness of the application. Basil is very clear about his attitude towards allegory. He says:

> I know the laws of allegory, though less by myself than from the works of others. There are those who do not admit the common sense of the Scriptures, for whom water is not water, but something else, who see in a plant, in a fish, what their fancy wishes, who change the nature of reptiles and of wild beasts to suit their allegories, like the interpreters of dreams who explain visions in sleep, to make then serve their own ends. For me grass is grass – plant, fish, wild beast, domestic animal, I take it all in the literal sense. For I am not ashamed of the gospel (Rom. 1:16) (9, 1).

And later on in the same section:

> Shall I prefer foolish wisdom to the oracles of the Holy Spirit? Shall I not rather exalt him who, not wishing to fill our minds with these vanities, has regulated all the economy of Scripture in view of the edification and making perfect of our souls? In my opinion, it is this which those who, giving themselves up to the distorted meaning of allegory, and having undertaken to give a majesty of their own invention to Scripture, have not under-

stood. It is to believe themselves wiser than the Holy Spirit, and to bring forth their own ideas under a pretext of exegesis. Let us hear Scripture as it has been written.

Basil's nine sermons are divided as follows:

1. *In the beginning God made the heaven and the earth.* In this sermon he begins by comparing the beauty of the creation account to the beauty of its human author, Moses. This may seem strange and extravagant to us, but Basil is comparing the text to its human author, whereas Philo compared it only to God himself. Of course, Basil believed that Moses was inspired by the Holy Spirit, but the change of emphasis is noticeable and significant. He then rehearses various pagan theories of cosmology, including the atomic theory of Democritus, to demonstrate that they are weak and contradictory when compared to the Genesis account. Basil does not adopt contemporary science as a buttress to his exegesis; on the contrary, he uses his exegesis to contradict the best that the science of his day had to offer.

He then posits a linear view of time, giving it a real beginning and an end. This Philo signally failed to do; he regarded the 'beginning' as figurative. But Basil follows the sweep of salvation in history, and has his eye as much on the last judgment as on the creation. He agrees with Philo that an order of things existed in the mind of the Creator before the beginning of the world, but he regards this as a mystery too deep to penetrate. However, he does recognize that the spiritual creatures were made outside of time, and were in existence when the material world was created.

Basil goes on to mention the elements of the created order, but says that these are not mentioned in Scripture. God does not want us to dwell on scientific theories, but on spiritual truths. Theories of the nature of matter are many and varied, and much in creation is a mystery beyond our understanding, Scripture speaks of these things in a poetic manner, in order to induce a spirit of awe and wonder in us. It is therefore a great mistake to read too much into biblical poetry. The truly Christian attitude is to worship the Creator, not to dissect the creation, and it is to this that Basil calls us in his concluding remarks.

2. *The earth was invisible and unfinished.* This is the Septuagint rendering of 'without form and void', and the use of the word 'invisible' inevitably affects Basil's interpretation. Basil is unwilling to accept that the earth was a spiritual idea; for him, 'invisible' means that it was hidden, either under water or under a cloud of dense air.

He is strongly critical of the allegorical school, which naturally understood 'invisible' in a Platonic sense. He is likewise strongly critical of those who said that the Creator merely fashioned an already existing matter; for Basil, creation is out of nothing (*ex nihilo*). In the same vein, he attacks those who would interpret 'light' and 'darkness' in a spiritual sense; for him, these are purely material realities, accessible to investigation by the senses. Any suggestion that evil might have its origin in God is firmly rejected. Evil is the result of human disobedience, not part of the divine plan, and it cannot be found anywhere in the material creation.

When dealing with the spirit which was borne upon the face of the waters (LXX), Basil considers the possibility that a kind of wind is meant, but comes down in the end in favour of the view that this is a reference to the Holy Spirit, as the church had always understood it. However, he relies for his interpretation on an unnamed Syriac writer (possibly Eusebius of Samosata) who claimed that there was an expression of this kind in the Syriac language, which, being closer to the original Hebrew, was most likely to be correct. Basil takes this interpretation over, and says that the text means that the Spirit 'cherished the nature of the waters as a bird covers its eggs', an interpretation not unfamiliar to modern readers.

Basil concludes with a discourse on the creation of light, and the separation of light and darkness into day and night. His interpretation is literal throughout, especially at the end, where he discusses why the first day is called 'one'. Basil's view is that God wanted to establish the relationship of this day, which was archetypal of time, to eternity. The day is a cyclical movement, like the week or the year. It is therefore the unit of time, which repeats itself in eternity, which Genesis is underlining here, not a spiritual realm above and beyond the material one.

3. *On the firmament.* Here Basil passes on to the wonders of the second day. He begins by referring again to the smooth character of the narrative, which he regards as evidence of its truth. Basil reflects that it was not necessary for God to speak his commands, since he could quite easily have created the firmament in silence. The fact that he does not do so indicates that he must have been speaking to somebody; obviously to the Son, who is the co-creator with the Father. He then goes on to rehearse various pagan theories, which he rejects, before returning to the theme of the firmament in the midst of the waters. Basil interprets this to mean that God has so ordered the universe that it will retain its stability until the end of time. The waters above the firmament are taken to refer to the rain and dew

which fall from heaven, and the suggestion that there is another world up there superior to this one is roundly condemned.

Basil concludes by praising the goodness and beauty of creation, which come directly from the hand of the Creator and Artist of matter.

4. *Upon the gathering together of the waters.* Basil uses this verse to develop a theory about the movement of water. Water that is spread everywhere is stagnant, he says; only when it is gathered together in one place does it start to flow. Basil realizes that it is impossible to take the words 'into one place' absolutely literally, but he pleads that here God is putting boundaries around the waters so that the dry land might appear. Both water and dry land are good in the sight of God, and both are equally necessary for human life.

5. *The germination of the earth.* This sermon is a detailed description of plant life, free of allegorical interpretation. Basil demonstrates in this sermon a great knowledge of his subject, which he delights to share with his hearers, who were no doubt also close to the land.

6. *The creation of luminous bodies.* Here Basil moves on to the fourth day, but there is no sign of Philo's numerology. The sun and the moon were created to be bearers of light, as a reminder to us that, in spite of appearances, they are not the source of light. He takes advantage of this verse to make a strong attack on astrology, which he regards as complete nonsense. The sun, moon and stars are signs, not of our spiritual destiny, but of God's providential ordering of the universe.

7. *The creation of moving creatures.* Basil takes this opportunity to dwell at length on the sea creatures, of which he knows a good deal. His description of nature is extremely vivid and memorable. Towards the end of the sermon there is a curious digression on to the subject of marriage, when Basil urges unhappy couples to stay together in the same way that a viper unites himself to a sea lamprey! As Basil says: 'What does this mean? However hard, however fierce a husband may be, the wife ought to bear with him, and not wish to find any pretext for breaking the union. He strikes you, but he is your husband. He is a drunkard, but he is united to you by nature. He is brutal and cross, but he is henceforth one of your members, and the most precious of all.'

8. *The creation of fowl and water animals.* This is a continuation of the previous sermon, with a similar attention to detail. In the middle of it, Basil turns to the phrase 'Let the earth bring forth a living soul', and concludes that creatures without reason have a soul which is part of their flesh and blood, and which perishes with them. This is an

important observation, which he promises to apply to humankind at a later stage, though the series of sermons breaks off before he gets there. The bulk of the sermon is given over to a detailed explanation of birds, where Basil demonstrates his usual skills of observation, and his deep interest in nature.

9. *The creation of terrestrial animals.* In this sermon Basil tackles the fantasies of the allegorizers (see the quotations above) before going on to describe the animals which roam over the face of the earth. At the very end of this sermon, Basil comes to the creation of humankind. He naturally refers the plural ('Let us make man . . .') to the Father and the Son, working together. For Basil it is the fact that humankind is created 'in our image' which excludes the possibility that God may have been talking to angels; we are created in the image of the Son, and so it is clear that here the Father must be talking to him. Basil intended to go on to expound the creation of humankind at greater length, but this sermon turned out to be the last in the series, which cuts off at this point.

The *Hexaemeron* of Basil was completed at a later date by his brother, Gregory of Nyssa, who wrote a treatise in thirty chapters called *De Opificio Hominis* (*On the Making of Man*). It is not a sermon, but a work of philosophy, with a style very different from Basil's. However, the exegetical method is the same as Basil's, and in this respect it differs greatly from Gregory's other hermeneutical works, which are largely allegorical.

After an opening résumé of Basil's work, Gregory goes on to discuss the creation of humankind in great detail. Like Philo, he believes that humankind was created last because God wanted to prepare the world and make it ready for them to dwell in. Gregory praises humankind as the supreme glory of the creation, and dwells on every aspect of their being at some length. He tends to assimilate the image of God to the dominion which men and women have been given over the creatures, though this is implied rather than clearly stated. The mind he regards as something which has been added to the image (9), to make it reflect God's nature more fully.

After a long discussion of the mind, and its relation to the soul, Gregory returns to the problem of the divine image (16). Gregory notices that Scripture says that the divine image embraces both male and female, which is a departure from the prototype, since in Christ Jesus there is neither male nor female (Gal. 3:28). Gregory concludes from this that human nature is a combination of the rational and the irrational. The former is the divine element, which does not admit the distinction of male and female; the latter is bound up with our sexuality and our animal nature. Naturally Gregory prefers the former, and the rest of the treatise is devoted to convincing us that life in God is far better than sexual or other forms of carnal indulgence.

When he gets to the fall, Gregory repeats the standard belief that the couple were beguiled by their senses, but he does not blame this on the woman any more than Philo does. According to Gregory, both male and female are deceived by the fruit of the tree; there is no attempt to portray woman as an evil temptress. The remainder of the treatise is a consideration of the resurrection, including what it means to say that the body will be raised. The focus is entirely on the end of time, the last judgment, and the life of the redeemed in heaven – an eschatological dimension which is characteristic of Christianity, and which cannot be ignored, because it explains the purpose of creation. In sharp contradistinction to Philo, both Basil and Gregory have their sights very firmly fixed on the end, as well as on the beginning, and their theology is soundly rooted in the eternal plan of God for the salvation of the human race.

Augustine

Augustine was fascinated by the creation account in Genesis, and wrote at great length about it. Early on in his career he adopted an allegorical approach to the text, and used it to combat the Manichees. Later, he wrote a long commentary on the same passage, in which he treated it according to the literal sense. In the last three books of his *Confessions* (written about 400), he combined both approaches, and it is that treatment which we shall look at briefly here.

Augustine devoted most of Book 11 and the whole of Book 12 to the very first verse: *In the beginning, God created the heavens and the earth.* This extraordinarily long treatment of a single verse can be subdivided into three major points: the relationship between time and eternity; the relationship between the invisible and the visible creation; and the proper interpretation of Scripture.

First, Augustine tried to explain how an eternal God can act in time. He was aware of how difficult it is to define time, and confessed ignorance as to how God can operate in both dimensions at once. He was strongly tempted to take the phrase 'in the beginning' as a metaphor meaning 'in the first place' (12.29), but refused to state categorically that that was the only possible interpretation. Second, he argued that if the phrase was to be taken figuratively, it would then be necessary to interpret 'the heavens and the earth' as 'the invisible and the visible worlds', because otherwise the rest of the chapter would be a repetition of what had already occurred. However, Augustine recognized that the opening verse might be a kind of heading, or introduction summarizing what was to follow, so that his preferred interpretation was not the only one possible.

Above all Augustine was concerned to avoid futile discussion about the 'correct' meaning, when many different meanings were equally possible. He made this point quite forcefully in 12.30–31:

> Let us also honour Moses your servant, who delivered your Scriptures to us and was filled with your Spirit, by believing that when he wrote those words, by your inspiration his thoughts were directed to whichever meaning sheds the fullest light of truth and enables us to reap the greatest profit. For this reason, although I hear people say 'Moses meant this' or 'Moses meant that', I think it more truly religious to say 'Why should he not have had both meanings in mind, if both are true?' And if others see in the same words a third, or fourth, or any number of true meanings, why should we not believe that Moses saw them all? There is only one God, who caused Moses to write the Holy Scriptures in the way best suited to the minds of great numbers of men who would all see truths in them, though not the same truths in each case.

Modern literary critics would not accept the notion that Moses knew of every possible meaning the text might have, but they are generally sympathetic to Augustine's belief that several different meanings are possible, and that it is wrong to restrict the text to only one interpretation.

In Book 13 of the *Confessions* Augustine dealt more briefly with the rest of the chapter, applying his theory of different levels of meaning as he went along. Here it becomes apparent that the literal sense gave way to a spiritual meaning more often than not. Augustine interpreted the famous command 'Let there be light' as applying only to the spiritual realm (13.3), because it was already in existence when the command was given. The light given to spiritual beings was the means by which they could turn to God and adore him as their creator. Later on, he identified the firmament as the Scriptures (13.15):

> And who but you, our God, made for us the firmament, that is, our heavenly shield, the authority of your divine Scriptures? For

> we are told that *the sky shall be folded up like a scroll* and that now it is spread out like a canopy of skins above us . . . Above this firmament of your Scripture I believe that there are other waters, immortal and kept safe from earthly corruption. They are the peoples of your city, your angels, on high above the firmament. Let them glorify your name and sing your praises, for they have no need to look up to this firmament of ours or read its text to know your word.

But the most striking feature in Book 13 is the way in which Augustine found the Trinity at work in it. It is not surprising that he connected the Spirit of Genesis 1:2 with the Holy Spirit, or that he thought of God primarily as the Father. But it is unusual, to say the least, to find the Son in the word 'beginning' – yet another example of how many different meanings the text could be made to have (13.5). The supreme self-manifestation of God as trinity in unity and unity in trinity is found in the creation of humankind (13.22):

> It is because you are the Trinity that you speak in the plural when you say *Let us make man*; yet in the next verse, which says *God made man*, the singular is used; and the phrase: *Wearing our own image and likeness*, in which the plural is used, is followed by the words *in his own image*, where you speak in the singular. This is how, when we learn to know God, we become new men in the image of our Creator.

Augustine went on to develop the idea that humankind was created in the image of the Trinity, by pointing out that the human mind possessed being, knowledge and will, in the same way that God does. In this respect his interpretation of Genesis 1:26 was unique among the fathers of the church, and his concentration on the interplay of forces within the human mind was one of the factors which eventually led to the development of modern psychology.

BIBLIOGRAPHY

Augustine, *Confessions* (London: Penguin, 1961).

Basil of Caesarea, *Hexaemeron*, in Library of Nicene and Post-Nicene Fathers (LNPF) second series vol. 8 (New York: Christian Literature Publishing Co., 1895), pp. 51–107.

Gregory of Nyssa, *On the Making of Man*, LNPF second series vol. 5, (1893), pp. 386–427.

Philo of Alexandria, *De Opificio Mundi*, Loeb Classical Library I, pp. 1–137.
G. A. Robbins, *Genesis 1 – 3 in the History of Exegesis* (Lewiston, NY: Edwin Mellen, 1988).

4

Medieval interpretation

The period and the subject

The medieval period of biblical interpretation is one of the most complex and difficult of all, and it has not received the attention it deserves from theologians or biblical scholars. Most of the work in this field has been done by medievalists, who cannot escape the all-pervasive role which the Bible played during those centuries. But medievalists have their own agenda, and it is not always possible for a theologian to gain ready access to their work. There is also the fact that centuries of training have made Protestant scholars particularly wary of the medieval period, which they have been inclined to think of as an age of darkness. As most modern biblical scholars have been Protestants, this prejudice has contributed to the relative neglect of medieval exegesis.

The transition from the ancient world to the Middle Ages took many centuries and occurred at an uneven rate. The process began with the fall of the western Roman Empire (476), but the real break with the past came in the eighth century, after North Africa, Egypt, Syria and most of Spain had been lost to Islam. As a result of the Arab conquests, the old Mediterranean culture broke up, and with it went the traditional links between Rome and the East. After 750, Rome looked increasingly to the Frankish kingdom in Gaul for support, and on Christmas Day 800, Pope Leo III crowned its ruler, Charlemagne, Emperor of the West. Charlemagne sponsored a revival of learning, which officially recognized that the ancient world had disappeared. Latin now had to be learned as a foreign tongue, even in Italy, and in 812 priests were given permission to preach in the vernacular (*lingua rustica*), an event which foreshadowed the rise of the modern Romance languages.

However, Latin remained the cultural language of western Europe, a development which was reinforced by a group of ninth-century theologians, who proclaimed what was known in the East as the 'three-languages heresy'. They claimed that there were only three languages in which God could be worshipped – Hebrew, Greek and Latin. But Hebrew had fallen into disuse because of the apostasy of the Jews, and the Greeks were prone to heresy. Only Latin remained pure, and therefore it was only in that language that God could be properly worshipped. Thus it was that the whole of western Christendom found itself worshipping God in a foreign tongue, a matter which was to cause a crisis in the sixteenth century. But a common language had its advantages, of course, and medieval Europe was a single cultural area. In particular, England and France were closely connected for much of the time, and English scholars made a notable contribution to Parisian intellectual life.

Having to work through the medium of a foreign tongue also forced scholars to study it carefully, and no period in our survey was more sensitive to the nature and possibilities of language than was this one. This had a great influence on biblical interpretation, which is only now beginning to be appreciated. Grammatical exegesis, which had been something of a luxury in patristic times, had become a necessity, and it was widely practised in spite of the overall dominance of allegory. Knowledge of Greek was rare until the fifteenth century, but a surprising number of medieval exegetes knew some Hebrew, and were able to make use of Jewish biblical interpretation.

The Middle Ages were also characterized by the generally felt need to appeal to ancient authority. Augustine of Hippo was the standard source for almost everything, and his methods of biblical interpretation, as outlined in the *De Doctrina Christiana* (*On Christian Doctrine*), became universal. In ancient times, the Bible had been one book among many, but it now became the only book of which many people had any knowledge. Medieval society created a culture that was Christian in every respect, not merely in its religious observances. Secular laws and government were reshaped along Old Testament lines. Art, literature and music were permeated with biblical themes, allusions and terminology. Often this meant baptizing the pagan past and recycling it in a new guise, but the fact that this was done shows how deeply Christianity penetrated European culture at this time. The Bible, though read only by scholars, became the unique source and guide for an entire civilization.

This new status for the written text of Scripture meant that it had to be carefully supervised and controlled. If society was to hold together, there had to be a common understanding about its basic document, so there could be no variant readings or interpretations of the Bible. Preachers who interpreted it for themselves were liable to provoke a political as well as a religious revolution, as happened on several occasions. Church and state had a common interest in suppressing biblically based reform, as John Wycliffe and his disciple Jan Hus discovered to their cost. The arbiter of this society was the papacy, an institution which in the Middle Ages developed from a purely ecclesiastical office into a major world power. From the time of the Cluniac reform in 1059, which made the papal elections free of secular control, until the so-called 'Babylonian captivity' of the pope at Avignon (1305–76), the papacy virtually ruled western Europe. On the whole, it tolerated a reasonable degree of academic freedom, but when it made a decision, it expected to be obeyed. The church, and not rational argument, was the ultimate authority in matters of controversy.

In the Middle Ages, most scholars and theologians looked backwards to a golden age which had disappeared, but which they were trying to preserve and explain to their own generation. Paradoxically, it was this desire which led them to seek new ways in which this could be done, and, in the process, to discover that the traditions which they had inherited were not perfect after all. This realization took a long time to dawn, and it did not happen everywhere at once, but when it occurred, medieval society was rocked to its foundations, and gave way to a new and more secular culture.

Periodization in the Middle Ages is difficult, because of the weight of traditionalism and the slow pace of change. Even so, it is possible to distinguish four major periods.

1. *The period up to 800.* This was one of transition from the ancient world, in which most people did not accept the permanence of the changes which had taken place since the fifth century. In theory, the Roman Empire continued to exist, with an Emperor at Constantinople, who would one day reclaim all the territories over which his forebears had ruled. This seems like a fantastic dream to us, but it is what most people at the time believed, and it deeply affected their outlook. Intellectual life during this period remained vigorous in the East, though increasing theological controversy led to a virtual ban on new biblical interpretation (at the Council *in Trullo,* 692). Scholarship also enjoyed a remarkable flowering in the British Isles,

where Irish and, later, Anglo-Saxon monks carried on the traditions of antiquity. Elsewhere, however, this period was known as the 'Dark Ages' because of the generally low standard of learning.

2. *The period from 800 to about 1150.* This was the Early Middle Ages, when western Europe began to forge a new culture and civilization. After about 1000 there was increasing stability, and centres of learning developed. A new scholarship came into being in the monasteries, and important schools were established, in which biblical exegesis was taught. These schools were attached to monasteries, and later to cathedrals. At first there was little originality in all of this, but that too appeared with time. By about 1150 western Europe was ready for intellectual take-off, and the golden age known as the High Middle Ages began.

3. *The period from about 1150 to about 1300.* This was the High Middle Ages, the time of a powerful papacy, of knights in shining armour and of courtly love. It was also the time when universities came into being, of which the most famous were at Paris, Oxford, Cambridge and Cologne. This period also saw the greatest flowering of medieval philosophy, theology and mystical writing. The medieval world received its first great intellectual jolt with the translation of Aristotle (from Arabic, not Greek!) in the twelfth century. This was perceived as such a threat to the existing order that the study of Aristotle was continually being banned – the last and most famous occasion being the condemnation of his works by the Sorbonne in 1277. By that time, however, Aristotle had been absorbed into the theological system of the church, thanks to the work of Thomas Aquinas (1226–74), and his writings were no longer such a danger to the established order.

4. *The period from about 1300 to 1500.* This may be called the Late Middle Ages. During this time Europe was devastated by the Black Death, and eastern Christendom (apart from Russia) fell under Muslim Turkish control. The church survived the exile of the pope in Avignon (1305–76) and the schism which followed (1378–1417), but by the fifteenth century new intellectual movements were appearing once more, and this time they proved to be uncontrollable. The scholastic system of Thomas Aquinas fell apart, and there was no generally accepted replacement. Scholars increasingly went their own way, and questioned the authorities they had accepted in the past. Ancient documents were rediscovered, and efforts were made to popularize the new learning, especially a knowledge of the Bible, which was still regarded as indispensable. Nationalism also made its appearance, and the consciousness of belonging to a single

civilization began to decline. Vernacular literatures now appeared, and, with the invention of printing, a vast new market for books opened up.

The Bible was at the heart of all this, and both translation and interpretation took on a new urgency. Greek scholars arrived from the East, fleeing a dying Byzantium, and they brought with them a Christian learning which had previously been unknown. Scholars once more began to study the biblical languages, and discovered that the Latin Vulgate was less than perfect. They also discovered that many ancient traditions, such as the belief that the pope had received his authority from the Emperor Constantine, were false. The church could not cope with such a threat to its authority, and by 1500 it was losing control of biblical interpretation, which was now firmly in the hands of the new breed of Renaissance scholar. That, more than anything else, marked the end of the medieval order, and the beginning of a new stage in the cultural life of western Christendom.

The interpreters and their work

Given the fact that the Bible was the central book of medieval culture, it is only to be expected that virtually every writer of the period should have written about it in one way or another. An enormous number of manuscripts, many of them unedited, survive to testify of this. The names which follow represent only a selection of the more significant interpreters of the Bible during this period. Basing ourselves on the periodization given above, we may distinguish the following stages.

Before 800

John Cassian (360–435). An Origenist monk who lived and worked during the golden age of patristic theology, Cassian was unexceptional in his own day. However, he became widely popular in the Early Middle Ages, thanks to the praise he received from Gregory the Great and Cassiodorus, and therefore belongs here rather than in his own time. Cassian was responsible for a different classification of the senses of interpretation, which became standard in medieval writing. To the three senses of Origen he added a fourth, the so-called 'mystagogical' or mystical sense, which soon became the most important of all.

Junilius (*fl. c.* 550). A Latin-speaking official at Justinian's court in

Constantinople, Junilius wrote a short introduction to the Bible (*Instituta Regularia Divinae Legis, Rules of the Divine Law*), in which he borrowed extensively from Theodore of Mopsuestia. The work survived Theodore's condemnation and was widely read in the West, where it was influential in maintaining an interest in the literal sense of Scripture.

Isidore of Seville (d. 636). He wrote introductions to several biblical books, but, even more important, left an encyclopedia (the *Etymologiae, Etymologies*) of names, numbers, dates and events, which he culled from earlier exegetes, notably Jerome. This became a standard reference work in the Middle Ages.

Maximus the Confessor (580–662). He was one of the greatest Byzantine theologians, whose remarkable synthesis of Neoplatonism and Christianity has become a subject of great fascination among scholars in recent years. He did not write biblical commentaries, but in his *Quaestiones ad Thalassium* (*Questions to Thalassius*) he dealt with sixty-five difficulties which his friend Thalassius encountered when reading the Scriptures. Maximus believed that there was a perfect harmony between God's revelation of himself in nature and his Word in Scripture, both of which found their meaning and fulfilment in Christ. To enjoy Christ fully, it was necessary to master even the hardest parts of the Bible, which concealed the deepest mysteries of the universe. Maximus played a prominent part in the development of the allegorical senses of interpretation, and his system later became standard in the eastern church.

Ambrose Autpert (d. 781). He wrote a massive commentary on Revelation in which he discussed the mystery of history and the destiny of both the church and the individual soul. This work was especially important for later Mariology because of his allegorical treatment of the woman with child (Rev. 12).

Beatus of Liébana (*c.* 750–*c.* 798). A Spanish cleric who lived a generation after the Muslim conquest of the peninsula, and who was deeply engaged in the struggles against both Islam and Spanish adoptionism. He is chiefly remembered today for his massive commentary on Revelation, which remained a favourite in Spain long after its original polemic purpose had been forgotten.

Of major importance during this time were the schools set up and staffed by Irish, and later also by Anglo-Saxon, monks. Many of these monks are unknown to us by name, but there are indications that they were more attracted to Antiochene exegesis than was customary in the West at that time. The most significant of the ones known to us were the following.

Aldhelm of Malmesbury (*c.* 640–709). A pupil of Theodore of Tarsus, the third Archbishop of Canterbury and an admirer of Theodore of Mopsuestia, Aldhelm may have derived his predilection for common-sense and literalistic interpretations from him, or from Junilius, whom he quotes. Alternatively, he may owe his approach to an Irish source, possibly to St Columban. His name is associated with the English-language version of the Paris Psalter, which follows the Hebrew-based 'Gallican' Psalter and not the Latin version (the Septuagint-based 'Roman' Psalter) which is parallel to it in the manuscript.

Bede (672–735). Best known nowadays for his famous *Ecclesiastical History*, Bede wrote a number of exegetical works, which stand out for their restrained use of allegory and the attention which he gave to matters of scientific detail. His biblical works were among the most popular during the Middle Ages, though they have largely been forgotten since. In some ways Bede was the 'last of the Fathers', but he was distinctly 'medieval' in his didactic methods. Bede was a strong supporter of Jerome's view of the Old Testament, and was the vehicle through whom much of his biblical learning was passed on to the later Middle Ages. The Cistercian Press (Kalamazoo, MI) has recently undertaken to publish translations of his biblical writings. To date, his commentaries on Acts (1990) and the catholic epistles (1985) have appeared, as has a two-volume edition of his *Homilies on the Gospels* (1991). Further volumes are projected.

From 800 to about 1150

Alcuin of York (*fl. c.* 796–*c.* 804). An English monk who became Charlemagne's chief educational adviser, Alcuin was a leading figure in the Carolingian Renaissance of the early ninth century. He wrote commentaries and undertook a revision of the Vulgate, which became the standard version used until the sixteenth century.

Claudius of Turin (d. *c.* 827). A Spaniard in the service of Charlemagne, he became Bishop of Turin about 816. He was subsequently accused of supporting the adoptionist heresy which had raged in Spain during his youth, but the accusation could not be sustained. On the other hand, he was an outspoken opponent of the veneration of the saints and of the idea of papal supremacy in the church. He wrote commentaries on Genesis, Leviticus, Joshua, Judges, 1 and 2 Samuel, 1 and 2 Kings, Matthew, Romans, 1 and 2 Corinthians, Galatians, Ephesians, Philippians and Philemon. It is also probable that he wrote commentaries on Exodus, Numbers,

Deuteronomy and Hebrews, which are now lost. His exegesis of Scripture was unoriginal and largely dependent on his predecessors, notably Gregory the Great, but in his own day he was widely admired for his learning.

Haimo of Auxerre (d. *c.* 855). He wrote commentaries on the Song of Songs, the twelve minor prophets, the Pauline epistles and Revelation, which until recently were erroneously attributed to his namesake, Haimo of Halberstadt (d. 853). Like most of his contemporaries, his work was almost entirely dependent on his patristic forebears.

Rabanus Maurus (*c.* 776–856). A pupil of Alcuin, he was a prodigious writer who produced commentaries on Genesis to Ruth, Chronicles, Proverbs, Jeremiah, Ezekiel, the Wisdom of Solomon, Maccabees, Matthew and the Pauline epistles. His work was not original, and was almost entirely dependent on earlier sources, especially Origen. However, he was very popular in his own day and was regarded as the founder of German scholarship.

Paschasius Radbertus (d. 865). Following a lead given by Eucherius of Lyon (d. 449), Paschasius added an element of theological discussion to his commentaries, a practice which would expand greatly in subsequent centuries. His work shows an originality frequently lacking in that of his contemporaries. He was also the first to state a theory of transubstantiation, which became official church teaching in 1215.

John Scotus Eriugena (d. *c.* 877). The most unusual of the Carolingians, John was an Irishman whose knowledge of Greek was sufficient to enable him to consult works written in that language. By doing this, he noticed a number of discrepancies between what the Greek fathers had taught and what was generally accepted in his day. This led him to question the accepted authorities, and he even admitted that the fathers, who could contradict each other, stood on a lower plane than Scripture, which could not be self-contradictory.

Remigius of Auxerre (d. 908). He aimed to write short and clear commentaries, which did not digress into theological discussions. His references to contemporary society in his commentary on the Psalms demonstrate his concern for applying the text to pastoral needs. He was something of a linguist, and may have known Hebrew as well as Greek. He was the first medieval writer who could properly be called a biblical scholar in the later sense.

Fulbert of Chartres (d. 1028). He seems to have been responsible for a revival of interest in biblical studies, after a lapse of more than a century. His method appears to have been that of the 'gloss', a kind of running commentary on the scriptural text.

Bruno of Würzburg (*c.* 1005–45). He was the author of a well-known commentary on the Psalms which reflects the standard Christological exegesis of the period.

Peter Damian (d. 1072). He used Scripture as a weapon in his efforts to reform both the church and the monastic orders. He also used it to settle points of doctrinal controversy, by comparing one text with another to produce agreement. His own biblical exegesis was highly allegorical, and concentrated heavily on the Song of Songs as the pattern of the union of the soul with God.

Othlo of St Emmeran (d. *c.* 1073). He regarded Scripture as the source of a spiritual ideal which he recommended to monks and clergy. He strongly recommended the devotional reading of the Bible as a way to promote personal moral and spiritual reformation.

Berengar of Tours (d. 1088). He was a pupil of Fulbert, and apparently the centre of a school of glossators which developed in the later eleventh century. Among his colleagues and imitators was Lanfranc of Bec (d. 1089), who became the first Norman Archbishop of Canterbury (1070).

Bruno the Carthusian (*c.* 1030–1101). Founder of the Carthusian order, he wrote a commentary on the Psalms and probably one on the Pauline epistles. His work reflects the allegorical exegesis of the time and was highly valued for its devotional content.

Anselm (d. 1117) and **Ralph** (d. 1134 or 1136) **of Laon**. These two brothers made great advances in developing a systematic form of Bible study, which was the direct ancestor of thirteenth-century scholasticism. Borrowing from earlier masters, they began to produce a gloss on the entire text of Scripture. They did not complete this work, but subsequent hands took it over and eventually published the *Glossa Ordinaria* (*Standard Gloss*) (*c.* 1135), which became the standard work of its kind.

Bruno of Asti or Segni (d. 1123). He wrote commentaries on several Old Testament books (Joshua, Job, Psalms, Song of Songs, Isaiah) and Revelation. He ensured that the study of Scripture played a prominent role in the monastic revival of the twelfth century. He was also one of the earliest exponents of 'political' exegesis, relating Scripture to the imperial claims of the papacy.

Guibert of Nogent (1053–1124). Though he lived and worked a generation before the great changes in biblical exegesis which took place after 1150, Guibert heralded them, and he belongs to that period more than to his own. He maintained that if theology was well taught, allegory became unnecessary, and was thus an early exponent of a return to the literal sense of Scripture.

Rupert of Deutz (1070–*c.* 1129). He wrote many works of biblical theology, which were strongly allegorical in tone and clearly dependent on Origen. He was one of the first to give the Song of Songs a Marian interpretation.

Hugh of St Victor (*c.* 1096–1141). A master of simple exposition, Hugh founded a tradition of scholarship at the Parisian monastery of St Victor, which was to bear fruit in the next generation. Hugh wanted to hold all knowledge together within the framework of biblical studies. His ideal was a system in which secular science would serve the literal interpretation of Scripture, while theology would teach the allegorical meaning. In this way, he thought, the life of the scholar and that of the monk could be blended in a higher synthesis.

Peter Abelard (1079–1142). He developed a distinction between the subject-matter (*materia*) of a text and its intention (*sensus*), which enabled him to look for a figurative sense within the literal sense of Scripture, not necessarily beyond it. His surviving commentary on Romans speaks of the Son of God becoming a man in order to set us an example of how to live. Abelard was very sensitive to the different ways in which the church fathers spoke and wrote, and tried to interpret each in his context. He was open to the idea that they might be in error, and even suggested that the same might be true for the prophets and apostles. They were not liars, of course, but merely human beings with an incomplete grasp of the truth.

William of St Thierry (*c.* 1085–1148). A disciple of Bernard of Clairvaux, he became Abelard's fiercest opponent after reading his commentary on Romans. In his own commentary on the same book, William struggled to show that there were no real contradictions between the various fathers of the church, in spite of appearances.

Zachary of Besançon (*fl. c.* 1150). This leading monastic biblical scholar composed a gospel harmony, on which he wrote a commentary. In the course of his researches, he consulted earlier works going back as far as Tatian.

Bernard of Clairvaux (1090–1153). A leader of monastic reform, his spirituality was most clearly manifested in his long series of sermons on the Song of Songs, which had an enormous influence in later ages, and which are now the only work of medieval exegesis which is still widely published and read.

Gilbert de la Porrée (*c.* 1076–1154). A disciple of the school of

Laon, Gilbert extended their work and wrote a number of biblical commentaries which still survive. He was condemned in 1148 for supposedly unorthodox views of the Trinity.

Peter Lombard (*c.* 1100–60). The greatest of the glossators, he recognized the inadequacies of the *Glossa Ordinaria* and sought to supplement it with exegetical work of his own. He gave special importance to background material relating to the authorship and composition of the various Bible books, and thought that the author's original intention was a key to understanding the meaning of the text. His *Sentences* (*Sententiae*) were an attempt to systematize this learning on a theological foundation, and they became the standard theological textbook for the rest of the medieval period. The sixteenth-century Reformers were largely brought up on him, and regarded him as the classical representative of medieval theology.

Robert of Melun (d. 1167). A transitional figure to the next stage of development, Robert of Melun wrote a commentary on the Pauline epistles in which theological questions become more important than the running exposition of the text. This was a prelude to the next phase, in which theology would be divorced from the text altogether, and would emerge as a discipline quite distinct from biblical exegesis.

Medieval Jewish exegetes. Hugh of St Victor and his school were able to take advantage of Jewish scholarship, which was enjoying a revival during his lifetime. The most prominent names associated with this are **Rashi** (1040–1105), **Ibn Ezra** (1089–1164), **Maimonides** (1135–1204) and **David Kimchi** (*c.* 1160–*c.* 1235). Rashi went beyond the traditional Talmudic distinction between halakic and haggadic interpretation, and added a third possibility: straightforward literal exegesis. He developed a great interest in comparative philology, history and geography, though he did not abandon the Midrashic tradition entirely. This occurred only slowly, partly through Rashi's pupil **Joseph Kara** (d. *c.* 1130) and even more through his disciples, all of whom were living and working in Hugh's lifetime. These included Rashi's grandson **Samuel ben Meir (Rashbam)** (*c.* 1080–1158), **Eliezer of Beaugency** (*fl.* *c.* 1150) and **Joseph Bekhor Shor of Orléans** (*fl.* *c.* 1150). It was from them and their associates that contemporary Jewish thought was passed on to Andrew of St Victor (see below).

Ibn Ezra is now famous because of his critical approach to the Pentateuch and Isaiah. This was known to a number of Christian scholars, but it was not until Spinoza reintroduced him to the

Christian world in the late seventeenth century that his theories became influential among Christians.

From about 1150 to about 1350

The Victorines. Pupils of Hugh of St Victor, the Victorines represented a distinctive strand of biblical exegesis. In theory, they tried to retain their master's dual emphasis on the life of the scholar and that of the monk, but in practice this broke down under the pressure of specialization. By 1200 St Victor was turning away from secular concerns, and the Paris schools were developing a theology independent of biblical exegesis. The main representatives of the Victorine approach were **Achard** (*fl. c.* 1155–71), **Andrew** (d. 1175), **Richard** (d. 1173) and **Walter** (*fl. c.* 1150–60).

Richard of St Victor was a prominent mystical theologian, but, thanks to the example of his master Hugh, he made some contribution to biblical studies as well. The real scholar of St Victor, however, was Andrew, an English monk who introduced completely new methods of exegesis. Andrew believed that the meaning of a text must be sought in the text itself, and not in external authorities, however venerable they might be. He had a strong preference for the literal sense of Scripture, and believed that Moses used earlier sources when writing the Pentateuch (as opposed to the general belief that he had been directly inspired to write).

Andrew's greatest originality, however, was his willingness to make use of contemporary Jewish exegesis. He believed that the Jews were closer to the atmosphere of biblical times than contemporary Christians were, and that their interpretation of the Old Testament offered a better insight into the original meaning. It is possible that he made some study of the Hebrew language himself, but more likely that he acquired his knowledge of the original text from Jewish scholars of his acquaintance. In any case, his many commentaries on the Old Testament reveal an awareness of Hebrew which was almost unique in the Middle Ages. Andrew was accused by his contemporaries of being a 'Judaizer', so great was his love for the literal sense of the Hebrew Old Testament, but he did not hesitate to criticize Jewish exegesis when it veered off into allegory.

Andrew's most extraordinary pupil was his fellow Englishman, **Herbert of Bosham** (*fl. c.* 1160–70), a member of the entourage of Thomas à Becket. Herbert left a commentary on Jerome's Hebraic Psalter which demonstrates a deep knowledge of Hebrew, and of Rashi's interpretative methods. Herbert was even prepared to accept that passages quoted in the New Testament as messianic may not have been so intended by the original author. He also seems to have been the first Christian scholar to have used a Hebrew dictionary. Unfortunately, his work never circulated, and was lost until it was discovered by accident in 1950.

Also within the Victorine orbit, though not members of the monastery, were **Peter Comestor** or **Manducator ('the Eater')** (d. 1179), so called because of his appetite for the Word of God, **Peter the Chanter** (d. 1197) and **Stephen Langton** (d. 1228). All of them worked to spread Victorine ideas and, as a result of their efforts, the literal interpretation of Scripture regained its place as the proper foundation for the spiritual exposition of the text. Peter the Chanter was especially interested in preaching, and wrote a manual on the subject. Together with Stephen Langton, he seems to have been largely responsible for the division of biblical books into chapters, which was standardized at Paris shortly after 1200.

Joachim of Fiore (d. 1204). He wrote a harmony of the two Testaments, and commentaries on Psalms, the gospels and Revelation, in which his main aim was to prophesy future historical events. His readiness to identify biblical prophecy with contemporary history remained very popular in non-academic circles, but its subversive character meant that it soon went underground.

Thomas of Chobham (*fl. c.* 1190–1210). He was a disciple of Peter the Chanter, and in his book, *Summa de Arte Praedicatoria* (*Handbook on Preaching*), argued that preaching was the highest form of biblical exegesis. His exposition of the preacher's art may be taken as a model for its time.

William of Auvergne (*fl. c.* 1220–28). He wrote a number of commentaries on the Old Testament wisdom literature, which specialized in the spiritual interpretation. Nevertheless, he was not afraid to bring his own philosophical insights to bear on the text, which gives him an originality lacking in many others of his time.

Hugh of St Cher (*fl. c.* 1230–35). One of the most important medieval commentators, he organized a movement of preaching friars, and provided them with a commentary which covered the entire Bible. He developed the traditional gloss into something more substantial, which he called a *postilla.* The origin of this word is obscure, but it soon replaced the word 'gloss' in the sense of 'commentary'. His postills continued to be published until the seventeenth century, and were widely studied and admired.

Robert Grosseteste (d. 1253). He taught in both Paris and Oxford, and continued the tradition of Victorine thought which he had inherited through Stephen Langton. He was a keen scientist, and wrote a number of commentaries on Scripture, notably one on the six days of creation, in which he displayed his scientific knowledge. He did his utmost to promote biblical studies, helping to create an English school of Scripture interpretation which produced an atmosphere favourable to the later work of John Wycliffe and the Lollards.

Thomas Aquinas (1226–74). The greatest medieval theologian, he also wrote commentaries and works on biblical exegesis. Following Aristotelian method, Aquinas argued that the unity of body and soul in the human person implied a similar unity of letter and spirit in Scripture, so that it was not possible to separate these two as had been the custom in allegorical exegesis.

Bonaventure (1221–74). He was contemporary with Aquinas, but opposed to the Aristotelian method. His much more traditional approach reflects the Victorines of the previous century more than his own time, though there are concessions to the new learning in his work. His postill on Ecclesiastes became a medieval classic.

Roger Bacon (*c.* 1214–92). He was a prominent English scientist like Robert Grosseteste, but more secular in his outlook. Nevertheless, he argued for the importance of studying Greek and Hebrew, and was not afraid to reopen questions of textual criticism.

Meister (Master) Johannes Eckhart (*c.* 1260–*c.* 1328). A Dominican friar of German origin, Eckhart became one of the most famous mystics of the Middle Ages. He wrote in German as well as in Latin, and made a major contribution towards the development of his native language as a literary medium. Today he is chiefly famous for his doctrine of mystical union with God, which was condemned by the pope at Avignon in 1329, shortly after Eckhart's death. His biblical works are different in style and tone, reflecting the scholastic influence of Thomas Aquinas. Eckhart wrote commentaries on Genesis, Exodus, the Wisdom of Solomon, Ecclesiasticus and John's gospel. He has also left us over 100 of his sermons, mostly on biblical themes.

Nicholas of Lyra (*c.* 1270–1340). He knew Hebrew and Jewish commentaries of the period, but was ignorant of Greek. His main aim was to establish the literal sense of Scripture and to reject allegory. In this he was following Andrew of St Victor, and a number of lesser and often anonymous exegetes, one of whom wrote a literal commentary on the Song of Songs about 1300. His postills were the first biblical commentary to be printed, and he remained popular until well into the sixteenth century.

Robert Holcot (d. *c.* 1349). He taught at Oxford and possibly also at Cambridge. He wrote commentaries on Wisdom, Ecclesiasticus and the twelve minor prophets, and was accused of 'Pelagianism' (literalism).

From about 1350 to about 1500

John Wycliffe (Wyclif, Wiclif) (*c.* 1329–84). One of the most outstanding biblical scholars of his day, he is usually hailed as the 'morning star' of the Reformation. Wycliffe wrote postills on the entire Bible, and strongly advocated its authority over against that of the church. After an initial period of scepticism, Wycliffe became convinced of the absolute truth of the literal sense of the Bible, a position which he defended in his great work *On the Truth of Scripture* (*De Veritate Sacrae Scripturae,* 1378). He undertook to translate the Bible into English for the first time since King Alfred's days. Although not concerned to start his own movement, he was followed by a number of itinerant lay preachers, who came to be called Lollards because of their supposed babbling. Wycliffe also exercised a great influence on the Czech reformer, **Jan Hus** (*c.* 1369–1415), who was eventually martyred for his beliefs.

Jean Gerson (1363–1429). In many ways he was the church's answer to Wycliffe. His allegorizing commentaries on the Magnificat and the Song of Songs were very influential on the young Martin Luther, and on a number of Counter-Reformation figures.

Paul of Burgos (*c.* 1351–1435). He compiled additions to the *Glossa Ordinaria,* which were subsequently printed with it, and often quoted, for instance by Luther.

John of Ragusa (d. *c.* 1443). He came to prominence at the Council of Basel (1431), at which he laid down a number of rules for biblical interpretation. His position is a mediating one between tradition and innovation, and his rules provide a good picture of the state of exegesis towards the end of the Middle Ages.

The issues

The issues which characterized medieval biblical interpretation as a whole may be outlined briefly as follows.

1. *It was necessary to determine both what the exact text of Scripture was, and how it should be interpreted.* The variant readings which had come down from antiquity were disquieting in a text which was divinely

inspired, and they could be dangerous if used against each other. Likewise, the apparent contradictions in the classical interpretations of the fathers had to be accounted for and somehow harmonized.

2. *It was necessary to have an agreed authority to mediate in matters under dispute.* When scholars differed with each other, someone had to provide an answer which would solve the difficulty and allow the church to go on living in peace. Who or what that authority was, was itself a matter of dispute, however. At one extreme were those who argued for Scripture alone (*sola Scriptura*). As it was the Word of God, it could not be subject to any human interpretation, but must convey its own meaning to the reader. What could not be read out of the text ought not to be read into it. At the other extreme were those who argued that the human mind was the measure of all things, and that reason could decide any question, even if it pronounced against the witness of Scripture. This was not a common view in the Middle Ages, but it did exist in some fairly isolated cases. In between these extremes was a range of views which gave greater or less prominence to the church. In principle, 'the church' meant the common witness of the fathers and the ecumenical councils, but in practice, during the Middle Ages the papacy claimed and largely acquired a right to interpret the Bible in a way which allowed of no further appeal.

3. *It was necessary to edify the church with biblical teaching.* The Bible could never be the preserve of scholars; it had to serve the spiritual needs of the ordinary believer as well. As the Word of God it had a power to feed people's souls on spiritual food, and if this was neglected the church would suffer the consequences. In this sense, the Bible was unlike any other book. Medieval scholars differed enormously about how the spiritual sense of Scripture was to be understood, but all agreed that it was there – and that it mattered more than any other aspect of the text.

4. *It was necessary to relate biblical teaching to other branches of knowledge.* To the medieval mind, truth was a unity, and therefore there could be no real discrepancy between what the Bible taught and what the laws of nature or the records of history revealed. Generally speaking, the Bible was presumed to be right in all scientific matters of this kind, but it was often recognized that its text was somehow 'wrong', either because it had been corrupted in the process of transmission, or because the biblical writer had other intentions when he wrote, and therefore distorted reality for one reason or another. But these difficulties were problems to be worked out; almost everyone agreed that a harmony could be found somewhere along the line.

The methods of interpretation

The methods employed in medieval biblical interpretation were at once extremely simple and extraordinarily complex. They were simple, because they followed the tradition laid down by patristic exegesis; indeed, for a long time, it would be regarded as almost heretical to depart from this. It is therefore possible, at one level, to state that medieval exegesis has little to contribute to the history of biblical studies. But such a conclusion would be highly misleading because, within the tradition established by the fathers, medieval exegetes were extremely active, and, in time, creative as well. It was during these centuries, in fact, that the groundwork was laid for the form which the interpretation of Scripture has taken ever since.

In discussing this subject, we shall begin with some general considerations which are valid for the period as a whole, and then look more closely at particular developments, following the periodization which we have already outlined.

General observations

The authority of Scripture as divine revelation was uncontested during the Middle Ages. Usually this meant that the text was held to be mechanically inspired, its authors having received what amounted to dictation from the Holy Spirit. At times this led some bolder commentators to question the Spirit's motives, as, for example, when he supposedly dictated errors to the prophets; but hardly ever did it force them to deny inspiration. Furthermore, this inspiration was 'verbal' in the strictest sense of the term, so that it was quite possible to take words and phrases out of context and use them as the 'word of God'.

The Bible was believed to have the form it does because of the fall of humankind. The fall broke the lines of communication between God and human beings, with the result that they became spiritually blind. It was therefore necessary for God to accommodate himself to human weaknesses in order to communicate with them. For this reason, God's revelation in the Bible is given in a way which fallen people can understand. But, for the same reason, the letter of the biblical text is inadequate as a guide to the spiritual life. The written text conceals a spiritual teaching which only the enlightened can grasp. To the medieval mind, spiritual enlightenment belonged not to scholars but to monks. Scholarship served only the outward form of the text, the part that could be understood by the unregenerate. Those who were born again of the Spirit would read it differently, as a source of spiritual nourishment. There were many places where the literal text could not offer this, and to get anything of value out of them it was necessary to resort to some kind of figurative interpretation. The matter is expressed very well by Bede in the prologue to his commentary on the books of Samuel:

> If we seek to follow the letter of Scripture only, in the Jewish way, what shall we find to correct our sins, to console or instruct us, when we open the book of the blessed Samuel and read that Elkanah had two wives; especially we who are celibate churchmen, if we do not know how to draw out the allegorical meaning of sayings like these, which revives us inwardly, correcting, teaching, consoling?

Bede here reveals an important fact about medieval exegesis, especially in its earlier stages. It was intended almost exclusively for the clerical élite. From the time of Gregory the Great onwards, there was no educated laity in western Europe, and lay people were regarded as little better than Jews, for whom the literal sense of Scripture was all they could manage. All learning was concentrated in the church, and most of it in the monasteries, so that parish clergy were often just as ignorant as their flocks. It was here that the tradition of 'spiritual reading' (*lectio divina*) was most ardently pursued, and it was thanks to the social conditions of the time that it became the basic, and often the only, form of Bible study. Indeed, for a long time it was the only form of theology, which was called the study of the sacred page (*sacra pagina*) until the thirteenth century. To the end of the medieval period the *lectio divina* retained its prestige, even among those exegetes who most strongly favoured the literal sense of the text. It was only when this spell was finally broken that the term 'spiritual reading' took on a rather different meaning and the nature of Bible study decisively changed.

The main features of *lectio divina* can be sketched briefly.

1. It involved spiritual preparation before reading the text. The Bible could be properly read only in an attitude of prayer.

2. It demanded of the reader a quiet receptiveness to the voice of the Holy Spirit, speaking in and through the text. Spiritually minded readers did not question what they read; they listened and obeyed.

3. It demanded a close attention to every detail of the text. Everything in the Bible was put there for our edification, and so

failure to listen to it carefully might result in losing some spiritual benefit.

4. It called for a deep appreciation of biblical imagery. *Lectio divina* stretched the imagination to the highest contemplation of God, and biblical imagery was one of the most precious ways in which this could be accomplished. A feeling for poetry and beauty was a distinct advantage in the service of God, because it pointed to the ultimate beauty and harmony of all things.

Medieval developments

Before 800

In this period of transition, the main development was the systematization of the spiritual senses of Scripture. To the traditional three senses of Origen, Cassian had added a fourth: the so-called 'mystagogical' or mystical sense. There had also been a certain development of the other figurative senses, notably by Gregory the Great who, in contrast to Cassian, preferred the moral (or tropological) sense as the highest of the original three. What this meant can best be illustrated by the classical example of the city of Jerusalem, whose meaning varied according to each of the four senses, as follows:

Literal: a city in Palestine; the capital of Israel.
Allegorical (typological): the church militant here on earth.
Moral (tropological): the soul of the believer.
Mystagogical: the heavenly city; the church triumphant.

We do not know for sure how Origen would have interpreted the different meanings of Jerusalem, but on the basis of what he said about the cleansing of the temple, a plausible reconstruction would go something like this:

Literal: a city in Palestine; the capital of Israel.
Moral: the soul of the believer.
Spiritual: the church (militant and triumphant).

It can be seen from this that in the Middle Ages the 'spiritual' sense of Origen practically disappeared, its place being taken by the 'allegorical' sense, which was identified with typology. The mystagogical sense partly supplied this lack, but it did so in a different way. For the mystagogical sense introduced history into the scheme of figurative interpretation, even if it is true that this history was basically prophetic and eschatological. The heavenly city already exists, of course, but it is also where we are heading, and the importance of this sense of interpretation was that it pointed believers towards their personal future, as well as towards the destiny of the church and the world.

It was in the area of commentary-writing that this period displayed the least originality. To Bede and his successors, a 'commentary' was little more than a selection of patristic writings, coupled with a guide to explain their use. This was also true of the Carolingians, whose main aim was to cull material from as many sources as possible.

From about 800 to about 1150

The main achievement of biblical scholarship during this period was the gloss (*glossa* or *glosa*). In the ninth century, biblical studies hardly progressed at all, except in quantity; and the tenth century is a complete blank, because theologians turned their attention to other matters, notably the development of the liturgy. It was only from about 1000 that a revival of interest in the scholarly study of the Bible began, and it took the form of short notes, mostly interwoven with the text or written in the margins. These notes were intended as guides to perplexed readers, so that they could understand what the text meant in places where it was otherwise difficult or incomprehensible.

From rather humble beginnings, the gloss developed until it became almost a parallel text in its own right. Some manuscripts were written in parallel columns – the text on the left, the continuous gloss on the right. In other cases, glosses were produced as separate manuscripts. The classic example is the so-called *Glossa Ordinaria*, which was the work of many hands and became a set text in the schools about 1150. It revealed a deep interest in other disciplines, particularly law, which had its own tradition of glossing going back to the time of Justinian I (527–65). It also revealed a common-sense approach to the text which was designed to remove mysteries as far as possible, and it revealed that the fathers of the church were not always in agreement about how a particular passage should be interpreted. This had the effect of lowering their authority, since truth must be one, and two contradictory opinions could not both be equally right.

Initially the purpose of the extended, or continuous, gloss was to provide a textbook explaining the text's meaning, but as time went on it gradually came to include theological questions (*quaestiones*) as well. These questions were frequently raised by monks and nuns who were puzzled by the text, and wanted to understand it more deeply. Commentators endeavoured to cater for them within the gloss framework, but this eventually became too unwieldy. The *quaestiones* gradually ousted the literal commentary, and this led to a division of labour.

In the final stage of development during this period, Peter Lombard took the step of extracting the *quaestiones* from his *Magna glosatura* ('Great Gloss'), and reordering them in a systematic way. This became his famous *Sentences*, a book which was used to teach systematic theology for the rest of the Middle Ages. It is important to bear in mind that systematics grew out of exegetics, and as long as Lombard was read, it continued to bear the stamp of its origin.

From about 1150 to about 1300

Pride of place during the earlier part of this period belongs to the Victorines, who strove to work out the plan of their master, Hugh of St Victor. Hugh was writing a generation earlier than his pupils, but he pointed the way for them to follow. He expanded the *lectio divina* to include a preparatory course of instruction, which was designed to give monks and nuns some background to biblical studies which they could then apply to their spiritual reading. This background involved consulting secular authors who wrote in biblical times, and the continuing tradition of Jewish interpretation, which Hugh and his disciples did much to rediscover. His prologue to Ecclesiastes gives us a good idea of his method, and the reasons for it:

> All Scripture, if expounded according to its own proper meaning [*i.e.* the literal sense], will gain in clarity and present itself to the reader's mind more easily. Many exegetes, who do not understand this virtue of Scripture, cloud over its stately beauty with irrelevant comments. When they ought to be disclosing what is hidden, they obscure even what is plain. I myself blame those who superstitiously strive to find a mystical sense and a deep allegory where there is none, as much as those who persist in denying it, when it is there.
>
> And so, in this work, I do not think that one should labour much to find tropologies or mystical allegorical meanings in every part of the argument, especially since the author himself aims less at improving, or at relating mysteries, than at moving the human heart to scorn worldly things by obviously true reasons and plain persuasion. I do not deny that mysteries are included in the argument, especially in the latter part. As he proceeds, the author always, with increasing contemplation,

> rises more and more above the visible. But it is one thing to consider the writer's intention and his argument as a whole, and another to think that some of his pronouncements, which have a mystical sense and must be understood spiritually, should not be passed over.

Hugh did not abandon the spiritual sense entirely, however, especially when it could be defended from Scripture itself. For example, he accepts fully that Joel 2:28, which is quoted in Acts 2:17, was intended as a messianic prophecy by Joel himself, and defended this position against Jewish exegetes. Of course, many subsequent exegetes would have agreed with Hugh on this point, even though they would not have placed their interpretation within the same fourfold scheme as he did.

The second generation of the Victorine movement made a number of further advances which characterized the next stage of development. The most creative work was done by Peter the Chanter and by Stephen Langton, who may have worked together at various times. They were partially responsible for the chapter divisions of the Bible as we now know them; it may seem hard to believe, but they had never existed before, making the work of a systematic commentator almost impossible. Verse divisions were made somewhat later, towards the end of the thirteenth century, but there was no standard system until the invention of printing (late fifteenth century).

The Chanter also compiled a manual for preachers, in which he divided the literal sense of Scripture into three parts: *lectio* (not now *divina*), *disputatio* (discussion) and *praedicatio* (preaching). These were further refined by Thomas of Chobham, for whom preaching was the highest form of biblical exegesis. Basic to Thomas's method was a distinction between the meaning of words and the meaning of things (including concepts). If we take Jerusalem as our example, Thomas believed that the word ('city of peace') could not be separated from the thing (a city in Palestine), and that any allegorical meaning could be based only on the second of these two. Otherwise there would be a complete separation from reality, which he was determined to avoid.

Thomas's analysis of the three parts of biblical study can be represented as follows.

1. *Lectio* ('reading'). This concentrated on grammatical and semantic questions. Thomas said that any given word might mean one thing only (example: dog); many things (right); nothing by itself (the); nothing in reality (leprechaun); or something implicitly ('on

high' = God). (Except for the last, these examples are modern ones.)

In reading the Bible, it was essential to know which of these categories any given word belonged to, so that it could be properly interpreted. Obviously there would be cases where a word would be used differently in different contexts, and perhaps even cases where a word would have more than one meaning in the same context. All this had to be worked out carefully before any spiritual interpretation was attempted.

2. *Disputatio* (discussion of difficult cases). This took place whenever there were uncertainties of interpretation. In principle, there could be no contradictions in Scripture, so apparent difficulties had to be ironed out by argument. More problematic were disagreements among the fathers, which were far more numerous. Scholars such as Thomas were well aware of these, and began to look for a solution which we today would call 'cultural context', or 'setting in life' (*Sitz im Leben*). Their grammatical bias led them to call this *usus loquendi* ('manner of speech'), according to which usage changed from place to place and from period to period. This was not really a very satisfactory solution to the problem, however, and as time went on, the authority of the fathers declined, because of their lack of inner harmony.

3. *Praedicatio* (preaching). This was the privileged domain of allegory, which got its impulse and vitality from the life of the cloister. The preacher was expected to unravel the divine mysteries, to open up heaven to those on earth, and to exhort his flock to persevere in the spiritual struggle for perfection. As long as preaching remained a monastic activity, this kind of exposition was both possible and expected. But when preachers began to turn their attention to the laity in the secular world, a different approach was required. It is not hard to see that in the secular context, moral exhortation soon gained the upper hand, and it was preaching more than anything else which encouraged medieval scholars to accentuate the moral sense over and above the allegorical or mystagogical ones.

By about 1200, the traditional *lectio divina* was undergoing a crisis. The need for basic instruction in the meaning of Scripture was leading exegetes to probe the literal sense more deeply, and there was an astonishing revival of Hebrew studies. The spiritual senses were not ignored, but they were increasingly reserved for the monastic élite. More and more commentators resorted to a false humility in order to disclaim any knowledge of allegory; that, they said, was for those who were perfect, not for them! Even in monastic circles, the imitation of Christ came to be taken much more literally than before, as can be seen in the career of Francis of Assisi. But before it left centre stage altogether, spiritual allegory had one last fling, in the sphere of predictive prophecy.

This had its roots, as we now know, in the exegetical work of monks such as Bruno of Asti (Segni), who were harnessed by a revived papacy to defend the power of the church against the emperors of the day. These exegetes used biblical allegory to demonstrate that the church was the kingdom of God, the new Jerusalem, and that the Holy Roman Empire was the kingdom of Satan, the new Babylon. The overtly political purpose of such allegorizing was obvious, and initially it failed to catch on as a method of interpretation. This changed, however, with the work of Joachim of Fiore.

Joachim tied political allegory to a universal scheme of redemptive history – the three ages of salvation. He revived the Montanist conception of a third age, in which the Holy Spirit, proceeding from both the Old Testament (the book of God the Father) and the New (the book of God the Son), would cast the letter of the biblical text aside and rule the world 'in Spirit and in truth'. He even prophesied that soon the first Antichrist would come, and in his wake a new contemplative order of monks would be founded. His followers quickly identified the Antichrist with Emperor Frederick II (1194–1250) and the monastic order with the Franciscans. There was enough plausibility in these identifications to give Joachim's scheme the publicity it needed to succeed. Political pressures soon drove it underground, but it continued to surface in different guises throughout the subsequent history of the church. Even today, there is a strong popular tendency to read current historical events into books such as Daniel and Revelation, and in this way Joachim's legacy lives on.

In the thirteenth century, a new rigour can be detected in commentary-writing. The gloss gave way to the postill (*postilla*), a word of uncertain origin (*post illa verba*?), which was a more strictly literal commentary interwoven with the scriptural text. In the course of this development, the term 'gloss' came to be restricted to marginal notes, and was often used of interpretation which was basically false. Francis of Assisi, for example, warned his followers not to 'gloss over' his rules, by which he meant that they should not be given a false interpretation. The great work of postillating was undertaken by Hugh of St Cher and his school, and the new method was in place by about 1235.

The final death of traditional theological study came with the work of Thomas Aquinas and his associates. Thomas rejected the notion that theology was no more than exegesis with an allegorical purpose, and established it as a separate science, based on the principles of Aristotelian philosophy. This led him to ground his theological speculation in natural reason as much as in divine revelation, and led to a vastly greater systematization of theological thought. The Bible was still the ultimate source book, of course, but now it was read with philosophical rather than mystical eyes.

One result of this was the rise of the literal sense of interpretation to undisputed prominence in the schools where the Thomists taught. For a start, the 'literal sense' was redefined, to include everything which appeared in written form, whether it was immediately clear to the reader or not. Textual difficulties had to be explained in a rational way, and not on the basis of allegory. The spiritual sense was completely separated from scholastic exegesis, although the Thomists continued to believe that it was given by God to charismatic interpreters, who said what came to them in a way which was beyond the reach of systematic enquiry. Of course, it was not long before this freedom was abused by unscrupulous 'spiritual' teachers, and by the late Middle Ages intellectuals were openly deriding monastic interpreters of Scripture as silly and ignorant dunces.

As an example of what this change of emphasis meant in practice, we may take the interpretation of Exodus 23:19: 'Do not boil a kid in its mother's milk.' Augustine regarded this verse as an allegory, because to him the literal sense was absurd, and unworthy of Scripture. He believed that it was a veiled prophecy that Christ would not perish in the slaughter of the innocents at Bethlehem (Mt. 2:16). Andrew of St Victor, on the other hand, with his knowledge of Judaism and his predilection for the literal sense, remarked that since the Jews of his day still maintained the ban on this practice, the Old Testament text must have a literal meaning. Stephen Langton added to this by saying that the prohibition had originally been given for hygienic reasons.

Thomas moved beyond this purely literal analysis, and found a theological principle in the verse, but without abandoning the literal sense. According to him, the prohibition was designed to avoid cruelty, and also to avoid a practice common among the Gentiles. It was therefore a form of spiritual instruction, since God's people must strive to avoid cruelty and pagan practices. In this interpretation, we feel that we have moved into the modern world, in that Thomas's exposition is one which could plausibly be given today, however much exegesis and theology have moved on since. This is a measure of his achievement, and a sign that the medieval church was moving into a new era.

From about 1300 to about 1500

The Late Middle Ages was a time when the forces of change which had slowly been building up in the previous period finally came to a head. The scholasticism of Thomas Aquinas went into decline, but it was replaced by a much more radical rationalism, associated with the name of William of Ockham (Occam) (*c.* 1285–1347). Ockham was not prepared to take anything on trust; everything had to be subjected to the most rigorous proof. He was also concerned to get to the point as quickly as possible, and excluded any evidence which was not pertinent to his argument. (This is his famous 'razor', which shaved off unnecessary accretions.) These concerns were not favourable to allegorical exegesis, and they had a revolutionary effect on the interpretation of the literal sense as well.

Just how revolutionary became clear in the work of John Wycliffe, who was the most prominent advocate of the view that Scripture alone sufficed for interpretation, and that any preacher who went beyond its plain meaning would be leading his flock astray. Wycliffe wanted a Bible study which was intellectually rigorous, yet accessible to the wider public at the same time. He was a strong advocate of the moral interpretation of Scripture, shorn of its allegorical tendencies. For him, the literal sense was moral enough, and he believed that a person would be justified in God's sight if he lived by the plain precepts of the gospel. He had no time for the sacramental excesses of the church, and denied the novel doctrine of transubstantiation, which he thought was unbiblical.

For Wycliffe, Scripture contained all truth, and human knowledge was useless by comparison. Nothing which could not be found in Scripture had any place in true religion, though he was forced to admit that there were many truths (such as the doctrine of the Trinity) which were implicit in the text rather than explicit. The fathers of the church he regarded as useless, unless what they said corresponded to what the Scriptures plainly taught – a tall order, given the allegorical inheritance! He also believed that Scripture must be read as a whole, the Old and New Testaments being taken together. In many ways, Wycliffe was the product of the philosophical currents of his time, but he was not an Ockhamist in the true sense. For him, all philosophy must be subordinate to the teaching of Scripture; logic was a tool to be used in defence of the Bible, not a weapon to be used for attacking it. Here we can see clearly that he was the forerunner of the Reformation, and its battle against the secularism of Renaissance humanism.

However, we should not forget that Wycliffe was still a child of the Middle Ages, and we must not be surprised to discover that his practice of biblical exegesis often fell short of his principles. He accepted figurative meanings in Scripture, and used allegory on occasion, in ways which would not be accepted a century or more later. Wycliffe was a pioneer of something new, but his ideas had to wait for nearly 150 years before they were able to bear lasting fruit.

The state of late medieval exegesis is perhaps best summed up in the rules of John of Ragusa (Dubrovnik), which he gave to the Council of Basel in 1433. John's rules are a fascinating mixture of the old and the new, and allow us to feel the spirit of transition which marked this period as a whole. The rules are as follows.

1. *All Scripture is inspired.* This was nothing new, of course, and as a doctrine it went back to the early church. But John was less confident than earlier expositors that he knew precisely how Scripture was inspired, and he did not elaborate on this theme.

2. *Nothing Scripture definitely asserts can mislead.* This was a restatement of the ancient doctrine of the perspicuity of Scripture, though in a context which makes it an attack on the excesses of allegorical exegesis. For John, Scripture asserted far more things 'definitely' than it did for an exegete such as Bede, for example.

3. *The teaching of Scripture accords with God's goodness.* This was another attack on traditional allegory, which claimed that Scripture was full of immoral statements which had to be allegorized away. John rejected this, and claimed that even the supposedly 'immoral' parts of Scripture (such as the divine command to murder the Amalekites) were manifestations of the goodness of God.

4. *Scripture has many senses, of which the literal is one.* The literal sense contained the figurative senses. This appears to be a concession to allegory, but the second part of the rule reveals John's true opinion. Any spiritual meaning to be derived from the text must come from the literal sense, and not be read into (or on top of) it.

5. *The literal sense is the one the author intended. It is infallible, and contains everything necessary for salvation.* This was a radically new proposition, more reminiscent of Wycliffe than of anything else. It put the previous rule into its proper context, and claimed spiritual authority for those who interpret the literal sense correctly.

6. *The reader must examine the context and the style of a passage.* This is Hugh of St Victor speaking, but John put him in a context where, thanks to the high value placed on the literal sense, his teaching had a spiritual significance which Hugh would not have dreamed of.

7. *Difficulties in the text are useful and necessary.* Scripture must be expounded. If everything were simple and obvious, argued John, nobody would bother to study the text of Scripture carefully, and there would be no need to expound it. This would mean in practice that it would not be read, or heeded.

8. *The fathers are to be preferred to the moderns as interpreters.* Here John's basic traditionalism shines through. He was not prepared to forsake the church's ancient heritage, even when it could be shown to be wrong. Of course, as in any age, the 'moderns' often went to extremes, and John was basically right to insist that they undergo the test of time before being taken too seriously. But a rule like this might also serve to negate many of the earlier ones, especially as the fathers could easily be shown to have favoured allegory over the literal sense in many parts of Scripture.

9. *Commentators should be compared and made to agree if possible. In case of disagreement, the one closer to Scripture is to be preferred.* The aim of commentary harmony was also a traditional one, rooted in the idea of the unity of truth and the authority of the fathers in expounding it. It was the second part of the rule which was new, because it gave Scripture a primary authority, whereas in earlier times preference would have been given to the opinions of the greater fathers, even if their interpretation was less literal.

10. *Heretics have interpreted Scripture falsely. The aim of biblical interpretation is to arrive at the truth.* This was a traditionalist statement, because it upheld the authority of the church (incarnated in the pope) to interpret Scripture. Although John was basically correct in what he said, everything depended on who decided what heresy was. Here we must remember the context; the 'heretics' he was most concerned about were the Lollards in England and the Hussites in Bohemia, both of whom followed the principles of Wycliffe.

Conclusion

We have now come to the end of our survey of medieval exegesis, and it is time to tie the threads together. Much of what we have surveyed seems strange to the modern reader, and it is important at this stage to draw out things in the medieval achievement which remain of permanent value. These may be summarized as follows.

1. We still compare textually similar usages in different parts of the Bible, an exercise which was originally systematized in the glosses and postills.

2. We still compare the views of earlier critics to decide what we can

learn from them, a practice which goes back to Bede, and even further, to Gregory the Great.

3. We still compare Scripture with the secular literature of the period, as the Victorines taught us to do.

4. We still use verse-by-verse commentary as the most usual type of written biblical exposition, and the sermon retains its place in oral exegesis. The work of Peter the Chanter and his followers thus remains a living reality in the life of the church today.

BIBLIOGRAPHY

B. Bischoff, 'Turning Points in the History of Latin Exegesis in the Early Middle Ages', in M. McNamara (ed.), *Biblical Studies: The Medieval Irish Contribution,* Proceedings of the Irish Biblical Association 1 (Dublin: Dominican Publications, 1976), pp. 74–77.

P. M. Blowers, *Exegesis and Spiritual Pedagogy in Maximus the Confessor: An Investigation of the* Quaestiones ad Thalassium (Notre Dame: University of Notre Dame Press, 1991).

G. H. Brown, *Bede the Venerable* (Boston, MA: Twayne, 1987).

W. Courtenay, 'The Bible in the Fourteenth Century: Some Observations', in *Church History* 54 (1985), pp. 176–187.

G. T. Dempsey, 'Aldhelm of Malmesbury and the Paris Psalter: A Note on the Survival of Antiochene Exegesis', *Journal of Theological Studies* new series 38 (1987), pp. 368–386.

R. K. Emmerson and B. McGinn (eds.), *The Apocalypse in the Middle Ages* (Ithaca, NY: Cornell University Press, 1992).

G. R. Evans, *The Language and Logic of the Bible: The Earlier Middle Ages* (Cambridge: Cambridge University Press, 1984).

———*The Language and Logic of the Bible: The Road to Reformation* (Cambridge: Cambridge University Press, 1985).

———'Thomas of Chobham on Preaching and Exegesis', *Recherches de théologie ancienne et médiévale* 52 (1985), pp. 159–170.

———'Wycliffe the Academic: The Old and the New', *Churchman* 98 (1984), pp. 307–318.

M. T. Gibson, 'Lanfranc's Commentary on the Pauline Epistles', *Journal of Theological Studies* new series 22 (1971), pp. 86–112.

———'The Study of the Bible in the Middle Ages', *Journal of Ecclesiastical History* 39 (1988), pp. 230–232.

A. G. Holder, 'Bede and the Tradition of Patristic Exegesis', *Anglican Theological Review* 72 (1990), pp. 399–411.

J. F. Kelly, 'Bede and the Irish Exegetical Tradition on the Apocalypse', *Revue Bénédictine* 92 (1982), pp. 393–406.

M. L. Laistner, 'Antiochene Exegesis in Western Europe during the Middle Ages', *Harvard Theological Review* 40 (1947), pp. 19–31.

————'Some Early Medieval Commentaries on the Old Testament', *Harvard Theological Review* 46 (1953), pp. 27–46.

G. W. H. Lampe (ed.), *Cambridge History of the Bible* 2 (Cambridge: Cambridge University Press, 1969).

R. Loewe, 'Herbert of Bosham's Commentary on Jerome's Hebrew Psalter: A Preliminary Investigation into its Sources', *Biblica* 34 (1953), pp. 44–77; 159–192; 275–298.

————'The Medieval Christian Hebraists of England', *Transactions of the Jewish Historical Society of England* 17 (1951–52), pp. 245–249.

H. de Lubac, *Exégèse médiévale: les quatre sens de l'Ecriture* (Paris: Aubier, 1959–64).

M. McNamara (ed.), *Biblical Studies: The Medieval Irish Contribution*, Proceedings of the Irish Biblical Association 1 (Dublin: Dominican Publications, 1976).

T. F. Merrill, 'Achard of St Victor and the Medieval Exegetical Tradition: Rom. 7:22–25 in a Sermon on the Feast of the Resurrection', *Westminster Theological Journal* 48 (1986), pp. 47–62.

R. Ray, 'What do we know about Bede's Commentaries?', *Recherches de théologie ancienne et médiévale* 49 (1982), pp. 13–18.

M. Reeves, 'The Originality and Influence of Joachim of Fiore', *Traditio* 36 (1980), pp. 269–316.

I. S. Robinson, 'Political Allegory in the Biblical Exegesis of Bruno of Segni', in *Recherches de théologie ancienne et médiévale* 50 (1983), pp. 69–98.

C. Scalise, 'The Sensus Literalis: A Hermeneutical Key to Biblical Exegesis', *Scottish Journal of Theology* 42 (1989), pp. 45–65.

B. Smalley, *The Gospels in the Schools c. 1100–c. 1280* (London: Hambledon, 1985).

————*The Study of the Bible in the Middle Ages* (Oxford: Blackwell, 3rd edn, 1983).

————'Use of the Spiritual Senses of Scripture in Persuasion and Argument by Scholars in the Middle Ages', *Recherches de théologie ancienne et médiévale* 52 (1985), pp. 44–63.

F. Stegmuller, *Repertorium Biblicum Medii Aevi* (Madrid, 1950–61); *Supplementum* (1976–80).

K. Walsh and D. Wood (eds.), *The Bible in the Medieval World* (Oxford: Blackwell, 1985).

B. Ward, *The Venerable Bede* (London: Geoffrey Chapman, 1990).

A case study: The Song of Songs

No book of the Bible received more attention during the Middle Ages than the Song of Songs. From the time of Hippolytus (*c.* AD 200) to that of Luther, there were at least sixty-four commentaries on the book, of which forty-five date from after 800. Virtually every major biblical expositor, and any number of minor ones, had something to say about this work, which remained a classic from one generation to the next. At the same time, there are some important commentators who did not write on it, among them Augustine, Hugh and Andrew of St Victor, and (much later) John Calvin.

No book of the Bible, with the possible exception of Revelation, has had so many divergent interpretations put upon it. From the rabbis who thought it was a saga of God's dealings with Israel, to those modern interpreters who see it as a treatise of women's liberation, almost every imaginable possibility has been canvassed at some time or other. Within this welter of variety, however, two basic modes of interpretation stand out: the literal and the allegorical. Before the advent of modern criticism, the literal interpretation was so rare as to cause scandal when it appeared. The only Christian writer of note to have adopted it was Theodore of Mopsuestia, and his work was conveniently lost. Allegory ruled the field in both Jewish and Christian interpretation, and so it remained until the first part of the nineteenth century.

Furthermore, it must be said that allegorical interpretations of this book are the only ones which have had much success in the life of the church. Even in our own anti-allegorical age, this is still true, as can be seen from Song 2:4: 'He brought me to the banqueting house, and his banner over me was love' (AV). In the original context, it appears that what the author had in mind was a night of sexual bliss following an orgy of heavy drinking, but no modern congregation singing the chorus based on these words ever thinks of that. To us, it is 'obvious' that here we have Christ, taking us into his church, and feeding us with his spiritual food and drink in holy communion. Scholars may protest all they like, but for most Christians, the traditional interpretation resurfaces almost without asking, and the literal sense is completely ignored.

This curious phenomenon leads us to ask whether the allegorical mode of interpretation is the right one to adopt in this case, or at least whether it is closer to the poem's intention than the 'literal' sense, as this is conceived by modern exegetes. What, after all, was the author's original intention? If we assume that the author was not Solomon, but someone working within the wisdom tradition associated with his name, what intention was he supposed to have had? The modern tendency to regard Proverbs as a collection of useful but rather boring advice, Ecclesiastes as the work of a jaded humanist and the Song of Songs as a piece of erotica shows how little the Wisdom tradition is understood or appreciated nowadays, in sharp contrast to earlier times, when these three books were regarded as among the choicest in the whole of Scripture. Literal interpretation has removed these books from everyday church use, and they have almost ceased to be a part of the canon for all practical purposes.

The Christian church inherited its allegorical interpretation from the Jews, and Christian expositors quickly tailored it to suit their own particular theology. From the time of Origen we meet with the two classical interpretations, the union of the Word of God with the human soul on the one hand, and the union of Christ with the church, his bride, on the other. These two interpretations represent different aspects of the church: the private, devotional life of the individual believer, and the collective witness and destiny of the spiritual communion of all the faithful. They are not mutually exclusive, and most allegorical commentaries contain elements of both, though they may tend towards one or the other.

It is certainly true, of course, that the discipline of celibacy imposed on the monastic orders created a very tense sexual situation, in which a book like the Song of Songs was potential dynamite. But it must be remembered that they did not invent the allegorical interpretation, which antedated the emphasis on celibacy by some centuries. The distaste felt by some for expressions of erotic love was at least matched by the confusion which the book's secular tone generated. Apart from Esther, whose canonical status was long questioned, the Song of Songs is the only book in the Bible which never mentions the name of God. To the medieval mind, this could only mean that it was the mystical text *par excellence*, for God had hidden himself behind its very words.

Of all the great commentaries on this book, none surpasses the eighty-six sermons of Bernard of Clairvaux, a devotional classic which is still widely read today. Bernard favoured the personal approach taken by the allegory of the Word and the soul, and it was on this that he concentrated. His sermons were written over a period of eighteen years, beginning in 1135 and continuing up to his death in 1153. In spite of the nearly 600 pages of text which resulted from this labour,

Bernard never got beyond the first verse of the third chapter. The first eight sermons are taken up with Song 1:2: 'Let him kiss me with the kisses of his mouth!' There are obviously an enormous number of digressions, but these are fascinating in their own right. For what Bernard does (and this is the main reason his work is still popular today) is to read the entire Bible through the prism which the Song of Songs offers. For Bernard the Song is not just a mystical allegory, but the key to understanding the Scriptures as a whole, and therefore the most perfect expression of the spiritual life. In the course of his sermons we meet the entire sweep of biblical revelation, from the creation of the world to the second coming of Christ.

The first sermon, which is a kind of introduction to the whole collection, sets the tone admirably. Bernard says:

> It is necessary to speak to you, Christian friends, about different truths from those truths which people need to hear who are in the world, or at least we have to speak about those truths in a different way. To people who are in the world, milk should be given and not meat, if a preacher wishes to follow the apostle Paul's method of teaching: *I gave you milk, not solid food, for you were not yet ready for it* (1 Cor. 3:2). Paul himself teaches us, through his own example, to offer more solid nourishment to spiritual people, as when he says: *This is what we speak, not in words taught us by human wisdom but in words taught by the Spirit, expressing spiritual truths in spiritual words* (1 Cor. 2:13). He also says: *We . . . speak a message of wisdom among the mature* (1 Cor. 2:6). So be prepared to be nourished not with milk, but with bread. There is bread in these words of Solomon, from the Song of Songs, which is full of nourishment. We now place it before us and break it as we have need of it.

And later in the same sermon:

> But who is going to break this bread? The Master of the House is present, so you must recognize him in the breaking of the bread (Lk. 24:35). Who else is capable of breaking the bread? As far as I am concerned, I am not rash enough to arrogate this to myself. If you are looking at me you will receive nothing. For I too, am with those who wait to receive their meat from God. I beg God, with you, for the food of my soul and the sustenance of my spirit. Poor and needy as I am, I knock at the door of the One who opens and no-one can shut (Rev. 3:7), so that I can receive a

> knowledge of the deep mystery which lies hidden in this book. The eyes of all look to you, and you give them their food at the proper time (Ps. 145:15). Your little children seek bread and there is no-one to break it for them. From your goodness we hope for that blessing. O most merciful One, break your bread to the hungry souls who are before you, through my hands, if you see fit, through the power of your grace!

So Bernard introduces his theme and prays to God for grace to expound the text as he should. Notice how he identifies the bread with the Word, not with the sacrament, which strikes us as a curiously 'Protestant' trait.

On the subject of the kiss, which takes up the sermons on Song 1:2, we can glean something of the flavour of his theological exposition from Sermon 8. Bernard says of this:

> I am sure that no creature, not even an angel, is admitted to such and so holy a secret of divine love. Does not Paul say from his own knowledge that that peace surpasses all understanding, even that of the angels (Phil. 4:7)? That is why the Bride, although she is bold in many things, does not dare to say: *Let him kiss me with his mouth,* for that is reserved for the Father alone. But she asks something less. *Let him kiss me,* she says, *with the kiss of his mouth.* See the new Bride receiving the new kiss, not from the Bridegroom's mouth but from the kiss of his mouth.
>
> He breathed on them, it says, and that certainly means that Jesus breathed on his apostles, that is, the primitive church, and said, *Receive the Holy Spirit* (Jn. 20:22). That was the kiss. What was it? A breath? No, but the invisible Spirit, who is so bestowed in the breath of the Lord that he is understood to have proceeded equally from the Son and from the Father (Jn. 15:26).
>
> The kiss is truly common to him who kisses and to him who is kissed. And so it satisfies the Bride to receive the Bridegroom's kiss, although it is not a kiss from his mouth. For she thinks it is not a small thing to be kissed by the kiss, for that is nothing but to be given the Holy Spirit. Surely if the Father kisses and the Son receives the kiss, it is appropriate to think of the Holy Spirit as the kiss, for he is the imperturbable peace of the Father and the Son, their secure bond, their indivisible unity.

So there we have it: the double procession of the Holy Spirit (the famous *Filioque* doctrine), which in Bernard's day was a hot topic of debate with the eastern church, is here revealed to us in Song 1:2!

For an example of how Bernard draws practical pastoral concern out of the text, we can do no better than turn to Sermon 61, where he comments on Song 2:13–14. This extract also demonstrates the way in which the two strands of allegory are mingled in a single exposition:

> 'Arise, come, my darling: my beautiful one, come with me.' The church does not flinch at the burning marks of the Saviour's passion, or run away from the discoloured marks of his wounds. The church even takes delight in them and wishes that her own death may be like these. The reason why the Bridegroom says to the Bride, *My dove in the clefts of the rock, in the hiding places on the mountainside, show me your face, let me hear your voice; for your voice is sweet, and your face is lovely,* is because she dedicated herself with single-minded devotion to the wounds of Christ and continually meditates on them. This is where the endurance which does not shrink from martyrdom comes from. This is the complete confidence that she has in the most high God. The martyr has nothing to fear if he can lift his eyes to that discoloured and bloodless face. He is healed by its paleness and is strengthened to become like his Master as he faced death, even to being as pale as gold. Why should we be fearful of the person who said: *Show me your face*? Why does he say this? I do not think it is so much that the Bridegroom desires to see the Bride as that he desires to be seen by her. For what exists that he does not see? He has no need that anyone should show themselves to him as he sees everything, even the hidden things. So what he wants is to be seen. The leader is full of kindness and wants his devoted soldiers to fix their eyes on his wounds so that they can draw strength from them. Then these soldiers will derive power from Christ's example.

The success of Bernard's allegorizing can be seen from the fact that it reappears down through the ages, and can be found as late as 1853, in George Burrowes' commentary. Even Martin Luther, who thought that he was interpreting the Song 'literally', *i.e.* within the context of God's relationship with Israel, saw the kiss in Song 1:2 as God's gift of his Word to his people.

Why, then, does the allegorical interpretation continue to find adherents even now? It may be the essentially poetic character of the book which lends itself to allegory, but it may also be that the alternative has failed to demonstrate that it is spiritually adequate. For a sample of modern literal interpretation, we may take Marvin Pope: 'Kiss. The root *nsq* has all the range of meanings of our word "kiss". There is in Ezekiel 3:13 the application to wings of the cherubim touching each other, but elsewhere it is a matter of at least one mouth applied to a variety of objects – mouth, lips, hands, feet, and idol, a calf.' After reading something as dry as that, it is perhaps easier to understand why the allegorical sense continues to exert its appeal.

BIBLIOGRAPHY

An almost complete guide to the history of interpretation of the Song of Songs will be found in M. H. Pope, *Song of Songs: A New Translation with Introduction and Commentary*, Anchor Bible Commentary 7C (New York: Doubleday, 1977).

H. Backhouse (ed.), *The Song of Songs: Bernard of Clairvaux* (London: Hodder and Stoughton, 1990). This contains sermons 1, 3, 6, 8, 13–15, 20, 28, 29, 31–33, 36, 38, 43, 45, 47, 50, 61, 69 and 85, in what is basically the Eales translation. Quotations in this chapter are from this translation.

S. J. Eales, 'Cantica Canticorum: Eighty-Six Sermons on the Song of Solomon', in J. Mabillon (ed.), *Life and Works of St Bernard, Abbot of Clairvaux*, 4 vols. (London: Catholic Standard Library, 1889).

G. R. Evans (ed.), *Bernard of Clairvaux: Selected Works* (New York: Paulist Press, 1987). This is a new translation, comprising sermons 1–5, 7, 8, 50, 62, 74, 80 and 82–84.

E. A. Matter, *The Voice of My Beloved: The Song of Songs in Western Medieval Christianity* (Philadelphia: University of Pennsylvania Press, 1990).

J.–P. Migne, *Patrologia Latina* 183, cols. 799–1198, contains the original text of Bernard.

5

The Renaissance and Reformation

The period and the subject

About 1450 a new spirit of enquiry was clearly discernible in western Europe. Mental horizons were expanding, and the invention of printing made it much easier to spread knowledge. At the same time, the arrival of Greek scholars fleeing a dying Byzantium, and the development of a more personal spirituality inside the church, created a new intellectual and spiritual climate. The papacy had suffered a number of crippling blows in the fourteenth century, from which it was making a remarkable recovery; but the old, unquestioned authority was gone for good. Papal attempts to mobilize Europe against the Muslim Turks proved to be expensive failures, and the infidel continued his advance for another century or more in the East. On the other hand, southern Spain was finally recovered from the Arabs, and Columbus's discoveries opened up a new world to conquer.

By 1500 a renaissance of learning and of culture was in full swing almost everywhere. The use of Latin as a common language meant that ideas spread very quickly; what was printed one month in Venice was read the next in Antwerp, Paris and London. Scholars such as Erasmus were in great demand everywhere, and they travelled from one country to another without difficulty. This meant that their criticisms of the existing order circulated with great ease. It was no longer possible for the authorities to conceal information or to prevent it from spreading. As the greatest authority of all, the papacy had the most to lose by this, especially since the behaviour of the Renaissance popes was not particularly edifying. The notion that Rome was a cesspool of corruption caught on, and criticism of the church became commonplace.

Modern researchers have shown that the picture of a corrupt church was not altogether fair, and that there were many signs of new life in it. Monasteries were becoming more popular, after a decline in the fourteenth and fifteenth centuries, and the appetite for devotional literature was enormous. Gifts of money for local shrines increased considerably in the years immediately after 1500, which shows that popular piety was growing all the time. Some argue from these facts that the Reformation was an unfortunate accident, which disrupted a church on the mend, but it is more likely that it was these very forces of recovery which made the Reformation inevitable, because they fuelled demands for a more genuine spirituality in the church.

The experience of the young Martin Luther may be regarded as typical. After a misspent youth, he had a spiritual experience and decided to enter a monastery. There he found a way of life which was supposed to lead him to perfection, but which in reality left him feeling even more depressed. He discovered that pious exercises and good works could not remove the deep sense of guilt which he felt for his sins, and this continued to trouble him. A visit to Rome did nothing to help; he was disgusted by the luxury and spiritual indifference of the Roman clergy, who were content to use their positions to reap as much financial benefit as they could. In 1512 Luther, still a young man of twenty-nine, became Professor of New Testament at the new university of Wittenberg. It was during the next few years that he discovered the doctrine of justification by faith alone, which transformed his whole outlook on life.

Luther found this doctrine in Romans 1:17, which is a quotation from Habakkuk 2:4: 'The just shall live by faith.' Suddenly he realized that good works could do nothing to earn salvation; only God himself, by implanting faith in our hearts, could bring this about. At first, Luther confined his discovery to the classroom, where he began to lecture on Romans. But soon he was drawn into conflict with the church, because of the campaign to sell indulgences in order to raise money for the rebuilding of St Peter's in Rome. An indulgence was an assurance from the pope that particular sins had been forgiven, and would not need to be atoned for in purgatory. Luther realized immediately that this idea was completely contrary to his own beliefs, and he attacked it publicly in his Ninety-Five Theses, which he published on 31 October 1517.

Publication of the theses, which were soon circulating all over Europe, unleashed a controversy which divided the continent. Most scholars were initially supportive of Luther, though as he became more radical in his demands, many of them refused to follow him any further. This was particularly true of Erasmus, who was critical of Rome but could never understand why Luther's doctrine of justification by faith alone was so vitally important. Others, who were of a more conservative bent, such as Henry VIII of England, reacted against Luther to start with, but later found themselves on his side – in this case, to their mutual embarrassment.

The watchword of the Reformation was *sola Scriptura* (Scripture alone), and this principle guided its theological development. Luther and the first generation of Reformers were still deeply immersed in medieval categories of thought, and they tended to interpret 'Scripture alone' in the traditional Christological way. In patristic terms, they had a certain 'Antiochene' leaning in theology, as can be seen from the fact that Luther was accused of Nestorianism and Calvin of Arianism, both regarded as Antiochene deviations. Soon, however, a new type of theology emerged, based exclusively on the Bible. This was covenant (or 'federal') theology, whose origins can be traced to William Tyndale in England and to some of Calvin's immediate followers in Germany. Calvin himself probably thought along these lines, though he did not create a defined hermeneutical system. Covenant theology gave the church a way of reading the Old Testament as a Christian book without lapsing into allegory, and it soon became the accepted framework for almost all Protestant biblical interpretation.

By 1560 the map of Europe had changed decisively. The Holy Roman Empire was split down the middle between Protestant and Catholic states, Scandinavia and England had broken with Rome, and there were strong Protestant movements in France, Hungary and Poland. The Roman church had at first tried to come to terms with this new movement, but eventually it gave up, and chose a policy of retrenchment instead. This was worked out at the Council of Trent, which met off and on from 1545 to 1563. By the time it ended, Roman Catholicism was a distinct fighting force, militantly opposed to the new Protestant powers, and fixed in a dogmatic mould which provided a model for the Protestants to emulate. This new Catholic militancy resulted in a long series of wars that did not finally end until the Treaty of Westphalia in 1648, which consecrated the religious division of western Europe. By that time, the different Protestant churches had also defined themselves: the Lutherans by the Formula of Concord (1577) and the Calvinists at the Synod of Dort (1618–19).

The division of Europe and the break-up of medieval civilization were most apparent in the emergence of national languages, which from the 1530s began to displace Latin in both state and (Protestant) church. The use of the vernacular in worship was one of the major demands of the Reformers, and it is thanks to their efforts that a number of European languages (*e.g.* Finnish, Slovak and Romanian) acquired a literature for the first time. The translation of the Bible into the different spoken languages of Europe was a major activity of this period, and it helped to define the national character of countries such as Germany, Holland and Britain. Latin, however, remained the international language of scholarship, and so the leading Reformers frequently published in it as well as in their native tongue. It was not until the late seventeenth century that French displaced Latin in this role, and then it was mainly in the secular, not in the religious, domain.

In the British Isles developments followed a slightly different course. After breaking with Rome in 1534, Henry VIII tried to forge an alliance with the Lutherans, but failed. He then entrenched a national Catholicism, which was not overturned until after his death in 1547. Under Edward VI (1547–53) England underwent a Reformation which was rapid and thorough. However, the king died before these policies could be properly implemented, and there was a period of reaction under his sister Mary I (1553–58). Mary's many failures demonstrated that a restoration of the old order was neither possible nor desirable, and her sister Elizabeth I (1558–1603) was able to establish a moderate, but clearly Protestant, settlement when she ascended the throne.

Despite pressures from more radical Protestants, the Elizabethan settlement survived until it was overthrown by the folly of Charles I (1625–49) and his henchman William Laud, who was Archbishop of Canterbury from 1633 to 1645. Their policies eventually led to the English Civil War (1642–49) in which the radical Protestants triumphed and the king was executed. The Protestants were not united, however, and they were unable to agree on a common policy for governing the state once they had captured it. Their initial idealism soon turned to tyranny, and the populace was disillusioned. By 1660 the monarchy could be restored to great rejoicing, in an atmosphere of increasing cynicism and indifference to matters of religion. English Protestantism would henceforth be divided into conformist and nonconformist parties, of which the latter was obviously the more committed – and the more radical.

The period from 1650 to 1700 was one of increasing intolerance among the devout, as dissidents were persecuted and expelled whenever possible. The French Protestants were finally sent into exile in 1685, an experience which radicalized some of them into opposition to all authority in religious matters. English Dissenters, as nonconformists were called, were also being squeezed, though not nearly as far. Official theological intransigence made it certain that university faculties of theology would have nothing creative to offer, and theological discussion moved elsewhere. As the passions aroused by the wars of religion spent themselves, a deep disillusionment set in, and religious indifference became widespread, especially among intellectuals.

Radical new ideas which had been muttered in secret since the 1630s now gradually made their appearance in open debate, and the spiritual climate changed dramatically. By the time the French king Louis XIV died in 1715, the religious fervour of 1685 had melted away, and a new era of scepticism had begun. It was a process which took a generation or more, and its spread was uneven. There was certainly no great, single event which marked the passing of the Reformation era and the dawn of a new age of so-called 'Enlightenment'. But that such a change occurred during the years around 1700 is now generally accepted by the leading historians of the period. The spiritual revolution which had begun with Luther was finally running out of steam, and a new era was taking its place.

The biblical scholars of the Reformation period are more easily classified by theological persuasion and interest than by chronology. In sharp distinction to the Middle Ages, intellectual movements in the sixteenth and seventeenth centuries were unable to carry the whole of Europe along with them. They were equally unable (or unwilling) to co-exist with each other. For this reason, virtually everything written during these centuries has an air of controversy about it, which has often seemed anachronistic and unattractive to later generations. It is only in our own time, when religious indifference is once more widespread, that scholars can work together in pursuit of a reasonably objective portrait of those years. It will not surprise us to discover that the Bible was frequently abused in these struggles; what is more important is that so much of lasting value was achieved. For whether we like it or not, modern Christianity in the West still defines itself by what happened during this period, and our churches remain tied to its legacy. There can be no escape from the Reformation, which remains the foundation stone of modern social, political and, above all, religious life.

The interpreters and their work

The humanists

These were the earliest of the new breed of interpreters to appear on the scene, and it is largely thanks to them that the Reformation was possible. However, although many early humanists sympathized with Luther, only a few actually followed him into rebellion. They were temperamentally at odds with him, and usually less passionately religious than he was. They shone in the study or in the lecture room more than in the pulpit, and some of them came to oppose Luther, because of his perceived fanaticism.

Lorenzo Valla (1407–57). The chief pioneer of the new humanism, Valla was an opponent of the temporal claims of the papacy, and spent many years demonstrating that these were based on forged documents. In his approach to Scripture, he wanted to go back behind the Latin Vulgate to the original texts, a move which in the context was equally subversive of papal authority.

Marsilio Ficino (1433–99). An Italian humanist of a definitely secular type. His esteem for the apostle Paul was based largely on the fact that the apostle demonstrated an awareness of secular literature!

Desiderius Erasmus of Rotterdam (*c.* 1466–1536). The best known of the humanists, universally recognized today as the most learned man of his age. He completely revamped the study of the classics, and was the first systematic student of textual criticism. His edition of the Greek New Testament, with a Latin translation (1516), created a sensation on the very eve of the Reformation. Luther happily made use of Erasmus's edition, which challenged Jerome's Vulgate in several places. Erasmus's devotion to textual criticism of the Bible made many people think that he would side with the Reformation, but he tried to stay out of the conflict, and eventually came to oppose Luther on the question of human free will. Particularly influential were his *Annotations* and his *Paraphrases* on the gospels, the latter of which were required reading among the English clergy in the first generations of the Reformation.

Jacques Lefèvre d'Etaples (*c.* 1460–1536). He wrote biblical commentaries in which it is possible to trace his progress towards Protestantism. In his first commentary on Romans (1512) he tried to reconcile Paul with James on the matter of good works, and revealed that he held a synergistic position, *i.e.* human beings co-operate with God in achieving their salvation. In his commentary on the gospels (1522) he was still synergistic in outlook, but he opposed the papal claims based on Matthew 16:19. However, in his commentary on the pastoral epistles (1527), he showed that he had embraced a more or less Lutheran position, which he held until his death.

Johann Eck (1486–1543). Professor of theology at Ingolstadt from 1510, Eck was a supporter of Luther until 1519, when the two men quarrelled. Eck became a leader of the Catholic reaction to Luther, and eventually produced a German-language Bible to rival Luther's translation (1537).

Johannes Reuchlin (1455–1522). A great-uncle of Luther's friend and disciple Melanchthon, Reuchlin was a leading Hebraist of his time. He encouraged students to work on their Hebrew as much as on their Greek, and published a grammar of the language for their use (1506). He was strongly opposed to the Reformation when it came, and tried to detach Melanchthon from it.

John Colet (*c.* 1466–1519). A great friend of Erasmus, Colet was responsible for bringing him to England for a few years. He himself delivered a series of lectures on the Pauline epistles at Oxford in 1497, which demonstrated his humanist learning and sympathies. He was the most outstanding English humanist of his time, and was later claimed by both Protestants and Catholics as one of theirs.

Guillaume Budé (1467–1540). A French humanist who persuaded the king of France to appoint secular lecturers who would expound the Greek and Hebrew Scriptures with a freedom denied them by the theological faculty of the Sorbonne. It was largely thanks to them that the young Calvin received a humanist training in scriptural as well as in secular exegesis.

Sebastiano Castellio (1515–63). This humanist professed Protestantism, but was deeply opposed to Calvin on many points of doctrine, especially on predestination. He is famous for his objections to the canonicity of the Song of Songs, which caused him to be denied ordination at Geneva. He later published elegant Latin and French translations of the Bible, which included the Song.

The Lutheran Reformers

Martin Luther (1483–1546). Martin Luther was such a towering figure in his own time that the entire Reformation of the sixteenth century is now indelibly associated with his name. His own theological output was prodigious, though some of his writings have been published only in the twentieth century. He is famous chiefly for his translation of the Bible into German, which he began in 1524, and which remains the basis of the most widely used modern

German translation. His exegetical works comprise slightly over half his total output – thirty volumes out of fifty-five in the American edition of his works. With a few exceptions, they are mostly lecture notes which have been written up for publication. The rest are mainly sermons. Because of their great importance, they are listed here in order of their composition.

1513–15	Psalms	1526	Ecclesiastes
1515–16	Romans (published in 1938)	1527	1 John
1517–18	Hebrews	1527–28	1 Timothy
1521	Luke 1:46–55 (Magnificat)	1527	Titus
1522	1 Peter (Sermons)	1527	Philemon
1523	2 Peter (Sermons)	1528	Isaiah
1523	Jude (Sermons)	1530–31	Song of Songs
1523	1 Corinthians 7	1531	Galatians
1523–25	Deuteronomy	1531–45	Psalms (selected)
1524	Hosea	1532	Matthew 5 – 7
1524	Joel	1534	1 Corinthians 15
1525	Amos	1535–45	Genesis
1526	Obadiah–Malachi	1543	1 Samuel 23:1–7

It will be seen from this list that a large part of Luther's exegetical work was done in the 1520s, when the doctrines of the Reformation were still being worked out. After 1535 he concentrated on a massive exposition of the Pentateuch, which was still a long way from completion when he died. The commentary on Genesis fills eight volumes, and represents nearly a quarter of his hermeneutical output. Considering that Luther was a professor of New Testament, it is surprising how little he wrote on it; most of his commentaries are on Old Testament books, and it was there that he concentrated his major effort towards the end of his life. Combating allegorical interpretations of the Old Testament, without losing its Christological significance, was a major preoccupation of the Reformers, because on that depended their belief that the literal sense of Scripture was the one which established true doctrine. In effect, Luther was explaining the harder parts of Scripture to a church which was once again asking whether the Old Testament had any significant place in Christian life and worship.

Luther is famous for his distinction between law and gospel, which he detected throughout Scripture. In his view, the epistle of James was almost completely law, and he therefore questioned its place in the canon. The notion that there is a fundamental incompatibility between James and Paul has often been refuted, but Luther's doubts on this score remain surprisingly influential, even today.

François Lambert (1486–1530). A Frenchman from the papal city of Avignon, Lambert migrated to Switzerland where he met Zwingli (1522), and then moved on to Wittenberg (1523). Converted to Lutheranism, he went to Hesse in 1526 and in the following year became Professor of Old Testament in the new university of Marburg. He was one of the most popular and persuasive of the early Lutherans, and his works enjoyed a wide circulation throughout Europe. After his death, however, his popularity declined, and today he is largely forgotten. His commentaries include works on the Song of Songs (1524), the minor prophets (1525–26) and Revelation (1528).

Andreas Althamer (*c.* 1500–*c.* 1539). An early convert to Lutheranism, he became the official preacher of the German city of Ansbach in 1528. He wrote a commentary on James (1527), but his claim to fame rests on his *Conciliatio Locorum Scripturae* (*Harmony of Scripture*) (1530), which was a harmony of difficult passages of Scripture, and was widely circulated throughout Europe.

Andreas Bodenstein von Karlstadt (Carlstadt) (*c.* 1477–1541). An early convert to Lutheranism, he wrote 380 theses on the supremacy of Scripture (1520). Later he adopted an extreme form of radical Protestantism, somewhat akin to later Puritanism, and broke with Luther. His theses are remarkable for the way in which they combine a reformed emphasis on Scripture, a humanistic love of languages and a knowledge of medieval rabbinic exegesis.

Johann Bugenhagen (1485–1558). Deeply influenced by Erasmus, he became a Lutheran in 1520 and later went to Denmark, where he was responsible for reorganizing the Danish church along Lutheran lines. He helped Luther translate the Bible into German, and wrote a commentary on the Psalms (1524) which became a classic. Among his other works were commentaries on Deuteronomy (1524), 1 and 2 Samuel (1524), Ephesians–Hebrews (1524), 1 and 2 Kings (1525), Jeremiah (1526), Romans (1527), 1 Corinthians 1 – 4 (1530) and Jeremiah (1546).

Philipp Melanchthon (1497–1560). A more systematic theologian than Luther, much of the work of establishing Lutheranism fell to him. He published a commentary on Romans which went through several revisions during the course of his life. The first edition came out in 1522, when a set of his lectures was published without his knowledge. He revised them thoroughly for a new edition in 1529, and produced further massive revisions in 1532, 1540 and 1556. It was this commentary, along with Luther's lectures on Galatians, which provided Lutheran theologians with their main scriptural source for the doctrine of justification by faith alone. Melanchthon was also responsible for expressing Luther's thought in terms of Aristotelian philosophy, a development which has been controversial ever since. His *Loci Communes Rerum Theologicarum* (*Commonplaces of Theological Matters*), which he wrote as early as 1521, became a standard textbook of Lutheran theology, and contributed greatly to the development of theological method among the later Reformers. His other commentaries were on Matthew (1520), 1 Corinthians and 2 Corinthians 1 – 3 (1522), John (1523; 1536), Genesis (1523), Proverbs (1524), Colossians (1527), 1 and 2 Timothy (1541), Daniel (1543), Ecclesiastes (1550), Zechariah (1553), Malachi (1553), Philippians (1554) and Psalms (1555).

Andreas Osiander (1498–1565). He was one of the first Reformers to attempt a thoroughgoing harmonization of the apparent discrepancies in Scripture. His *Harmonia Evangelica* (*Harmony of the Gospels*) (1545) demonstrates his method, which was to say that the simplest way to reconcile apparent contradictions was to insist that similar events occurred as often as was necessary to harmonize the differences. Thus, in the passion narratives, Osiander believed that Christ was crowned with thorns twice, and that Peter warmed himself at the fire no less than four times! Luther was unimpressed by this effort, but later generations used Osiander as a model for their own efforts at harmonization.

Johannes Brenz (1499–1570). He studied under Oecolampadius at Heidelberg, and had become a Lutheran by 1521. In 1537 he led the Reformation in Tübingen, and in 1550 he did the same in Stuttgart. In his later years he was a staunch defender of classical Lutheranism against the perceived innovations of both the Calvinists and Melanchthon. He was a prolific commentator on Scripture, and enjoyed a huge reputation in Germany for a century after his death. Many of his books were republished annually in the sixteenth century, but since then he has been unjustly neglected. However, a new edition of his complete works is now being prepared and has been forthcoming from Tübingen since 1986. His commentaries include works on Job (1527), John (1527), Ecclesiastes (1528), Amos (1530), Hosea (1531), Acts (1535), Judges (1535), Ruth (1535), Luke (1537), Exodus (1538), Leviticus (1542), Philemon (1543), Esther (1543), Galatians (1547), Philippians (1548), Psalms (1548), Joshua (1549), Isaiah (1550), 1 Samuel (1554), Romans (1564), Jonah (1566) and Matthew (1567).

Reformers influenced by Luther

Wolfgang Capito (1478–1541). A native of Alsace, he became a leader of the Reformation at Strasbourg. He wrote commentaries on parts of Scripture, notably Hosea and Habakkuk, which were widely circulated during his lifetime, but which faded into oblivion thereafter. He is chiefly remembered today as an early associate of Martin Bucer.

Martin Bucer (1491–1551). An early convert to Lutheranism (1518), Bucer was the leader of the Reformation at Strasbourg, capital of his native Alsace. Though sometimes classified as a Lutheran, he was one of the great Reformer's more critical followers, and before long he adopted other ideas as well. He was host to Calvin during the latter's sojourn in the city (1538–41), and had already drawn closer to the Swiss Reformers, whose views on the eucharist he had come to appreciate. For a long time he attempted to mediate between the Lutherans and the Zwinglians over this issue, but his efforts were unsuccessful. In 1548 he was exiled and went to England as the guest of Archbishop Cranmer. There he participated in the revision of the 1549 *Book of Common Prayer* and the Ordinal of 1550. He died as Regius Professor of Divinity at Cambridge, in 1551. Bucer's many contacts made him the most ecumenical of the Reformers, a fact which has been appreciated only in recent years. His work has long been neglected, but is now coming to be seen as of seminal importance. He wrote commentaries on Zephaniah (1528), Psalms (1529), Ephesians (1527) and John (1530), before embarking on the synoptic gospels (1536) and Romans (1536), which was meant to be part of a project covering all the Pauline epistles, which he did not live to complete. He also wrote a commentary on Judges (1544).

William Tyndale (*c.* 1494–1536). Tyndale belonged to the first generation of English Reformers, and was attracted to Lutheran ideas about 1522, when he proposed an English translation of the Bible to Cuthbert Tunstall, Bishop of London. Receiving no encouragement, he left England in 1525, and spent the next ten years at Antwerp. In 1535 he was betrayed to agents of the Emperor Charles V, and taken to Vilvoorde, near Brussels. There he was tried for heresy and put to death the following year. He had completed a translation of the New Testament, and embarked on the Old, but did not live to complete it. His New Testament of 1526 was accompanied by an important introduction, *A Pathway into Scripture*, which is the oldest hermeneutical study in English, and often regarded as the ultimate source of later covenant theology. Like Bucer, he was theologically independent of Luther, and in some ways closer to the Swiss Reformers.

Miles Coverdale (1488–1569). Like Tyndale, a convert to Lutheranism (1528) and afterwards closer to Calvin and the Swiss, he helped his fellow countryman revise his translation of the Pentateuch. Later (1535) he published an entire Bible, using Tyndale's work as a basis and supplementing it from various Latin and German versions. He was later prominent in the production of the Great Bible of 1539 and of Cranmer's Bible of 1540. He became Bishop of Exeter in 1551, but was exiled in 1554 and went to Geneva, where it seems likely that he worked on the Geneva Bible (1560). He returned to England in 1559, but took little part in public affairs.

The Swiss Reformers

Ulrich (Hulderych) Zwingli (1484–1531). The chief Reformer of Zürich, he was not a noted biblical commentator, but produced a number of sermons and expositions in the Erasmian style. Unlike Luther, he made no distinction between the law and the gospel, so the epistle of James presented no problem for him. The other Swiss Reformers, and notably Calvin, followed Zwingli in this respect. Zwingli is chiefly famous for his 'symbolic' interpretation of the bread and wine of holy communion, though recent research has shown that towards the end of his life he moved towards a position closer to that of Luther, whom he had previously opposed.

Johannes Oecolampadius (1482–1531). He was a German disciple of Erasmus, whom he helped to publish his New Testament of 1516. He was later attracted to Luther, and became Professor of Holy Scripture at Basel in 1523, where he worked to introduce the Reformation. During these years he moved away from Luther's understanding of the eucharist to that of Zwingli, which he defended at the Colloquy of Marburg (1529). He wrote commentaries on 1 John (1524), Romans (1525) and Haggai–Malachi (1525), following the lines laid down by Erasmus and Reuchlin. He was also concerned to emphasize the importance of biblical study for the establishment of true doctrine and discipline in the church.

Conrad Pellican (1478–1556). A noted Hebraist long before the Reformation, Pellican was the first Christian to write a grammar of that language. Between 1532 and 1539 he wrote commentaries on the whole Bible, including the Apocrypha. He aimed his work at the edification of local ministers, who had to preach from a Bible of which they understood little.

Peter Martyr Vermigli (*c.* 1500–62). An Italian by birth, Vermigli became Swiss by adoption only towards the end of his life (1556), when he was invited to become Professor of Hebrew at Zürich. The main influence on his earlier development was that of Bucer. He taught at Strasbourg (1542–48) and accompanied Bucer to England, where he remained until the accession of Mary I (1553). As Regius Professor of Divinity at Oxford he lectured on Romans and on 1 Corinthians, though his main area of concentration was the Old Testament, on which he wrote a number of commentaries.

Wolfgang Musculus (Mäuslein) (1497–1563). An early convert to Lutheranism (1518), he moved to Strasbourg in 1527 to work with Bucer. Later he went to Augsburg (1531) and finally settled in Bern (1549), where he supported the right of the local magistrates to control the church. As a commentator he was prolific and original. He wrote on Genesis, Psalms, Isaiah, Matthew, John and the Pauline epistles, giving first the meaning; second, a thorough examination of grammatical and historical matters; and third, doctrinal and practical conclusions in the medieval form of 'questions'.

Theodor Bibliander (*c.* 1504–64). A follower of Zwingli and professor at Zürich, he was a noted Hebrew scholar and biblical exegete, who, like Pellican, was mainly interested in the education of the clergy. He had a great interest in foreign missions, and produced an edition of the Qur'an (1543) which was nearly banned.

Johann Heinrich Bullinger (1504–75). A supporter of Zwingli, Bullinger was called to continue the Reformer's work at Zürich after Zwingli's untimely death. He gradually moved closer to Calvin's views on predestination, but resisted his theory of church–state relations, which in his view gave too much independence to the ecclesiastical arm. It was partly for this reason that he was popular in Elizabethan England, where his *Decades* (fifty sermons on Christian doctrine) were required reading. He was a voluminous writer and correspondent, and wrote commentaries on all the New Testament epistles (1525–37) and on Revelation (1557).

Jean (John) Calvin (1509–64). With Luther, he was the greatest of the Reformers, and by far the most outstanding biblical exegete of his time. Calvin is the one Reformer whose commentaries still stand comparison with what is produced today, and in a real sense he may be called the father of modern biblical scholarship. His output was overwhelmingly biblical, though it was anchored in his great doctrinal work, the *Institutes of the Christian Religion* (*Institutio*

Christianae Religionis), which went through a number of editions in the course of his career, from 1536 to 1559. It is the last of these which is now the standard text.

Calvin, a Frenchman educated in the humanist tradition at the Sorbonne, joined the Reformers about 1533, after he had already published a commentary on Seneca's *De Clementia* (*On Mercy*). He soon had to flee the country and eventually went to Geneva, where he was welcomed by Guillaume Farel. Geneva proved to be unreceptive to his ideas, and he left for Strasbourg, where he spent three years with Martin Bucer (1538–41). In the meantime, the situation in Geneva changed dramatically, and Calvin was invited back. He spent the rest of his life in the city, preaching and teaching the Scriptures, and working out the basis for a Christian state.

His biblical works take different forms. There were the commentaries, which were the fruit of his exegetical labours. These covered all of the New Testament except 2 and 3 John and Revelation, and slightly more than half the Old Testament. Many of the commentaries were based on lecture notes, given either at the theological school (*leçons*) or to pastors of the church (*congrégations*). The crowning glory of his labours were the Sunday sermons, which, however, occasionally show a degree of independence from the commentaries. This makes it difficult to establish their precise relationship. Because of the enormous importance of Calvin's exegetical works, they are all listed here in biblical order, with the appropriate correspondences.

	Commentary	**Sermons**	***Leçon/congrégation***
Genesis	1554	1559–61	1550 (L)
Exodus	1564		1559 (C)
Leviticus	1564		1560 (C)
Numbers	1564		1561 (C)
Deuteronomy	1564	1555–60	1562 (C)
Joshua	1564		1563 (C)
Judges		1561	
1 Samuel		1561–2	
2 Samuel		1562–3	
1 Kings		1563–4	
Job		1554–5	
Psalms	1557	1549–54	1552 (L) 1555 (C)
Isaiah	1551	1556–9	1549 (L)
Jeremiah	1563	1549–50	1560 (L)

	Commentary	Sermons	*Leçon/congrégation*
Lamentations	1563	1550	1562 (L)
Ezekiel (1 – 20)	1565	1552–4	1564 (L)
Daniel	1561	1552	1559 (L)
Minor prophets	1559	1550–52	1557 (L)
Synoptic gospels	1555	1559–64	1553 (C)
John	1553		1550
Acts	1552	1549–54	
Romans	1540		
1 Corinthians	1546	1555–7	
2 Corinthians	1547	1557	
Galatians	1548	1557–8	1562–3 (C)
Ephesians	1548	1558–9	
Philippians	1548		
Colossians	1548		
1 Thessalonians	1550	1554	
2 Thessalonians	1550	1554	
1 Timothy	1548	1554–5	
2 Timothy	1548	1555	
Titus	1549	1555	
Philemon	1551		
Hebrews	1549	1549	1549 (C)
James	1551		1549 (C)
1 Peter	1545		1549 (C)
2 Peter	1545		1549 (C)
1 John	1551		1549 (C)
Jude	1545		1549 (C)

From this list it can be seen that Calvin worked his way through the New Testament and then started on the Old, which he was unable to complete before he died. It should be pointed out that the commentaries on Exodus–Deuteronomy and on the synoptic gospels are really harmonies of those books, which seek to present a single, coherent narrative of events. Some claim that he wrote a commentary on Revelation, but nothing of it survives, and it is unlikely that he wrote one. A large number of his sermons remain unpublished, in particular most of those on Genesis.

Robert Estienne (Stephanus) (1503–59). A French printer who became a Protestant and fled to Geneva in 1551, he published Bibles in Latin, Hebrew and Greek. His large edition of the New Testament (1550) was the first to contain a critical apparatus, and the next year it was reissued with verse divisions which have now become standard.

His text formed the main basis of the *Textus Receptus*, which was first printed as such in 1633.

Augustin Marlorat du Pasquier (*c.* 1506–62). A disciple of Calvin and minister in Switzerland, he became leader of the Protestant community at Rouen in 1559, and was executed there following an unsuccessful bid to take over the city. He wrote a commentary on the entire New Testament (*Novi Testamenti Catholica Expositio Ecclesiastica*) (1561), portions of which were later translated into English, as well as commentaries on Genesis (1561), Song of Solomon (1562), Isaiah (1564) and Job (1585). He was also the author of a Latin concordance which was published after his death (1574).

The Catholics

Tommaso de Vio (Cajetan) (1464–1534). A prodigious writer, he turned his attention to biblical commentaries in 1525, after doing battle with Luther. He was steeped in the scholastic tradition of Peter Lombard and Thomas Aquinas, and his commentaries reflect their influence. His first work was a treatise on difficult passages in the New Testament, from which he graduated to commentaries on the Psalms (1527), the gospels (1527–8) and the Acts (1529). These were all published together at Venice in 1530. He then wrote commentaries on the epistles, which were published at Paris in 1532. He refused to write a commentary on Revelation, because he could not interpret it according to the literal sense. His last years were taken up with works on the Pentateuch (1531), Joshua (1531–2), Job (1533) and Proverbs, Ecclesiastes and Isaiah 1 – 3, which appeared some years after his death (1542). Cajetan was the best and most renowned Catholic commentator of his time, and his works were very influential at the Council of Trent.

Francis Titelmans (*c.* 1498–1537). Little-known defender of the Vulgate text of Romans (1529) and then of all the New Testament epistles (1532), he appears to have been a traditionalist in an age of reform, though he stuck as closely as he could to the literal sense of the text. He was a popular writer, and his books went through several editions.

Jacopo Sadoleto (1477–1547). A cardinal in the Curia from 1524 to 1527, Sadoleto was a leading exegete of his time. He published a controversial commentary on Romans in 1535, which many thought was almost indistinguishable from a Protestant work. His work is very much in the Erasmian humanist tradition, and his professed aim in writing was to show that Romans supported the papal position against that of Luther, though in an eirenic spirit.

Jean de Gagny (Gagnaeus) (d. 1549). Rector of the University of Paris from 1531, he wrote commentaries on the Pauline epistles. His commentary on Romans appeared in 1533 and was followed by a complete edition of the epistles in 1543. Gagny followed the literalistic tradition of Chrysostom and Nicholas of Lyra, and defended the Pauline authorship of Hebrews, largely on the ground that its author was zealous for the conversion of the Jews.

Claude Guilliaud (1493–1551). A Parisian like Gagny, he wrote commentaries on Paul (1542), John (1550) and Matthew, which appeared posthumously (1562). He was well disposed towards the Protestants, and his commentaries reflect the influence of Bucer among others. In 1545 he was accused of heresy, and was forced to revise his Pauline commentary in a more 'Catholic' direction.

Ambrosius Catharinus Politus (1483–1553). He wrote a commentary on all the New Testament epistles, which was published in 1551. He was a conservative, opposed to innovators like Cajetan, and represented the medievalist spirit which was to triumph at the Council of Trent and later.

Jean Arboreus (d. *c.* 1569). Author of commentaries on the difficult passages of Scripture (1540) and on the Pauline epistles (1553), he was a disciple of Erasmus who was extremely widely read in patristic and other sources. Nevertheless, he was more conservative than his master, and opposed to what he saw as the liberalism of Cajetan and others.

Sixtus of Siena (1520–69). A converted Jew, he produced a complete guide to the Bible, the *Bibliotheca Sancta* (1566), in which he refers to the Old Testament Apocrypha as 'deuterocanonical' for the first time. His style of interpretation closely resembled that which was practised in scholastic circles, though he was not fond of elaborate theological arguments being built on single words or verses of Scripture. On the other hand, he continued to find room for the spiritual sense in his interpretation, and thus retained a medieval distinction which the Reformers were doing their best to abolish.

Andreas Masius (1514–73). He wrote a commentary on Joshua (1574), in which he raised the question of the book's authorship. He suggested that Ezra might have written it, along with Judges, and 1 Samuel to 2 Kings. He was the first biblical scholar to speak of a 'compilation' of material which underwent a 'redaction' at a late stage. Masius thus implicitly rejected the traditional belief that Joshua himself had written the book, and accepted that it might contain elements reflecting a much later period.

Alfonso Salmeron (1515–85). One of the original Jesuits, his commentaries on the New Testament were published in sixteen volumes in 1597. These were mostly notes of sermons which he had preached to a general audience over a period of more than forty years.

Benito Arias Montano (1527–98). A biblical scholar who was responsible for a polyglot edition of the Bible, which he published between 1568 and 1572. This work was basic to the achievement of the Jesuit school of exegetes, many of whom are listed below.

Juan Maldonado (1534–83). He taught for many years in Paris and later compiled a commentary on the gospels, which was completed and published after his death (1597). His exegesis strongly reflected the patristic tradition.

Francisco Toleto (Toletus) (1532–96). A Jesuit commentator, who published works on John and Luke, he was the first post-Tridentine Catholic expositor to publish commentaries which were more than sermon notes.

Francisco Ribera (1537–91). The confessor of St Teresa of Avila, he wrote extensively on the Old Testament. His main work was a commentary on the minor prophets (1587), but further commentaries on John, Hebrews and Revelation appeared after his death. In the last of these he developed a theory of futurism, which was designed to counteract Protestant attacks on the papacy as the Antichrist.

Bento Pereira (1535–1610). A pupil of Andreas Masius, he wrote on Genesis, Exodus and Daniel, and later on Paul and Revelation as well. He was aware of critical problems in the Pentateuch, and not convinced that it was entirely the work of Moses. His work later inspired that of Richard Simon, a pioneer of biblical criticism in the modern sense.

Willem Hessels van Est (Estius) (1542–1613). He was a Professor at Douai from 1582 and a leading Catholic exegete. His commentaries on the Pauline epistles were widely used, and display vast erudition and fine judgment.

Robert Bellarmine (1542–1621). A controversialist, his main work (*Disputationes de Controversiis Christianae Fidei, Discussions of the Controversies of the Christian Faith*) was printed in three volumes at Louvain (1586–93) and contained a long section on the Bible and its relationship to the teaching authority of the church. He was also influential in the preparation of the Clementine Bible (named after

Pope Clement VIII) which appeared in 1592. This was a major revision of the Vulgate, and remained the official Bible of the Roman Catholic Church until the Second Vatican Council (1962–5). Later he published a commentary on the Psalms (1611).

Leonard Lessius (1554–1623). He moved away from the theory of the verbal inspiration of the Scriptures, and suggested that 'a book such as 2 Maccabees, written by human industry without the aid of the Holy Spirit, may afterwards, if the Holy Spirit give testimony that it contains nothing false, be ranked as Holy Scripture'. Under pressure from conservatives, he later withdrew the remark, claiming that he was talking about what God might have done, and not about what he actually did.

Cornelius a Lapide (van den Steyn) (1567–1637). The most popular Catholic commentator of his age, he laid down rules of interpretation which were influential for more than two centuries. Among other things, he said that Paul's negative statements must be understood literally, while his positive ones usually have some qualifying factor which must be taken into account. He tried to include as many possible interpretations of individual passages and books as he could manage, and his work covers the entire Bible, except for Job and the Psalms.

Jacques Bonfrère (1573–1642). He revived the theory of Lessius regarding the inspiration of Scripture, and added that the church was empowered by the Holy Spirit to give such approval to a book that it might become part of the Bible, even though it was not originally inspired by God. This error was condemned at the First Vatican Council (1870), on the ground that a council of the church, however authoritative, did not have the same inspired character as a writer of Scripture.

The defenders of Protestant orthodoxy

Joachim Camerarius (Kammermeister) (1500–74). A Greek scholar and friend of Melanchthon, he was a professor at Tübingen and later at Leipzig. He wrote a Latin commentary on the four gospels (1573), which outlined their literary structure and was influential in the later development of literary and textual criticism.

Matthias Flacius (Vlacić) Illyricus (1520–75). A Croatian Lutheran who became Professor of Hebrew at Wittenberg in 1544, his main work was a key to the Scriptures (*Clavis Scripturarum*), which is a major hermeneutical study. Flacius was faithful to Luther's inspiration, and it is from him that we get the clearest idea of what the great

Reformer intended in his biblical exposition. Flacius maintained that an exegete must examine each biblical passage in its context, and determine its author's original intention. He was particularly concerned to highlight the perspicuity of Scripture, and Luther's identification of the spiritual with the literal sense of the text.

Kasper Olevianus (1536–87) and **Zacharius Ursinus** (1534–83). These colleagues collaborated in the outworking of covenant theology. Ursinus also wrote the Heidelberg Catechism (1562), which is still widely used today.

Girolamo Zanchi (Zanchius) (1516–90). A follower of Calvin who did much to restructure Reformed thought along Thomist and Aristotelian lines. He was quite prepared to go beyond Scripture in his theology, especially when it came to the question of the nature of God, about which the Bible had little to say. At the same time, though, he believed that Scripture was the only infallible source of divine truth, and that faith meant, above all, assent to everything which it contained. He harmonized his devotion to Aristotle with his faith in Scripture by maintaining that Aristotle used the same methods as the biblical writers, for instance in the description of the creation of the world in Genesis.

Robert Rollock (*c.* 1555–99). First Principal of Edinburgh University (1585), and a popular preacher in Scotland, he was one of the main disseminators of covenant theology in that country. He wrote a number of Latin commentaries, some of which were published only after his death. They include Ephesians (1590), Daniel (1591), Romans (1594), 1 and 2 Thessalonians (1598; Eng. trans. 1606), John (1599), Psalms (1599; Eng. trans. 1600), Colossians (1603) and Hebrews (1605).

Niels Hemmingsen (1513–1600). A Lutheran commentator on the New Testament epistles (1572). He distanced himself from Luther quite considerably, especially in his understanding of the law. For Hemmingsen it was not the entire law, but only its ceremonial aspect, which was abolished in Christ. This approach makes him much closer to Théodore de Bèze and the second generation of Calvinists than to Luther and his contemporaries. He also introduced humanistic principles of literary criticism into his exposition, and developed a deep interest in problems of historical background and so on.

Giles Hunnius (1550–1603). A Lutheran who bitterly attacked Calvin for his refusal to accept allegory as a valid form of biblical interpretation, Hunnius represents the tendency of the later Reformers to return to a spiritualizing exegesis of the Bible, which subsequently became a prominent feature of 'orthodox' Protestant commentaries.

Théodore de Bèze (Beza) (1519–1605). He was Calvin's successor at Geneva, and the main architect of systematic Calvinism, as this is now understood. His chief importance as a biblical scholar lies in his textual work on the New Testament. He is the only Reformer to have a manuscript named after him (*Codex Bezae*). His editions of the Greek New Testament (1565 and 1582) had a wide influence, and became one of the chief sources for the translation of the Authorized Version of 1611.

Thomas Brightman (1562–1607). This Anglican divine was a leading authority on Revelation. He was one of the first Protestants to apply the book to the church politics of his day, and interpreted it to favour the Calvinists over against the Lutherans and High Church party in England. Some of his views later worked their way into Puritan exegesis.

Robert Boyd (1578–1627). This Scotsman taught for many years in various French Protestant colleges (1599–1614) before becoming Principal of Glasgow (1615) and of Edinburgh (1622–3) Universities. He wrote a Latin commentary on Ephesians, which was published many years after his death (1652). It is full of systematic theology in defence of Calvinist orthodoxy.

Johann Gerhard (1582–1637). His *Loci Theologici* (*Theological Commonplaces*) (1610–22) represent the apogee of Lutheran dogmatic theology. In this work, Gerhard maintained that Scripture was adequate as a basis for developing a science of theology. He therefore made Scripture the basis of his theological system, and regarded its infallibility as the guarantee of the truth of the other articles of faith.

Johann Heinrich Alsted (1588–1638). An important Calvinist commentator on Revelation, he believed that the millennium would come in 1694 and be followed by the reign of an invisible Christ. Alsted did much to resurrect historical interpretations of the Apocalypse, and his influence was widely felt in both Germany and England.

Joseph Mede (1586–1638). Fellow of Christ's College, Cambridge, he appropriated Alsted's ideas about Revelation. Though not politically minded himself, his ideas had a special appeal to those who were opposed to Charles I and his ecclesiastical policies. Most of the millenarians of the English Civil War acknowledged their debt to Mede as the principal interpreter of the Apocalypse in their time.

Constantijn L'Empereur (1591–1648). Hebraist and notable rabbinical scholar, he was Professor of Hebrew and Theology at

Leiden and a staunch defender of orthodox Calvinism against attacks from younger humanists. His works are not original, but give a good idea of how rabbinical studies were used to support Protestant orthodoxy in the seventeenth century.

Johannes Cocceius (1603–69). A German Calvinist who rejected the more rigorous systematizations of his school, he wanted to devise a purely biblical theology, of which his major work *Summa Doctrinae de Foedere et Testamento Dei* (*Sum of Doctrine on the Covenant and Testament of God*), which appeared in 1648, is the chief monument. Cocceius's exposition of covenant theology, which drew on both German and English sources, became the standard for later generations. Cocceius was able to develop his idea of the covenant in terms of a succession of historical periods and events, and is thus the ancestor of both salvation history and modern millenarianism.

François Turretin (1632–87). The most outstanding Calvinist dogmatician of the later seventeenth century, he was largely responsible for codifying the doctrine of Scripture which became the hallmark of later orthodoxy. For him, the form of the words in the text, reaching even to the Hebrew vowel points, was supernatural and above criticism. His method of debate was in the scholastic tradition of Thomas Aquinas and Aristotle, and he recognized the danger that critical methods of enquiry would have for his type of theology. His was the moving spirit behind the Consensus Formula of 1675, in which the Swiss churches bound themselves to accept a very rigid interpretation of biblical inspiration. This Formula was severely attacked, however, and was rejected at Geneva in 1706. It became a dead letter soon after that date.

Early English Puritans. This name may be given to those members of the Churches of England and Ireland who tried to encourage them to move in a more purely Calvinistic direction. Some of them were occasionally out of favour with the authorities, but most did not want to establish independent churches of their own. In terms of theological method, they followed the early Reformers quite closely, and were not greatly affected by the neo-scholasticism which was then developing on the Continent. The great monument of their theology was the Westminster Confession of Faith (1646).

Typical of these theologians and expositors were **Thomas Adams** (*fl.* 1612–53), who wrote a commentary on 2 Peter (1633), **Nicholas Byfield** (1569–1622), who wrote on 1 Peter and Colossians, and **William Perkins** (1558–1602), generally reckoned to have been the leading theologian of his day, and the author of commentaries on Galatians, Jude and Revelation, as well as the Sermon on the Mount

(Mt. 5 – 7). Also important was **William Ames** (1576–1633) who contributed greatly to the development of a distinctively English form of covenant theology which spread widely on the Continent, thanks to his professorship at Franeker in Friesland (1622–33).

Among those who were more radical in their views were **William Whitaker** (1548–95), who was one of the architects of the orthodox doctrine of Scripture, **Thomas Cartwright** (1535–1603) who was often in trouble with the authorities and wrote commentaries on Ecclesiastes, Colossians and Revelation, and **Henry Ainsworth** (*c.* 1569–*c.* 1623), a leading rabbinical scholar who became head of the separatist congregation at Amsterdam, and wrote notable commentaries on the Pentateuch, the Psalms and the Song of Songs. He is generally reckoned to be the most unjustly neglected scholar of his age. Finally, we ought to include **John Cotton** (1584–1652), who left for New England in 1633 after having penned works on the Song of Songs, Ecclesiastes and Revelation.

Standing somewhat apart from these were **Hugh Broughton** (1549–1612) and **James Ussher** (1581–1656). Both were deeply interested in biblical chronology, which Broughton tried to work out in his book, *A Consent of Scripture* (1588). His work provided the basis for Ussher's further researches, among which was the 'discovery' that the creation of the world occurred on 26 October 4004 BC. Ussher's chronology, which he worked out in his *Annales Veteris Testamenti* (*Annals of the Old Testament*) (1650) is still sometimes printed as the standard one in the Authorized Version of the Bible.

Later English Puritans. These were men who either fought in the Civil War or who were marked by its consequences. They were more influenced by Continental developments towards a neo-scholastic theology than their predecessors had been, though they generally avoided the extremes of people like Turretin. Among them we may mention **Thomas Manton** (1620–77), who was ejected from St Paul's, Covent Garden, in 1662. He wrote on James and Jude. **John Owen** (1616–83) was Dean of Christ Church, Oxford, from 1651 to 1660, and wrote a large commentary on Hebrews (1668). Even more important for our purposes was **Matthew Poole** (1624–79), whose great *Synopsis Criticorum* (1669–76) is a compendium of biblical scholarship. This was followed by *Annotations upon the Holy Bible,* a work which was completed by his friends after his death.

Scottish theologians. They were partial allies of the English Puritans, whom they resembled at many points, but the situation of the Reformed and strictly Calvinist Church of Scotland was significantly different from that of the Church of England, and so it is inappropriate to describe them as Puritans. In terms of biblical study, their leading light was **David Dickson** (*c.* 1583–1663), who was Professor of Divinity at Glasgow (1640) and Edinburgh (1650–60). He wrote important commentaries on Hebrews (1635), Matthew (1647), Psalms (1655) and the Pauline epistles (1659). He inspired a series of commentaries which were intended to cover the entire Bible, and present a clear, straightforward application of the text along Calvinist lines. **James Fergusson** (1621–67) produced Philippians and Colossians (1656), Galatians and Ephesians (1659) and 1 and 2 Thessalonians (1674). **James Durham** (1622–58) contributed Revelation (1658) and the Song of Solomon (1668), as well as an exposition of Job which did not appear in print until 1759. **George Hutcheson** (1615–74) wrote on the minor prophets (1654), John (1657) and Job (1669), and **Alexander Nisbet** (1623–69) tackled 1 Peter (1658) and Ecclesiastes (1694). But for the unsettled state of the church during this period, the series would have been completed with works by other leading divines. Somewhat outside this circle was **John Brown of Whamphray** (*c.* 1610–79), who was the author of a highly doctrinal commentary on Romans, which remained unpublished until 1766.

Among conformist writers in England, **John Trapp** (1601–69) stands out for his erudition and wit, combined with an orthodox Calvinism which he used to good effect in his extensive commentaries, which cover both Testaments in outline, and Ezra, Proverbs, the minor prophets, John and the epistles in more detail. In Scotland, **Robert Leighton** (1611–84), the conforming Archbishop of Glasgow (1670–4), wrote a commentary on 1 Peter (1693–4) which was highly prized in the nineteenth century. Also of interest is **Simon Patrick** (1626–1707), Thomas Manton's successor at Covent Garden and later Bishop of Chichester and Ely. He was the author of a substantial commentary on the Pentateuch.

Last but by no means least we must mention the nonconformist **Matthew Henry** (1662–1714), whose magnificent *Exposition of the Old and New Testaments* (1704–14) was completed by others after his death. It remains a classic, and is still widely used today in various abridgments. Henry not only sought to explain the spiritual significance of every passage in Scripture; he also provided sermon outlines on them for preachers. Later evangelicals were deeply indebted to his work, though it must be admitted that many of his interpretations verge on the allegorical, a fact which distances him from the Reformers of an earlier period.

The issues

The Reformation era was a time of intense theological debate, so that it often seems that those who were involved in the controversies had little in common with each other. It is true that as time went on there was a division between Protestants and Roman Catholics which was serious enough for us to be able to say that theologians on either side were moving in different mental and spiritual worlds. But equally, it is easy to forget that for a long time that was not so, and that for much of the sixteenth century the common theological universe of the Middle Ages continued to function. Only after about 1560 did it give way, and even then the humanist 'republic of letters' kept theological issues at the centre of European intellectual life until about 1650, when it gradually became secularized.

The issues which every theologian and biblical scholar during this period had to contend with may be summarized as follows.

1. *It was necessary to find a principle of authority on which Christian faith and experience could be credibly grounded.* The unsettling influence of the new learning had brought ancient authorities into question. The Roman church's power had been undermined by internal divisions, the exposure of the False Decretals, with their claims to universal jurisdiction, and endemic corruption. The rediscovery of Scripture, which everyone agreed was the Word of God, led to the proposition that it, and not the pope, should be the final authority in matters of faith and morals. Whether Scripture was adequate to this task, or whether it had to be supplemented by other factors, such as tradition and human reason, became a major subject of debate.

The Protestants gradually defined themselves more clearly in terms of their adherence to Scripture alone (*sola Scriptura*), and sought to base their theology exclusively on the Bible. This in turn led them into lengthy discussions about the nature of Scripture and the limits of its authority, and these eventually produced a doctrine of biblical inspiration which defended the absolute infallibility and inerrancy of the written text.

2. *It was necessary to expound the Bible in a way which would make its true meaning clear.* There was a general rejection of allegorical and other forms of spiritual interpretation in the early sixteenth century, though it is not difficult to find examples where practice lagged behind principle. Nevertheless, all scholars of the period were concerned to produce editions of the Bible which would faithfully represent the original text, cleansed of its ancient corruptions. Protestants believed that translating the Scriptures into the

vernacular languages was an essential part of this process, and they did not believe that any right-minded person would have undue difficulty in understanding the plain meaning of the sacred text. Commentaries served mainly as textbooks for preachers and theologians, and were often taken up more with doctrinal controversy than with matters of textual criticism.

3. *It was necessary to defend a particular theological position on the basis of scriptural teaching.* Here there was a major division between those of a more 'Catholic' outlook, who thought of Scripture as providing evidence for a theological position which was also grounded in ecclesiastical tradition and philosophical reason, and those who insisted that the principle of 'Scripture alone' meant that the Bible contained its own theological system, which ought to be developed independently. This issue was fought out most thoroughly in Britain, where the two principles vied for control of the national churches. At first it seemed possible that the principle of 'Scripture alone' would lead to a commonly accepted covenant theology, and it was on this basis that reformed Protestants were able to unite and win the Civil War. However, it soon became apparent that within a broadly covenantal framework, there were a number of practical disagreements which could not be settled by an appeal to 'Scripture alone', because theologians read the Bible in different ways, and were not prepared to accept that some of their conclusions were matters of indifference on which Christians should be allowed freedom of conscience. The spectacle of Bible-believing Christians discriminating against each other because of differences over matters which were unclear in the Bible itself persuaded many that such dogmatism was harmful to the cause of true religion and led to demands for a more tolerant and liberal approach to biblical interpretation.

The methods of interpretation

With the Renaissance and Reformation, biblical interpretation entered a new era of sophistication. Until the middle of the nineteenth century, it was commonly supposed that it represented the beginnings of modern critical exegesis, and even today most scholars of the subject have to take this period into account, if only as an introduction to what they want to say. The Reformers developed methods of textual analysis which are still in use, and conservative Protestants continue to look at them as a source of inspiration. Calvin is still taken seriously as a scholar and exegete, and his commentaries continue to be reprinted. Those of Luther have recently been translated into English, and are now being studied once more as well.

Nevertheless, the exegetes of this period lived in a mental climate different from our own. Like their medieval forebears, they were accustomed to receiving things on authority, and the Bible was never seriously questioned in this respect. When the Reformers attacked the church it was not because they were anti-authoritarian, but because they believed that the authority of Scripture was superior to that of the ecclesiastical hierarchy. They never doubted that the Bible was comprehensible; to them, the 'plain meaning' of the text could be made available to everyone by translations which were faithful to the original. It was obviously necessary to study the grammar and vocabulary of the original languages, but nobody seriously doubted that this was an objective science which did not depend on theological prejudice.

At the same time, the interpreters of this age almost all believed that the Bible had to be read within a theological context, and their commentaries are full of debates about doctrinal questions of one kind or another. Whether this context was imposed from without (as in 'Catholic' theology) or discovered within the text (the 'Protestant' view), the underlying approach was the same. The Bible reflected a coherent system of thought, which was the faith of the church. Outside this context it had no real meaning, and what later generations would call a properly 'critical' attitude to the text was regarded as a sign of unbelief. The very few commentators who indulged in such criticism did so in isolation, and became significant only when later scholars picked up their ideas and developed them in a different philosophical and theological atmosphere.

To understand the biblical interpretation of this period, it is necessary to grasp the implications of the Reformed doctrine of *sola Scriptura.* Only then can we proceed to particular types of exegesis, and to the system of theology which Protestants believed they could find in the pages of the Bible itself.

Sola Scriptura

This doctrine was the watchword of the Reformation, and had been inherited from late medieval theologians, especially John Wycliffe. It was enunciated as early as 1519, and was a characteristic element of all Protestant theology after that time. In general, it meant that Scripture was the only rule in matters of faith, so that whatever could not be proved by it could not be required as an article of belief necessary for salvation. This moderate opinion, which Archbishop Cranmer wrote into his Forty-Two Articles of Religion (1553), and which survives in Article 6 of the current Thirty-Nine Articles (1571), was interpreted in different ways. At one end of the spectrum were radical Protestants, who insisted that only things clearly allowed by Scripture could be tolerated in the church. This was a rather unrealistic attitude, and soon had to be modified in practice, but it left them open to constant criticism from within their own ranks, as various forms of 'compromise with the world' were detected.

At the other end of the spectrum were a number of High Church Anglicans, in particular Richard Hooker (*c.* 1554–1600) and the followers of Archbishop William Laud (1573–1645), who believed that it was possible, and even necessary, to allow practices which were not expressly forbidden by Scripture and which could be justified on the basis of tradition or reason. For them, Scripture was an ultimate court of appeal against abuse rather than a handbook outlining daily life and practice.

The key issue which distinguished Protestants from Catholics was whether Scripture was self-interpreting, or whether it required the teaching authority of the church to make it plain. In this respect, all Protestants, including the Laudians in the Church of England, agreed that the Bible was its own interpreter (*sui ipsius interpres*). This was put most clearly by Laud's godson and protégé, William Chillingworth (1602–44), who, in a book commissioned by the Archbishop, *The Religion of Protestants: A Safe Way to Salvation* (1638), uttered the memorable phrase: 'The Bible, I say, the Bible only is the religion of Protestants.' Chillingworth went on to defend the right of free enquiry into the meaning of the text – a clear attack against all forms of authority imposed on it from outside.

In theory, the principle of self-interpretation was simple. Most of the Bible was held to be clear in its meaning, and therefore could and should be interpreted in the literal sense. This was agreed by almost everyone, from Erasmian humanists to radical Protestants. Only traditionalist Catholics continued to maintain the old distinction between the literal and the spiritual (allegorical) senses, and they were under considerable pressure to minimize this as much as possible. In most cases, allegory was defended either because it was used in the New Testament, or because it had been consecrated in certain special cases by the consensus of the fathers of the church, not because it was an acceptable method in itself.

Those parts of the Bible which were not clear were to be interpreted according to what was called the analogy of faith. This meant that whatever was said about them should be in agreement with what the clearer parts of Scripture already made plain, and that nothing should be inferred from an unclear passage which could not be proved from another, more obvious, text. In practice, of course, things were not as simple as they seemed. As usual, the Old Testament caused the biggest problems, since it was unclear how it should be read in a Christian context. Parts of the New Testament were also problematic, notably the book of Revelation, which did not lend itself to self-interpretation in this way. Other matters of controversy, like the proper form of church government, or the propriety of infant baptism, could not be settled by a simple appeal to Scripture, because the text did not speak clearly to issues of that kind. Protagonists in these arguments picked passages which suited their case, and either ignored evidence to the contrary, or dismissed it as 'unclear'.

Having said that, however, it should not be forgotten that there was a large measure of agreement among the Reformers. In particular, the key doctrines of the Trinity and the divinity of Christ were upheld by a literal reading of the text against those who tried to deny them on the ground that they were 'unscriptural'. Calvin, in particular, was vehement in his criticism of those who refused to use words such as 'person' and 'Trinity' simply because they were not in the Bible, when the things which they were designed to express were clearly present in the text. He therefore accepted that the language of systematic theology might be derived from outside the Bible, but not its substance.

The early Reformers were very conscious that there was a distinction to be made between understanding the meaning of a text and being convinced of its truth. As good humanists, they knew too much about the myths and legends of antiquity not to appreciate this. Calvin, in particular, maintained that a conviction of the Bible's truth could come about only through what he called 'the inner witness of the Holy Spirit' (*testimonium internum Spiritus Sancti*). This was not a subjective experience, as we might imagine today, but an objective conviction that what was plain in the text was also true in experience. The idea that the inner witness might somehow lead to a private (and off-beat) interpretation of the Bible was the farthest thing from his mind, as his writings make abundantly clear.

The next problem faced by defenders of *sola Scriptura* was the extent of the biblical canon. All the Reformers agreed with Jerome that the Hebrew canon was the one which should be used by the church, without the apocryphal additions found in the Septuagint.

Here the Roman church found itself in a dilemma. Tradition dictated that the Septuagint canon be retained, but scholarship was on the side of Jerome. The Council of Trent upheld the traditional canon, but Catholic theologians were soon referring to the parts not present in the Hebrew as 'deuterocanonical', which in practice confined them to a secondary position.

More serious were the attacks launched against the Hebrew canon, and even against the New Testament. The example was set by Luther himself, who disliked Esther because it was too 'Jewish', James because it did not preach the gospel, and Revelation because it was too unclear. Whether a book was of apostolic origin or not did not worry him; the test of true canonicity was whether a book proclaimed Christ. In a characteristic burst of exaggeration, Luther said: 'That which does not preach Christ is not apostolic, though it be the work of Peter or Paul, and conversely that which does teach Christ is apostolic even though it be written by Judas, Annas, Pilate or Herod.' In the end, however, nothing was done and Luther managed to come to terms with the canon as it stood. Subsequent attacks, on the Song of Songs for instance, also failed, and the canon remained as it was.

Once this was accepted, the next stage was to ensure that the text of the canonical books was reliable. This was a major activity of humanist scholarship, and great advances were made during this period. Everyone came to accept that Jerome's Vulgate was less than perfect, and even the Roman church authorized an official revision of it. Behind that lay a century of textual study, during which it was firmly established that the Greek and Hebrew originals must take priority over the traditional Latin version. At the same time, there was widespread translation activity, in which it was believed that a literal rendering of the original was possible. To some extent this was achieved by reshaping the modern European languages into a pattern which conformed to Hebraic idiom. There was precedent for this in the Septuagint and in the New Testament, where the Greek has a strange feel about it, because of its Semitic substratum. It is largely because of that that much of what we think of now as 'religious English' came into being. When concessions had to be made to the language into which the Bible was being translated, this might be indicated in the text, as it is in the Authorized Version of 1611, where the italicized words are additions which the translators had to make in order for the sense to be conveyed properly in English.

The Hebrew text of the Old Testament caused little difficulty; even today, there are not enough manuscripts available to make textual criticism a major problem. In the case of the New Testament, the situation is now very different, but in the sixteenth and seventeenth centuries only a limited number of Greek manuscripts were available and these could be harmonized without too much trouble on the basis of the text used in the Greek Orthodox Church (known as the Byzantine or Ecclesiastical Text). This text was issued by the Dutch printer Elsevier in 1633, with the subheading *Textus Receptus* ('Received Text'), which it remained for nearly 250 years.

Translation presented its own problems, particularly when certain words became the subject of theological controversy. Early attempts to render the Greek word *ekklēsia* as 'congregation' met with opposition from those who saw that as a threat to a supra-congregational national church. The word 'bishop' was retained for *episkopos* for similar reasons, though the Authorized Version of 1611 has 'elder' and not 'priest' for *presbyteros*. Other words which caused trouble were *agapē* ('love' or 'charity') and *metanoia* ('repentance' or 'penance'). In each case, the second of these options suggested a righteousness obtained by good works within a Catholic sacramental system. The Authorized Version chose the middle way; 'charity' would be allowed, but not 'penance'.

The divine inspiration of Scripture

Once a doctrine of *sola Scriptura* took root, the nature of the sacred text became a matter of considerable urgency. If an entire church was to be built on that basis, it was necessary to ensure that the foundation was adequate to support the theological superstructure. The church had always believed that Scripture was divinely inspired, but little attempt had been made to clarify what this meant. Some of the church fathers held to a 'dictation' theory of inspiration, according to which the writers of the Bible were passive instruments in the hands of the Holy Spirit; while others believed that the human writers of Scripture played a more active role in its composition. To a large extent, these views were correlated with Christology. Those who stressed the divine activity of the Son of God in human flesh were more inclined to a 'dictation' model of inspiration, whereas those who put their emphasis on the true humanity of Christ preferred the alternative, or 'co-operation', model. At the time of the Reformation, Luther and Calvin were both identified with this alternative, and it is that which characterizes their understanding of biblical inspiration.

For the first generation of Reformers, Scripture was the voice of Christ, who spoke through the text to his church. The question of errors and discrepancies in the Bible was resolved along these lines. Christ would not have been less divine had he lost an arm or a leg, nor indeed would he have been less human. Imperfection of this kind was a natural concomitant of human nature and was to be expected. If God had truly spoken in human terms, then it was only right that he should have accommodated himself to the limits of human nature. An unnatural perfection would not be truly human, and would in practice amount to a denial of the incarnation. At the same time, of course, Christ was without sin, and therefore incapable of leading his followers into spiritual error. For this reason, both he and the Bible could properly be regarded as infallible.

This way of looking at the matter had the sanction of church tradition and caused few problems. As long as the message was clear, it mattered little if there were a few verbal blemishes in the text. Attempts to harmonize different accounts of the same event were brushed aside as unnecessary; they bore witness only to the well-known fact that everyone sees things from a slightly different angle, and could not be regarded as 'error' in any real sense. This outlook changed, however, as Protestantism became increasingly scholasticized. The use of the Bible as an infallible textbook suited the theologians and jurists of the later sixteenth century, because it supported their elaborate theological constructions. In their minds, infallibility could only mean total inerrancy; that is to say, there are no errors or discrepancies of any kind, on any matter whatsoever, in the biblical text. Evidence to the contrary must be explained either by appealing to corruption in the process of textual transmission (which could be corrected), or by saying that the intention of the author had been misunderstood.

Somewhat more controversially, this doctrine also implied that the biblical books were written by the men to whom they were attributed. The Pentateuch was universally regarded as the work of Moses, though a few brave souls were prepared to consider that he might have used earlier sources, and some wondered how he could have composed the account of his death in Deuteronomy 34. The Psalms were attributed to David, even though some of them (*e.g.* Pss. 126; 137; *etc.*) clearly spoke about events long after David's time. This was explained by saying that David was a prophet, who foresaw what would happen to Israel. The gospels were written by the four evangelists in the order given in the New Testament, Hebrews was the work of Paul, and the apostle John was the author of Revelation. The fact that the Bible does not actually say any of these things was overlooked – a clear case of tradition being accorded the authority of the text itself.

By the early years of the seventeenth century, the ancient doctrine of 'verbal inspiration' had reappeared with a vengeance. This doctrine held that every word of Scripture was given by God, and therefore reflected his perfection in every aspect. On the ground that religious truth could not be divorced from secular truth, it came to be accepted that the Bible must be 'true' in a precise and scientific sense, even to the point of insisting that the numbers quoted in Scripture were exact, and not merely approximations; for instance, if 23,000 men were killed on a certain day, Scripture meant what it said and there could be no question of suggesting that the real number might have been 22,999 or 23,001!

As a result of this approach, statements of Scripture could be taken out of their context and used to elaborate theories on matters far removed from the original intention of the writers. The most notorious case, of course, was the creation account in Genesis, which was held to contain a perfectly valid scientific explanation of the way the universe came into being. Biology, astronomy, geology and history were all subject to the authority of the Bible, which came to be regarded as the revealed foundation of all knowledge and truth.

This concept of inspiration reached its highest point in the Swiss Consensus Formula of 1675, where the Mosaic authorship of the Pentateuch and the infallibility of the Hebrew vowel points received particular attention. By that time, however, there was a growing realization that things had been taken too far, and a reaction set in. A number of otherwise orthodox churches and theologians refused to agree to the Consensus, and within a generation it had become a dead letter. Meanwhile, a much more radical attack on its presuppositions had been launched, which heralded the end of Protestant orthodoxy as the dominant theological system, and the rise of the historical-critical method of biblical interpretation.

Luther's hermeneutic

Luther was deeply indebted to both the humanist and the monastic traditions of the later Middle Ages. However, in the course of his Reformation, he elaborated the principles which he had inherited in a new and compelling way. Most of what he said can be found elsewhere, in one predecessor or another, but the combination is Luther's own. The main aspects of his interpretation of the Bible may be outlined as follows.

1. *The literal sense of Scripture is also the spiritual sense.* This is the starting-point for any analysis of Luther's hermeneutical method. In

his lectures on the Psalms, which he gave at the very beginning of the Reformation (1518–21), he said:

> It was very difficult for me to break away from my habitual zeal for allegory. And yet I was aware that allegories were empty speculations and the froth, as it were, of the Holy Scriptures. It is the historical sense alone which supplies the true and sound doctrine.

On occasion, Luther could push the principle of literal exegesis too far, as in the famous controversy over the meaning of Jesus' words at the Last Supper: 'This is my body' (Mt. 26:26), which he used to justify a doctrine of the real presence of Christ in the sacrament. The notion that Jesus may have been speaking symbolically he described as rationalism; for him, the real presence was a matter of faith, however hard it might be to justify it logically.

At the other extreme, however, Luther frequently resorted to allegory in his exposition of the biblical text. He did this partly because he believed that Paul also did it (as in Gal. 4:22ff.), and partly because he believed that every part of Scripture should proclaim Christ – by allegory, if nothing else would suffice. However, Luther did not believe that allegory could be used to prove anything by itself. For him, it could serve only to apply already known truths to passages of the Bible which would otherwise be incomprehensible.

There are times when Luther's use of allegory breaks with the tradition of the church, as, for example, in his lectures on the Song of Songs. He avoids the traditional Christological interpretations, and suggests instead that the poem is about the relationship between God and Israel. Once that is established, he goes right back to allegory, but in a purely Old Testament context, thereby maintaining the historical dimension. Luther's allegory is one which the writer of the Song could have understood, and not something imposed by later church speculation.

2. *The Bible is the Word of God in written form, which points to the Word of God incarnate in Jesus Christ.* For Luther the Bible is not simply a catalogue of truths, but a record of God's saving purpose, which came to fulfilment in Jesus Christ. Everything in Scripture pointed towards him, and anything which was not read in the light of Christ was fundamentally misinterpreted. Luther understood this revelation in a historical sense, in that he did not believe that the Old Testament contained the fullness of truth hidden in mystery. He accepted that God revealed his truth in stages, and that the Old

Testament was a progressive unveiling of his purposes for humankind. But at each stage of this unveiling, we learn something more of the meaning of Christ for the church, and it is in this sense of Christological fulfilment that we must read the text.

Luther's doctrine of the Word of God extended also to his concept of the importance of preaching. In his mind, a believer was supposed to receive the oral Word in preaching, based on the written Word in Scripture, so that his heart might be prepared to receive the living Word in the sacrament. In this way, preaching, the Bible and the life of the church were all held together in a unity expressed by the concept 'the Word of God'.

3. *The Bible contains two opposed but mutually complementary elements, the law and the gospel.* This is the most important single principle of Luther's hermeneutic, which sets it apart from the Calvinist tradition. For Luther the law was the principle of condemnation, which sent Christ to death on the cross for our sins. The gospel, in contrast, was the word of forgiveness and restoration. Just as the crucifixion of Christ (law) had no meaning without the corresponding resurrection (gospel), so the manifold condemnations in Scripture meant nothing apart from the promise of forgiveness and new life in Christ.

It is easy to conclude, on the basis of the law–gospel distinction, that Luther is separating the Old Testament from the New. But that is much too simple an analysis of his thought. Luther believed that there were parts of the New Testament which contained more law than gospel – the epistle of James, for example – and in the promises of redemption in the Old Testament he continually found signs of the gospel at work. What changed in Christ was that the promise gave way to fulfilment, the gospel was fully revealed, and the power of the law was broken for ever.

Luther's relations of opposition (law–gospel, promise–fulfilment, *etc.*) have provided a fundamental theme of biblical interpretation among Lutherans ever since. Even today, this often lies at the heart of German theology, however greatly its biblical exegesis may have moved away from Luther's methods and conclusions. It fits well with an existentialist emphasis on passing from darkness into light, on being born again, and so on. Furthermore, there is no doubt that here Luther has captured an important biblical idea. The contrast between the righteous and the unrighteous, between the saved and the lost, is certainly a very prominent theme in Scripture, and Luther's pastoral sense and personal experience of conversion gave him a deep understanding of this. As long as the opposing forces are held together and given their proper weight, the balance of biblical teaching will hold and the Word of God will be proclaimed. It is when that balance is lost that things can go dangerously wrong, and the message from the pulpit becomes either a loveless legalism or a gospel of 'cheap grace', which has no moral content or spiritual challenge.

Tyndale's hermeneutic

A somewhat surprising companion of the giants of Reformed biblical interpretation is William Tyndale. He wrote no commentaries, and even his translation of the Bible was unfinished. But Tyndale did something which was all too rare then and is not altogether common now: he prefaced his New Testament with a guide to the Scriptures which is unique in its simplicity, and did more to help people along the pathway of Bible reading than many a learned treatise. Tyndale clearly stood in the Lutheran tradition, and it was with Luther's theology that he was mainly concerned. Yet there are subtle differences between the two men. These point to a new understanding of Scripture which would become the special hallmark of Reformed thought – covenant theology.

Tyndale's hermeneutical principles may be stated as follows.

1. *The Old Testament is the law and the New Testament is the gospel. Both belong together in the Christian Bible.* Tyndale was more categorical on this subject than Luther was, but he recognized that there is no neat distinction between the Testaments:

> In the Old Testament are many promises, which are nothing else but the Evangelion, or Gospel, to save those that believed them from the vengeance of the Law. And in the New Testament is oft made mention of the Law, to condemn them which believe not the promises. Moreover, the Law and the Gospel may never be separate, for the Gospel and promises serve but for troubled consciences, which are brought to desperation, and feel the pains of hell and death under the Law, and are in captivity and bondage under the law.

The novelty here is that the gospel does not abolish the law but reaffirms it and declares its true purpose. To abolish the law would inevitably entail abolishing the gospel as well. Not only that, the true Christian rejoices in the law and sees in it the character of God being revealed.

2. *The Christian is both a child of (fallen) Adam by nature, and a child of Christ by grace.* This is a standard belief of the church in all ages, but for Tyndale, the two things were simultaneous in the experience of a Christian. It was not enough to say that in Christ we have passed from darkness into light, as if the darkness had thereby vanished. The darkness remains in us as long as we are children of Adam, and for this reason, the law also has a saving purpose to fulfil in us. Christians are bound by the law because of the grace of God, and they must use it as a guide to right behaviour. Luther's ironic cry to Melanchthon ('Sin boldly!'), which he justified on the ground that in Christ we have full salvation, does not fit into Tyndale's scheme at all. Rather, a believer was to demonstrate the truth of his faith by living out the law in love.

Tyndale's hermeneutic presents a picture of the Old Testament which made it a guidebook of the Christian life for the first time in Christian history. The great men of the Old Testament were models of faith for us to emulate just as much as those of the New. By linking the two Testaments in this way, Tyndale prepared the way for the development of a covenant theology which would integrate them on a firm theological footing, and provide a workable alternative to the law–gospel dichotomy of Luther.

Calvin's hermeneutic

In sharp contrast to both Luther and Tyndale, Calvin learned his hermeneutical method at the Sorbonne, among some of the leading humanists of the time. His work lacks the passion and deep sense of spiritual turmoil which we find in Luther, but it is more systematic and logical. His hermeneutical principles may be stated as follows.

1. *In the Bible, believers have a personal encounter with God which convinces them of the truth of the message contained in it.* This was basic to Calvin's understanding, for without it there could be no genuine interpretation of the Bible at all. In essence, of course, he was merely repeating what Tertullian had said in his attacks on the heretics, who distorted the Bible because of the false spirit within them. But unlike Tertullian, Calvin undertook to demonstrate what this meant by a detailed verse-by-verse commentary. For him, the purpose of all true interpretation was to edify the church and the individual believer, on the ground that Scripture had been given for correction and for training in godliness (2 Tim. 3:16). To lose the sense of God's presence, and of his voice speaking when the text was being read, was to lose the text itself. Here the inner witness of the

Holy Spirit was the ultimate guide, and Calvin never strayed from that principle.

2. *The chief virtues of a good commentary are clarity and brevity.* He believed that the text not only stood above the interpreter, but that the interpreter must demonstrate this by serving the text to his readers, not by concealing it in obscurity or long-windedness. He was critical of Melanchthon for doing the former, because Melanchthon concentrated on difficulties in Scripture, which he solved in a piecemeal fashion. For Calvin that was confusing, because readers could not easily jump from one problem to the next, ignoring the clear parts of Scripture in between. He also criticized Bucer for his long-winded approach, saying that readers would get lost in Bucer's analysis and fail to understand the point. A balance must be struck between saying enough on the one hand, and saying it in a way which could be absorbed without undue strain, on the other.

3. *The author's intention must be the guiding principle of interpretation.* No text should be interpreted without regard for the way in which the author intended it to be read. This was particularly important in the Old Testament, where Calvin castigated many Christian interpreters for their determination to find a reference to Christ in every verse, however far-fetched that might be. The author's intention could be discovered by examining the historical circumstances in which he wrote, the audience and situation which he was addressing, and the grammatical form in which he expressed himself. To go beyond these in the interests of piety was to disparage the way in which God had chosen to give his Word to his people.

4. *The literal sense of interpretation is paramount, but we are not expected to follow it slavishly.* Calvin was well aware that context and meaning might oblige an interpreter to go beyond what was written in the actual text, and he insisted that this be done when necessary, as long as the meaning of the whole was not thereby altered. For example, the sixth commandment, 'Thou shalt not kill', can hardly be allowed to stand without comment; there are times when killing is not wrong, and the Bible itself gives many examples of that. A strict literalism in this case would be unfaithful to the general meaning of the Bible as a whole. Another instance is the one already mentioned in connection with Luther. When Jesus said, 'This is my body', he did not mean (and could not have meant) it to be taken in the strictly literal sense, because he was sitting there with his body intact. A literalistic abuse of the literal sense undermined it, and destroyed the credibility of the method, a danger which Calvin was determined at all costs to avoid.

5. *The Christological interpretation of Scripture must be historical as well as theological.* In this respect, Calvin broke with the spiritual interpretations of the past, and even with Luther's idea of 'Christ in all the Scriptures'. For him, Christ was the fulfilment of the Old Testament and the theme of the New, but that did not mean that every verse necessarily contained some hidden reference to him. Rather, the interpreter must be careful to relate every passage of Scripture to Christ, whatever it actually said in itself, and not to interpret it in a way which would destroy the gospel. Thus, the Levitical sacrifices were types of Christ's sacrifice, in that they illustrated the principles underlying his death on the cross, but they were not thereby unhistorical, or merely allegorical. Finding Christ in the Old Testament was for Calvin a more subtle business than it was for most of his contemporaries and predecessors, and in this respect he set a standard for biblical interpretation which was altogether new in Christian circles.

6. *Biblical interpretation passes through three distinct but related phases. If any one of these phases is omitted, the text will not be interpreted properly.* The three phases are *exegesis* (represented by his commentaries); *dogmatics* (represented by his *Institutes*); and *preaching* (represented by his sermons).

Exegesis is logically the first of these, because unless we understand what a text means it is impossible to apply it. Calvin felt free to use all the means needed to get at the true sense of a text, and it is here more than anywhere that we find his humanist training at work. As an exegete Calvin is noted for his scrupulous honesty; he resisted the temptation to read Christological meanings into even such 'obvious' passages as Genesis 3:15.

Dogmatics comes next, because it represents the framework in which exegesis is to be interpreted. Calvin avoided the medieval tendency, evident still in Peter Martyr, Melanchthon and Bucer, to overload his commentaries with theological digressions. However, we should not conclude from that that he thought theology was of little importance. On the contrary, he spent most of his life perfecting his *Institutes*, which remain the most succinct and systematic treatment of Reformed dogmatics.

Preaching comes last, because this is meant to be the application of exegesis and dogmatics to everyday life. Preaching could only be expository, because congregations needed to hear the Word of God, proclaimed to them from the biblical text. At the same time, it was more than mere lecturing, because it contained an exhortatory element which added a subjective dimension to an otherwise purely objective presentation of the facts. If preaching did not change people's lives it was a failure, and the Bible had not been rightly interpreted. Calvin never lost sight of the practical side of biblical hermeneutics, and his sermons remain models of their kind even today.

Perhaps the best way to appreciate the necessity of holding these three things together in harmony is by looking at what happens if one of them is left out. Exegesis and dogmatics without preaching are dry and academic; there is no application. Exegesis and preaching with no dogmatics are subjective and contentless; a passage of Scripture will be interpreted without regard for its proper context in the Word of God as a whole. Finally, dogmatics and preaching without exegesis are mere propaganda; they are not based on a proper assimilation of the facts. Only as all three are held together in proper balance can the message of Scripture be properly applied to the life of the church, and God's people be edified as they are meant to be.

Looking for a biblical hermeneutic: the development of covenant theology

In Calvin we find a balance between the text, its meaning and its application which has seldom if ever been equalled in the life of the church. But in spite of his greatness, it was left to his disciples to work out the implications of his teaching for hermeneutics as a whole. The relationship between Calvin and what we now call covenant theology is a complex one, and frequently controversial. There is no doubt that the German theologians and English Puritans who were largely responsible for it believed that they were walking in his footsteps, and merely explaining what he had already taught in his commentaries and in the *Institutes.* At the same time, most independent observers today would say that there is a definite evolution from one to the other, even if elements of covenant theology are present in Calvin himself. What happened was that there was a new systematization, based on the events of Scripture itself, which tied together the different parts of the Bible under the heading of the one covenant which God had made with his people Israel. Covenant theology developed slowly over a generation or more, but its full flowering can be seen in the writings of Johannes Cocceius, whose principles can be outlined as follows.

1. *The Bible is the story of God's relationship to humankind.* In spite of all the developments which this has undergone since the beginning,

there is one concept which describes the whole process – that of covenant. The word 'covenant' (Heb. *b^e^rît*; Gk. *diathēkē*; Lat. *testamentum*) is often used in the Bible, but especially in the Pentateuch, to refer to the special alliance which God made with Abraham, and the promises which he gave to him and to his descendants. Everything else in the Bible unfolds on that basis. The 'Old' and 'New' Testaments (= covenants) are not separate, but merely two aspects (dispensations) of the same thing. There is in reality only one covenant between God and humankind, the covenant of grace.

2. *God's first covenant was with Adam in the Garden of Eden. It was a covenant of works.* Covenant theology did not confine itself to the biblical usage of the term, but began its exposition of Scripture much farther back than Abraham – with Adam himself. In the beginning, it was claimed, God intended that Adam should earn his salvation by exercising his dominion over creation, and working to keep the commandments which had been given to him. (It was later disputed that this was really a covenant of 'works', and in the nineteenth century some Calvinist theologians spoke of Adam's covenant as being one of 'common grace', as opposed to the 'special grace' given to Abraham; but that is another story.)

3. *Adam disobeyed God, and his covenant was broken. However, God spoke to fallen humankind a second time, in the covenant made with Noah.* The human race was to be destroyed in the flood apart from Noah, who was chosen to survive and carry on the inheritance of Adam. Noah's covenant was one of preservation, in which God committed himself to allowing the human race to continue in spite of its sinfulness. Furthermore, God gave Noah a sign (the rainbow) which served as a pledge that he would keep his promises.

4. *The covenants made with Adam and Noah were inadequate for salvation. At a later time, God chose Abraham to be the father of all who believe.* The role of Abraham in the history of salvation was crucial. Like Noah, he was chosen out of the entire human race to fulfil God's purpose. But unlike Noah, he was not called to be a kind of second Adam. Instead, he was destined to be the ancestor of a special people who would live in the world, but not be of it. The sign of this covenant was circumcision. Abraham's covenant was one of separation, of election to a special destiny. This covenant was renewed in his son Isaac, and in his grandson Jacob, who was given the name Israel. These patriarchs were the ancestors of the prophets, who maintained an awareness of Israel's special calling in later centuries.

5. *The covenant made with Abraham was preserved in the law of Moses.*

Just as it was impossible for Adam's descendants to keep their covenant with God, so it proved impossible for Abraham's descendants to maintain their original relationship with God. But this time, God's reaction was somewhat different. Rather than destroy the people in a second flood, he brought them through the waters of the Red Sea, in which their enemies were drowned instead. He then sealed the covenant at Mount Sinai, when he gave the law to Moses and Aaron. By this law, the sacrificial priesthood was established, and the principles of atonement, which would eventually determine Christ's sacrifice on the cross, were laid down. Moses was himself a prophet, but his law was the charter of the priests, who, in association with the prophets, would serve the covenant purposes of God within the nation of Israel.

6. *God renewed his covenant with Israel a second time, in David.* Even after granting the law to Moses, Israel was not strong enough to ensure that it could be kept in the right way. Only after the establishment of a strong monarchy, and the capture of Jerusalem, was it possible to implement the law of Moses. David himself was not allowed to do this, but had to consign the work to his son, Solomon, who built the temple in which the atoning sacrifice was made. However, David was promised that his descendants would reign for ever on the throne of Israel, and that in him the destiny of the people would ultimately be realized. The covenant with David was the charter of the kings, who would be specially anointed to preserve the nation from harm, and bring glory through their rule to the name of the God of Israel.

7. *Christ came to be the fulfilment of the covenant promises made to Abraham, and also of those made to Adam.* The covenant promises made to Abraham, Moses and David were all temporary in character. They contained within them the promise of a future fulfilment, when God would send his anointed one, the Messiah, to restore Israel once and for all. The New Testament makes it plain that Jesus of Nazareth was this Messiah. By the word which he preached, he showed himself to be the last and greatest of the prophets. By the sacrifice which he made at Calvary, he accomplished the role of the priests, and put an end to their ministry. By his triumphant return from the dead and ascension into heaven, he claimed a kingdom far greater than that of his human ancestor David, and fulfilled God's promise that the house of David would rule for ever.

However, the New Testament also says that Christ is the new Adam, who has come to restore the entire human race. Salvation is no longer to be restricted to the Jews, but is granted to anyone who believes. More precisely, salvation now belongs to those Gentiles who, like the Jews of old, have been chosen and predestined to share in the election of the children of Abraham. Far from being anti-Jewish, covenant theology was the strongest Christian affirmation of the special place which belonged to ancient Israel. Where it took root, attitudes towards Jews changed dramatically. In England, for example, Jews had been expelled in 1290, but thanks to covenant theology they were readmitted in the 1650s, on the ground that England was home to all God's chosen people.

Within Christian theology itself, the emergence of covenant theology led to a reappropriation of the Old Testament, which now became the historical record of the church before Christ. The Old Testament enjoyed a revival of interest among Christians seldom seen before or since. Theologians spoke quite happily of the 'Jewish church' and looked upon the law as still valid, in some sense, for Christians. Old Testament names were frequently given to places of worship (Bethel, Ebenezer), and children were often given the names of prophets rather than of Christian saints (Abraham, Joshua, *etc.*). The Psalms, sometimes in metrical form, became a staple of Protestant worship, and later hymnwriters also relied heavily on Old Testament imagery, as can be seen in such favourites as 'The God of Abraham praise' and 'Guide me, O thou great Jehovah'. Covenant theology became the characteristic hermeneutic of traditional, 'orthodox' Protestantism, which dominated the churches until the first half of the nineteenth century. Even today, it is still widespread among the conservative elements in Protestantism, and as a way of reading the Old Testament as a Christian book it has never been adequately superseded.

The strong Old Testament bias of covenant theology quickly led to the belief that Protestant states were in some sense heirs of ancient Israel. This belief was especially strong in Holland and in Britain, where it helped to shape the national self-understanding in the seventeenth century. The Puritans who went to America, for instance, believed that they were God's chosen people, called to do his work in the world, and they were convinced that their settlements were a beacon of light similar to Israel among the nations of old. The English Civil War was fought and won by men who professed this belief, and it was Oliver Cromwell's greatest desire to establish a 'godly commonwealth' which would be the foretaste of the new Jerusalem.

It was this sense of mission which gave both Dutch and British imperialism their special quality – that peculiar combination of 'bearing the white man's burden' of responsibility towards other peoples and races, and rigid exclusivism, which created an apartheid long before the word was invented. Evangelism, which is at least partly the desire to include in the blessings of the covenant others who are not like ourselves, was no more a feature of covenant theology than proselytism was a characteristic of the Jews. When mass evangelism began in England in the 1740s, it had to be reconciled with covenant theology, a task which did not appear to be all that obvious or desirable at the time. Even now, objections to this type of theology are most likely to come from those who have a strong evangelistic commitment, and the impression remains that covenant theology is not particularly friendly to the idea that the gospel should be preached to those who have never heard it.

A note on Counter-Reformation Catholic hermeneutics

When studying the Reformation period, it comes as a surprise to discover that, despite the Reformers' great emphasis on the principle of 'Scripture alone', most of the commentators of the period were Roman Catholics, or at least humanists who never broke with Rome. They also played a considerable role in establishing the text of the Bible in the original languages, and even undertook some translation work, though not on the same scale as Protestants. Why is it, therefore, that in spite of this productivity, their works have faded into oblivion? To some extent, of course, fashion is to blame for this. Most biblical research in modern times has been done by Protestants, and they are not particularly interested in post-Reformation Catholicism. Since the general abandonment of Tridentine theology following the Second Vatican Council (1962–5), much the same can also be said for contemporary Catholics.

But fashion does not explain everything. There were no Catholic giants to match Luther or Calvin, and in an age which looked for authority this was a serious handicap. The first generation of Catholic expositors and controversialists was also much closer to the Reformers than most people today realize. Until the 1540s, it was possible for them to borrow extensively from Protestant writers, which many of them did. The methods which they used, and many of the conclusions which they came to, were not very different from those of their 'schismatic' contemporaries, not least because both had been trained in the humanistic traditions of Erasmus. Then again, both sides had been part of a single church before 1520, and the lines between them were not clearly drawn. As long as there was still hope of a reconciliation, Catholic writers found it difficult to distinguish themselves clearly from their Protestant opponents.

By the time a distinctive Catholic theology emerged, after the Council of Trent (1545–63), it was anti-humanistic and ultra-traditional. Later Catholic writers repudiated their predecessors such as Cajetan, and they turned back more and more to patristic and medieval interpretation. This conservatism was coupled with a defensive mentality which ensured that any originality of thought would be suspected of heresy. In such a climate, biblical scholarship was a dangerous activity, and it quickly declined into propaganda for the Roman cause. There was an enormous amount of that, to be sure, and it was more successful than many people would like to think, but it was not creative. There was no Catholic equivalent of covenant theology, and no real encouragement to read the Scriptures, even among the clergy. It was not until the end of the nineteenth century that this state of affairs began to change, and then it took a generation for real biblical scholarship to be accepted once more in Catholic circles.

BIBLIOGRAPHY

Texts

J. Calvin, *Opera quae Supersunt Omnia* (Braunschweig and Berlin: Corpus Reformatorum, 1863–1900).

———*Commentaries* (Grand Rapids: Baker, 1948; frequently reprinted).

———*New Testament Commentaries* (Edinburgh: St Andrew's Press, 1959–).

M. Luther, *Collected Works*, American edition (St Louis: Concordia, 1957–).

W. Tyndale, *Works* (London: Parker Society, 1848).

General studies

J. W. Aldridge, *The Hermeneutic of Erasmus* (Richmond, VA: John Knox Press, 1966).

E. Armstrong, *Robert Estienne, Royal Printer* (Cambridge, MA: Harvard University Press, 1954).

J. Bentley, 'Erasmus' *Annotationes in Novum Testamentum, Archiv für Reformationsgeschichte* 67 (1976), pp. 33–53.

H. Bornkamm, *Luther and the Old Testament* (Philadelphia: Fortress, 1969).

C. L. Cohen, 'Two Biblical Models of Conversion: An Example of Puritan Hermeneutics', *Church History* 58 (1989), pp. 182–196.

R. M. Douglas, *Jacopo Sadoleto (1477–1547), Humanist and Reformer* (Cambridge, MA: Harvard University Press, 1959).

G. E. Duffield (ed.), *John Calvin: A Collection of Distinguished Essays* (Grand Rapids: Eerdmans, 1966), pp. 19–37.

H. Eells, *Martin Bucer* (New Haven and London: Yale University Press, 1931).

E. H. Emerson, 'Calvin and Covenant Theology', *Church History* 25 (1956), pp. 136–144.

G. R. Evans, *The Language and Logic of the Bible: The Road to Reformation* (Cambridge: Cambridge University Press, 1985).

H. J. Forstman, *Word and Spirit: Calvin's Doctrine of Biblical Authority* (Palo Alto: Stanford University Press, 1962).

M. H. Franzmann, 'Seven Theses on Reformation Hermeneutics', in *Concordia Journal* 15 (1989), pp. 337–350.

R. C. Gamble, 'Exposition and Method in Calvin', in *Westminster Theological Journal* 49 (1987), pp. 153–165.

B. Gerrish, 'Biblical Authority and the Continental Reformation', in *Scottish Journal of Theology* 10 (1957), pp. 337–360.

S L. Greenslade, *The Cambridge History of the Bible* 3: *The West from the Reformation to the Present Day* (Cambridge: Cambridge University Press, 1963).

K. Hagen, 'From Testament to Covenant in the Early Sixteenth Century', *The Sixteenth Century Journal* 3 (1972), pp. 1–24.

————*Hebrews Commenting from Erasmus to Bèze 1516–1598* (Tübingen: Mohr, 1981).

I. J. Hesselink, 'Calvin's Understanding of the Relation of the Church and Israel, based largely on his Interpretation of Romans 9 – 11', *Ex Auditu* 4 (1988), pp. 59–69.

————'Luther and Calvin on Law and Gospel in their Galatians Commentaries', in *Reformed Review* 37.2 (1984), pp. 69–82.

A. Hoekema, 'The Covenant of Grace in Calvin's Teaching', *Calvin Theological Journal* 2 (1967), pp. 133–161.

W. J. Kooiman, *Luther and the Bible* (Muhlenberg, PA: Muhlenberg Press, 1961).

H. J. Kraus, 'Calvin's Exegetical Principles', *Interpretation* 31, pp. 8–18.

P. J. Lambe, 'Critics and Skeptics in the Seventeenth Century Republic of Letters', *Harvard Theological Review* 81 (1988), pp. 271–296.

P. L. Lehmann, 'The Reformers' Use of the Bible', *Theology Today* 3 (1946), pp. 328–344.

R. McCutcheon, 'The Responsio ad Lutherum: Thomas More's Inchoate Dialogue with Heresy', *The Sixteenth Century Journal* 22 (1991), pp. 77–90.

D. K. McKim, 'John Owen's Doctrine of Scripture in Historical Perspective', *The Evangelical Quarterly* 45 (1973), pp. 195–207.

V. N. Olsen, *The New Testament Logia on Divorce: A Study of their Interpretation from Erasmus to Milton* (Tübingen: Mohr, 1971).

J. Pelikan, *Luther's Works. Companion Volume: Luther the Expositor* (St Louis: Concordia, 1959).

T. H. L. Parker, *Calvin's New Testament Commentaries* (London: SCM, 1971).

———*Calvin's Old Testament Commentaries* (Edinburgh: T. and T. Clark, 1986).

———*Calvin's Preaching* (Edinburgh: T. and T. Clark, 1992).

———*Calvin's Sermons on Isaiah's Prophecy of the Death and Passion of Christ* (London: James Clarke, 1956).

L. Puckett, *John Calvin's Exegesis of the Old Testament* (Louisville: Westminster, 1995).

A. Rabil, *Erasmus and the New Testament: The Mind of a Christian Humanist* (San Antonio: Trinity University Press, 1972).

B. Rekers, *Benito Arias Montano (1527–98)*, Studies of the Warburg Institute 33 (London: Warburg Institute, 1972).

J. T. E. Renner, 'Some Thoughts on Luther and the Old Testament', *Lutheran Theological Journal* 25 (1991), pp. 157–165.

J. B. Rogers and D. K. McKim, *The Authority and Interpretation of the Bible: An Historical Approach* (San Francisco: Harper and Row, 1979).

M. Ruokanen, 'Does Luther have a Theory of Biblical Inspiration?' *Modern Theology* 4 (1987), pp. 1–16.

W. Schwarz, *Principles and Problems of Biblical Translation: Some Reformation Controversies and their Background* (Cambridge: Cambridge University Press, 1955).

D. C. Steinmetz, 'Calvin and Abraham: The Interpretation of Romans 4 in the Sixteenth Century', *Church History* 57 (1988), pp. 443–455.

T. Torrance, *The Hermeneutics of John Calvin* (Edinburgh: Scottish Academic Press, 1988).

P. T. Van Rooden, *Theology, Biblical Scholarship and Rabbinical Studies in the Seventeenth Century: Constantijn L'Empereur* (Leiden: Brill, 1989).

J. Wicks, 'Thomism between Renaissance and Reformation: The Case of Cajetan', *Archiv für Reformationsgeschichte* 68 (1977), pp. 9–31.

A. S. Wood, *The Principles of Biblical Interpretation as Enunciated by Irenaeus, Origen, Augustine, Luther and Calvin* (Grand Rapids: Zondervan, 1967).

P. F. M. Zahl, 'E. P. Sanders' Paul vs Luther's Paul: Justification by Faith in the Aftermath of a Scholarly Crisis', *St Luke's Journal of Theology* 34 (1991), pp. 33–40.

A case study: Romans

There can be few periods of church history which have been so clearly marked by the influence of a single book of the Bible than that of the Reformation. It is true that Luther also stressed the importance of Galatians, but Galatians is in many ways a preparation for Paul's more ambitious exposition of the gospel in Romans. It was through reading and commenting on this great epistle that Luther came to his understanding of justification by faith, so that it is not wrong to say that the Reformation owed its origin to it. More recently, T. H. L. Parker has shown that between 1529 and 1542, commentaries on Romans came out at the rate of one a year, and that at least half of these were by Roman Catholics – not at all what we would expect! Yet because the differences between Protestants and Catholics at this time were more subtle and complex than they were to become later, it is not possible to make a neat distinction between them along purely confessional lines. At the same time, Calvin's greatness as a commentator stands out against the efforts of his contemporaries, and we can begin to see why his work has survived the test of time in a way that that of others has not.

In looking at this epistle, we shall first take Luther and Calvin themselves, and compare what they say on key verses in Romans with the views expressed by modern exegetes. Then we shall follow Parker and look at a selection of Reformation commentaries, and examine how they interpreted certain important texts.

We shall begin with the all-important Romans 1:17: 'For in it [*i.e.* the gospel] the righteousness of God is revealed through faith for faith; as it is written, "The one who is righteous will live by faith" [Hab. 2:4].'

In commenting on this passage, Luther makes the following points.

1. The righteousness of God stands in sharp contrast to human righteousness. The latter is by works, the former comes by faith. Luther quotes Aristotle (*Nicomachean Ethics* 3.7) in support of what he says about human righteousness.

2. The term 'righteousness of God' does not refer to God's own nature, but to the righteousness which he gives to us. Luther supports this by a quote from Augustine (*On the Spirit and the Letter* 11.18): 'It is called the righteousness of God because by imparting it he makes righteous people.'

3. Luther denies that righteous works performed by unrighteous people have any saving significance. He says that they are 'like the works of a person who performs the functions of a priest and bishop without being a priest; in other words, such works are foolish and tricky and are to be compared with the antics of hucksters in the marketplace'. (The same thought is expressed with considerably more decorum in Article 13 of the Church of England which, however, adds that such works 'have the nature of sin'.)

4. He notes that the expression (literally) 'from faith to faith' has been taken in different ways. He quotes two different interpretations, which he refutes, before giving his own. The first of these is that of Nicholas of Lyra, who understood it as meaning 'from unformed faith to formed faith'. Luther rejects this on the ground that 'unformed faith' is meaningless; faith either exists or it does not. He then quotes the opinion of 'others', which we can trace to the medieval *Glossa Ordinaria*, according to which the phrase means 'from the faith of the fathers of the old law to the faith of the new law'. Luther rejects this on the ground that nobody lives by the faith of past generations, and he rejects the idea that Old Testament faith was of a lower quality than New Testament faith.

In place of these views, Luther holds that the phrase means that faith makes its appearance in the heart in such a way as to become clearer as time goes on, and he compares this to the degrees of glory in 2 Corinthians 3:18 ('changed from glory into glory') and of strength in Psalm 84:8 ('they go from strength to strength'). He concludes with a polite refutation of Augustine's view that the phrase means 'from the faith of those who confess with their mouth to the faith of those who are obedient', and the view of Paul of Burgos, who in his addition to the *Glossa Ordinaria* stated that it meant 'from the faith of the synagogue (as a starting-point) to the faith of the church (as a goal)'.

Calvin's interpretation of the same verse dovetails Luther's to a large extent, but has its own characteristic emphases. Calvin explains it as follows.

1. God's righteousness must be understood in the context of salvation, because that is what the gospel is all about. It is because we want to be saved that we look for righteousness, since that is the only

way that we can be reconciled to him and enjoy eternal life. At once we see how Calvin tries to situate his exposition in a wider context; in this case, the whole matter of our salvation in Christ.

2. Calvin defines 'the righteousness of God' as being that which is approved by him when he judges us. He accepts that some commentators see it as something which God actually gives us, and he admits that the words of the text can bear this meaning, but he does not prefer it himself. He treats this question as of secondary importance, but reminds us that righteousness must be understood primarily in terms of forgiveness of sins and reconciliation to God, not in terms of a thing implanted in us by the grace of regeneration.

3. Calvin accepts Luther's interpretation of 'from faith to faith', and does not discuss earlier commentators, except for a brief allusion to the opinion of Paul of Burgos, which he rejects.

4. Calvin remarks that Paul bases his doctrine on Habakkuk, whom Luther does not mention. He regards Habakkuk's intention, which was to say that faith is the basis of everlasting life for the godly, as directly relevant to Paul's purpose in quoting him here. Calvin returns to the theme of the gospel, and reminds his readers that it is the source of eternal life.

When we compare Luther and Calvin on this passage, we discover that Luther is more involved in theological controversy. Like a good medieval teacher, he quotes Aristotle as his authority in human affairs, and the fathers of the church for theology. At the same time, he is careful to distinguish the true from the false in the fathers, and is not afraid to reject Augustine when necessary. He is also very much preoccupied with the question of good works, and the nature of the righteousness which comes from God. Calvin, on the other hand, shows less concern for this, and avoids theological controversy as much as possible. He never quotes from any authority outside of Scripture, and determines the meaning of the text from its context. This he develops much more than does Luther, and he also considers the context of Habakkuk, which Luther ignores.

When we turn to a modern commentator on this verse, we discover a new set of problems which set the Reformers over against us today. In his monumental summary of the different views which one might take of this verse, C. E. B. Cranfield (1975, 1979) begins by examining the question of translation. There are two major points where modern exegetes would question the Reformers' understanding of this. The first is over the meaning of the phrase 'righteousness of God'. Does this righteousness belong to God himself (*i.e.* is it objective?) or is it given to us (*i.e.* is it subjective?)?

Cranfield recognizes that there has been a vast amount of informed debate on this subject, and he gives a detailed analysis of the various arguments which have been used to support both positions. Interestingly enough, however, he eventually comes down on the side of Calvin, and for much the same reasons; it fits the context better, it is closer to Habakkuk, *etc.*

The second area of debate is over the phrase 'from faith to faith'. Here Cranfield argues, on the basis of linguistic evidence, that Paul is not talking about two different types of faith, or even about two stages in the development of a single faith. He claims that the whole phrase is a rhetorical device, common in Hebrew, intended merely to strengthen the meaning of the term 'faith'. It should therefore be translated more or less as 'by faith alone'. The Reformers did not adopt this conclusion, because they did not understand the grammatical construction, but it is fascinating to observe how they stumbled towards it nonetheless. For both Luther and Calvin saw, as Cranfield says, that the verse is not talking about two different kinds of faith. They prefer the idea that there is a growth in faith, but are somewhat hesitant even about that. It seems probable that had they been aware of the linguistic device being used, they would have plumped for Cranfield's solution with relief, since it certainly corresponds to their overall theological position.

Cranfield differs most obviously from Calvin in his interpretation of the Habakkuk quotation. Whereas Calvin associates 'by faith' with 'shall live', so that faith becomes the means of life, Cranfield takes it with 'the righteous', so that faith becomes the basis of righteousness, by which we shall live. The difference can be illustrated like this:

Calvin: The righteous person has faith so that he may live.

Cranfield: Faith makes a person righteous so that he may live.

This is not a trivial difference, for in it is contained the distinction between what in the eighteenth century were called 'Calvinism' and 'Arminianism'. The first of these presents faith as a gift from God to the righteous person, who is righteous because God has decreed it. The second makes faith the condition of righteousness, and thus runs the risk of turning it into a work. It is interesting in this connection to note that Cranfield's interpretation was first suggested by Théodore de Bèze, who is usually credited with the 'scholasticization' of Calvin's thought.

When we turn to a modern translation of the verse (NIV), we discover the following: 'For in the gospel a righteousness from God is revealed, a righteousness that is by faith from first to last, just as it is written: "The righteous will live by faith."' In this translation, the view of God's righteousness common to the Reformers and to Cranfield is adopted and made explicit, while Cranfield's view of the meaning of 'from faith to faith' is chosen, though the other (more literal) rendering is given in a footnote. However, his interpretation of the Habakkuk passage is rejected, which demonstrates that the translators of the NIV were not persuaded that it was necessary to alter the traditional understanding of the text at this point.

Another key verse which we must look at in this connection is Romans 5:12. It reads as follows:

According to Luther: 'Therefore as through one man sin came into this world, and through sin death, and so death spread to all men, in which all men sinned . . .'

According to Calvin: 'Therefore, as through one man sin entered into the world, and death through sin, and so death passed to all men, for all have sinned . . .'

Luther makes very great play of this verse, which is central to his whole understanding of salvation. For him, there is a fundamental difference between original sin, which is the subject of this verse, and actual sins, which are committed daily by every individual person. He quotes Augustine and Chrysostom at great length to prove that Adam's sin was something unique and of universal significance, and not like the actual sins which each one of us commits. It is therefore wrong to say, as the Pelagians did, that our sins are imitations of Adam's sin, which we fall into because of an inherent tendency in that direction. The presence of death in the world is proof of this, since even those who have not committed actual sin will die. If it is true, as Paul says, that it was through Adam's sin that death entered the world, then that sin cannot just be personal to Adam; it must have a wider meaning.

Luther goes on to define original sin as an inherent bias and desire towards wrongdoing, in contrast to the scholastic theologians of the Middle Ages, whom he accuses, not altogether fairly, of having reduced it to a mere lack of original righteousness – in other words, the absence of good rather than the presence of evil. He is aware of the textual difficulty in the final phrase, but although he adopts the Erasmian translation, based on the Greek text, he shows no awareness of the Byzantine theology underlying it. The Greek fathers generally held that death was the cause of sin, but Luther does not consider that possibility. Rather, he discusses whether the phrase *eph' hō* (Lat. *in quo*) should be taken to read 'in him' (*i.e.* Adam) or 'in it' (*i.e.* Adam's sin). Perhaps realizing that it does not make a great deal of difference which he chooses, he plumps for both; Paul is being deliberately ambiguous here.

Calvin spends far less time on this verse than Luther does. He is just as anti-Pelagian as Luther, and agrees with him that the reference to sin in this verse is to be taken to mean our original depravity, and not any act of the will by which we may have committed a particular sin. Calvin is quite specific that we have all inherited this depravity, since after Adam lost his original righteousness, that was all he had to pass on to his descendants. Calvin furthermore says that we have all sinned because we are imbued with this deep-seated original corruption, and he specifically interprets the verb 'to sin' as meaning 'to be corrupt'. He is untroubled by the difficulty in translating the last phrase, and does not mention it.

Cranfield, in sharp contrast to this, pays enormous attention to the grammatical difficulties of this verse, which he recognizes as of key importance to the interpretation of the whole passage. Cranfield believes that the irregular construction comes about because Paul is reluctant to press his comparison of Adam with Christ beyond the actual point at issue, which is that Christ's death has the same universal significance as Adam's sin. Moreover, he devotes most of his attention to the final clause, and the many possible meanings of *eph' hō*. Unlike Calvin, who saw only one interpretation of this phrase, and Luther, who managed two, Cranfield distinguishes no fewer than six possibilities, all of which have had their supporters at one time or another. Luther's second alternative is listed as the second possibility by Cranfield, who ignores Luther's other choice. The first possibility listed is the traditional Greek Orthodox view, while the Pelagian view is included as the fifth. Calvin's view is the fourth one listed. The third is the same as the second, except that the Greek word *epi* (*eph'*) is taken to mean 'because of' rather than 'in'.

The sixth view, which is the one Cranfield himself prefers, is similar to Calvin's, except that the verb is taken to refer to actual sins, not to the state of corruption, although of course it is recognized that that is the cause of actual sins. The difference may be outlined as follows:

Calvin: 'Death has come to all men because all are corrupt and therefore sin whether they want to or not.'

Cranfield: 'Death has come to all men in their turn because all men have sinned voluntarily.'

Once more, Cranfield comes across as being more 'Arminian' in tone, though not in a polemical, or even in a conscious, way. The truth is probably that most modern Protestants in the English-speaking world subscribe to a modified 'Calvinism' which occasionally appears to be 'Arminian' when compared with the master himself.

Turning to the NIV, we find the following translation: 'Therefore, just as sin entered the world through one man, and death through sin, and in this way death came to all men, because all sinned . . .' Here it is Calvin's view which has triumphed, and the translators show the same indifference to the problem of translation as he did; no alternative is given in a footnote.

When we turn to those exegetes who were contemporary with the great Reformers, we find a wide range of interpretations in key verses. Some of these have been very carefully examined by T. H. L. Parker, and we rely on his judgment for what follows.

The first verse we shall look at is Romans 1:18, which may be translated: 'For the wrath of God is revealed from heaven on every impiety and injustice (unrighteousness) of those who hold the truth in injustice (unrighteousness).'

On purely exegetical matters, there is a fairly broad measure of agreement. All accept that 'revelation' means 'unveiling', and that 'the wrath of God' refers to his vengeance. There is some disagreement about the coupling of 'impiety' with 'injustice' (or 'unrighteousness'). Bucer and Bullinger related the former to sins against God and the latter to sins against people, but Melanchthon and the Catholic exegetes refer both terms to sins against God. Calvin accepts this also, and regards the two words as being different aspects of the same thing. This has an implication for translation into English, since 'injustice' would suit sins against people, whereas 'unrighteousness' fits more naturally with sins against God.

There is greater disagreement, as one might expect, on the meaning of the final clause. Most commentators accept that 'the truth' refers to knowledge of God, though there are subtle differences here. At one extreme is Bucer, who takes it to mean knowledge of what we owe to God, and at the other Bullinger, for whom it is nothing less than the truth about God himself. As for the meaning of 'unrighteousness', opinion varies from Bucer's view that acts of violence are involved, to Calvin's assertion that Paul is referring mainly to a suppression of the truth. Most exegetes, however, lean towards Calvin's position.

On the matter of the general interpretation of the verse in the light of the epistle as a whole, there is considerable disagreement about whom Paul is addressing. Most assume that Paul had the Greek philosophers in mind, but Calvin firmly rejects this, and says that it is addressed to everyone, whether they philosophize about their sin or not. In the context of the argument about justification by faith, it is evident that the Catholics generally have an easier time of it than the Protestants. These verses can easily be slotted into a Catholic scheme of redemption, in which justification is an element in the ongoing process of salvation. The Protestants rejected this, of course, but found it hard to interpret this and the following verses in the context of a once-for-all justifying act of God. It was only when Calvin interpreted it within the wider context of human inexcusability in the face of divine judgment for sin that this difficulty was overcome, and the passage settled down to what has now become its traditional place in the Protestant scheme of salvation. When we turn to Cranfield we discover that this is taken for granted; the critical debate has moved on to matters on which the sixteenth-century exegetes were agreed, such as the meaning of the phrase 'the wrath of God'.

A final example comes from Romans 3:20, which reads (literally): 'For by the works of the law is no flesh justified before him. For through the law is knowledge of sin.'

The sixteenth-century exegetes could not agree about the meaning of the word 'law' in this context. Some, such as Bullinger, Cajetan, Calvin, Melanchthon and Sadoleto, take it to refer to the law as a whole. Others, however, notably Bucer and most of the Catholics, take it to refer to the ceremonial law only. Otherwise there is general agreement, although one or two of the Catholic interpreters, including Sadoleto, are inclined to see 'no flesh' as restricted in its application to those who live according to the flesh, and therefore as being inapplicable to the saints.

On the theological question of the value of works in justification, there is, as might be expected, considerable disagreement. Cajetan says that we must distinguish between the righteousness of the work, which is sufficient to justify both it and the doer of it, and the righteousness of God, which is far above any human righteousness. The former cannot be compared to the latter, but that does not mean that it is without value. The law, of course, can give only knowledge of sins, not forgiveness, and it is for this reason that we are worse off with it than we were before it was given.

It is this distinction between human and divine righteousness which is common to Catholic interpreters, and opens the way to an interpretation which permits them to say that justification cannot simply be God's forgiveness of human sins; there must be a human contribution in relation to humankind's capacity for righteousness. In sharp contrast to this, the Reformers insisted that there is no human righteousness at all, and that works performed by human effort alone were inevitably useless and even sinful. The verse itself does not decide the issue for us, but the overall context of Paul's argument in the epistle surely does. Here we have a classic case of an alien theology being imposed upon the biblical text, and then defended in a piecemeal fashion. The Reformers, and Calvin in particular, responded to this by appealing to the general thrust of the epistle, and argued out the meaning of individual verses in relation to that. They were therefore not imposing an external system, but elucidating the inner meaning, which is what a good commentator is (after all) expected to do.

BIBLIOGRAPHY

J. Calvin, *Romans* (London: Oliver and Boyd, 1960).
C. E. B. Cranfield, *Romans,* 2 vols. (Edinburgh: T. and T. Clark, 1975, 1979).
M. Luther, *Lectures on Romans, Works* 25 (St Louis: Concordia, 1972).
T. H. L. Parker, *Commentaries on Romans 1532–1542* (Edinburgh: T. and T. Clark, 1986).

Part 2

The historical-critical method

The five chapters in this section deal with the development of historical criticism, which is the name usually given to a particular method of biblical interpretation which gives primary importance to the historical context in which the texts were originally composed and subsequently redacted, developed and supplemented. Those who practise historical criticism often attack the exegesis of earlier times as unscientific and ignore it, apart from passing glances at the Antiochene tradition in antiquity and the humanists of the Reformation. Opponents of historical criticism, on the other hand, have frequently been tempted to regard it as a massive attack on the church's theological tradition, which is grounded in what they misleadingly call 'pre-critical' hermeneutics.

These opposing judgments reflect the difficulties which the historical-critical method has faced in establishing itself as the norm in biblical studies. For a long time, it was strenuously combated by both church and state establishments, and sympathetic historians of its development regard its pioneers as martyrs for their cause. Those on the other side write the same history in terms of a series of lost battles, in which one bastion of orthodoxy after another has succumbed to the corroding influence of the critical approach, and in which they have become pariahs on the fringe of the academic establishment. Because deep-seated religious convictions are involved in this, feelings run high, and even now it is hard to find a dispassionate discussion of the subject.

The historical-critical method starts from the belief that any text or religious movement must be understood in its original context. This principle was accepted by the Renaissance humanists, but they applied it with little awareness of the effects which historical development had on the emerging tradition. For example, however critical Erasmus or Calvin may have been, they had little difficulty accepting that Moses was the author of the Pentateuch. The thought that Moses lived at a time and in a society in which the writing of such a document would have been impossible never occurred to them. They would not have been hostile to the idea that Moses used earlier sources, nor would it have disturbed them to think that later hands might have made a few additions, such as the account of Moses' death at the end of Deuteronomy, but in the humanistic perspective, the final product was essentially his, and there was no real reason why it should not have been.

The emergence of the historical-critical method changed all that. Textual anomalies which had been ignored or explained away by earlier generations now became essential clues in the attempts to reconstruct the historical evolution of both the written text of Scripture and the religion which it proclaimed. The suspicion grew that all was not what it seemed, especially in the Old Testament. Behind the self-evident monotheism of the present texts may have lain layers of a more primitive polytheism, which have since been obscured. Israel was not as unique as its official history makes out; it was part of a general middle-eastern culture which could be discerned by the critical eye. What earlier generations ascribed to divine revelation could be explained by an evolutionary process which had parallels in other cultures, even if Israel had developed farther than most.

Of course, if Israel was not unique, and the claims it made about the divine inspiration of the Scriptures were either false or unverifiable, its religion could not make any special claims either, and it was this which produced a headlong clash with the church. Historical criticism began to suggest that Israel's faith evolved out of a much lower (and more widespread) form of religion, traces of which could be found throughout the Bible. The principle of atoning sacrifice, for example, came to be regarded as a survival from a primitive cult, which was inconsistent with the philosophical monotheism of a later time. That the two things co-existed was regarded as irrational; in the service of true religious development, the church ought to purify its doctrine and practices by removing such survivals (or accretions from other sources).

The historical-critical method thus very soon acquired a theological agenda – or perhaps it would be more accurate to say that those with a particular theological agenda very quickly adopted the historical-critical method. Whichever way one looks at it, the two phenomena certainly went together, and it was not until well into the nineteenth century that theologically orthodox scholars were able to demonstrate that they could use the techniques of historical criticism without changing their doctrinal position. However, many scholars have continued to believe that a conservative theology is bound to have a negative effect on academic freedom and integrity. Conservatives have therefore laboured under the need to demonstrate their scholarly credentials to a sceptical academic community, without losing the confidence of their churches – not an easy task.

Historical criticism made its first appearance in the middle of the seventeenth century, and it fought for recognition for over two hundred years. By 1850 it had established itself in Germany and it became common in the English-speaking world about 1890, but it continued to encounter a lively and active conservative opposition well into the twentieth century. By 1945, however, virtually all professional biblical scholars had accepted its principles, though some still continued to draw conservative conclusions from them. The historical-critical method had triumphed and become the general consensus in academic circles.

At the time there was no reason to suppose that this situation would not continue indefinitely, but just as historical criticism finally triumphed, it began to be called into question – and not just by conservatives. Since about 1970, there have been increasing calls for a reassessment of biblical scholarship, partly because the historical-critical method appeared to be running out of steam, and partly because it had little impact outside the academic world, except perhaps to turn people away from the church. At a time when science was more highly valued than ever before, the academic study of Scripture was increasingly being seen as irrelevant to the spiritual and social needs of the Christian community. Could it therefore be possible that historical criticism was the wrong method to use in reading the Bible? Were there alternatives which could be defended with academic integrity? It is still too early to say whether this new self-criticism will become dominant, but it is sufficiently widespread to merit a section on its own.

The historical-critical method can now be examined with an objectivity which until recently was lacking, and which is still hard for many professional biblical scholars to accept. It may be too early to say that the method has come to an end; after all, it is still dominant in university faculties everywhere, and very productive in its research. But much the same could have been said for the conservative orthodoxies of the late seventeenth century, which to contemporaries appeared to be fixed and immutable, as well as academically productive. We cannot exclude the possibility that, just as those orthodoxies withered and died in a generation, so the current orthodoxy may also collapse with a speed which is scarcely imaginable today. What we cannot predict is whether (or when) it will be replaced by a new scholarly orthodoxy, or whether we are entering a phase of academic (as well as religious) pluralism in which different approaches, including the historical-critical method, will be allowed to co-exist. For the moment, we can only consider what has happened so far, and wait to see what the future will bring.

6

The beginning of the historical-critical method

The period and the subject

Historical criticism of the Bible first appeared in the so-called 'Age of Reason', which may be dated from the end of the Thirty Years War (1648) to the outbreak of the French Revolution (1789). It was an age in which the *philosophe* replaced the theologian as the fount of all wisdom, and 'enlightenment' became the order of the day. Members of the intellectual élite belonged to a 'republic of letters' and moved freely around the various royal courts, where French was replacing Latin as the universal language of culture and diplomacy.

The intellectual history of the period is best understood in terms of the countries where it developed. Britain came first, perhaps because Anglicans had a special need to justify their theological position on rational and historical grounds. British scepticism was soon adapted by the leading French thinkers of the time and repackaged for European consumption. Thus it was that British liberalism penetrated Germany, where it was well received. By 1750 Enlightenment thought was dying out in its country of origin, but in Germany it had taken root and was about to produce an intellectual revolution.

Biblical scholarship during this period was mainly pursued in these three language areas, though the contribution of smaller countries, notably of Holland, cannot be ignored. As long as theological works continued to be written in Latin, Dutch scholarship competed with its European counterparts on an equal footing; only when that ceased, in the course of the eighteenth century, was the Dutch intellectual scene no longer followed by other Europeans. Perhaps it was for this reason that the use of Latin lingered longest in smaller countries like these.

In England, the Elizabethan Settlement of 1559 tried to include as wide a variety of theological opinions in the church as it could. The logic of comprehension theoretically encouraged tolerance, but in practice different views could not live together easily. Successive British régimes imposed their own forms of orthodoxy, and persecuted those who disagreed with them – always a numerous group. Only after 1688 was there a relative degree of toleration, which allowed dissenting views to be expressed fairly openly.

These dissenting views were of two distinctly different kinds. On the one hand there were rationalistic critics who opposed any authority other than that of human reason. They objected to the religious establishment as well as to the political one, and wanted as much freedom for dissent as possible. The other group consisted of religious nonconformists who had been pushed out of the establishment in 1662. They were just as opposed to the authorities as the freethinkers were, but for different reasons. They wanted to establish their own versions of orthodoxy, and attacked the state church as corrupt and misguided. After about 1700, however, nonconformity went into decline. Many of its more intellectual elements became freethinkers, while others joined the Church of England. It might have died out altogether, had it not been for the new wave of pietism, which reached England from Germany in the 1720s. By 1740 this had produced the conversion of John Wesley, and led to the Methodist, or Evangelical, Revival.

Initially, the defenders of traditional Protestant orthodoxy distrusted the evangelicals, because the latter preferred the uncertain emotions of religious experience to the doctrines of official confessional statements, but by 1800 religious enthusiasm had become a factor to reckon with in the mainline churches. This enthusiasm was categorical in its rejection of rationalistic biblical criticism, which made little headway in Britain until the end of the nineteenth century.

The French scene was more complex. In theory, France became the first European country to accept religious pluralism, when Henri IV promulgated the Edict of Nantes (1598), which gave limited toleration to Protestants. Quite soon, though, this toleration was whittled away until finally the Edict itself was abolished (1685). This did not stifle intellectual dissent; it merely served to secularize it. Within a generation, French thinkers were in the forefront of a battle against Christianity, which reached the highest circles in the land. They were very interested in England's relatively liberal atmosphere, and did much to popularize the work of the English radicals of their time. It was much the same with Dutch thinkers, who found a ready market for their ideas in France, in spite of the difference in religion between the two countries. Ironically, by the time the French Revolution broke out (1789), the main achievement of the *philosophes* was already over. The enthronement of the goddess Reason in Notre-Dame in 1794 was its last gasp, and France soon reverted to an orthodox Catholicism, tinged with Romantic notions. Liberalism came back in the middle of the nineteenth century, as it did in Britain, but it had just as hard a time imposing itself in Paris as it did in London or Oxbridge. In neither country did it represent an unbroken tradition of religious free thought stemming from the seventeenth century.

Things turned out rather differently in Germany. In the eighteenth century all educated Germans knew French, and a surprising number had been to study in England. English books circulated with particular ease in Hanover, which was united to the British Crown from 1714 to 1837, and its new University of Göttingen (founded by George II in 1734) soon became a major centre for biblical scholarship. Germany also had the advantage of being so decentralized that censorship of new ideas was virtually impossible. An Englishman or a Frenchman who expressed unorthodox views might easily go to prison; a German merely had to decamp to the neighbouring principality, which was rarely more than a few hours' journey away. Princely rivalries and religious divisions led to the creation of an extraordinarily large number of universities, where theology – of the local ruler's preferred type – was an essential part of the curriculum. This created a market for new ideas and an intellectual diversity which was unknown in other European countries. While Oxford, Cambridge and the Sorbonne declined into intellectual torpor, the German universities made great strides forward in all fields. In 1648, Germany was backward and devastated by war, but by 1800 it was beginning to dominate the scholarly world, and to set an agenda which still remains influential today.

During this period the study of the Bible was closely linked to the development of western philosophy. The orthodox theologians of the post-Reformation era had tied their doctrine of biblical inspiration to philosophical criteria for determining the nature of truth. They had also insisted that all knowledge could be based on biblical principles, which was to cause trouble when modern science began to discover evidence which did not accord with the data of biblical revelation.

Reformation theologians had generally believed that Scripture and reason were in harmony with each other, because God was the author of both. In the seventeenth century, when disputes over the right interpretation of Scripture were dividing the church, many theologians believed that the matters under debate could be resolved by appealing to reason, which set an objective standard above and beyond the demands of party or church politics. They developed what they called a 'rational orthodoxy', which sought to harmonize basic Christian doctrine with the findings of natural science, and they used this very effectively in debates with those whose rationalism was essentially anti-theological. Their approach became very popular, and was supported by the founders of the Royal Society (1660), who believed that scientific investigation could put an end to most theological arguments, and provide a sure guide to truth.

Only at a later stage, and somewhat to the dismay of orthodox rationalists such as John Locke, was this weapon turned against the church. The eighteenth century witnessed a great debate between rationalists who denied the validity of a supernatural revelation, and rationalists who maintained that the divine revelation of Scripture was entirely reasonable. The former focused very largely on the question of miracles, which they regarded as irrational. This naturally led them to deny the truth claims of Scripture, which was full of miraculous accounts. Denial of miracles was obviously also a denial of the claims of Jesus Christ to be the Son of God, and thus the advocates of pure rationalism were open enemies of Christian orthodoxy.

It was in this climate that other questions, such as discrepancies in the biblical text, came to be investigated in a scientific way. Every suggestion that the Bible might be less than totally accurate was seized upon by the rationalist critics of Christianity as evidence which supported their case. This ulterior motive inevitably brought biblical scholarship under a suspicion from which it has never fully recovered. By the end of the eighteenth century it would be fair to say that those who defended orthodox theology were opposed to biblical criticism of any kind, which they identified with heresy.

In this chapter, our concern is to study how critical scholarship emerged and came to maturity in the German universities. We shall begin with a consideration of the early British rationalists, who did so much to create the climate of scepticism in which critical study later flourished, and take the story up to the point where the study of the Old Testament was recognized as a separate discipline from that of the New Testament. Because of the increasing influence of nationalism, and the tendency of each country or cultural area to go its own way, we shall divide our study of the period along national lines, beginning with the British and the Dutch, who led the way towards the new ideas, passing through France, which was the intellectual clearing-house of Europe, and finishing with Germany, the new academic power on the horizon.

The interpreters and their work

British

Thomas Hobbes (1588–1679). Extraordinarily long-lived, and difficult to place within any of the periods of his life, Hobbes can fairly claim to have been the first of the modern biblical critics. His most famous work was *Leviathan* (1651), a searching critique of political power which was rooted in biblical and theological concepts. But on reading him, it becomes clear that Hobbes was an atheist, for whom religious language was merely a vehicle of expression. He doubted the historicity of parts of the Old Testament and tended to deny the traditional attributions of authorship in the case of Moses and of Solomon, though his main concern, which was to insist that the Israelite kings were subject to the rule of the law (a point not without its bearing on political events in his own time), mitigated the effects of this. He did not hesitate to state that the law of God was valid only because it conformed to the dictates of reason – a clear sign of a shift in the basis of authority, which was to have tremendous consequences for the future.

John Wilkins (1614–72). He attempted to defend Christianity against the criticism of irrationality by insisting that the Bible was not a source of scientific truth, but of religious principle. This distinction, which was to become very prominent in nineteenth-century rationalism, was regarded by his scientific contemporaries as an important aid to their own freedom of investigation, which they were nevertheless concerned to harmonize with the claims of revealed religion.

John Lightfoot (1602–75). This Hebrew scholar was deeply interested in rabbinical studies and the relationship of Jesus to contemporary Judaism. In his major work, the *Harmony of the Four Evangelists among Themselves and with the Old Testament* (1644), he raised a number of chronological issues which would later become the standard stuff of gospel criticism. Lightfoot is frequently honoured today as a pioneer of Jewish studies in relation to the New Testament.

John Spencer (1630–93). Another noted Hebraist, he advanced the theory that the religious laws of the Old Testament had originated in Egypt. He was one of the first to suggest that a study of comparative religion would shed light on the origin of Israel's monotheism.

John Locke (1632–1704). Best known nowadays as a philosopher, Locke was an accomplished theologian who believed that reason was supreme in all religious matters. He defended his position in his *Essay Concerning Human Understanding* (1690) and in *The Reasonableness of Christianity* (1695). He himself was an orthodox Anglican, and denied that he shared the ideas of the Deist critics of Christianity who claimed him as their model, but there seems to be little doubt that his rationalistic approach was congenial to the Deistic way of thinking and contributed to it. He wrote a series of notes and paraphrases of Galatians, 1 and 2 Corinthians, Romans and Ephesians, which were published after his death (1705–07).

John Mill or **Mills** (1645–1707). He was a leading New Testament scholar, whose critical edition of the *Textus Receptus* was the first to draw attention to variant readings in other manuscripts. His work launched the modern academic study of the New Testament text.

Isaac Newton (1642–1727). Now regarded as the greatest mathematician of his age, Newton was also an accomplished theologian of the traditional school of 'rationalist orthodoxy'. His *Principia Mathematica* (1687) established the law of gravity, and in the process asserted that cause and effect were part of a single process. This meant that everything could be explained in a rational way, without recourse to supernatural causes or authorities. Newton believed that this inner consistency in the universe was the product of the orderly mind of the Creator, and wanted to affirm Christianity rather than deny it, but the inherent tendency of his thought was to equate God and Christ with the abstract concepts of eternity and reason. His theories were therefore of more help to the Deists than to the defenders of orthodox belief.

The English Deists. These were a diverse group of thinkers who did not form a well-defined school of thought. Rather, they represented a particular attitude, one of scepticism towards the Bible and Christianity. They believed that reason was the only criterion of truth, and that much of what was found in Scripture was irrational. Deism's origin is usually associated with the name of **Lord Herbert of Cherbury** (1583–1648), who, in common with a number of friends, met privately during the 1620s and 1630s at the estate of Lord Falkland just outside Oxford. This group is usually known nowadays as the Great Tew Circle, after the name of Lord Falkland's estate. It was broken up by the outbreak of the Civil War in 1642.

Charles Blount (1654–93). He wrote *The Oracles of Reason* (1693) in which he showed a very sceptical attitude towards the Bible, especially the Old Testament. He suggested that Deuteronomy, or a large part of it, was forged by Hilkiah the Priest (*c.* 622 BC) and passed off by him as the work of Moses.

John Toland (1670–1722). Deism resurfaced in the writings of John Toland. His most famous work was *Christianity not Mysterious* (1696), in which he put forward the primacy of reason and argued that Scripture was both subordinate to it and in harmony with it. Toland was well acquainted with apocryphal writings on the fringe of early Christianity, and in 1718 he published *Nazarenus*, in which he used them to distinguish Jewish from Gentile Christianity.

Anthony Collins (1676–1729). Collins wrote a number of important works, of which the most notorious was his *Discourse of Freethinking* (1713), in which he defended the rationalistic principles of Deism. His later *Discourse of the Grounds and Reasons of the Christian Religion* (1724) outlined the theory that the New Testament writers adapted the Old Testament by means of allegory to the claims of the Christian religion. He believed that a literal reading of the Old Testament would uphold the anti-Christian position of the Jews, rather than the claims of the church, but he did not pursue this idea to the point of constructing an alternative theology. Like most Deists, he was content to demolish the prevailing orthodoxy, and it was left to others to work these ideas into a viable system of thought.

Matthew Tindal (1655–1733). Another Deist, Tindal wrote *Christianity as Old as the Creation* (1730), in which he discounted the idea that the Supreme Being could possibly have revealed himself only to an obscure tribe in a remote corner of the world. For him, the gospel was the same as natural law, a fact which made Scripture superfluous.

Thomas Woolston (1670–1733). He wrote six *Discourses on the Miracles of our Saviour* (1727–29), which are so disconnected in their thought that modern critics have doubted his sanity. At the time, however, he provoked a furious reaction from churchmen who took him seriously, and he was eventually imprisoned for his impiety. Woolston thought the miracle stories in the gospels were absurd, and insisted that they must be read as allegories of the spiritual union between Christ and the believer. The effect of his writing was to unsettle many previously orthodox people, and his work contributed greatly to the spread of Deistic ideas.

Thomas Morgan (1680–1743). He was a bitter opponent of the

Jews, whom he blamed for the corruptions which he found in the Bible. His book, *The Moral Philosopher* (1737), contained an indictment of the immoral behaviour of King David, which he regarded as typical of Judaism. He claimed that Paul was a freethinker, though he believed that the apostle had ultimately failed to liberate the gospel of natural religion from the clutches of the Judaizers. He also believed that the Gnosticizing heretics of the second century were the true disciples of Jesus, whom an apostate church eventually succeeded in stamping out.

Thomas Chubb (1679–1749). He denied the literal truth of the Scriptures and criticized both the Old and the New Testaments for their many inaccuracies. Though not a great scholar, he was a fluent writer and defended Deistic views in an attractive and sympathetic manner. His best-known work was *The True Gospel of Jesus Christ, Asserted* (1738), in which he defended the kind of moralistic Christianity advocated by Morgan.

Peter Annet (1693–1768). Generally reckoned to have been the last of the Deists, his book *The Resurrection of Jesus Examined by a Moral Philosopher* (1744) puts forward the hypothesis that the resurrection was a fraud perpetrated by the disciples of Jesus after his death.

Opponents of the Deists. From the very beginning, Deistic thought met with strenuous opposition in Britain. Working from a similar rationalistic base, but drawing different conclusions, these thinkers tried to prove that Christianity is true and that the Scriptures are reliable by demonstrating that the 'contradictions' between the Bible and nature are more apparent than real. Some were philosophers, working to create a natural theology based on reason; others were pietists, whose main concern was to emphasize the supernatural character of the Scriptures. But whether they started from faith or from nature, they were all concerned to achieve a universal harmony rooted in religion. In their own time, these apologists were remarkably successful, and their arguments became the stock answers to liberalism in the nineteenth century. But nowadays it is often doubted whether they were really as successful as they appeared. Their main argument was that philosophy could not answer every question about the nature of the universe; science left just as many things unexplained as revelation did. But science was for ever making new discoveries which helped to resolve its problems, which revelation was incapable of doing, and merely denying the absolute character of natural science did not necessarily support the absolute claims of revelation. On the contrary, it might just as easily lead to a denial of any absolute truth claims whatever.

The Cambridge Platonists. These were a group of Cambridge philosophers who sought to base their rationalism on the works of Plato instead of (as was common) those of Aristotle. They were opposed to Deism, which they believed was unable to cope adequately with the mystical dimension of human experience. The leading representatives of this school of thought were **Ralph Cudworth** (1617–85), **Henry More** (1614–87), **John Smith** (1616–52) and **Benjamin Whichcote** (1609–83).

Daniel Whitby (1638–1725). Elected a Fellow of Trinity College, Oxford, in 1664, Whitby became a leading voice of moderate orthodoxy within the Church of England. His major work in the field of biblical studies was *A Commentary on the Gospels and Epistles* (1703), which continued to be reprinted for about 150 years. He believed that the writers of Scripture were divinely inspired and preserved from fundamental error, though he was prepared to accept that not everything in the Bible was dictated by the Holy Spirit. He defended the biblical miracles on historical grounds, and argued for the apostolic origin of all the books of the New Testament. His writings may be taken as typical of the 'establishment' view of the Bible, before the rise of historical criticism.

Samuel Clarke (1675–1729). An early opponent of the Deists, Clarke nevertheless showed some sympathy with their views. His book, *The Scripture Doctrine of the Trinity* (1712), questioned the biblical basis of that most fundamental of Christian doctrines, and he was accused of unitarian leanings. His career demonstrates how difficult it was to combine rationalistic thought with traditional Christian doctrine.

Richard Bentley (1662–1742). A prominent classicist and defender of orthodoxy against the Deists, Bentley wrote *A Confutation of Atheism* (1692), against the rising Deism of the age, and his *Remarks upon a Late Discourse of Freethinking* (1713) were a powerful demolition of the slipshod scholarship of Anthony Collins. Bentley made a great contribution to the development of textual criticism, for which he is still remembered.

William Whiston (1667–1752). This Cambridge mathematician was troubled by the inaccuracy of the New Testament's quotations from the Old. He advanced the theory that the New Testament's quotations are the original ones, and that the Jews later tampered with the Old Testament to make it less favourable to the Christian argument. Whiston's views were easily refuted by Anthony Collins, but his suspicion that the Massoretic tradition of the Hebrew Bible is not the only one, and that texts closer to the New Testament renderings existed in ancient times, has recently been confirmed by the discoveries at Qumran.

Joseph Butler (1692–1752). Author of an important *Analogy of Religion* (1736) which was written as a frontal attack on Deism, he appealed to the facts of both nature and revelation in support of his argument that the two were closely interrelated. His work was sufficiently powerful to refute the Deists, and has influenced later generations up to our own time. Butler was also a strong opponent of John Wesley, whose revivalist brand of 'enthusiastic' religion he regarded as irrational and dangerous.

Thomas Sherlock (1678–1761). A conservative opponent of all innovations in church and state, Sherlock's *Discourses on the Use and Intent of Prophecy* (1726) were intended as a counterblast to the scepticism of Collins. Sherlock posited the absolute perfection of God on the one hand, and the total depravity of humankind on the other, and claimed that the link between these two is not philosophy but biblical prophecy. Prophecy is a message of hope to those who are perishing in sin and unbelief, and its fulfilment can be witnessed in the broad sweep of biblical history. By focusing on sin and human depravity, Sherlock put his finger on one of the Deists' main weaknesses: their optimism about human nature and the possibilities of reason.

Nathaniel Lardner (1684–1768). A Presbyterian Dissenter, Lardner's main achievement was *The Credibility of the Gospel History*, of which the first two parts appeared in 1727 and the rest in 1757. In this work he undertook to refute the scepticism of Thomas Woolston by adducing convincing historical explanations for the apparent discrepancies which Woolston had noted. His work was basically conservative, though it is important to note that he employed the same rationalist techniques as his Deist opponents, which demonstrates how deeply the Enlightenment had penetrated the eighteenth-century mind.

Alexander Cruden (1699–1770). This Scottish bookseller in London is known for his *Concordance* (1737), which has frequently been republished, sometimes in an abridged form, and is still used today.

David Hume (1711–76). A famous Scottish philosopher, Hume was the heir of the Deist tradition, though he moved beyond it to a higher level of sophistication. He was a proponent of natural religion, and the best-known critic of miracles. His essay on that subject was written between 1735 and 1737, but he delayed its publication for ten years because of the reception its radical ideas were likely to get.

John Brown of Haddington (1722–87). A popular Scottish preacher who wrote *The Self-Interpreting Bible* (1778), which is noted for its tendency to compare one part of Scripture with others in a way which foreshadows the later technique of cross-referencing. This work, which to some extent was a reworking of his earlier *Dictionary of the Holy Bible* (1769), became extremely popular, and was widely used for up to a century after his death.

Robert Lowth (1710–87). He is famous for his great work, the *Lectures on the Sacred Poetry of the Hebrews,* which he published in Latin in 1753. (An English translation by Richard Gregory appeared in 1787.) Lowth discovered that much of the Old Testament, and notably the Psalms, was in verse form, and this dramatically altered his reading of the text. To his mind, poetry was the oldest and most suitable form of divine revelation, and he therefore inclined to attribute greater antiquity and authority to the poetic parts of the Old Testament. His work was soon circulating in Germany, where it made a great impression, and Lowth can be regarded as an important contributor to the growth of the Romantic movement of the late eighteenth century. In 1779 he produced a new translation of Isaiah, in which he used the latest critical methods in conjecturally emending the text. This work was translated into German by J. B. Koppe (1780), who remarked in his introduction that the latter chapters of the book dated from the Babylonian exile. In this way, the theory that there were two Isaiahs was first circulated among the educated reading public.

Benjamin Kennicott (1718–83). A leading Hebraist and close associate of Lowth, whose work he annotated, Kennicott embarked on the systematic study of Old Testament manuscripts. He demonstrated that the number of variant readings in them was so slight as to be of no real importance in Old Testament study, and his conclusions remained valid until the discovery of the Qumran Scrolls in 1947.

John Wesley (1703–91). Famous preacher and evangelist, Wesley had a generally conservative view of the Bible, which he regarded as both divinely inspired and infallible. He was not averse to textual criticism, however, and in 1754 he retranslated the Bible (though his version did not appear in print until 1775). He also published *Explanatory Notes upon the New Testament* (1755), which was reprinted as recently as 1983. In this work, his dependence on J. A. Bengel is obvious, though his own theological interests should not be understated. Wesley interpreted the Bible according to the 'analogy of faith', which led him to find references to justification and sanctification on almost every page, and which also influenced him in translating the text in such a way as to avoid an emphasis on election and predestination, ideas to which he was formally opposed.

Alexander Geddes (1737–1802). An anomaly if ever there was one, Geddes was a Scottish Roman Catholic versed in the critical theories of J. G. Eichhorn, who became a pioneer of Old Testament literary criticism. He was suspended from the priesthood in 1793 because of his translations of the Bible, which leaned towards a mythical interpretation of Genesis. Geddes adopted a rationalistic approach to the supernatural elements in the Old Testament, and refused to accept that God could have ordered the 'immoral' killings attributed to him in the text. His work was avidly read in Germany, and in turn provided an important channel by which German critical ideas came to be introduced into Britain.

The Unitarians. These were the chief inheritors of the Deist tradition, and in the later eighteenth century they kept an interest in critical questions alive. As heretics in the eyes of most British Christians, they and their views were not well received, and they probably contributed as much to the refusal of the mainline churches to take critical scholarship seriously as they did to its promotion. Their main representatives were **William Frend** (1757–1841), **Robert Robinson** (1735–90), **George Dyer** (1755–1841), all of Cambridge; and **Joseph Priestly** (1737–1804), **Theophilus Lindsey** (1723–1808), **Thomas Belsham** (1750–1829) and **Thomas Beddoes** (1760–1808).

William Paley (1743–1805). This philosopher-theologian defended the truth of Christianity in his *Evidences of Christianity* (1794), and in his great work, *Natural Theology* (1802), argued that God's goodness could be proved from the natural order. Paley argued from the design of the universe that God must be a rational and beneficent creator. He seems to have been attracted to the unitarian heresy, but generally he remained a conservative supporter of Anglican orthodoxy, and was much used by other similar conservatives in the debates of the later nineteenth century.

Thomas Scott (1747–1821). The most famous exegete of the Evangelical Revival, whose *Commentary on the Bible* appeared in weekly instalments from 1788 to 1792. He ignored critical questions and concentrated on the spiritual lessons to be learned from the Scriptures. His approach was generally warm-hearted and personal, and his work became very popular.

Dutch

Dutch biblical interpretation in the seventeenth century was marked by the struggles between Calvinists and Arminians for control of the church. The victory of the former at the Synod of Dort (1618–19) settled the question of orthodoxy, but this could not be imposed with the same thoroughness as elsewhere, and dissident voices enjoyed a freedom unknown in the rest of Europe. This was particularly important in the publishing industry, where Holland led the world, and many new and radical works from England or France came out in a Dutch edition. After the expulsion of the Huguenots in 1685, Holland became a major centre of French Protestantism, and the debate with the Catholic theologians of Louis XIV was carried on from there.

Konrad von der Vorst (Vorstius) (1569–1622). A German from Cologne, Vorstius succeeded Arminius as Professor of Theology at Leiden in 1610. His rationalistic *Tractatus Theologicus de Deo, sive de Natura et Attributis Dei* (*Theological Treatise concerning God, or concerning the Nature and Attributes of God*) (1610) earned him the reproach of the Calvinists, and he was censured by James I of England, among others. He was later condemned as a heretic, and banished in 1619. He wrote a commentary on Paul's epistles, which was published after his death (1631).

Hugo de Groot (Grotius) (1583–1645). Internationally famous as a jurist, Grotius was also a prominent theologian of staunch Arminian principles. His most important theological work was *De Veritate Christianae Religionis* (*On the Truth of the Christian Religion*) (1622), which he wrote in Paris. Towards the end of his life he published his *Annotationes in Vetus et Novum Testamentum* (*Notes on the Old and New Testaments*) (1644), in which he discarded the reigning theory of the divine inspiration of the Scriptures, and insisted that the Bible be interpreted along the lines of established philological criticism, albeit with some regard for ecclesiastical tradition. His reading of the Old Testament was based on what he called the 'primary sense' of the text, by which he meant its pre-Christian meaning. Thus he interpreted passages such as Isaiah 53 in the light of the prophet's own life, and not as prophecies of the coming Messiah. His secular outlook led him to interpret the biblical text entirely within the context of contemporary history, an approach which at that time was startlingly novel.

Gerhard Jan Vossius (1577–1649). A German, he studied at Leiden, where he became a close friend of Grotius. He was more circumspect in his theology, but was nevertheless suspected of Arminianism and forced to resign temporarily in 1619. Later he became a close associate of Archbishop Laud, and in 1629 was made a non-residential prebend of Canterbury Cathedral. His approach to the Bible was similar to that of Grotius.

Isaak Vossius (1618–89). Son of the former, he went to England in 1673, where he was noted as a defender of orthodoxy against the rationalism of the Frenchman, Richard Simon.

Baruch (Benedict) Spinoza (1632–77). A Jew of rationalistic tendencies, he was able to use the relative freedom of Holland to publish his critical views. He denied the divine inspiration of Scripture, and urged that the Bible should not be used as the foundation of all learning. Along with his rationalist contemporaries in England, he asserted that religion must never contradict reason, which was superior to it. In biblical criticism, he denied the Mosaic authorship of the Pentateuch, and argued that the doctrine of election was merely a projection of human pride and selfishness, and the very opposite of true religion. He was thus deeply opposed to the religious basis of his own people's existence, as well as to the prevailing Calvinism of the time.

Campegius Vitringa (1659–1722). He was an orthodox Calvinist, whose exegesis was marked by an unusual freshness and penetration. His most important work was a commentary on Isaiah (1714–20), but he also wrote a commentary on Revelation (1705) which introduced millenarianism into pietistic circles, where it became very popular.

French

In the seventeenth century, the French theological scene was a battleground between Protestants and Catholics to a degree unknown elsewhere. The revocation of the Edict of Nantes (1685) had a traumatic effect on France, from which the study of the Bible never recovered.

Jean Morin (Morinus) (1591–1659). A Protestant who became a Catholic in 1617, he was ferociously anti-Semitic, and argued that the Hebrew text of the Old Testament was completely wrong. In the course of his polemic he noticed certain problems with the text which were later to become themes of critical study, but his perverse attacks on the Jews, and his equally bizarre preference for the Septuagint in spite of contemporary research, make his work more of a curiosity than anything else.

Louis Cappel (Cappellus) (1585–1658). A French Protestant, he opposed both the extremely orthodox inspiration theories of François Turretin and the scepticism of Morin with regard to the Hebrew text. Cappel was one of the first to put the study of the Hebrew Bible on a solid critical foundation, rooted in the careful study and evaluation of the variant textual readings. He did not accept the then current idea that differences in the text were the result of (deliberate) Jewish corruption, but saw them instead as the natural result of human infirmity in the long process of copying.

Issac de la Peyrère (*c.* 1600–76). A French Protestant who later converted to Catholicism, de la Peyrère developed a belief in the existence of 'pre-Adamites', a kind of proto-human race, in order to explain such problems as where Cain got his wife. He was tried for his heresy and imprisoned in Brussels, but was released when he recanted.

Pierre Bayle (1647–1707). A French Protestant exiled to Holland, Bayle published a *Dictionnaire historique et critique* (1697), in which he sought to remove religion from the realm of rational discourse altogether. His attacks on the immorality of David, who was supposedly the Lord's anointed, made a great impression on a generation prone to confuse piety with morality. His arguments were quickly picked up by the English Deists, who made considerable use of them.

Pierre Jurieu (1637–1713). A Protestant polemicist, he wrote bitter attacks against Catholicism and all forms of religious orthodoxy, apart from his own strict Calvinism, from his exile in Holland. More of a controversialist than a thinker, he did not seem to realize that his arguments could be turned against his own views with as much ease as he turned them against others. His *Histoire critique des dogmes et des cultes* (1704) did much to introduce critical thinking into the French Protestant community.

Richard Simon (1638–1712). He was the greatest biblical scholar in seventeenth-century France, and a leading liberal, despite his professed Catholicism. He was a pupil of Morin, from whom he seems to have acquired his sceptical attitude towards the Hebrew text, but he rejected Morin's preference for the Septuagint. He believed that the Old Testament was compiled on the basis of the earlier work undertaken by public scribes, who had existed, he claimed, from early times among the Jews. His *Histoire critique du Vieux Testament* (1677) was condemned, and Simon was exiled to a country living. Simon himself related his belief that the Old Testament was the product of an ongoing tradition to the Catholic doctrine of the relationship between tradition and Scripture, and argued that they were much the same thing. The fact that he perceived that behind the Hebrew text as we now have it, there lay a long prehistory of distinct documents, makes him undoubtedly one of the most important forerunners of modern critical research.

Jean Le Clerc (Clericus) (1657–1736). A French Protestant in Dutch exile, Le Clerc composed his critical work in the form of an open letter to Richard Simon. He objected to Simon's theory of textual development on the ground that if Moses was the founder of the scribal tradition, the Pentateuch could not contain earlier sources. He pointed out a number of weaknesses in Simon's theory, and offered alternative explanations, but he agreed with Simon that Moses was not the author of the Pentateuch. Instead, he suggested that it was the work of the unknown priest who is mentioned in 2 Kings 17:28 as having returned from exile to Samaria (*c.* 720 BC). This was Le Clerc's way of explaining how the Pentateuch could be common to both Jews and Samaritans. He also suggested that the evangelists had used earlier sources, an idea which was first developed a generation later in Germany.

Jean-Alphonse Turretin (1671–1737). Son of the extremely orthodox François Turretin, Jean-Alphonse belonged to the school of rationalist orthodoxy which paved the way for the introduction of critical method in the following generation. In particular, he insisted that the Bible was a book which had to be interpreted by exactly the same criteria as applied to any other book, and that reason was the only judge of sound exegesis. Turretin is an important transitional figure, whose views were taken to the most radical extremes a generation after his death.

Augustin Calmet (1672–1757). This French Catholic scholar wrote a commentary on the whole of Scripture (1724). He was mildly adventurous in some of his conclusions, notably the suggestion that the Book of the Law which Hilkiah found in the temple was Deuteronomy 28 – 31. This idea had some currency in the eighteenth century before being finally abandoned.

Jean Astruc (1684–1766). Court physician to Louis XV, he was an amateur theologian and disciple of Richard Simon. He was long credited with having been the first to assert that the Pentateuch contained separate E (Elohist) and J (Jahwist) documents, though modern research has revealed that this distinction belongs to an otherwise unknown pastor from Hildesheim, Henning Bernhard Witter, who published his findings in 1711. However, this is of no significance in the history of biblical criticism, since it was Astruc's independent discovery of the same thing which marked the true beginning of a development which would climax over a century later, in the documentary hypothesis of Julius Wellhausen.

François-Marie Arouet (Voltaire) (1694–1778). Though not a Bible scholar, Voltaire was a powerful critic of the supernatural and 'irrational' elements in the Bible, which he believed completely discredited Christianity. It was thanks to him that the work of the English Deists and their associates was recycled and circulated throughout Europe. Of course, Voltaire did not mention those philosophers and apologists who were opposed to Deistic thought, so Europe, and especially Germany, had a rather one-sided digest of the British theological scene.

Charles Chais (1701–88). A Huguenot exile who was French pastor at The Hague, he wrote a number of Old Testament commentaries, in which he argued for traditional solutions to critical problems. He was conversant with the Deist literature of his time, and his arguments against them later influenced German scholars such as Michaelis.

Italian

Giovanni Bernardo de Rossi (1742–1831). A Roman Catholic scholar who taught at Parma from 1769 to 1821, he was an expert at Hebrew, and wrote extensively on linguistic matters. He was also involved in controversy with Jews over Old Testament interpretation. He recognized textual problems and sought to resolve them within a traditional dogmatic framework, but counts as a 'liberal' in the Catholic climate of his time.

German

Philipp Jakob Spener (1635–1705). He was the leading spirit of pietism, which was a devotional movement opposed to the rationalistic rigidity of contemporary Protestant 'orthodoxy'. His major work was *Pia Desideria* (*Pious Requirements*) (1675), in which he advocated a thoughtful interpretation of the Scriptures based on the literal, original meaning of the text, and freed as far as possible from dogmatic assumptions. However, Spener was basically conservative, and he accepted the main outlines of classical Reformation teaching. He also published a commentary on Galatians (1697), a book which he insisted must be interpreted in its historical context.

August Hermann Francke (1663–1727). A disciple of Philipp Spener, Francke was one of the most important exponents of pietistic biblical interpretation. He believed that individual passages of Scripture must be read in the context of the whole, which was the person and work of Christ. Historico-grammatical exegesis was the key to a deeper, inner understanding of the text, which would automatically lead to holy living. His major works were *Manducatio ad Lectionem Scripturae Sanctae* (*Guide to the Reading of Holy Scripture*) (1693), *Einleitung zur Lesung der Heiligen Schrift* (*Introduction to the Reading of Holy Scripture*) (1694), *Einfältiger Unterricht* (*Simple Instruction*) (1694) and *Christus, der Kern Heiliger Schrift* (*Christ, the Marrow of Holy Scripture*) (1702).

Johann Jakob Rambach (1693–1735). A disciple of Semler and the early pietists, he ranks with Francke and Bengel among the leading biblical exegetes of his time. His early commentaries on Ruth, 2 Chronicles, Nehemiah, Esther and Ecclesiastes were collected and published as *Ulteriores Annotationes in Hagiographa* (*Further Notes on Holy Scripture*) (1720). In that year he began to lecture at Jena, but he soon went to Halle (1723), where he published his famous *Institutiones Hermeneuticae Sacrae* (*Institutions of Sacred Hermeneutics*) (1724). Academic politics forced him to leave Halle for Giessen (1731) where he died. Rambach was also a noted poet and hymnwriter, and he exerted a considerable influence on his students, many of whom were to become leading biblical scholars of the next generation.

Johann Albrecht Bengel (1687–1752). The founder of modern New Testament textual criticism, Bengel started with J. Mill's edition, which troubled him because of its large number of textual variants. He studied these in order to regain his faith in the inspired nature of the text, and in his own edition made a few cautious emendations to the *Textus Receptus* where he could find printed support for them (*e.g.* in Erasmus). His real achievement, however, was his critical apparatus, in which he distinguished manuscripts by 'families', and listed the variant readings according to whether they were 'superior' or not. The soundness of Bengel's judgment can be seen from the fact that many of his decisions are still accepted by textual critics today.

Johann Jakob Wettstein (1693–1754). He advanced beyond Bengel in textual studies, and wanted to abandon the *Textus Receptus* altogether. However, he was removed from the ministry for daring to suggest this, and he had to content himself with an even more elaborate critical apparatus. Wettstein included cross-references to classical and Jewish literature with a diligence which has never been surpassed. By doing this he demonstrated a desire to read the text in its contemporary setting, an idea which took a generation to catch on.

Nikolaus Ludwig von Zinzendorf (1700–60). The leading exponent of pietism after Spener, Zinzendorf was preoccupied with the problem of 'practical atheism'; *i.e.* daily life without reference to Christian faith and values. After his conversion, he turned to the Bible as the book which revealed the living Christ. He was completely opposed to rationalism, whether in its Deistic or in its 'orthodox' form. This led him to challenge the 'orthodox' belief in the verbal inspiration of Scripture, and to admit the existence of (minor) errors in the sacred text. He even saw these errors as proof of divine inspiration, on the ground that the Holy Spirit uses fallible human beings as his instruments. His position provoked much opposition from his fellow pietists, notably from J. A. Bengel, though it was to prove influential after his death.

Hermann Samuel Reimarus (1694–1768). He wrote an extensive critique of Christianity based largely on the writings of Peter Annet, the English Deist, but kept it to himself. However, G. E. Lessing heard of its existence, got hold of it, and published some of it anonymously as the Wolfenbüttel Fragments (1774–78). The full version was not published until 1972. Reimarus has frequently been credited with starting a new era in New Testament studies, one which tried to find the 'historical Jesus' behind the gospel accounts, but that is too generous an assessment. Reimarus believed that Jesus was a political agitator who had been put to death by the Romans for treason, and that the resurrection had been fabricated by his disciples. His views were soon rejected, but they raised the question of how far the teaching of Jesus is reflected in the preaching of the early church, and of what role should be ascribed to Jesus in the separation of that church from the Jewish synagogue. These questions would form dominant themes in later German scholarship, and in that sense Reimarus's pioneering work ought to be recognized.

Gerhard Tersteegen (1697–1769). Of Dutch origin, Tersteegen became one of the best-known German pietist preachers and hymnwriters. He made a clear distinction between the eternal, inner Word of God which anyone could grasp in his soul, and the temporal, outer manifestation of this Word, which was the Bible. He fought constantly against contemporary 'orthodoxy', which he accused of turning the Bible into a 'paper pope'. He always insisted on the primacy of the living Word, though he saw no real contradiction between that and the written text of Scripture. However, Tersteegen's distinction between the letter and the spirit of the Word was to be the forerunner of later nineteenth-century German liberalism.

Gotthilf Traugott Zachariae (1729–77). He wrote a *Biblical Theology* (*Biblische Theologie*) in 1771, in which he tried to relate Christian doctrine to biblical passages in a way which would subject dogmatics to criticism on the basis of Scripture. In this attempt he was a pioneer, but he did not take the historical development of the Bible into account, and treated all parts of it as equal in significance.

Gotthold Ephraim Lessing (1729–81). A German philosopher, writer and freethinker, he brought Reimarus's work to the attention of the public. He made a literary study of the gospels, and on the basis of patristic testimony to the existence of a gospel belonging to a group of Jewish Christians he deduced that all three synoptists based their work on an Aramaic original, which is now lost. Mark, because it is shorter and more concise than the others, was supposedly closest to this original document. The hypothesis of a lost original robbed the existing gospels of their aura of divine inspiration, as Lessing intended. Lessing gave John's gospel a higher rating than the synoptics, though he did not raise the question of its historical reliability.

Johann August Ernesti (1707–81). Professor at Leipzig, and author of *The Biblical Interpreter* (1761; Eng. trans. 1826), Ernesti concentrated on the New Testament to the exclusion of the Old, and insisted that the two parts of the Bible must be treated separately. His interpretation was purely historical and grammatical, and ignored the church's theological tradition as much as possible. However, he continued to believe in biblical inspiration, and did not accept the idea that the Bible should be read like any other book.

Johann Georg Hamann (1730–88). He was a German who studied in England, where he was converted through contact with the evangelical revival. On his return to Germany he introduced the writings of David Hume to Immanuel Kant, thereby setting the philosopher off in a new direction. He also had a great influence on J. G. Herder, whom he taught at Königsberg. For Hamann, the critical details of biblical study sank into insignificance when set against the deeper issues of faith, in which the incarnation of the Word played a central role. In this way, he was close to the traditions of the early church and the Reformers, who read the Scriptures as the written presence of a divine voice, analogous to the incarnation of Christ.

Johann Salomo Semler (1725–91). With Semler, a new era in biblical studies began. He wrote a number of New Testament commentaries, and in his epoch-making *Free Research on the Canon* (1771–75) he broke with the doctrine of inspiration and moved over to a purely historical approach to the Bible. This approach, which he developed in conjunction with J. D. Michaelis, came to be called 'neology'. He wanted the Bible to be read in its original context, which he believed would provide an objective basis for determining its true meaning. Semler was the first to discover a difference of quality between the mass of later manuscripts of the New Testament and the few earlier and more reliable witnesses, though he attributed the difference to geography (the better manuscripts being 'western'; the others 'eastern') and not to the history of transmission. He also believed that there was a sharp difference between Jewish and Gentile Christianity, and attempted to divide the New Testament books according to which of these communities they belonged to. Semler was soon accused of trying to destroy Christianity, but he defended himself on the ground that his historical investigations had nothing to do with true faith – another sign of how far he had departed from tradition.

Johann David Michaelis (1717–91). Professor of Oriental Languages at Göttingen, he studied in England, and revised Lowth's book in 1768. He also published *Paraphrases of the Old Testament* (1769–86), and *Old Testament Introduction* (1787) which he never completed, *Introduction to the New Testament* (1750) and *Commentaries on the Laws of Moses* (1770). These went through several editions, and established Michaelis as one of the foremost biblical scholars of his day. Michaelis took over where Semler left off, and virtually initiated the rigorously historical study of the biblical documents. He was deeply indebted to Richard Simon, but he went further than his mentor, and developed the scientific discipline of biblical introduction. Unlike Semler, he wanted to hold to the doctrine of biblical inspiration, though he did this in a peculiar way. As far as the New Testament was concerned, Michaelis would recognize only an apostolic book as canonical, which left out Mark, Luke, Acts, James, Jude and possibly Hebrews and Revelation as well. He also discounted Matthew, on the ground that it was a translation from Aramaic. Michaelis was unorthodox in his theology, but he did not reject the prophetic dimension of the Old Testament, and argued for its inspiration. He was also influenced by pietism, and firmly believed that the Bible was a book with the power to change people's lives.

Johann Benjamin Koppe (1750–91). Professor at Göttingen, he translated Robert Lowth's version of Isaiah into German (1780), and later published an important study of the gospels (1782), in which he held that Mark had not abbreviated Matthew, as Augustine had maintained. Koppe argued from the texts that the evangelists copied from earlier documents, rather than from each other. His views were similar to those of Lessing's, but more sophisticated. He was the first to notice that when Mark deviates from Matthew he is closer to Luke. Why this should be so subsequently became a matter for intense scholarly debate.

Johann Christoph Döderlein (1746–92). Professor of Theology at Altdorf, he is widely thought to have been the first to have proposed a composite authorship for the book of Isaiah (1775), though this seems to have gone largely unnoticed at the time.

Karl Friedrich Bahrdt (1741–1792). Though belonging to the eighteenth century, Bahrdt has a fair claim to have been the first biographer of Jesus in the nineteenth-century sense. He believed that Jesus was a tool of a secret society, which he identified with the Essenes, of whom Nicodemus and Joseph of Arimathea were supposed to be examples. His main works were *Ausführung des Plans und Zwecks Jesu* (*Development of the Plan and Goal of Jesus*) (1784–92), and *Die sämtlichen Reden Jesu aus den Evangelien ausgezogen* (*The Collected Speeches of Jesus taken out of the Gospels*).

Johann Gottfried Herder (1744–1803). Hamann's pupil, he took his master's theory and turned it inside out. Herder believed that the Bible was a unique book which bore witness to the religious feeling in humankind. Its greatness could not be limited by the canons of historical and critical research, but must be sought more widely, within the category of literature, folk tales and myth. His book *The Spirit of Hebrew Poetry* (1782) was an attempt to develop his essentially aesthetic approach. However, he retained his interest in the historicity of the biblical events, and in this respect must be carefully distinguished from later mythologizers.

Immanuel Kant (1720–1804). Not a biblical scholar or critic, Kant was a philosopher whose views were to have a great influence on subsequent theology and biblical studies. He believed that true Christianity was a moral message, and that what could not be understood by reason alone must be interpreted in the light of the moral teaching it intended to convey. The resurrection of Jesus was the supreme example of this. Clearly there could be no bodily return from the dead, but Kant understood this as a way of teaching the immortality of the soul, and therefore of the permanence of moral values. His inconsistency appears from the fact that though he objected to telling lies in order to promote morality, that is what he thought the biblical writers had done.

Gottlob Christian Storr (1746–1805). Professor at Tübingen, he was generally reckoned to have been the founder of 'supernaturalism', in opposition to the prevailing rationalism of the time. Supernaturalism involved taking miracles seriously, and recognizing the limitations of the human mind when it comes to evaluating spiritual matters. In his gospel criticism, he was a strong believer in Marcan priority, which he defended against Griesbach (1786).

Christian Gottlieb Heyne (1729–1812). He was the first person to define 'myth' as a literary category, and produced a means whereby the Bible could be interpreted without resorting to Deist and rationalist assertions that the biblical writers had practised deliberate deception. His method was quickly adopted by others, and became of foundational importance in later biblical studies.

Johann Jakob Griesbach (1745–1812). Professor of Theology at Halle (1773) and then at Jena (1775), he tended towards orthodoxy in his theology but was an active textual critic. In 1783 he published his now famous synopsis of the gospels of Matthew, Mark and Luke, in which he demonstrated their close relationship and argued that this was because Mark had copied both Matthew and Luke, while Luke had used Matthew as a source in writing his own gospel. Griesbach's views were controversial and were rejected after about 1835, but they have enjoyed a new lease of life in recent years.

Franz Volkmar Reinhard (1753–1812). Despite a strong anti-mystical streak, he accepted the miracles of Jesus as historical events. For him, morality was the key to religion, and Jesus owed his status to his elevated ethical teaching, not to his supernatural powers. Reinhard, however, could not answer the vital question: how did a moral teacher (of whom there were obviously many) come to be acclaimed as the only-begotten Son of God? He wrote a book in which he claimed to show why Christianity was the best of the world's religions (1798).

Karl August Gottlieb Keil (1754–1818). He taught in Leipzig from 1787, and campaigned incessantly for recognition of the fact that the grammatico-historical method was the only one suitable to biblical studies. His views were adopted by H. A. W. Meyer, but opposed by many of his contemporaries, including F. Schleiermacher.

Johann Christian Karl Nachtigall (1753–1819). He published two articles in 1794 and 1796, under the pseudonym Othmar, in which he argued for a late dating of some of the material relating to sacrifices in the Pentateuch.

Erhard Friedrich Vogel (1750–1823). He attempted to prove (1801–04) that the gospel of John could only have been written after the apostle's death. He strongly criticized earlier commentators on the gospel, claiming that their views on authorship and date were wholly arbitrary, and concluded that the text was largely inexplicable.

Johann Gottfried Eichhorn (1752–1827). A student of Michaelis and Heyne, he was also influenced by Semler and Herder. He was the first to make a systematic study of the Bible using the category of myth, a concept which he developed in his *Urgeschichte* (1779). He wrote a major introduction to the Old Testament (1780–83) and to the New Testament as well (1804–12). He also wrote a work on the prophets (1816–19), among many other historical books. He was one of the last scholars to be equally at home in both Testaments. In his introduction to the Old Testament, Eichhorn laid the foundations for the later development of the documentary hypothesis concerning the origins of the Pentateuch. Unlike many later proponents of the theory, however, Eichhorn remained a conservative in matters of dating, and was prepared to subscribe to a generally Mosaic authorship of the first five books of the Bible.

Johann Philipp Gabler (1753–1826). A pupil of Eichhorn, he was the first to make a clear distinction between biblical theology and dogmatics. The former he regarded as fixed for all time, while the latter is constantly changing to keep pace with developments in the world at large. For Gabler, biblical theology was a necessary prelude to dogmatics, since the latter cannot be justified otherwise than by an appeal to its source. Gabler's assertion marked an important reversal of roles, since for a long time dogmatics had been used as a means of controlling and censoring the work of biblical scholars. Gabler showed that this was nonsensical, and after his time insistence on the priority of dogmatics gradually declined and disappeared.

Georg Lorenz Bauer (1755–1806). He wrote a theology of the Old Testament (1796), an introduction to biblical hermeneutics (1799) and a theology of the New Testament (1800–02). In his method he adopted and expanded the mythological views of Heyne, Eichhorn and Gabler, and he was the first to treat the two Testaments as separate entities, as Ernesti had originally wished.

Johann Severin Vater (1771–1826). He wrote an important commentary on the Pentateuch, in which he picked up the theories of Alexander Geddes and reworked them. This commentary was to have an important influence on subsequent theories of the origins of the Pentateuch.

Johann Jakob Hess (1741–1828). He harmonized the four gospels, using John as his base. He found the miracles a problem, and tried to interpret them in ethical terms, but he accepted the raising of Lazarus. In general, John was a better source than the synoptic tradition. He wrote a 'history of the last three years of Jesus' life' (1768).

Carl Friedrich Stäudlin (1761–1826). He taught at Göttingen from 1790. He accepted the necessity of employing the grammatico-historical method of biblical exegesis, but insisted that it was not enough. A rational acceptance of divine inspiration was also necessary, so that the text might be read in the spirit in which it had been written.

Georg Konrad Horst (1767–1832). This pastor took his lead from E. Vogel. He suggested (1804) that the Christological 'contradictions' in John are due to the fact that the author used several sources, and that the Alexandrian cast of his theology indicated that the gospel was written long after the apostle's death.

Karl David Ilgen (1763–1834). He made a great contribution to Pentateuchal studies, suggesting that the first five books of the Bible were put together from archives in the temple at Jerusalem (1798).

The issues

The main issues which confronted the interpreters of this period can be summed up as follows.

1. *It was necessary to determine how truth could be known, and what role the Bible played in discovering it.* Seventeenth-century Protestant orthodoxy had said that all truth was compatible with the Bible, because it was divinely inspired. Scripture was therefore accurate on matters of biology, history, geography, *etc.*, and no statement which contradicted it could be true. The Deists and other rationalists challenged this assumption, and as scientific knowledge advanced, most people realized that it was not a tenable theory. But if the Bible was not an encyclopedia of science, what was it? What kind of truth did it contain, if any?

These questions were answered in radically different ways, ranging from the most extreme Deists who thought it was complete fiction, to the more pious rationalists who believed that the Bible could be shown to be factually accurate, even in small details. Slowly, however, it came to be understood that the Bible could not be read as a scientific textbook. It was a work of literature which had to be interpreted in literary, not in scientific, categories. That raised questions of style (genre) and context which led to a much deeper analysis of the text than had hitherto been practised. Classical scholars and orientalists led the way, and applied to the Bible methods they were developing in their own disciplines. It was as this happened that the modern critical study of the Bible began.

2. *It was necessary to determine the nature and necessity of religion, and how the Bible related to it.* In a world governed by reason, what role did religion have to play? During this period, it was sometimes assumed that reason and true religion were virtually the same thing; anyone who thought straight about the world around him, who read 'the book of nature' properly, had all the religion he would ever need. Anything apart from that was superstition, based on the ignorant traditions of past ages, and was best forgotten as quickly as possible.

On a slightly more elevated plane, religion came to be seen as the necessary bulwark of morality. The picture of a science blind to the evil it could engender was beginning to penetrate the minds of late eighteenth-century thinkers. The horrors of the French Revolution drove home the lesson that the animal instincts in humankind had not all been abolished by the Enlightenment. The rise of Romanticism, with its emphasis on the value of feelings, reminded people of culture that mathematics could not explain everything. Mystery, which in 1700 was being persecuted and driven underground at every turn, was making a big comeback a century later. In this climate, religion could be used to explain the non-rational side of human nature, which was just as important as the rational one. The Bible played a key role in this, speaking to the human heart in a way which defied logic, but which transformed people's lives. That was what mattered in the end, and biblical studies entered the nineteenth century on a more positive note than might have been thought possible a hundred years earlier.

The methods of interpretation

When looking at the methods of interpretation used during this period, we are struck by the vast difference between what was going on at the beginning and what was happening at the end. Earlier ages had witnessed great changes, but they were more like swings of a pendulum than like progress to a new and different way of doing things. Jerome, Andrew of St Victor and Calvin would have been at home with each other – speaking the same language, reading the same classics and honouring the same methods of study. We might choose to call one tradition 'Antiochene' and the other 'Alexandrian', but these labels mean less than we might think. In spite of the many differences, there was one world, one mental universe, which forty generations of Christians had shared.

In the eighteenth century all that came to an end. The break with the past was less brutal than it might seem to us, and there were many people who accepted the new ideas only partially, so that inconsistencies and anomalies abound when we look at particular individuals. But the mental climate changed decisively, and the theologians mentioned above were all relegated to a past which was no longer fully relevant. The dialogue of kindred spirits through the ages was replaced by an interest in new discoveries which would reveal the past for what it was, and in so doing distance it from the present. A small but significant sign of this was that the classical languages, which had been pronounced like their modern descendants, now acquired a 'reconstructed' pronunciation (ultimately due to Erasmus) and died through fossilization.

In the initial phase of this great change, critical methods were fairly crude. Like children learning to walk, the scholars of the late seventeenth century had a tendency to stumble in all directions, and a good deal of what they wrote seems embarrassingly naïve today. But their writings nevertheless contained the seeds of future developments, and it is important to understand them, if only to see how their blind spots caused problems for later generations and hindered the growth of biblical studies as a critical science in its own right.

By the end of the period, we are on the threshold of modern times, and the language of criticism begins to sound familiar. This is understandable, of course, but it carries its own dangers with it. For although the theories of Griesbach and Eichhorn may still be with us, they have developed a long way since their time, and we are liable to misunderstand and misrepresent them if we fail to take this evolution into account. Apparently familiar things can be far more deceptive for the student than clearly foreign ones.

The influence of rationalism

Rationalism was basic to the critical methods of all scholars of this period, whether they were orthodox or not. Only towards the end did it begin to be called into question, and even then the questioning was rationalistic in form and intention. Rationalism took many forms, and could be used to defend quite different theological positions, but at its heart were the following common assumptions.

1. *Reason is a human faculty which is adapted to the natural environment.*

This means that it is capable of studying and making critical judgments on things and events in the external world. This definition may seem obvious, but it was not taken for granted in the seventeenth century, nor is it beyond criticism now. Orthodox contemporaries of the early rationalists believed that human reason was an image of the divine, but that it had been corrupted by the fall, and was therefore no longer capable of discerning the truth. This was why revelation was needed. The rationalists removed sin and the fall from their calculations, and insisted that the right use of reason was both possible and essential. Mathematics was the supreme manifestation of rational science, and it is not surprising that many of the greatest rationalists were mathematicians.

2. *The universe is constructed according to rational principles, known as scientific laws.* This was a revolutionary idea in the seventeenth century, and it did a great deal to wean people off superstitions of various kinds. We too easily forget that as late as the sixteenth century serious theologians and scientists could be deeply concerned with astrology, witchcraft and alchemy, all of which fell into disrepute with the rise of modern science. This belief had enormous implications for Christian faith, especially when it came to evaluating miracles and other signs of supernatural activity. The rationalists came to believe that the universe was a closed system, which worked by its own internal laws, and that it was not subject to intervention from outside forces. It was therefore irrational to believe that God might have suspended the laws of nature to suit his own purposes.

3. *The universe has a maker in the same way that a clock has a maker.* It was assumed by almost everyone that a system as complex as our universe could not have come into being by chance. The rationalists called this maker the Supreme Being. Whether he (or it) could be identified with the God of the Bible was a more difficult question. In theory, the Israelites, and later the Christians, worshipped the Supreme Being, whom they called Yahweh (Jehovah). But other peoples and religions also worshipped the Supreme Being under different names. Furthermore, the biblical picture of Yahweh was far from satisfactory. Quite apart from errors which might be ascribed to the human limitations of the biblical writers, there were serious moral doubts about Yahweh's suitability to be identified as the Supreme Being without qualification.

4. *It is the duty of every person to live a moral life.* Morality might be defined as conformity to the laws of nature, in what would now be called 'enlightened self-interest'. Viewed in this light, however, Yahweh appeared to be highly immoral. First, he had chosen a single

individual, Abraham, and revealed himself exclusively to him, leaving the rest of the world to perish in darkness. Then, he had protected his chosen people by ordering the periodic slaughter of their enemies, who were otherwise innocent, and by encouraging his people to seek bloody revenge (*e.g.* Ps. 137). Lastly, he had honoured certain individuals among the chosen people whose conduct was far from meritorious, King David being the classic example of this.

5. *Religion and the Bible must be purified of irrational and immoral elements.* According to many rationalists, Jesus and Paul had tried to do this, but failed, and it was the duty of the modern rationalist to complete their work. True Christianity was adherence to the moral code of nature, and in theory Jesus had tried to inculcate this in his disciples. Later, the apostle Paul had tried the same thing, but Jewish pressures and prejudices were too strong. The Christian church could not break free of its Old Testament roots, and continued to develop a theology which contained such primitive and irrational elements as human sacrifice in atonement for sin. Given that the rationalists did not take sin very seriously, it is hardly surprising that they should have been so shocked by the official remedy for it.

Rationalist critics delighted in pointing out what to them were 'errors' in the Bible, but it must be remembered that they were not interested in these as scholars. Their aims were more philosophical, and they used evidence of this kind to demonstrate to their satisfaction that the Bible could not be trusted. That there were complex textual questions lying behind the discrepancies which they noticed scarcely occurred to most of them, and would not have mattered very much in any case. In the history of biblical interpretation, rationalism is important mainly because it sowed the seeds of doubt in minds which had previously accepted orthodoxy (in either its Protestant or its Catholic forms) without question.

The rise of textual criticism

Textual criticism was a discipline practised by the humanists at the time of the Reformation, but it had run out of steam in the early seventeenth century. Almost by accident, a *Textus Receptus* emerged, which was really no more than a publisher's version of Robert Estienne's Greek New Testament, touched up with readings from the *Codex Bezae* and one or two other sources. Yet such was the spirit of orthodoxy that this text was accepted without question as the Word of God, and any tampering with it could land a scholar in prison. The result was that as more manuscripts of the New Testament were discovered, and new variant readings became available, scholars had to resort to an ever larger critical apparatus to explain readings which were not in the official text. Eventually, things got to the point where in Wettstein's New Testament, for example, the apparatus was several times longer than the text itself.

This situation was never fully resolved during this period, and the *Textus Receptus* retained its official position until the latter part of the nineteenth century. But in spite of this handicap, great progress with the text was made, specifically in the following respects.

1. *It was discovered that manuscripts could be classified according to 'families'.* This meant that it was possible to determine which manuscripts had been copied from which other ones, and thus a history of textual development became possible. It is true that this did not develop as much as it might have done, because Bengel thought in terms of geography (western and eastern families) rather than of history (earlier and later manuscript traditions), but an important beginning had been made.

2. *It was recognized that the most common reading was not necessarily the best one.* Here techniques which were being developed in classical studies were applied to the Bible as well. The most important single 'rule' of the new criticism was the so-called *lectio difficilior.* This was the belief that a more difficult (and therefore less probable) reading was likely to be more authentic. The reason for this is that a later copyist would naturally try to reproduce something comprehensible to him, and would therefore simplify a text which he could not understand. Of course, this is not always the case; any typist knows that a *lectio difficilior* can be produced by accident. But as a general principle, this proved to be sound, and it led to the recovery of a substantially earlier text than had previously been known.

3. *It was accepted in scholarly circles that the divine inspiration of Scripture could not be understood in a mechanically literalistic way.* This was a clean break with the excesses of Protestant orthodoxy, as typified in the Helvetic Consensus Formula of 1675, and some scholars went so far as to deny inspiration to the text altogether. More commonly, textual criticism was undertaken in the hope of recovering the original text, which most people still believed was literally, or 'verbally', inspired.

The textual criticism of this period made an extremely important contribution to later developments, not only because it pointed out the need for better editions of the original biblical texts, but also because it showed that it was possible to use rational critical methods without imbibing the ideology of the Deists and their friends. In other words, it was possible to be an acute textual critic and remain dogmatically orthodox, as both Bengel and Lowth did, or at least to dissociate oneself from the cruder ideas of the Deists. By the end of the eighteenth century, textual criticism was in full flower, but in a completely different intellectual milieu from the one in which it had been revived a century earlier.

The effects of Romanticism

Towards the end of the eighteenth century a new current of Romanticism arose, which sought to counterbalance the one-sided approach to human affairs which had characterized the rationalists. Romanticism maintained that human nature is not purely mechanical, and that there are a number of factors for which rationalism cannot account, such as beauty and love. The Romantics were also aware of the evil side of nature 'red in tooth and claw', though most of them did not believe in the total depravity of humanity any more than the rationalists had done. On the other hand, there were some Romantics, whom we now call 'pietists' or 'evangelicals', who took sin seriously, and as a result of their preaching, saw mass conversions, frequently of an emotional kind. Evangelicals clung to Protestant orthodoxy in the face of rationalism, but this did not mean that they had a well-defined theological system. Protestant orthodoxy in the English-speaking world was strictly Calvinist, but many evangelicals were not. Wesley and his followers were openly Arminian, and their theology led evangelicals away from the doctrinal precision of an earlier age, just as other Romantics were abandoning the cool logic of their rationalist predecessors.

The leading theorist of romanticism was J. G. Herder, whose interests extended to comparative anthropology, of which he was a leading exponent. Herder realized that the Bible could not be reduced to a historical or legal document. The stories of the Bible had a power to move the heart which did not depend on their historical accuracy, or on the morality which they conveyed. There was something deeper at work here, which rationalism had missed. Herder was attracted to Lowth's idea that much of the Old Testament was poetry, and belonged to a very primitive stage of literary development. What the rationalists criticized as immoral or inconsistent could be seen as a subtle device of composition, engaging the hearer at many different levels of his being.

Herder was not indifferent to the historical claims of the Bible, though these were secondary to his main concerns, which were literary. For example, nobody would claim that Shakespeare's *Henry*

VIII is a greater play than *Hamlet* on the ground that Henry VIII is a well-known historical figure whereas Hamlet is not. In that sense, the historicity of the Bible cannot determine its literary value. On the other hand, if Shakespeare had given Henry VIII (or Hamlet, for that matter) a walk-on part in *Julius Caesar*, something would have been seriously wrong, and it would have been noticed. In that sense, the historicity of the Bible was important, since without it the story would lack consistency. (The question of how credibly *Henry VIII* may have interpreted the life of Henry VIII did not bother Herder nearly as much.)

The Romantics were not great biblical scholars; they did not have the mental bent for detailed investigation which great scholarship requires. They were largely reacting to a position which they felt had been wrongly stated, rather than proposing any radically new method of their own. Yet they had important things to say which future generations would take note of. These may be summarized as follows.

1. *The Bible is a literary work which must be understood in literary, not in scientific, terms.* Things which were not 'true' in the scientific sense might well contain truths of another kind, which were equally important. An obvious and uncontroversial example is the story of the good Samaritan. This man probably never existed, and the details of the story are almost certainly not 'true' in a historical sense. But the good Samaritan remains an important figure in the moral heritage of Christian civilization, and no-one would deny him that place simply because he never existed in historical fact. The Romantics extended this principle to the whole of the Bible, and thereby sought to undercut the radical opposition to its teaching which had grown up in rationalistic circles.

2. *The Bible's greatness lies in its proven capacity to change people's lives.* Rationalists had made a mistake when they accused the Bible of 'immorality'. This was because their outlook on life was too superficial. The Bible contains the whole range of human emotion, and deals with matters of justice, as well as of good behaviour. Its message speaks to all sorts and conditions of people, and not just to scholars in their ivory tower. If this is forgotten, the text withers and dies, whether it is interpreted in a conservative or in a very radical way. The true expositor of Scripture must be in tune with the Spirit who wrote it. Only in this way, and not by a minute examination of historical and scientific details, would it be possible for him or her to appreciate its divine origin and character.

Neology: a synthesis?

By the end of the eighteenth century rationalism of the Deistic sort had vanished, to be replaced by something more subtle. There were still some rationalists around, but they were no longer brash in the Deist mould. They verged on overt atheism, and many believed that they were taking Deism to its logical conclusion. But they had become cautious and exacting textual critics of the Bible, determined to support their conclusions by solid evidence, and less sure about the philosophical underpinnings of their scholarly enterprise. A new breed of scholars, influenced by pietism and Romanticism, had come to the fore, and was making the running in most German universities. These were called neologists, because people believed that the way they read the Bible was fundamentally new. In reality, they and the surviving rationalists were virtually identical when it came to the use of critical method; the only real difference was that the neologists were more receptive to miracles and other supernatural elements in the Bible, which the rationalists found hard to swallow.

In the face of rationalism, the neologists were 'conservatives', though not in any sense acceptable to orthodox Protestants. The founder of the movement, J. S. Semler, openly denied the divine inspiration of the Bible, a doctrine which he regarded as a hindrance to scientific study of the text. On the other hand, Semler was not as sceptical as this denial might seem. He was quite prepared to take the text as it stood, and investigate its claims, regardless of whether or not they seemed plausible at first sight. This did not mean that he was ready to accept every miracle, but that he was prepared to consider what the text was trying to say, without prejudging it in the rationalist manner. By accepting the validity of a pre-scientific worldview in its historical context, Semler was reviving the ancient notion of accommodation, the idea that God accommodated himself to human weakness and limitation in revealing himself to us.

Semler also believed that the Old Testament contained passages which pointed forward towards the coming of the Messiah, whom he naturally identified with Jesus Christ. He was therefore prepared to accept that there was a Christological element in the Old Testament, though he limited this to a few well-known and fairly 'obvious' passages. The rest he regarded as a record of Israel's history, and treated it accordingly. But although this may be taken as further evidence of Semler's 'conservatism', appearances are deceptive. Semler's basic principle was that the Scriptures must be examined without dogmatic presuppositions. What this meant in practice was that systematic theology had no place in biblical exegesis, either as a presupposition or as a conclusion. Semler did not believe that there was any coherent system of theology in the Bible, and thought that attempts to find one could result only in a distortion of the text's true meaning. Neology therefore divorced exegesis from dogmatics, a position which came to characterize nineteenth-century biblical interpretation.

As neology was developed by its greatest exponents, J. G. Eichhorn and his pupil J. P. Gabler, Semler's principle of accommodation was extended farther, to include the 'oriental mentality' which they believed the biblical writers possessed. This was a period when the Orient was being 'rediscovered', and there was a growing awareness of the vast cultural gulf which separated East from West. We now know how simplistic this 'discovery' actually was, but to the people of Eichhorn's generation it seemed logical enough that if the Bible was set in its own cultural context, it would make perfectly acceptable sense. They were therefore prepared to accept that the opening chapters of Genesis were a mythical account of creation which was perfectly 'accurate' within the terms of oriental mythology.

It is best to understand neology as an attempted synthesis of contemporary thought. From the rationalists, the neologists got their critical spirit, their refusal to recognize the Bible as divinely inspired, and many of their theories. But they abandoned the rationalist ideology, and were prepared to accept that Scripture had more to say than an approach based on natural science would allow. From the Romantics, they got the idea that the Bible was a literary monument to be interpreted in literary categories. And from the tradition of pure textual criticism, they got their concern for detailed analysis of the text, from which their critical theories had to be justified.

Whether neology was a successful synthesis of these disparate elements or not is another matter. Historically speaking, it vanished within a single generation, overtaken by a renewed rationalism on the one hand, and a new 'supernaturalism' on the other. The accusation that neology was little more than rationalism with a human face may be somewhat harsh, but it is true that the neologists were unable, and probably unwilling, to move away from rationalist presuppositions in any decisive way. In the end, they could not separate critical methods from the ideology which lay behind them, and their attempts to do so made them appear inconsistent with their own principles. The supernaturalism which replaced neology claimed to be more wholeheartedly committed to traditional theology, but it also relied on rationalistic explanations for miracles and similar events, and in the end proved to be equally inconsistent.

On the other hand, many of the principles of neology remained influential, and others have been resurrected in more recent times, with a firmer theological and philological grounding than they had in Eichhorn's day. The commitment to a rigorous textual analysis based on the best manuscript text has remained unaltered. The insistence that the Bible is a literary document which must be read within its own context and presuppositions has come and gone, but is now once more firmly established and accepted. Above all, the refusal to accept that rationalism is the only sure guide to truth is now more widely shared, and has recently been more consistently applied to biblical studies than was the case in Eichhorn's day. The only major tenet of neology which is widely disputed today is its divorce of exegesis and dogmatics. In the late twentieth century more and more critical scholars are asking themselves whether that is really a viable option, since without theology so much exegesis appears to be sterile. That aspect of the neologist heritage, widely accepted for over 150 years, has once more come under attack. Perhaps the best judgment on neology is to say that it was not so much a failure at synthesis as a first attempt, which needed considerable revision, but which established basic principles that still play their part in biblical interpretation today.

Neologist textual criticism

In their textual criticism, the neologists concentrated on two major areas of research: the Pentateuch and the gospels. They dabbled in other parts of Scripture as well, of course, but it was to these two fundamental portions of the canonical text that they devoted the bulk of their efforts and attention. We shall look at each one in turn.

The Pentateuch

To begin with, the neologists recognized the doubts which had been expressed by various rationalists about such matters as the dating and authorship of the Pentateuch. In 1780–83 Eichhorn consciously revived the theory which he (wrongly) believed had first been put forward by Jean Astruc in 1753. This was that the Pentateuch was a compilation of earlier documents, whose identity could be determined according to whether they used the name Elohim or Yahweh (Jahweh) for God. These are the documents which we now call E and

J respectively. Eichhorn applied this theory to Genesis, and divided the book in a way which is remarkably close to the classical documentary theory put forward nearly a century later by Julius Wellhausen (1878). In the course of his investigations, Eichhorn discovered that Genesis 2:4 – 3:24, though closer to J than to E, was not really part of either. This opened the way to the possibility that there might be a third document, which did not rely on a distinctive name of God for its identity.

Further progress was made by K. D. Ilgen, who published his researches on Genesis in 1798. Working from headings which indicated breaks in the material, from repetitions and differences of style, and from perceived differences of content and outlook, Ilgen divided the E document in two, and discovered two major cruces of interpretation which were to remain constant throughout the nineteenth century. He claimed that Genesis 37:28 revealed two sources, which had been combined in a single verse, and that Genesis 39:1 was the work of a later redactor. Ilgen was the first scholar who consciously sought to reconstruct the textual history of the Pentateuch by positing sources in the archives at Jerusalem, which were later combined to produce the text we now have.

Shortly afterwards, the theory of A. Geddes was introduced into Germany by J. S. Vater (1802–05). Geddes maintained that behind the Pentateuch there lay a series of fragments (rather than complete documents), and that Astruc's E–J division represented different traditions, rather than two particular authors. This theory threw Pentateuchal criticism wide open, and the challenge to work out a new synthesis was soon taken up by W. M. L. De Wette (1806–7). With his work, modern Pentateuchal criticism began.

In spite of the radical criticism of Pentateuchal origins which the neologists encouraged, they did little or nothing to explain its theological development. No doubt their lack of interest in theology accounted for some of this, and it is also true that an investigation of that kind would have provoked very serious opposition in both church and state. Yet that cannot be the whole story. Eichhorn was quite prepared to believe that Moses had used earlier sources in his redaction of the Pentateuch, and that its theology was therefore as primitive as it claimed. Whatever religious evolution there had been in Israel had taken place at an earlier stage; from the time of the exodus, the Hebrew people were monotheistic and grouped round the law and the sacrifices of the tabernacle. It was only when that belief was challenged that the charge of impiety would be made against the scholars who propounded it.

Beyond the Pentateuch, Old Testament criticism was still in its infancy at the end of the eighteenth century. Eichhorn wrote on the origin of Chronicles, but did not get very far beyond denying that its author had used Samuel and Kings as a source. Study of the prophetic literature remained deeply affected by Lowth's assertion that much of the text was poetic in form, but although there were tentative assertions that Isaiah and Zechariah were composite works, nothing much was done to pursue these lines of investigation. That still lay in the future, when neology had given way to a more sophisticated form of historical criticism.

The gospels

In the New Testament, the late eighteenth century saw the rise of gospel criticism on a large scale. There had always been a recognition of a certain problem of dating in the gospels, and the traditional view, put forward by Augustine, was that Matthew had written first (originally in Aramaic, according to Eusebius), that he had been abridged by Mark, that Luke had used both in writing his gospel and that John was later and more or less independent of the other three. The second-century Greek writer Papias has stated that Mark contained the memoirs of Peter, thereby giving it an authority which the other gospels, apart from John, lacked. Clement of Alexandria had also divided the gospels into Matthew/Luke on the one hand and Mark/John on the other, though in a way directly opposed to Papias. According to Clement, the first two were earlier, and the others were written in the light of them.

The Augustinian view generally held the field for most of the Middle Ages and the Reformation period, as can be seen from Calvin's commentaries. Calvin wrote a harmony of the gospels, combining Matthew, Mark and Luke on the basis of Matthaean priority, and he treated John separately. It was only with the pioneer work of G. E. Lessing that a serious attempt was made to unravel the confusion about gospel dating which had been inherited from the ancient world.

Lessing assumed that there was an original text which lay behind all four gospels as we now have them. In his view Mark was closest to this original text, because it was the least elaborate of the gospels, and because it could be shown that Matthew and Luke were expansions of Mark, or something like it. John was the gospel most distant from this source, and was therefore the last to be written.

This theory received some confirmation in the work of J. B. Koppe

(1782), who argued against the Augustinian view that Mark had abridged Matthew. He pointed out that Mark's literary method was not that of an abridger, and that the order of his gospel, where it differed from that of Matthew, was frequently closer to Luke. This could be accounted for on Augustine's theory that Luke had copied Mark, but it was not clear why Luke would have preferred Mark's order of events, if he knew that Matthew was Mark's original source. The only logical conclusion was that Luke did not know this, and assumed that Mark, not Matthew, was the earlier text.

The assertion of Marcan priority, backed by the testimony of Papias, quickly caught on, and was enthusiastically defended by G. C. Storr (1786) and J. G. Herder (1797). But they both had to contend with a new hypothesis, developed by J. J. Griesbach (1783), who must be considered the true father of modern gospel criticism. Griesbach recognized the peculiar nature of John, and virtually excluded it from his synopsis of the gospels. Taking Koppe's thesis seriously, Griesbach proposed that Mark was dependent on Luke, as well as on Matthew, and that Luke had used Matthew independently. We thus find ourselves returning to Matthaean priority, but with a new twist to the plot. To help see our way more clearly, we may place the different theories in a table as follows.

	Augustine	**Griesbach**	**Lessing *etc.***
1	Matthew	Matthew	Mark
2	Mark	Luke	Matthew
3	Luke	Mark	Luke
4	John	John	John

From this table it can be seen that by 1783 there were three competing views about which gospel had been written second, and general agreement only that John had been written last. Griesbach's hypothesis had the advantage of discounting the need to posit an earlier, unknown source for the gospels, but it left critics wondering why Mark had bothered to write at all, since his gospel is almost entirely identical with one or other of the supposedly earlier ones. For this reason, the tradition initiated by Lessing came to be preferred, with reservations about the exact nature of earlier source material. The Griesbach hypothesis faded into oblivion, to be resurrected by W. R. Farmer as recently as 1964, since when it has once more become a matter of scholarly debate.

The consensus of these critics on John was much greater than it was on the synoptics. All believed that John was a late gospel, almost certainly written in a Hellenistic atmosphere some time after the apostle's death. There were degrees of emphasis here, of course, and some scholars preferred John to the other gospels because it was more obviously theological in content, but as a purely historical source its reputation was not very high. As with the synoptic tradition, this period laid the groundwork for an approach to the fourth gospel which has endured, with many modifications (mostly in a more conservative direction), to the present day.

As for the rest of the New Testament, apart from doubts about the authorship of Hebrews and Revelation, neologist scholarship remained at an essentially pre-critical stage.

BIBLIOGRAPHY

G. Allison, 'Giovanni Bernardo de Rossi (1742–1831): A Sketch of his Life and Works, with Particular Attention Given to his Contribution to the Field of Biblical Criticism', *Trinity Journal* 12 (1991), pp. 15–38.

C. J. Betts, *Early Deism in France, from the So-called 'Déistes' of Lyon (1564) to Voltaire's* Lettres philosophiques *(1734)* (The Hague: M. Nijhoff, 1984).

T. K. Cheyne, *Founders of Old Testament Criticism* (London: Methuen, 1893).

W. L. Craig, *The Historical Argument for the Resurrection of Jesus during the Deist Controversy* (Lewiston, NY: Edwin Mellen, 1985).

J. Drury, *Critics of the Bible 1724–1873* (Cambridge: Cambridge University Press, 1989).

W. R. Farmer, *The Synoptic Problem* (Dillsboro: Western North Carolina Press, 1976). (Reprint of 1964 edition.)

R. C. Fuller, *Alexander Geddes 1737–1802: A Pioneer of Biblical Criticism* (Sheffield: Almond, 1984).

S. E. Johnson, *The Griesbach Hypothesis and Redaction Criticism* (Atlanta: Scholars Press, 1991).

P. J. Lambe, 'Critics and Skeptics in the Seventeenth-Century Republic of Letters', *Harvard Theological Review* 81 (1988), pp. 271–296.

F. Laplanche, *L'Ecriture, le sacré et l'histoire: Erudits et politiques protestants devant la Bible en France au XVIIe siècle* (Amsterdam: APA – Holland University Press; Lille: Presses Universitaires, 1986).

H. D. McDonald, *Theories of Revelation: An Historical Study 1700–1960* (Grand Rapids: Baker, 1979).

J. E. Marshall, *Thomas Scott (1747–1821) and the Force of Truth (1779)* (London: Evangelical Library, 1979).
J. C. O'Neill, *The Bible's Authority: A Portrait Gallery of Thinkers from Lessing to Bultmann* (Edinburgh: T. and T. Clark, 1991).
B. Orchard, *The Griesbach Solution to the Synoptic Question* (Manchester: Koinonia, 1977).
C. A. Patrides (ed.), *The Cambridge Platonists* (Cambridge: Cambridge University Press, 1980).
H. G. von Reventlow, *The Authority of the Bible and the Rise of the Modern World* (London: SCM, 1984).
H. G. von Reventlow, W. Sparn and J. Woodbridge, *Historische Kritik und biblischer Kanon in der deutschen Aufklärung* (Wiesbaden: Harrassowitz, 1988).
K. Scholder, *The Birth of Modern Critical Theology: Origins and Problems of Biblical Criticism in the Seventeenth Century* (London: SCM, 1990).
R. E. Sullivan, *John Toland and the Deist Controversy* (Cambridge, MA: Harvard University Press, 1982).
C. M. Tuckett, *The Revival of the Griesbach Hypothesis* (Cambridge: Cambridge University Press, 1983).
J. Van den Berg, 'Thomas Morgan versus William Wharburton', *Journal of Ecclesiastical History* 42 (1991), pp. 82–85.

A case study: Deuteronomy

The centrality of Pentateuchal research for eighteenth-century critical interpretation of the Bible has already been observed. A key role in this was played by the book of Deuteronomy, the 'Second Giving of the Law', which from a very early date was recognized as having a place apart. From Jewish exegetes in the time of Jesus, the early Christians took over the tradition that the Book of the Law found by Hilkiah in the temple during Josiah's reformation (622–621 BC) was none other than Deuteronomy. How it got there was uncertain, though Nicholas of Lyra introduced the rabbinic notion that it was hidden there when King Amon tried to burn the books of the law (an event not recorded in the canonical text).

Thomas Hobbes wrote in his *Leviathan* (1651) that Deuteronomy 11 – 27 (not the whole book) was the Book of the Law which Hilkiah had found in the temple, though he continued to ascribe the authorship of this part of Deuteronomy to Moses himself. As far as Hobbes was concerned, it was the rest of the Pentateuch which was written, or at least put together in its present form, long after Moses' time. Although Hobbes did not say so, his theory suggested that the core of Deuteronomy was the most primitive (and the most authentically Mosaic) part of the Pentateuch.

Hobbes also rejected the idea that Moses could have written Deuteronomy 34:6, which states that no-one knows 'to this day' where he was buried, and for a long time this verse was a favourite weapon in the hands of those rationalists who argued against the extreme orthodox Protestant understanding of the divine inspiration of Scripture. But as with other rationalist arguments, this one tended to be quoted in isolation, with little thought being given to its wider implications for the history of the biblical text.

The next stage was reached in 1693, when the Deist Charles Blount published his work, *The Oracles of Reason.* In this book he wrote the following about Deuteronomy 11 – 27:

> It may be also questioned, whether the aforesaid was that very law which Moses delivered, since having been a long time lost, Hilkiah pretended to find it again, and so sent it to King Josiah (2 Ki. 22:8; 23:1–3) so that we have only Hilkiah's word for it.

This launched a new spate of critical doubt, in which it became commonplace to regard the Book of the Law, and therefore much of Deuteronomy, as the work of Hilkiah, which he conveniently 'discovered' and passed off as the work of Moses. This was the opinion of Voltaire, who believed he was only repeating what scholars generally thought. At the very end of the eighteenth century, the famous Anglo-American freethinker Thomas Paine (1737–1809) could write in *The Age of Reason* (1797):

> There is every apparent evidence that the books called the books of Moses (and which make the first part of what are called the Scriptures) are forgeries contrived between a priest and a limb of the law, Hilkiah, and Shaphan the scribe, a thousand years after Moses is said to have been dead.

Of the book of Deuteronomy, Paine wrote:

> My belief in the perfection of the Deity will not permit me to believe that a book so manifestly obscure, disorderly, and contradictory can be his work. I can write a better book myself. This belief in me proceeds from my belief in the Creator.

Seldom was the Deist spirit more clearly and accurately expressed than this! Paine was not particularly interested in what Hilkiah wrote; whether it was the whole of Deuteronomy or only a part of it was a secondary issue to him. But many scholars continued to believe that the Book of the Law was Deuteronomy as a whole (with the possible exception of the last chapter), and one or two thought that Hilkiah had discovered the entire Pentateuch. At the other extreme was the view of A. Calmet, who restricted Hilkiah's find to Deuteronomy 28 – 31, an opinion which was shared by a number of scholars who followed him.

When we turn to the neologists, however, we enter a completely different world from that of the Deists. Both Michaelis and Eichhorn believed that virtually the entire Pentateuch was Moses' work. According to them, he might have used earlier sources, but of course, this completely excluded Hilkiah, who they believed found the entire Pentateuch (or almost) in the temple.

The neologist picture was taken to pieces by J. S. Vater, who worked from the thesis of A. Geddes. Vater believed that before the exile the Pentateuch existed only in fragments, and that it was one or more of these which Hilkiah found in the temple. That this fragment later became the core of Deuteronomy Vater could scarcely doubt, though he continued to insist that Deuteronomy was the last of the Pentateuchal books to be written – after the exile. He reconciled this contradiction by saying that Hilkiah's fragment remained unattached to any wider sources until after the other books of the Pentateuch had been compiled. His position was not a very satisfactory one, because he also recognized that there were Deuteronomic elements in Samuel and Kings, and concluded that parts of the text must have existed from the time of Solomon, if not before.

Vater's views might have collapsed from their own inconsistency, had it not been for the brilliance of W. M. L. De Wette (1780–1849). De Wette's main career as a scholar belongs to the next period in our study, but as a young man he tackled the problem of Deuteronomy in a Latin thesis (1805) and then in his famous *Beiträge* or *Contributions* to the study of the Old Testament (1806–7).

De Wette accepted the fragments hypothesis of Vater, but tackled the whole question of Deuteronomic origins from a different perspective. He argued that Chronicles was a late composition, which is therefore unreliable on the subject of Israel's worship before the exile. In particular, the centralization of the cult in the Jerusalem temple was unknown during the monarchy or before, when, as

Samuel and Kings make abundantly clear, there were altars all over the place. Earlier critics, who had of course noticed this, argued that these altars were built in exceptional circumstances and did not detract from the Mosaic principle that sacrificial worship should be in one place only. In this way he demonstrated to his own satisfaction that Deuteronomy 12 could not be Mosaic, or even pre-exilic, because it contained injunctions which went completely against standard Israelite practice before the exile.

De Wette's importance was that he was the first to present a global picture of Israelite origins which was completely different from the record given in the Old Testament itself. De Wette regarded the Old Testament text as a fictitious back-projection of post-exilic Israelite life into the period of the settlement in Canaan and the monarchy. Moreover, he did this not as a Deist but as a scholar, concerned with minute textual analysis. As for the book found by Hilkiah, De Wette was prepared to believe that it was substantially part of what is now Deuteronomy, but he did not exclude the possibility that fragments now included in other Pentateuchal books may have been found as well. Deuteronomy was not as special as had been made out, and the origin of the Pentateuch was a more complex issue than had thitherto been imagined. A lot more work remained to be done, but the ground had been prepared for seeing Deuteronomy as part of a process of Pentateuchal formation, in which it was neither the beginning nor the end. A new era in Pentateuchal criticism had indeed begun.

De Wette's arguments, presented in his *Dissertatio* of 1805, went as follows:

1. *The history of Moses is complete by the end of Numbers, including the appointment of Joshua as his successor.* De Wette followed Eichhorn in believing that Genesis was a compilation of two sources, and Vater in accepting a multiple authorship for Exodus to Numbers. Deuteronomy, however, seems like a new beginning to the story, just when it has reached its conclusion.

2. *The opening verses of Deuteronomy paraphrase what has been fully recounted in Numbers.* This seems strange if Deuteronomy is merely the continuation of an ongoing story, and doubly strange when we realize that in some ways it appears to contradict what was said earlier.

3. *Deuteronomy has a distinctive style.* Single verses found elsewhere in the Pentateuch get vastly expanded: *e.g.* Exodus 20:18 becomes Deuteronomy 5:22–27, and Leviticus 26:29 becomes Deuteronomy 28:53–57. De Wette discovered ten examples of this.

4. *There are over thirty words and phrases which are peculiar to Deuteronomy.* The notion that this was because Deuteronomy was a speech and not originally a written document is refuted by comparing Leviticus 26, which is also a speech, with its counterpart in Deuteronomy 28, which exhibits Deuteronomy's particular style.

5. *Deuteronomy has a more advanced concept of religion than the rest of the Pentateuch.* De Wette believed that it was more subtle, and more theological in its approach to questions like the miracle of the manna. It also contains laws of later origin, such as the law of the king (17:14–20), of the prophets (18:9–22) and of divorce (24:1–4).

6. Lastly, and most importantly, *Deuteronomy contains instructions that worship is to be offered at a single sanctuary.* In this it is highly innovative, and contradicts Exodus 20:24–25. It also goes against the normal practice in Israel in early times, as can be seen from the fact that Samuel, Saul, David and Solomon sacrificed quite happily in many different places.

De Wette concluded that Deuteronomy was designed to supplement the earlier books in the light of a new ideology, in which the Jerusalem temple played a central role. In a footnote, he added that it was the book found by Hilkiah in 622 BC, though he did not speculate further about its ultimate origin. Nevertheless, the gist of his arguments, and his evident belief that Deuteronomy revealed a development of Israelite religion over time, indicate that he must have accepted a dating of Deuteronomy near to the time of Hilkiah, even if he did not believe that Hilkiah was himself the author.

BIBLIOGRAPHY

J. A. Bewer, 'The Case for the Early Date of Deuteronomy', *Journal of Biblical Literature* 47 (1928), pp. 305–321.

P. C. Craigie, *The Book of Deuteronomy* (Grand Rapids: Eerdmans, 1976).

E. Day, 'The Promulgation of Deuteronomy', *Journal of Biblical Literature* 21 (1902), pp. 197–213.

W. M. L. De Wette, *Dissertatio Critico-Exegetica qua Deuteronomium a Prioribus Pentateuchii Libris Diversum, alius cuiusdam Recentioribus Auctoris Opus Esse Monstratur* (Jena, 1805).

————*Beiträge zur Einleitung in das Alte Testament* (Halle, 1806–7).

S. Japhet, 'The Historical Reliability of Chronicles: The History of the Problem and its Place in Biblical Research', *Journal for the Study of the Old Testament* 33 (1985), pp. 83–107.

R. H. Kenneth, *Deuteronomy and the Decalogue* (Cambridge: Cambridge University Press, 1920).
N. Lohfink (ed.), *Das Deuteronomium* (Leuven: Leuven University Press, 1985).
J. G. McConville, *Law and Theology in Deuteronomy* (Sheffield: JSOT Press, 1985).
E. W. Nicholson, 'The Centralisation of the Cult in Deuteronomy', *Vetus Testamentum* 13 (1963), pp. 380–389.
M. J. Paul, *Het Archimedisch Punt van de Pentateuchkritiek* ('s Gravenhage: Boekencentrum 1988).
J. Reider, 'The Origin of Deuteronomy', *The Jewish Quarterly Review* 27 (1936–7), pp. 349–371.
G. J. Wenham, 'The Date of Deuteronomy; Linch-pin of Old Testament Criticism', *Themelios* 10.3 (1985), pp. 15–20, and 11.1 (1985), pp. 15–18.

The nineteenth century (1800–1918)

The nineteenth century was a time of enormous social, political and scientific development. After the upheaval caused by the French Revolution and the Napoleonic Wars (1789–1815), a new order of society emerged in Europe. In the Americas and in Russia, new powers came into being, with a potential which was as yet only dimly realized. In the course of the century, European civilization was extended to most of Africa and Asia, so that by 1900 western Christian culture was dominant almost everywhere. The churches were part of this expansion; by 1900 Protestant missions, which a century earlier were virtually non-existent, had established indigenous churches in many parts of the globe. This involved a massive effort at Bible translation, which was to have considerable implications for biblical studies.

The French Revolution and its aftermath produced a strong reaction in Roman Catholic countries which effectively stifled biblical studies for nearly a century. In Germany, Napoleon made a clean sweep of the old order, by abolishing the Holy Roman Empire (1806) and reorganizing the hundreds of mini-states into which the country was divided. This reorganization (or 'mediatization' as it was called) also affected the universities, where German biblical scholarship was concentrated. Seven Protestant faculties disappeared: Altdorf (1807), Rinteln and Helmstedt (1809), Frankfurt-an-der-Oder (1811), Erfurt (1816), Wittenberg (1817) and Duisburg (1818). Wittenberg, Luther's university, was merged with Halle, and Frankfurt-an-der-Oder was moved to Breslau, which opened in 1811. In partial compensation, new theological faculties were opened at Berlin (1810) and Bonn (1818).

Because nineteenth-century biblical scholarship was largely dominated by Germans, it is important to understand how the German academic world was organized. For most of the period there were twenty-one Protestant theological faculties training German-speaking pastors. Of these, seventeen were on traditional German soil. They were at Berlin, Bonn, Breslau, Erlangen, Giessen, Göttingen, Greifswald, Halle, Heidelberg, Jena, Kiel, Königsberg, Leipzig, Marburg, Rostock, Tübingen and Würzburg. To these must be added Strasbourg (Strassburg), which was German from 1871 to 1919. Outside the German Reich were Basel and Zürich in Switzerland, and Dorpat (Tartu) in Estonia. Dorpat was Russified in 1893 (before becoming Estonian in 1918), and so moved out of the German orbit.

These universities enjoyed a high degree of internal autonomy, as long as they did not threaten the order of the state. This could be a serious problem for those universities in the kingdom of Prussia, but it did not weigh heavily on the others. Professors generally stayed in their posts for life, and became identified with the tradition of the university they were at. This was especially true at Tübingen, Göttingen and Berlin, though the same principle could be applied almost anywhere. Students, on the other hand, moved freely from one faculty to the next, and often attended several universities in the course of their undergraduate career. This meant that there was real competition between the universities, and that popular new ideas could not long be kept quiet. The German intellectual scene had an openness which was unknown elsewhere, and this was a major factor contributing to its phenomenal development in the nineteenth century.

Censorship of unorthodox opinions was still practised after 1815, even in Protestant countries; indeed, it was not until about 1890 that a holder of radical new ideas could feel relatively safe from persecution. In Germany, the state played an active part in this, while in the English-speaking world it was left to the churches, which made frequent use of the lawcourts to resolve their problems. The nineteenth century was a time of theological struggle between the liberals, who were the heirs of eighteenth-century critical scholarship, and the conservatives, who dominated most of the church establishments. As time went on, the liberals gradually gained control of the universities and excluded conservative scholars from them.

German academic scholarship dominated the Scandinavian countries, with their Lutheran background, and the same was true of the Protestant minorities in France and in Austria-Hungary. The Netherlands maintained an independent tradition to some extent, but German influence was strong there also. Only in the English-speaking countries was there any effective counterweight to German domination, but that crumbled as the century wore on. Whereas in 1800 British ideas were still being exported to Germany, a century later the trend had been reversed to such an extent that most British scholars were unaware of how 'German' liberalism had originated.

Between 1805 and 1815 the face of German biblical scholarship changed beyond recognition. Neologism gave way to a new critical school, which turned the Old Testament on its head. It took longer for the same thing to happen in New Testament studies, but by 1840 that process was well under way. At the time, very few people in England understood this. German was not a well-known language, and those who championed the Germans were often on the margins of church life, associated with Unitarians and other freethinkers. It is said that when E. B. Pusey (see p. 290) wanted to study in Germany in the 1820s, he could find no-one in Oxford to teach him German, and he later claimed that there were only nine people in the whole country with the required ability. That must be an exaggeration, but it gives an accurate impression of the general knowledge of things German at the time.

Pusey went to Germany, where he studied under Friedrich Schleiermacher, generally reckoned today to be the father of German liberal theology. Pusey was horrified, and returned to England as a staunch conservative, even a reactionary, in theological and biblical matters. As Regius Professor of Hebrew at Oxford from 1828 until his death in 1882, he ensured that no liberal ideas would be tolerated in Old Testament studies. In Scotland there was a similar trend, backed not by Pusey's catholic type of conservatism, but by dissenting Presbyterians. The result was that British biblical scholarship retained a strongly conservative streak far longer than was the case in Germany. The American scene was even more conservative than the British, and the battles between conservatives and liberals there were not finally won by the latter until the 1920s.

Because this struggle was so important, it is essential to consider what the words 'liberal' and 'conservative' implied in the nineteenth century. A 'liberal' may be characterized as follows.

1. He was devoted to the historical-critical method as the only sure and objective way of arriving at truth. The Bible was a human book written within a given historical and religious context. Even if its authors were somehow inspired by God, they were writing to commend a religious position which could be explained by any number of factors quite apart from divine revelation. Scholarly

investigation could uncover the process by which this had occurred, and pronounce judgment upon it. Many critical scholars were convinced that the Old Testament was largely fiction, and that many of the people and places described in it had never existed. The New Testament had more credibility, but its picture of Jesus was historically inaccurate. Christianity, including the New Testament documents, was the product of diverse and competing forces within the early church. The victorious party, which came to the fore about AD 200, simply anathematized the rest and suppressed their writings.

2. 'Liberals' were suspicious, and often contemptuous, of pre-Enlightenment scholarship and tradition. In particular, anything which could be called 'catholic' was disliked and opposed. Liberals thought of the Reformation as a great breakthrough to personal intellectual freedom, and they waged what sometimes amounted to open war against the papacy and the Roman church. The New Testament church did not have a religious hierarchy, and any signs of its development could be branded 'early catholicism' and relegated to the post-apostolic period.

3. The liberal was usually attracted to a spiritual experience unencumbered by dogma. Systematic theology was the result of the corruption of the early church by Hellenistic ideas, and did not correspond to the original teaching of Jesus. Jesus was a man who taught morality and spiritual freedom; he was not God in human flesh. Dogma had turned important intellectual principles into unfathomable mysteries, and was therefore the great enemy of science.

A 'conservative' may be characterized as follows.

1. He was convinced that the Bible is the divinely inspired Word of God. This was the basic unifying principle for all conservatives in the nineteenth century. Some were prepared to admit that earlier generations had not expressed this as well as they might have done, and in their zeal may have gone too far in making their claims. Others clung rigidly to the position of the Helvetic Consensus Formula of 1675, as this had been interpreted by François Turretin. But all were agreed that divine inspiration was of the essence of Scripture, and that without it, Christianity would collapse.

2. He was convinced that dogmatic theology was necessary to explain the teaching of Scripture. Nineteenth-century conservatives were not usually pietistic in their understanding of theology. On the contrary, they frequently blamed the pietistic movements for adopting an air of indifference to doctrinal questions which presaged the introduction of liberalism into the churches.

3. He believed that if scholarly methods were properly applied, the

liberal case would be shown to be faulty. Liberalism was based more on prejudice than on evidence, most of which could legitimately be interpreted in a conservative way. Liberalism was not a science but a belief, which in its essence was anti-Christian. The most encouraging field of development for the conservatives was archaeology, and it was they who led the great expeditions to Palestine, Egypt and Mesopotamia. It must be remembered that these countries were largely unknown in 1800, and nobody could say for sure whether cities such as Nineveh or Babylon had ever existed. Such scepticism was widespread, and extended well beyond the Bible; most scholars doubted the existence of Homer's Troy until Heinrich Schliemann discovered it. Archaeology undoubtedly had a sobering effect on the wilder liberal speculations, and ultimately made much nineteenth-century critical scholarship seem hopelessly outdated and out of touch with historical reality. Not every archaeological discovery supported the conservative position, but enough did to make a radical revision of many liberal positions essential.

In conclusion, we may add that the nineteenth century witnessed the development of specialization within what had previously been a single field of biblical studies. After 1800 it became increasingly rare to find a scholar who was equally at home in both Testaments. It is therefore appropriate to divide our study at this point into Old and New Testament scholarship, and to look at each in turn.

7

The Old Testament from De Wette to Wellhausen

The period and the subject

The new era in Old Testament scholarship opened with the career of W. M. L. De Wette (1780–1849), who broke with the neologist tradition, and embarked on a path which would lead him to a total reworking of Israelite history and religion. De Wette was as sceptical as any eighteenth-century rationalist could wish, but he tied his opinions to careful and exacting scholarship. Those who disagreed with him could not dismiss his arguments out of hand, but had to prove their own case on equally exacting scholarly grounds.

De Wette's heirs expanded his views and reworked them, but in spite of any number of minor revisions and corrections to De Wette's thesis, some of which caused fairly heated scholarly discussion, the overall direction was plain enough. De Wette's method had won the day; the rest was merely detail.

Among the new breed of critical scholars, it was recognized that the historical books of the Old Testament had a strong Deuteronomic flavour, and were somehow related to that book, though the modern theory of a 'Deuteronomic History' was not developed until 1943. It was also asserted that Isaiah could not all be the work of the prophet who lived in the time of Hezekiah (*c.* 715–686 BC), and that the later chapters were the work of one or more prophets living in or just after the exile. Several other books, notably Daniel and the wisdom literature attributed to Solomon, were given dates much later than the ones traditionally assigned to them.

Textual criticism was generally more conservative, if only because the limited number of variants made new departures very difficult. The most promising developments were in the field of comparative philology, which became a major discipline as other Semitic languages were discovered. A number of conjectural emendations were made to the Hebrew text, on the basis of etymologies derived from cognate languages, but although some words of uncertain meaning were clarified in this way, they were not numerous enough to cause a major revolution in our knowledge of the text. The main legacy of this period was a series of excellent Hebrew grammars and dictionaries, which have remained models of their kind.

Towards the end of the century archaeology began to be developed, and its results came to the aid of conservatives in their struggle against the liberals. Not surprisingly, it was in the most conservative country of all, the United States, that archaeology received the greatest support and encouragement. There, and to a large extent in Britain also, it became a bulwark of conservative scholarship and one of the main scientific resources of conservative theology. So powerful was its impact that by the early years of the twentieth century even liberal German academics were being swayed towards a more conservative position by this new source of evidence.

By that time, however, Old Testament scholarship had been transformed by the theories of Julius Wellhausen. Wellhausen's researches on the Pentateuch established a documentary hypothesis of its origins which was so successful that it virtually displaced earlier theories, so that many people now think that Pentateuchal criticism began with him. The documentary hypothesis has frequently been challenged, but in spite of its problems, it remains the starting-point for all modern study of the Pentateuch.

The interpreters and their work

The German sphere

Wilhelm Martin Leberecht De Wette (1780–1849). By most accounts the founder of modern critical Old Testament scholarship, De Wette fell under the influence of J. G. Herder at an early age. When he was still only twenty-five, he published his dissertation on Deuteronomy, which set a new standard in the critical study of that book. A year later he began publishing his *Beiträge zur Einleitung in das Alte Testament* (*Contributions to Old Testament Introduction*) which appeared in 1806–7. In this ground-breaking work, De Wette argued that much of the Old Testament was mythical, and of little or no historical value. But De Wette was not a rationalist; he thought of myths as important vehicles for the expression of philosophical and religious ideas in an essentially poetic form. In this he followed the main opinions of the leading scholars of his day, including Herder. He was also deeply influenced by the religious philosophy of J. F. Fries (1773–1843), for whom theology was a contemplation of the 'highest' (*i.e.* most intellectual and 'spiritual') elements in religion. He later wrote a number of works on the Psalms (1811, 1819, 1836) and a dogmatic theology in which he included his critical insights (1813).

Wilhelm Gesenius (1786–1842). He is best known for his detailed philological analysis of the Hebrew text, which he conducted along rationalist lines. He defended the late dating of both Chronicles and Deuteronomy, and developed a more subtle treatment of the category of 'myth', dividing concrete examples of it into historical, philosophical and 'mixed' categories. His commentary on Isaiah (1820–21) was outstanding in its grasp of critical detail, and firmly established scholarly belief in the multiple authorship of the canonical text. He remains famous for his Hebrew dictionary, which first appeared in 1810–12.

Carl Peter Wilhelm Gramberg (1798–1830). He published a critical history of the religious ideas of the Old Testament (1829–30) in which he anticipated many of the ideas of Wellhausen, but he died too young to have much impact on the development of historical critical scholarship.

Friedrich Bleek (1793–1859). His main work was an introduction to the Old Testament, which did not appear until after his death (1860). In this book he moved decisively away from De Wette's radical views, towards a belief that the priestly code in the Pentateuch was of Mosaic origin. He believed in the right use of critical tools, which for him implied obtaining conservative results.

Christian Carl Josias von Bunsen (1791–1860). This German diplomat and scholar spent much of his life in England, and was chiefly responsible for introducing German critical methods of biblical study to the English-speaking world. So much was this the case that in *Essays and Reviews* (1860), Rowland Williams devoted a forty-page essay to him, while other German scholars of the time were virtually ignored. He was highly regarded by H. Ewald and returned the compliment. Bunsen held an evolutionary view of the development of religion, and interpreted Genesis against an Egyptian background (1845–57). His fame in Germany largely rests on his *Bibelwerk für die Gemeinde* (*Bible for the Parish*) (1858), in which he made the findings of critical scholarship accessible to the average churchgoer.

Friedrich Wilhelm Karl Umbreit (1795–1860). He taught at Heidelberg from 1820, and was Professor of Old Testament there from 1829 until his death. He wrote a number of commentaries, which pursued a middle way between conservative orthodoxy and radical criticism. In many ways he was the intellectual child of Eichhorn, whose strict philological approach he followed closely, and also of Herder, who gave him an understanding of the spiritual quality of the Old Testament. He saw the text both as a remarkable record of human development, and as a fundamental part of divine revelation, leading up to its fulfilment in Christ.

Anton Günther (1783–1863). He was a Roman Catholic priest from Vienna whose philosophical theology had a considerable influence on Franz Delitzsch. He believed that the Hebrew theocracy had originally been a living organism, in which sin and forgiveness were proclaimed in the sacrificial cult and supported by the prophetic movement. But in the course of time the cult became purely formal, and the prophets began to look forward towards the future restoration of the world. The Old Testament did not produce the desired healing, and only in Christ were the promises finally fulfilled. Günther's views were not radical by contemporary standards, but they were enough to have him condemned by Rome in 1857. Some of his followers continued to fight for his ideas, and many were instrumental in forming the breakaway Old Catholic Church after 1870.

Hermann Hupfeld (1796–1866). He was a faithful follower of De Wette and, like him, an admirer of Herder. For him the Bible was a living witness to the eternal religious spirit, not a record of Israel's history. His most important book was *Die Quellen der Genesis und die Art ihrer Zusammensetzung* (*The Sources of Genesis and the Manner of their Conflation*), which appeared in 1853. He distinguished two types of E source, one which was older and priestly (now the priestly document), the other which was newer and more legal in orientation. Furthermore, he insisted that the priestly document was the basis of the Pentateuch (its so-called *Grundschrift*), to which the other sources were subsequently added.

Karl Heinrich Graf (1815–69). His great book *Die geschichtlichen Bücher des Alten Testaments* (*The Historical Books of the Old Testament*) appeared in 1866 and at once broke new ground in Old Testament criticism. The first part dealt with Genesis to 2 Kings, the second with Chronicles. He argued that there was no *Grundschrift* in the Pentateuch. According to him, the Deuteronomic redactor had combined J with what were supposed to be the narrative sections of the *Grundschrift* and his own additional material to form the backbone of the Pentateuch. The priestly material was composed in imitation of the narrative parts of the so-called *Grundschrift* and added to the rest after the exile.

Gustav Friedrich Oehler (1812–72). A staunchly conservative scholar, he published an introduction to the theology of the Old Testament (1845). He rejected attempts to Christianize the Old Testament, though he saw it as preparatory to the New. However, the connections between the Testaments are apparent mainly from hindsight; the Old Testament writers themselves were not consciously looking forward towards a future fulfilment of their writings.

Johann Friedrich Ludwig George (1811–73). His main work was a study of early Jewish festivals in relation to the Mosaic law (1835), in which he claimed that all the official festivals were of post-exilic origin. He also believed that Deuteronomy, whose origin in the time of King Josiah he accepted, was earlier than large parts of Exodus–Numbers, an idea which later led to the theory that the latter were the work of a previously unidentified 'priestly source'. George took De Wette's ideas to their logical conclusion, and believed that pre-exilic Israelite religion was one of cultic freedom. In many respects he was the precursor of Wellhausen, with whom he briefly overlapped at Greifswald (1872–73), though it is not known whether he influenced the younger man directly or not.

Heinrich Ewald (1803–75). Associated with Göttingen for most of his life, he spent eleven years in exile at Tübingen (1837–48) in protest against the suspension of the Hanoverian constitution, and in 1868 he was forced out of the university for refusing to take the oath of loyalty to Prussia. He is universally recognized as having been one of the greatest Old Testament scholars of all time. Ewald appears as a radical when compared to someone like Eichhorn, but in the company of De Wette and his followers he seems like a conservative, and was criticized for this by Wellhausen. However, it can be said that he anticipated the theories of twentieth-century scholars such as A. Alt and M. Noth, and his views receive greater acceptance now than in his own lifetime. He was the first person to write a history of Israel, which appeared between 1843 and 1859. He also published large works on the poets (1835–9; 1866–72) and prophets (1840–41; 1867–8) of the Old Testament, and regarded the text as of great value for reconstructing Israelite history.

In the course of his work on these subjects, Ewald developed a highly complex theory of the literary origins of the documents, which he believed went through several stages of redaction before reaching their final form. In his view, the historical books of the Old Testament could be divided into three great works. The first of these was the 'Great Book of Origins', which comprised the Pentateuch and Joshua. This was completed before the exile. The second book was the 'Great Book of Kings' extending from Judges to 2 Kings, which appeared during the exile, and finally, the 'Great Book of Universal History' which comprised Chronicles, Ezra and Nehemiah, and was written about 323 BC by a Levite. Another note of originality was his view that there were two Deuteronomists.

In 1848 Ewald published *Die Alterthümer des Volkes Israel* (*The Antiquities of Israel*) in which he gave his account of the origins of the priestly rituals and festivals. Ewald's reconstruction of Israel's origins claimed that although the Genesis account was highly stylized, it contained more than a core of truth. In particular, he was prepared to accept, on critical grounds, that Israel had migrated in patriarchal times from northern Mesopotamia. Ewald combined criticism, tradition and theology in a unique blend, which made his views accessible to all schools of thought. At the same time, it distanced him from any one of them, and he cut a lonely figure on the German scene during his lifetime. It was only after his death that his pupils came to realize how important he was and how much they owed to him.

Ferdinand Hitzig (1807–75). He was professor at Zürich from 1833 to 1861, and then at Heidelberg. He was a prolific commentator, and advanced some very radical proposals for dating, such as the suggestion that Psalms came from the second century BC. According to him, Israel's great achievement was to have developed a transcendental religion while avoiding pantheism. In his view, this was because the Israelites preferred truth to beauty, and so avoided the worship of nature. Otherwise, he believed that early Israelite religion had been strongly influenced by surrounding cults, especially by those of Persia.

Ludwig Diestel (1825–79). Professor at Greifswald (1862), Jena (1867) and finally Tübingen (1872), he is chiefly remembered today for his history of Old Testament scholarship (*Geschichte des Alten Testamentes in der christlichen Kirche*) which appeared in 1869 and remains the starting-point for all histories of Old Testament exegesis.

Johann Karl Wilhelm Vatke (1806–82). He published a radical *Biblical Theology* in 1835, which, unfortunately for him, coincided with a conservative reaction in Berlin. He was deeply influenced by Hegel, though his critical work can stand independently of his philosophical ideas, and did so. His most fundamental idea was that religion is continually developing from a lower to a higher stage, which is why he rejected De Wette's theory that post-exilic Judaism represented a falling away from a high point under Moses and the early prophets. Vatke rejected the historical pretensions of Israelite literature before the eighth century BC, and based many of his conclusions about the earlier period on a study of comparative religion in Canaan and Egypt. His opinion of Moses was necessarily low, although he continued to believe that he was the initiator of the Yahweh cult, which supposedly replaced Israel's earlier, astral religion.

The orthodox confessionalists. The union of Lutheran and Reformed churches, which was consummated in 1830, brought about a revival of interest in the Reformation Confessions, particularly among those who were determined to protect the Lutheran tradition in the united church. These men were motivated by a religious experience connected with the spread of the Evangelical Revival from Britain to the Continent, and were devoted to the Augsburg Confession of 1530, which they regarded as the most adequate expression of their faith. Old Testament scholars were prominent among them, and they mounted a long and partially successful campaign against the proponents of the new critical methods. In approaching the text, these men accepted the faith claims which it made, and regarded the history in which they were presented as basically accurate. They therefore used their scholarship to defend the authenticity of the Old Testament, particularly in its historical aspects.

A prominent member of this group was **August Tholuck** (1799–1877). In a speech made in London in 1825, he attacked the unbelief of the Halle theological faculty, and launched a controversy which was soon to embroil scholars all over Germany. He was supported by a number of like-minded academics, who thought that the critical methods adopted by De Wette, Gesenius and others were undermining Christianity.

Other prominent confessionalists included the following.

Ernst Wilhelm Hengstenberg (1802–69). Professor of Old Testament at Berlin from 1828 until his death, he became the most prolific and highly regarded of the confessionalist scholars. Hengstenberg's greatest works were his *Beiträge zur Einleitung ins Alte Testament* (*Contributions to Old Testament Introduction*) which appeared in three volumes from 1831 to 1839, and his *Christology of the Old Testament*, published in German in 1829, translated into English in 1858 and periodically reissued ever since. His chief theological concern was to defend the atoning work of Christ, and he therefore took a very conservative view of the Old Testament sacrifices. He played a prominent part in church and academic controversies, and tried his best to prevent scholars who used critical methods from gaining important university positions.

(Johann) Karl (Carl) Friedrich Keil (1807–88) and **Franz Delitzsch** (1813–90). These two scholars are indelibly associated with each other, thanks to their magnificent and extremely detailed commentaries on the Hebrew text. Keil remained staunchly conservative all his life, but Delitzsch became slightly more accommodating to the critical method after his move from Erlangen to Leipzig in 1867. His Isaiah commentary of 1866 defended the traditional authorship of all sixty-six chapters, but later editions revealed a modification of this position, and he appears to have accepted multiple authorship of the text by the time he died. Because of the great importance of their commentaries, which are still widely used today, they are listed here by year of publication, with K or D to indicate the author:

1851	Song of Songs (D)
1852	Genesis (D)
1857	Joshua (K)
1864	Exodus and Leviticus (K); Job (D)
1865	Deuteronomy and Joshua (K)
1866	Isaiah (D)
1868	Judges, Ruth, minor prophets (K)
1870	Esther (K)
1871	Psalms (D)
1872	Daniel and Chronicles (K)
1873	Proverbs (D)
1875	Samuel (K)
1876	Kings (K)
1877	Ecclesiastes (D)
1880	Jeremiah and Lamentations (K)
1882	Ezekiel (K)
1887	Genesis, revised edition (D)
1888	Ezra and Nehemiah (K)
1889	Isaiah, revised edition (D)

Delitzsch was also a renowned theologian, and his *System of Biblical Psychology* (1855) was a notable attempt to demonstrate the unity of the biblical picture of humanity, and its essential conformity to Christian teaching.

Johann Christian Konrad von Hoffmann (1810–77). A confessionalist who later departed from strict orthodoxy, Hoffmann was deeply influenced by the historicism of L. von Ranke (1795–1886), which gave him a clear appreciation of the balance which had to be struck between the motives of individuals and the underlying processes of history. He believed that human history was the outworking of the love of the triune God manifested to his creation. This reality could be known only through personal conversion to Christ, after which the Bible would confirm it. His historical method can be seen most clearly in *Prophecy and Fulfilment* (1841–42), a work in which he placed the prophets in their own time and saw their role as pointing from one age to the next in Old Testament history, and not primarily as foretellers of Christ (in sharp contrast to Hengstenberg).

Johann Heinrich Kurtz (1809–90). The last of the great confessionalist scholars, he was Professor at Dorpat from 1850 to 1870. He wrote a number of works defending traditional views against the critics, including a history of the old covenant (1848–55), and a book on the sacrificial worship of the Old Testament (1862). It is significant that his main interest lay in church history, on which he also wrote extensively.

Eduard Riehm (1830–88). He wrote an important introduction to the Old Testament (1889), in which he criticized Wellhausen's documentary hypothesis of Pentateuchal origins for its author's failure to recognize that J and E were not always as closely connected as he assumed. He himself believed that the priestly *Grundschrift* dated from early monarchical times, and that it had been combined with J and E in a single-stage operation, some time around the eighth century BC. The Deuteronomic redaction finally put the whole Pentateuch together as it now stands.

Edouard (Eduard) Reuss (1804–91). Born in Strasbourg, and writing mainly in French, Reuss nevertheless studied in Germany and remained in Strasbourg after it became German. As early as 1834 he was maintaining that the priestly law was post-exilic, and therefore later than the major prophets. Even Ezekiel, according to Reuss, predates the composition of the ritual laws of the Pentateuch. Reuss kept this idea to himself, and it did not become public until one of his pupils, August Kayser, developed it in his *Das vorexilische Buch der Urgeschichte Israels und seine Erweiterungen* (*The Pre-exilic Book of Israel's Earliest History and its Expansions*) (1874).

Abraham Kuenen (1828–91). This Dutch scholar and Professor at Leiden was closely in touch with developments in Germany. His view of Old Testament history was distinctly reductionist, and he repudiated any concept of 'salvation history' (*Heilsgeschichte*), according to which the text presented the development of God's saving purpose for Israel. He also proposed to Graf, on the basis of his reading of Colenso, that the entire *Grundschrift* was post-exilic.

August Dillmann (1823–94). A student of Ewald's, he advanced critical arguments on the Pentateuch very similar to those of Riehm. As far as he was concerned, the closeness of J and E in original content was enough to explain why they were so interwoven in the final redaction; it was not necessary to posit two stages in the editorial process.

Bernhard Stade (1848–1906). Professor at Giessen from 1857, he wrote a great history of Israel (1905) fully supporting Wellhausen's position. However, he also believed that the Old Testament was preparatory to the New, and that a discipline of biblical theology was both possible and necessary.

Adolf Kamphausen (1829–1909). Employed by Bunsen as his private secretary, Kamphausen began his career as his assistant. In 1859 he went to Bonn and in 1868 he succeeded Delitzsch at Erlangen, where he remained until 1900. He was strongly critical of Wellhausen's historical scepticism, and he struggled to correct it. He was an excellent student of the Hebrew text, and a good judge of his material. On the whole, his scholarship was conservative for the time, though he did not believe in the historicity of Daniel, for instance. He wrote little, but was influential in updating Luther's translation of the German Bible.

Rudolf Smend (1851–1913). Professor in Basel from 1881 and then in Göttingen from 1889 until his death, he was a colleague of Wellhausen's in the latter post and supported him fully.

Julius Wellhausen (1844–1918). Professor at Greifswald (1872), then at Halle (1882), Marburg (1885) and finally Göttingen (1892), he is universally recognized today as the classical exponent of the documentary hypothesis of the Pentateuch. He published his main work in 1878, as *The History of Israel*. This was revised in 1883. He also published a brief sketch of the history in 1880, which formed the basis for the article on 'Israel' in the ninth edition of the *Encyclopaedia Britannica* (1881) which provoked a scandal in the English-speaking world, then still largely immune to German critical scholarship. Wellhausen had a low view of the reliability of the Pentateuch as history, though he accepted that a shadowy figure called Moses had in some sense been the founder of Israelite religion. He gave greater credence to the history of the people under the judges and early kings, and his views on that period are broadly similar to what can be found in critical histories of Israel today.

Friedrich Delitzsch (1850–1922). A fanatical liberal, in sharp contrast to his father, Delitzsch went as far as to say that archaeological discoveries, which most people thought supported the historicity of the Old Testament narrative, destroyed their uniqueness, and therefore made them relatively unimportant. He was a major advocate of the theory that much of the Old Testament had a Babylonian background, a view which was reinforced by the discovery of the Code of Hammurabi (1902). His main positive contribution was in the realm of philology, where he carried on and developed the work of Gesenius.

Wolf Wilhelm Graf von Baudissin (1847–1926). Professor at Strasbourg (1880), Marburg (1881) and Berlin (1894), he gave a lecture in 1884 in which he stated that although the priestly document (P) was published in the time of Ezra, it represented a revival of pre-exilic practices, so that its contents were much earlier. He believed that early Israelite religion contained distinctive prophetic, priestly and Deuteronomic elements.

Bernhard Duhm (1847–1928). Professor at Basel from 1889 until his death, Duhm wrote a *Theologie der Propheten* (*Theology of the Prophets*) in 1875, in which he prepared the way for Wellhausen. His best-known work is his commentary on Isaiah (1892), in which he effectively isolated the different 'servant songs' and posited a Third Isaiah as the author of chapters 56 – 66, as well as confirming Eichhorn's view that there was a Second Isaiah who composed chapters 40 – 55.

Rudolf Kittel (1853–1929). Professor at Breslau from 1888 to 1898, and then at Leipzig, Kittel developed Wellhausen's notion that P was a composite source, and traced its earliest elements to Davidic times (1888). He thought it had been put together in the eighth century BC, and criticized Wellhausen for ignoring the importance of Hezekiah's reform. At first he believed that the entire Pentateuch was composed during the exile, though, as a result of archaeological discoveries, he was converted to a much more conservative position (1906). After that, he developed a more positive approach to the text, especially to the so-called 'succession narrative' in 2 Samuel.

Theodor Nöldeke (1836–1930). Professor at Kiel (1864–1872) and then at Strasbourg (1873–1906), Nöldeke developed Graf's hypothesis in his *Untersuchungen zur Kritik des Alten Testaments* (*Investigations in the Criticism of the Old Testament*), which appeared in 1869. His main aim in this was to demonstrate the unity of the *Grundschrift* – in opposition to Graf – and to argue that it was pre-exilic. He argued that it was the Deuteronomist who had made the final redaction of the text.

Karl Budde (1850–1935). Professor at Bonn from 1879, Strasbourg from 1889 and Marburg from 1900, he wrote *Die biblische Urgeschichte* (*Biblical Prehistory*) in 1883, in which he subdivided the J source of the Pentateuch, thereby heralding modifications to the documentary hypothesis which have been picked up in twentieth-century research. In a later work on the history of Israel's religion (1899), he suggested that Israel's Yahwism came from Moses' marriage (Ex. 2:16–22), and had therefore been adopted from the Kenites. This became known as the Kenite hypothesis of the origin of Yahwism.

Johannes Meinhold (1861–1937). The last of the great nineteenth-century German Old Testament scholars, he taught at Greifswald from 1885, and then in Bonn from 1889, where he remained until his retirement in 1928. From a very conservative background, he was converted to the Wellhausen position after many years of research on his findings. He wrote at some length on Daniel and Isaiah, and tried to show that Israel's festivals were mostly post-exilic in origin. He held to an evolutionary view of Israelite religion, which culminated in the teaching of Jesus. But at the same time, he distinguished Jesus' teaching quite sharply from its Old Testament roots, because in him Meinhold saw the perfection of true spiritual love. Meinhold lived to see his brand of liberalism overthrown in Germany, and he felt out of place in the theological atmosphere of the 1920s and 1930s – a clear sign that an age in scholarship had come to an end.

The English-speaking world

Adam Clarke (*c.* 1760–1832). An orthodox commentator on the Bible, his work on Genesis appeared in 1810. In it, he felt free to say that not everything in the Pentateuch derived from Moses, though he upheld the overall Mosaic authorship of the text. He was also at great pains to tie the creation account to current scientific opinions, and he showed a keen awareness of textual difficulties. His solutions were always conservative in intention, and sometimes produced ingenious results.

Hugh James Rose (1795–1838). A scholar of Trinity College, Cambridge, he went to Germany in 1824 and came back the following year, when he preached a series of sermons before the university on the state of Protestantism in that country. These were subsequently published, and contained a surprisingly good survey of current German biblical scholarship. Rose knew all about Eichhorn, Gabler and De Wette, and described their views reasonably accurately, though in a superior and hostile tone.

Thomas Arnold (1795–1842). He was not an Old Testament scholar, but a liberal Anglican who believed in progressive revelation, and wanted the Old Testament to be read in that light. He did a great deal to prepare the general Christian public to accept an evolutionary view of the origins of biblical religion.

Moses Stuart (1780–1852). He taught at Andover Seminary in the

USA from 1810, and developed American Old Testament scholarship during that time. He was a great admirer of contemporary German scholars, especially Eichhorn and Herder, and tried to interpret them within the bounds of Calvinist orthodoxy. When he met critical difficulties which he could not explain, he relied on the concept of divine inspiration to account for them. Oddly enough, he came to accept a degree of progressive revelation in the Old Testament, which was generally regarded as heretical in the circles in which he moved. His most influential work was *A Critical History of the Defence of the Old Testament Canon* (1845), and he also wrote commentaries on Daniel (1850) and Ecclesiastes (1851).

Theodore Parker (1810–59). The most radical American biblical critic of his day, Parker was a Unitarian minister who believed that critical scholarship would eventually destroy the Bible's authority – an event to which he looked forward in anticipation. He translated De Wette's introduction to the Old Testament and annotated it in an even more radical direction. His ultimate aim was to transplant the whole of German critical scholarship to American soil. Interestingly enough, he was the only American Old Testament scholar whose work was noticed in Germany at that time.

Joseph Addison Alexander (1809–60). He taught at Princeton Seminary from 1834, and was a prolific Bible commentator. His commentaries have remained classics of their kind, representing the best in orthodox Calvinist biblical exposition, and they are frequently reprinted even today. Of particular note are his commentaries on the Psalms (1850) and on Isaiah (1846–7).

Essays and Reviews (1860). A collection of seven essays by six liberal clergymen in the Church of England and a Cambridge don, which is widely claimed to have been the effective beginning of modern Anglican liberalism. Four of the essays have a direct bearing on Old Testament criticism. They were by **Frederick Temple** (1821–1902), **Benjamin Jowett** (1817–93), **Rowland Williams** (1817–70) and **Charles Goodwin** (1817–78). Jowett's essay on the interpretation of Scripture has become famous, and is frequently reprinted in anthologies even today, though after the controversy he gave up writing on religious matters and went back to classical studies. His main argument was that the Bible is a book like any other book, and should be read with the same critical approach as was taken to any other work of classical antiquity. According to him, the Bible was the record of the progressive education of the human mind, which reached its culmination in the teaching of Jesus.

Temple argued in a somewhat similar vein, that the Old Testament was a book of rules (law) designed to educate the human race to the point where it could accept the freedom of the Spirit given in Christ, with the prophetic tradition pointing the way forward to this. He compared the legalism of the Old Testament to the dogmatic tradition in Christianity, and argued that humankind had now reached a stage of development in which neither was necessary any longer.

Williams dealt with contemporary German scholarship, which for him meant almost exclusively the work of Bunsen, a minor figure on the German scene. Goodwin's essay is perhaps the best. He tackled the Genesis account of creation, and said that it was written in the light of the scientific knowledge available to the author. Viewed in that perspective, it is a remarkable piece of work, but not comparable to the complex theories of modern science. To argue, as defenders of Genesis were doing, that the biblical account of creation was entirely compatible with the findings of modern science was not only false, it was untrue to the writer's intention.

Essays and Reviews caused an enormous scandal in England, and some of its contributors were prosecuted for heresy. The official replies were invariably strong defences of the traditional belief in the divine inspiration of Scripture, and the complete concordance between its teaching and modern scientific discoveries. Neither the *Essays* nor the replies were of a very high standard; in terms of German scholarship, they scarcely got beyond the position of Eichhorn. But the controversy served to embitter the atmosphere and colour the whole issue of biblical criticism for another generation.

Josiah Willard Gibbs (1790–1861). He taught at Yale from 1824, and developed Hebrew textual studies there. He wrote little himself, but influenced a generation of scholars and pastors in a more liberal direction.

Thomas Hartwell Horne (1780–1862). He is chiefly known for his *Introduction to the Critical Study and Knowledge of the Holy Scriptures* (1818), which went through a number of editions and revisions until 1860, and became one of the main textbooks on the subject. His views were more conservative than those of Clarke, but he did not hesitate to suggest textual emendations and rearrangements where he felt them to be necessary.

Edward Robinson (1794–1863). He had a strong interest in biblical criticism, but from an essentially conservative standpoint. He retained a belief in a single Isaiah, following Hengstenberg, a position which was even more conservative than that of his teacher,

Moses Stuart, who (perhaps surprisingly) followed the most traditional view on this point. He translated Gesenius's lexicon (1833), and was a pioneer of biblical archaeology. After a visit to Palestine, he produced *Biblical Researches in Palestine* (1841), the first scientific survey of the archaeological evidence and still regarded as a masterpiece. It was this experience which confirmed Robinson's conservatism, and led him to assert confidently that the Bible could and should be interpreted in its original context.

Henry Hart Milman (1791–1868). He was author of *The History of the Jews* (1829–30; second edition 1863), which makes occasional references to German scholars such as Michaelis, but is on the whole a traditional account of Israelite history. Occasional suggestions made in it that the biblical account may need to be corrected were enough to cause a storm of controversy when the book first appeared. By the time of the second edition his views were becoming acceptable, but they were still about as radical as the British reading public was prepared to accept.

George Rapall Noyes (1798–1868). Professor of Hebrew and Sacred Literature at Harvard from 1840, he was noted for his translations of Old Testament poetry, and wanted to produce a new translation of the entire text, as well as a series of critical commentaries. He was a strong critic of contemporary conservatives such as Hengstenberg, and thought that Christian faith could never be defended on a rational basis.

Frederick Denison Maurice (1805–72). This theologian converted from Unitarianism to the Church of England. Like Arnold, he was a progressive in religious matters, and wanted to encourage liberal thought. However, he maintained a conservative view of the historicity of the Old Testament, and later fell out with J. W. Colenso (see p. 291) over this. His main work in the field of Old Testament studies was *Patriarchs and Lawgivers of the Old Testament* (1851).

Henry John Rose (1800–73). Brother of Hugh (p. 286), he continued to maintain a conservative position on Old Testament matters. He was one of the main opponents of *Essays and Reviews* (see p. 287).

Patrick Fairbairn (1805–74). Free Church of Scotland preacher and teacher, his greatest work was his *Typology of Scripture* (1845–7), followed by a sequel, *The Interpretation of Prophecy* (1856), in which he argued that typology in the Old Testament was more prevalent than the New suggests, though it should not be pushed to extremes. He also edited *The Imperial Bible Dictionary* (1864–6), and wrote commentaries on Jonah (1849) and Ezekiel (1851), as well as a *Hermeneutical*

Manual (1858). Though mainly an Old Testament scholar, he also published a commentary on the pastoral epistles (1874).

James Bowling Mozley (1813–78). Regius Professor of Divinity at Oxford from 1871, he opposed both *Essays and Reviews* and Colenso, but felt that a more considered reply was required than the ones which were commonly being given at the time. He developed his own opinions in his *Ruling Ideas in Early Ages and their Relation to Old Testament Faith* (1877). In this book, he maintained that the chief difference between Old Testament times and our own was the fact that ancient peoples had no conception of individual responsibility or morality. Everything was collective in their experience, which explains why mass tribal killings, which seem immoral to us, were perfectly acceptable to them. To understand the Old Testament, it is first necessary to enter its thought world; only then will we be in a position to judge the rightness or wrongness of what the text says.

Arthur Penrhyn Stanley (1815–81). Regius Professor of Ecclesiastical History at Oxford from 1856 to 1863, he published three series of *Lectures on the History of the Jewish Church* (1863, 1865, 1876). From the point of view of critical scholarship, the lectures are eclectic and unsatisfactory, but they represent the first attempt in English to write a critical history of Israel along the lines of Ewald, whose work Stanley greatly admired. His position on the Pentateuch is hard to discern, though he opposed Colenso's scepticism. It appears that he was willing to accept that the laws did not assume their present shape until a much later period than the one to which they were theoretically assigned. At the same time, Stanley believed that the priestly system was a borrowing from non-Israelite sources, and represented a lower form of religion than that proclaimed by the prophets. The chief value of the priesthood was its staying power; after prophetic inspiration had died away, the sacrifices in the temple carried on as a reminder of Israel's religious identity.

Edward Bouverie Pusey (1800–82). Regius Professor of Hebrew at Oxford from 1828 until his death, he wrote his *Historical Enquiry into the Probable Causes of the Rationalist Character lately Predominant in the Theology of Germany* in 1828. Even more hostile to the Germans than Hugh Rose, Pusey denounced Michaelis and Eichhorn as virtual infidels. He was less condemning of De Wette, though by no means favourable to his Friesian philosophy. In Oxford he defended extremely conservative views, as his commentary on Daniel (1865) makes plain. Pusey was deeply involved in the Anglo-Catholic revival, and his name almost became synonymous with it. Much of his later life was devoted to controversy over this, and he was not very productive as a biblical scholar.

John William Colenso (1814–83). A graduate of St John's College, Cambridge, and a friend of the liberal clergyman F. D. Maurice, he was appointed Bishop of Natal in South Africa in 1853. His views on the Bible were naïvely conservative at that time, but were shaken by questions about the true meaning of the text posed by one of the Zulu converts to whom he had been called to minister. About 1861 he began to study the Pentateuch seriously, with the help of works by the leading German scholars of the day, both conservative and liberal. Soon he was denying biblical infallibility, and attacking conservatism, which he associated above all with the rising Anglo-Catholic movement. In 1862 he was charged with heresy because of a commentary which he had written on Romans, and he returned to England to face trial. There he read Samuel Davidson's *Introduction* (see p. 293), which he declared was the most able work in England on the subject of biblical criticism.

At the end of 1862 Colenso published *The Pentateuch and the Book of Joshua Critically Examined*. In this book he tackled the problem of the high numbers of the Israelites who apparently marched through the wilderness: 600,000 according to Exodus 12:37–38, and 603,550 according to Numbers 1:46. This would have made a total population of over two million! To serve their religious needs, there were apparently only three priests: Aaron and his two sons, who would have had to work round the clock to perform the rituals allotted to them in Leviticus. These criticisms were similar to those already made by the Deists, and Colenso was saying little that was new. Later he expanded his researches into the questions of authorship and composition. He argued that E was the *Grundschrift* in the Pentateuch and that it had been composed by Samuel, since the name Yahweh was not used before his time. Colenso supported this argument from the Psalms, which he believed offered evidence that David had used Elohim as the name of God for the earlier part of his life and then switched to Yahweh. (Today, as a matter of interest, many scholars believe that the 'Elohist' psalms originally contained the name Yahweh and were later altered.)

Colenso subsequently concentrated his attention on Deuteronomy and on Genesis 1 – 11, which he examined as thoroughly as he could. To some extent he was dependent on contemporary German critical exegesis, particularly that of Hupfeld, but many of his conclusions were reached independently. In particular, he thought that the Second Elohist was probably identical with the Yahwist, and that the change in the use of the divine name was deliberate on his part. This had the effect of dissociating the writer from the use of a particular divine name, and represented a major advance in critical understanding. Colenso then went on to posit the existence of four separate Yahwists, who lived and worked in the early monarchic period. Much of the Pentateuch was therefore in existence at the time of Solomon, with Deuteronomy being added by Jeremiah, parts of Leviticus by Ezekiel, and the final touches by various priestly writers up to the time of Ezra, when the whole work was complete.

Colenso was constantly in trouble with the ecclesiastical authorities, not least because he combined critical with Low Church views. He regarded the late dating of the Levitical parts of the Pentateuch as a support to those who were battling against the rise of ritualism in the Anglican Church. He also fell out with F. D. Maurice, whose liberalism did not extend to criticism of the Old Testament as historical fact. His solutions to critical problems were often simplistic, but the issues he raised have remained part of the discipline of Pentateuchal study ever since.

Marcus Kalisch (1825–85). This German Jew emigrated to England in 1848. He wrote a four-volume commentary on Genesis (1858), Exodus (1855) and Leviticus (1867, 1872), as well as a Hebrew grammar. His views on Genesis and Exodus were fairly traditional, though he recognized the existence of critical problems. On Leviticus, however, he was much more radical, and believed that the priestly system did not fully develop until after the exile. However, he resisted contemporary attempts to tie this view to a theory of religious development, and based his conclusions as far as possible on textual evidence alone.

Hugh Martin (1822–85). This Free Church of Scotland minister defended traditional covenant theology and the inspiration of Scripture against the rising trends of liberalism. He wrote a commentary on Jonah (1866) along highly traditional lines.

Edward Hayes Plumptre (1821–91). He was Professor of Exegesis at King's College, London from 1864 to 1881, and a leading conservative scholar. In his *Biblical Studies* (1869), he rejected the Second Isaiah theory. He also published a commentary on Ecclesiastes in 1881.

Andrew Alexander Bonar (1810–92). Prominent Free Church of Scotland preacher, he wrote a commentary on Leviticus (1846) in which he interpreted the ceremonial law as an allegory of the work of Christ.

Charles Haddon Spurgeon (1834–92). The greatest preacher in a century of giants, Spurgeon preached in London from 1854 until his death, leaving a mountain of sermons which were published weekly until 1917. As a biblical commentator, his fame rests on *The Treasury of David*, a seven-volume study of the Psalms (1888–91). He also strongly attacked contemporary critics in *Commenting and Commentaries* (1876).

Francis William Newman (1805–97). Younger brother of John Henry Newman, he moved from an orthodox faith to a position of extreme radicalism. In his book *A History of the Hebrew Monarchy from the Administration of Samuel to the Babylonish Captivity* (1847), he developed his critical opinions, among which was a late dating of the Pentateuch. He showed some acquaintance with contemporary German scholarship, but it does not seem to have influenced him very much, and his approach was largely original.

Samuel Davidson (1806–98). Born in Northern Ireland, he became Professor of Biblical Criticism at the Belfast Academical Institution in 1835, and moved to the Lancashire Independent College in 1843. In 1857 he was forced to resign because of his liberal views, expressed in *The Text of the Old Testament Considered* (1856). In 1862 he took up a post in London, where he began to associate with Unitarians from about 1870. His *Introduction to the Old Testament* was published in 1863. From an early date, he showed a great sympathy with contemporary German critical thought, and in his *Sacred Hermeneutics* (1843) wrote a detailed and generally fair assessment of it. He was quite critical of Kant's tendency to judge the Bible according to his ideas of morality, even when the Bible itself was not making moral judgments. He was also critical of Eichhorn and the neologists for pushing the ancient principle of accommodation too far. Davidson was prepared to accept that the Bible employed formal accommodation (*i.e.* the use of appropriate forms, such as parable or allegory) but not that the biblical writers had adapted their message to the ignorance and prejudices of their age. His critical views largely followed those of Keil, and could hardly be called radical by German standards, but they were unacceptable to conservative opinion in Britain. Today he is remembered as the 'martyr' of 1857, rather than for his largely unoriginal biblical scholarship.

Andrew Bruce Davidson (1831–1902). He was Professor of Old Testament at New College, Edinburgh, from 1863, and the author of a number of critical commentaries published at Cambridge. These included Job (1884), Ezekiel (1892) and Nahum, Habakkuk and Zechariah (1899). He studied under Ewald at Göttingen, and largely shared his outlook. He also taught William Robertson Smith (p. 294), but stayed out of the controversy caused by the latter's views.

William Robertson Smith (1846–94). He was Professor at the Free Church College, Aberdeen, from 1870 to 1881, and then successively Reader and Professor of Arabic at Cambridge from 1883 until his death. His best-known works are *The Old Testament in the Jewish Church* (1881) and *The Prophets of Israel and their Place in History to the Close of the Eighth Century* BC (1882). Robertson Smith was a strong evangelical, who believed that a critical reading of the Old Testament along the lines laid down by Wellhausen was the only way in which it could be vindicated as the Word of God. His importance lies in the fact that he tackled the opinion that biblical criticism was a rationalistic attack on Christianity, and tried to show that it was compatible with a fervent devotion to the gospel message.

Robertson Smith argued that the Bible spoke to the heart, through the working of the Holy Spirit, in order to bring the reader to a living faith in God. In this way, he was convinced that his position was that of the leading Reformers, who had also spoken of the 'inner witness of the Holy Spirit'. For him, the Old Testament was the record of God's gracious dealings with Israel, and was therefore a progressive unfolding of the divine love. He dealt with the apparently false historical claims of certain Old Testament books (notably Chronicles) by appealing to the outlook of the writer(s), for whom such claims would have seemed natural. The key to his interpretation was that the Old Testament speaks of a religion which offers 'access to God'. The developed Levitical priesthood hedged this access about with all kinds of cultic and legal restrictions, but it was still appropriate in its own time and place.

Robertson Smith's importance for subsequent history is that he was able to integrate an understanding of divine revelation with Wellhausen's critical theory and method. By claiming that one could be a pious Christian and a radical critic at the same time, he disarmed the attacks of the former and opened the way to acceptance of the latter. The British intellectual climate was in any case being prepared for the acceptance of an evolutionary approach to human development, and Wellhausen's theories dovetailed neatly with that. Robertson Smith provided the bridge, and the link which combined his scholarship with the spirit of the age in Britain, and thus introduced a new era in Old Testament studies.

William Gordon Blaikie (1820–99). Professor at the Free Church College, Edinburgh (1868–97), he wrote *David, King of Israel* (1856), *Bible History* (1859), *Bible Geography* (1861) and *Heroes of Israel* (1894). His approach was popular and widely influential. On the whole he stuck to a conservative interpretation of Old Testament characters and events, though he was not opposed to biblical criticism and made some use of it where appropriate.

John James Stewart Perowne (1823–1904). He was Hulsean Professor of Divinity at Cambridge from 1875 to 1878, and first editor of the Cambridge Bible Commentary, which, after an initially conservative start (1872–84), became one of the chief vehicles of critical scholarship in England.

William Rainey Harper (1856–1906). Professor of Semitic Languages and Literatures at Chicago from 1891, he wrote a number of works on Hebrew syntax, and a well-known commentary on Amos and Hosea (1905). His views were those of the critical mainstream which had penetrated Anglo-American thought in the 1880s.

Samuel Rolles Driver (1846–1914). He was Pusey's successor at Oxford (1883). The development of his views on Old Testament criticism mirrors the progress made by the radical German critics in the decade after 1880. In a sermon preached in Oxford on 21 October 1883, Driver accepted that there were two creation accounts in Genesis, which had been influenced by outside sources, especially Babylonian ones. Yet Driver remained convinced that the Bible was the inspired Word of God, and unassailable at the level of moral and spiritual truth. In 1882 his attitude towards textual criticism was still cautious and therefore conservative, and he did not hesitate to object to German views, including those of Wellhausen. However, it seems that he had a more cerebral view of revelation than Robertson Smith's; for Driver, revelation was not so much the presence of God in the heart as the imparting of spiritual information to the mind, which raised acute problems for his view of the trustworthiness of the biblical text.

By 1885, Driver was prepared to accept that there were priestly, prophetic and Deuteronomic streams of narrative in the Pentateuch, and in 1887 he ascribed progress in Israelite religion to the role of the prophets – a view which had been put forward in Germany by B. Duhm in 1875. But in 1891, in his book *An Introduction to the Literature of the Old Testament,* Driver showed a complete acceptance of Wellhausen's position. From that time onwards, it became increasingly common in British academic scholarship. Driver further developed his views in his commentary on Genesis (1904).

Thomas Kelly Cheyne (1841–1915). Grandson of T. H. Horne and Oriel Professor at Oxford from 1885 to 1908, he began as a disciple of Ewald, but later accepted the post-exilic dating of the Pentateuchal *Grundschrift.* After 1880 he became more evangelical in his outlook, though mainly along the lines of Robertson Smith. In old age he became eccentric in his scholarship, and was not taken seriously. He is chiefly remembered today for his book *Founders of Old Testament Criticism* (1893), which chronicled the rise of critical scholarship in England.

Crawford Howell Toy (1836–1919). He was Professor of Old Testament at the Southern Baptist Seminary, Louisville (1869–79), and subsequently Professor of Oriental Languages and Biblical Literature at Harvard (1880–1909). He resigned from the Louisville Seminary because of his liberal views, but went on to become a leading exponent of German higher criticism from his base at Harvard. His main works include *A History of the Religion of Israel* (1882), *Quotations in the New Testament* (1884), *Judaism and Christianity* (1890), *An Introduction to the History of Religions* (1913) and a commentary on Proverbs (1899).

George Buchanan Gray (1865–1922). Tutor and Professor at Mansfield College, Oxford, he made notable contributions to Old Testament scholarship in his commentaries on Numbers (1903), and Isaiah 1 – 27 (1912). His posthumous work, *Sacrifice in the Old Testament* (1925), was a major work of Old Testament theology.

John James Lias (1834–1923). A conservative scholar, he wrote *Principles of Biblical Criticism* (1893), in which he strongly attacked both Wellhausen and Driver. He also wrote a commentary on Judges (1884).

John Skinner (1851–1925). Professor at London from 1890, and later at Cambridge, he wrote a commentary on Isaiah 1 – 39 in the Cambridge series (1896).

Charles Fox Burney (1868–1925). He taught at Oxford, where he was Oriel Professor from 1914. His main Old Testament works were *Notes on the Hebrew Text of the Book of Kings* (1903), *Israel's Settlement in Canaan* (1918), and a commentary on Judges (1918).

Herbert Edward Ryle (1856–1925). Hulsean Professor of Divinity at Cambridge from 1887 to 1901, he was the son of the most prominent conservative evangelical bishop of the day, John Charles Ryle (1816–1900). However, he developed strong critical opinions, which became evident in his books, *The Early Narratives of Genesis* (1892) and *The Canon of the Old Testament* (1892). His commentaries on Ezra and Nehemiah (1893) and Genesis (1914) were published in the Cambridge series. After 1892 he was estranged from his father, who would not allow him to teach or preach in the diocese of Liverpool.

Henry Preserved Smith (1847–1927). He taught at Lane Seminary (1874–93), Amherst College (1898–1906), Meadville Seminary

(1907–13) and Union Theological Seminary, New York (1913–25). He wrote *Inspiration and Inerrancy* (1893), *Old Testament History* (1903), *The Religion of Israel* (1914), *Essays in Biblical Interpretation* (1921) and a commentary on 1 and 2 Samuel (1899). In all these writings he advanced the views of Wellhausen and his associates, becoming one of the leading advocates of classical liberalism in the English-speaking world.

Arthur Samuel Peake (1865–1929). The first Rylands Professor of Biblical Criticism and Exegesis at Manchester (1904), he wrote *The Problem of Suffering in the Old Testament* (1904). He is best remembered today for his editorship of a famous *Commentary on the Bible* (1919), which still bears his name, though the latest edition (1962) is completely different from the original.

Robert Henry Charles (1855–1931). Professor of Biblical Greek at Trinity College, Dublin (1898), and then Lecturer in Oxford (1905), he is chiefly known for his magisterial collection of apocrypha and pseudepigrapha (1913). He also wrote commentaries on Daniel (1929) and Revelation (1920).

Robert Lawrence Ottley (1856–1933). His Bampton Lectures of 1897, published the same year as *Aspects of the Old Testament*, attempted to combine critical scholarship with traditional theology. He was basically conservative, and argued that the religious traditions of the Old Testament were older than the written records.

William Emery Barnes (1859–1939). He taught at Cambridge from 1885, and became Hulsean Professor of Divinity (1901–34). He wrote a commentary on Chronicles (1899) in the Cambridge series.

Alexander Francis Kirkpatrick (1849–1940). Regius Professor of Hebrew at Cambridge from 1882 to 1903, he was author of a famous critical commentary on the Psalms (1892, 1895, 1912), which is full of devotional insights. He also wrote *The Divine Library of the Old Testament* (1891), which is a modified version of Robertson Smith's history of Israel (1881).

Frederick John Foakes-Jackson (1855–1941). Fellow of Jesus College, Cambridge (1886) and Professor of Christian Institutions at Union Theological Seminary, New York (1916–34), he wrote a *Biblical History of the Hebrews* (1903) and a *Biblical History for Schools* (1912–13). His later work was mainly in the New Testament field (see pp. 348–349).

George Adam Smith (1856–1942). Professor of Old Testament at the United Free Church College, Glasgow (1892) and Principal of the University of Aberdeen (1909), he wrote commentaries on Isaiah (1888–90), the minor prophets (1896–7), Deuteronomy (1918) and

Jeremiah (1923). His *Historical Geography of the Holy Land* (1894 and many subsequent editions) is a classic which has never been surpassed. In 1912 he also delivered the Schweich Lectures on *The Early Poetry of Israel*. Publication of his Yale Lectures in 1901 (*Modern Criticism and the Preaching of the Old Testament*) led to threats of a heresy trial, but the climate had changed sufficiently in less than a decade to allow Smith to continue to expound his liberal critical views under the umbrella of the United Free Church.

The issues

In spite of the atmosphere of controversy which surrounded the study of the Old Testament in the nineteenth century, there was a clear unity of purpose among scholars of a kind which had never existed before. The scholarly world was a single intellectual space in which everyone participated on more or less equal terms. Academic debates took place within a common framework of ideas, even though the solutions proposed to particular problems might vary widely. In Old Testament studies, the main issues of the time can be summarized as follows.

1. *It was necessary to establish the right relationship between the Old Testament and 'secular' history.* To what extent was the Old Testament a reliable historical source? This question plagued all nineteenth-century scholars, and had to be answered one way or another. The tradition which flows from De Wette to Wellhausen answered it in a negative manner – the Old Testament was unreliable as history, and could be used only if it was radically reinterpreted. Others were more positive in their assessment, including such critical scholars as Eichhorn and Ewald. They might not accept everything as it stood, but the general lines of historical development presented in the text were true as far as they went. The tendency towards radicalism was held in check by the natural conservatism of the churches, and later by archaeological discoveries. In spite of everything, it was probably easier to defend traditional views in a scholarly manner in 1900 than it had been in 1800.

2. *It was necessary to explain the nature of Israel's origin and development.* The historical awareness of the nineteenth century inclined scholars to accept the idea that cultures evolve over time. In some sense, that was obvious in the Old Testament, since the coming of Christ led Israel into a new stage of religious development. But to what extent could a 'progressive' form of revelation be envisaged in the Old

Testament? How authoritative could a text now be, if it had been superseded at a later stage? Was it right to picture Israel as having grown out of an early polytheism and idolatry into a sophisticated monotheism? Did moral standards change along with this development? Here again, solutions varied widely. Extreme radicals dismissed the Old Testament entirely, as unworthy of serious consideration on a moral and spiritual level. Extreme conservatives, on the other hand, refused to accept that anything in the Old Testament could be on a lower plane than what is to be found in the New, because the same God had revealed himself in both.

Most people fell somewhere between these extremes. As the century wore on, more came to accept that there had been a series of changes in Israelite religion, connected with the wilderness journey, the establishment of the monarchy, and (above all) the reforms of Josiah, the subsequent exile and the restoration. It was the nature of these changes which continued to cause divisions. On the one hand were the radicals, who believed that pre-exilic Israelite religion had been a chaotic affair, with no centralized cultic organization. Instead, there had been a series of ecstatic prophets, who had taught the people. This prophetic tradition was snuffed out during and after the exile, to be replaced by a priestly dictatorship which kept the nation alive while at the same time paralyzing its religious development. Some conservative scholars continued to insist that the sacrificial practices described in Leviticus and Chronicles were of ancient origin, but the rough scheme of pre-exilic prophets and post-exilic priests continued to dominate the discussion.

3. *It was necessary to relate the development of Israel to that of the surrounding nations.* This aspect of Old Testament history was virtually a blank area in 1800. Little or nothing was known of the other middle-eastern peoples, apart from what could be gleaned in sources like Herodotus. But as archaeology and comparative linguistics got into their stride, the picture was filled in rapidly. From being virtually the only source of our information about the ancient Middle East, the Bible came to be seen as one witness among many. Empires which had long been forgotten were rediscovered, and their civilizations were exposed to view for the first time in millennia. Israel, it transpired, was a small and generally insignificant nation in the context of the time. It was rather as if a modern student of European history had been forced to concentrate on the Low Countries until suddenly presented with evidence pointing to the greatness of Britain, France and Germany.

The readjustment of perspective which these discoveries entailed was naturally taken to extremes. Just as the Low Countries have played an important role in European history because of their geographical position, so too, Palestine occupied a key position in the ancient Middle East. But this was forgotten in the rush to embrace evidence from Egypt and Mesopotamia. Scholars quickly found parallels to Old Testament ideas in these civilizations, and automatically attributed this to the 'fact' that Israel must have borrowed heavily from one or other of them. Here fashions changed as the century wore on. At first, Egypt was the preferred source of everything significant in Israel; later, it was Babylonia, and even Persia. That influences might have gone in the opposite direction was scarcely considered.

In one important respect, this development altered Old Testament studies for ever. Whereas in 1800 it had been possible to doubt that Israel could have reached the level of sophistication it supposedly had in the time of Moses (anywhere from 1400 to 1200 BC), by 1900 it was becoming clear that this was not so. On the contrary, a man like Abraham was no longer regarded as a primitive, half-civilized nomad, but as the inheritor of an ancient and highly developed Mesopotamian culture. A knowledge of writing and of law-making was now seen as entirely compatible with an early dating of the patriarchal narratives. The conclusions of radical scholars such as Wellhausen were not thereby overturned, but at least it became possible to put forward a viable alternative along traditionalist lines.

4. *It was necessary to redefine the relationship of the Old Testament to the New Testament.* The older view that the two Testaments were one was gradually abandoned, as ideas of progress in religion became common. By 1900 only the most conservative theologians still held it, and they had mostly opted out of the critical enterprise. The Old Testament was seen by almost everyone as an earlier stage of religious development, superseded by the teachings of Christ. But did Christ fulfil the Old Testament, or abolish it? Those who inclined to the former view thought of the Old Testament as a prelude to Christ's coming, and therefore saw nothing wrong in detecting 'Christological' themes in it. There was a big difference, to be sure, between those who thought of this in terms of actual prophecy, and those who regarded it more as a matter of religious patterns which had no specifically prophetic purpose, but either way it was possible for Christians with this outlook to give the Old Testament abiding spiritual value.

Opposed to it was the attitude that Christ had abolished what had gone before and replaced it by something infinitely better. There might be some foretaste of this in the prophets, but on the whole the Old Testament had little to offer the Christian. Within this perspective, there were some who argued that it had once been valid, and others who insisted that it had been wrong from the start. But either way, it was hard to see what justified a Christian scholar in spending so much time on a text which had little moral or spiritual value, especially if he was expected to be teaching future ministers of the churches. Because of this, even scholars inclined to this position might find themselves arguing against their own theories, insisting that the Old Testament does have something to say to us today, in spite of the vast distance in time and sophistication which separates us from it.

The methods of interpretation

In the nineteenth century, the dominance of the historical-critical method was such that other forms of interpretation appeared to be anachronisms. There were some commentators who continued to produce conservative works, including allegorical interpretations of the Bible, but they were on the sidelines of academic scholarship, where the most liberal theories reigned unchecked. Most of these have now been repudiated, but the main methods of enquiry developed during the nineteenth century remain valid for historical criticism.

Old Testament critical method

The main principles of nineteenth-century historical criticism, as applied to the study of the Old Testament, can be stated as follows.

1. *Interpretation must be based on a solid knowledge of the original documents, the language in which they were written and the context in which they were composed.* The intense study of Hebrew, which was such a feature of neologist exegesis, continued unabated throughout the nineteenth century. Other versions of the Old Testament, notably the Septuagint, faded out of the picture, though curiously enough Robertson Smith thought it was a better text than the original Hebrew. The historical context presented a greater problem, because for a long time the Bible appeared to be isolated in its literary milieu. There was no other ancient Hebrew literature to speak of, and archaeology had not yet developed sufficiently to be able to provide much material for comparison. Nevertheless the goal

remained, and the enthusiasm which greeted the discovery of documents such as the law-code of Hammurabi (1902) shows that this concern was a real one.

2. *A reasonable explanation must be sought for every phenomenon.* This meant that a scholar should seek to explain his evidence on the basis of reliable data. Any hypothesis must be meticulously tested against the available evidence, to see whether it would stand up. The lack of external sources for comparison forced Old Testament scholars to rely on internal phenomena, which meant that there was no objective means of testing whether a hypothesis was 'true' or not. However, it was clear to the critics that any explanation which required divine intervention, or which could be defended only by an appeal to Christian doctrine, was inadmissible. Thus it was inevitable that the straightforward Old Testament record would be disregarded at many points.

3. *Evidence gleaned indirectly from a text is of more value than direct statements or claims, because it is less likely to have been concocted to make propaganda.* The effects of this can be seen most clearly in the debates over the sacrificial cult and its priesthood. According to Deuteronomy and Chronicles, this was established by Moses, but the evidence of Samuel and Kings indicated that there was a great deal of freedom about who sacrificed, and where they built altars. The centralization of the cult and its submission to the control of a single priesthood appears to be a post-exilic (or at least, a post-Josianic) reform, because only after that does the indirect evidence accord with what Deuteronomy and Chronicles openly state. The conservative argument was that these texts set out principles which were either disregarded from time to time, or not faithfully observed until much later, but this was generally reckoned to be special pleading, and was not accepted by most critical scholars.

4. *There is an evolutionary drift from the simpler to the more complex; therefore, more complex ideas and practices date from a later time.* This was, and still is, the most controversial of all the assumptions of the critical method. It is demonstrably false in linguistics, since the grammatical structure of English, for example, is much simpler now than it was a thousand years ago, and no-one would claim that this represents a decline in civilization. That primitive peoples are incapable of very complex structures, especially in their worship and religious life, is now known to be false also. It is in the western world that people want religion to be straightforward, because they have little time to spare for it. Elsewhere, this may be the one sphere of activity where the human mind is given free rein to be as convoluted as it likes.

Nevertheless, the belief that the more primitive a religion was the simpler it would be was generally held by most nineteenth-century critics, which explains why there was such general agreement that the complex laws of Leviticus and the ceremonies of Chronicles must be late in date, whereas the relative simplicity of prophetic religion could be placed much earlier.

5. *Monotheism is a 'higher' form of religion than polytheism, and therefore it developed later.* This may seem to contradict the last principle, because to us monotheism seems at first sight to be simpler than polytheism. This however, is only superficially apparent. In reality, monotheism is more complex, because it demands a unified system of knowledge and perception which can take account of all reality. Polytheism is disconnected in this respect, with different activities being assigned to different gods, and it is therefore 'simpler'. In terms of Israelite religion, this means that any sign of polytheism is a sign of its primitive cult. Similarly, the more absolute the monotheism, the later in date the text will be. Many Old Testament theologians came to think in terms of an Israelite 'henotheism' – the belief that Israel worshipped only one God but did not deny existence to other deities – as a kind of halfway house. The idea was first put forward by F. Max Müller (1823–1900), who was a specialist in Sanskrit and Indian religions, and it caught on as the century progressed. Gradually it came to be thought that Israel was not strictly monotheistic until the time of Hezekiah (eighth century BC) or even later.

Pentateuchal criticism

Old Testament interpretation in the nineteenth century was entirely dominated by Pentateuchal criticism. This does not mean that other books were not studied and commented on; of course they were. But often the critical issues which they raised assumed importance largely because of the bearing which they had on Pentateuchal origins – the case of Chronicles being the most obvious example of this. To those who held to a late dating of the priestly material and to the priority of Israel's prophetic tradition, the prophets also had to be interpreted in a way which would fit this scheme. The historical books were understood to be connected to Deuteronomy, and so they too were an appendage to the Pentateuch.

At the heart of Pentateuchal criticism was the question of its sources. There were three main theories in the nineteenth century, which may be categorized as follows.

1. *Mosaic authorship.* This traditional view was still maintained by many, including a number of critical scholars. Generally, they held that Moses had used earlier material available to him. They also allowed that there had been subsequent redactions of the material. However, their main belief was that Moses was the founder of Israelite religion, and the source of Israel's laws and cultic practices.

2. *The fragments hypothesis.* This was the theory propounded by Geddes, Vater and De Wette. The basic belief was that the Pentateuch had been composed out of a number of distinct fragments, and had no unity other than the one given it by the final redactor(s), who lived either during or shortly after the exile. One of the fragments which went to making up the Pentateuch was the Book of the Law found by Hilkiah; this made up part of Deuteronomy, and may have contributed something to Leviticus as well.

3. *The documentary hypothesis.* This could be held in conjunction with Mosaic authorship (Eichhorn), or not (Wellhausen). The documentary hypothesis was less flexible than the fragments one, and obliged those who held it to develop some very complex theories about how the various documents were put together before the final redaction, since it was clear that there must have been a lengthy process of cut-and-paste before the Pentateuch as we know it now came into being. But in spite of these difficulties, the documentary hypothesis won the day in the nineteenth century, and was stated in its classical form by Julius Wellhausen (1878).

To understand the issues at stake, it is perhaps best to begin with the four documents posited by Wellhausen's immediate successors, and work from there. These were the *Elohist* (E), so called because its author(s) referred to God as El; the *Yahwist* or *Jahwist* (J), so called because its author(s) referred to God as Yahweh; the *Deuteronomist* (D), composed *c.* 622 BC from the Book of the Law found by Hilkiah in the temple; and the *Priestly* (P), composed by a group of priests after the exile.

E was widely regarded as the basic document (*Grundschrift*) to which the others had been added. It was often thought that there were in fact two Elohists, an older one and a younger one, whose work was so intertwined with J that it could no longer be disentangled. The dating of E was a major problem in critical studies. Some said it was early (tenth century BC), and others that it was post-exilic. Graf (1866) maintained that it was not a unity, and that its narrative sections were early, while its legal sections were post-exilic.

J was the first redactor of the Pentateuch, because he was supposed to have taken the *Grundschrift* and added his own material to it.

D was connected to Hilkiah, and had been added to a previously existing E-J combination. This did not necessarily mean that E-J was older than D, but only that when the Pentateuch was finally put together in its present form, D was added to E-J, which at that time existed as a distinct document.

P had no separate existence until Graf (1866) isolated it from E and declared that it has been added to E-J and D after the exile.

Wellhausen took this situation and transformed it as follows.

The *Grundschrift* was not a unity. Its basic core was a Priestly Code, which was a substantial part, though not all, of P. To this was added Q, a compilation of four different covenant books. Once Q was added to the Code, additional material was incorporated, notably Leviticus 17 – 26, to give P. This was the *Grundschrift* in its final form, which could not have been extant before the exile. P was thus based on previous existing written sources, not on oral tradition.

Independently of the *Grundschrift*, there were the 'younger' Elohist and the Yahwist, whose work was ultimately based on oral tradition and had gone through two stages of redaction before being combined by a third party, the so-called Jehovist, at some point during the later monarchic period. This E-J unit was subsequently combined with the *Grundschrift*, but not before it had already been combined with D.

D had originally existed as two separate editions, which were first combined into one and then added to E-J. The narrative sections of D are dependent on E-J, which shows that D used the earlier work as source material. D could be dated to the period of Josiah's reform, and was somehow connected to Hilkiah's discovery in the temple.

At some point after the exile, E-J and D were combined with each other and then with P, to form the Pentateuch as we know it today.

This may be expressed diagrammatically as overleaf.

Subsequent critics of Wellhausen were most concerned with his late dating of the *Grundschrift*, or P. They were inclined to think that it must have been completed much earlier, possibly even in the time of David or Solomon. This, however, made no difference to the final redaction, which they were still inclined to place in the time of Ezra, nor did it alter Wellhausen's fundamental scheme. After 1878, earlier theories of Pentateuchal criticism gradually faded out, and Wellhausen's hypothesis became the basis on which further investigation was made. There were plenty of modifications as to what belonged to which strand of tradition, and there were many attempts to redate the material in a more conservative direction, but the basic structure survived intact.

Written sources			Oral sources	
Priestly Code	D1	D2	Tradition	
+ 4 covenant books (Q)			E	J
+ additional material			E-J	
	D			
EXILE ------------------------------------				
P (*Grundschrift*)			D + E-J	
	Pentateuch			

Non-critical exegesis

This played a minor role in the nineteenth century, once historical criticism took over the universities, but it remained influential in the churches, and at the popular level generally. It was virtually universal in the Roman Catholic Church, which anathematized historical criticism, and in the Protestant churches it became the identifying mark of conservative evangelicals. It retained the traditional distinction between the literal and the 'spiritual' senses of the text, but with a new and pronounced emphasis on the latter. Perhaps this was a reaction to historical criticism, which many thought was the logical consequence of following the literal sense too exclusively; but, just as probably, it demonstrated a thirst for spiritual meaning, which was not satisfied with the hermeneutical methods then common in academic circles.

The move away from the literal to the spiritual sense(s) of Scripture can be seen by comparing the work of three conservative exegetes of the time, E. W. Hengstenberg (1842), J. A. Alexander (1850) and C. H. Spurgeon (1888–91), all of whom wrote on the Psalms. This is what they have to say about Psalm 22, whose opening line, 'My God, my God, why hast thou forsaken me?' is famous as Jesus' cry of dereliction on the cross (Mt. 27:46; Mk. 15:34).

Hengstenberg wrote:

> The view which has always obtained throughout the Christian Church is that which refers the psalm directly and exclusively to

> Christ. The author by no means regrets that he adopted this view in his Christology.

He went on to repeat the view of Calvin and Melanchthon, that David was inspired by a spirit of messianic prophecy, and explained why he could not accept it:

> David, it is maintained, according to this hypothesis, in fleeing to the Lord on the ground of a particular case of distress, transfers, elevated by the spirit of Messianic prophecy, his own being into the extreme sufferings of the hoped-for Messiah, and speaks as the present type of the coming deliverer. Although the author acknowledges that in this attempt justice is done to those considerations which may be pleaded in favour of opposing expositions, yet he cannot but regard it as an unsuccessful attempt at reconciliation. Such a view of the way in which the psalm was produced appears to him as psychologically altogether inconceivable. How David could extend his consciousness to that of his offspring cannot be conceived without confusion of the life of souls and destruction of personal identity.

He then said that the psalm refers to the ideal person of the Righteous One, whose exact identity was unknown to David. David composed the psalm on the basis of his own experience, and any righteous man, in so far as he is truly righteous, may appropriate it to himself, as an expression of his own suffering. But because no-one is perfectly righteous, the psalm remained unfulfilled until the coming of Christ, who alone could truly and finally appropriate it to himself. But although these were his remarks in his introduction to the psalm, when Hengstenberg came to commenting on the actual verse he stated categorically: '. . . the assertion . . . that these words are suitable only on the lips of Christ is altogether erroneous'. So in commenting on the text, he kept his Christological interpretation in check, and did not allow it to control his exegesis.

Alexander, who based his commentary on Hengstenberg's, had this to say:

> The subject of this psalm is the deliverance of a righteous sufferer from his enemies, and the effect of this deliverance on others. It is so framed as to be applied without violence to any case belonging to the class described, yet so that it was fully

> verified only in Christ, the head and representative of the class in question. The immediate speaker in the psalm is an ideal person, the righteous servant of Jehovah, but his words may, to a certain extent, be appropriated by any suffering believer, and by the whole suffering Church, as they have been in all ages.

In this passage the Christological interpretation is admitted, but kept to a minimum. The emphasis is very much on the believer, whoever he may be, and on the church as a whole. There is no mention of David, although Alexander clearly accepted that he was the human author of the psalm. It is almost as if this were an irrelevance for him; the true speaker of the words is the believing Everyman.

Spurgeon knew both Hengstenberg and Alexander, but he did not mention either of them in connection with this psalm. Instead, he referred to the Roman Catholic commentator A. Calmet (1672–1757) and to A. Clarke (*c.* 1760–1832), of whom he approved. His Christological bent is apparent from his introduction:

> It is the photograph of our Lord's saddest hours, the record of his dying words, the lachrymatory of his last tears, the memorial of his expiring joys. David and his afflictions may be here in very modified sense, but as the star is concealed by the light of the sun, he who sees Jesus will probably neither see nor care to see David. Before us we have the description both of the darkness and of the glory of the cross, the sufferings of Christ and the glory which shall follow. Oh for grace to draw near and see this great sight! We should read reverently, putting off our shoes from off our feet, as Moses did at the burning bush, for if there be holy ground anywhere in Scripture it is in this psalm.

When we turn from the introduction to the commentary on the verse itself, we read:

> *Why hast thou forsaken me?* We must lay the emphasis on every word of this saddest of all utterances. *Why?* What is the great cause of such a strange fact as for God to leave his own Son at such a time and in such a plight? There was no cause in him; why then was he deserted? *Hast.* It is done, and the Saviour is feeling its dread effect as he asks the question; it is surely true, but how mysterious! It was no threatening of forsaking which made the great Surety cry aloud; he endured that forsaking in very deed.

> *Thou.* I can understand why traitorous Judas and timid Peter should be gone, but thou, my God, my faithful friend, how canst thou leave me? This is worst of all, yea worse than all put together. Hell itself has for its fiercest flame the separation of the soul from God. *Forsaken.* If thou hadst chastened I might bear it, for thy face would shine, but to forsake me utterly – ah, why is this? *Me.* Thine innocent, obedient, suffering Son, why leavest thou me to perish? A sight of self seen by penitence, and of Jesus on the cross seen by faith will best expound this question. Jesus is forsaken because our sins had separated between us and our God.

Here, after a generation of critical scholarship which denied the very possibility, we have the most deeply Christological interpretation of all. Spurgeon far surpasses Alexander and Hengstenberg in his application of the psalm to Christ; he goes so far in this that David and his circumstances are totally obscured. Even when we make allowances for the rhetoric of a preacher, this is surely taking matters too far! On the other hand, Spurgeon is not merely Christological; he is Christocentric. His interpretation does not talk about our suffering, but of Christ's. In spite of all the extravagant language, this is an objective portrayal of what he has done, not a subjective application of David's feelings to ourselves. In that respect, there is a greatness in Spurgeon's interpretation which can easily be missed by the critical mind, and it is not hard to see why his approach appealed to those who wanted to understand more of Christ as they read the Scriptures.

Is this type of interpretation justified? Here we meet the great divide between the critical scholar and the pious traditionalist. To the former, what Spurgeon is saying is anathema. Hengstenberg is more tolerable but still wrong; Alexander might just pass the test of acceptability. But to the traditionalist, the order of preference may well be reversed! It may be Spurgeon who comes closest to the heart of the matter, and Alexander who is farthest from it, though still within acceptable bounds. The real question then becomes something different: is the Bible meant to be the preserve of critical scholars working from rationalist presuppositions? Or is there room for the believer to meet his Lord and Saviour in the words of the psalm which he chose for himself at the moment of his death?

BIBLIOGRAPHY

A. Alt, 'Edward Robinson and the Historical Geography of Palestine', *Journal of Biblical Literature* 58 (1939), pp. 365–372.

T. O. Beidelman, *W. Robertson Smith and the Sociological Study of Religion* (Chicago: Chicago University Press, 1974).

J. Bewer, 'Edward Robinson as a Biblical Scholar', *Journal of Biblical Literature* 58 (1939), pp. 355–363.

J. W. Brown, *The Rise of Biblical Criticism in America, 1800–1870* (Middletown, CT: Wesleyan University Press, 1969).

N. M. de S. Cameron, *Biblical Higher Criticism and the Defense of Infallibilism in 19th Century Britain* (Lewiston, NY: Edwin Mellen, 1987).

R. E. Clements, *A Century of Old Testament Study* (Guildford: Lutterworth, 1976).

J. E. Dirks, *The Critical Theology of Theodore Parker* (New York: Columbia University Press, 1948).

J. Drury (ed.), *Critics of the Bible 1724–1873* (Cambridge: Cambridge University Press, 1989).

I. Ellis, *Seven against Christ: A Study of 'Essays and Reviews'* (Leiden: Brill, 1980).

W. B. Glover, *Evangelical Nonconformists and Higher Criticism in the Nineteenth Century* (London: Independent Press, 1954).

J. Herbst, *The German Historical School in American Scholarship* (Ithaca, NY: Cornell University Press, 1965).

P. Hinchliffe, *John William Colenso* (London: Nelson, 1964).

E. G. Kraeling, *The Old Testament since the Reformation* (London: Lutterworth, 1955).

H.–J. Kraus, *Geschichte der historisch-kritischen Erforschung des Alten Testaments* (Neukirchen-Vluyn: Neukirchener Verlag, 3rd updated edn, 1982).

H. D. McDonald, *Theories of Revelation 1700–1960* (Grand Rapids: Baker, 1979).

J. Moore, *The Post-Darwinian Controversies* (Cambridge: Cambridge University Press, 1979).

R. R. Nelson, 'The Theological Development of the Young Robertson Smith', *Evangelical Quarterly* 45, (1973), pp. 81–99.

J. C. O'Neill, *The Bible's Authority: A Portrait Gallery of Thinkers from Lessing to Bultmann* (Edinburgh: T. and T. Clark, 1991).

R. A. Riesen, *Criticism and Faith in Late Victorian Scotland: A. B. Davidson, William Robertson Smith and George Adam Smith* (Lanham, MD: University Press of America, 1985).

J. W. Rogerson, *Old Testament Criticism in the Nineteenth Century: England and Germany* (London: SPCK, 1984).
———— *W. M. L. De Wette: Founder of Modern Biblical Criticism* (Sheffield: JSOT Press, 1992).
R. J. Thompson, *Moses and the Law in a Century of Criticism since Graf* (Leiden: Brill, 1970).
D. Williams, *The Andover Liberals* (New York: King's Crown Press, 1941).

A case study: Isaiah

Until 1775 it was generally agreed that the book of Isaiah was substantially the work of a single author, the prophet who had lived at Jerusalem in the time of Hezekiah (eighth century BC). This Isaiah had been specially privileged by God, in that to him had been given a unique insight into the future destiny of the people of Israel. He was enabled to foresee the exile, the restoration and the eventual coming of the Messiah, not as a triumphant ruler, but as a suffering servant, who would bring the good news of salvation from sin (Is. 52:7 – 53:12).

During the course of the nineteenth century, this unity was exploded by the 'discovery' that what appeared to be the work of a single author was in fact a compilation of different writings, which might be ascribed to two or more distinct prophets. The reasons given for this were rooted in the rationalistic rejection of predictive prophecy, which had enormous theological implications for the fate of the messianic texts. In many ways, the critical study of Isaiah and the reaction to it typify the hermeneutical struggles of the nineteenth century.

The first critical scholars to insist that there had to be a Second Isaiah were Döderlein (1775), Eichhorn (1780–83) and Gesenius (1820–21). They were following a suggestion first put forward by the medieval rabbi Ibn Ezra in the twelfth century, though it had not been developed by either Jews or Christians since then. The division of Isaiah into two parts was followed by the further researches of Duhm (1875, 1892), who subdivided Second Isaiah and produced a third prophet, who wrote after the return from exile. This was (and is) more controversial than the thesis of Eichhorn and Gesenius, and some scholars have preferred to see 'Third Isaiah' as a collection of separate documents by different authors, but this argument is of relatively little importance for the great nineteenth-century debate.

Critical views were introduced to the English-speaking world in the commentaries of G. A. Smith (1890) and T. K. Cheyne (1893), as well as in the important introduction to the book by S. R. Driver (1891).

The arguments they put forward for a late dating of chapters 40 – 66 were as follows.

1. The historical setting of 40 – 66 pictures a time after the fall of Jerusalem and the exile of the captives to Babylon. The Persian King Cyrus is actually mentioned by name (44:28; 45:1). It is true that the same historical background can sometimes be found in the earlier chapters (*e.g.* 13:1 – 14:23; 21:1–10) but this is an argument supporting Duhm's thesis that 'First Isaiah' is a composite document reflecting many strands of later development, not an argument in favour of the overall unity of the book.

2. There are great differences in language, style and concepts between the two parts of the book of Isaiah, and this points to different authors. In particular, the name of Yahweh is exalted high above all heathen idols, and an exclusive monotheism, supposedly unknown before the exile, is proclaimed with great vigour and power. The universal character of his rule and the expectation of a messianic fulfilment at some future time are also signs of late dating.

3. Hebrew prophets were expected to address contemporary issues in the light of God's law. Predictive prophecy was not part of their task, though this concept of prophecy became common among the Jews in post-exilic times. It is therefore impossible for 40 – 66 to be the work of the historical Isaiah, but perfectly comprehensible that later Jewish compilers should attribute it to him in his (historically inaccurate) predictive capacity.

This last point was stated with great clarity by S. R. Driver (1891):

> The prophets, one and all, stand in an intimate relation to the history of their times. Whatever be the truth which they announce, it is never presented by them in an abstract form; it is always brought into some relation with the age in which they live, and adapted to the special circumstances of the persons whom they address. Of course, the principles which the prophets assert are frequently capable of a much wider range of application; their significance is not exhausted when they have done their work in the prophet's own generation; but still his primary interest is in the needs of his own age.

Conservative defenders of the traditional authorship included Hengstenberg and Delitzsch in Germany, as well as Alexander and others like him in the English-speaking world. Great play was made by liberal scholars of the fact that Delitzsch, who defended the single authorship of Isaiah as late as 1880, changed his mind towards the end of his life, and admitted a Second Isaiah in the fourth and last edition of his commentary (1889). After that, there were virtually no critical scholars left who upheld the traditional view with any conviction. However, the defence of the ancient position was not entirely abandoned, and in the mid-twentieth century it enjoyed a revival among conservative scholars connected with Princeton Theological Seminary (until 1929) and then Westminster Theological Seminary (Philadelphia). Their great monument is the three-volume commentary by E. J. Young (1965–72). The unity of Isaiah was also defended, though less strongly, by the conservative Roman Catholic scholar, E. J. Kissane (1941–3), and most recently by the conservative evangelical Anglican, J. A. Motyer (1993).

Conservative scholars attacked the liberal arguments with the following three points.

1. The book has always been a unity in the manuscript tradition, and been accepted as such by Jews and Christians alike. The predictive nature of chapters 40 – 66 is not out of keeping with the role of an eighth-century prophet.

2. The language and concepts of 40 – 66 are similar enough to what goes before to permit a single authorship. The differences can be explained by the change in subject-matter, and the predictive nature of these chapters.

3. A late dating of 40 – 66 compromises the divine inspiration of the text, which is particularly important in view of its messianic dimension.

A typical statement of this position can be found in J. A. Alexander (1846–7), commenting on chapter 40:

> The specific application of this chapter to the return from Babylon is without the least foundation in the text itself. The promise is a general one of consolation, protection, and change for the better, to be wrought by the power and wisdom of Jehovah, which are contrasted, first, with those of men, of nations, and of rulers, then with the utter impotence of idols. That the ultimate fulfilment of the promise was still distant is implied in the exhortation to faith and patience. The reference to idolatry proves nothing with respect to the date of the prediction, although more appropriate in the writings of Isaiah than of a prophet in the Babylonish exile. It is evidently meant,

> however, to condemn idolatry in general, and more particularly all the idolatrous defections of the Israelites under the old economy.

Alexander passes over the references to Cyrus almost without comment; he accepts them as prophetic, but does not dwell on the fact, and treats the text as a detailed account of his conquests and career. It is very different with O. T. Allis (1950), for whom the problem of Cyrus is central to the interpretation of the whole book. Allis wrote:

> The mention of Cyrus by name as the Lord's shepherd who will order the rebuilding of the cities of Judah and the restoration of Jerusalem and of the temple which is desolate is one of the most remarkable single phenomena in the entire book of Isaiah. It may properly be said of it that it either offers conclusive proof of the unique inspiration of the prophet who uttered it more than 140 years before its fulfilment or that it furnishes equally conclusive proof that this prophetic utterance and probably other and extended portions of the book we call 'Isaiah' must date from a time long after the ministry of the son of Amoz. At the risk of being accused of trying to simplify the problem unduly, it may be said that if the Cyrus prophecy can be regarded as by Isaiah there is little if any warrant for denying to him the authorship of the entire book which passes under his name.

To the objection that Isaiah 44 – 45 speaks with a vividness which suggests an eye-witness account of events which are already past, Allis answered:

> In claiming that the Cyrus Poem indicates clearly that Cyrus belongs to the future, we are not unmindful of the fact that in most of the passages which refer to him, he is described with a vividness which suggests that he is already present to the mind of the prophet. This we hold to be quite consistent with, indeed to be an example of, that feature of prophecy to which attention has already been directed and of which other examples will shortly be given, the tendency to represent future events as present or already past. But we hold that here in the Cyrus Poem, in view of the remarkable definiteness and vividness with which Cyrus is introduced, the Spirit of prophecy deemed it

needful to make clear that the coming of this mighty deliverer belonged to a distant future.

It is apparent that the main point at issue between critics and conservatives was the nature of prophecy, and the bearing this had both on the inspiration of Scripture and on the unity of the Old and New Testaments. The position was clearly stated by Allis:

> . . . the supremely important issue . . . is as to whether there is any close and vital connection between the Old Testament and the New, whether the great historic events of which we read in the Gospels can really be said to be the fulfilment of predictions recorded in the Old Testament. A. B. Davidson declared many years ago . . . that there must be a connection between prophecy and fulfilment. To anyone who accepts the statements of the New Testament at their face value, such a statement is so obvious as to be axiomatic. The Christian Church has accepted and defended this position, as clearly implied, for example, in the words, that it might be fulfilled, which was spoken by the prophet. But we have seen that the unmistakable trend in critical circles has been to weaken or destroy that connection, to do this by adopting a definition of prophecy which makes prediction *ex hypothesi* practically impossible.

Matters came to a head over the identification of the Servant of the Lord. Jewish tradition from the time of Rashi, if not before, had identified this figure with the nation of Israel as a whole. Christians, of course, had always seen him as a prophecy of Christ, and Isaiah 53 was thought of as one of the most detailed accounts of Christ's atoning sacrifice in the entire Bible. The traditional position was well stated by Alexander in his commentary:

> Notwithstanding these and other prophecies of the Messiah, he is not recognized when he appears.
>
> v. 1. He is not the object of desire and trust for whom the great mass of the people have been waiting.
>
> v. 2. Nay, his low condition, and especially his sufferings, make him rather an object of contempt.
>
> v. 3. But this humiliation and these sufferings are vicarious, not accidental, or incurred by his own fault.
>
> vv. 4–6. Hence, though personally innocent, he is perfectly unresisting.

> v. 7. Even they for whom he suffers may mistake his person and his office.
>
> v. 8. His case presents the two extremes of righteous punishment and perfect innocence.
>
> v. 9. But the glorious fruit of these very sufferings will correct all errors.
>
> v. 10. He becomes a Saviour only by becoming a substitute.
>
> vv. 11–12. Even after the work of expiation is completed and his glorious reward secured, the work of intercession will still be continued.

This was the theology and the interpretation of this key chapter which conservative commentators were determined at all costs to uphold, because in them was contained the essence of the gospel message. Critical scholars, by contrast, took a rather different view. On the identity of the Servant with Christ, G. A. Smith (1890) had this to say:

> . . . the external correspondence between this prophecy and the life of Jesus Christ is by no means perfect. Every wound that is set down in the fifty-third [chapter] of Isaiah was not reproduced or fulfilled in the sufferings of Jesus. For instance, Christ was not the sick, plague-stricken man, whom the Servant is at first represented to be . . . Christ was no Job.

Smith certainly did his best to recognize that there were striking resemblances to Christ in these lines; indeed, his commentary is positively oozing with expressions of piety and devotion to the man who suffered and died for us. But there is a lingering suspicion that it is all overdone, and that behind these professions of faith there lurks a deeper sense of doubt. This was stated clearly by Driver:

> The prophet always, in using the term my servant, means Israel; but sometimes, as he speaks, he thinks merely of the literal historic nations; at other times he has in view the true Israel, Israel as it has been gradually trained by God to respond to its intended vocation and destiny, the Israel which from the beginning has been latent in idea in the historic nation, and has sometimes, in the godly kernel of the people, been manifested (approximately) in reality, but which, as it seems, he conceives will in the future be realized completely upon the

> stage of history. Israel, from this point of view, is delineated by him as an ideal personality, and projected upon the future as a figure displaying the most genuine characteristics of the nation, and realizing them in action with an intensity and clearness of aim which the historic Israel had never even remotely attained.

The notion that the Servant of the Lord is the nation of Israel, in however idealized and attenuated a form, runs completely counter to Christian doctrine and tradition, and amounts to an acceptance of the Jewish interpretation of the passage. Yet it is intriguing how Smith, Driver and Cheyne all contrived to avoid a verse-by-verse analysis of the text, speaking only in general terms about the 'servant songs'. Evidently even they were not prepared to stir up the hornets' nest which such an analysis would inevitably have entailed. But how, asked Allis, is this kind of interpretation possible for a scholar claiming to be a Christian? Is such a person not committed by his faith to a wholehearted acceptance of the messianic prophecy which Isaiah 53 contains? Can an acceptance of Jewish exegesis be regarded as legitimate in his case?

The theological issue posed by this and other traditional messianic texts in Isaiah is an important one which will not go away, as Brevard Childs (1979) has reminded us. On the achievements of critical scholarship, which he accepts and praises for what they are, Childs says:

> Nevertheless, from the perspective of the community of faith and practice which confesses a special relationship to the Bible, the critical study of Isaiah has brought with it a whole set of new problems which have grown in size rather than diminished over the years.

Childs itemizes the problems as follows.

1. Critical scholarship has atomized the book into so many distinct fragments that the coherence of its message has been lost from view.

2. Critical exegesis now rests on a very tentative historical reconstruction of events, which gets less solid still as more fragments are distinguished. Large sections of the book have become quite undatable as a result of this process.

3. The more the book is anchored in ancient Israelite history, the harder it becomes to appropriate its message for the life of the church today.

Though he broadly accepts the 'three Isaiahs' formula of Duhm and his successors, Childs is keen to emphasize the conservative point that the canonical text is, and probably always has been, a unity. Whoever redacted it in its present shape took great care to mix up prophecies from different periods, so that the entire book would reflect a single message. 'Second Isaiah' is the fulfilment of the promises given to 'First Isaiah', and the book's unity is built around this basic promise-fulfilment theme. Chapters 36 – 39, far from being the original ending of First Isaiah, perform an important linking role between these two theological principles, and were inserted in their present position quite deliberately.

On the critical approach to prophecy Childs takes Westermann's view (identical to Driver's) as typical, and complains:

> This modern hermeneutical theory can probably be explained as an existential rejection of the concept of eternally valid ideas which was popular in the idealistic philosophy of the nineteenth century. However, Westermann's exegetical rule renders virtually impossible the task of taking seriously the canonical shape of the biblical text. Specifically in terms of Second Isaiah, the final form of the literature provided a completely new and non-historical framework for the prophetic message, which severed the message from its original historical moorings and rendered it accessible to all future generations. Although the canonical shaping of the Isaianic traditions allowed a great variety of different forms to continue, the various witnesses hold in common a concern to testify to the ways of God with Israel and the world, both in judgment and in redemption.

On the vexed question of the Servant, Childs accepts the critical view that this must refer to Israel in the first instance, but he draws attention to the personification of the nation, and points out that the Servant is not portrayed as the fulfilment of anything in First Isaiah. He must therefore refer to someone new, who is to come in the future. Childs says:

> . . . the canonical process preserved the message in a form, the significance of which was not fully understood. The diversity within the witness could not be resolved in terms of Israel's past experience, rather the past would have to receive its meaning from the future.

Childs also points out that in New Testament times, both Jews and Christians worked from the same presuppositions regarding Isaiah, and that both saw the Servant as an eschatological figure. The disagreement between Jews and Christians remains a theological one, which cannot be solved by appeals to an 'objective, scientific exegesis'.

Though basically a critical scholar himself, Childs holds out hope for a possible resolution of the nineteenth-century divide between liberals and conservatives over the question of Isaiah. If his proposals were to be carried through, something like the following might emerge as a general consensus.

1. The book is a unity, pieced together out of different prophetic material, whose inner link is the principle of prophecy and fulfilment. 'First' Isaiah would be the former; 'Second' (and possibly 'Third') Isaiah would be the latter.

2. Historical references to Cyrus would have been written after the event, but along the lines of prophecy fulfilment; many passages relating to Israel's exile and restoration were genuinely predictive of future events.

3. The Servant of the Lord is a figure who recapitulates the historic destiny of Israel, but who cannot be identified with any Old Testament person. He remains an eschatological hope, which Christians naturally believe was fulfilled in Christ.

As it happens, a consensus on this basis has recently been worked out in detail by J. D. W. Watts (1985; 1987), though it remains to be seen whether it will catch on among scholars in general.

A somewhat similar attempt to do justice to the unity of Isaiah, while respecting its internal diversity, has recently been proposed by Hugh Williamson (1994). Working from 'Second Isaiah', he tries to show how this prophet incorporated earlier material into a wider but coherent whole. Williamson does not tackle the problem of 'Third Isaiah', though perhaps a solution along his lines can be extended to cover it as well. What is becoming increasingly clear is that the issue of Isaianic unity will not go away. Whatever the process of redaction may have been, there is a single book which holds together remarkably well, and which has come down through time as the work of a single author. Whether a scholarly consensus can be found which respects this unity is too early to say, but one thing is certain: the issue is far from dead, even among those who accept the tripartite division of the book.

BIBLIOGRAPHY

J. A. Alexander, *Isaiah Translated and Explained* (Philadelphia: Presbyterian Board of Publication, 1846–7).

O. T. Allis, *The Unity of Isaiah* (London: Tyndale, 1950).

T. K. Cheyne, *Introduction to the Book of Isaiah* (London: A. and C. Black, 1893).

B. S. Childs, *Introduction to the Old Testament as Scripture* (London: SCM, 1979), pp. 311–338.

S. R. Driver, *Isaiah: His Life and Times* (London: Francis Griffiths, 1891).

J. A. Motyer, *The Prophecy of Isaiah* (Leicester: IVP, 1993).

T. H. L. Parker, *Calvin's Sermons on Isaiah's Prophecy of the Death and Passion of Christ (Is. 52:13 – 53:12)* (London: James Clarke, 1956).

G. A. Smith, *The Book of Isaiah* (London: Hodder and Stoughton, 1890).

J. D. W. Watts, *Isaiah,* 2 vols. (Waco: Word, 1985, 1987).

H. G. M. Williamson, *The Book Called Isaiah* (Oxford: Oxford University Press, 1994).

E. J. Young, *The Book of Isaiah,* 3 vols. (Grand Rapids: Eerdmans, 1965–72).

8

The New Testament from Schleiermacher to Schweitzer

The period and the subject

In the nineteenth century historical-critical study of the New Testament ranged more widely and eventually penetrated church life even more deeply than that of the Old Testament. This was because the New Testament occupied a place in Christianity so central that any change in its status, or in popular perception of its importance, was bound to send shock waves through the Christian community. Old Testament critics inadvertently contributed to the high esteem in which the New Testament was held, because they often argued that the gospel was a far higher revelation than what was given in the Old Testament. To question the New Testament was to attack the essence of Christianity, and the very basis of the moral and spiritual order of western civilization.

Scholars such as Semler and Michaelis had a more reverent attitude towards the New Testament, and though they used critical methods, they were less inclined to probe deeply into it. The few radicals, such as Reimarus, walked in fear of their reputations, and possibly even of their lives. It was not until 1835 that the dam burst, with the publication of David Strauss's *Life of Jesus.* Strauss was not an academic, but he raised issues which had been quietly debated in academic circles for two generations, and which could no longer be concealed.

The main architect of a new understanding of the New Testament text was F. C. Baur. Working in Tübingen, where he and a handful of disciples developed a 'school' of interpretation which has been famous ever since, Baur attempted to rewrite early church history, using the New Testament as his source. His basic conviction was that the New Testament had relatively little to do with the historical Jesus of Nazareth, in spite of the fact that he was its central character. Its true value lay in the witness which it bore to the development of the first Christian communities. In these communities, or churches, there were a number of competing tensions which spilled over into the pages of the New Testament. The epistles and the Acts of the Apostles (obviously) and the gospels (less obviously) were written against the background of these competing forces, and tell us more about them than they do about Jesus. The Apocalypse was a tougher nut to crack, and was generally ignored or disparaged in the early stages of research, because its form and meaning were not properly appreciated.

Once Baur got to work, the whole task of textual criticism changed. The gospels, which had been the main focus of attention in the eighteenth century, now had to share attention with the rest of the New Testament. In fact the focus shifted to a later period – AD 50–100, rather than AD 1–30. The 'historical Jesus' now became a hidden figure, buried under layers of theological tradition and debate. Recovering him was still thought to be possible, but it was not an easy task. The energy which had already been spent on trying to solve the 'synoptic problem' now turned in a new direction, with the quest for the historical Jesus becoming the main motive for gospels research.

Thanks to Baur and his disciples, the epistles came to be recognized as the most important primary sources for our knowledge of early Christianity. The Acts of the Apostles, which purports to tell the church's history, was said to be a later composition, and generally unreliable. But the epistles, written in the heat of controversy and intended for immediate use, were an unrivalled source of information. At the same time, they were incomplete, because they gave only one side of the story. A reader of Paul, Peter, James or John would have to reconstruct the situation which gave rise to the epistle in the first place – its so-called *Sitz im Leben* ('setting in life'). Normally, the best way to do this would be to find external evidence which would give us another side to the story.

Unfortunately, however, evidence of this kind was meagre. Pagan writers said little about Christians, and Jewish sources were scarcely more informative. Apocryphal and post-apostolic writings were available, but they were generally regarded as late in date and of doubtful reliability. Occasionally someone would suggest that a sect such as Montanism, which flourished in Asia Minor about AD 170, was a lingering vestige of apostolic Christianity which the church of the day was doing its best to stamp out. Marcion was also sometimes looked on in this way. But these witnesses were late, and of uncertain value in reconstructing the first generation of Christianity.

Real progress in this could be made only by examining the New Testament text itself. By doing that, Baur concluded that there were three circles in the early church which were competing for influence. First, there was the circle of Palestinian Judaism. This was the one closest to Jesus himself, and therefore most likely to have retained authentic memories of him. Next there was the circle of Diaspora Judaism, which was more open to external influences. The apostle Paul was a member of this group, and fought for its interests against the Palestinians. Finally, there was the Hellenistic Gentile circle, which initially lay on the outer fringe of the New Testament church but which soon took it over completely. The fall of Jerusalem in AD 70 ended the independent existence of Palestinian Jewish Christianity, and the Diaspora communities, which then became estranged from the synagogues, merged with the Gentiles to form a new church.

With so many disparate sources contributing to it, this new church had a great internal variety, but this could not survive the process of self-definition and struggle for recognition which ensued. In the face of persecution, the church hardened its theological stance, and gradually an 'orthodox' party emerged which drove out the 'heretics'. These 'orthodox' were the most Hellenized group of all, and they imposed a system of doctrine on the church which was heavily influenced by Greek philosophical models. Among the 'heretics' were those who protested against this, often because they retained elements of primitive Christianity which the Great Church (as the 'orthodox' party claimed to be) was trying to get rid of. A major example of this was the so-called 'parousia hope', or eager expectation of the imminent second coming of Christ. Heretical groups were supposed to have kept this hope alive long after the Great Church had abandoned it.

Also among the 'heretics' were those whose Hellenization of the gospel was crude and unsuccessful – the so-called 'Gnostics'. These were a disparate group of people, whose approach to the Bible was basically mythical and allegorical, with little appreciation of its historical dimension. The Great Church outflanked them by tying the myths to history, and insisting that Jesus of Nazareth was the dying and rising God who had brought salvation to his chosen people. The 'mystery' of faith was not confined to an élite group within the chosen community, but was shared with all its members, who collectively constituted a separate society. It is true that the Great Church had a hierarchy and a system of internal control which was foreign to the New Testament, but this did not depend on degrees of spiritual initiation – at least not to begin with. It was only when Christianity was legalized and took over the Roman Empire that there developed within the church a spiritual élite of 'religious' people, who controlled the community until Luther's great revolt in the name of spiritual and religious freedom.

This rewriting of church history took place with little reference to Jesus, who remained a shadowy figure. Distinguishing him from the myths surrounding his name became a major preoccupation, but suffered from lack of reliable evidence. One theory after another was put forward, with few positive results. By the end of the nineteenth century it was frequently assumed that Jesus had been a particularly successful rabbi, who had internalized the moral demands of the Mosaic law and thereby incurred the wrath of the Jewish establishment, which tried to get rid of him. This they eventually succeeded in doing, possibly because Jesus was somehow connected to groups which sought to get rid of the Romans. What they could not have foreseen was that Jesus' followers would resist this, and create of him not just a martyr but a living Saviour and God who had come back from the dead and gone up to heaven.

This picture remained relatively undisturbed until 1906, when Albert Schweitzer published his remarkable book, *The Quest of the Historical Jesus*. This was a history of nineteenth-century attempts to find the 'historical Jesus', which Schweitzer regarded as entirely misdirected. The real Jesus, according to him, was a fanatical, apocalyptic figure who had looked for the imminent end of the world. The Jewish establishment could not cope with such a figure any more than we could today. When they got rid of him, his disciples reconstructed his life and teachings, domesticating them for a wider audience and turning them into the combination of moral precept and miracle which we find in the gospels. The real key to the spirit of Jesus lay in those parts of the New Testament which nineteenth-century scholarship had found hardest to understand – the 'Little Apocalypse' of Mark 13 (paralleled in Mt. 24 and Lk. 21), and of course, the great Apocalypse of John. New Testament scholarship had been turned on its head, and a whole new era of research had begun.

British New Testament scholars put up greater resistance to trends in Germany than their Old Testament colleagues did, although they were prepared to embrace certain aspects of the critical method.

There were a number of reasons for this. The English-speaking world was generally more cautious and conservative, and more resistant to philosophical pressures than German and other continental countries were. Church life had also been deeply influenced by the Evangelical Revival and by Anglo-Catholicism. The former contributed an emphasis on the atonement which continued to dominate much theological discussion. The latter contributed a corresponding emphasis on the incarnation of Christ, which was deeply hostile to the 'myth' theories of the Tübingen school and its successors.

Anglican ecclesiology also had a vested interest in demonstrating that it was not a late corruption, but something which could be justified by early tradition. Anglicans were not tied to a Roman Catholic type of fundamentalism, which would have obliged them to look for the papacy in the gospels (Mt. 16:18), and so they could accept that church structures had developed over a period of time. But unlike other Protestants, they were committed to upholding the legitimacy of that development, which involved demonstrating that it went back to early times. This they did with remarkable success, and in the process shifted the timescale of New Testament origins back into the first century. That in turn made it more difficult to argue that the New Testament contained traditions radically different from the teaching of Jesus, since the time available for their development was scarcely more than a generation, in which people who had known Jesus were still alive and active in the church.

British conservatism was closely tied to minute textual study, and here again, New Testament critics lived in a different atmosphere from their Old Testament colleagues. Far from being dependent on a single manuscript tradition, New Testament scholars had a vast range of texts and fragments to choose from. The *Textus Receptus* could not survive the renewed study of these documents, and in 1880 it was abandoned for good, when a new Greek text, based on a careful choice of readings from the best manuscripts available, made its appearance. That set off a new round of textual studies, which in the course of a century was to produce an agreed text of the New Testament which is as close to the original as we can hope for on the basis of the evidence currently available. This was a major achievement, and can be justly regarded as the one truly assured result of modern criticism.

The interpreters and their work

The German sphere: the forerunners of Baur

Friedrich Daniel Ernst Schleiermacher (1768–1834). Professor at Halle (1804) and Berlin (1810), he is now recognized as the father of liberal German theology in the nineteenth century, and most of his work was in that field. His liberalism was different from the older rationalism of the Deists, and was strongly opposed to it. He combined a critical approach to textual and historical questions with a religious sensibility inherited from pietism. In his speeches on religion (1799), he argued that religion was the study of the non-rational side of human beings, which was just as important as the rational side, and that Christianity was the highest form of religion which had yet evolved. He was the first person to lecture on the life of the historical Jesus, but his thoughts on the subject were not published until 1864, when they were severely criticized by Strauss. In his own lifetime, he published little in the field of New Testament studies, apart from commentaries on 1 Timothy (1807) and Luke (1817).

Hermann Heimart Cludius (1754–1835). He claimed (1808) that John's gospel represents a Christianity very different from that of the synoptics, and therefore cannot be the work of an eye-witness. According to him, inner contradictions in the text make it clear that the gospel was worked over by a series of different redactors.

Hermann Olshausen (1796–1839). He taught at Königsberg (1821) and Erlangen (1834), and wrote prolifically on New Testament themes, mainly from a doctrinal point of view. His works include *The Genuineness of the Four Canonical Gospels* (1823), *Ein Wort über tieferen Schriftsinn* (*A Word about the Deeper Meaning of Scripture*) (1824), *Die biblische Schriftauslegung* (*Biblical Scriptural Exposition*) (1825) and his great *Biblical Commentary on the New Testament* (1830–40; Eng. trans 1847–60), parts of which have been republished in recent years (1983–4). Olshausen was a staunch defender of historical criticism, but he used it to reach very conservative conclusions. For example, he believed that Peter dictated both his epistles in Hebrew; the differences between them could be attributed to different Greek translators, the second of whom made use of Jude in the course of his work.

Johann Leonhard Hug (1765–1846). The most important Roman Catholic biblical scholar of the early nineteenth century, he taught at the Catholic seminary in Freiburg im Breisgau (1792). His major work was his magisterial *Introduction to the New Testament* (1808; Eng. trans. 1827). This makes full use of historico-critical methods, but comes to predictably conservative conclusions in every case. Even so, Hug must be credited with having opened the Catholic Church to contemporary Protestant biblical criticism. Towards the end of his life he became a major opponent of David Strauss, arguing that Strauss's secular presuppositions and basic misunderstanding of the nature of myth had led him to undervalue the reliability of the New Testament records.

Karl Gottlieb Bretschneider (1776–1848). Writing in Latin so as to avoid giving offence to the general public, Bretschneider suggested (1820) that John was a gospel of Hellenistic origins, far removed from the atmosphere of Palestinian Judaism. This view was to become widespread in the nineteenth century.

Karl Heinrich Venturini (1768–1849). He took over Bahrdt's thesis (see p. 246) and perfected it. According to him, Jesus could only make himself understood by clothing his spiritual message in flesh. His 'miracles' were just normal cures, and the resurrection of Lazarus was from a coma, not from death. On Palm Sunday Jesus proclaimed himself Messiah in order to try to destroy popular superstition, but this ploy failed and he was crucified instead. His main work was *Die natürliche Geschichte des grossen Propheten von Nazareth* (*The Natural History of the Great Prophet of Nazareth*) (1800–02).

Heinrich Eberhard Gottlob Paulus (1761–1851). He taught at Jena from 1789, at Würzburg from 1803 and at Heidelberg from 1811, and was an important link between the eighteenth-century neologists and rationalists and the next generation of critics, notably De Wette. He wrote a number of commentaries, including three volumes on the synoptic gospels (1830–33), but is chiefly remembered today for his *Life of Jesus* (1828), in which he dismissed the miracles as natural events. He remained a classical rationalist of the old school until the end of his life.

Wilhelm Martin Leberecht De Wette (1780–1849). See pp. 276–277. His New Testament work included eleven short exegetical studies, covering the whole text, which appeared between 1836 and 1848.

Karl Lachmann (1793–1851). He was Professor of Classical Philology at Königsberg (1825) and then at Berlin (1827). Lachmann's techniques of textual criticism introduced a new era in biblical studies. His classification of manuscripts is still the generally accepted one, and his editions of the Greek New Testament (1831 and 1847–50) were the first to be based entirely on the most ancient manuscript traditions. In this respect, his work was a forerunner to that of Westcott and Hort. He also argued, on the basis of a minute study of the textual evidence, that Mark was the earliest gospel to have been written.

Johannes Martin Augustinus Scholz (1794–1852). A student of J. L. Hug, he became the Dean of the Catholic faculty at Bonn. He was a pioneer in research on the Greek text of the New Testament, though his bias was towards acceptance of the *Textus Receptus*, a fact which made later scholars disregard much of his work. However, Scholz was not entirely bound to the ecclesiastical tradition, and towards the end of his life he repudiated many of his earlier views in favour of contemporary scientific opinion.

Christian Gottlob Wilke (1786–1854). A pastor until he was dismissed in 1837, he wrote a book called *Der Urevangelist* (*The Primary Evangelist*) in 1838, in which he advocated the priority of Mark, followed by Luke and then Matthew. In 1846 he became a Roman Catholic.

Johann Carl Ludwig Gieseler (1792–1854). He was Professor at Bonn (1819) and Göttingen (1831). He took up Herder's suggestion that there was an oral 'primal gospel' extant in Aramaic, but in developing this hypothesis he managed to reveal its grave difficulties, notably the fact that it could not account for the verbal similarities between the synoptic gospels in Greek. His main work on the subject was published in 1818.

Gottfried Christian Friedrich Lücke (1791–1855). He taught at Bonn from 1818 and at Göttingen from 1827. He published commentaries on the gospel of John, the Johannine epistles and the Apocalypse, but his most important work was an outline of New Testament hermeneutics (*Grundriss der Neutestamentlichen Hermeneutik*) which appeared in 1817 and was a faithful reflection of Schleiermacher's ideas. Lücke argued that grammatico-historical exegesis was not enough to understand the New Testament; the religious element also had to be accounted for. He therefore rejected the idea that the Bible could or should be read 'like any other book'.

The German sphere: Baur and his legacy

Ferdinand Christian Baur (1792–1860). Possibly the greatest New Testament scholar of the nineteenth century, he was certainly one of the most influential. From 1826 he was Professor of Church History and Dogmatics at Tübingen, where he formed an entire generation of scholars. He was a follower of G. W. F. Hegel's philosophy, and believed that early Christianity was a synthesis created out of the conflict of opposing forces. He developed this theme in his *Untersuchungen über die sogenannten Pastoralbriefe des Apostels Paulus* (*Investigations concerning the So-called Pastoral Epistles of Paul*), which appeared in 1835. Later, he wrote another book on Paul, *Paulus, der Apostel Jesu Christi* (*Paul, Apostle of Jesus Christ*), which came out in 1845 but was not translated into English until 1873–5. In this book, he denied the Pauline authorship of all the epistles except Galatians, 1 and 2 Corinthians and Romans. He also denied the apostolic origin (and therefore the basic historicity) of Acts. In 1847 he published his last work of New Testament criticism, *Kritische Untersuchungen über die kanonischen Evangelien* (*Critical Investigations concerning the Canonical Gospels*). He believed that Matthew was the first of the gospels to have been written, because it reflected the Jewish background of Christianity best. On the other hand, he believed that John's gospel reflected the Gnostic and Montanist controversies of the late second century, and had no historical value.

Albert Schwegler (1819–1857). A representative of the Tübingen school, his book *Das nachapostolische Zeitalter in den Hauptmomenten seiner Entwicklung* (*The Post-apostolic Period in the Chief Moments of its Development*) (1846) interpreted the whole of early Christian literature in terms of Baur's conflict theory, and became the classic expression of the Tübingen position.

Matthias Schneckenburger (1804–48). Professor at Bern from 1834, he died young. He wrote a number of New Testament studies, including one on Acts (1841), in which he followed the Tübingen school's position. He was a more careful scholar than Baur, however, and backed up his arguments with a great deal of evidence which Baur ignored.

Christian Hermann Weisse (1801–66). He taught at Leipzig from 1828, apart from a brief interruption (1837–41), and was an idealist philosopher at a time when idealism was going out of fashion in Germany. In his *Gospel History* (1838) he advocated the two-source hypothesis of gospel origins in which Mark and another source were both used by Matthew and Luke. This was the first time someone had proposed the existence of a document which we now call Q (*Quelle*, the German word for 'source'). He regarded John as unhistorical, but claimed that it was mainly Hebraic in tone, not Hellenistic. He also believed that Jesus had rejected Jewish apocalyptic by spiritualizing it. According to Weisse, Jesus became aware that he was the Messiah when he was baptized. The resurrection however, was a psychological belief of the early Christian community, not a historical fact.

Heinrich August Wilhelm Meyer (1800–73). He wrote a commentary on the New Testament which he took as far as Philemon (1829–47), but which has continued to appear up to the present day under a number of successive authors. The commentary claimed to be based exclusively on grammatico-historical principles, and thus acquired a reputation for conservatism, though Meyer was by no means hostile to critical theories which could be supported by textual evidence.

David Friedrich Strauss (1808–74). A student at Tübingen, he was called to a professorship at Zürich in 1839, but because of opposition from conservatives, he was pensioned off before being allowed to teach. He spent the rest of his life as a freelance writer. His most famous book, and the one which aroused the opposition to him, was his *Life of Jesus* (1835). In this work, he demonstrated a marked preference for supernaturalist interpretations of Jesus over rationalist ones, and stated that it was impossible to write a normal history of his life. In any case, Strauss argued, history is unimportant. What matters is the myth surrounding the man, because it is this which has changed the world. He claimed that Mark was an epitome of Matthew which tried to turn the gospel story into history, but failed. He attacked the rationalists for their high opinion of John, which he regarded as inconsistent with their principles, since John was the least historical gospel of all. Because of his preference for non-historical mythology, Strauss had no interest in eschatology – an important point, as Schweitzer later remarked. Strauss had little critical sense, and completely ignored the problem of the origin of the church. Nevertheless, his book raised new questions, and forced scholars to re-examine their presuppositions in gospels research. It marked a turning-point in New Testament studies, equal in importance to Schweitzer's plea for an eschatological approach, made nearly two generations later.

August Wilhelm Neander (1789–1850). An eminent church historian, he entered New Testament studies late in life, in an attempt to find an answer to Strauss (1836; 1837). His general approach was conservative and rationalistic. He took the miracles of Jesus seriously, but interpreted them as a kind of psychic power to influence nature, both human and material.

Christoph Friedrich von Ammon (1766–1850). He was another elderly rationalist who entered the fray against Strauss (1840; 1842–7). His approach was entirely rationalistic, and he preferred John as a historical source over the synoptics because of its idealism.

August Friedrich Christian Vilmar (1800–68). Author of a six-volume commentary on the Bible (*Collegium Biblicum*), Vilmar occupies an important place in the history of interpretation. Long before Albert Schweitzer, he objected to the commonly held idea that historical criticism could provide a better understanding of Scripture than that held by earlier generations. He drew a clear distinction between theology, as the study of God and his works, and exegesis, which he regarded as primarily a literary technique. This distinction was not widely appreciated in his own day, and Vilmar was severely criticized for making it, but it has become more widely accepted in recent times.

Constantin Tischendorf (1815–74). Famous for his manuscript researches, he published twenty-four editions of the Greek New Testament during his lifetime and made a major contribution to textual criticism and research.

Friedrich Wilhelm Ghillany (Richard von der Alm) (1807–76). His views were close to those of the Tübingen school, though he dated Mark after Luke. He had no time for John. He believed that Jesus came to be worshipped because of a syncretistic blend of Judaism and Gnostic influences. He claimed that Jesus believed that he was an eschatological Messiah, and that he provoked the Romans into killing him in order to usher in an eschatological kingdom of brotherly love. On the strength of this belief, he tried to found his own church, based on Deistic principles, but failed.

Johann Tobias Beck (1804–78). Professor of Systematic Theology at Tübingen from 1843, but the very antithesis of Baur, Beck was a traditional conservative in the style of J. A. Bengel, and upheld confessional Lutheranism. This is especially apparent in his posthumous commentary on Romans (1884). His position was later defended, though in a modified form, by A. Schlatter and even by K. Barth.

Karl Theodor Keim (1825–78). He published a history of Jesus (1867), in which he claimed that there had been a Galilean phase to Jesus' ministry before he moved to Judaea. In the former period, his message was still idyllic and moral in tone; only later did it become political and eschatological. This view later became the standard liberal picture of Jesus' life.

Karl Christian Planck (1819–80). A member of the Tübingen school, and intimate of Baur, he devised an extremely complex philosophical system, which nobody but he could understand. His main contribution to New Testament research came in two articles (1843, 1847) which raised the question of Jesus' relationship to Judaism for the first time.

Bruno Bauer (1809–82). He believed that John was a work of art, not a historical record, and that the gospel had been strongly influenced by Philo. The synoptic gospels were not historical either, though they were obviously different from John. Mark was the earliest, and the only literary source of the others. The birth narratives of Jesus were fictitious, and the messianic idea was an invention of the early church. He introduced the idea of a messianic secret, later developed by Wrede. He believed that miracles represented a false victory over nature; true victory lies only in death. Christianity, he maintained, was a Stoicized Judaism, the product of the dying cultural agony of Greece and Rome. As for Jesus, Bauer eventually concluded that he had never existed. His work on John was published in 1840, and that on the synoptics shortly afterwards (1841–2), to be followed by a work on the gospels as a whole (1850–51). He also wrote on Acts (1850) and on the Pauline epistles (1850–52). His two works on the wider cultural scene came later; the one dealing with Philo appeared in 1874, and the one on the Graeco-Roman crisis theory came out in 1877.

Johann Peter Lange (1802–84). Professor at Zürich from 1838, and the conservative replacement for D. Strauss, he wrote a theological commentary on the history of the early church (1853–4) in which he defended traditional views against the Tübingen critics.

Johannes Henricus Scholten (1811–85). Professor at Leiden from 1843, he belonged to the modern school of criticism and published commentaries on Mark (1868) and Luke (1870).

Gotthard Victor Lechler (1811–88). He wrote a massive work on the apostolic age (1851), in which he sought to show the essential unity between Paul and the other apostles. He accepted that there were differences of emphasis in the apostolic band, but resisted the Tübingen urge to find conflict everywhere. His work remains valuable for the way in which he distinguished different strands within the New Testament church.

Timothée Colani (1824–88). He came from Alsace and wrote in French. In 1864 he asserted that there were different messianic theories in Judaism, and that Jesus could not be identified with any one of them with absolute certainty. He was convinced that Jesus never envisaged a second coming, but believed that his work would be complete at his death. It therefore lacked any eschatological dimension.

Michael Baumgarten (1812–89). A severe critic of the Tübingen school, he wrote a three-volume commentary on Acts (1852) which bristled with venom against his opponents. However, his argument that Baur had misunderstood Paul's concept of 'freedom from the law', and had turned it into a new law, was valid and profound.

Albrecht Benjamin Ritschl (1822–89). One of the greatest liberal New Testament scholars of the period, he established ideas which determined the shape of liberal Protestantism until after 1918. He was Professor of Systematic Theology at Bonn from 1852 and then at Göttingen from 1864. His book on the origin of the early catholic church (1850) broke with the thesis of Baur, and represented the first revolt from within the Tübingen school. He also wrote a great theological work on justification, which appeared in two volumes (1870, 1874).

Karl August Hase (1800–90). He taught in Jena from 1830. His major field was church history, but he also wrote on New Testament subjects. He was the first person to write a life of Jesus from a purely historical base. He accepted only the miracles recorded in John, and perhaps the virgin birth as well. He divided the career of Jesus into two distinct parts. In the first period of his ministry, Jesus supposedly accepted popular messianism, and conformed to its apocalyptic demands for a restoration of Israel, but in the second period he branched out on his own, and developed other views. According to Hase, the apostles remained wedded to the first of these phases, apart from John, who understood Jesus's psychological development and responded to it. Hase published *Das Leben Jesu* (*The Life of Jesus*) in 1829 and *Die Geschichte Jesu* (*The History of Jesus*) in 1876. His interpretation of Jesus' life became standard in the 1830s, and remained so for half a century.

Edouard (Eduard) Reuss (1804–91). See p. 283. He wrote a history of the New Testament writings (1842), a Johannine theology (1847) and a history of Christian theology in the apostolic age (1852), all of which appeared in French.

Gustav Volkmar (1809–93). He was an extremist member of the Tübingen school, whose works have now been forgotten. He took Baur's thesis to its logical conclusion, and found Jewish–Hellenistic conflict almost everywhere in the New Testament. Most of his associates thought he was taking things too far, and in their reaction to him they sowed seeds of doubt about the school's methods as a whole.

Karl Heinrich von Weizsäcker (1822–99). He succeeded Baur at Tübingen (1861). His most famous works were *Untersuchungen über die evangelische Geschichte* (*Investigations concerning Gospel History*) (1864) and *Die apostolische Zeitalter* (*The Apostolic Age*) (1886).

Augustus Hermann Cremer (1834–1903). He was professor at

Greifswald from 1870 and a strong Lutheran. His most famous work is *Die Paulinische Rechtfertigungslehre* (*The Pauline Doctrine of Justification by Faith*), which appeared in 1899).

Franz Overbeck (1837–1905). He taught at Jena from 1864 and then at Basel (1870). He revised De Wette's commentary on Acts in the light of the beliefs of the Tübingen school, and wrote several works on the canon (1880), post-apostolic literature (1882) and John (1911). He was a declared unbeliever, and much of his work was designed to disprove the claims of Christianity. A great deal of it has never been published.

Willem Christiaan van Manen (1842–1905). Professor at Leiden, he was the main representative of the radical Dutch school of New Testament criticism. He was not as bitterly opposed to orthodoxy as were Baur and his associates, but was more radical than they were. Arguing from the developed, and therefore 'Hellenized', theology of Romans and Galatians, van Manen concluded that they could not have been written by Paul, whose background was much too Jewish. Van Manen therefore concluded that none of the Pauline epistles was genuine.

Adolf Hilgenfeld (1823–1907). He taught at Jena from 1847. He was a critical adherent of the Tübingen school, and wrote a number of studies on the Jewish cultural background to the New Testament. In 1857 he drew attention for the first time to the importance of Jewish apocalyptic for Christian origins. He also wrote important works on the canon (1863) and on various extracanonical writings (1884).

Eduard Zeller (1814–1908). A member of the Tübingen school, and a close associate of Baur's, Zeller taught at Bern from 1847 and at Marburg from 1849. In 1862 he went to Heidelberg and then to Berlin in 1872. He wrote little, but supported Baur and Strauss in controversy. His own beliefs were pantheistic, and he did not believe in life after death. For him, Christianity was the supreme moral code, and little more.

Heinrich Julius Holtzmann (1832–1910). He taught at Heidelberg (1858) and then at Strasbourg (1874–1904). He wrote a classic study of the synoptic gospels (1863), which established the two-source theory, an introduction to the New Testament (1885) and a New Testament theology (1896). He was opposed to the views of Wrede, whom he criticized in *Jesus' Messianic Self-Consciousness* (1907). He also wrote commentaries on Ephesians and Colossians (1872), the pastoral epistles (1880), the synoptic gospels and Acts (1889) and John (1890).

Emil Schürer (1844–1910). He taught at Leipzig (1869), Giessen

(1879), Kiel (1890) and Göttingen (1895). His most famous work is his *History of the Jewish People in the Age of Jesus Christ*, which began to appear in 1874 and was completed in 1887. It is still a basic resource for the study of Judaism in New Testament times, and the English translation (1885–91) was updated and reissued as recently as 1973–86.

Martin Kähler (1835–1912). He taught at Halle from 1860, except for a short period at Bonn (1864–7). He was a conservative Lutheran theologian and biblical scholar, and highly productive. He wrote a stinging attack on the liberal approach to the life of Jesus, which was published in 1892, though not translated into English until 1964. His main line of argument was that there are no historically reliable documents relating to the life of Jesus, apart from the gospels, which are not histories in the usual sense of the term. Looking for the 'historical Jesus' was therefore a big mistake, and should be replaced by a concentration on the preaching and teaching ministry which the gospels record. His views became influential in twentieth-century criticism, though they were not well received when they were first published.

Carl Friedrich Georg Heinrici (1844–1915). He taught at Berlin (1871), Marburg (1874) and Leipzig (1892). In the 1880s, he was the first to make extensive use of parallels between Hellenistic and Pauline thought, but was careful to emphasize that Paul's Old Testament background ensured that his approach was original. Later (1911), he opposed Reitzenstein's suggestion that Christianity was basically a mystery religion, and argued that it triumphed over its rivals because of its unique combination of religion and morality.

Rudolf Sohm (1841–1917). This jurist argued in his book *Kirchenrecht* (*Church Law*) (1892) that the early church was primarily a spiritual and not a legal organization. He advocated a theological approach to church history, and in that sense was a forerunner of the 'history of religions' school.

Bernhard Weiss (1827–1918). Professor at Königsberg (1857), Kiel (1863) and Berlin (1876), he wrote many of the volumes in Meyer's commentary, a biblical theology of the New Testament (1868), a life of Jesus (1882) and an introduction to the New Testament (1889), which was widely read in its day, and almost immediately translated into English. Weiss was the father of Johannes, and a very conservative interpreter of the Bible.

Johannes Weiss (1863–1914). Son of Bernhard, and son-in-law of Albrecht Ritschl, he predeceased his father. He taught at Göttingen from 1888, at Marburg from 1895 and at Heidelberg from 1908. He was associated with the 'history of religions' school and became a pioneer of what would later be known as form criticism. His views on Jesus as an eschatological figure were developed in his book, *Jesus' Teaching on the Kingdom of God* (1892), and they were later popularized and circulated to a wider public by A. Schweitzer, who acknowledged Weiss's insight. Weiss also wrote commentaries on Luke (1893) and 1 Corinthians (1910), and at his death left an unfinished work on early Christianity, which was published posthumously (1917).

Paul Wilhelm Schmiedel (1851–1935). He was professor at Zürich from 1893 to 1923, and the last major representative of the radical tradition of Baur. His views were very similar to those of F. Overbeck, and he had an extremely low opinion of the historicity of the New Testament documents.

The German sphere: the 'history of religions' school and after

Hermann Usener (1834–1905). Professor of Classical Philology at Bern (1861), Greifswald (1863) and Bonn (1866), he was a leading scholar in the field of comparative religions and the history of the early church, and his work paved the way for the 'history of religions' approach to the New Testament. His book on the Christmas festival (1899) drew on Egyptian magic as the main source of the birth narratives of Jesus.

Otto Pfleiderer (1839–1908). He taught at Tübingen (1864–8), at Jena (1871–5) and then at Berlin. His most important works of biblical criticism were his famous *Paulinism* (1873) and his *Primitive Christianity* (*Das Urchristentum*) (1883). He argued that John was wholly conditioned by eschatology, that Mark was a work of theology, not history, that Paul was heavily influenced by Hellenism and that the sacraments were influenced by mystery religions. He also believed that there was a radical difference between Jesus and Paul.

Adolf Hausrath (1837–1909). He taught at Heidelberg from 1867. Although he was a church historian, he wrote on the influence of Hellenistic ideas on Paul and produced a history of New Testament times which reflected the views of the Tübingen school (1868). He was a precursor of the 'history of religions' school, but failed to connect the New Testament to early post-apostolic Christianity in any constructive way.

William Wrede (1859–1906). He taught at Göttingen (1891) and then at Breslau (1893). He was a founder of the Göttingen 'history of religions' school, and wrote a number of important works. *The Task and Methods of New Testament Theology* appeared in 1897, followed by studies on John (1903) and Paul (1904) which still remain significant today. His most significant work was *The Messianic Secret* (1901), which was not translated into English until 1971. His main argument was that Jesus hid any claim to be the Messiah, but that the early church read this claim back into his ministry.

Wilhelm Bousset (1865–1920). He taught at Göttingen from 1896 to 1916, and then in Giessen. He published a large number of works on Judaism and early Christianity, as well as on patristic studies of various kinds. His most important works were on the book of Revelation (1896), Judaism (1902), apocalyptic (1903) and Gnosticism (1907), and his famous *Kyrios Christos* appeared in 1913, though it was not translated into English until 1970. Bousset was one of the founding members of the 'history of religions' school at Göttingen, and most of his work reflects that orientation. He believed that the early church was a worshipping community held together by sacred rites, and that 'Kyrios' was a mystical power felt to be present during this worship.

Albert Eichhorn (1856–1926). He taught at Halle (1886) and at Kiel (1901–13), but had to retire because of illness. He published little, but influenced many others by his teaching. His most famous work is his theses (*Thesen*), which appeared in 1886, and dealt mainly with Christ's passion and death. He later wrote on the Last Supper in *Das Abendmahl im Neuen Testament* (*The Lord's Supper in the New Testament*) (1898). He was a prominent follower of the 'history of religions' approach to New Testament criticism.

Wilhelm Heitmüller (1869–1926). He taught at Göttingen (1902), Marburg (1908), Bonn (1920) and Tübingen (1924). A close associate of Bousset and the 'history of religions' approach, he wrote a commentary on John (1907), as well as works on baptism and the Lord's Supper.

Hans Heinrich Wendt (1853–1928). He revised Meyer's commentary on Acts (1899) and insisted that Luke was a historian first and foremost, even if some of the details of his history are inaccurate. He thus did his best to undercut the arguments of the Tübingen school, and to restore the question of historicity to the agenda of New Testament interpretation.

Adolf von Harnack (1851–1930). He taught at Leipzig (1874), Giessen (1879), Marburg (1886) and Berlin (1888–1921). Though mainly a church historian, he covered New Testament matters as well, and was the most prominent representative of liberal German criticism until his death. His support for Germany's war aims in 1914 disillusioned the young Karl Barth, and helped to set him on a theological journey away from liberalism. His main work was the *History of Dogma* (*Dogmengeschichte*), which came out in several volumes between 1886 and 1889, and was soon translated into English (1894–9). He also wrote on Luke, Acts and Q. His lectures on the essence of Christianity (*Das Wesen des Christentums*), given in 1900, were immediately popular, and were translated into several languages. He developed his theory of Christian origins in a work on that subject (1902), and later tried to rehabilitate Marcion (1921), as one of the last representatives of 'true' Christianity.

Richard Reitzenstein (1861–1931). He taught classics at Breslau (1888), Rostock (1889), Giessen (1892), Strasbourg (1893), Freiburg im Breisgau (1911) and finally at Göttingen (1914). He wrote many works of classical philology, and stressed the non-Jewish inheritance of early Christianity. In his work on the Hellenistic mystery religions (1910), he claimed that Paul had been heavily influenced by them, an idea which he later developed in further studies of Iranian mystery religions (1921) and the pre-history of Christian baptism (1929). He strongly influenced W. Bousset, and later R. Bultmann.

Hermann Gunkel (1862–1932). He taught at Göttingen (1888), Halle (1889), Berlin (1905), Giessen (1907) and again at Halle (1920). His life's work was in Old Testament, but as a young man he wrote on New Testament subjects as well. His book on Genesis and Revelation (*Schöpfung und Chaos in Urzeuit und Endzeit*; *Creation and Chaos in the Beginning and End-time*) which appeared in 1895, drew attention to the importance of the Apocalypse, and paved the way for a revival of apocalyptic studies. Another work of major importance was *Zum religionsgeschichtlichen Verständnis des Neuen Testaments* (*On the History-of-Religions Understanding of the New Testament*) which appeared in 1903.

Theodor Zahn (1838–1933). He was professor at Göttingen from 1871, at Kiel from 1877, at Erlangen from 1878, at Leipzig from 1888, and back at Erlangen from 1892. He was an important historian of the canon and wrote at great length on it (1888–1916), an introduction to the New Testament (1897–9) and nine commentaries in his own series (1903–26). His outlook was conservative and deeply scholarly. He was one of the first Germans to appreciate the importance of the archaeological discoveries made by Anglo-American scholars, especially Sir William Ramsay.

Hajo Uden Meijboom (1842–1933). This Dutch scholar wrote *A History and Critique of the Marcan Hypothesis* (1866; Eng. trans. 1992) which contains a penetrating critique of the presuppositions underlying much modern synoptic research. He is particularly critical of the arguments in favour of Marcan priority, and in the end comes down in favour of the Griesbach hypothesis. For good measure, he adds that the high Christology of Mark must be a sign of its lateness, thereby revealing that he too, has not escaped the kinds of presuppositions which governed the thought of those whose views he so strongly opposed.

Paul Feine (1859–1933). Taught at Göttingen (1893), Vienna (1894), Breslau (1907) and Halle (1910). His textbooks on New Testament theology and introduction attacked the 'history of religions' approach and became standard works in German universities, going through several editions.

Ernst von Dobschütz (1870–1934). He taught New Testament at Jena (1893), Strasbourg (1904), Breslau (1910) and Halle (1913). In his book *Probleme des Apostolischen Zeitalters* (*Problems of the Apostolic Age*), which appeared in 1904, he criticized the 'history of religions' approach to Christian origins, and insisted that the triumph of Christianity could only be explained by what distinguished it from other religions of antiquity, not by what it had in common with them.

Adolf Deissmann (1866–1937). Professor of New Testament at Heidelberg (1897–1908) and then at Berlin, he had a deep interest in political and ecumenical questions, as well as New Testament studies. He was the first to draw attention to the significance of the formula 'in Christ' in the New Testament, an issue which is still debated today. In 1911 he wrote a major work on Paul, which was translated into English in 1926. He also proved that New Testament Greek was not a special language, or a corruption of classical Greek, but the ordinary spoken tongue of the time.

Adolf Schlatter (1852–1938). Professor of New Testament at Greifswald (1888), Berlin (1893) and Tübingen (1898), he was by far the most notable conservative New Testament scholar of his day, and has achieved classical status as such in Germany. He wrote on faith in the New Testament (1885), following Cremer and attacking scholars who tried to drive a wedge between Jesus and Paul. He later produced a New Testament theology (1909), and from 1930 until his death wrote commentaries on every book of the New Testament.

Adolf Jülicher (1857–1938). Professor at Marburg from 1888 to 1923, he was a noted textual critic, and wrote a classical work on the parables (1888–9) in which he argued against allegorical interpretations of them. He also wrote an introduction to the New Testament (1894) and a commentary on Romans (1907). He was an inheritor of the Tübingen school, but dissented from it at many points, and found little evidence of radical conflict between Judaizers and Hellenists in the New Testament.

Paul Wernle (1872–1939). He taught at Basel from 1897. Most of his New Testament works were published early in his career, including *Der Christ und die Sünde bei Paulus* (*The Christian and Sin in Paul*) (1897), *Die Anfänge unserer Religion* (*The Beginnings of our Religion*) (1901) and *Die synoptische Frage* (*The Synoptic Question*) (1904). In 1916 he published *Jesus*, but later turned to dogmatic and historical works. He was deeply influenced by the 'history of religions' school, but was not entirely tied to that view.

Kurt Deissner (1888–1942). He taught at Greifswald from 1915. He was a lifelong opponent of the 'history of religions' school, and wrote a number of works against their approach, of which the best known is *Paulus und die Mystik seiner Zeit* (*Paul and the Mysticism of his Time*) which appeared in 1918.

Albert Schweitzer (1875–1965). He lectured at Strasbourg from 1902 to 1913, when he became a medical missionary in Gabon. His main works include *The Mystery of the Kingdom of God* (1901), *The Quest of the Historical Jesus* (1906) and *Paul and his Interpreters* (1911), which was later expanded into *The Mysticism of Paul the Apostle* (1930). He also wrote a book on the Lord's Supper (1901). Schweitzer is famous for the way in which he dissected nineteenth-century German New Testament scholarship, and showed that its main premisses were based on false assumptions about the nature of Jesus and his teaching. Schweitzer picked up the eschatological theories of J. Weiss, and brought them to the attention of a wider public. He was convinced that Jesus himself believed that he would return in the very near future, but that he got this wrong. In Schweitzer's view, Christianity as we know it is a highly diluted version of what Jesus originally taught, which in its pure form would have been incredible even in his own time. After the publication of his great works on Jesus and on Paul, New Testament studies in Germany entered a new era.

The English-speaking world

Joseph Stevens Buckminster (1784–1812). Probably the first liberal critic of the Bible in the United States, he tried to show that the New Testament did not support orthodox Calvinism, and that only those books which could claim undoubted apostolic authority should be recognized as canonical. He died too young to make any scholarly contribution to the subject, but his theories and example remained to inspire a generation of critics in New England.

Samuel Taylor Coleridge (1772–1834). Well known as a Romantic poet and literary critic, Coleridge's theological views were essentially Unitarian. He objected to theories of the divine inspiration of Scripture, claiming instead that the biblical text was a work of art which expressed in symbols a reality which went beyond the senses and appealed primarily to the imagination of the reader.

Charles Simeon (1759–1836). The leading Anglican evangelical of his time, his *Horae Homileticae* (1840) contain twenty-two volumes of sermon outlines which have been widely used ever since, and which reflect a traditional orthodox Protestant exposition of the Scriptures.

Herbert Marsh (1758–1839). Lady Margaret Professor of Divinity at Cambridge (1807), he was the first theologian at that University to lecture in English instead of Latin. He later became Bishop of Llandaff (1816) and Peterborough (1819). His lectures were printed between 1810 and 1823, and reflect a traditional orthodoxy, bolstered by the use of historical evidence. He translated J. D. Michaelis's *Introduction to the New Testament* (1802), and included in it an essay on the synoptic problem, which he had already published separately (1798). Marsh argued for a common Aramaic source for the gospels, but held that each of the three synoptists used a different version of it. He also believed that there was a supplementary Aramaic document used by Matthew and Luke, which he called *Beth*, and which is effectively identical to the later Q hypothesis.

Robert Haldane (1764–1842). Scottish Congregationalist and (after 1808) Baptist, he was a leading evangelical of the early nineteenth century. He wrote extensively on the subject of biblical inspiration, and even defended the orthodox position on this subject against August Tholuck (1838). His commentary on Romans (1836–9) has become a classic.

Thomas Arnold (1795–1842). A disciple of Coleridge, Arnold did much to popularize his views, though he never managed to complete a biblical commentary. He was strongly opposed to the Tractarian movement, and this pushed him in the direction of greater liberalism. He was prepared to accept a wide range of late datings for different biblical texts, and also accepted the possibility of errors in them. His ideas were later taken up and developed by A. P. Stanley and Benjamin Jowett.

Moses Stuart (1780–1852). See pp. 286–287. His New Testament works included commentaries on Hebrews (1827), Romans (1832) and Revelation (1851).

Andrews Norton (1786–1852). A Unitarian minister and professor at Harvard from 1813, he played a major role in introducing biblical criticism to the Harvard Divinity School, and from there to the rest of the USA. He published a three-volume work, *The Evidences of the Genuineness of the Gospels* (1837, 1844).

William John Conybeare (1815–57) and **John Saul Howson** (1816–85). They were joint authors of a well-known commentary on *The Life and Epistles of St Paul* (1852), which is still widely read today. They demonstrated that archaeological knowledge of the Middle East contributed more to an understanding of Paul than tendentious reconstructions of divisions within the early church. Their work is now out of date in many details, but it remains influential in its overall approach to the subject.

John Brown of Edinburgh (1784–1858). Scottish dissenting Presbyterian minister and theologian, he was noted for his defence of liberal views of the atonement. He was a prolific author of biblical commentaries, in which he stressed the need to ensure that everything a preacher gleaned from a text was actually there in it. His commentary on 1 Peter (1848) marked a turning-point in Scottish exegesis, and was followed by other works on Galatians (1853), Romans (1857) and Hebrews, which appeared posthumously (1862).

William Lindsay (1802–66). Scottish dissenting Presbyterian theologian, he is chiefly known for his lectures on Hebrews (1867).

James Smith (1782–1867). A Scottish layman and amateur archaeologist, he demonstrated that Luke's account of the sea voyage in Acts 27 was not a literary fiction, but a true account of sailing conditions in the area. His researches, published in 1848, did much to convince British scholars of the unsoundness of the Tübingen reconstruction of Acts.

John James Tayler (1797–1869). A Unitarian, he taught for many years at Manchester College, which during his time there moved from York to Manchester to London. (It is now in Oxford.) He wrote *An Attempt to Ascertain the Character of the Fourth Gospel* (1867), in which he defended the spiritual value of the text in spite of admitted difficulties over its authorship and provenance. He strongly doubted its accuracy as a historical record, but still maintained that it was a spiritual revelation of the living God.

Henry Alford (1810–71). Fellow of Trinity College, Cambridge, he was author of a four-volume commentary on the Greek New Testament. Alford was open to German critical ideas, but not mesmerized by them. His commentary is judicious and lucid, and has been the model for all subsequent English-language commentaries of its kind.

James Eadie (1810–76). This Scottish dissenting Presbyterian scholar was noted for the conservative views of the inspiration of Scripture which undergirded all his exegetical work. He is remembered today for his commentaries on Ephesians (1854), Colossians (1856), Philippians (1859), Galatians (1869) and 1 and 2 Thessalonians (1877).

Charles Hodge (1797–1878). One of the founders of Princeton Seminary (1820), he is chiefly noted today for his *Systematic Theology* (1872–3). However, he also wrote a notable commentary on Romans (1835), in which he maintained a strictly Calvinist position. Hodge's views on the inspiration of Scripture were those of the orthodox Protestant dogmatician, F. Turretin, and it is largely because of him that this position became the hallmark of Princeton and of conservative American evangelicalism generally.

Arthur Penrhyn Stanley (1815–81). A pupil of Thomas Arnold, he taught at Oxford from 1838. He was mainly a church historian, but he was forced to adopt a position on New Testament matters as well. This appears in his *Sermons and Essays on the Apostolical Age* (1847) and later in his posthumous *Lectures on the History of the Jewish Church* (1902). He also wrote an important commentary on 1 and 2 Corinthians (1855). In his view, the early church was plagued by Judaizers, who later developed into full-blown Gnostics. He defended the historicity of the apostles and their mission, but failed to find any support for the 'Catholic' views of the Tractarians. He was appreciative of contemporary German scholarship, and adopted many of its conclusions, but never lost the conviction that all biblical interpretation should have a practical application to the life of the church and the individual believer. In this respect, he represented a typically English blend of liberal scholarship and conservative churchmanship, which was to mark much of Anglicanism for the next century.

Matthew Arnold (1822–88). Poet and literary critic, he was the son of Thomas Arnold (see p. 341). He wrote at length on religious questions, especially about the interpretation of the Bible, which he regarded as primarily a literary document. He was very critical of his contemporaries who failed to see this, and who tried to read into Scripture scientific and historical theories which the text itself was not concerned with. His works were controversial in their day, but have proved fruitful in the twentieth century, with the great rise of interest in literary criticism. His main religious works were *St Paul* *and Protestantism* (1870), *Literature and Dogma* (1873), *God and the Bible* (1875) and *Last Essays on Church and Religion* (1877).

Joseph Barber Lightfoot (1828–89). He was Professor of Theology at Cambridge from 1861 and Bishop of Durham from 1879. The most outstanding English New Testament scholar of his generation, he wrote commentaries on Galatians (1865), Philippians (1868) and Colossians and Philemon (1875) which have retained their importance ever since. He is also noted for his work on post-apostolic literature, especially Clement of Rome (1869) and Ignatius of Antioch (1885). The fact that he was able to prove that seven of the Ignatian Epistles were genuine was a major advance in dating the New Testament documents. Lightfoot successfully demonstrated that these could not have been produced after AD 100, thereby knocking a large hole in Baur's theories.

Edwin Hatch (1835–89). Lecturer in Church History at Oxford from 1867, he was a leading representative of liberal thought in British theology. He was an enemy of the Anglo-Catholics, but much admired by Harnack, who translated his work into German. In 1880 he gave the Bampton Lectures on *The Organization of the Early Christian Churches* (published 1881). He also wrote an influential book on *The Influence of Greek Ideas and Usages upon the Christian Church*, which was published in 1890 and reissued as recently as 1957. Today his fame largely rests on the concordance of the Septuagint which he edited with H. A. Redpath, and which appeared some years after his death (1897).

Alfred Edersheim (1825–89). A Jew converted to Christianity, he entered the Church of Scotland (1846) and later the Church of England (1875). He wrote an enormous amount on Judaism at the time of Jesus, and his classic work was his two-volume *Life and Times of Jesus the Messiah* (1883). His books are very informative and entertaining, though not always very critical of their source material. His work is conservative in tone, and is still widely read in Jewish Christian circles.

Fenton John Anthony Hort (1828–1892). Professor of Theology at Cambridge from 1871, he wrote *Judaistic Christianity* (1874), *The Christian Ecclesia* (1897) and commentaries, which were edited and published after his death, on 1 Peter (1898), Romans and Ephesians (1895) and James (1909). He is chiefly famous, however, for his work as a textual scholar. In 1881 he published, together with B. F. Westcott, the first modern critical edition of the Greek New Testament. He was also a major contributor to the Revised Version of the English Bible (1881).

Benjamin Jowett (1817–93). Regius Professor of Greek at Oxford from 1855 and Master of Balliol from 1870, he wrote a two-volume commentary on the Pauline epistles (1855), but withdrew from theology after the controversy caused by *Essays and Reviews* in 1860 (see pp. 287–290). His approach was basically liberal and critical.

Alexander Balmain Bruce (1831–99). This Scottish Free Church scholar wrote extensively on different aspects of New Testament theology. He actively engaged with the Tübingen school, and his writings were widely respected in Germany. He also wrote a commentary on Hebrews (1899).

John Charles Ryle (1816–1900). Bishop of Liverpool from 1880, his conservative expositions of the gospels are still being printed and are widely read among those who share his evangelical outlook.

Brooke Foss Westcott (1825–1901). He was Professor of Divinity at Cambridge (1870–84), and subsequently Canon of Westminster and Bishop of Durham (1890–1901). In 1851 he wrote an *Introduction to the Study of the Gospels*, which helped to introduce critical methods into England. He also wrote a *History of the Canon* (1855) at about the same time. From 1853 until 1881 he worked closely with F. J. A. Hort on their edition of the Greek New Testament. Later he produced commentaries on John (1881), the Johannine epistles (1883) and Hebrews (1889). He was a Platonist in philosophy and a socialist in politics, and by far the most left-wing of the Cambridge trio of Westcott, Lightfoot and Hort.

Frederic William Farrer (1831–1903). Fellow of Trinity College, Cambridge, and pupil of J. B. Lightfoot, he wrote a classic study of *The Life and Work of St Paul* (1879), in which he defended the historical reliability of both the Pauline epistles and Acts. He is also well known for his 1885 Bampton Lectures, published as the *History of Interpretation of the Bible* (1886).

Charles John Ellicott (1819–1905). He taught at King's College, London (1848) and briefly at Cambridge (1860–61), before becoming Bishop of Gloucester (1863). He was a prolific author, and wrote commentaries on Galatians (1854), Ephesians (1855), Philippians, Colossians and Philemon (1857), 1 and 2 Thessalonians (1858), the pastoral epistles (1858) and 1 Corinthians (1887). His main contribution, however, and the one he is remembered for today, was his massive commentary on the entire Bible. The New Testament section appeared in stages from 1877 to 1882, followed by the Old in 1882 to 1884.

Marcus Dods (1834–1909). A Scottish scholar who was equally at home in both Testaments, he wrote commentaries on Genesis

(1882), 1 Corinthians (1889) and John (1891). He also gave a series of lectures which were later published as *The Bible, its Nature and Origins* (1909). In this, as in a number of earlier works, he rejected the orthodox doctrine of biblical inspiration and defended a view which restricted infallibility to matters of substance, and not to every detail of the text.

Richard Belward Rackham (1868–1912). He wrote a commentary on Acts (1901) which is essentially theological rather than philological in outlook.

Henry Barclay Swete (1835–1917). He carried on the textual tradition of Lightfoot, first at King's College, London (1882) and then at Cambridge (1890–1915). He was a founder of the *Journal of Theological Studies* (1899), and wrote extensively on early church doctrine. His New Testament work included commentaries on Mark (1898) and Revelation (1906). He also edited the Septuagint in three volumes (1887–94).

James Hope Moulton (1863–1917). This student of New Testament Greek was author, together with G. Milligan, of a famous grammar. He also published studies of Greek papyri and revealed an underground world of magic and mystery religions, which he connected with early Christianity.

Richard John Knowling (1851–1919). He wrote a famous commentary on Acts (1900), which is outstanding for its careful treatment of the linguistic and historical evidence.

Handley Carr Glyn Moule (1841–1920). He was the first principal of Ridley Hall, Cambridge (1881) and later Professor of Divinity (1899) and Bishop of Durham (1901). He wrote commentaries on almost all the New Testament epistles, and these are still read today by conservative students, who appreciate their elegant style and careful exegesis.

William Sanday (1843–1920). New Testament Professor at Oxford from 1882, he was one of the main channels through which German biblical criticism entered the Church of England. He delivered the Bampton Lectures on the subject of inspiration in 1893, and the following year started a seminar on the synoptic problem which eventually resulted in the Oxford Studies of 1911. In 1895 he wrote a commentary on Romans with A. C. Headlam, which is still in common use today. Later, between 1905 and 1910, he wrote a number of books on Christology and the life of Christ in which he followed the German scholarship of the day.

Vincent Henry Stanton (1846–1924). Regius Professor of Divinity at Cambridge from 1916 to 1922, he wrote extensively on the gospels.

He is chiefly known today for his three-volume work, *The Gospels as Historical Documents* (1903, 1909, 1920), which went through a number of editions. He was a strong defender of Marcan priority, which he backed up by close philological discussion.

Ernest De Witt Burton (1856–1925). American theologian and biblical scholar, he taught at Chicago for many years. He wrote an important study entitled *Principles of Literary Criticism and the Synoptic Problem* (1904), in which he showed a willingness to question the prevailing assumption of Marcan priority.

Edwin Abbott Abbott (1838–1926). He wrote extensively on the literary and philological problems of the gospels. He is especially noted for his article on the subject in the 1879 edition of the *Encylopaedia Britannica,* in which he developed his own theory of synoptic origins. He also published a book, *The Corrections of Mark* (1901), dealing with the same subject.

Alfred Plummer (1841–1926). After teaching at Cambridge (1865) and at Durham (1874), he became one of the editors of the International Critical Commentary series. He was an extremely prolific biblical commentator himself, and wrote on 1 and 2 Peter and Jude (1879), John and the Johannine epistles (1880), Luke (1896), James and Jude (1903), the pastoral epistles (1903), Matthew (1909) and 2 Corinthians (1915). Together with **Archibald Robertson** (1853–1931) he also wrote a commentary on 1 Corinthians (1911). Several of these commentaries went through a number of editions, and one or two are still in print today.

John Caesar Hawkins (1837–1929). He was author of *Horae Synopticae: Contributions to the Study of the Synoptic Problem* (1898), which is noted for its very careful examination of the linguistic evidence of the texts. He also demonstrated the essential unity of Luke-Acts as a single piece of historical work.

Cuthbert Hamilton Turner (1860–1930). He was a Fellow of Magdalen College, Oxford, from 1889, and Dean Ireland's Professor of Exegesis from 1920. He wrote a series of articles on Mark in the *Journal of Theological Studies* (1924–5), followed by a full commentary (1928) and a number of works of church history.

George Foot Moore (1851–1931). He was Professor at Harvard from 1904 to 1921. His work on *Judaism in the First Centuries of the Christian Era* (1927) is a classic. In many ways his approach to the subject anticipated the later work of K. Stendahl and E. P. Sanders.

Benjamin Wisner Bacon (1860–1932). Professor of New Testament at Yale (1897–1927), he wrote extensively on Mark (1919, 1925) and Matthew (1930). He was a faithful follower of German source criticism, and helped to introduce its methods into the English-speaking world.

Joseph Armitage Robinson (1858–1933). A Cambridge scholar in the Lightfoot tradition, he published a commentary on Ephesians (1903), in which he defended Pauline authorship. He also published a number of works on church history.

Harry Angus Alexander Kennedy (1866–1934). Professor of New Testament at Knox College, Toronto (1905) and then at New College, Edinburgh (1909–25). His greatest work was *The Theology of the Epistles* (1919), which became a minor classic of Pauline theology. He was one of the first scholars to insist that the Greek of the New Testament was the common spoken language of the time, and his work reflects a careful analysis of the critical scholarship of his day.

Francis Crawford Burkitt (1864–1935). Professor of Divinity at Cambridge from 1905, he is noted for a number of studies in the Syriac and Old Latin versions of the New Testament. He published a large number of works on different aspects of early Christianity, among them *The Gospel History and its Transmission* (1906), *Christian Beginnings* (1924), and *Church and Gnosis* (1932).

Burnet Hillman Streeter (1874–1937). He was Fellow of Queen's College, Oxford, from 1905 and Provost from 1933. He was a prominent modernist critic of the gospels, and his 'solution' to the synoptic problem, which he published in *The Four Gospels* (1924), remained the standard one for a generation. He also wrote a book on *The Primitive Church* (1929).

Edwyn Clement Hoskyns (1884–1937). He taught at Cambridge from 1919. Originally a liberal scholar, he was converted to a more conservative position, and became a leading exponent of 'biblical theology'.

William Mitchell Ramsay (1851–1939). A pioneer archaeologist of Asia Minor, he came to regard Luke as a most careful historian, and did much to undermine the theses of the Tübingen school. Most of his writing was done before 1900, but it bore its greatest fruit later on. His commentary on Galatians (1900) introduced the so-called 'South Galatian' theory in support of an early dating for Acts. Thanks to him, it is now generally accepted that the 'Galatians' of the New Testament were inhabitants of the Roman province of Galatia, and not, as had formerly been supposed, ethnic Galatians (who lived in 'North Galatia').

Frederick John Foakes-Jackson (1855–1941). Already mentioned in connection with his early work in Old Testament studies, he wrote *St Luke and a Modern Writer* (1916), *St Paul, the Man and Apostle* (1926), and *Peter, Prince of Apostles* (1927), and, together with Kirsopp Lake, edited a five-volume study of Acts (1931). His work reflects the reverent use of historical criticism common among Anglican scholars of the period.

French-speaking writers

Michel Nicolas (1810–86). Born to a Protestant family at Nîmes, he studied at Geneva and from 1839 taught at Montauban. From 1858 he began to introduce German criticism to France, and published a number of articles on the New Testament canon and the fourth gospel. His major literary monument was a two-volume critical study of the Bible (*Etudes critiques sur la Bible*), of which the Old Testament volume was published in 1862 and the New in 1866.

Edmond Scherer (1815–89). Born in Paris to an Anglo-Swiss family, he was converted to evangelical faith in England in 1832. He then studied at Strasbourg and went to Geneva in 1846, where a crisis of faith led to his resignation three years later. He is chiefly remembered for the significant contribution which he made towards the establishment of Marcan priority in the synoptic gospels.

Ernest Renan (1823–1892). He was the first person to write a life of Jesus from an essentially Catholic standpoint, though he was far from orthodox in his beliefs. He rejected the Johannine discourses, but accepted the narrative parts as history. He tried to write a fifth gospel, in which he portrayed Jesus as a teacher who persuaded himself that he was especially close to God, and became a mystic. He was not really sincere or profound as a New Testament scholar, though his *Life of Jesus* (1863) had an enormous influence in literary circles. It was translated into English by George Eliot (1864) and it also influenced Tolstoy.

Frédéric Godet (1812–1900). A Swiss Protestant pastor from Neuchâtel, he wrote commentaries on Luke, John, Romans and 1 Corinthians. Godet was extremely conservative, though he was not afraid to confront the problems which the texts posed. His own conclusions were dogmatic and forcefully made, but he is still widely read and appreciated today in conservative circles.

Albert Réville (1826–1906). Born in Dieppe, he studied at Strasbourg, probably under Reuss and Colani. From 1851 to 1873 he was pastor of the Walloon Church at Rotterdam, and in 1862 he published an important study of Matthew. From 1880 he taught at the Collège de France in Paris.

Marie-Joseph Lagrange (1855–1938). This French Roman Catholic biblical scholar founded the Ecole Biblique at Jerusalem in 1890. He wrote widely on biblical subjects, and is now regarded as the father of modern Roman Catholic biblical studies.

Alfred Loisy (1857–1940). A French Roman Catholic scholar who was a major protagonist in the modernist controversy. In 1893 he was removed from his teaching post at the Institut Catholique because he accepted critical methods in biblical studies, and in 1908 he was excommunicated for his book *L'Evangile et l'Eglise* (*The Gospel and the Church*), which had appeared in 1903. He also wrote important commentaries on the synoptic gospels (1907–8) and Acts (1920).

The issues

The issues in New Testament interpretation which most characterize the nineteenth century may be set out as follows.

1. *It was necessary to determine the relationship between the New Testament and historical fact.* In one sense, this was a less serious problem than for the Old Testament, since the period covered by the text was much shorter and better known. But in another sense it was more difficult, because of the claims made for Jesus by orthodox theology. Few people doubted that he had existed, and most were prepared to accept that he was an extraordinary teacher and prophet. But there agreement ended. What Jesus believed about himself, and whether he did the extraordinary things attributed to him in the gospels, were matters of endless controversy. The boundary between history and myth was unclear, and constantly shifting among scholars according to their own theological presuppositions.

The rise of the church presented a further problem. Here most scholars were prepared to accept that the epistles were the best sources of information, but that made many doubt the reliability of Acts. There was also the problem of internal division in the church between Jewish and Gentile Christians, to which the epistles were supposed to bear witness. Closely allied to this was the question of how far Christianity had suffered from 'Hellenization', even before the New Testament was written, and what the significance of that was.

2. *It was necessary to determine what the source of New Testament theology was.* Was it the teaching of Jesus, or had his message been distorted in the next generation, notably by the apostle Paul? If the Pauline epistles are older than the gospels, are they not more reliable as an indicator of what the church really thought at the time, and do they not reveal a diversity of opinion which is not found in the gospels?

The main issue at stake here was the relationship between the orthodox theology of the church and the beliefs of Jesus. To what extent would Jesus have recognized the Christological claims of a later generation, or even the messianic claims of his Jewish contemporaries? Another important matter was the origin of the church's hierarchy and sacraments. Did the New Testament give any comfort to the 'Catholic' position on these matters, or was the hierarchy a later invention, and were the sacraments an import from various mystery religions or other pagan cults?

3. *It was necessary to establish an accurate text from which to work.* This was a major problem in New Testament studies, quite without parallel in the Old Testament, where there was a single manuscript tradition. The vast number of New Testament manuscripts and their many divergences demanded an intense and laborious work of textual criticism which occupied the minds of some of the greatest scholars of the day. The *Textus Receptus* was abandoned in favour of an 'eclectic' text, drawn from many different sources, a move which required the most careful presentation of the evidence and reasons for choosing one reading over others. In many respects this labour has lasted to the present day, and represents the permanent contribution of nineteenth-century scholarship to the history of biblical interpretation.

The methods of interpretation

Comparison with the Old Testament

When we come to look in detail at the history of New Testament interpretation in the nineteenth century, we are struck by the fact that the historical-critical method was applied to the New Testament in a way very different from the way it was applied to the Old. Historical criticism assaulted both Testaments on the ground that they were not straightforward reports of events. It tended to apply the same criteria to each Testament as far as supernatural phenomena were concerned. Miracles were a particular difficulty, and were explained by some other means if at all possible. Theophanies and the like could also be dismissed, either as illusions or as poetic ways of reporting deep psychological experiences.

Beyond that, however, the approach to each Testament differed. The Old Testament was regarded as unreliable because of the vast distance in time which supposedly separated it from the events it described. It was generally assumed that most of the present text was put together between about 700 BC and about 200 BC, a period of 500 years. The events described, however, took place over a much longer period, and many of them were ancient history when the first texts were written. Even without Genesis 1 – 11, Old Testament scholars were still talking about events stretching from about 2000 BC to about 400 BC, and it was only in the period of overlap – the 300 years from Hezekiah to Ezra – that there was any chance of having a first-hand historical record. On the other hand, there was little consciousness of a cultural gap between the Hebrews and their neighbours. Discoveries in Egypt and Mesopotamia were eagerly applied to the Old Testament, and cognate languages were scoured for words which might help interpret obscure Hebrew ones. Historical criticism debunked the uniqueness of the Old Testament by showing how closely it was connected to the cultural milieu beyond the boundaries of Israel.

With the New Testament, the approach was so different as to be almost the exact opposite. The timescale was much shorter – not more than a century from beginning to end, and the distance between the events described and the first record of them was no more than a generation, well within living memory. The chances of accuracy were therefore infinitely greater, but here New Testament critics introduced the cultural factor as one which divided the texts from their subject. Jesus may have lived only a few years before Paul was preaching to the Gentiles, but his cultural universe was far away from theirs. Palestinian Jews inhabited a mental world vastly different from that of Greeks and Hellenized Jews in the Diaspora, and the conflict between these two elements was one of the most salient features of the early church. The man who was a political Messiah in the first context became a dying and rising Redeemer God in the second, because cultural norms and expectations demanded it. The Hebrew mind could not come to terms with a divine incarnation, whereas its Hellenic counterpart found that quite natural.

Greek culture was much better known than the ancient middle-eastern cultures were, and points of linguistic and conceptual comparison were many. If John spoke of the Logos as the creator of the universe, scholars were bound to think of the Logos of Plato and his followers. That the two concepts might have been quite independent of one another was scarcely thought to be possible. The mere fact that the apostles and their associates had chosen to write in Greek, which was not their native language, proved that there had been a cultural assimilation of an originally Hebraic religion to the Graeco-Roman world. Then too, there was the fact that most of the New Testament epistles were addressed to communities in Greek-speaking cities, and the epistles were generally thought to be the oldest and most authentic Christian records. It was therefore not difficult to suggest that the historical Jesus had been buried under a cultural avalanche which had taken over the Christian church at a very early stage in its development.

Theological considerations also played a more important role than they did in Old Testament interpretation. Nobody seriously doubted that Hebraic monotheism was superior to the surrounding paganism, and although there were differences of opinion about how this monotheism had come into being, the final result was accepted as legitimate by everyone concerned. In the case of the New Testament, the situation was once again exactly the opposite. Here the assumption was that the primitive teaching of Jesus was infinitely superior to the subsequent corruptions and misunderstandings which resulted from the spread of Christianity in an alien environment. How much of this primitive teaching could be recovered became the main question in gospels criticism, and the suggestion that it could be 'purified' by abandoning the orthodox dogmatic formulations of the church was bound to provoke the strongest opposition from confessional theologians.

The figure of Jesus could not be studied in detached isolation from the life of the church, and the gulf between what liberal critics were suggesting and what the church confessed in its creeds and other confessional documents grew wider as the century progressed. The 'historical Jesus' turned out to be a caricature of nineteenth-century liberal moralism, with little connection either to the church or to historical reality. Traditionalists naturally believed that a return to that reality would vindicate the church's theology, while J. Weiss and A. Schweitzer advocated an alternative which would commend itself to a later generation of liberals – the belief that the historical Jesus was an apocalyptic figure whose outlook would be incomprehensible now, and who had to be domesticated for mass consumption even then. But whether one follows the older liberals, or the eschatological approach of Weiss and Schweitzer, the result is similar; the New Testament is a text which is inferior to the original teaching of Jesus, and therefore represents a decline, not an advance, in religion.

The grammatico-historical method

The first method of interpretation which we have to consider is the one which is called 'grammatico-historical'. This was a form of historical criticism, but one which avoided the deeper philosophical and theological questions which came to be associated with the latter. The mainstay of this type of criticism was textual analysis, for which there was a great deal of scope in the New Testament. Deciding which of the variant readings was the best involved a considerable amount of detective work, not only in manuscript study but also in theological judgment, since it was often the case that variants represented one theological position or another. The most famous example of this was 1 John 5:7, which in the *Textus Receptus* contained a clear reference to the Trinity. However, careful study of the manuscripts revealed that this addition was very late and confined to a small number of texts. A truly critical edition of the New Testament would therefore have to leave it out, and trinitarian doctrine lost what had been one of its principal supporting texts. Even if the doctrine of the Trinity did not depend on this one verse, the thought that it was unauthentic was bound to unsettle earlier convictions that the Trinity was a New Testament doctrine, and increase the likelihood that it was a post-apostolic (and therefore corrupt) development of the original teaching of Jesus.

Grammatico-historical criticism relied heavily on exegetical principles which had been worked out since the time of Erasmus and which continue to be regarded as valid today. The belief that the meaning of a word was to be determined from its context and from usage elsewhere remained basic to this approach. The assumption that the original text must have made sense to the writer and to his first readers was also accepted without question. Lastly, the recognition that later scribes tended to simplify difficulties which they did not understand also played an important part in textual analysis, giving rise to a predilection for the so-called *lectio difficilior* ('more difficult reading') as the more probable one.

Because of its close attention to detail and its refusal to move away from the actual texts themselves, grammatico-historical criticism came to be regarded as the most conservative form of biblical study practised in an academic environment. For this reason, those with a naturally conservative bias also tended to choose it as the most objective and scientific form of critical study open to them. However, it would be a mistake to think that those conservatives were necessarily 'orthodox' in the traditional sense of that term.

Protestant orthodoxy was a confessional stance, adopted in relation to the doctrinal position(s) approved by the main Protestant churches at the time of the Reformation and after.

In continental Europe and in Scotland, these confessions were detailed and demanding, and many biblical scholars felt that adherence to them as a starting-point would compromise their academic freedom and integrity. Even many of the conservatives among them preferred to base their conservatism on the conclusions of their research rather than on an ecclesiastical confession adopted in advance, and therefore they were not 'orthodox' in their methods. The practical difference was that if the evidence of the texts led away from the confessions, a conservative scholar would follow the evidence, whereas his 'orthodox' colleague would seek to interpret the evidence in the light of his church's confession. Because of this, conservative scholars who could be persuaded to adopt critical positions on various matters compromised their orthodoxy in the eyes of the confessionalists.

In this climate, Anglicans had a distinct advantage, because they lacked a detailed confession of faith. Anglican scholars could follow the grammatico-historical method to its logical conclusions without coming up against opposition from confessionalists within their own church. The result was that Anglicans made a distinctive contribution to textual criticism which was highly conservative without being tied to a confessional 'orthodoxy' in the Lutheran or Reformed sense.

The main weakness of the grammatico-historical approach was its philosophical and theological superficiality. By effectively ruling these issues out of consideration, proponents of the method were often unable to answer the theological assertions of the more radical critics. Minute textual exegesis did not explain how the text itself had come into being, nor did it tell anyone what it meant. Those who practised this method also came up against the objection which had been made since Philo's day to the literal sense of the text: by itself, it was 'unspiritual' and therefore unedifying to the soul of the believer. This was put very clearly by F. Lücke as early as 1817:

> Since by the literal sense only individual ideas and conceptual relationships can be fully and directly expressed, never the whole of a discourse or a document, much less religious ideas and feelings, it follows that the grammatical principle of interpretation is not adequate completely to ascertain and present the content of the New Testament records of religion . . . Since in the New Testament not only the external historical

> beginnings but also the inner ideological origin of Christianity is set forth, the historical interpretation, which is concerned only with the former, must be regarded as insufficient . . .

A deeper analysis of these factors required another method, based on grammatico-historical principles as far as possible, but going beyond them in certain vitally important respects.

The Tübingen school

It was at least partly in answer to this need that F. C. Baur and his pupils developed their own distinctive method of interpretation. Baur based his approach on the philosophy of G. W. F. Hegel, according to which all human development was the result of conflict between opposing forces, which Hegel called *thesis* and *antithesis*. Out of this conflict would eventually emerge a higher *synthesis*, combining elements of the thesis and the antithesis, but producing a fundamentally new reality. There is an obvious human analogy here in the process of procreation: the male (thesis) enters into 'conflict' with the female (antithesis) to produce a child (synthesis), who in turn grows up to become a new thesis, repeating the process in the next generation.

Applied to the study of the New Testament, Hegel's thought produced in Baur's mind a conflict between Judaism (thesis) and Hellenism (antithesis), which eventually led to a new synthesis, which Baur called 'early Catholicism'. According to Baur, this conflict was in full swing in the early church, and can be documented from the Pauline epistles. Paul comes across as the champion of the Gentile party, whereas Peter is the representative of the 'Judaizers'. Signs of the emerging 'Catholic' synthesis can be found in the Acts of the Apostles and in the pastoral epistles (which Baur regarded as post-Pauline). The synoptic gospels, James, Jude and Revelation stand as witnesses of Jewish Christianity. Furthermore there is an important difference between the synoptic gospels and John, because John represents a more advanced stage of synthesis, in which the earlier conflicts had all but been forgotten. For this reason, John must be quite late in date, and has no value as a historical source for the life of Jesus. Baur thus insisted that every New Testament book represented a 'tendency' which had to be discerned before it could be properly interpreted. Only when this was done would it be possible to place each book of the New Testament in its proper historical context, and so reconstruct the inner development of New Testament theology.

Baur's understanding of this can be grasped quite clearly if we consider his approach to New Testament Christology. He thought that the synoptic gospels presented Jesus as a purely human Messiah, and that the transition from the human to the divine was represented by the ascension, an idea which is only hinted at at the end of Matthew and Luke, and not present at all in Mark. John, on the other hand, presents a Christ who came down from heaven at the beginning – a very different perspective. And Paul stands somewhere in the middle; for him, Christ is a man, but something more as well, though not yet the divine Son come down to earth. As Baur says:

> First, we have the Christology of the Synoptic Gospels, and here it cannot be contended on any sufficient grounds that they give us the slightest justification for advancing beyond the idea of a purely human Messiah. The idea of pre-existence lies completely outside the Synoptic sphere of view . . . In contrast to this point of view stands that of the Johannine Logos-idea. According to this, the substantial conception of the person of Christ is the conception of his essence as divine in itself. Here the thought travels, not from below upwards, but from above downwards, and the human is therefore only a secondary thing, and added afterwards.
>
> Between these two opposing points of view, the Christology of Paul occupies a place of its own, and we cannot fail to see that it gives us the key of the transition from the one to the other. On one side Christ is essentially man, on the other he is more than man; and his humanity is already so enhanced and idealized, that the sense in which he is man is certainly inconsistent with the Synoptic mode of view, which stands on the firm basis of his historical and human appearance.

Baur was the first to state openly the contrast between 'Christology from below' and 'Christology from above', a contrast which was later to play a great role in twentieth-century theology and biblical interpretation.

Baur's critical methods became so important for subsequent New Testament study that it is essential to have a clear grasp of their strengths and weaknesses. Their strengths may be outlined as follows.

1. *Baur was able to account for the historical and theological development of the New Testament as a whole.* He recognized the interdependence of the various texts, and the need to provide a theory of Christian

origins which could explain all the evidence. All subsequent theories of New Testament origins have had to follow Baur in this.

2. *Baur recognized that Christology was the key to understanding the development of the New Testament.* The more 'advanced' the Christology of a book was, the later it must be dated. Working on this basis, it was possible to discern the different strands of New Testament Christianity with the utmost clarity.

3. *Baur recognized the importance of the author's intention in deciding when and to whom any particular New Testament book was written.* He was one of the first to recognize the diversity within the apostolic community, and to devise a theory to account for it.

The weaknesses of his approach can be outlined as follows.

1. *Baur was tied to a philosophical approach which forced him to reduce the teaching of Jesus to its purely moral dimension.* He therefore overlooked the importance of Jesus as a person, and the meaning of his eschatological expectations. This made it difficult to understand how the ministry of Jesus was transformed into the founding of the church, and removed the historical Jesus from theological discussion.

2. *Baur's approach was far too schematic, and made the evidence fit his presuppositions.* His opponents were subsequently able to demolish virtually every one of his conclusions, a fact which inevitably called his overall method into question. In particular, Baur's conflict model was inadequate as an interpretation of the growth of New Testament Christianity, and it contradicted his own intentions. For the conflict model, as Hegel presented it, was a model of progress, whereas in Baur's application of it, it was a model of decline. Baur did not think that the 'early Catholicism' which resulted from the synthesis of Jewish and Gentile Christianity was an improvement on what had gone before; on the contrary, he believed that it was a distortion of the true message of Jesus. Baur wanted to get back to the simple thesis, which his own researches showed was a historical impossibility.

A somewhat aberrant form of the Tübingen approach was that of D. Strauss, whose *Life of Jesus* (1835) maintained that the gospels could be understood only on the basis of myth. Strauss borrowed this concept from the neologists, but pursued it more systematically, by extending it to the gospels as a whole and not restricting it to certain phenomena such as parables. Influenced by the rationalism of H. Paulus, Strauss also included the miracles of Jesus in his category of myth. Strauss undoubtedly went too far in applying this principle to the texts, but he made the point that it was necessary to find an overall principle which could be used to interpret the meaning of the gospels. Strauss also believed that Jesus thought of himself as the

Messiah, and could therefore be credited with having authorized the appropriation of the myth (which in itself was of earlier Jewish origin) to himself. It was Strauss, for example, who first suggested that John's gospel was an advanced form of this myth, and therefore a much later document than the synoptics.

Baur's relationship to Strauss is problematical. Strauss had been a pupil of his at Tübingen, and had therefore imbibed some of his principles. When the *Life of Jesus* appeared, Baur acknowledged it as a contribution to understanding the New Testament which was fundamentally similar to his own work on the Pauline epistles. But later on, Baur began to object to Strauss's 'negative' approach. In 1847 he published his own study of the gospels in which he maintained that the synoptic tradition was historically reliable to the extent that it portrayed a non-divine Jesus. John was of no historical value, but Baur did not believe that it was 'mythical'; rather, he suggested that it was philosophical and idealistic in tone and intention. It was ideology which distinguished John from the others, not a predilection for mythology.

Strauss's mythological approach was to have a great future, but it did not fit very well with the historical rationalism of the Tübingen school, and so it was either attacked or ignored for much of the nineteenth century. Strauss himself never occupied an academic post, which is a sign of his alienation from the mood of the time. Yet the questions which he raised remained to haunt the scholarly world, and even Baur was aware that his own researches were to some extent an answer to Strauss. Strauss's voice remains an important one in the history of nineteenth-century biblical interpretation.

The demolition of the Tübingen approach

Baur's researches were highly controversial from the beginning, and were soon being attacked on all sides. Conservatives naturally rushed to defend the traditional picture of the New Testament as a unified structure, built round the teaching of Jesus given to the apostles, including Paul. One of the most valuable contributions which they made to further research was that they effectively destroyed Baur's concept of 'Jewish Christianity' as a single entity. They pointed out that the first Jewish Christians were not simply Jews; a separation between them and the synagogue had occurred from the beginning of the proclamation of the gospel. Likewise, they were not to be identified with heretical Jewish-Christian sects such as the Ebionites, who appeared only later and were not representative of mainstream

Jewish Christian thought. Baur had lumped all these together in a way which was confusing and tendentious.

Next, Baur's opponents tackled his understanding of the New Testament source material. Like many others of his time, Baur accepted the view that there had been an Aramaic gospel, now lost, which formed the basis for all three of the synoptics. However, by painstaking textual research, the classical scholar K. Lachmann showed that Mark was almost certainly the oldest gospel, and that Matthew and Luke were both dependent on it in its written (*i.e.* Greek) form. This destroyed the idea that the gospels were different interpretations, within a Hellenistic milieu, of primary Hebraic material, and forced scholars to accept that there had been a development of the synoptic tradition within a purely Hellenistic context.

Finally, a former pupil of Baur's, A. Ritschl, demonstrated (1857) that Baur's picture of the origins of 'early Catholicism' could not be supported from the available evidence. Catholic Christianity was not the fruit of conflict between Jewish and Gentile variants, but the descendant of a purely Gentile Christianity. He understood the teaching of Jesus to imply a radical break with Judaism, which was carried through by all the apostles. It was therefore wrong to suggest that Paul was in conflict with the others to any significant degree. The 'Judaizers' within the church were reactionaries out of tune with the mainstream, even though Peter, in a moment of weakness, had apparently given in to their wishes. They did not constitute a 'party' in Baur's sense of the term, and had no organized theology which they could articulate in opposition to the teaching of Paul.

Yet for all the many points on which Baur could be shown to have been wrong, his opponents did not succeed in eliminating his overall picture of the development of Christianity through a series of historical stages. In particular, the formative influence of the apostle Paul on the church came to be almost universally recognized, as did his 'mediating' position between the earlier apostles and the later church. Within the historical critical approach, Baur's theory was taken apart in detail, but the structure survived to accommodate a more rigorous examination of the evidence by later generations.

A more fundamental critique of Baur's position came from opposite ends of the theological spectrum. On the one side were the conservatives, including the orthodox confessionalists, who wanted to maintain the ideological uniformity of the New Testament. In practice, this meant opposing Baur's interpretation of Paul as a Hellenized Jew. Scholars such as A. Schlatter maintained that Paul was fully conversant with Palestinian Judaism, and developed his theology in relation to it. His was the world of the rabbis, not of the Greek philosophers, and it is in relation to rabbinical studies that his thought must be understood. Within this context, it soon became clear that faith is Paul's most important concept, in opposition to the legalistic tendencies of the Jewish establishment, and that he shared this idea with Jesus, presumably because he got it from him. On theological grounds, therefore, the Jewishness of Paul was apparent, and the essential unity between his thought and that of the earlier apostles could be made clear.

The other fundamental objection to Baur's theory came from the sceptical position of F. Overbeck. Overbeck completely rejected Baur's Hegelianism and his lingering attachment to theology. He claimed that the fact that the first Christians expected Christ's imminent return ruled out the possibility that such a theology could ever have existed. He also pointed out that the decisive shift away from primitive Christianity towards a more Hellenistic model occurred some time after the end of the New Testament period, because for a generation or so the bishops who succeeded the apostles continued to write letters in the apostolic style. There were therefore grounds for extending the apostolic age until about the middle of the second century, and positing a post-biblical period within it. On that basis, the Hellenization of the church and the 'early Catholic' synthesis could not be dated to New Testament times, and Baur's understanding of the 'tendency' of books such as Acts and the pastoral epistles must be mistaken.

The 'history of religions' approach: first phase

This approach to historical-critical problems was first developed by O. Pfleiderer (see p. 336). Its basic starting-point was the belief that early Christianity was the product of a development shared with other religions of the time. Pfleiderer himself believed that Pauline theology, which for him was the foundation of early Christianity, was a combination of Pharisaic and Diaspora Judaism, whose inconsistencies were ironed out by Paul's successors as they progressively purged Pauline thought of its Pharisaic element. He was also prepared to find in Paul influences from contemporary mystery religions, and to regard him as the product of a development in the spirit of classical antiquity. In this way, Pfleiderer thought that he could remove theological questions entirely from the history of early Christianity, and explain it in the light of what amounted to religious syncretism.

The idea that the first Christian churches were more like Greek religious associations than like synagogues was developed by E. Hatch, whose views were to have a great influence in Germany as well as in England. The discovery of the *Didache* in 1883 forced A. von Harnack to modify these ideas considerably, by recognizing that the offices of apostle, prophet and teacher were intended for the use of the whole church, and not just the local congregation, so that the 'club' model was inappropriate. However, Harnack never deserted Hatch's main thesis, in spite of this evidence which appeared to contradict it.

The break with Hatch's views, and with the 'history of religions' approach in its first phase, came only when R. Sohm (1892) insisted that the church was a universal, charismatic organization, in which the idea of the local church as a legal association had no place. For Sohm, the church was a divine body, not a human creation, and therefore manifested a spiritual unity which transcended local conditions. This essentially theological and anti-historical approach to the New Testament evidence was taken further by M. Kähler, who virtually discounted the significance of the historical Jesus altogether. As Kähler wrote in 1892:

> The historical Jesus portrayed by modern authors conceals from us the living Christ . . . What is the effect that Jesus has left behind? According to the Bible and church history, it is none other than the faith of his disciples, the conviction that in him we have the victory over guilt, sin, the tempter and death. All other effects flow from this one; we measure them by it; with it they rise and fall, stand and fall. And this conviction is summed up in the single confession: 'Christ the Lord'. With this confession, the history of New Testament times had nothing to do, and the theology of Judaism still less . . . The risen Lord is not the historical Jesus behind the Gospels, but the Christ of the apostolic proclamation, of the entire New Testament . . . The real Christ is the Christ who is preached.

Kähler's views mark the effective end of the first phase of the 'history of religions' approach, and point the way to new developments which would not come to fruition until after the First World War. Meanwhile, however, the study of the history of religions entered a second, and more sophisticated, phase.

The 'history of religions' approach: second phase

In its second phase, the 'history of religions' approach moved from being a set of related ideas and became a fully fledged system, which attracted a number of scholars to it and can legitimately be called a 'school'. Its centre of gravity was Göttingen, and its main journal was the *Theologische Rundschau,* founded in 1898 by W. Bousset and W. Heitmüller. The second phase of this approach was distinguished by the attention which it paid to the whole phenomenon of apocalyptic. Apocalyptic had been the stepchild of New Testament studies for generations, since, except to religious fanatics of various kinds, who used it for their own ends, it seemed to be incomprehensible. It certainly did not fit well into the rationalist approach of the eighteenth century, and had therefore largely been ignored.

Taking his cue from Gunkel (1895), Bousset (1896) developed the idea that the Antichrist portrayed in Revelation was a reworking of the primeval dragon myth into the expectation of a pseudo-Messiah. Nevertheless, Bousset resisted the notion that Revelation was a composite work pieced together out of the myths of the surrounding nations. To his mind, what really mattered about it was the extent to which it differed from contemporary works of that kind, and he attributed this difference to the influence of the gospel, which was singularly free of mythical accretions. The book of Revelation demonstrated what a Christian writer could and would do with sacred myths; he would transform them into something new in the light of the revelation of Christ.

This theme was pursued further by Gunkel (1903), who argued that Christianity, at least in its Pauline and Johannine forms, had been born out of a syncretistic Judaism. He wrote:

> Early Christianity is like a river that is the confluence of two great source streams: the one is specifically Israelite, it originates in the Old Testament; the other, however, flows through Judaism from foreign, oriental religions. Then added to this in the West is the Greek factor . . . It is not the Gospel of Jesus, as we know it predominantly from the Synoptics, but the early Christianity of Paul and John which is a syncretistic religion.

Meanwhile, Bousset had also taken up the theme again and applied it specifically to apocalyptic (1903). Bousset now claimed that Jewish apocalyptic was the seedbed of the Christian gospel, and that it explained a great deal of what was found in the New Testament, including in the teaching of Jesus. He wrote:

> On the one hand we have seen that it is probable that the Jewish apocalyptic is not a genuine product of Israelite religion, but that rather, Iranian apocalyptic played some part in its genesis. On the other hand, we have become aware of a far-reaching influence of Jewish apocalyptic on the New Testament.

The theological consequences of this were far-reaching. Bousset maintained that alien accretions could and should be expunged from the gospel when it was apparent that they had never really been assimilated by the Christian tradition. As an example of this, he cited belief in the devil and in evil powers generally, which he regarded as a form of Iranian dualism. But this principle was not universally valid. As Bousset wrote:

> The rule that all that has come in from alien sources is to be removed is not a universally valid one. It holds true only where what is alien has remained alien, unassimilated. But it does not hold where what was perhaps once alien has amalgamated completely with the spirit of the Gospel to form an essential and fundamental part of it. In this category belongs above all the Gospel faith in the beyond. That is part of its indispensable deposit of truth.

Later on, in his famous *Kyrios Christos* (1913), Bousset brought this line of thinking to a climax, taking on board the researches which had been done in the field of Iranian studies by R. Reitzenstein, among others. In this classic work, Bousset abolished the distinction between the New Testament canon and other early Christian writings. As far as he was now concerned, there was only one literary tradition in the early church, part of which was later canonized, and therefore preserved, but in a condition removed from its historical context. The early Christians, Bousset maintained, had a theology which they had taken over from a form of Judaism in which the Son of Man motif played a prominent role. But it was the Gentile church, and not the Jewish one, which pushed matters to their logical conclusion. They were the ones who began to worship Christ as Kyrios ('Lord'), and to claim that he was spiritually present among them, a claim opposed to the eschatological belief of Jewish Christians, which was that Jesus had gone away and would return only at the end of time. On the origin of this Kyrios cult, Bousset was quite clear:

> A survey shows that the title 'Lord' encompasses an area in the history of religions that can still be delimited with some confidence. The title penetrated the Hellenistic-Roman religion from the East. Syria and Egypt were actually its native habitats. That it plays the major role in the Egyptian-Roman worship of rulers is only one aspect of the general phenomenon . . . It seems as if the title 'Lord' was given especially to the divinities which stood at the centre of the cult of the fellowship with which we are concerned . . . Antiochene Christianity and that of the other primitive Hellenistic congregations came into being and developed in this atmosphere.

Thus for Bousset and the 'history of religions' school, the emergence of Christianity is entirely explicable in the context of Hellenistic religious history. Christian theology is an appropriation of pagan mythology, imperfectly assimilated to a select form of Judaism. Its uniqueness, and presumably also its success, can be explained by the degree to which its synthesis matched the spiritual yearnings of contemporary Greeks and Romans.

The end of this particular road can be found in the writings of W. Wrede, who pushed historical criticism to its radical limits. In his classic book, *The Messianic Secret* (1901), Wrede argued forcefully that Jesus never claimed to be the Messiah. The fact that this idea is so prominent in Mark's gospel, which is supposedly the most 'historical' of the four, Wrede explained by saying that Mark reflects the church's theological concept of the 'messianic secret', which was then read back into the teaching of Jesus. Mark came to his task as an evangelist with the tradition that Jesus was a great teacher, and also a miracle worker. He tied the two together and turned Jesus into a secret Messiah, whose true career did not begin until after the resurrection. Indeed, the real identification of Jesus with the figure of the Messiah was almost certainly the work of the apostle Paul. Writing on this subject in 1904, Wrede said:

> What was the origin of the Pauline conception of Christ? For those who see in Jesus what Paul saw, a supramundane, divine being, no problem arises. But those who take Jesus for what he was – a historical human personality – perceive an enormous gulf between this man and the Pauline Son of God. Not a

> generation has passed away since the death of Jesus, and already his form had not only grown into the infinite, but had been utterly changed. How did that come to pass? The picture of Christ did not originate in an impression of the personality of Jesus. This view has often been maintained, but never proved . . . There remains only one explanation: Paul believed in such a celestial being, in a divine Christ, before he believed in Jesus . . . Paul is to be regarded as the second founder of Christianity.

With Wrede, radical historical criticism reached its logical limit. It soon provoked serious opposition, not least from A. von Harnack (1909), who regarded its method as fundamentally flawed. By neglecting theology, Harnack claimed, the 'history of religions' school overemphasized the place of myth in the development of Christianity, and neglected the fact that the higher religions were all demythologizations of an earlier primitivism. This objection was amplified by A. Jülicher (1907), who particularly attacked Wrede's understanding of Paul. For Jülicher, it was clear that Paul had not founded a new religion, but rather had probed the logical conclusions to be drawn from Jesus' teaching. In applying them to his inherited Judaism, Paul had broken down barriers and cleared away myths; he had not constructed new ones.

The final word on the subject properly belongs to K. Deissner (1918). Deissner accepted that Paul often used terms and concepts common to the mystical mystery religions of his time, but argued that in taking them over, the apostle demythologized them. Deissner wrote:

> . . . the gnosis of mysticism is fundamentally ahistorical; it has no inner relation to the events and occurrences of history. The Pauline gnosis, on the contrary, originates . . . in the historical fact which, for the Apostle, is the focal and turning-point of all history: in the crucified Christ. As a result of this close connection with history the Apostle's gnosis is from the first divested of all mystical magic . . .

In other words, the notion that Christianity must be understood against the background of contemporary religiosity is a valuable one, but the 'history of religions' school applied it too uncritically, and in a way which ignored Christianity's basic commitment to historical realities. Its insights could therefore bear fruit only as and when they were refined and detached from a portrait of early Christianity which attributed too much to the surrounding culture and not enough to the originality of the life and teaching of Jesus himself.

Eschatology

Our survey of nineteenth- and early twentieth-century biblical interpretation must conclude with the rediscovery of the importance of eschatology in the life and ministry of Jesus. This discovery completely altered the traditional liberal view of the Messiah, because it introduced the theory that Jesus' self-understanding was radically different from what the moral philosophers of modern times could possibly imagine. This emphasis on eschatological matters began with J. Weiss, who initially (1892) followed his father-in-law A. Ritschl's views on Jesus and the 'kingdom of God' as a moral and spiritual order. But by the time the second edition of his book had appeared (1900), it was clear that Weiss had changed his mind. Weiss wrote in his introduction to that edition that 'Ritschl's idea of the kingdom of God and the idea by the same name in the proclamation of Jesus are two very different things'. Weiss went on to outline his conviction that when Jesus spoke of the kingdom of God, he envisaged the imminent arrival of the end of the world, and the beginning of an entirely new age of the Spirit. In particular, his ethical demands were but a prelude to the coming of the kingdom, and entirely subordinate to it. To quote Weiss:

> . . . the kingdom of God as Jesus saw it is a wholly supernatural entity that stands completely over against this world. It follows from this that in Jesus' thought there cannot have been any place for a development of the kingdom of God within the framework of this world. On the basis of this result it seems to be the case that the dogmatic religio-ethical use of this idea in recent theology, which has divested it completely of its originally eschatological-apocalyptic meaning, is unjustified.

Weiss attracted the ire of the liberals because his statements could not be harmonized with the spiritual kingdom of God, as portrayed by them, without attracting conservative support, which was still wedded to the idea of a kingdom of God in the present. Conservatives appreciated Weiss's stress on the future, to be sure, but were not prepared to accept that the kingdom was exclusively future in orientation. Weiss's view was shared by R. Käbisch (1893), who pointed out the eschatological dimension of Paul's preaching and tied it to contemporary Judaism.

The views of Weiss and Käbisch were tied together and popularized by A. Schweitzer (1906, 1911), who excluded any possibility that either Jesus or Paul had been influenced by forces from outside the Jewish tradition. To Schweitzer, the eschatological emphasis of the New Testament was wholly (and only) explicable from within Jewish apocalyptic. As he said (1911),

> The solution must therefore consist in leaving out of the question Greek influence in every form and in every combination, and risk the 'one-sidedness' of trying to understand the doctrine of the Apostle to the Gentiles entirely on the basis of Jewish primitive Christianity.

A more complete rejection of the 'history of religions' approach would be hard to imagine. Schweitzer may have gone too far in his reaction to nineteenth-century liberal attempts to turn Jesus into a moral bourgeois religious teacher, but slowly his contemporaries began to appreciate the force of his arguments. After the First World War the old-fashioned liberalism rapidly died out, and a new way of thinking, much more in tune with the eschatological vision, began to make its impact on New Testament interpretation.

BIBLIOGRAPHY

J. Drury (ed.), *Critics of the Bible 1724–1873* (Cambridge: Cambridge University Press, 1989).

I. Ellis, *Seven against Christ: A Study of 'Essays and Reviews'* (Leiden: Brill, 1980).

M. Granquist, 'The Role of "Common Sense" in the Hermeneutics of Moses Stuart', *Harvard Theological Review* 83 (1990), pp. 45–64.

H. Harris, *The Tübingen School* (Leicester: Apollos, 2nd edn, 1990).

W. G. Kümmel, *The New Testament: The History of the Investigation of its Problems* (London: SCM, 1972).

S. Neill and N. T. Wright, *The Interpretation of the New Testament 1861–1986* (Oxford: Oxford University Press, 1988).

J. C. O'Neill, *The Bible's Authority: A Portrait Gallery of Thinkers from Lessing to Bultmann* (Edinburgh: T. and T. Clark, 1991).

H. G. Reventlow and W. Farmer (eds.), *Biblical Studies and the Shifting of Paradigms 1850–1914* (Sheffield: Sheffield Academic Press, 1995).

H. Rottmann, 'From Baur to Wrede: The Quest for a Historical Method', *Studies in Religion/Sciences religieuses* 17 (1988), pp. 443–454.

A. Schweitzer, *The Quest of the Historical Jesus* (London: SCM, 1981) (reprint of 3rd edn of 1954).

A case study: the synoptic gospels

It was J. J. Griesbach (1774–5) who invented the term 'synoptic' to describe the close relationship between Matthew, Mark and Luke, and who made the first systematic attempt to determine what the connections between them were. Of course these similarities had been noticed long before, and been commented on. Augustine, for example, writing about AD 400, clearly distinguished the first three gospels, which 'were for the most part engaged with those things which Christ did through the vehicle of the flesh of man, and after temporal fashion', from John, who 'had in view the true divinity of the Lord in which he is the Father's equal, and directed his efforts above all to the setting forth of the divine nature in his gospel in such a way as he believed to be adequate to men's needs and notions' (*De Consensu Evangelistarum* 4).

Calvin, writing about 1555, also remarked that John was very different in style from the other three gospels, and commented on the latter as follows:

> . . . we will not say that the diversity which we perceive in the three Evangelists was the object of express arrangement, but as they intended to give an honest narrative of what they knew to be certain and undoubted, each followed that method which he reckoned best. Now as this did not happen by chance, but by the direction of Divine Providence, so under this diversity in the manner of writing the Holy Spirit suggested to them an astonishing harmony, which would almost be sufficient of itself to secure credit to them, if there were not other and stronger evidences to support their authority.

He went on to explain that in writing a commentary on the harmony of the three gospels, rather than on each one separately, he was following a method already developed by others, notably Martin Bucer. Calvin explained his approach like this:

> First, it is beyond all dispute that it is impossible to expound in a proper and successful manner, any one of the Evangelists, without comparing him with the other two; and accordingly,

> faithful and learned commentators spend a very great portion of their labour on reconciling the narratives of the three Evangelists. But as it frequently happens that persons of ordinary abilities find the comparison to be no easy matter, when it is necessary to pass at every turn from the one to the other, I thought that it might prove to be a seasonable and useful abridgement of their labour if I were to arrange the three histories in one unbroken chain, or in a single picture, in which the reader may perceive at a glance the resemblance or diversity that exists. In this way I shall leave out nothing that has been written by any of the three Evangelists; and whatever may be found in more than one of them will be collected into one place.

From there, Calvin went on to develop a scheme, based largely on the assumed priority of Matthew, according to which the synoptic gospels could be read together. Minor differences among them were explained by the different outlook of the evangelists themselves, of which Calvin was quite aware.

The first attempt to explain the origin of the synoptic gospels in a scientific way was made by J. Le Clerc (1716), but his views were ignored. Nearly two generations later, G. E. Lessing proposed (1778; published 1784) that the evangelists had independently copied an Aramaic original, now lost, which was known to the church fathers as the *Gospel of the Hebrews*, or *of the Nazarenes*. He picked up Eusebius's statement that Matthew had originally composed his gospel in Aramaic (*Hist. Eccl.* III.24.6) and claimed that the gospel we now known as Matthew was the most faithful replica of this text.

In 1782 J. B. Koppe demonstrated that Mark was not an abridgement of Matthew, and he was followed by Griesbach (1783), who claimed that Luke wrote in dependence on Matthew, and Mark in dependence on both. This was contested by G. C. Storr (1786) and by J. G. Herder (1797), both of whom argued for Marcan priority, but in general Griesbach's views prevailed among critical scholars until the 1830s.

Various suggestions were made about the possibility that the evangelists had had access to more than one source, but this idea did not really take off until 1832, when F. Schleiermacher, following the testimony of the second-century writer Papias, argued that the primal gospel was a version of what we now know as Mark, in addition to which there was a separate collection of 'sayings' of Jesus (*logia*) which did not constitute a gospel but had been used by Matthew to supplement the pre-Marcan material (and later copied by Luke).

This idea was later to form the basis of the so-called two-document hypothesis, though Schleiermacher did not think in such terms, and accepted Griesbach's solution as the most satisfactory one.

Schleiermacher was soon followed by K. Lachmann (1835), who employed detailed textual arguments to demonstrate that Mark was most likely to have been the earliest of the gospels, though probably not quite in its present form. A few years later, C. H. Weisse perfected the two-document hypothesis (1838), which he maintained were Papias's Mark (not identical with our Mark) and the Matthaean *logia.* After a number of attempts, Weisse finally came to the conclusion that Matthew, Mark and Luke had all copied Papias's Proto-Mark, and that Matthew and Luke had also made use of the *logia.* The existence of the *logia* was part of the argument that 'Mark' was the earliest gospel, since, without them, it would have been impossible to account for the great body of material common to Matthew and Luke, but absent from Mark.

This argument was helped along by the radicalism of the Tübingen school, which combined Griesbach's hypothesis of Matthaean priority with the assertion that Matthew was written after the end of the eye-witness period, and was therefore unreliable as a historical source. That drove people to look for earlier sources, and made Weisse's theory more attractive. The Tübingen school made one further contribution to synoptic criticism which must be mentioned. By positing a fundamental conflict between Jewish and Gentile Christianity, and by arguing that the synoptics stood for the former while John represented the latter, the men of Tübingen forced the academic world to choose between two traditions, only one of which had any claim to historicity. The synoptics might be erroneous in any number of respects, but they were more likely to contain historical truth than was John, which came out of an entirely different cultural context.

The next great advance in synoptic criticism was made by H. J. Holtzmann (1863), who carried on where Weisse had left off. Holtzmann produced a synthesis of contemporary German research on synoptic origins, and as able to convince most scholars that there were two basic documents underlying the three gospels: Mark, or a Proto-Mark very much like it, and a *logia* source which Holtzmann called Lambda but which Harnack would later dub 'Q' for *Quelle* (the German word for 'source'). The success of Holtzmann's theory was due not to his scholarship, which was faulty at many points, but to the prevailing mood of the time. This was the real key, as Schweitzer pointed out, to the widespread acceptance of Marcan priority. As

W. R. Farmer, the leading modern advocate of the Griesbach hypothesis, states it,

> This liberal life of Jesus [*i.e.* Proto-Mark], unencumbered by embarrassing birth legends and contradictory resurrection stories, provided the historical basis on which liberal theologians could ground their faith while they pressed with devastating effect their historico-critical attack on the two most vulnerable pillars of nineteenth century orthodoxy – the Virgin Birth and the physical Resurrection. It was therefore the Marcan hypothesis which provided the liberals a critical basis for their defense of the citadel of Faith against the attack of nineteenth century radicals like Bruno Bauer from the left, while they themselves carried on their battle with the Orthodox to the right.

After Holtzmann's time, the focus of interest in the synoptic gospels shifted to England. This was natural in a sense, because the English tradition had always stuck closely to textual and philological problems, and the synoptic question was nothing if it was not one of these. It was William Sanday who introduced Holtzmann's theory to the English-speaking world, and it was he who provided the impetus for an eventual 'solution' to the problem. Sanday was intrinsically hostile to the Tübingen approach, which was too speculative for his liking. His own theological position was closer to that of Holtzmann, who wanted to combine traditional views with critical methods in so far as this was possible, and who recoiled from the extremes of Baur and his disciples.

Sanday started a seminar in Oxford in 1894 to consider the synoptic question, and subsequent English scholarship was largely dependent on it. Among its more notable achievements were Sir John Hawkins's *Horae Synopticae* (1898, 1909) and a symposium on the issue published in 1911. The seminar's last great representative was B. H. Streeter, whose 'solution' to the synoptic problem (1924) was to become the standard one.

The first main contribution of this 'Oxford school' was to eliminate the distinction between Mark and 'Proto-Mark'. As Holtzmann was simultaneously coming to the same conclusion independently, this new theory carried the day immediately. By 1900 it was universally agreed that Mark was the earliest of the gospels, and that the other synoptists had used it, in its final form, as a source for their own work. This hypothesis was not entirely satisfactory, as there are minor divergences between Mark on the one hand, and Matthew-Luke on the other, in material which is otherwise common to them both, which make a Proto-Mark theory attractive. Nevertheless, these considerations were not regarded as significant enough to prevent the adoption of the theory that Mark as we now have it was the source of the other synoptics. It also came to be accepted that Matthew and Luke had used Mark independently of each other, just as they had also used the Q document independently.

By 1900, the material common to Matthew and Luke was generally recognized as a distinct Q source, though what this document might originally have been was not agreed. Most scholars felt that in its present form, Q is merely a series of extracts from a larger document, which may have overlapped with Marcan material. As the original Q was not available for inspection, this hypothesis remained unprovable. But as a convenient term for material common to Matthew and Luke, but absent from Mark, Q has now successfully established itself, regardless of any connection it may have with an actual document.

B. H. Streeter (1924) recognized that Q provided the biggest headache for those who wanted to maintain Marcan priority. For why would Matthew and Luke have agreed with each other against Mark, if they had both copied from him independently? That each of them differed from their model was understandable, but not that they differed in the same way. Explaining that was the problem! Streeter solved it by abandoning the two-document hypothesis in favour of a much more complex theory of synoptic origins. Working within the main lines laid down by Holtzmann and the 'Oxford school', he produced the following scheme.

1. Mark and Q were basic sources, which overlapped to some extent, though we cannot say by how much. In very broad terms, it would appear that Mark was narrative history whereas Q was a more theological source.

2. Matthew began by taking Mark and adding his own material (M). He then rearranged parts of Q in the shape of five great discourses.

3. Luke, on the other hand, started with his own material (L), to which he added extracts from Q. After that, he integrated as much of Mark as would fit.

4. Agreements between Matthew and Luke against Mark were explicable by accident and coincidence in most cases. When this would not work, Streeter maintained that Matthew and Luke may have been faithfully copying Q, from which Mark had deviated in minor particulars.

Students of the synoptic problem today are frequently bewildered by the vast range of possibilities which open up once we start to examine and compare these gospels, and many wonder whether it is really worth the effort spent on it. After all, the variations are so minor, and have so little effect on the meaning, that Calvin's solution to the problem seems closer to reality than many of the complex charts which later scholars have devised. It is perhaps because of this that more recent scholarship has given greater weight to the individual evangelists, and has tried to explain their agreements and differences in the light of their theology and purpose in writing.

This now seems to be a more fruitful avenue of research than the synoptic problem itself, but we must remember that it was a product of its age as much as anything else. It was closely paralleled by contemporary Pentateuchal criticism, so much so that 'Proto-Mark' was sometimes referred to as the *Grundschrift*. Those who pursued it most avidly were not just playing games with the text, as some recent critics have alleged. They were concerned to isolate the earliest and therefore the most authentic historical source for the life of Jesus. The fact that it seemed to be possible to find such a source, which was unconnected to any particular 'theology', supported the view that Jesus was not a theological figure in his own right, and that later developments of this kind were alien intrusions.

In this context, the character and status of Q assumed disproportionate significance. Here was a collection of sayings apparently going back to the time of Jesus himself, and probably older even than Mark. Where had Q come from? Was there a great unknown writer, of the stature of 'Second Isaiah', or were scholars merely dealing with a collection of sayings which might have been collected by the apostles and attached to the name of Jesus in their attempt to rehabilitate him after his death?

Synoptic criticism was conducted following the most exacting philological principles, but it was never detached from the theology of its age. It was the exegetical frontline of the search for the 'historical Jesus', and every conclusion it came to must be seen in that light. It was only when the 'historical Jesus' faded into myth and was abandoned that the old approach to the synoptics could be substantially reworked from a different theological perspective. What we learn from this episode is that there is no purely 'scientific' research; everything has a theological foundation, however little it may be acknowledged, and however much 'rational' criteria are used to defend a position. That lesson was to be learned again many times over in the twentieth century. The history of synoptic studies therefore stands both as a monument to the great age of historical criticism and as a foretaste of what was to come.

BIBLIOGRAPHY

A. J. Bellinzoni *et al.*, *The Two-Source Hypothesis: A Critical Appraisal* (Macon, GA: Mercer University Press, 1965).

G. W. Buchanan, 'Has the Griesbach Hypothesis been Falsified?', *Journal of Biblical Literature* 91 (1972), pp. 550–572.

R. A. Edwards, *The Theology of Q* (Philadelphia: Fortress, 1971).

W. R. Farmer, *The Synoptic Problem: A Critical Analysis* (New York: Macmillan, 1964; Dillsboro, NC: Western North Carolina Press, 1976).

S. E. Johnson, *The Griesbach Hypothesis and Redaction Criticism* (Atlanta: Scholars Press, 1991).

P. Parker, *The Gospel before Mark* (Chicago: Chicago University Press, 1953).

B. H. Streeter, *The Four Gospels: A Study of Origins* (London: Macmillan, 1924).

C. M. Tuckett, *The Revival of the Griesbach Hypothesis* (Cambridge: Cambridge University Press, 1983).

The mid-twentieth century (1918–1975)

The First World War (1914–18) marked an important turning-point in the history of the western world. The horror of the destruction demonstrated that the evil in human beings, which the progressives of the nineteenth century believed had been banished for ever, lurked just beneath the surface still. The optimism which had reigned before 1914 was gone, and few were listening to the liberals who had promoted it. As an old man, Adolf von Harnack could fulminate against Karl Barth, his former pupil and now opponent, but to little avail. Barth's call for biblical preaching based on sin, righteousness and judgment was the message which spoke to the mood of the postwar years.

The eclipse of the old-style liberalism in Europe was not paralleled in America, where the battles of the previous century were still being waged. During the 1920s, the conservatives lost control of the major denominations, and were driven from Princeton Theological Seminary, which had been their great stronghold. In Britain too, the older liberalism lasted longer, and outside Scotland the message of Barth was heard only patchily. On the other hand, Britain and America continued to lead the field in philological studies, which kept scholars close to the biblical texts, and in archaeology, which became the main bastion of conservative thought. Throughout this period, archaeologists made discoveries which appeared to confirm the biblical record, and many of those who had begun as sceptics came to accept the essential reliability of the scriptural texts.

Another important feature of the period was that scholars with very different kinds of expertise began to enter the field of biblical studies, and to propose new answers to old questions. Anthropologists, in particular, acquired a respectability which would have been scarcely imaginable before 1914, and theories of cultural development, which had been politely ignored when put forward by Herder, now returned with a new lease of life. Sociologists also made their appearance, as did economists and political scientists. Eventually, experts in these fields would make a contribution to biblical interpretation which would challenge the dominance of historical criticism, but in the 1920s that day was still a generation or more away.

The postwar world also witnessed an increasing secularization of everyday life. The churches no longer commanded the following which they had had before the war, and there was less interest in religious questions. Matters which had enthralled or divided the general public in the nineteenth century no longer interested most people. This gave professors of theology a much greater freedom than they had ever enjoyed before, but at the price of losing their audience. When nobody is listening, academics can say what they like and get away with it!

Another important feature of this period was the growth of ecumenism. By 1920 it was coming to be accepted that Protestants, at least, could and should work together at the academic level. The old confessionalism gave way to the divide between 'liberals' and 'conservatives'. The 'conservatives' had scarcely changed from what they had been a century earlier, but the 'liberals' had become much less ideological in their approach. The rise of neo-orthodoxy, which adopted a traditional confessionalism but combined it with an acceptance of modern biblical criticism, provided a bridge between the two camps, even as it was rejected by the purists in both. In reality, biblical studies were becoming increasingly secular in tone, and it ceased to matter very much what a professor's own beliefs might be.

The Second World War (1939–45) marked another important milestone in the development of biblical studies. The dominance of the German university world was shaken by the rise of Hitler and the subsequent annihilation of Germany, and it had to compete with a much expanded university network elsewhere. Even so, the huge advantage enjoyed by Germans in the field of historical criticism remained unchallenged for another generation, and when it finally gave way, the dominance of the historical critical method went with it. Yet there is no doubt that the years after 1945 witnessed the preparation of a new era in biblical studies, which became apparent in the 1970s.

These years also saw the broadening of biblical studies to include Roman Catholic and Jewish scholars on equal terms with Protestants. Roman Catholics were able to take advantage of the papal encyclical

Divino afflante Spiritu (*By the Breath of the Divine Spirit*) (1943), which gave them permission to engage in critical study of the Scriptures, provided that they remained within the dogmatic framework of the Roman church. This restriction proved to be a light one, and soon Catholic scholars were taking their place as equals alongside Protestant ones. Much the same could also be said for the Jews. The founding of the state of Israel naturally gave Jewish scholars an interest in exploring the nation's biblical past, which was an essential part of the new country's ideology. The fortuitous discovery of the Dead Sea Scrolls in 1947 gave this interest a new impetus, since for the first time a substantial body of Jewish literature, dating from New Testament times, had been discovered.

Jewish scholars quickly made their mark on both biblical studies and archaeology, and although they were generally conservative in their approach, they were by no means 'fundamentalistic'. Gentile scholars, meanwhile, were drawn to Judaism for other reasons. The terrible destruction of European Jewry during the war affected many Christians, who felt that the rediscovery of Judaism was part of their own spiritual rehabilitation. In the process they realized once more just how Jewish Jesus and his disciples had been. Contact between him and the Qumran community may have been slight, but the similarities were there for all to see. Theories put forward, more or less as guesswork, by J. Weiss and A. Schweitzer, now appeared to be confirmed by hard evidence.

Before long, Christians and Jews were working alongside each other to put together a mutually acceptable picture of first-century Judaism, a sure sign that old religious antagonisms were virtually dead. At the same time, conservative Christians were recovering from the defeats of the interwar years, and they were once more a force to be reckoned with in the scholarly world. However, there was an important difference between postwar conservatives and their forebears of a generation or more earlier. Whereas the latter had based their views on doctrinal orthodoxy, the new conservatives played by the rules which the critics had established. If they maintained conservative positions, they did so by using the same methods and style of argument as their opponents. In one sense their task was fairly simple; nineteenth-century liberals had not always been too careful about assessing the evidence properly, and had too often accepted any conclusion which discomfited the orthodox, whether it was justified or not. The new conservatives could happily point this out, and bring the academic world back to a more balanced assessment of the data.

At the same time, conservatives were suspect because their scholarship was religiously motivated. After 1945, secularization became the order of the day, and for a time it began to seem as if any religious allegiance was a hindrance to scholarly objectivity.

However, this was an artificial situation which could not last. It gradually became clear that religiously committed scholars were divided among themselves, and that the conservative revival in the churches was more apparent than real. Before long, doctrinally orthodox scholars were once more fighting for survival in their own institutions, as one conservative bastion after another felt the pressure of a new liberalism arising from within.

Some time after 1970 it became apparent that the world in which biblical scholarship had lived for over a century was no longer the same. The giants of historical-critical method, who had been trained by the classical liberals of the late nineteenth century, began to die off, and their place was taken by people who did not share the same concerns. Many of the old arguments now appeared to be boring or irrelevant; it was time to break new ground, which could be done only by entering other fields of research. The tentative interdisciplinary efforts of the 1920s now became increasingly common. New philosophies, including Marxism, began to influence the thinking of scholars, and social trends also invaded their domain. What nineteenth-century scholar could have imagined that his Greek word studies, for example, would be put to use in the service of radical feminism? This was indeed a new era, in which historical-critical scholarship lost its academic monopoly, and found itself competing with a wide range of alternatives.

9

Old Testament criticism after Wellhausen

The period and the subject

Twentieth-century Old Testament criticism has been distinguished by the important place it has given to archaeology. Before 1900, archaeology had been a weapon used against the theories of the radical critics, but it had not been integrated into a coherent interpretation of the Old Testament. To scholars trained in the tradition of De Wette, this was not to be expected. They believed that Israel had developed its religious particularity at a fairly late stage, and that the documentary records had little historical value before about 800 BC.

Once archaeological discoveries were brought to bear on Old Testament study this picture changed radically. In 1902 Friedrich Delitzsch made a celebrated speech in which he claimed that much of the material in the Pentateuch had literary parallels in Babylonian documents going back to 2000 BC and beyond. He concluded that the Israelites had borrowed cultic material from the Babylonians at a very early stage, an assertion which was anathema to many scholars, including Wellhausen, who insisted that the religion of the Bible was a unique development. The result was a 'Bible–Babel' controversy which continued for about twenty years, until it was recognized that although Delitzsch had overstated his case, his basic claims about dating were correct.

The most important representative of the new way of thinking was Hermann Gunkel. Gunkel had published his researches on the subject as early as 1901, but because of Wellhausen's opposition, his theories were largely ignored. Gunkel associated himself with the 'history of religions' school at Göttingen, and applied its methods to the Old Testament. He concluded that the documentary hypothesis, though fundamentally sound as an analysis of the present state of the text, was inadequate as a theory of Pentateuchal origins. Gunkel believed that each of the four 'documents' had a prehistory which stretched back many centuries, into an ancient oral tradition which faithfully reflected many of the conditions of Babylonia about 2000 BC. This in turn lent plausibility to Israel's claim that its patriarchs had migrated from there about that time.

Further archaeological research uncovered a 'patriarchal' society in which Abraham, Isaac and Jacob could be regarded as genuine historical figures. The early history of Israel had to be completely rewritten, taking into account the civilization and literary traditions of Babylonia, which included creation and flood stories similar to those found in Genesis. It was certainly true that the Israelites had modified these stories to suit the religion of Yahweh, but the basic pattern had an unmistakably Babylonian, and very ancient, pedigree.

Gunkel's work was supplemented by that of Albrecht Alt and Martin Noth, both of whom conducted extensive research into the origins of Israel in Palestine, and concluded that it was under Egyptian hegemony that the Hebrews established their first communities. According to them, the early Israelites banded together as a tribal confederacy, united by religious shrines. This pattern, known as an 'amphictyony', had parallels in Greece and Italy, as well as among the Philistines. Discoveries in Egypt further revealed that much of Israel's wisdom literature had parallels there, and was probably related to Egyptian sources. Even Israelite monotheism had an Egyptian parallel in the strange, ephemeral cult of Ikhnaton.

Alt and Noth, along with a number of colleagues, were also able to demonstrate that the historical books of the Old Testament were a reliable account of events from the time of David. The 'Succession Narrative' in 2 Samuel 9 – 20 was taken to be an eye-witness report, and the whole of Joshua to 2 Kings came to be classified as the 'Deuteronomic History' (1943), because of its close links with the last book of the Pentateuch.

The overall result of this was that Israel was firmly placed in its ancient near-eastern context. Egypt and Mesopotamia were shown to have had much closer links with Palestine than had previously been supposed, and a good deal of the Old Testament could be illuminated, if not entirely explained, by drawing on these sources. The result was a picture of Israelite origins which was diametrically opposed to that given by Wellhausen and his associates at two crucial points.

1. The Old Testament records were shown to be far more ancient and historically reliable than Wellhausen had imagined. Even if it could not be proved that source documents had existed before the time of Israel's monarchy, it was evident that a series of traditions, many of them undoubtedly oral, had preserved the memory of a far earlier time. It could therefore no longer be assumed that these texts represented only social and religious conditions at the time when they were put together in their present form.

2. Israelite religion was shown to be far less unique than had been previously thought. It was not the creation of a priestly caste at Jerusalem, working just before, during and shortly after the exile, but the product of a long period of development and borrowing from many sources. At first this caused considerable disquiet in the churches, because of the suspicion of syncretism, but further research soon demonstrated that Israel had not just borrowed from other religions; it had transformed the material into something which could exist only in the context of a full-blown Yahwism. In particular, scholars began to reassess the role of the Prophets. It was now agreed that they were the real creators and sustainers of Yahwism, who guaranteed the uniqueness of Israel in its cultural and historical setting.

Another very important development of this period was the spread of critical research to the Psalms. Nineteenth-century scholars had recognized that it was almost impossible to date these, and to a large extent they were ignored. One or two scholars had tried to place them very late, even as late as the time of Jesus. Here Gunkel's researches provided a new departure. By working from principles of literary criticism, Gunkel was able to classify the psalms in a way which made sense, and allowed them to be integrated into the religious life of Israel at a much earlier stage of its historical development. In particular, the traditional association of many of the psalms with David came to seem less improbable than it had been in Wellhausen's day.

The general impression left by the Old Testament critical scholarship of this period is that Israel was a fully integrated part of middle-eastern culture, and that it could trace its historical roots back to Babylonia about 2000 BC, as Genesis claimed. Its religion had ancient ties with neighbouring cults, but retained a distinctiveness which grew over time, and by the end of the exile had become absolute. The importance of archaeology and of literary and oral tradition was fully accepted, in a way which profoundly modified the standard liberal picture of a generation before. Nevertheless,

Wellhausen's basic analysis of the different sources continued to be recognized, and it provided a basic framework into which these new developments were integrated.

The interpreters and their work

The heralds of a new approach

Edward Burnett Tylor (1832–1917). This English anthropologist made a special study of 'animism', which he defined as belief in, worship of, and contact with, the souls of the departed. He wrote a number of anthropological works in the years 1865–81, which were frequently reprinted and translated into German, where they had considerable impact on the 'history of religions' school. Tylor believed that the Old Testament was the classic example of how primitive animism had developed into a sophisticated monotheistic religion.

Emile Durkheim (1858–1917) and **Max Weber** (1864–1920). Working separately, but along similar lines, Durkheim and Weber maintained that religion was a social function which provided cohesion in primitive communities. The concept of the 'holy' was a projection of community values which had to be maintained if it was to stay together. Weber was the founder of a specifically religious sociology. He reinterpreted the history of Israel by arguing that it had begun as a confederation of tribes, in which Yahweh was the link-deity. The original tribal law was eventually theologized by the prophets, in order to give it supreme authority over this tribal grouping. In Weber's view, the exile was a major social crisis, which led Israel to a new self-understanding, in which the Jews came to be regarded as outcasts and sojourners on the earth.

Wilhelm Wundt (1832–1920). This younger contemporary of Wellhausen represented a new spirit in critical research. Wundt was mainly concerned to define the nature of Israelite prophecy and examined the relationship between prophetic utterances and personal psychology. His conclusion was that the prophets were distinctive largely because of the way in which they manifested a psychological interplay between 'vision' and 'reality'. His main work, entitled *Völkerpsychologie* (*Folk Psychology*), was published in 1906.

Albert Eichhorn (1856–1926). He was a pioneer in relating the ideas of the 'history of religions' school to the Old Testament.

Eichhorn argued that it was not enough to trace source material back to its origin; one must also account for the development of the traditions over time. He was especially interested in the history of ideas, and developed this approach in a famous public disputation (1886).

James George Frazer (1854–1941). He was a British amateur archaeologist and literary critic, whose work *The Golden Bough* (1890) is still famous for the way in which it developed the folkloric approach to religion, using animism, magic, fetishism, mana and taboo as typical concepts. Today Frazer's work is regarded as pseudo-anthropology, with little scientific value, though its literary impact has been considerable. He applied his theories to the Old Testament in *Folklore in the Old Testament* (1918).

Gunkel and his followers in Germany

Hermann Gunkel (1862–1932). Originally a New Testament scholar (see p. 338), he turned to the Old Testament after 1900. In 1901 he produced a commentary on Genesis, but is now chiefly remembered for his pioneering work on the Psalms (1933), in which he expounded his literary-critical theories. Gunkel was unable to make much headway with his ideas as long as Wellhausen was alive, but after 1918 he was widely recognized as an original new voice in Old Testament scholarship. In terms of critical method he opened up a number of new paths which have continued to prove fruitful for researchers.

Gunkel believed that it was essential to examine the concept of genre (*Gattung*) to understand how the Old Testament had been constructed. In his view, the Israelites were wedded to cultural forms inherited from neighbouring peoples, which they subsequently used to express their belief that Yahweh had revealed himself uniquely to them. He believed that the early legends of Genesis could be explained as 'saga', and that the Psalms could be classified according to certain types. He also maintained that exegesis was an art, not a science, and that it was necessary to appreciate the spirit which had motivated the original writers. This spirit had nothing in common with the doctrines of Christianity; it was a practical piety closely related to the demands of everyday life.

In sharp contrast to Wellhausen, Gunkel believed that the Pentateuchal traditions reflected very ancient stages in the development of Israel. In his view it was necessary to dissect the 'documents' which Wellhausen had isolated to find their true historical context, which he called their *Sitz im Leben* ('setting in life'). This concept was to become extremely important in subsequent research.

Justus Köberle (1871–1908). This brilliant theologian died too young to make a major impact on biblical studies. He nevertheless pointed the way towards a new development of salvation history. He believed that the role of God in history had been overlooked in nineteenth-century scholarship, which was too human-centred. In his view, the uniqueness of Israel's religion was not the faith of the people (as Gunkel maintained) but the fact that God had revealed himself to them. Köberle's views had little influence at the time they were published, but became more significant with the rise of neo-orthodoxy after 1918. His major works were on sin and grace in Israel's religion (1905) and salvation history (1906).

Hugo Gressmann (1877–1927). He was a close friend of Gunkel's and, like him, a follower of the new methods of research introduced by the 'history of religions' school. He believed that Gunkel's critical methods needed further refinement, and proposed to write a history of the literary genres which Gunkel had identified. Gressmann insisted that content must be carefully studied, as well as form, and that Israel's religious uniqueness could and should be traced back to an early period. He was also in favour of using the insights of religious sociology as expounded by Weber.

Albrecht Alt (1883–1956). Professor of Old Testament at Basel (1914) and then at Leipzig (1922), his name is associated with the 'historico-geographical method', which he used in investigating the land of Palestine and its close cultural relations with Egypt. He tried to root Gunkel's theories in a Palestinian context corresponding to his theories about Israel's historical development. Among other things, he suggested that there was a covenant renewal ceremony every seven years, and that a number of the Psalms had originally been composed in connection with this. He is also known for an important study of Israelite law (1934).

Martin Noth (1902–1968). A pupil of Alt's, and later Professor at Königsberg (1930) and Bonn (1968), Noth made major advances in the 'history of traditions' research begun originally by Gunkel. His first major work was a commentary on Joshua (1938). In 1943 he suggested that Israel's tribal structure could be compared to Greek amphictyonies, and that it was a religious confederation gathered round the cult of the ark of the covenant. In 1948 he wrote a history of Pentateuchal traditions, based on this theory, and he later produced commentaries on Exodus (1959), Leviticus (1962) and Numbers (1966).

Gerhard Von Rad (1901–71). He was another pupil of Alt's, and Professor at Jena (1934), Göttingen (1945) and Heidelberg (1949). In 1938 he published a book on the form-critical problem of the Hexateuch, which pioneered the development of redaction criticism. Von Rad's main interest was to explain how the various traditions lying behind the Pentateuch had been put together, and on what principles. He exposed Gunkel's weaknesses along lines already indicated by Gressmann, and argued that the development of traditions was more important for hermeneutics than their ultimate origin. Von Rad believed that Israel's faith was the determining factor in the selection of traditional material for inclusion in the canon. This resulted in a kind of creed, expressed in the form of saga. Following the lead given by Köberle, Von Rad asserted that the entire canonical text was salvation history (*Heilsgeschichte*), and that it was futile to try to understand it in any other way.

Otto Eissfeldt (1887–1973). A pupil of both Wellhausen's and Gunkel's, he was Professor of Old Testament at Halle from 1921 to 1957. He attempted to piece together the fruits of his teachers' research in a synopsis of the Hexateuch, and was aware of the need to integrate literary criticism into a coherent history of genres. His best-known work was an introduction to the Old Testament (1934; Eng. trans. 1965).

Other German scholars

Walther Eichrodt (1890–1978). Professor at Basel from 1922, Eichrodt reacted against Gunkel's approach to the Old Testament. He focused his attention on the covenant as the central theological principle around which the Old Testament had been composed. His main concern was to uphold the doctrine of divine revelation, and to explain how God had been at work in the history of Israel. In this sense, he too was an inheritor of the mantle of Köberle.

Walter Zimmerli (1907–1983). Professor of Old Testament at Göttingen from 1951, Zimmerli wrote commentaries on Ecclesiastes (1962) and Ezekiel (1969), as well as an outline of Old Testament theology (1972). Zimmerli also believed that it was important to draw the Old Testament material together into a coherent theological whole, and he attempted to do this by isolating themes common to the text as a whole, *e.g.* the land, the priesthood and the kingship, all of which were seen as gifts of God to the nation. As a textual critic, he drew conclusions which were radical. In particular, he attempted to show that Ezekiel was a composite work put together long after the prophet's death and was only a partial reflection of his life and work.

Wilhelm Rudolph (1891–1987). Professor in Giessen (1933) and later in Münster (1946), he was a prolific commentator, and wrote works on Numbers (1934), Jeremiah (1935), Lamentations (1938), Judges (1947), Kings (1951) and Esther (1954). He was strongly opposed to the anti-Semitic tendencies of the Third Reich, but he persisted in keeping Old Testament studies alive and free from ideological pressures during that time. Like Eichrodt, he was a strong critic of the 'tradition history' approach of Gunkel and his followers, which he regarded as far too schematic in its approach to the data.

Claus Westermann (1909–). He was professor at Berlin (1949) and later at Heidelberg (1958). His major field of study has been in the prophets and in Genesis, on which he has written a major commentary (1974–82). His general approach is similar to that of Alt and Noth.

Georg Fohrer (1915–). A follower of Eissfeldt on the whole, he has been critical of attempts to push a 'history of traditions' approach to Pentateuchal criticism beyond what the texts will bear. He is the author of a significant book on the basic theological structures of the Old Testament (1972), in which his main concern has been to demonstrate that the intellectual world of ancient Israel was distinct from that of the neighbouring peoples, and that it prepared the way for the subsequent emergence of Christianity, with its demythologization of religion and its concept of a personal God.

Hans-Joachim Kraus (1918–). Professor of Old Testament at Göttingen (1968) and a pupil of Von Rad's and Noth's, he is chiefly known for his magisterial history of Old Testament criticism (1956), now in its third edition (1982), and for a commentary on the Psalms (1961).

The Scandinavians

Johannes Pedersen (1883–1977). Professor of Semitic Philology at Copenhagen (1916–50), he was deeply influenced by contemporary anthropological theories. In his four-volume history of Israel (1920, 1934) he developed his psychological and anthropological theories in a way which appeared to go against the general picture of Israel's development previously sketched by Wellhausen. He was particularly influenced by the thought that the Pentateuch might reflect Israel's worship, and interpreted Exodus 1 – 15 as a Passover liturgy, a suggestion which has been overturned by G. Fohrer.

Aage Bentzen (1894–1953). Professor of Old Testament at

Copenhagen, he studied under Pedersen. His approach to the Old Testament continued the cultic tradition, and his main works were a commentary on Daniel (1953) and an introduction to the Old Testament (1941).

Ivan Engnell (1907–64). He was a Swedish Old Testament scholar who wrote a detailed refutation of Wellhausen, using tradition-historical criticism borrowed from Noth. He rejected the idea that there were extensive documents lying behind Genesis–Numbers, and regarded 'P' as the virtual author of the text as we now have it. Engnell successfully demonstrated a number of weaknesses in Wellhausen's theory, but was not able to overturn it successfully. His main work on the Old Testament was published in Swedish in 1945.

Sigmund Mowinckel (1884–1965). A pupil of Gunkel's, he taught at Oslo from 1922. He wrote a number of works, on Jeremiah (1914), Isaiah (1921 and 1925), the Ten Commandments (1927) and prophecy (1946). However, he is chiefly famous for his work on the Psalms (1921–4 and 1951), in which he pursued Gunkel's theories and developed a full-blown theory of the liturgical origins supposedly lying behind them. His work is now regarded as a classic of its kind, though most of his conclusions have been disputed by other scholars.

The English-speaking world

Henry Wheeler Robinson (1872–1945). He taught at Rawdon Baptist College (1906) and was then Principal of Regent's Park College from 1920 until his death. He embraced critical methods and ideas, but remained firmly within the traditional framework of Baptist theology and piety. His influence on the younger generation was immense, and continued long after his death. Among his works are *The Religious Ideas of the Old Testament* (1913), *The Old Testament, its Making and Meaning* (1937) and *Inspiration and Revelation in the Old Testament* (1946). In 1935 he gave two lectures on the subject of 'corporate personality', a device which he used to try to explain the sudden shifts from singular to plural, particularly in the Psalms. The lectures were published together as *Corporate Personality in Ancient Israel* (1964), and fuelled a debate about the Hebrew perception of human personhood. Robinson suggested that the nation of Israel could project itself as a single individual, an idea which would find its fulfilment in the identification of Jesus Christ with the Jewish people. This view is no longer widely accepted, but many traces of it can be found, especially in the writings of scholars trained in the interwar period.

James Alan Montgomery (1866–1949). He taught at the Philadelphia Divinity School (1906–35) and was editor of the *Journal of Biblical Literature* (1909–13). He wrote commentaries on Daniel (1927) and on 1 and 2 Kings (1951). Perhaps his most enduring contribution to scholarship was his recognition of and support for younger scholars, notably W. F. Albright.

William Oscar Emil Oesterley (1866–1950). Professor of Hebrew and Old Testament Exegesis at King's College, London (1926–36), he was a prolific author of many standard works, including *The Evolution of the Messianic Idea* (1908), *The Religion and Worship of the Synagogue* (1911), *The Books of the Apocrypha* (1914), *Studies in Isaiah 40 – 66* (1916), *Hebrew Religion* (1930), *A History of Israel* (1932) and *An Introduction to the Books of the Old Testament* (1934). The last two works were written in conjunction with T. H. Robinson (see below). Oesterley's fluency of style and ability to synthesize complex data made his works a kind of canonical source for liberal Old Testament interpretation in mid-twentieth century Britain and America.

Leonard Elliott Elliott-Binns (1885–1963). An ordained Anglican clergyman (1915), he wrote *From Moses to Elisha* (1929), *The Jewish People and their Faith* (1929), and commentaries on Numbers (1927) and Jeremiah (1919). His work represents a typical synthesis of contemporary liberal Old Testament scholarship.

Theodore Henry Robinson (1882–1964). He taught at University College, Cardiff (1915–44), and was one of the main founders of the Society for Old Testament Study (SOTS). He was well known through his association with W. E. O. Oesterley (see above), but also wrote a number of independent works. Among them were *Prophecy and the Prophets in Ancient Israel* (1923), *The Poetry of the Old Testament* (1947), *Job and his Friends* (1954), and commentaries on Amos (1923), Matthew (1928) and Hebrews (1933).

Harold Henry Rowley (1890–1969). Professor of Hebrew Language and Literature at Manchester (1949–1959), he wrote a number of significant works, including *The Aramaic of the Old Testament* (1929), *Darius the Mede* (1935), *The Relevance of Apocalyptic* (1944), *The Missionary Message of the Old Testament* (1945), *The Rediscovery of the Old Testament* (1946) and *The Old Testament and Modern Study* (1951). He followed the main lines of the liberal orthodoxy of his time, but his work was distinguished by careful exegesis and comparison of the material with other near-eastern sources.

Godfrey Rolles Driver (1892–1975). Professor of Semitic Philology at Oxford (1938–62), he was the son of S. R. Driver. He wrote extensively on Old Testament background, including *Problems of the*

Hebrew Verbal System (1936), *Semitic Writing* (1948), *Aramaic Documents of the Fifth Century* BC (1955) and *Canaanite Myths and Legends* (1956).

Henry Snyder Gehman (1888–1981). He taught at Princeton after its reorganization along liberal lines in 1929, and is chiefly known as the editor of the *Westminster Dictionary of the Bible* (1944, 1970).

Mitchell Joseph Dahood (1922–1982). This leading Roman Catholic Old Testament scholar specialized in questions of philology. He wrote *Proverbs and Northwest Semitic Philology* (1963), *Ugaritic and the Old Testament* (1968) and a commentary on Psalms (1966–70).

John Gray (1913–). Professor of Hebrew at Aberdeen (1961–80), he has written extensively on a number of Old Testament themes, ranging from archaeology to theology. His main works include *The Legacy of Canaan: The Ras Shamra Texts* (1957, 1965), *Archaeology and the Old Testament* (1962), *The Canaanites* (1964), *A History of Jerusalem* (1969) and *The Biblical Doctrine of the Reign of God* (1979) as well as commentaries on Joshua, Judges and Ruth (1967) and on 1 and 2 Kings (1970).

The Anglo-American archaeologists and their followers

The development of archaeology in Palestine and the Middle East was the fruit of international co-operation on a vast scale between about 1890 and 1945, but there is no doubt that pride of place belongs to English-speaking scholars, who were often motivated by a desire to 'rediscover' the Bible in its original setting. The general conservatism of the English-speaking world, and the widespread public interest in archaeological research (which appeared to be 'objective' enough to overcome denominational barriers), served to equip and finance two generations of scholars, before the wider academic community took them on board. In a history of biblical interpretation, it is impossible to do justice to all these men and women, and we can include only those whose work has proved most fruitful for biblical studies as such. Nevertheless, it must be remembered that this was a major enterprise, backed by the churches, and deeply influential on English-speaking Old Testament scholarship at every level.

Palestine before 1945

The leading archaeologists of this period were **Sir Flinders Petrie** (1853–1942), **Archibald Henry Sayce** (1845–1933), **Sir John Garstang**

(1876–1956), **William Foxwell Albright** (1891–1971) and **Nelson Glueck** (1901–71). Petrie was the first systematic excavator of a Palestinian site, which he believed to have been ancient Lachish, but which is now thought to have been Eglon instead. Sayce was one of the first popularizers of the idea that the critical theories of Wellhausen and his associates had been disproved by archaeology, a view which he put forward with great vigour in *The Higher Criticism and the Verdict of the Monuments* (1894). Sayce did not prove his case in the eyes of the critics themselves, as S. R. Driver was quick to point out, but the general lines of future conflicts and developments were established by his work.

Sir John Garstang was the first director of the Palestine Antiquities department (1920–26), and under his supervision the main lines of Palestinian exploration were established. Later he conducted a series of well-publicized excavations at Jericho (1930–36), as a result of which he claimed that the city had been destroyed by the Israelites about 1400 BC, about 200 years earlier than had generally been supposed.

W. F. Albright spent most of the interwar years in Palestine, and set the tone of American scholarship for a generation. Having begun with a fairly open mind towards biblical criticism, Albright became more conservative as time went on. He was sensitive to the ambiguities often found in the biblical texts, but he regarded them as essentially trustworthy, and used them as a guide for his own archaeological research. His support for the establishment of the state of Israel in 1948 gave him a privileged position in the new order, and he was extremely influential among the first generation of Israeli archaeologists. He also took up the cudgels against the higher critics, more or less at the point where Sayce had left off. Among his many works, *The Archaeology of Palestine and the Bible* (1932) and *From Stone Age to Christianity: Monotheism and the Historical Process* (1940) remain classics. Towards the end of his life he published *Yahweh and the Gods of Canaan* (1968), a conservative study of Old Testament religious ideas in the light of the archaeological evidence.

Nelson Glueck was one of the first Jewish scholars to develop a deep interest in Palestinian archaeology, and he specialized in the nations of the surrounding desert: Ammon, Moab and Edom. He travelled constantly between 1932 and 1947, and pioneered work in these areas. His two books, *The Other Side of the Jordan* (1940) and *The River Jordan* (1946), are classic defences of the conservative view of biblical dates established by Garstang and Albright.

Egypt and Mesopotamia before 1945

The leading Egyptologist of the time, apart from Sir Flinders Petrie, who began there, was the American **James Henry Breasted** (1865–1935). Egyptology had been a flourishing discipline since the time of Napoleon, whose troops had discovered the Rosetta Stone (1799), enabling scholars to decipher hieroglyphics. Breasted tied Egyptology to the wider Orient, and contributed significantly to the view that Israel had borrowed extensively from classical Egyptian civilization. He also showed, in *The Dawn of Conscience* (1933), that there was a close connection between the book of Proverbs and the Egyptian *Teaching of Amen-em-ope*, which may have been as much as a thousand years older. This discovery forced upon scholars the realization that Israel's morality had not developed slowly over the course of time, but had probably been imported from the surrounding world. Another important Egyptologist of the period was **George Reisner** (1867–1942), who set the highest possible standards of investigation, and demonstrated their use in his work at Samaria (1908–10).

In Mesopotamia the leading role was played by **Henry Layard** (1817–94) whose excavations at Nimrud and Nineveh unearthed a huge number of cuneiform tablets which still remain one of the most important sources for biblical archaeologists, outside the Bible itself. His pioneering work was carried forward by **Sir Charles Leonard Woolley** (1880–1960), whose much-publicized excavations of Ur of the Chaldees yielded remarkable evidence in support of the biblical flood (1929).

After 1945

The period since the Second World War has seen a vast development of biblical archaeology, in which the field is less dominated by Anglo-Americans than was the case before the war. Nevertheless, some very significant names have made an important contribution to the subject, both in Palestine and elsewhere in the Middle East.

Pride of place must go to **George Ernest Wright** (1909–74), the pupil and heir of Albright. Wright founded *The Biblical Archaeologist* in 1938, and that remains the main journal in the field, with both a popular and an academic readership. From 1959 until his death, Wright's influence on American archaeology was all-pervasive, and he directed or encouraged a number of new excavations, notably at Gezer (1964–71).

Of equal importance was the work of **Kathleen Kenyon** (1906–78), whose major excavations at Jericho and Jerusalem overturned many earlier conclusions, and reopened such issues as the sack of Jericho by Joshua. Another important archaeologist of the period was **Joseph Callaway** (1920–1988), who achieved remarkable results at Ai (1972, 1980).

Further work of great significance was undertaken by **James Leon Kelso** (1892–1978), and **Paul Lapp** (1930–70). Kelso excavated Bethel (1954–60) and Lapp continued Glueck's work in Jordan. But for his early death, it is probable that he would have assumed the place of Albright and Wright in due course. His work on the edges of ancient Palestine was complemented by that of the British scholar, **Crystal Bennett** (1918–87), who added a great deal to our knowledge of Edom and the Edomites. Another prominent American, though not in the Albright mould, was **James Bennett Pritchard** (1909–), who excavated Gibeon (1956–62) and has written extensively on the subject of Old Testament archaeology.

The fruits of Anglo-American research were made known to the English-speaking world in the famous *History of Israel* by Albright's pupil **John Bright** (1908–), which has appeared in three different editions (1960, 1972, 1980). In this work, Bright wrote Israel's history along quite conservative lines, especially in the earliest periods. In sharp contrast to Wellhausen and his school, it was the post-exilic period which Bright found most difficult to analyse historically. In the third edition to his work, however, he did accept that Albright's view of Israel's origins had been questioned by the most recent research. Bright also wrote an important study, *The Authority of the Old Testament* (1967), which dealt with the use of the text in the Christian church and the ways in which it could be preached today. As with his other work, this is essentially a conservative introduction to the subject.

Another American scholar who has done much to popularize archaeological findings is **Bernhard Word Anderson** (1916–). Professor of Old Testament Theology at Princeton from 1968, he has written a number of works, including *The Living World of the Old Testament* (1957), *The Old Testament and Christian Faith* (1963), and *Creation versus Chaos* (1967). Somewhat less conservative than Bright, he has nevertheless been deeply influenced by the Albright tradition, which is clearly reflected in his work. Finally, mention should be made of **Donald John Wiseman** (1918–), whose career at the British Museum (1948) and the School of Oriental and African Studies in London (1961) did much to further the development of Assyriology and to relate it to the world of the Old Testament.

Other archaeologists

The dominance of Anglo-Americans in the archaeological field should not be allowed to obscure the very important contribution made by those of other nationalities. Among the Germans who were particularly active before the First World War, **Gustaf Dalman** (1854–1941), who directed the German Institute in Jerusalem from 1902 to 1917, must claim pride of place. Dalman's research concentrated on the daily life of the people of ancient Palestine, and he was the first to use this material as evidence in supporting his biblical studies. His massive documentation of every aspect of Palestinian culture was begun in 1928 and has still not been completed.

French archaeology was almost on a par with British, and in some areas was far ahead. The French had pioneered the study of Egyptology in the nineteenth century, and conducted widespread excavations in Syria after the First World War. Pioneer work in Palestinian archaeology was undertaken by **Louis Hugues Vincent** (1872–1960), who was long associated with the Ecole Biblique in Jerusalem, and whose *Canaan* (1907) was the most judicious assessment of the fieldwork which had been undertaken up to that date. His most famous successor was **Roland de Vaux** (1903–71), who was director of the Ecole Biblique from 1945 to 1965, and largely responsible for the investigation of Qumran, the home of the Dead Sea Scrolls. The French also undertook digs at the ancient site of Mari on the Euphrates (1933), which Albright regarded as an important link in the chain stretching from Mesopotamia to Palestine, and above all at Ugarit (from 1929), where the local language, now called Ugaritic, turned out to be one of the closest relatives of biblical Hebrew, and an invaluable source of linguistic information relating to the Old Testament.

After 1948, Israeli archaeology also became significant, and here the leading figures were **Yigael Yadin** (1917–84) and **Yohanan Aharoni** (1919–76). Working in the Albright tradition, they laid the groundwork for subsequent Israeli scholarship. Yadin became famous for his excavations at Hazor in the 1960s and early 1970s. Aharoni, who became a bitter rival of Yadin, is chiefly remembered for his close attachment to the land of Israel and its historical geography, which he related to his archaeological work. He may be compared with Alt and Noth in Germany, though his approach to the Old Testament was more conservative than theirs.

The issues

The main issues for Old Testament scholarship in the mid-twentieth century can be stated as follows.

1. *It was necessary to identify what kind of literature the Old Testament was.* Once it was agreed that the Old Testament had been pieced together at different times and from a number of sources, it had to be explained why it eventually assumed its present shape. To what extent was it 'literature', and what did that rather vague word mean in this particular context? Could it be interpreted along literary lines, in a way which was not entirely dependent on historical origin(s)? This was the question which lay at the root of the disagreement between Wellhausen and Gunkel, and it assumed greater importance as time went on. The existence of distinct literary genres, each with its own tradition and history, was increasingly regarded as the main clue to the ultimate origin of Israelite religion.

2. *It was necessary to define the proper place of archaeology within the discipline of Old Testament studies.* Here the main tensions were between those conservatives who believed that archaeology provided conclusive proof that the radical critics were wrong, and those same critics, who at first ignored archaeology altogether and then argued that because archaeological evidence was open to a variety of interpretations, it proved nothing one way or the other. Towards the end of the period there were growing signs that a broad consensus was emerging. Most scholars came to accept that archaeological evidence was important, and in the case of written materials, virtually indispensable to any reconstruction of Israelite history, but the conservatives among them were forced to admit that they could not just impose their own agenda on the evidence. Even so, however, archaeology continued to be a conservative influence on scholarship generally.

3. *It was necessary to decide the nature of the relationship between Old Testament texts and Old Testament religion.* The older view was that the religion of Yahweh had given rise to the texts, which represented a fairly late stage of Israel's development. But Gunkel's researches opened up the problem of early tradition, and its relationship with (or dependence on) non-Israelite religions. The notion that at least some of the texts might have been older than the religion, and that this religion may have adapted foreign writings to its purposes, caused great disquiet in the Christian community, because it brought into question the uniqueness of Israel and the reality of divine inspiration. Here as elsewhere, it seemed that a kind of compromise

solution would probably emerge as time went on. It would be admitted that Israel had borrowed concepts, and possibly even texts, from other cultures, but that in the process it had transformed them to suit the demands of its own religious faith. Whether this transformation took place under divine inspiration or not, was a theological matter which continued to divide those who accepted the texts as the Word of God and those who did not.

The methods of interpretation

Gattungsgeschichte *(form criticism)*

This was the type of interpretation most closely associated with H. Gunkel and his followers. The German word means 'history of genre', which is a more accurate description, but in English the term 'form criticism', which technically refers to a branch of *Gattungsgeschichte*, has been used to describe this method in general. Form criticism must be understood as a response to the source criticism which had been the mainstay of biblical studies until Wellhausen. In the nineteenth century, the main critical effort had been expended on textual analysis, which had revealed a number of different strands lying behind the canon as we now have it. Of course, this was not an accident, and Wellhausen developed a very clear idea of what these sources were, as we have seen. But he showed little appreciation of the fact that the written documents which he uncovered were literary creations, following their own internal rules of composition, and bearing witness to their own historical development.

By taking such matters into consideration, Gunkel believed that he could take the history of the canon back beyond the redactional stages in the late monarchic and exilic periods, and trace Israel's cultural growth from a much earlier time. The discoveries of ancient Babylonian and Egyptian documents similar to those found in the Old Testament, but of an undoubtedly very ancient date, strengthened Gunkel's case. It also supported his contention that Israel's religious literature was fundamentally similar to that of the surrounding peoples. In trying to assign dates and record changes in Israel's religious experience, Gunkel concentrated on what he called the text's *Sitz im Leben*, its social and historical context.

Gunkel's approach to the Old Testament had its roots in comparative religion. As far as he was concerned, the study of the Bible belonged to the study of religious phenomena in general, and 'revelation' was a concept by which peoples everywhere related their cultic, mythic and moral heritage to a divine source. To that extent, he was a late product of the religious Romanticism which had inspired J. G. Herder in the eighteenth century. At the same time, Gunkel was prepared to recognize Israel's uniqueness on the ground that the Israelites believed that there was a single God who had revealed himself to them in the course of their national history. This was the 'theological' factor which gave rise to the Israelites' faith in their own peculiar destiny. It should be noted that this kind of 'theology' eschews the metaphysical; since Gunkel did not believe that religion was about abstract philosophical speculations, he did not think that Israel was interested in them either! For him, the dogmatic teaching of the church was basically irrelevant; what mattered was the practical wisdom needed to live life as it was, on an everyday basis.

In examining the literary background of the Old Testament, Gunkel found three major areas on which he could fruitfully concentrate his attention. First, there was the legendary material of Genesis. Gunkel believed that this corresponded to the literary category which scholars call 'saga', in imitation of the Old Norse poems of that name. 'Saga' was supposed to be an art form which combined historical facts with a poetic tradition reaching deep into the ancient folklore of the nation, which had been preserved by oral tradition. The resulting literary creation served to define the nation's identity, give it a sense of purpose, and point it forward to a glorious future.

In evaluating the claims Gunkel made for 'saga', it is important to remember that he believed that such a concept existed as a literary genre, which had been consciously employed by those who created the legends. This was undoubtedly true of the Norse bards who composed the classical Scandinavian sagas, but whether the same could be said for ancient Israel was less clear. Among the first to point this out was his friend and colleague H. Gressmann. In a searching criticism of Gunkel's methods, Gressmann argued that the sagas were poetry, whereas the Pentateuch was mostly written in a kind of elevated prose. For someone as deeply concerned with form as Gunkel was, this should have been a serious difficulty, but he seems to have ignored it. Secondly, the sagas were independent literary creations with their own integrity, whereas in the Old Testament any saga-like material had been reworked into something different long before it had been committed to writing. There were therefore distinct limits to what could be claimed for 'saga' as written, rather than as oral, tradition behind the Old Testament.

There was also the problem of religion, and it was here that Gunkel was at his weakest. Quite apart from his one-sided assumptions about Israel's cult, it was not at all clear that the Norse sagas were 'religious' in any sense comparable to the Pentateuch. The Norse gods had walk-on parts in a story of great men, but this could hardly be said of the God of Israel, whose hand was the guiding factor in the movement of the Old Testament patriarchs. Gunkel himself recognized this, as when he accepted that Genesis 1 was a Babylonian creation story which had been demythologized by a priestly writer, who had made Israel's God the one supreme creator. The relationship between the divine and the human in Israel's literature was so different from anything found in 'saga' that the genre was not a helpful category to use when interpreting Genesis 1 – 11.

Gunkel's second area of interest was prophetic literature. He became convinced that prophecy was a literary genre, and not the ecstatic utterances of particularly gifted, charismatic figures. He claimed that the spoken word of prophecy crystallized on paper into recognizable forms, such as threats, scoldings and warnings. The basic genre was 'oracle', which underlay most prophetic utterances. 'Oracle' was a form in which God spoke directly to the people, using the prophet only as a means of communication. 'Oracle' was also predictive in character, and here Gunkel parted company with the liberal scholarship of an earlier generation. He was not content to portray the prophets as teachers and guardians of an established moral and cultic order; for him they were also, and necessarily, heralds of future events, both good and evil.

Gunkel recognized that not everything in the prophetic literature could be explained in this way, and that the prophets had borrowed widely from the literature and folk traditions of their time. In particular, they had made considerable use of songs, both sacred and profane. In the course of adapting these, however, the prophets had imbued them with their own spirit. This in turn had the effect of giving Hebrew lyric style a decidedly prophetic tinge, which can be seen in the Psalms.

Gunkel further believed that some of these prophetic utterances had been made in the context of public worship. For example, he accepted that Joel 1 – 2 was a cultic lament presented in the form of prophecy, which showed that Joel had made use of liturgical elements in his work. But Gunkel did not develop his ideas on the subject very far. That was to be the work of his pupil and disciple, S. Mowinckel, who recognized Gunkel's hesitation in this area and admonished him for it, claiming that it was due to the lingering influence of Wellhausen (and others like him) on his mind. Mowinckel pursued Gunkel's idea that there was an intimate connection between prophecy and worship, and this governed his approach to both the prophets and the Psalter. Mowinckel thought that there were 'temple prophets' in Jerusalem who were disciples of Isaiah, and that they were responsible for many of the liturgical elements in that prophetic book. He also believed that these prophets had contributed to books such as Nahum, Micah and Habakkuk, by drawing on similar cultic and legal material.

Mowinckel succeeded in demonstrating that there were a number of intimate connections between prophetic literature on the one hand, and both the Pentateuch and the Psalter on the other, but his suggestion that this was because of the overriding influence of 'temple prophets' at Jerusalem is more doubtful. What is more likely is that the temple cult provided the different writers with a common focus, so that when they composed their material they had it in mind as an important backdrop. To that extent, Mowinckel's work represented a genuine advance in Old Testament study.

Subsequent scholarship has both modified and extended Mowinckel's insights. On the one hand, it has been generally recognized that some prophecy may originally have been written, not oral. This eliminated the need to posit a period of oral transmission, but it did not seriously alter the approach of form criticism. More significant was the rush to demonstrate that everything in the prophets was connected to a cultic source, as if prophecy could be explained entirely within the context of Israel's worship. By going against the nineteenth-century view of the prophets, which had seen them as free and somewhat wild spirits frequently opposed to the priestly cult, there is no doubt that the new emphasis served to correct an imbalance. But when prophetic utterances about warfare were interpreted as references to mythological themes transmitted to the prophets through the medium of cultic imagery, things had gone too far. The relationship between the prophets and the cult was undoubtedly closer than had previously been recognized, but that did not mean that the prophets were entirely dependent on what happened in the temple at Jerusalem.

Gunkel's third area of concentration, and the one which proved to be most fruitful for his theories, was the Psalter. He was convinced that the prophetic use of lyrical texts from early Israel had so transformed the genre that by the time the Psalter came to be written Hebrew lyric was permeated by the prophetic spirit. The Psalter was a part of the Old Testament which had more or less been ignored by

Wellhausen and his followers because of the extreme difficulty in applying historical criteria to most of the individual psalms. By using form criticism, Gunkel found a way to explain the Psalter in terms of its *Sitz im Leben* in the religious life of Israel. Precise dating would still cause problems, but at least it could be suggested how and when the various literary types came into being. This would make it possible to reconstruct an overall picture of psalm development which mirrored the religious evolution of the nation in general.

Gunkel's analysis of the Psalter produced the following categories of psalm.

1. *Hymns.* These are songs of praise, and constitute the oldest layer of Israel's lyric poetry, as can be seen from the Song of Miriam (Ex. 15:21), and the Song of Deborah (Jdg. 5). The prophets, especially Isaiah, have many examples of such hymns. In the Psalter itself are Psalms 19:1–6; 29; 33; 40; 47; 96 and 103 – 105. Of them, Gunkel wrote:

> The predominant mood in all the Hymns is the enthusiastic but reverent adoration of the glorious and awe-inspiring God. To a certain extent, it might be said that the purpose of the Hymns was to give pleasure to Yahweh, whom they extol with such exuberance. For just as the king at a festive meal would not dispense with songs sung in his praise, so Yahweh was offered songs whenever one celebrated his festivals or offered him sacrifice. But also for the singers themselves the songs were beneficial. The religious idea, when expressed vocally, became stronger, and the individual was caught up in the mood of the throng.

A special subset of this type was the Eschatological Hymn, of which Gunkel found several examples. These hymns looked forward to the end of time, and were composed late in Israel's history. Indeed, they were still being written in New Testament times, as the hymns recorded in Luke 1 demonstrate. Examples in the Psalter include Psalms 46; 82; 85; 126 and 149.

2. *Community Laments.* Second in age to the Hymns are the Laments of the community, which were called forth by the various calamities which it occasionally suffered. This type is also well represented in the Prophets, who frequently had to call on the people to lament for their sins. Gunkel claimed that special days were set aside each year for lamentation, which thus assumed a ritual character very early (*cf.* 1 Ki. 21:9). It should be noted, however, that

of the Lamentations of Jeremiah, only the fifth was regarded as a Community Lament by Gunkel. In the Psalter there are examples in Psalms 44; 60:1–5; 74; 79; 80; 89:38–52 and 94.

3. *Songs of the Individual I: Thanksgivings.* Here Gunkel was forced to argue that individual psalms were possible. It had been argued by R. Smend (1888) that the 'I' of the Psalter was a personification of the community, and not the expression of a single individual. Gunkel admitted that there were cases where this was so, but argued that most of the time the 'I' ought to be read in its natural sense, as the voice of the poet himself. Once again there were prophetic examples of this type, though they were few (*cf.* Jon. 2:2–9). Nevertheless they were of great antiquity, and were almost certainly borrowed from the surrounding nations. As Gunkel said,

> Arguing in support of the great antiquity of this entire literary type is the fact that the Egyptian inscriptions and the Phoenician votive tablets, as well as the so-called 'Job Psalm' (which is really a Thanksgiving Song), contain the same narrative structure. One can see from such examples that in the case of this type of cultic poem we are not dealing with distinctively Israelite structures but with a type of poetic composition that was shared with the nations surrounding Israel and was certainly practised in Israel from earliest times.

In the Psalter they are represented by Psalms 18; 30; 40; 66; 100; 107; 116; 118; 136 and 138.

4. *Songs of the Individual II: Laments.* This type also occurs quite frequently in the Psalter, and according to Gunkel it exhibits a very pronounced literary style. The same images recur, for example, of a suppliant who in the middle of some illness must at the same time complain of his enemies who are persecuting and slandering him. In general, the psalmists assert their innocence in the face of these trials (*e.g.* Pss. 17; 26), though occasionally they confess their guilt instead (Ps. 51). The order of the psalms is also characteristic, beginning with a lament, followed by a prayer of passionate intensity, and concluding with the certainty of deliverance, uttered in a jubilant tone. Examples of this type are Psalms 3; 6; 17; 22; 51; 69; 88; 94; 121; 123 and 130.

5. *Minor types: Entrance Liturgies, Torah Songs, Blessings.* Psalms 15 and 24 are examples of these, being characterized by a call to purity as the holy place is approached.

6. *Royal Psalms.* These find parallels in both Egypt and Babylonia,

and were originally prayers offered for the king. Some followers of Wellhausen had dated them late, arguing that the 'king' is a poetic figure for the nation of Israel, but Gunkel rejected this on the ground that parallels in other literature made an early date more likely. In the Psalter they are Psalms 2; 18; 20; 21; 45; 72; 101; 110; 132 and 144:1–11. Gunkel recognized that they contained a good deal of variety, representing, as they did, different aspects of royal life. The identification of the Royal Psalms led to a great reappraisal of the role of the king in Israel. No longer was he seen as a purely secular ruler, but as a cult figure in his own right. At the same time, attempts to link this new awareness with kingship elsewhere in the Middle East were less successful. Different nations had different customs, and Israel could not be directly compared with its neighbours. So the Royal Psalms were typical in showing how Israel borrowed foreign ideas; they were also distinctive, in that there was nothing quite like them elsewhere.

7. *Non-liturgical psalms.* Gunkel dubbed these 'Spiritual Songs' and regarded them as the last to be written and the closest to the spirit of the gospel. Psalm 50, in which Yahweh states explicitly that he does not want sacrifice and ceremonies, is a typical example of these.

8. *Mixed types.* A number of psalms are mixed types, containing elements taken from two or more of the above categories. Most typical of these are the psalms depicting Yahweh's enthronement, which combine the Hymns with the Royal Psalms, and elevate praise for the earthly monarch into praise to the heavenly one. Psalms 47; 93 and 95 – 99 are all examples of this. In some cases they overlap with other types; Psalm 18 is also an individual thanksgiving, and Psalms 89:46–51 and 144:1–11 are also individual laments. Other psalms combine lamentation with thanksgiving (Ps. 22) or lamentation with a hymn (Pss. 44; 104). Very occasionally, a psalm will be combined with a different genre altogether, as for example Psalm 32, which is a mixture of a thanksgiving and a wisdom poem.

Gunkel was followed by Mowinckel, who developed these ideas still further. Mowinckel was deeply influenced by anthropological ideas, and looked for signs of a primitive cult in many of the psalms. He believed that all but a few of the psalms had been composed for public worship, and therefore tried to link them with a particular cultic practice. He concentrated on the Royal Psalms, which he thought reflected the semi-religious status of the king. Mowinckel singled out the psalms in which Yahweh was enthroned as king, and argued that these were sung at an annual New Year festival, when Yahweh was ritually 'enthroned'. Mowinckel drew on Babylonian analogies to prove that such a festival existed, and he even argued that aspects of it contributed to the origin of eschatology in Israel. But in spite of his pleas, few scholars have followed him in this, and the idea of a New Year enthronement festival has generally been rejected.

Mowinckel differed from Gunkel in his belief that it was the Psalter which had inspired the prophets, and not the other way round. In Mowinckel's view, even the so-called Eschatological Hymns were manifestations of the temple cult, which the prophets later borrowed. Such a reconstruction meant that the Psalter had to be dated relatively early, and the prophets relatively late – an idea which did not commend itself to everyone.

We may therefore conclude by saying that the work of the form critics was most fruitful in the prophets and the Psalter, especially in the latter, where it opened up a whole new avenue of research, but has proved to be of rather limited usefulness elsewhere.

The impact of archaeology

We have already noted that archaeology exerted an enormous influence on Old Testament research in the mid-twentieth century. When trying to evaluate this, we must always remember that archaeology is an independent discipline, governed by canons and standards which may not be directly applicable to biblical studies. This was not always clearly understood by those archaeologists who went to the Middle East with the specific intention of 'digging up the Bible'. From a strictly archaeological point of view there is no such discipline as 'biblical archaeology', because each of the countries mentioned in the Bible has its own history, which must be interpreted as such. But the early explorers of the Middle East did not see things in that way. For them, Mesopotamia and Syria were of interest only because the Bible mentioned them, and everything they discovered was interpreted in that light. This produced a number of serious distortions from which the archaeology of the region has only slowly recovered.

For one thing, it meant that sites mentioned in the Bible were looked for and dug up for that reason, and nobody bothered to consider how they fitted into the wider culture of the time. It is only because of its prominence in the Bible that Jericho is the most excavated site in Palestine; it is far from having been the most important city. For the same reason, the sites of Ur, Babylon and Nineveh were excavated long before lesser-known places, although the finds from Mari or Ugarit are just as important for a proper reconstruction of the patriarchal age. It is only because they were not mentioned in the Bible that nobody took an interest in them until much later.

It is also true that archaeological techniques were not perfected for a long time. The methods of digging, the importance of pottery as evidence, and the criteria used to date the various historical layers of debris were being worked out even as the discoveries intended to support the historicity of the Bible were being made. This sometimes produced confusion, as for example at Jericho, where faulty techniques led some scholars to conclude that they had found evidence for Joshua's sack of the city, when in fact they had not. Given that these scholars were deliberately looking for such evidence, and were determined to interpret whatever they found in a way which would support their quest, we can begin to understand how problematic the use of archaeology was. Only very slowly, and very painfully, has it become possible to disentangle the evidence from the propaganda of those who discovered it, and make a reasoned assessment of the value of the finds.

At the same time, we must also remember that there was a scholarly prejudice against archaeology which had to be overcome. Wellhausen and his associates dismissed it as irrelevant; they had no understanding of the importance of things such as pottery, and laughed at their colleagues for taking such 'trivia' seriously. Rooted as they were in a literary and philological tradition, they could not break out of it far enough to realize the significance of non-linguistic evidence for the study of the Bible. If it is possible to accuse the early archaeologists of naïveté, it is equally possible to accuse contemporary biblical scholars of snobbish ignorance.

After 1918 this situation began to change, thanks mainly to the work of A. Alt and M. Noth. Alt realized early on that it was wrong to suppose that the main influence on ancient Israel had come from Mesopotamia. There were certainly contacts in that direction, though most of them were either very early (*i.e.* dating back to patriarchal times), or quite late (exilic and post-exilic). In the formative centuries of its national existence, Israel had been much more closely linked with Egypt, a fact testified to by the Bible itself. Alt therefore believed that it was more important to look for Egyptian influences on Israel's development than for Mesopotamian ones. Alt also had a deep sense of the importance of Palestinian topography for Israel's economic and political relations. The links between the hill-country and the coastal plain, between the Jordan valley and the desert, were ancient and constant. Alt had the additional advantage of being able to visit Palestine and observe how commercial relations worked just before the ancient patterns were disturbed by modern development in the region. He was therefore able to observe at first hand how trade routes, for example, determined the evolution of social organization.

By applying his theories to the biblical text, Alt was able to suggest that Israel and Judah had originally existed as separate tribal confederacies, which banded together temporarily under David and Solomon before going back to their original state. He further suggested that the two kingdoms had different conceptions of monarchy. Judah was a dynastic state, tied to the fortunes of the house of David. But Israel had an elective monarchy, in which any charismatic figure might be chosen king.

Alt's methods also had a special importance for the examination of the vexed question of Israel's invasion of Canaan. Because of the ambiguities surrounding the excavations at Jericho, most scholars were coming to believe that Israel had invaded the land in two stages, and from different directions. The first wave of invaders had come from the south, directly out of the Sinaitic desert. A second wave, led by Joshua, had come from the East somewhat later. Alt completely altered this view by his study of Egyptian sources and the relationship which existed between Egypt and the Canaanite cities. His contention was that the Israelite 'invasion' was in fact a very slow penetration by sheep-farming bedouin, who gradually occupied more and more territory until they came to be the principal inhabitants of the land. It was for this reason, argued Alt, that the tribal structure retained such great importance, even after the apparent consolidation of the nation into a single monarchy. In reality, he argued, the scattered tribes continued to form the basis of society for a very long time afterwards.

Alt's researches were taken up and developed further by M. Noth. Noth argued on the basis of philological evidence that the names of the different tribes could have arisen only on Palestinian soil. The tribal organization was therefore one which had been created *after* the invasion (if indeed there had really been an invasion) and not before it. Noth also realized that the unity of Israel as a nation could be explained only in religious terms, and he therefore developed the theory that Israel had originally been a religious confederacy grouped around the Ark of the Covenant. The Ark itself moved from place to place, until it finally came to rest at Jerusalem, which then became the centre of Israel's national life. But earlier resting-places of the Ark were not forgotten, and cultic observances continued at different places with which it had once been associated (Shechem being Noth's chief example).

Noth's method has suffered both from lack of evidence to support his theories and from the enthusiasm of his many disciples, who have sought to portray every aspect of Israel's life in terms of a loose religious confederacy. This has resulted in a number of distortions, which have made it more rather than less difficult to disentangle Israel's origins from those of the surrounding peoples. As so often in Old Testament research, comparisons made with other nations led some scholars to impose a pattern on Israel which did not fit the evidence. Israel was a nation *sui generis*, with no real counterparts elsewhere. To compare its institutions with those of ancient Greece, for example, could only lead to misunderstanding. Nevertheless, Noth's method did underline the fact that Israel was conscious of its existence as a religious community with no fixed centre long before it acquired the attributes of a nation state. Because of this prior consciousness, the nation state was never fundamental to Israel's existence, and this enabled it to survive not only the exile, but centuries of dispersion, when other ancient nations collapsed and disappeared.

A curious side-effect of Alt's and Noth's historical researches was that they revealed to what extent the 'historical' books of the Old Testament were really religious compositions. The more these scholars probed their evidence in an attempt to relate it to the archaeology of Palestine, the more they realized that it reflected a very particular interpretation of events. There was a great deal more to the history of the period than what the Old Testament revealed, and a modern 'history of Israel' would use the biblical texts only as one piece of evidence among many. A notorious example of this is the case of Omri, who was one of the most important kings of Israel, but who is dismissed in a mere eight verses in 1 Kings 16:21–28. Likewise, the biblical record gives only a very incomplete account of the reign of Josiah, who seems to have reconquered most of the Davidic kingdom, and who played an important role on the stage of international politics. It is not that what the Bible says about these kings is untrue; it is merely that it reflects priorities different from those of most modern historians.

These priorities could only be religious ones, of course, and so archaeology inadvertently contributed to a rediscovery of the importance of religion for Israel's chroniclers. This is turn reintroduced theological considerations to Old Testament study in a way which had become slightly unusual, and led to the next important stage in the development of critical research. From the archaeological standpoint, the most important contributor to this development was W. F. Albright. Albright firmly believed that archaeology offered important clues to the evolution of intellectual ideas, and he tried to demonstrate this by showing how Israel's monotheism had developed first out of primitive Babylonian sources, and had later been strengthened by the curious episode of Ikhnaton (Akhnaten) in Egypt (fourteenth century BC). Moses, who may have been a refugee escaping from the persecution which befell the followers of Ikhnaton's monotheism after his death, was certainly the founder of Israel's faith, which maintained itself against the intrusion of Canaanite practices for several centuries. Such a view of Israel's religious history was almost directly contrary to Wellhausen's, and it greatly strengthened the position of those conservatives who viewed Old Testament monotheism as divine revelation and not as the product of lengthy historical evolution.

Redaction criticism and Old Testament theology

The increasing emphasis on religious factors in Old Testament interpretation led to a number of new developments. For a start, literary criticism played a much greater role. The recognition of different sources and genres drew attention to the way in which the diversity of material had been put together. Following a number of studies which showed the importance of the religious theme for different parts of the historical narrative, a synthesis was attempted by G. Von Rad in 1938. Von Rad demonstrated how important was the theological outlook of the text's final redactors, who had evidently chosen and adapted their material for a particular purpose. In the 'historical' books this was fairly obvious; they wanted to demonstrate how the cult had been centred on Jerusalem since the time of David, and thus how important the Davidic monarchy was to Israel's national identity. What we would today call the link between 'church and state' was their chosen theme, and they endeavoured to show how it worked to the advantage of both. The deeds of the various kings were therefore recorded only to the extent that they affected this link; other things were more or less ignored.

This new approach inevitably focused sharply on the theological views of the redactors, which is why redaction criticism, as Von Rad's method is now called, led to a new interest in Old Testament theology. Wellhausen and his contemporaries, including Gunkel, had also been interested in this subject, but in a different way. For them, it was not the internal consistency of the Old Testament which mattered, but the contribution which Israel had made to the development of universal religious insights. These critics had believed that the end-product of Israel's religious history was an ethical monotheism, which in post-biblical times had produced the most important of the great world religions. For them, the moral code was more important than the theology, since their practical bent led them to regard dogmatics as a tiresome irrelevance. Of course, there was a great deal in the text which by our standards would be considered 'immoral', and not a little of this was associated with Yahweh; in particular, his commands to Israel to slay its (and his) enemies. However, Wellhausen and his contemporaries believed that these episodes could be written off as unfortunate aberrations.

The inadequacy of this approach became apparent when the discoveries of Egyptology were applied to Old Testament study. If Israelite writers had 'purified' their Babylonian inheritance, and created a higher and more consistent moral code out of it, the same could not be said for the Egyptian contribution to Israel's literature. It came as a great surprise to J. Breasted when he realized that Egypt had moral standards higher than those of the Ten Commandments at least a thousand years before Moses! Discoveries of this kind made it impossible to base Israel's uniqueness on its moral superiority, and this undercut the traditional liberal approach to religious concerns.

At the same time, scholars also developed an appreciation of Israel's distinctiveness rooted in its historical self-understanding. Von Rad argued that the earliest theological statements in Israel could be found in a number of short passages (*e.g.* Dt. 6:20–24; 26:5–9 and Jos. 24:2–13) which constituted a kind of 'creed'. This 'creed' was not a philosophical statement of various abstract doctrines, but a record of the great acts of Yahweh in the history of the nation. What sustained Israel was its belief that God had intervened in history on its behalf, and that he continued to guide and direct the nation's fortunes. The Pentateuch was thus fundamentally a *Heilsgeschichte* ('salvation history'), in which historical events and religious faith blended into one. This salvation history was given in its most basic form in the Pentateuch, which remained the fundamental statement of Israel's faith. The prophets were familiar with this tradition, and saw their own activity in the light of it. In the years up to and including the exile, they interpreted the decline in the nation's fortunes in terms of disobedience to Yahweh's commands as revealed in the Torah. Later, they changed their tune to some extent, and interpreted the restoration under Cyrus as a new beginning for Israel, in which God showed that his ancient promise of election had not been forgotten. Now, however, it was interpreted on a different basis, and with a more explicitly eschatological hope. Von Rad saw this hope as having been realized in Jesus Christ, and in this way he sought to integrate the Old Testament with the New in an overarching biblical theology.

Von Rad's essentially historical approach was complemented by that of W. Eichrodt, who started from a more systematic angle. Eichrodt disliked the way scholars had carved up the Old Testament into scarcely related fragments, and he sought to find the underlying principle of unity which could explain the theology of the text as a whole. For him, this principle was the covenant, which he proceeded to develop. It is a measure of how far Protestant Old Testament research had grown away from the insights of the Reformation that so few scholars noticed that the covenant concept was really a return to the theology of the seventeenth century, with the results of biblical criticism thrown in for good measure. Other scholars were quick to point out that the word 'covenant' occurred very unevenly in the Old Testament, but Eichrodt sensibly refused to allow his research to depend on the use of a single word. Instead, he used the term as a convenient label to describe something which was all-pervasive in the Old Testament – Israel's sense of its deep-seated personal relationship with God. Through all the ups and downs of its historical existence, Israel retained this fundamental belief, which could legitimately be regarded as the constant factor linking very different historical situations and beliefs.

However, it must also be recognized that the legitimacy of constructing a single Old Testament theology continued to be questioned, and from two diametrically opposite angles. Critical scholars were constantly afraid that theologians might be trying to impose a logical system on data which resisted any such neat classification, whereas conservative Christians could not accept any theology which was not ultimately Christological in emphasis. Of course, the historical-critical analysis of the Old Testament virtually excluded that, since to read it in its original context ruled out the Christ theme, except perhaps as an eschatological, messianic hope. Yet the fact remains that there is no religious tradition which now rests exclusively on the Old Testament as its authoritative source material. Judaism has the Mishnah and the Talmud to guide it, and in practice these are of greater importance than the Torah. Christianity has the New Testament, which both fulfils and abolishes the Old. Islam has the Qur'an, which claims to supplement and replace both the Old and the New Testaments, and sects of more recent origin, such as Mormonism, also modify the Old Testament in similar ways.

For the Christian teacher and preacher, the issue was very clearly stated by J. Bright in his book *The Authority of the Old Testament* (1967). After reviewing the problems posed by critical research and the solutions offered by the different Christian traditions, both liberal and conservative, Bright opts for an essentially conservative approach which nevertheless takes modern critical study seriously. His main focus is on the needs of the preacher, who must find in the text a message of contemporary relevance without distorting the original meaning. Individual interpreters will disagree with this or that aspect of his thesis, but his main line of approach is helpful in the way in which it seeks to integrate traditional concerns with modern discoveries and needs. Bright sums it up thus (p. 201): 'The Old Testament is the history of our own heritage of faith – but before Christ; it is the record of the dealings of our God and a revelation of our God – but before Christ.' He goes on to develop what he means as follows (p. 202):

> Neither aspect of this twofold relationship is for a moment to be lost from view in attempting to interpret the Old Testament. To do so is ruinous. To ignore the continuity is to forget that the New Testament has claimed the Old, to rip the Gospel from its anchorage in history and, thereby, to mutilate it. To ignore the discontinuity is to forget the claim of the New Testament to be 'New'; it is also to level the Testaments, stop history dead in its tracks, and ignore the fact that we do not and cannot practice the religion of old Israel. Both aspects are to be held in view in dealing with all parts of the Old Testament. It is not as if some of its texts were continuous with the New Testament, others discontinuous – though it is true that now one feature predominates, now the other. In each of its texts the Old Testament stands with the New in a relationship both of continuity and of discontinuity. At no place may we forget either of these aspects, for under both the Old Testament is a book that points to Christ and, at the same time, speaks its indispensable word to men in Christ.

With this statement we return to the classical theme of Christian biblical interpretation: the relationship of the New Testament to the

Old in Christ. Even after two centuries of historical criticism, the ancient challenge to the would-be preacher of the gospel remains fundamentally unaltered.

BIBLIOGRAPHY

J. Bright, *The Authority of the Old Testament* (Nashville: Abingdon, 1967).

R. E. Clements, *A Century of Old Testament Study* (Guildford: Lutterworth, 1976).

A. H. J. Gunneweg, *Vom Verstehen des Alten Testaments* (Göttingen: Vandenhoeck und Ruprecht, 2nd edn, 1988).

M. R. Hauge, 'Sigmund Mowinckel and the Psalms: A Query into his Concern', *Scandinavian Journal of the Old Testament* 2 (1988), pp. 56–71.

W. Klatt, *Hermann Gunkel* (Göttingen: Vandenhoeck und Ruprecht, 1969).

E. G. Kraeling, *The Old Testament since the Reformation* (London: Lutterworth, 1955).

H. J. Kraus, *Geschichte der historisch-kritischen Forschung des Alten Testaments* (Neukirchen and Vluyn: Neukirchener Verlag, 3rd edn, 1982).

D. Kvale and D. Rian, *Sigmund Mowinckel's Life and Works: A Bibliography* (Oslo: University of Oslo Press, 1984).

R. Moorey, *A Century of Biblical Archaeology* (Cambridge: Lutterworth, 1991).

J. C. O'Neill, *The Bible's Authority* (Edinburgh: T. and T. Clark, 1991).

J. D. Smart, *The Past, Present and Future of Biblical Theology* (Philadelphia: Westminster, 1979).

G. W. Van Beek (ed.), *The Scholarship of William Foxwell Albright* (Atlanta: Scholars Press, 1989).

C. Westermann, *Essays on Old Testament Interpretation* (Richmond, VA: John Knox, 1964).

A case study: the Psalms

There can be no doubt that one of the major achievements of twentieth-century Old Testament criticism was a radically new way of reading the Psalms and the wisdom literature of Israel. The rise of historical criticism in the nineteenth century had led to certain difficulties where these books were concerned, because they could not readily be placed in a particular historical context. Once it was agreed that David was not the author of the Psalms, or Solomon the author of the wisdom literature, the field was open to any number of suggestions regarding the date and original purpose of that literature. We may illustrate this by presenting the approach of a historical critic writing before the rise of form criticism, and then look at the changes which that produced.

In Oxford in 1889 T. K. Cheyne delivered a series of Bampton Lectures on the Psalms, and these were published in 1891. Cheyne had a particular religious motivation behind his work; he was an evangelical churchman, concerned to demonstrate and apply the authority of Holy Scripture as the supreme rule of faith and life in the church. In the context of the time, this meant that he was an opponent of Anglo-Catholicism, with its emphasis on tradition and church doctrine. In his introduction to the lectures, Cheyne wrote:

> It is, I suppose, of the essence of evangelical Protestantism that the religious teaching received from without should be submitted by the individual Christian to the test of its agreement with the 'living oracles' . . . It is incumbent upon him to take nothing upon authority, but in humble reliance upon the Spirit's all-powerful help, by the critical study of the Scriptures and by personal experience, to discover for himself, and to help his fellows to discover for themselves, what are the really vital elements of Church doctrine. I do not say that he will soon come to an end of that study, but I do say that, from the Protestant point of view, he must begin it. And that which is the duty of ordinary evangelical Churchmen must surely be still more the duty of those who are in High-church positions. It is for them not to be continually appealing to the letter of Church-formularies, but first to study the Scriptures both critically and spiritually, and then to initiate a higher exegesis of the formularies to correspond to the higher criticism and exegesis of the Scriptures . . . A true Evangelical begins, not with the Prayer-book and Articles, but with the Holy Scriptures. And a reforming Evangelical should prove his Protestant sincerity by adopting modern historical principles of Bible-criticism.

For Cheyne, as for Robertson Smith and other evangelicals of their type, the historical criticism of the Bible was an essential ingredient of their faith. Cheyne returned to this theme in his sixth lecture, where he comments as follows:

> Should anyone still ask, What has the historical origin of the Psalter to do with the defence of Christian truth? I need only reply, How could we possibly use the Book of Psalms as a record of Church theology until we had critically proved that it belonged to the period of the Jewish Church? Now that this proof has been given (the 18th being, as it would seem, the only possible pre-Exile psalm – and even this is late enough to be called in a certain sense a Church composition), we can venture to say that it is the consciousness of the Church, or of some leading members of the Church, which finds a voice in every part of the Psalter.

To the modern reader, it comes as something of a surprise to discover that Cheyne, who rejected church authority when it applied to Christian times, was prepared to accept it – and indeed, to insist upon it – when it came to the 'Jewish Church', by which he meant post-exilic Judaism. In insisting on such a late date for the entire Psalter, Cheyne was adopting a position more radical even than that of many contemporary German critics. For example, he rejected Ewald's suggestion, made in 1835, that Psalm 50 was connected with the Josianic reform of 622 BC. Ewald had argued his case on the basis of similarities between the psalm and the teaching of Jeremiah, but although Cheyne accepted this to some extent, he rejected the suggestion that Jeremiah's theology could have been absorbed in such depth before the exile. In favour of a post-exilic date, he mentioned a number of features found in the psalm, such as the description of a theophany, the importance of Jeremiah's ideas, and the widespread formalism and hypocrisy which were supposed to have characterized the post-exilic period. To the objection that Ezra and Nehemiah would hardly have had an opponent of this calibre among the temple poets, Cheyne had this to say:

> Perhaps; but history does not follow the course prescribed by theory. We must allow for the varieties of religious sentiment. Ezra at any rate (as the books of Ruth and Jonah prove) was not an autocrat, and the author of Psalm 50 may have belonged to a somewhat different school than that of the great reformer . . . Suffice it to remark that while the psalmist admits the temporary validity of the established legal system, he looks forward to the realization of nobler visions than those of Ezra.

Of course, a post-exilic date for the Psalter created special problems for interpreting the 'Royal Psalms', since it was not clear who could have occupied the throne as a second David. The fashionable view in Cheyne's day was to attribute this role either to Cyrus, who allowed the Jews to return to Palestine, or to his successor Darius, who continued the same policy. Cheyne, however, rejected this possibility in favour of a much later identification. As he put it:

> But was there no prince less remote but not less powerful than Darius, for whom the Jews had the strongest feelings of loyalty and gratitude? Yes, there was one - Ptolemy Philadelphus, who 'to the Jews became as a Jew, that he might gain the Jews', and who, almost better in some respects than Cyrus or Darius, deserved a Hebrew poet's encomium. He was in fact the second Cyrus of Israel, not only because he continued the privileges granted by his father to the Jews, but because he redeemed at his own cost a multitude of Jewish captives.

This identification, based on some remarks in the late Jewish chronographer Aristeas, would have dated the psalms to the reign of Ptolemy II (285–246 BC) or even later. More significantly, it would have attributed to him a role which his activities hardly deserved, however grateful contemporary Jews may have been for his assistance to them. What is missing from Cheyne's analysis is any sense of the religious dimension of the king's position in Israel. Even Cyrus, chosen and anointed by God as he undoubtedly was, could not take the place of David, because he was not a covenant king. This aspect of the matter was simply not present in Cheyne, who appears to have thought that any remotely plausible identification in post-exilic times would do – and the later it could be placed, the better.

The emergence of form criticism completely altered this picture of the Psalter, because it revived the long-dormant idea that the psalms were intimately linked to the worshipping life of Israel. That this discovery had implications for modern church life was freely acknowledged by Mowinckel, who wrote:

> In the meantime, the comparative study of religions had brought to the fore the important place of the cult in religion in general. The rediscovery of the old oriental cultures showed Biblical scholars that exactly the same was true of the religions of the peoples that surrounded Israel, from whose culture and religion Israel had taken over many important customs and conceptions. Even in Protestant Christianity a better under-

> standing of the value of ordered worship has emerged – although in some circles it is still branded as a 'high church' tendency. This change in the scholarly and spiritual situation has necessarily influenced also the interpretation of the Old Testament and especially of the psalms.

Mowinckel went on to praise Gunkel, who had 'proved beyond doubt that in Israel also the origin of psalm poetry is to be found in the public cult: the different types of psalms have come into existence in connexion with different cultic situations and acts to which they originally belonged'.

Gunkel's discovery, said Mowinckel, made it possible to lay the foundation for a real historical and literary understanding of the psalms, which would lead to a substantial revision of critical views about Old Testament religious history and a revaluation of the disparaged 'cult religion' of the Old Testament. But Gunkel spoiled his theory, Mowinckel argued, by saying that the psalms as we now have them are not original cultic compositions, but private imitations composed at a later date. Gunkel cited similar examples in the prophetic literature as proof of this claim, but Mowinckel was able to point out that prophetic 'borrowings' from cultic poetry were adapted to a different purpose, and were not simply imitations. He therefore argued that Gunkel was wrong to draw this comparison, and suggested that the psalms were originally cultic texts.

Linking the psalms to the cultic life of Israel was a major change in critical perception. As Mowinckel pointed out, the cult was among the most ancient and constant features of Israel's life, reaching back into the distant prehistoric past. There may well have been theological developments within the cult, and it may have acquired various accretions and changed outwardly from time to time, but forms of religious observance are notoriously conservative in all societies, and this produced an *a priori* argument in favour of an early dating for much of the Psalter. The fact that it was poetic in form contributed to this assumption, since in most societies poetry and song preceded the development of prose literature. There was therefore a good case for saying that at least parts of the Psalter were considerably older than the Pentateuch or the historical books of the Old Testament.

Gunkel and Mowinckel agreed that there was a fundamental division between the 'we' psalms and the 'I' psalms. The former reflected the life of the community, including the ancient view that the individual lost his identity in the tribe. The latter were more difficult to interpret, though there were two main possibilities. The first was that the 'I' was a personification of the nation, a view which had some adherents. But neither Gunkel nor Mowinckel was prepared to make this a universal principle of interpretation. They generally preferred the second option, which was that the 'I' psalms reflected the prayer and spiritual life of a particular individual whose life reflected the common experience.

The 'I–we' alternation is most apparent in the so-called 'royal psalms'. Mowinckel believed that the traditional ascription of the Psalms to David made them all 'royal', and he regarded this as a significant indication of their meaning and place in the cult. The king played a prominent role in worship, though he was not deified in the Egyptian or Mesopotamian way. Nevertheless, the king's role was such that the royal psalms must reflect a real cultic situation, and therefore date from the time of the Davidic monarchy, if not from the time of David himself.

Mowinckel was thus quite happy to date most of the psalms to the time of the monarchy or to the very early exile. He also recognized that a good number undoubtedly stemmed from the post-exilic period, and he regarded these as particularly profound in their spiritual insight (in sharp contrast to Cheyne). However, he categorically rejected the suggestion that any of the canonical psalms could be dated as late as the Maccabean period (second century BC). But Mowinckel was careful not to be dogmatic about dating. As he wrote:

> . . . within this period [*i.e.* of the monarchy and early exile] it is not possible to write any history of psalmography. Most datings of the individual psalms are too uncertain for that, and we find so many typical, common features recurring in earlier as well as in later psalms that it is not possible to arrange the material so as to produce anything like a clear line of development between the comparatively scarce fixed points.

According to Mowinckel, the association of the royal psalms with the Davidic dynasty was a major factor in the way in which their use was transformed after the exile. The dynasty had disappeared, but it gave way to a messianic hope, in which a future Son of David would arise and claim his ancestral inheritance. The royal psalms were therefore reinterpreted and regarded as prophecies of the coming Messiah. It was on this basis that they were eventually collected and included in the canon, so that the way they were used in the New

Testament was consistent with their function in later Israelite worship.

A major side-effect of the identification of the psalms with the cult was the increased interest shown in their theology. This comes out very clearly when we compare what Cheyne had to say with what can be found in more modern commentaries. We shall take as our example the interpretation of Psalm 22, to which we have already referred. Cheyne said that it had been composed just before the mission of Nehemiah, and reflected the persecution that the Jews were experiencing at the hands of Sanballat and his friends. There was no note of salvation to be sounded other than that offered by the appearance of Nehemiah and his rescue operation, which Cheyne naturally understood largely in secular terms.

Form-critical analysts, on the other hand, were frequently tempted to link Psalm 22 to the royal psalms, by maintaining that in the cultic ritual the king represented the dying and reviving deity. According to this interpretation, put forward by A. Bentzen and others, the man abandoned by God was the dying king, and the man who gives thanks (vv. 22–31) was the reviving ruler, portrayed in a drama of worship. At a later stage, when the psalm had finally been redacted in its present form, there had been a process of 'democratization' which allowed individual worshippers to appropriate the experience of the representative king figure.

More recently, C. Westermann (1984) has interpreted Psalm 22 in the light of form criticism, but without linking it to the royal psalms. Like earlier interpreters, he regards its present form as a redaction of an older psalm, though he seems to accept the basic framework as one of a 'lament which had been turned round'. It therefore cannot be regarded as a combination of an original lament with a later thanksgiving; both these elements were there from the start. Westermann agrees with his immediate predecessors that the psalm was very carefully put together. He analyses it as follows:

vv. 1–21: the lament

1–3	the lament or complaint to God
4–5	God's dealings with his people
6–8	an 'I' lament (about the enemy from v. 7)
9–10	God's dealings with the suppliant
11	a petition to God
12–13	an 'I' lament about the enemy
14–15	an 'I' lament

16–18	an 'I' lament about the enemy
19–21	a petition to God

vv. 22–31: the thanksgiving

22	a transitional utterance of praise
23	a summons to praise
24	another transitional utterance of praise
25–26	the redeeming of the vow (final end of the lament)
27–32	descriptive praise

Westermann goes on to interpret the all-important first verse by saying that it describes a relationship with God which cannot be broken, despite the intense suffering which the psalmist has experienced. Westermann puts it like this:

> It is to be noted that, in this opening of Psalm 22, there is a fundamentally different understanding of man's relationship with God from the one that has grown up since the period of the Enlightenment. We describe that relationship as 'belief' and equate the term with religion itself. But in a relationship with God viewed as belief, it is man who is the subject; one either believes in him or not. In this respect the relationship with God in the psalms is quite other; there God is the subject, he it is who initiates the relationship. So even when a man despairs of God, he can never break free from him, as we see clearly in Psalm 139.

In his concluding remarks on the psalm, Westermann states:

> The centre of all the Old Testament's theological discourse is found in a verbal clause: God has acted. That can only be said by one who has actually experienced what God has done, in this case the speaker of Psalm 22. His experience has been shaped by the contrast which determines the progression of the psalm from its first to last verse. Only because he had experienced God's remoteness and God's silence could he experience their reversal; and because he had experienced this reversal, he had to recount it. What he had to recount had to advance even further, for God has acted. It is of God's actions that Old Testament theology speaks, and in so doing it speaks of the divine–human relationship, past, present, and future.

Finally, we may look at the interpretation of the psalm given by a contemporary evangelical scholar, Peter Craigie (1983). Craigie has an analysis of the psalm different from that of Westermann, and one which is more closely tied to a liturgical model. He breaks it down as follows:

2–22b	Lament. The sick man declares his sorrow	
	2–11	he is forsaken by God and mankind
	12	his prayer for help
	13–19	he is surrounded by trouble
	20–22b	his prayer for deliverance
22c	Response. This presupposes an oracle	
23–27	Thanksgiving (declared by the sufferer)	
28–32	Thanksgiving (declared by the congregation)	

Craigie sees the psalms as primarily individual in tone, though set in the context of a public liturgy. For him, the whole process of lament, prayer and thanksgiving would have taken place during a single act of worship, which may have been connected with a royal ritual of some kind, though this hypothesis must remain uncertain.

Of the opening verse, Craigie writes:

> The worshipper begins by expressing the darkest mystery of his suffering, namely the sense of being forsaken by God. It is a mystery because it appears to be rooted in a contradiction, namely the apparent contradiction between theology and experience. Theology, based upon the tradition and experience of the past, affirmed unambiguously that trust resulted in deliverance. Indeed, it was of the essence of the covenant faith that those who trusted in the holy God would not be disappointed . . . But experience was altogether at odds with theology; whereas the fathers trusted and were delivered, the essence of the psalmist's complaint was 'the distance of my salvation'. The God of covenant, who was believed not to have deserted his faithful people, appeared to have forsaken this worshipper who, in sickness, faced the doors of death. And it was the sense of being forsaken by God that was the fundamental problem – more grave than the actual condition of sickness and the threat of death.

It is extremely interesting to note the contrast between Craigie and Westermann. Craigie's view of faith as trust is clearly more subjective than Westermann's; in traditional Protestant theology Craigie's approach would be described as 'Arminian' and Westermann's as 'Calvinist'. On the other hand, Craigie mentions the covenant theme, reflecting both traditional Calvinism and Eichrodt, in a way in which Westermann does not. However, neither makes any reference to the use of this verse in the New Testament, at least not in the course of the commentary itself. Craigie does, however, add this at the end:

> Though the psalm is not messianic in its original sense or setting, it may be interpreted from a New Testament perspective as a messianic psalm *par excellence.* It is clear from the recorded words of Jesus on the cross that he identified his own loneliness and suffering with that of the psalmist. And it is clear that the evangelists interpreted the crucifixion in the light of the psalm, utilizing its words in their description of the scene . . . It is not without reason that the psalm has been called the 'Fifth Gospel' account of the crucifixion.

Craigie goes on to draw out the implications for this for Christology:

> What is most significant about the New Testament perspective is the self-identification of Jesus with the suffering psalmist, for it provides an insight into one part of the meaning of the crucifixion. The sufferer of Psalm 22 is a human being, experiencing the terror of mortality in the absence of God and the presence of enemies. In the suffering of Jesus, we perceive God, in Jesus, entering into and participating in the terror of mortality; he identifies with the suffering and the dying. Because God, in Jesus, has engaged in that desolation, he can offer comfort to those of us who walk now where the psalmist walked. But there is also a remarkable difference between the experience of the suffering psalmist and that of Jesus. The psalm concludes with praise because the sufferer escaped death; Jesus died. Yet the latter half of the psalm may also be read from a messianic perspective. The transition at v. 22 is now understood not in deliverance from death, as was the case for the psalmist, but in deliverance through death, achieved in the resurrection.

Craigie's Christological application of the psalm may be as far as it is legitimate to go in the light of historical criticism, but the Protestant theologian will immediately notice the missing element in it. Craigie talks at great length about suffering and death, and about how Christ shared with us in these things. But at no point does he mention the atonement; there is no suggestion that Christ was our substitute on the cross, that he endured these things for our salvation. In this respect, his Christological application is unsatisfactory, because it misses the main point of the gospel. Whether this is due to careful exegesis, or to latent 'Arminianism' (or both) is not easy to decide. What it does show, however, is that the theological application made in the above examples is unsystematic in character. It has grown out of the biblical scholar's desire to relate the text to his own faith perspective, and not from a concern to tie it to a systematic framework of Christian doctrine.

BIBLIOGRAPHY

T. K. Cheyne, *The Origin of the Psalter* (London: Paul, Trench, Trübner and Co., 1891).

P. C. Craigie, *Psalms 1 – 50* (Waco: Word, 1983).

H. Gunkel, *The Psalms* (Philadelphia: Fortress, 1967).

H. J. Kraus, *Psalms 1 – 59* (Minneapolis: Augsburg, 1988).

S. Mowinckel, *The Psalms in Israel's Worship* (Oxford: Blackwell, 1962).

C. Westermann, *The Living Psalms* (1984; Eng. trans. Edinburgh: T. and T. Clark, 1989).

10

New Testament criticism after Schweitzer

The period and the subject

New Testament criticism after the First World War was dominated by a neo-orthodox revival inspired by Karl Barth (1886–1968). Barth had been a student under A. von Harnack at Berlin, where he had absorbed the most advanced liberal theories of his day. In 1912 he became a pastor in the Swiss town of Safenwil, and there he began to realize that the theology he had learned at the university could not be preached in the parish. In 1914 he received a further shock, when his former professors announced that they were supporting the German war aims. Barth began to realize that there was something wrong with liberal theology, and during the war years he made an intensive study of Paul's epistle to the Romans, which had given the Reformers their main theological inspiration. The fruit of his labours appeared in 1919, as a commentary on that epistle.

Barth's work shook the German theological world. Coming hard on the heels of national defeat, and pointing back to an era which the great minds of the day had long since rejected, Barth's commentary struck the mood of a disillusioned generation. The war also created a mental climate in which apocalyptic and eschatology could flourish. Here the way had already been prepared by J. Weiss and A. Schweitzer, but it was after 1919 that their message really began to hit home.

Outside Germany, the impact of neo-orthodoxy was uneven, especially in the English-speaking world, which had never fully absorbed prewar German liberalism. Anglo-Saxon pragmatism was also resistant to it. Neo-orthodoxy was basically a philosophical movement, rooted in systematic theology, and this had never appealed to the English mind. Only in Scotland, and to some extent in the USA, did it make much headway. Its main contribution was in the rise of biblical theology, which attempted to expound the theology of the biblical writers independently of traditional dogmatics.

Biblical theology is often thought of as a movement, but it lacked internal cohesion. Archaeologists, not theologians, played the major role in backing up its conservative stance. At first, there was little New Testament archaeology, since the New Testament did not lend itself to it in the way that the Old Testament did. The major exception to this was the work of Sir William Ramsay in establishing the historical reliability of Luke-Acts, and in locating the various churches established by Paul and the other apostles in Asia Minor. His findings came to be regarded as of great importance, and still continue to influence scholarly assessments of Luke's writings.

At the same time, other forces at work often supported a conservative outlook, even if that was not their primary intention. For example, in 1922 Paul Billerbeck published the first part of his four-volume commentary on the New Testament, based on Midrashic and Talmudic sources. Though he was not the first scholar to point out the importance of the Jewish background for Jesus' thought, Billerbeck was by far the most systematic. Working from what was essentially a 'history of religions' approach and not from a traditional conservative position, he turned the presuppositions of the school on their head. Almost overnight, studies of the relationship between the New Testament and various pagan cults came to seem irrelevant, as the world of contemporary Judaism was unfolded. Billerbeck did not live to see it, but the discovery of the Dead Sea Scrolls at Qumran pushed New Testament scholarship even farther in the same direction. The Jewishness of Jesus and his disciples became so important that by the 1970s some scholars were wondering whether there was any fundamental difference between New Testament Christianity and Judaism at all!

Almost as important as the discovery of the Qumran scrolls was the discovery of the Gnostic papyri at Nag Hammadi in Egypt (1946). For the first time scholars had access to a large body of heretical Christian literature which definitely had not been tampered with by the orthodox of a later time. This allowed them to reconstruct a coherent picture of Gnosticism, which soon led to debate about how far various New Testament epistles were combating Gnostic tendencies. Some scholars thought that Gnosticism was a pre-Christian phenomenon, which confronted and to some extent influenced the growth of the New Testament church. Others believed that Gnosticism emerged only towards the end of the New Testament period, as the church broke out of its Jewish milieu and began to confront the wider world of Hellenism.

The next question was: how soon did the Christian community begin to define its beliefs in a way which excluded Gnostic and other groups? Was it true to say that there was a primitive pluralism in the church, which was gradually branded as 'heresy' by a narrow group of self-declared 'orthodox' believers? This was the thesis of W. Bauer, which he attempted to defend from a wide range of epigraphic evidence, in addition to the usual textual sources. Bauer was ably opposed by H. W. E. Turner, but doubts about the nature of orthodoxy in the early church would not go away. The 'conflict' between the Judaizers and the Hellenists continued to provide material for more than one theory of Christian origins. As with the nineteenth-century debate, its twentieth-century equivalent was not unconnected with church politics. Those who tried to prove that the first Christians lived in a pluralistic church also wanted to recommend that model for the present day – not least because then they could feel at home in it!

While all this was going on, modern literary criticism began to make its mark on biblical scholarship. Form criticism was applied to the New Testament, though with less satisfactory results than the ones Gunkel had obtained in the Old Testament. 'Epistle' was quickly recognized as a genre, and 'apocalyptic' was accepted for the first time as a type of literature with parallels outside the canon. 'Gospel' was also regarded as a special genre, though it was harder to decide what its distinctive characteristics were. The gospels were neither history nor biography in the strict sense, though they had traditionally been regarded as both. Whether they could be read as a mythologization of history was a matter of dispute, although many scholars believed there were mythical elements derived from Jewish apocalyptic sources, such as the book of Daniel, embedded in the gospel portrayal of Jesus. More successful was the isolation of 'parable' as a literary type, though here too there were problems of definition which were not as straightforward as they might seem. What parables were for thus became a major question in New Testament research, and it has still not been resolved satisfactorily.

Another legacy of form criticism was the problem of the *Sitz im Leben* (historical context) of the gospels. Did they represent conditions in the life and ministry of Jesus himself, or were they mirrors of life in the early church? This was not a matter which could be resolved easily, and things got still more complicated when the standpoint of the individual evangelists was added, creating even more historical contexts to be considered. This development came about as a result of the emergence of redaction criticism after 1945. Its proponents had sympathies with biblical theology, and concentrated heavily on the theological outlook of the individual evangelists. They tried to go beyond the old synoptic problem, by showing that the redactional characteristics of each gospel reflected its author's particular theological concerns. This approach had the great merit of demonstrating what A. Schweitzer had already claimed, *viz.* that Mark's presentation of the life of Jesus was primarily theological rather than historical.

At the same time, however, the quest for the historical Jesus continued to occupy scholars' attention. Schweitzer's criticisms of the nineteenth-century approach were accepted, but they were not enough to diminish interest in the man behind the gospel 'myth'. In its first phase, the renewed quest for the 'real' Jesus followed a conservative bent, in line with the prevailing neo-orthodoxy. The gospels were regarded as historical to a significant extent, and the crucifixion was thought to be of central importance in understanding Jesus. Theology assumed a prominent place in this kind of research, and other considerations were relegated to second place. Later on, the mood changed, and there emerged a 'third quest' of the historical Jesus. This minimized the historical value of the gospels and looked more towards external evidence. Judaism played a prominent part in this, and the politics of Palestine were once again regarded as an important clue in understanding Jesus. Theological considerations were thought to be less significant, though they were not totally disregarded.

During this period scholarly perception of the close links between the gospels and the early church was reinforced, though in a different way from what had been the case earlier. Paul and the other apostles were now seen to have been just as Jewish as Jesus was, so that Jewish–Christian relations in New Testament times took on fresh importance. Looming large in this discussion was the Jewish revolt of AD 66–73, which climaxed in the destruction of Jerusalem (AD 70). This revolt is not mentioned in the New Testament, except perhaps obliquely in a warning given by Jesus (see Mk. 13). Yet it came to be regarded as a key factor in the process by which the church ceased to be a Jewish and became a largely Gentile movement, for it must have been about that time that the synagogue and the church finally parted company. The historical reliability of Acts was a major factor in this discussion, since Luke placed this separation considerably earlier, and did not connect it with Palestinian politics. Was his account historically accurate, or merely the reflection of early Christian propaganda?

Finally, the uniqueness of Paul's theology also came to be questioned. He had always been regarded as the 'apostle to the Gentiles', the archetypal anti-Judaiser. But in the 1970s some scholars began to suggest that his theology was just as Jewish as that of his opponents; the difference was that his perspective was that of Diaspora Judaism, not that of the Palestinian rabbis. With this suggestion, it may be said that the re-Judaizing of the New Testament reached its zenith. For the first time since the death of the apostles, a thorough knowledge of rabbinic and other Jewish sources was regarded as essential for interpreting the New Testament, and the impact of Hellenism was pushed into the background. The climate of New Testament studies in the 1970s was radically different from what it had been for nearly 200 years, and it seemed possible that a new era in biblical scholarship was about to dawn.

The interpreters and their work

The German sphere

Paul Billerbeck (1853–1932). He is best known for his four-volume commentary on the New Testament (1922–28), which is generally (though incorrectly) referred to as 'Strack-Billerbeck', because H. Strack agreed to help with the publication and got his name on the title page, although he did not write a single word of the text. Billerbeck was a noted rabbinic scholar, and his commentary is of great value because it contains a wealth of background information on the period.

Hans Windisch (1881–1935). He was Professor of New Testament at Leiden (1914), Kiel (1929) and Halle (1935). His work on the Sermon on the Mount (1929) was a reply to Bultmann from a 'history of religions' perspective. He also wrote commentaries on the catholic epistles (1911), Hebrews (1913) and 2 Corinthians (1924).

Rudolf Otto(1869–1937). Professor of Systematic Theology at Göttingen (1897), Breslau (1914) and Marburg (1917–29), he is now chiefly remembered for his famous study of comparative religion, *The Idea of the Holy* (1917). However, he also wrote on New Testament themes, notably in *The Kingdom of God and the Son of Man* (1934).

Hans Lietzmann (1875–1942). Professor of Church History at Jena (1908) and Berlin (1924), he wrote commentaries on Romans (1906), 1 and 2 Corinthians (1907) and Galatians (1910), all parts of a series which he founded on the whole New Testament. He is chiefly remembered today for his work on early church history, including his well-known *Mass and the Lord's Supper* (1926).

Hans Freiherr von Soden (1881–1945). He taught at Breslau (1918) and Marburg (1924) and was a prominent anti-Nazi. His main works concentrated on textual criticism and church order. He tried to fuse both Hellenistic and Jewish insights into a deeper understanding of Christianity, which for him was always a practical ethic as well as a philosophical theology.

Friedrich Buchsel (1883–1945). Professor of New Testament at Rostock from 1917 until his death, he was a conservative scholar who wrote commentaries on the Johannine epistles (1933) and John (1934). He also wrote a book on the Christology of Hebrews (1922) and another on John and Hellenistic syncretism (1928). He rejected the common assumption that John had been deeply influenced by Hellenistic models and concepts, and argued that everything in the fourth gospel came from a Palestinian Jewish context, making it more historically reliable than had previously been thought.

Ernst Lohmeyer (1890–1946). Professor at Breslau from 1920 to 1935, he was dismissed for his anti-Nazi views. He was murdered by Russian troops in 1946. He anticipated redaction criticism in *Lord of the Temple* (1942), and wrote a number of commentaries, on Revelation (1926), Philippians, Colossians and Philemon (1930) and Mark (1937). A commentary on Matthew was published after his death (1956). His interpretation of Paul demonstrates a depth of insight into the text unequalled by his contemporaries in Germany.

Martin Dibelius (1883–1947). A student of both Harnack and Gunkel, he was Professor of New Testament at Heidelberg from 1915. He was a leading representative of the 'history of religions' approach in New Testament criticism, and a pioneer of form criticism. He wrote commentaries on the shorter Pauline epistles (1912), the pastoral epistles (1913), the gospels (1919) and James (1921). Later he wrote popular works on Jesus (1939) and Paul (1951), and his collected *Studies in the Acts of the Apostles* (1951) were published posthumously. He opposed the theologizing tendencies of redaction criticism, and seemed rather old-fashioned in the climate of the 1930s and later.

Julius Schniewind (1883–1948). He taught at Halle (1921), Greifswald (1927), Königsberg (1929), Kiel (1935) and Halle

(1936), but was dismissed in 1937 for anti-Nazi views. He was restored to his post in 1945. He wrote a number of articles on the synoptic gospels and on New Testament theology, in which he demonstrated that the concept of 'good news' had its origin in post-exilic Jewish hopes of the coming Messiah, rather than in Hellenism. Schniewind continued the conservative, theological tradition of Martin Kähler and August Tholuck, which, thanks to him, became known in Germany as the 'Hallenser Theologie'. For Schniewind, theology, like faith, came from hearing the Word, and the Bible was a voice calling to be heard, not a text waiting to be dissected. He made a conscious attempt to revive the Reformers' principles of biblical exegesis in the face of modern historical criticism, and was one of the main representatives of the biblical theology movement in Germany.

Gerhard Kittel (1888–1948). Professor of New Testament at Tübingen (1926–45), he is most famous for his *Theological Dictionary of the New Testament* (1933–74). In spite of his work on the problems of 'late Judaism' and early Christianity (1926), in which he outlined the influence of the former on the latter, he became a Nazi and was removed from his teaching post in 1945.

Karl Ludwig Schmidt (1891–1956). He was Professor of New Testament at Giessen (1921), Jena (1925), Bonn (1929) and Basel (1935–53). His main work was on the synoptic gospels (1919) and their literary character (1923).

Walter Bauer (1877–1960). He was Professor of New Testament at Göttingen (1916–45). His work forms the basis of the standard dictionary of New Testament Greek, which is now in its sixth edition. (The fourth edition, 1952, was translated into English and is usually known as 'Arndt and Gingrich', after the names of the translators.) He also wrote a commentary on John (1912) and a very important study *Orthodoxy and Heresy in Earliest Christianity* (1934). In this book he sought to prove that 'orthodoxy' was a late concept, developed as part of the gradual centralization of authority in the church, and that 'heresy' represented more authentic (*i.e.* more primitive) forms of Christianity.

Karl Barth (1886–1968). A Swiss Reformed theologian, he taught at Göttingen (1921), Münster (1925), Bonn (1930) and finally Basel (1935). His major work was his *Church Dogmatics*, a massive systematic theology which he composed over several decades and left unfinished at his death. He also wrote theological commentaries on Romans (1919, 1921), 1 Corinthians (1924) and Philippians (1928). Barth's blend of theological conservatism and critical methods came to be known as 'neo-orthodoxy', which inspired a whole generation of Reformed theologians. However, he met with considerable opposition from Catholics, who objected to his radical denunciation of natural theology. It is also doubtful whether 'neo-orthodoxy' will be able to maintain itself as a theological synthesis, once the generation of Barth's pupils has passed from the scene.

Rudolf Karl Bultmann (1884–1976). He was Professor of New Testament at Marburg (1921–51), and his form-critical approach to New Testament studies came to dominate the field in Germany. In the English-speaking world his methods and conclusions were more controversial, and he was often pilloried as the archetype of an unbelieving critic. The classic study in which he developed his theories was *The History of the Synoptic Tradition* (1921), a book which reveals his debt to Gunkel. Other important works were *Jesus and the Word* (1926), *Primitive Christianity* (1949) and *History and Eschatology* (1957). He also wrote commentaries on John (1941), the Johannine epistles (1967) and 2 Corinthians (1976).

Bultmann is famous for maintaining that the gospel message is essentially a proclamation (Gk. *kērygma*) which can be universalized by removing the outer layer of myth which encapsulates it. This is the process known as 'demythologization', which Bultmann regarded as essential if the kerygma was to be successfully preached to 'modern man'. Criticism of his work has centred around his concept of 'myth', which clearly goes back to D. F. Strauss, and which many have regarded as an inappropriate category to describe the content of the gospels. Bultmann has also been attacked for making the kerygma a disembodied abstraction, which in theological terms amounts to a denial of the incarnation.

Leonhard Goppelt (1911–73). He was Professor of New Testament at Hamburg from 1954, and at Munich from 1967. His approach was conservative, though still within the critical tradition. His best-known works are *Typos: The Typological Interpretation of the Old Testament in the New* (1939) and *Apostolic and Post-Apostolic Times* (1962). At his death he left an incomplete theology of the New Testament (1975, 1982) and a commentary on 1 Peter (1978), both of which were published posthumously.

Joachim Jeremias (1900–79). Professor of New Testament at Greifswald (1929) and Göttingen (1935), he remained committed to the traditional quest for the historical Jesus, as opposed to the kerygmatic Christ of Bultmann. By using 'history of religions' methods, he believed he could identify the very words (*ipsissima verba*) of Jesus in the gospels. His books, *The Eucharistic Words of Jesus* (1935), *The Parables of Jesus* (1947) and *The Theology of the New*

Testament (1971), were well received outside Germany, and helped to spread his methods to other countries.

Heinrich Schlier (1904–82). A pupil of Bultmann, he was Professor of New Testament at Bonn (1946). He wrote extensively on Pauline subjects, including commentaries on Galatians (1949), Ephesians (1957) and Romans (1977). His last work was a detailed study of Paul's theology (1978).

Günther Bornkamm (1905–90). A pupil of Bultmann's, he was Professor of New Testament at Heidelberg from 1949 to 1971. His *Jesus of Nazareth* (1956) is the classic statement of the 'new quest' for the historical Jesus, and his book on Paul (1969) has also become a standard work. He pioneered the redaction criticism of Matthew (1963, 1968), and defended the classical Protestant view of the centrality of justification by faith in Pauline theology, against the attacks of Ernst Käsemann.

Willi Marxsen (1919–93). Professor of New Testament at Zürich, he wrote widely on New Testament theology, largely from a redaction-critical perspective. His study of Mark (1959) is a classic of this type of interpretation. He also wrote commentaries on 1 Thessalonians (1979), 2 Thessalonians (1982), an introduction to the New Testament (1964) and books on Christology (1969) and early catholicism (1958).

Georg Ewald Strecker (1929–94). Professor of New Testament at Göttingen (1964), he was a leading redaction critic of Matthew's gospel. His main work is *The Sermon on the Mount* (1984).

Werner Georg Kümmel (1905–). He was Professor of New Testament at Zürich (1932), Mainz (1951) and Marburg (1952). His *Introduction to the New Testament* (1963) is an excellent guide to modern New Testament research.

Ernst Käsemann (1906–). A pupil of Bultmann's and one of his most profound critics. He was Professor of New Testament at Mainz (1946), Göttingen (1951) and Tübingen (1953). He was the chief instigator of the 'new quest' for the historical Jesus (1953). His work was noted for its ability to stir up controversy, and many (if not most) of his conclusions have been rejected by as many scholars as have accepted them. It is largely because of him that the canon, 'orthodoxy', John's gospel, 'early catholicism' and apocalyptic as 'the mother of Christian theology' have figured so prominently in modern research. He challenged the traditional Protestant emphasis on justification by faith in Pauline theology, and attributed Paul's teaching on the subject to apocalyptic influence. Most of his work is in the form of essays in other collections, but he has written an important commentary on Romans (1973).

Nils Alstrup Dahl (1911–). A Norwegian student of Bultmann's, he taught at Oslo (1946) and at Yale (1965–82), and is therefore a bridge between the German, the Scandinavian and the English-speaking worlds. He was one of the initiators of the 'new quest' for the historical Jesus. His many essays on different New Testament themes have been published in various collections: *The Crucified Messiah* (1974), *Jesus in the Memory of the Early Church* (1976) and *Studies in Paul* (1977).

Heinz Schürmann (1912–). Professor of New Testament at Erfurt (1952), and a leading Roman Catholic representative of the 'history of religions' approach, he specialized in the gospels, and has written a two-volume commentary on Luke (1969, 1993) which is incomplete.

Eduard Schweizer (1913–). A student of Bultmann's, he was Professor of New Testament at Zürich from 1949 to 1978. He has written at great length on New Testament studies. After early works on *Lordship and Discipleship* (1955), *Church and Church Order in the New Testament* (1959) and *The Church as the Body of Christ* (1965), he turned to commentaries. He has written on Mark (1967), Matthew (1973), Colossians (1976) and Luke (1982).

Kurt (1915–) and **Barbara** (1937–) **Aland**. A husband-and-wife team who have made a major contribution to the textual study of the New Testament. Their book on the subject (*The Text of the New Testament*) was published in 1982 and is a standard work. They have also revised W. Bauer's lexicon (1988), and he has written on the problem of the canon (1962).

Hans Conzelmann (1915–). A pupil of Bultmann's, he taught at Zürich (1954) and then at Göttingen (1960). He was a pioneer of redaction criticism, as can be seen in his classic work, *The Theology of St Luke* (1956). He has also written commentaries on Acts (1963) and 1 Corinthians (1969), and was involved in the 'new quest' for the historical Jesus.

Ceslaus Spicq (1901–93). A leading French-speaking, conservative Roman Catholic biblical scholar, he is especially noted for his classical commentary on Hebrews. More recently, he edited a theological dictionary of the New Testament (1985; Eng. trans. 1995).

The English-speaking world

John Martin Creed (1889–1940). He taught at Cambridge from 1914, and was a leading liberal. He wrote a commentary on Luke (1930) and a doctrinal study of the divinity of Christ (1938). He played a prominent part in attempts to weaken the traditional doctrine of the Church of England.

Shailer Mathews (1863–1941). He was Dean of the Chicago Divinity School (1908–33), where he developed a generation of scholars concerned with social interpretations of the gospel. Initially he followed the liberalism of his day, but in *The Messianic Hope in the New Testament* (1905) he adopted the eschatological perspective of J. Weiss. Later he wrote a number of works in which he tied New Testament interpretation to contemporary sociological study.

James Moffatt (1870–1944). A Scottish biblical scholar, he was deeply influenced by A. B. Bruce. After teaching in Glasgow (1915), he went to Union Theological Seminary, New York (1927–39). He was a noted Bible translator, bringing out a New Testament in 1901 and an Old Testament in 1924. The whole work was revised in 1935. In addition, he contributed commentaries on the general epistles (1928) and on 1 and 2 Corinthians (1938) to a commentary series based on his own translation.

Kirsopp Lake (1872–1946). A follower and popularizer of W. Bousset, he related the mystery religions to his own high view of the eucharist as the centre of Christianity.

Arthur Cayley Headlam (1862–1947). He regarded the Jesus of the gospels as a coherent historical figure, and argued that it was necessary to treat the texts as historically reliable. His main work in this area was *The Fourth Gospel as History* (1948). He also published a commentary on Romans with W. Sanday (1920), and other works on Paul (1913) and miracles (1915).

Shirley Jackson Case (1872–1947). Professor of New Testament at Chicago (1908–38), he was a leading liberal of his generation. He specialized in social history, and attempted to write biographies of Jesus on that basis (1927, 1932).

Wilfred Lawrence Knox (1886–1950). This conservative Anglo-Catholic scholar wrote extensively on *Paul and the Church of Jerusalem* (1925), as well as on *Paul and the Church of the Gentiles* (1939). His study of the sources of the synoptic gospels appeared posthumously in 1953–57.

Robert Henry Lightfoot (1883–1953). Professor of New Testament at Oxford (1934), he introduced form criticism to England in *History* *and Interpretation of the Gospels* (1935), and was a forerunner of redaction criticism. He wrote commentaries on Mark (1950) and John (1956); the latter appeared posthumously.

William Ralph Inge (1860–1954). He argued against Baur and his school that the New Testament cannot be explained in terms of an opposition between Judaism and Hellenism, a theory which was already out of date in his view. He wrote numerous works, mainly on ancient Greek philosophy and mysticism.

Charles Cutler Torrey (1863–1956). Professor of Semitic Languages at Yale, he wrote a number of important works of biblical criticism, including a study of *The Composition and Date of Acts* (1916), in which he argued that an Aramaic original underlay the biblical text.

Thomas Walter Manson (1893–1958). He taught at Oxford (1932) and Manchester (1936), where he succeeded C. H. Dodd. His main works were *The Teaching of Jesus* (1931) and *The Sayings of Jesus* (1939). He was strongly opposed to form criticism, and clung to the philological approach traditional in England.

Arthur Darby Nock (1902–63). He taught at Cambridge (1926) and Harvard (1930). His anthropological approach to religion meant that his interpretation of the New Testament was very liberal and anti-dogmatic. He is chiefly remembered today for his study of *Conversion* (1933), though he also wrote on the Hellenistic background of Christianity (1928) and on St Paul (1938).

Vincent Taylor (1887–1968). He taught at Leeds (1936) and wrote voluminously on New Testament themes, from a moderately critical standpoint. He produced a commentary on Mark (1952) and on the passion narrative of Luke (1970), as well as several studies in New Testament theology, including *Jesus and his Sacrifice* (1937), *The Atonement in New Testament Teaching* (1940), *Forgiveness and Reconciliation* (1941) and *The Person of Christ in New Testament Teaching* (1958).

Samuel George Frederick Brandon (1907–71). A student of comparative religion, and generally liberal in his approach, he wrote a major work on the fall of Jerusalem in AD 70 (1951) and its significance for the Christian church. His work on *Jesus and the Zealots* (1967), which portrayed Jesus as a revolutionary sympathizer, has not received general approval.

Charles Harold Dodd (1884–1973). Professor of New Testament at Manchester (1930) and Cambridge (1935–49), his most important work was on John, but he wrote widely on the New Testament and is generally regarded as the greatest scholar of his generation in Britain. He wrote commentaries on Romans (1932) and the

Johannine epistles (1946), in addition to his classic *The Interpretation of the Fourth Gospel* (1953) and *Historical Tradition in the Fourth Gospel* (1963). Other significant works included *The Parables of the Kingdom* (1935, revised in 1961), *The Apostolic Preaching and Its Developments* (1936) and *The Founder of Christianity* (1967). His theological stance was liberal, and he is well known for his objections to the 'wrath of God' concept. He also advocated a 'realized eschatology' in his interpretation of the parables, and broadened Bultmann's concept of kerygma to include the idea of historical fulfilment.

Henry Joel Cadbury (1883–1974). He made a major contribution to the study of Christian origins by insisting that Luke-Acts be treated as a single work. His most important book was *The Style and Literary Method of Luke* (1916).

Norman Perrin (1921–76). He was Professor of New Testament at Emory University (1958) and at Chicago (1964). He developed the approach of T. Manson and J. Jeremias in his *The Kingdom of God in the Teaching of Jesus* (1963). Later he published a more sceptical work, *Rediscovering the Teaching of Jesus* (1967). In his last book, *Jesus and the Language of the Kingdom* (1976), he advocated a literary approach to the gospels.

William Barclay (1907–78). Professor of Divinity at Glasgow (1963–74), he is chiefly famous for his commentaries on the New Testament, which are widely used by preachers. They represent a conservative approach to biblical criticism but a fairly liberal attitude to matters of Christian doctrine.

John Arthur Thomas Robinson (1919–83). This well-known New Testament scholar held conservative exegetical but wildly radical theological views. His book, *Redating the New Testament* (1976), was a sustained attempt to demonstrate that the entire New Testament was written before AD 70. Though much criticized by liberal scholars, its thesis has not been convincingly refuted.

Stephen Charles Neill (1900–84). A very wide-ranging scholar of fairly conservative leanings, his chief contribution to New Testament studies was his highly readable account of New Testament interpretation from 1861 to 1961 (1964).

George Bradford Caird (1917–84). A last representative of the old Cambridge school of exegesis, he wrote careful commentaries on Revelation (1966), Luke (1968) and Paul's prison epistles (1976). His last work was *Language and Imagery of the Bible* (1980), which is a minor classic.

Arthur Michael Ramsey (1904–88). He taught at Durham (1940) and Cambridge (1950), and became successively Bishop of Durham

(1952) and Archbishop of York (1956) and Canterbury (1961–74). His stance was that of a liberal catholic, and he defended this position in a number of works, including *The Gospel and the Catholic Church* (1936), *The Resurrection of Christ* (1945) and *The Glory of God in the Transfiguration of Christ* (1949).

John Knox (1900–90). Professor of New Testament at Union Theological Seminary (1943–66), he wrote a number of liberal critical studies on New Testament themes, including *Christ the Lord* (1945), *Chapters in a Life of Paul* (1950), *The Death of Christ* (1958), *The Church and the Reality of Christ* (1962) and *The Humanity and Divinity of Christ* (1967). He also wrote commentaries on Romans (1954) and Philemon (1959).

Matthew Black (1908–94). He taught in a number of British universities before becoming Principal of St Mary's College, St Andrews (1954–78). His early training was in Old Testament and Semitic languages, an expertise which he was to use to good effect when he switched to the New Testament after 1945. His *Aramaic Approach to the Gospels and Acts* (1946) was a major study of Jewish influences on the New Testament, and was to be of seminal importance in directing research into this area. He later wrote on Qumran (*The Scrolls and Christian Origins,* 1961), and produced a commentary on Romans (1973). His last major work was another commentary, on *1 Enoch* (1985).

Charles Francis Digby Moule (1908–). He was Professor of New Testament at Cambridge from 1952 to 1976 and a leading scholar of conservative tendencies. He wrote commentaries on Mark (1965) and Colossians (1957) as well as two fine books on the New Testament in general: *The Birth of the New Testament* (1962) and *The Phenomenon of the New Testament* (1967). He was also a prominent opponent of those who would demythologize the divinity of Christ, and countered their arguments in a major study of the origin of Christology (1977).

Christopher Francis Evans (1909–). Professor of New Testament at King's College, London (1962) and a well-known liberal, he has objected to the imposition of canonical limits on early Christian literature (1971) and has written a commentary on Luke (1990).

William David Davies (1914–). He was Professor of New Testament at Union Theological Seminary in New York (1949) and at Duke University (1966). His classic work on *Paul and Rabbinic Judaism* (1949) was a major contribution to a reassessment of Paul in his Jewish context. Further studies on the Jewish background of the New Testament include *The Setting of the Sermon on the Mount* (1964) and *The Gospel and the Land* (1974). He has also written the first volume of a commentary on Matthew, in co-operation with D. C. Allison Jr (1988).

Bruce Manning Metzger (1914–). Professor of New Testament at Princeton (1938), he is an outstanding conservative scholar of the Greek New Testament. His books *The Text of the New Testament* (1964) and *A Textual Commentary on the Greek New Testament* (1971) are classics in their field.

Charles Ernest Burland Cranfield (1915–). He is a renowned conservative exegete and New Testament commentator. Early works of his were commentaries on 1 Peter (1950) and Mark (1959). His major production is his two-volume commentary on Romans (1975, 1979), which has rapidly established itself as a standard work on that epistle.

Reginald Horace Fuller (1915–). He was professor at Lampeter (1950), Chicago (1955), Union Theological Seminary, New York (1966) and finally Virginia Seminary (1972–86). His fairly radical approach can be seen in his well-known book, *The Formation of the Resurrection Narratives* (1971). He was also largely responsible for translating R. Bultmann's major works into English.

Charles Kingsley Barrett (1917–). This major British New Testament scholar was Professor at Durham (1958–82). His stance was critical, but generally on the conservative side, in the philological tradition of Cambridge. His commentary on John (1955, revised edition 1978) has become a classic. He has also written commentaries on Romans (1957) and 1 and 2 Corinthians (1968, 1973). Among his many other books are *The Holy Spirit and the Gospel Tradition* (1947), *From First Adam to Last* (1962), *Jesus and the Gospel Tradition* (1967), *The Signs of an Apostle* (1970) and *The Gospel of John and Judaism* (1975). He has also published a number of essays on the New Testament (1972), Paul (1982) and John (1982).

Ernest Best (1917–). Professor at Glasgow (1974–8), he has written widely on Mark and Paul, and his commentaries on Romans (1967), 1 Peter (1971) and 1 and 2 Thessalonians (1972) are concise statements of a moderately critical position.

The issues

The main issues confronting the critical study of the New Testament during this period can be summed up as follows.

1. *It was necessary to determine the relationship between Jesus and the*

Christian church. This was a fundamental question, left over from the nineteenth century. At its heart lay the problem of the 'historical Jesus', the man behind the gospel story. Conservative interpreters regarded the gospels as historically reliable records, and portrayed Jesus as the great founder and teacher of the faith which now bears his name. More liberal scholars tended to see Jesus in a passive role, as the one around whom the legends and doctrines of Christianity collected. Most study of the gospels was ultimately concerned with this question. As time went on, it became increasingly clear that Jesus had to be seen primarily against his Jewish background. Any distance between him and later Christianity was connected with the separation of the church from its Jewish roots, which took place sometime around AD 70 or shortly thereafter. There was also the important question of eschatology, raised by J. Weiss and A. Schweitzer. To what extent was the New Testament a realized eschatology, *i.e.* a fulfilment of Old Testament promises, and to what extent did it point forward to a future hope? Did the disciples water down this aspect either to make their preaching more acceptable, or to take account of the failure of the future hope to materialize as expected? These questions remained matters of fundamental debate during this period.

2. *It was necessary to determine the relationship between the Christian church and Judaism.* This question is closely linked to the former one, and it assumed much greater importance after 1945. There was a general reaction throughout this period to the picture of Christianity as a Hellenized Jewish sect, which had grown up in the nineteenth century and had been promoted by the early representatives of the 'history of religions' approach. Instead of this, it was asserted with ever greater boldness that Christianity was a perfectly comprehensible form of Judaism, at least in the form in which it was proclaimed by Jesus. Even Paul came to be understood more and more in terms of his Jewish origins, until finally he was regarded by some as little more than a mildly eccentric rabbi. This was clearly an extreme view, but by the late 1970s it was setting the pace for scholarly discussion.

3. *It was necessary to decide to what extent Christian theology as it now exists is rooted in the New Testament.* The traditional claim that all Christian theology was based on the teaching of Scripture was increasingly questioned. Some liberal Protestant theologians asserted that the New Testament contained a variety of theological positions which could be harmonized only in very general terms (*e.g.* by saying that Jesus was of 'central significance' for our understanding of God). Others maintained that certain orthodox Christian doctrines,

especially those concerning the divinity of Christ and the concepts of sin and judgment, were distortions of the biblical record, and they wanted to modify the dogmatic tradition on the basis of a new exegesis of the texts. Still others, fundamentally more conservative, insisted that the New Testament was part of a wider Scripture which contained a coherent theological message; they were identified as the so-called 'biblical theology' movement. In the mid-twentieth century these views vied with one another among critical scholars, and none could be said to have established itself as definitive.

4. *It was necessary to absorb the most recent archaeological discoveries into the study of the New Testament.* Until 1945 this was a fairly minor problem, apart from the history of Acts and the location of the churches of Asia Minor. But after the discovery of the Nag Hammadi texts, and the Qumran Scrolls, New Testament archaeology acquired much greater significance. It became possible to recreate the background of the early church, and evaluate the vast store of papyri which had been found in Egypt. The Greek of the New Testament was finally recognized as the standard vernacular of its day – not quite the 'spoken language' but a written norm approximating to it. The discovery and examination of a large number of New Testament manuscripts and fragments enabled scholars to piece together what amounted to a definitive Greek text, thus completing as far as possible the work begun by Lachmann in the early nineteenth century.

The methods of interpretation

Form criticism

The outstanding representative of the tradition of Gunkel and Von Rad in New Testament studies was R. Bultmann. To a considerable extent, he combined their critical achievements with a philosophical and theological perspective, which linked him to contemporary existentialism and the theories of M. Heidegger, in particular. Bultmann therefore provoked considerably more opposition than Von Rad, but his remained the dominant ideology in New Testament criticism until the early 1970s. Today it can be said that Bultmann's approach is fading away, though his critical achievement remains.

Bultmann began by applying Gunkel's methods to the synoptic gospels. By analysing each minute bit of tradition, he believed he could demonstrate from the way they were preserved how they had been used in the first Christian communities. In this way, he thought he could uncover their *Sitz im Leben* and so fill in the blank period between the life of Jesus and the writing of the gospels. It should be emphasized that Bultmann was not interested in the sociological insights which this method might provide; history remained his sole concern. For Bultmann, there were two dimensions to history – the one in which the text was composed, and the one about which the text spoke. The first of these was the more important, since its interests and priorities would inevitably determine what it selected from the earlier period.

Because of this, Bultmann believed that the search for the 'historical Jesus' was doomed to failure. What the New Testament really bore witness to was the proclamation of the gospel, which was only tangentially related to the life of the historical Jesus. Bultmann tied his critical theories to the theological opinions of M. Kähler and K. Barth, both of whom stressed the 'preached Christ' as opposed to the Jesus of history, though without denying the latter as Bultmann did. From there it was but a short step to claiming that the gospel traditions had developed in accordance with the church's preaching, and that the historical record had been adapted to suit that aim. This in turn underscored the legitimacy – even the necessity – of making further adaptations to the text so as to accommodate it to the modern worldview. It was this procedure which Bultmann called 'demythologization', and which formed the basis of so much of his work.

Among scholars who understood the 'history of religions' approach, Bultmann's ideas found a ready audience and were soon taken up. Elsewhere, however, there was confusion, misunderstanding and rejection. The great weakness in Bultmann's theory was the short timespan between the life of Jesus and the composition of the gospels; comparison with folk culture elsewhere suggested that developments which would normally take generations were compressed by Bultmann into the space of a few decades. Demythologization was not a concept readily absorbed by those whose understanding of 'myth' was less sophisticated than his, and it was rejected by everyone who took the gospels to be a reliable historical record. It is true that when the philosophy underlying 'history of religions' research was more widely understood, especially in the English-speaking world, Bultmann's ideas gained greater favour, but by then discussion had moved on and his views were pressed into the service of sociological and other similar interpretations, which he himself avoided.

Bultmann's understanding of 'myth' was close to that of his nineteenth-century predecessor, D. F. Strauss, though there were significant differences as well. The similarities can best be outlined as follows.

1. Both believed that myth had emerged as an expression of religious consciousness.

2. Both believed that myth was no longer an acceptable category of thought for 'modern man'.

3. Both believed that myth must be interpreted, not simply eliminated.

4. Both believed that ideas are more important than historical events. For them, the gospels are a record of the former, not of the latter.

Their differences can best be described as follows.

1. Strauss used historical criticism as a weapon to destroy a conservative, supernaturalist theology. Bultmann, by contrast, used it to destroy the liberal 'life of Jesus' theology initiated by Strauss.

2. Strauss abandoned all contact with the historical Jesus of Nazareth, claiming that the divine idea could not possibly have been restricted to the life of a single individual. Bultmann, on the other hand, continued to focus on Jesus, and the uniqueness of the 'Christ event', even though this had little historical content.

3. Strauss adopted a Hegelian philosophy which could not be harmonized with the biblical texts because the former was a metaphysical system while the latter were not. Bultmann's existentialism was no more metaphysical than the texts themselves, and could be adapted to them under the common denominator of 'spiritual experience'.

In spite of all the criticism of Bultmann's views from conservative sources, it must be stressed that within his own context, he was a conservative theologian. In his theology of proclamation he wanted to preserve a genuine continuity between his own beliefs and those of the New Testament. He believed that Paul would have agreed with his approach, but not with that of many contemporary exegetes who were more 'literal' but less theological. By developing his theology of the proclaimed Word, Bultmann thought he had found an acceptable criterion for distinguishing between what was fundamental to the gospel and what was not. The former he hung on to; the latter he felt free to criticize. Thus, if he found something in a text which he disagreed with, he would dispense with it, claiming that it was inconsistent with what the writer himself believed in his better moments. In other words, Bultmann thought that the New

Testament documents were inconsistent with themselves, but that he had found the key for deciding what could be rejected and what must be retained.

This type of interpretation was called by Bultmann *Sachkritik* ('substance criticism') and was applied by him to such matters as the resurrection of Jesus described in 1 Corinthians 15:1–11. Bultmann maintained that this belief was inconsistent with the general tone of Paul's writings elsewhere, and therefore claimed that in writing this passage, Paul had had an 'off day'! Of course, such argumentation is ludicrous, in that Paul did not dash off his letters without thinking about their contents, especially not when the subject-matter was as serious as this. Bultmann's problem was that he was trying to express his own beliefs through the medium of an ancient text with which he claimed to be in historical continuity, but with which he in fact disagreed. His work was a last attempt among liberal scholars to hold personal belief within the canon of Scripture, and it resulted in a complete distortion of the latter. In this connection we may add in passing that as Bultmann did not regard his faith as continuous with that of the Old Testament, he had little to say about that part of the Bible.

Bultmann's total indifference to history was another serious weakness which could not long survive criticism. For Christianity was a historical religion. There was a well-known historical time when it did not exist, and another well-known historical time when it had appeared. Between these two stood the figure of Jesus of Nazareth, who simply would not go away, or allow himself to be transformed into a 'Christ-event' divorced from the historical process. Sooner or later the historical Jesus was bound to resurface, and when it did, Bultmann's theological construction began to melt away.

Redaction criticism

Bultmann's own pupils were among the first to detect the weaknesses in his approach, and they began the search for a better synthesis of the Bible as both history and theology. Bultmann had shown little interest in the evangelists as theologians; for him, the gospels were a collection of theologically informative fragments which had to be isolated and examined separately. But his pupils soon found it more interesting to discuss how and why these fragments had been pieced together in their present form. It is important to understand that the primary motive for this was theological, rather than exegetical. Bultmann's own theological position can be outlined as follows.

1. Faith must not be bolstered by rational argument, because this might make it less than all-sufficient for salvation.

2. Faith cannot be exposed to the risk of rational investigation, and is therefore best kept separate from historical claims. We cannot expect to change or abandon our faith simply because of some archaeological discovery.

3. Faith is a relationship with God, who cannot be understood in human terms; it is therefore wrong to try to lower him to a level we can cope with.

4. Faith is centred in Jesus, who for a Christian is a unique revelation of God. This is a matter of conviction which is not open to proof by rational means because it goes far deeper than human reason.

The redaction critics who followed Bultmann (G. Bornkamm, E. Käsemann, H. Conzelmann) tended to agree with him on all these points, with the partial exception of the last. It is obviously impossible to 'prove' anything about Jesus by rational enquiry, but that does not make it undesirable to find out as much as we can, because historical facts will shape our faith to a larger degree than Bultmann was prepared to recognize. For example, Christianity would not be what it is had Jesus never been crucified; that historical fact lies at the very heart of the proclamation.

The redaction critics were also aware that there was a vital link between the Jesus of history and the Christ of faith. They were not content to let these two things drift apart, because the early church proclaimed their identity and made it the basis of its faith. Without the resurrection, there would have been no Christianity. They were aware that the evangelists were writing in the light of the 'Easter event', as the resurrection came to be called, and did not believe that it was possible or desirable to go back beyond this. For them, the 'historical Jesus' was essentially Jesus as he was perceived in the light of Easter, with the benefit of hindsight. The details might be hidden from the view of modern believers, just as the roots of a tree are invisible to those who lie in its shade, but they are there – and they matter. This was the essence of the 'new quest' for the historical Jesus, which took shape in the 1950s and 1960s.

From a literary point of view, there can be no doubt that redaction criticism was much more satisfactory than the old source criticism, which had merely analysed the text, or even than form criticism, which had examined the resulting pieces to see whether there were common patterns or structures. But the 'new quest' theologians were not literary analysts; they were historians, interested in 'facts'. It is probably because of this that they were ultimately unsuccessful. Their method, which was highly promising from a literary point of view, was put to the service of a different end – historical criticism. This would not work in the long term, and the 'new quest' did not survive beyond the initial attempts to demonstrate its potential.

The historical question

Redaction criticism clearly raised the question of how much historicity there is behind the gospel accounts, and we have seen that it was less sceptical about this than Bultmann had been. Even so, redaction critics were not generally prepared to abandon Bultmann's assertion that the *Sitz im Leben* of the gospels must be sought in the early church, not in the life of Jesus of Nazareth. This is a vitally important point, which determines all modern New Testament exegesis. Ever since the time of F. C. Baur it has been accepted that the Pauline epistles (and to a lesser degree the catholic epistles as well) are the most historically reliable of all the New Testament documents. The reason for this is simple. They were letters, written to particular people and dealing with particular problems. It is well known that letters are among the most valuable sources of information we possess; examining them is always a major task of any historian. So putting the epistles first was good historical method, quite apart from anything else.

Problems arose, however, when the epistles were used as a yardstick by which Acts and the gospels could be measured. To say, for example, that the birth narratives represent a later theology simply because there is nothing like them in the epistles is taking this method too far. We do not know why they are not mentioned in the epistles, and an argument from silence is always a dangerous one. Saying nothing might mean anything. The point would be valid only if it could be shown that the epistles somehow contradict the birth narratives of the gospels, and this, of course, they do not do. A number of biblical scholars, especially in the English-speaking world, were prone to use arguments of this kind to demonstrate that the new methods of critical research were faulty, and that they did not destroy the historical credibility of the gospels. That might be difficult to prove, and it would usually be a question of believing the text to be right until (and unless) it could be shown to be wrong – but that was another matter.

The real problem of historicity showed itself in the epistles themselves, and in Acts. Sir William Ramsay had discovered that

Luke was historically reliable to a degree which had previously been undreamt of, and this gave Acts a new credibility among historians. The epistles, however, became increasingly difficult to situate in their historical setting. Nobody doubted that they had one; the problem lay in trying to describe it adequately. In some cases, notably 1 and 2 Corinthians, it was disputed whether the epistles as we now have them are original texts, or conflations of earlier documents, reflecting a different *Sitz im Leben.*

Pauline authorship of the epistles attributed to him was less widely denied than it had been in the nineteenth century, but there were still a number of scholars who doubted the authenticity of Colossians and the pastorals, and Ephesians hovered on the brink of recognition. In general, it was felt that the situations these letters described were too 'advanced' historically to be placed in the time of Paul; they must have reflected the work of his disciples in the next generation. Of course, this cannot be proved, and a case can be made out the other way, as J. A. T. Robinson showed so clearly (1976). But old ideas persisted in spite of these arguments, and it is still difficult to find a critical scholar who readily accepts the Pauline authorship of the pastorals, in spite of the great amount of research which has gone into demonstrating this.

Even in the undoubtedly Pauline epistles, however, there were a number of important historical questions which remained unanswered. The precise identity of the Galatians still caused problems, although the 'South Galatian' theory of Ramsay seemed by far the more probable of the alternatives. The nature of the 'conflict' between Jew and Gentile was still debated, even though several scholars warned that a rigid division between them was too simplistic. Only in the 1970s was it conclusively proved, by archaeological research at Aphrodisias, that the 'God-fearers' mentioned in Acts (*i.e.* Gentiles who believed in the God of Israel and lived on the fringes of the synagogues) actually existed, and even then some scholars continued to doubt it.

The existence of the God-fearers has some importance for the whole question of Gnostic influence, which has been a major question in New Testament research since before 1850. It has now been generally agreed that Christianity was not a Gnostic sect, and radical views of this kind no longer carry any conviction. At the same time, it is still uncertain to what extent a form of Gnosticism can be found in the New Testament. Who, for example, were the opponents of Paul at Corinth? What was the problem at Colossae? The origins of Gnosticism remain mysterious, and in any case it was never a single sect or movement, but a way of thinking which had many manifestations.

By the second century some of these manifestations had developed into recognizable 'theological' systems, in which a central role was played by a heavenly Redeemer. The analogy with Jesus is clear enough, but the old view, that Christianity absorbed this myth and applied it to Christ, is now untenable. If anything, it was the other way round; others took the story of Christ and interpreted it against a philosophical background which was human-centred and inward-looking. The Gnostic systems may be compared to some pseudo-Christian and New Age sects today. Like them, they combined an unsystematized welter of spiritual themes and experiences in a way which purported to be an improvement on mainstream Christianity, and like them they were parasitic; without Christianity they would not have existed. It seems quite possible that something approaching a kind of proto-Gnosticism existed in the church at the time of Paul, but if so, it lacked inner coherence and could not maintain itself as an independent system.

Judaism

Closely tied to the question of the historicity of the New Testament has been the rediscovery of contemporary Palestinian Judaism. This has opened up a number of perspectives which were occasionally hinted at in earlier research, but which were generally regarded as unprovable. Among them was the belief that Judaism in Jesus' day was pluralistic to a degree unknown later. The greatest monuments to this belief have been written since the mid-1970s, but the seeds were sown a generation before. Very little, if anything, in the gospels has not been matched from one Jewish source or another, so that a theory of Gentile influence is superfluous. Many scholars now assume that Christianity grew out of Judaism almost exclusively, and that the 'Hellenistic' influences which may be detected in the New Testament – most obviously the use of Greek to write it – had been thoroughly absorbed by the Jews before Christianity appeared on the scene.

The variety of Judaism in the time of Jesus makes it easier to find a place for him as a Jewish teacher. There is no need to make him an Essene, or a Zealot, in spite of S. G. F. Brandon's attempt to do so (1967). If Judaism was genuinely pluralistic, there would have been plenty of room for him. The exegetical methods of the New Testament writers have now been shown to have had close parallels in contemporary Judaism, particularly at Qumran, where so-called 'Pesher' exegesis was just as popular as it is in the New Testament. By the mid-1970s, it was taken for granted that Judaism was an essential ingredient in Christianity, but it was still generally thought that Jesus, or at least Paul, preached a gospel quite different from anything the rabbis could have accepted. Only later, and then in quite a radical way, was this assumption challenged, and the role of Judaism in the rise of Christianity extended to become even more pervasive than before.

Perhaps the most important single fact which has emerged from the study of Judaism is that Jesus made significant use of Jewish apocalyptic concepts. His preferred title for himself, 'Son of Man', is clearly one of these, being derived from Daniel 7. Likewise, his preaching of the 'kingdom of God' has been shown to have a Jewish apocalyptic background, though the precise meaning of the term remains somewhat obscure. But it also seems fairly clear that the historical Jesus was not the wild apocalyptic figure portrayed by A. Schweitzer. Jesus used apocalyptic imagery in a careful and deliberate way, and integrated it into a different agenda. Jesus may have employed familiar Jewish concepts, but if so, he used them in an original and compelling way.

The fruits of historical criticism for New Testament study

We may now summarize what historical criticism in its different forms had contributed to the study of the New Testament by the 1970s. The list given here is similar to that of Bishop Stephen Neill (1964).

1. The New Testament is now freely studied in a non-confessional, even in a non-religious, atmosphere. Anyone who possesses the appropriate academic tools is, in principle, welcome to participate in scholarly research. If anything, there is a bias against those who may be suspected of religious presuppositions which might influence the course of their research.

2. A text of the Greek New Testament has been reconstructed which is as close to the original as it is possible to get. There may be new developments in this area, but at the moment that seems unlikely.

3. The Greek language of the New Testament period has been thoroughly studied. We now know that the New Testament is written in the vernacular, but with a particular flavour all its own.

4. The entire New Testament must now be dated in the first century, and possibly before AD 70. This considerably reduces the

time available for oral tradition to have developed, and is a pointer to the greater historical accuracy of the text.

5. The Pauline epistles are the earliest and most historically reliable parts of the New Testament.

6. Mark's gospel was probably the earliest to have been written, in spite of the arguments put forward in favour of Matthaean priority. However, it is now clear that the synoptic problem cannot be resolved in any schematic or artificial way, and it seems most likely that the three gospels grew up alongside each other to some extent.

7. The shape and content of the gospels were strongly influenced by the needs of the early church, though precisely how remains uncertain.

8. At the heart of Jesus' message was his proclamation of the 'kingdom of God', a phrase which must be understood against a background of Jewish apocalyptic, though, again, it is not agreed how this can best be done.

9. The New Testament reflects both Jewish and Hellenistic influences, with the former predominating. However, its message cannot be reduced to a combination of these two factors; there is something radically new about it as well.

10. The fourth gospel is distinct from the synoptics, but this does not mean that it has no historical value. In some ways, it may reflect traditions which are even older than those recorded in the synoptic gospels.

These points sum up the main achievements of historical criticism, and with few modifications they may be said to be still valid today. However, in the meantime the discussion has moved on to other matters, and the great debates which lie behind some of these 'conclusions' have been not so much resolved as shunted to one side.

BIBLIOGRAPHY

F. W. Dillistone, *C. H. Dodd: Interpreter of the New Testament* (London: Hodder and Stoughton, 1977).

F. Donadio, *Critica del mito e ragione teologica: Saggio su Rudolf Bultmann* (Naples: Guida Editori, 1983).

W. J. Hynes, *Shirley Jackson Case and the Chicago School* (Chico, CA: Scholars Press, 1981).

W. G. Kümmel, *The New Testament: The History of the Investigation of its Problems* (London: SCM, 1972).

R. Morgan with J. Barton, *Biblical Interpretation* (Oxford: Oxford University Press, 1988).

S. Neill and N. T. Wright, *The Interpretation of the New Testament 1861–1986* (Oxford: Oxford University Press, 1988).
J. C. O'Neill, *The Bible's Authority* (Edinburgh: T. and T. Clark, 1991).
J. Painter, *Theology as Hermeneutics: Rudolf Bultmann's Interpretation of the History of Jesus* (Sheffield: Sheffield Academic Press, 1987).
R. E. Parsons, *Sir Edwyn Hoskyns as a Biblical Theologian* (London: C. Hurst, 1985).
J. D. Smart, *The Past, Present and Future of Biblical Theology* (Philadelphia: Westminster, 1979).
P. Stuhlmacher, *Historical Criticism and Theological Interpretation of Scripture* (Philadelphia: Fortress, 1977; London: SPCK, 1979).
————*Vom Verstehen des Neuen Testaments* (Göttingen: Vandenhoeck und Ruprecht, 1979).
D. Way, *The Lordship of Christ: Ernst Käsemann's Interpretation of Paul's Theology* (Oxford: Oxford University Press, 1991).

A case study: Revelation (the Apocalypse)

With the possible exception of the Song of Songs, no book of the Bible has been subjected to more diverse and fantastic interpretations than the Relevation to John, sometimes known by its Greek name, the Apocalypse. In a recent study of how the book was interpreted in the Renaissance, C. A. Patrides listed no fewer than 1,313 commentaries on all or part of the book in the period up to 1979, and added that this list was incomplete. From the beginning of church history, the special character of the book was recognized, and there were debates about how it should be read. Origen interpreted it allegorically, and it certainly lends itself to that kind of treatment. But many ancient commentators also read the book literally, as a prophecy of the end of the world. A certain Bishop Nepos, somewhere in Egypt, apparently thought that there would be a millennium on earth, when the saints would be able to indulge in hedonistic pleasures.

It was left to the Bishop of Alexandria, Dionysius, to refute this idea, which he did in a book called *On Promises,* which is now lost. According to Eusebius, Dionysius also gave three reasons why John the apostle was not the author of the Apocalypse. First, the Apocalypse names him as John, unlike either the gospel or the epistles ascribed to him. Second, the style and construction of the Apocalypse are very different from those of the other Johannine writings. The Apocalypse is written in very peculiar, almost barbaric,

Greek, whereas the gospel and epistles show an elegant mastery of the language. Third, its character is different from that of the other Johannine writings; its theology and content are quite unique, and unlike anything else in the New Testament. Dionysius's arguments were perceptive, but his was a lone voice until the rise of historical criticism appeared to vindicate his judgment.

Today, Dionysius's views are widely held, but the question of authorship is far from being settled and modern scholars are sharply divided on the question. For if Dionysius's case is strong, so is that of the traditionalists. They argue that no other early Christian writer would have dared to call himself 'John' without qualification. The book's style can be explained by its genre; on that score, the differences between the gospel and the epistles are just as great. The 'barbaric language' which so displeased Dionysius has been shown to belong to apocalyptic as a genre; John's solecisms were deliberate, and put there for stylistic effect. As for the content and theology, there are more links than one might imagine between John's gospel and the Apocalypse. The recent rediscovery of the essential Jewishness of the fourth gospel has helped here, since the Apocalypse is deeply impregnated with Old Testament and Jewish folk imagery. But it is also true that the Apocalypse concentrates on certain Johannine themes, of which the most obvious and important are the Lamb of God and the heavenly descent of Jesus. Johannine authorship of the Apocalypse is therefore not to be ruled out.

The struggle between Dionysius and Nepos demonstrates the dilemma which interpreters of Revelation have encountered for hundreds of years. If the book is interpreted historically, it must be a future prophecy of the coming end. Political events can therefore be assumed to lie behind the apocalyptic imagery, which points towards a coming judgment. In the ancient world this approach was called 'chiliasm' after the Greek word *chiliae* (thousand) – a reference to the thousand-year reign of Christ forecast in Revelation 20. Later on, this came to be known by its Latin name, 'millenarianism', which is how we normally describe it today.

Chiliasm developed against the background of fear which permeated the persecuted church of the second and third centuries. Its message of judgment on the secular order following the triumphant return of Christ, and the vindication of the suffering saints, was a great comfort to people who had neither the desire nor the means to rebel against their situation. Rather than attempt the impossible, Christians merely had to learn to read the signs of the times, and discern in them the approaching end. But, as it turned out, the 'end' was rather different from what they had been led to expect. Instead of a terminal conflict between the kingdom of Christ and the Roman Empire, the Empire came to terms with the church, and embraced Christianity within its system. Somehow, it became clear that traditional chiliasm would no longer work, and a new interpretation of the Apocalypse had to be devised. Many theologians put their minds to this task, with varying degrees of success, but the interpretation which became standard was that of Augustine.

Augustine did not adopt an allegorical position pure and simple. Instead, he interpreted the whole of human history as a vast conflict between the forces of good and evil, represented by the two 'cities', Jerusalem and Babylon. These 'cities' could not simply be identified with their earthly counterparts, though of course there were points of resemblance. Rather they were symbols, used to represent spiritual powers at work in the world. In his own time, Augustine recognized Jerusalem in the church and Babylon in the civil power, though the correspondence was far from complete. Good and evil could not be pinned down quite as easily as that. As for the thousand-year reign, Augustine believed that this referred to the present age of the church, an interpretation which removed the eschatological element. During this age, the forces of evil would be held in check, until at some future time Christ would return to redeem his people.

Augustine's interpretation was generally followed in the centuries after him, though even in his time there were endless variations as to detail. A good example can be found in the interpretations put on Revelation 4:7, which describes the vision of the four living creatures around the throne of God. Most writers seemed to believe that they represented the four evangelists, but they could not agree as to which creature represented which evangelist. The following comparative table gives some idea of the range of opinions which were held.

	Irenaeus	**Primasius**	**Jerome**
lion	John	Matthew	Mark
ox	Luke	Luke	Luke
man	Matthew	Mark	Matthew
eagle	Mark	John	John

Students of medieval art history will recognize that Jerome's view eventually became the 'standard' one.

As time went on, there was an increasing tendency to equate Jerusalem with the church and Babylon with the state, especially during the great controversies of the high Middle Ages. Some people thought that judgment would come in the year 1000, but it passed without incident. In the eleventh century it seems that the papacy itself encouraged a chiliastic interpretation, to serve its own political ends, though without much success. The real breakthrough in interpretation came with the work of Joachim da Fiore, a Calabrian monk who lived in the second half of the twelfth century. Joachim revived the economic trinitarianism of the second-century church, according to which each person of the Godhead was associated with a particular age of human history. Joachim did not simply take over the ancient scheme, though; indeed, he may not have known about it.

According to Joachim, the first age began at the creation and continued into the Old Testament life of the people of Israel. The second age started with the messianic hope in the Old Testament, and overlapped with the first until the coming of Christ. The third age had not yet begun. It would be characterized by a full revelation of the Holy Spirit, who would usher in an age of progress and illumination. Joachim related the vision of the Apocalypse to this scheme, and discovered parallels between the opening of the seven seals, and the tribulations associated with them, and the history of Israel before the coming of Christ. The same pattern was being repeated in the history of the church, which he believed was then entering the tribulations of the sixth seal. When that time came to an end, the seventh seal would be opened and the church would enter into the Sabbath rest of God, represented in Revelation 8:1 by the half-hour of silence.

Joachim's views were soon popularized, and spread far and wide, causing social disturbances for many decades afterwards. The official church authorities condemned his works and tried to suppress them, but with only limited success. A new twist was now added to the familiar arguments – that of the coming of the Antichrist. At first, this figure was identified with Frederick II (1194–1250), but when he died without any great upheaval, speculation ran rife. The thirteenth century was an age of great prophetic expectation, which of course failed to materialize.

The figure of the Antichrist developed still further in the fourteenth century, when for the first time he was identified with the pope. Joachim and many others of his time had hoped for an angelic pope, and they had interpreted passages such as Revelation 20:1 as a reference to the papacy. But although this interpretation was to survive until the sixteenth century, it was eventually superseded by the exact opposite. The first person known to have denounced the papacy as Antichrist was the Emperor Frederick II, though his political motives were too obvious for him to be taken seriously. But by 1300 a number of Franciscans and their supporters were condemning the worldliness of the Roman court in apocalyptic terms, and a negative evaluation of both individual popes and the institution of the papacy became common in the fourteenth century. The definitive identification of the papacy with the Antichrist was made by the Lollard followers of John Wycliffe, and from there it spread to the Hussites in Bohemia. After that it became a commonplace of popular folklore, and resurfaced with a vengeance at the Reformation.

It must of course be stressed that interpretations of this kind were largely confined to the popular level; they were not shared by the educated élite. Luther's opinion of the Apocalypse was surprisingly similar to that of Dionysius of Alexandria, and Calvin never wrote a commentary on it. Both Luther and Calvin used the Apocalypse from time to time, as a source of instruction and consolation, but neither seems to have had a systematic view of it. As far as we can tell, they tried to read it historically, as a prophecy of the trials which the church would suffer, and of the ultimate victory which it would win. The circumstances of the time made the identification of the papacy with the Antichrist very tempting, and Luther actually called the pope the Antichrist in his response to the Bull which excommunicated him (1520). Later, in the so-called Smalcald Articles (1537), this identification was confirmed, and it subsequently entered official Lutheran theology. It also appeared in the Westminster Confession of Faith (1647), though again as an isolated tenet, unrelated to any overall interpretation of the Apocalypse.

The relative restraint of the Reformers did not last, of course, and in the heat of the religious controversies which broke out in the late sixteenth and early seventeenth centuries, apocalyptic imagery became a commonplace of political debate. The precise identification of the Antichrist changed with the circumstances: sometimes it was the pope, sometimes the Holy Roman Emperor, and sometimes the king of either England or France. The common thread which united all these identifications was that the Antichrist was the upholder of an established order which revolutionary forces were trying to overturn. Once this political pattern was established, it repeated and renewed itself from one generation to the next. The French Revolution and the many upheavals of the twentieth century were all regarded in this light by certain groups of Christians, though interpretations of this kind were seldom if ever accepted by the official church establishments.

What characterized them most of all was the increasingly elaborate systematization which they underwent, especially after the events of the French Revolution. Beginning with the work of John Nelson Darby (1800–82) and continuing through a succession of conservative interpreters, a new form of 'dispensationalism' emerged which purported to explain the Apocalypse in terms of the fulfilment of prophecy. As with earlier interpretations, this new form focused on the millennium rather than on the figure of the Antichrist, though there was certainly no shortage of candidates for his role. Dispensationalism enjoyed its greatest triumph in the Scofield Reference Bible, which was published by Oxford University Press in 1909. The editor of this edition, C. I. Scofield (1843–1921), championed a form of millenarianism which soon came to be regarded as 'orthodox' in fundamentalist circles, particularly in the USA, and this has frequently remained the case even today. At the present time, dispensationalism is still a doctrinal issue in many American churches, and is closely associated with Dallas Theological Seminary, in particular.

To outsiders, millenarianism seems much of a muchness, but to those within the dispensationalist framework there are any number of subtleties which distinguish one group of interpreters from the others. It is impossible to list all the variations in a short space, but the main ones can be outlined as follows.

1. *The historic premillenarians.* They stick to the 'natural' reading of Revelation 20:1–6, according to which Christ's second coming precedes his thousand-year reign. At the end of the millennium there will be the final consummation and judgment. During the millennium, Satan will be bound and his power will be curtailed. The saints will rise from the dead, in what is known as the first resurrection. At the end of the thousand years, Satan will be let loose to do battle with God. He will lose this battle, of course, and be destroyed. There will then follow the second resurrection and the final judgment. Historic premillenarians are careful to interpret the Old Testament in the light of the New. They insist that the church is the inheritor of the millennial promises, and that it is inappropriate to apply them to the historic Israel, except in a secondary sense. It may be true, as Paul suggests in Romans 11, that the Jews will be saved as part of the final consummation, but this does not imply that they have a separate destiny apart from the Christian church.

2. *The dispensational premillenarians.* They believe that the destinies of Israel and the church are separate, because each belongs to a different dispensation. For this reason, the promises made to Israel in the Old Testament must still be fulfilled, including the return of

the Jews to Palestine and the re-establishment of the state of Israel. It is because of this view that dispensational premillenarians strongly support modern Zionism. Dispensationalists also make a distinction between the 'kingdom of heaven' and the 'kingdom of God' as these terms are found in the New Testament. According to them, the kingdom of heaven is an eternal reality, whereas the kingdom of God is a promise to be fulfilled within a temporal future. It must be admitted, however, that this distinction is obscure, and little understood outside the circles in which it is proclaimed.

More significant for dispensationalists is the question of the great tribulation in Revelation 7. According to the standard view, the saints will be taken up into heaven before the tribulation, and thus escape the suffering which is due to follow. This event is known as the rapture. At a later stage there will be a resurrection of those saints who endure the tribulation, and still later, another resurrection of those who die during the millennium. The idea of a series of resurrections is difficult to harmonize with the text of the Apocalypse, and has been the source of considerable criticism of the dispensationalist theory.

Dispensationalism of this kind has penetrated a very wide circle of conservative evangelicals in the USA, and is regarded as an essential component of 'orthodoxy' by many of them. It combines the view that the general movement of creation is upwards, and is therefore able to come to terms with modern notions of progress, but at the same time it insists that this will be interrupted by a sudden catastrophe, and is therefore basically pessimistic. In the midst of prosperity and affluence, say the dispensationalists, judgment is at hand. This view has an obvious echo in some of the Old Testament prophets, and in that sense it may be said to be continuing an ancient biblical tradition.

3. *The post-millenarians.* These are now a minority group, but they were once quite powerful and articulate, and may one day be so again. Post-millenarians believe with Augustine that the present age must be equated with the thousand-year reign of Christ. They maintain that in spite of apparent reverses, the triumphant progress of the gospel cannot be stopped. The kingdom of God is not a future hope but a present reality, which is daily being extended by the preaching of the gospel. According to this theory, the world will be fully Christianized before Christ comes again after a long period of peace and prosperity. Many post-millenarians reject the crisis mentality of the dispensationalists in favour of what is sometimes known as a 'prosperity gospel'. This type of millenarianism has close

affinities with the liberalism of the late nineteenth century, and its followers are frequently classed with them by their opponents.

4. *The amillenarians.* These are the people who believe that the millennium is a spiritual symbol which has no direct historical reference point. To some extent they agree with the post-millenarians, in that they tend to identify the blessings of this age with the current life of the church. Christ has already won the decisive victory over Satan, sin and death, and so it is impossible to look upon this as a future event. There is no distinction between the kingdom of heaven and the kingdom of God; both terms refer to a reality which is equally temporal and eternal. Amillenarians also reject the distinction between Israel and the church, at least as far as future destiny is concerned. There will be only one resurrection, and only one fulfilment of the promises – in and through Christ. The second coming of Christ will therefore be a single event, in which the last resurrection, the rapture and the judgment will take place simultaneously.

In so far as the mainline Christian churches may be said to have a position on the matter, it has traditionally been amillenarian. However, it must be added that the question has seldom been raised as a matter of urgency outside circles which may be loosely described as 'fundamentalist'; the true position of most mainline Christians is one of cautious agnosticism, not to say open indifference to something which in the final analysis appears to them to be unclear.

When we turn from popular beliefs to scholarly theories, a different picture emerges. It hardly seems necessary to state that the Apocalypse had no appeal to the rationalists of the seventeenth and eighteenth centuries, almost all of whom regarded it as barbaric, and even insane. This negative estimation carried over into the academic scholarship of the nineteenth century, where the general opinion was that, although the book had certain literary and theological merits, it was generally inferior to the rest of the New Testament and could safely be ignored by the church. Given that these same theologians had a high regard for the moral and theological qualities of the fourth gospel, it is not surprising that the nineteenth century witnessed a widespread rejection of the traditional Johannine authorship of Revelation.

One of the astonishing results of twentieth-century biblical study has been the scholarly discovery of apocalyptic as a way of thinking characteristic of Judaism in New Testament times. Perhaps there is no better single instance of how the liberal consensus of the 1800s has been almost completely overturned. This change of direction was already foreshadowed in the work of J. Weiss and A. Schweitzer, who portrayed the historical Jesus as an eschatological prophet whose message would be completely incomprehensible to most people today. Since that time, the rediscovery and analysis of other apocalyptic texts from the ancient world has helped scholars put the canonical Apocalypse in a literary and historical context which has greatly aided the whole course of interpretation. Not everyone would want to go as far as E. Käsemann (1960), who declared that apocalyptic was the mother of all Christian theology, but this view of the centrality of apocalyptic for our understanding of the mentality of the early church is much more common now than it once was, and is largely the fruit of a form-critical analysis of recent textual discoveries and research.

Apocalyptic has now been recognized as a genre in its own right. This means that there are certain literary rules to which it conforms. Behind the form lies the message of apocalypticism, which is greater than the content of the actual apocalypses. In the form-critical analysis of apocalyptic, we can observe two basic distinctions. The first is between apocalypses in which the seer goes on an extraterrestrial journey and those in which he does not. The canonical Apocalypse belongs to the former type (see Rev. 4). The second is between apocalypses which present a review of history, complete with the coming crisis and transformation; those which present the crisis and transformation without the review of history, and those which are purely personal in their understanding of eschatology. The canonical Apocalypse belongs to the second of these categories, though some interpreters would put it in the first.

It must always be remembered that, as in most form-critical analyses, there are texts which do not fit neatly into the definition of the genre. These may be regarded as containing apocalyptic elements, and in some cases (*e.g.* the *Apocalypse of Moses*) may even carry the official title, without being apocalypses in the literary sense of the term. General features common to most, if not all, literary apocalypses are as follows.

1. The revelation is conveyed to humankind through the agency of a heavenly mediator. In Jewish apocalyptic there is always an angel, and many Christian apocalypses are similar in this respect. However, some, including the canonical Apocalypse, have Christ as the mediator of the message.

2. The revelation is made to a human sage, who is pseudonymous. In Jewish apocalyptic, he is usually a figure from the remote past, such as Enoch, Daniel or Moses. Christian apocalypses are sometimes

exceptional, in that the seer is a figure of the new covenant, though the question of his identity remains unresolved, as we have already seen in the case of John. If the John of Revelation is the apostle, his Apocalypse is a prominent exception to the established rule in this matter.

3. The revelation may be made visually or orally. In the apocalyptic texts there is almost always some combination of these, with the result that the visionary aspect is invested with a heavy degree of symbolism. Here the canonical Apocalypse is no exception.

4. The revelation is almost always connected with a book of some kind. It may have come in the form of a book sent down from heaven, or it may be the seer's duty to write what he has seen (as in the canonical Apocalypse), but either way, the 'scriptural' character of apocalypse is quite striking. It is meant to be conveyed to its prospective audience in written rather than in spoken form – a feature which distinguishes it from traditional prophecy.

5. The revelation is concerned with historical destiny. This may be heavily overlaid with allegorical symbolism, but underneath it there is a concern to demonstrate how divine providence controls the historical process, which is rapidly heading towards its predetermined end. This end will be catastrophic, but in the sense that a divine judgment will break in at some point to overturn the established order. Central to this is the cosmic battle between good and evil, which will be won by the forces of good. The precise relationship between this cosmic reality and historical events as we understand them is seldom clarified, and it is difficult to link specific incidents with apocalyptic fulfilment – another important difference between apocalyptic and prophecy. Nevertheless, events in human history typify the overall struggle being waged at the spiritual level, and the wise person will be able to read the signs of the times.

When we compare the results of this scholarly investigation, we are struck by the many similarities and differences between its conclusions and the traditional interpretations of the church. It is certainly too simple to dismiss the classical traditions of interpretation as mistaken; many of them have elements in common with recent scholarly analysis. Historical premillenarianism has been vindicated in the sense that apocalyptic clearly points to a future fulfilment of history, which is viewed as a unitary concept under the control of God's sovereign will. Dispensational premillenarianism has been upheld in its insistence on the catastrophic nature of the end, which is a clear feature of the genre as a whole. And amillenarianism has been justified in its insistence that the movement of the apocalypse cannot be readily equated with events in human history, to which the revelation is linked in a much more subtle and undefinable way. Even post-millenarianism, which is the interpretation furthest removed from historical apocalyptic, can claim some validity by linking its understanding of the kingdom of God with the providential ordering of history to which the apocalypses bear witness.

In terms of biblical interpretation, therefore, it seems that the traditional views are not so much wrong as inadequate to do justice to all the features of apocalyptic, which are now much better understood than they used to be. Perhaps the church will someday find scholars who will be able to integrate all these perspectives on the basis of what is now known about the genre, and produce an interpretation of the canonical Apocalypse which will command the general assent of Christians.

An encouraging move in that direction can be seen in recent books by Richard Bauckham, who has made apocalyptic a major area of his own research and expertise. For him, the book is Christian prophecy, intimately connected with the entire Jewish and early Christian prophetic inheritance. As he says in *The Theology of the Book of Revelation* (1993):

> Revelation's claim to be prophecy must be understood in relation to its claim to continuity with the whole biblical prophetic tradition . . . Like biblical prophecy in general, Revelation as prophecy may be said to comprise three closely related elements. First, there is *discernment* of the contemporary situation by prophetic insight into God's nature and purpose . . . Secondly, there is *prediction.* In John's vision he sees not only 'what is', but also 'what must take place after this' (1:19, *cf.* 4:1, 1:1). Essentially, the prediction consists in seeing how God's ultimate purpose relates to the contemporary situation as it is perceived by the prophet. What *must* take place is the coming of God's kingdom – or God would not be God . . . Thirdly, prophecy demands of its hearers an appropriate *response* to its perception of the truth of the contemporary world and its prediction of what the working-out of God's purpose must mean for the contemporary world.

Bauckham goes on to point out that, just as the promises made by other biblical prophecy were frequently only partially fulfilled in the time when the prophecy was given, so Revelation retains an element of unfulfilled, eschatological hope. The book's ultimate purpose is to give the reader an understanding of the meaning of human history by opening up a new and deeper vision of God. Revelation is primarily *theology* in the strictest sense; it is a deeper penetration into the mystery of the Divine Being. To quote Bauckham again:

> Revelation has the most developed trinitarian theology in the New Testament, with the possible exception of the Gospel of John, and is all the more valuable for demonstrating the development of trinitarianism quite independently of hellenistic philosophical categories. It has a powerful, apophatic perception of the transcendence of God which entirely avoids and surmounts current criticism of monarchical images of transcendence. At the same time as it withholds the glory of God from a world in which the powers of evil still hold sway, it recognises the presence of God in this present world in the form of the slaughtered Lamb and the seven Spirits who inspire the church's witness. By placing the Lamb on the throne and the seven Spirits before the throne it gives sacrificial love and witness to truth the priority in the coming of God's kingdom in the world, while at the same time the openness of the creation to the divine transcendence guarantees the coming of the kingdom.

BIBLIOGRAPHY

R. J. Bauckham, *The Climax of Prophecy: Studies on the Book of Revelation* (Edinburgh: T. and T. Clark, 1993).

———*The Theology of the Book of Revelation* (Cambridge: Cambridge University Press, 1993).

R. G. Clouse, *The Meaning of the Millennium: Four Views* (Downers Grove, IL: IVP, 1977).

N. Cohn, *The Pursuit of the Millennium* (London: Secker and Warburg, 1957).

R. K. Emmerson and B. McGinn, *The Apocalypse in the Middle Ages,* (Ithaca, NY: Cornell University Press, 1992).

S. J. Grenz, *The Millennial Maze: Sorting out Evangelical Options* (Downers Grove, IL: IVP, 1992).

D. Hellholm (ed.), *Apocalypticism in the Mediterranean World and the Near East* (Tübingen: Mohr, 1983).

K. Koch, *The Rediscovery of Apocalyptic* (London: SCM, 1972).

G. Maier, *Die Johannesoffenbarung und die Kirche* (Tübingen: Mohr, 1981).

F. D. Mazzaferri, *The Genre of the Book of Revelation from a Source-Critical Perspective* (Berlin and New York: De Gruyter, 1989).
L. Morris, *Apocalyptic* (London: IVP, 1972).
C. A. Patrides and J. Wittreich (eds.), *The Apocalypse in English Renaissance Thought and Literature* (Manchester: Manchester University Press, 1984).
D. S. Russell, *Apocalyptic: Ancient and Modern* (London: SCM, 1978).
A. W. Wainwright, *Mysterious Apocalypse: Interpreting the Book of Revelation* (Nashville: Abingdon, 1993).

Part 3

The contemporary scene

From the end of the nineteenth century until the 1970s, it was taken for granted among academics that the historical-critical method was the only scientifically respectable way to study the Bible. Of course there were 'fundamentalists' and other traditionalists about, who rejected the method and applied different criteria to the biblical texts, but they were not taken seriously. The scholarly battle for the historical-critical method had been won, to all appearances definitively. Yet suddenly everything was thrown into the melting-pot again. Historical criticism came under attack from many different sources, including from within the discipline itself. Alternative methods of interpretation were put forward and were taken seriously by scholars, many of whom were beginning to participate in interdisciplinary research. The relevance of the Bible to social and political issues was rediscovered, somewhat to the surprise of a public which had grown used to associating Christianity with political conservatism.

Religious issues also made a comeback of a sort. For a long time religious commitment was on the decline among scholars, and this process seemed to be accelerating after 1945. The notion that a scholar could or should be judged by his theology was becoming increasingly obsolete, and discussion of theological issues in the Bible was conducted on the assumption that scholars would keep their personal convictions, if any, to themselves. The acceptance of historical criticism among Roman Catholics broke down the last major confessional barrier, and unified the scholarly world on a religiously neutral 'scientific' basis. But just as this was happening, a new type of religiously committed scholarship made its appearance. This was the revived form of conservative evangelicalism which began to grow rapidly in the 1950s and was set to become the largest single branch of Protestantism by the end of the century. The new evangelicalism was less dogmatic than its older counterpart, but it was also more exclusively 'biblical' than ever before. William Chillingworth's famous statement that 'the Bible only is the religion of Protestants' was never truer than among post-1945 evangelicals.

Faced with all these pressures, the monolithic structure of historical criticism began to crack. The historical-critical method has certainly not disappeared; in spite of prophecies of its demise, it remains the standard form of biblical interpretation in all major universities and in most textbooks and commentaries. It has not ceased to grow and develop, and the student of the contemporary scene cannot ignore it. It has changed in any number of subtle ways from what it was in 1945, but it is still there.

The secular climate of modern biblical studies means that it is perilously easy for scholars to miss the central point of the Bible, and to take refuge in technical studies which are of no great interest to anyone. The proliferation of PhD theses on highly technical matters provides ample evidence of this. The issues may be important, and may even change the course of scholarship, but they are liable to seem quite irrelevant to anyone less specialized.

The need to relate the findings of biblical specialists to those of colleagues in other disciplines has produced new types of interpretation which cannot be considered 'unscholarly' but which are hard to relate to traditional critical methods. The first and most natural of these is the literary approach. It is obvious that the Bible is part of the world's literature, and foundational for much of it. Yet literary theories have not often been taken very seriously by biblical scholars in modern times. Benjamin Jowett's insistence in *Essays and Reviews* (1860) that the Bible be read 'like any other book' never really got beyond the level of textual criticism. Profounder philosophical questions concerning the nature of language and the social function of literature were not explored in depth until much more recently.

In the 1920s the emergence of form criticism, and later of its offshoot, redaction criticism, prepared the way for a more searching literary analysis of the Bible. Cultural anthropology also reached maturity as a scholarly discipline, and was being applied to Scripture. Finally, new linguistic theories and existential philosophy were also taken on board, so that by the 1970s there had developed a 'new hermeneutic' which sought to analyse the Bible in an entirely new way. Practitioners of the new hermeneutic drew liberally on the surrounding literary culture, many of whose representatives approached the Bible from the disciplines of classical or modern literature or both. As a result of this, literary works from many different cultures, which nobody had thought relevant to biblical studies before, came to be used as examples to illustrate principles of composition in various books of the Bible.

In a completely different sphere, scholars were also turning their attention to questions of politics and social injustice. It was noticed that the Old Testament prophets had a good deal to say about these things, and the exodus of Israel from Egypt could easily be portrayed as a liberation from economic injustice. Marxism challenged the social conscience of the church in Third World countries, just as it was itself challenged by the churches whenever it was in power. The notion that the Bible had a message for economic and political life once more became common, with the difference that now the word 'theology' was used to describe this. Thus we have become familiar with such expressions as 'liberation theology', 'black theology' and 'feminist theology', none of which has much to do with God or with theology in the traditional sense.

The collapse of Marxist regimes in eastern Europe suggests that interpretations of the Bible which have attempted to engage with Marxism are unlikely to have much future, but things are very different with 'black' (*i.e.* non-European) and feminist theologies, both of which are buttressed by the appearance of non-European and female scholars in larger numbers than ever before. The former make great play of the fact that academic scholarship has hitherto been almost exclusively conducted from the standpoint of (white) western European civilization (which for this purpose includes North America, Australia and New Zealand), while the geographical and demographic balance of the church is rapidly shifting in favour of the Third World, and of historically marginalized groups such as the African Americans. There is truth in this perception, but it is difficult to say whether historically 'oppressed' peoples really have something unique to contribute to academic scholarship, or whether what is happening is that they are progressively being integrated into what has been the European, but is now the global, mainstream. At the present time it seems most likely that the emergence of the 'global village' will create a single world culture, in which regional variations will be reduced to the level of folklore.

Feminism presents a different challenge, because there are real differences between men and women which transcend racial and cultural issues. The difficulty is to know how far these can (or should) influence the development of biblical scholarship. The 'rediscovery' of neglected female theologians of the past such as Hildegard of

Bingen, or Julian of Norwich, is interesting, but has not done much to change our general perception of the Middle Ages. It is also uncertain whether there are specifically female concerns in Scripture which male scholars have thus far failed to address. The problem is not so much to focus on neglected areas, of which there are many, but to demonstrate that they are somehow peculiarly 'feminine' concerns. The danger of subjectivity is very great, and it has to be said that the issue has not yet been addressed with sufficient seriousness by the academic world at large.

Finally, the revival of conservative evangelicalism injected a new religious impulse into the scholarly study of the Bible. Some conservative evangelicals became noted critical scholars, fully accepted as such by their more liberal colleagues. But even when this was the case, there remained a fundamental difference of purpose between evangelical academics and their colleagues. At a time when critical scholarship was becoming increasingly esoteric, evangelicals were reminding people that the Bible was meant to be expounded in the teaching ministry of the church. The new evangelicals did not major on systematic or confessional theology as their forebears had done, though they were often suspected of this. Instead they preferred to create a new kind of conservative ecumenism, based on a reductionist understanding of the Reformation principle of *sola Scriptura* ('Scripture alone'). Where someone such as Calvin had a three-stage progression from exegesis to dogmatics to exposition, the new evangelicals omitted the dogmatics and tried to practise exposition on the basis of exegesis alone. This often produced flabby sermons, but the fact that they were concerned with exposition at all set them apart from mainstream critical scholarship.

The new generation of conservative evangelicals also possessed a self-awareness and a group identity which are unique in the history of biblical interpretation. Never before had a minority consciously bound together to challenge an accepted consensus. Few scholars were in any doubt about who was in the movement and who was not; both its supporters and its enemies recognized evangelicals clearly enough when they saw them, even if it was frequently difficult to define them precisely. Their doctrinal flexibility allowed them to embrace conservatives holding a wide range of theological positions, some of which were contradictory (*e.g.* baptist and paedobaptist views of baptism), but it also made it possible for them to exclude anyone who disagreed with certain shibboleths – the single authorship of Isaiah being a prime example. In the 1950s no true conservative evangelical could have accepted the existence of a 'Second Isaiah' and anyone who did so was regarded with deep suspicion. This attitude was challenged in the 1970s, but with limited effect. All that really happened was that a previously united evangelicalism began to split into a more 'liberal' and a more 'conservative' wing, a process in which each side has suspected and mistrusted the other. Whether this was a side-effect of an inevitable coming of age, or the sad result of clashes which could and should have been avoided, is hard to say, but the evangelical world cannot now be defined as easily as it could have been a generation ago.

The contemporary scene thus presents a pluralism of approaches in biblical studies which would have been inconceivable in 1945. The chapters which follow examine the three major groupings outlined above, considering the debates and problems proper to each of them. The dividing lines are far from absolute; for example, among conservative evangelicals there are many scholars who participate fully in critical debates, and there are also a considerable number who are deeply concerned with social and political issues. Nevertheless, there are at least three different worlds of discourse in contemporary biblical studies, and justice must be done to each of them, however much overlap there may be in individual cases. In the following chapters, there is no attempt at inclusive coverage, because contemporary scholarship covers too vast a range. Only the main trends and movements are dealt with, and a selection of representative writers and works is given.

In cultural and linguistic terms, the contemporary scene is distinguished by the emergence of English as the dominant language of biblical study. Even as the Bible itself is being translated into virtually every known human tongue, the languages in which advanced scholarship is written are becoming fewer. English has long dominated in the natural sciences, but its progress in the humanities has been slower. However, since the mid-1970s English-language publications have outstripped all others, and there is little sign that this trend is about to alter. Perhaps the best way to measure it is to look at the percentage of English-language articles published in journals intended for a largely non-Anglophone readership. For this purpose, we have compared four journals of international reputation: the *Zeitschrift für die alttestamentliche Wissenschaft* (*ZATW*), the *Zeitschrift für die neutestamentliche Wissenschaft* (*ZNTW*), *Biblica* (*B*) and the *Revue Biblique* (*RB*). The percentages of English-language articles published in them since 1945 are as follows.

	ZATW	*ZNTW*	*B*	*RB*
1945–54	20	5	14	0
1955–64	22	11	27	0
1965–74	33	13	40	4
1975–84	55	23	53	9
1985–94	50	23	65	28

When we consider that English-language journals seldom publish in any other language, and also that they are far more numerous overall, we can begin to measure the effect of this enormous change, which is taking place before our very eyes.

11

Academic trends in interpretation

Introduction

The first world of discourse in contemporary biblical interpretation is that of academic scholarship, which carries on the historical-critical tradition inherited from the last century, and seeks to integrate new approaches into its established norms. Representatives of this approach tend to believe that it is the only legitimate one, and regard the others as 'subjective' and 'unscientific'. Some of them have a deep-seated dislike of conservative evangelicals, whom they deliberately – but mistakenly – label as 'fundamentalists'. On the other hand, there are conservative evangelicals who are distinguished scholars in this tradition, and who are widely respected by those who do not share their religious convictions. Similarly, some critical scholars are in the forefront of interdisciplinary research, while others have held back and may even have been critical of their more adventurous colleagues. Thus it is that the academic establishment now manifests a degree of pluralism which is relatively new and which holds exciting possibilities for the future.

The interpreters and their work

Literary critics and philosophers

Erich Auerbach (1892–1957). He was a pioneer of modern literary criticism, whose classic work *Mimesis* (1947) claims that the gospels stand out as literature because of the depth of their realism. Auerbach had few links with academic biblical scholarship, and was little read in those circles during his lifetime.

Clive Staples Lewis (1898–1963). A popular apologist for orthodox Christianity, he basically followed Auerbach's approach. He was especially critical of biblical scholars who tried to apply literary categories such as 'myth' to their material without really understanding what these categories were. He has had considerable influence as a critic of the methods traditionally employed by biblical scholars.

Martin Heidegger (1889–1976). He was Professor of Philosophy at Marburg from 1923, where he had a great influence on R. Bultmann, and later at Freiburg (1928). His classic work is *Being and Time* (1927), which remains fundamental for modern hermeneutics. Though not a biblical scholar in any sense, Heidegger has provided a philosophical framework which underpins modern interpretation of the Bultmannian type, and which has proved to be very fruitful in the development of current hermeneutical theories.

Ernst Fuchs (1903–83). This student of Bultmann's taught at Berlin from 1955, and at Marburg from 1961 to 1970. Most of his work is profoundly philosophical, and he was a leading representative of the new school in hermeneutics. Unfortunately, most of what he wrote is also obscure and difficult to understand. His most noted work is a study of the historical Jesus along the lines of the 'new quest' (1960).

Hans Wilhelm Frei (1929–89). He taught at Yale from 1957. His major work was *The Eclipse of Biblical Narrative* (1974), which made a significant contribution to literary study of the Bible. Frei argued that the Bible is mainly 'realistic' in its portrayal of events, even when the events themselves were not 'historical' by modern criteria. He explains this apparent realism as a literary device, which scholars have too often ignored. By mistaking it for 'history', they have been forced to argue that the Bible is not true, and have therefore missed its main message. Literary 'realism', on the other hand, can do justice to the narrative quality of the text without prejudging the historical issue one way or the other.

Northrop Frye (1912–91). This leading literary critic has pioneered the application of semantic theory to the Bible. His main works of biblical criticism are *The Great Code: The Bible and Literature* (1982) and *Words with Power* (1990). Frye was one of the leading advocates of the view that the Bible uses literary symbolism to convey its message, and that this symbolism can be detected in particular words (*e.g.* 'mountain'), which are used as signs representing spiritual truth.

Amos Niven Wilder (1895–1993). He taught at Chicago (1943) and Harvard (1954–63). He was the founder of literary criticism of the New Testament in North America, and has written a number of important studies on religious language, including *Eschatology and Ethics in the Teaching of Jesus* (1939).

Hans George Gadamer (1900–). A pupil of both Heidegger and Bultmann, he was Professor of Philosophy at Heidelberg from 1949 to 1968. His classic work, *Truth and Method* (1960), ranks with Heidegger's *Being and Time* as one of the main foundations for modern hermeneutical studies.

Gerhard Ebeling (1915–). Professor at both Tübingen and Zürich (1946), he was a major exponent of biblical hermeneutics in the 1960s, and contributed greatly to the revival of interest in the philosophical aspects of the discipline. His many books include *The Nature of Faith* (1959), *Word and Faith* (1960) and *The Truth of the Gospel* (1981), which is actually a study of Galatians. He also wrote a *Dogmatics* (1970).

Paul Ricoeur (1913–). He is a well-known French Protestant thinker, whose hermeneutical theories have been widely influential in the field of modern literary criticism. He has also written on biblical themes. His most significant books in this area are *The Symbolism of Evil* (1967) and *Essays on Biblical Interpretation* (1981).

Professional biblical scholars

Joseph Augustine Fitzmyer (1920–). Professor of Biblical Languages and Literature at the Catholic University of America, Washington DC (1976), he is a leading representative of modern Roman Catholic critical scholarship. In addition to many contributions on Qumran and Aramaic studies, he has written an outstanding commentary on Luke (1981, 1985), and another on Romans.

William Farmer (1921–). Professor at Dallas (1964) and a strong advocate of the Griesbach hypothesis of synoptic origins in his book *The Synoptic Problem* (1964), he is chiefly responsible for having reopened the synoptic question after a generation, although his own preference for Matthaean priority remains highly controversial.

Dennis Nineham (1921–). Professor at London (1954), Cambridge (1964) and Bristol (1979–86), he has written widely on hermeneutical questions from the standpoint of cultural relativity. He has also published a well-known commentary on Mark (1963).

Krister Stendahl (1921–). He taught at Harvard (1958–79) before returning to Sweden as Bishop of Stockholm (1980). His work on *The*

School of Matthew (1957) was one of the first to make use of Qumranic material in interpreting the New Testament. A later work, *Paul among Jews and Gentiles* (1976), has contributed to the recent revisionist movement in Pauline studies.

Savvas Agouridis (1921–). He taught at Athens (1954), Thessalonica (1960) and again at Athens (1980). He has written a number of books on different biblical themes, as well as commentaries on the Johannine epistles (1973) and 1 Corinthians (1985). He was largely responsible for raising the scholarly level of biblical studies at Thessalonica, making it the leading Orthodox faculty in the world today. He also founded the *Greek Bulletin of Biblical Studies* and has been the leading spirit behind the efforts to produce a modern Greek translation of the Bible.

Brevard Springs Childs (1923–). Professor at Yale (1966–88), he is a leading exponent of biblical theology and canonical criticism. In developing these themes, he has tried to integrate the traditional theological concerns of the church with the findings of critical scholarship. His work has often been criticized (from both ends of the spectrum), but it seems likely that the main thrust of his approach will be very influential in the years to come. His main books include *Biblical Theology in Crisis* (1970), *Introduction to the Old Testament as Scripture* (1979), *The New Testament as Canon: An Introduction* (1984), *Old Testament Theology in a Canonical Context* (1985) and *Biblical Theology of the Old and New Testaments* (1992). He has also written an outstanding commentary on Exodus (1974).

James Barr (1924–). He taught at Montreal (1953), Edinburgh (1955), Princeton (1961), Manchester (1965) and Oxford (1976–90). He has written extensively on biblical interpretation, and is well known as an iconoclast. His work has demonstrated that the traditional distinction between 'Hebrew' and 'Greek' ways of thinking is vastly exaggerated, and of little importance. He has also been a savage critic of the 'word-study' approach to biblical theology typified by G. Kittel. More controversially, he has attacked conservative evangelicals in a series of books and articles denouncing 'fundamentalism'. His main works are *The Semantics of Biblical Language* (1961), *Old and New in Interpretation* (1966), *The Bible in the Modern World* (1973), *Fundamentalism* (1977), *The Scope and Authority of the Bible* (1980) and *Holy Scripture: Canon, Authority, Criticism* (1983).

Martin Hengel (1924–). Professor of New Testament at Erlangen from 1967, and at Tübingen from 1971, he developed the Jewish context of the New Testament in his classic work *Judaism and*

Hellenism (1969), and is noted for his opposition to sharp distinctions between Palestinian and Hellenistic Jewish ideas in the New Testament. He has been prominent in the so-called 'third quest' for the historical Jesus, and is noted for his positive evaluation of the gospels and Acts as historical documents.

James McConkey Robinson (1924–). He popularized the 'new quest' for the historical Jesus (1959) and Bultmannian theology. His name is associated with the publication of *The Nag Hammadi Library* (1977). His own theological position is radical and secular.

Geza Vermes (1924–). This Jewish scholar is known for his work on the Dead Sea Scrolls and *Jesus the Jew* (1973). He has made a major contribution to our understanding of the Jewish background to the New Testament. His own belief is that Jesus was a mainline Jew, and that the development of the Christian church was a Hellenistic aberration.

James Louis Martyn (1925–). He was professor at Union Theological Seminary in New York (1959, 1967–86). His *History and Theology in the Fourth Gospel* (1968, revised in 1978) marks a turning-point in Johannine studies.

Arthur William Wainwright (1925–). After a brief teaching spell in Birmingham and a career as a Methodist minister in England, he went to Emory University in Atlanta in 1965. He is the author of a classic study of *The Trinity in the New Testament* (1952), and also wrote *Beyond Biblical Criticism* (1982). In 1985 he edited John Locke's *Paraphrase and Notes on the Pauline Epistles,* and recently he has published an introduction to the book of Revelation, entitled *Mysterious Apocalypse* (1993).

Robert Walter Funk (1926–). His own works include *Language, Hermeneutics and the Word of God* (1966), *Jesus as Precursor* (1975) and *Parables and Presence* (1982). His approach to the Bible is purely secular, and he has advocated a completely new gospel shorn of any theological connotations. His main contribution to scholarship has come through the founding of Scholars Press, which has become a major publishing outlet for works of radical biblical hermeneutics.

Helmut Koester (1926–). A pupil of Bultmann, Bornkamm and Käsemann, he has been at Harvard since 1964. Through his teaching and his *Introduction to the New Testament* (1980) he has transplanted the 'history of religions' approach to the USA.

Ben Franklin Meyer (1927–). He taught at McMaster University, Hamilton, Ontario, where he was a colleague of E. P. Sanders (see below). His main works are *The Aims of Jesus* (1979), generally held to be the pioneer study of the 'third quest' for the historical Jesus, *The*

Early Christians (1986) and *Critical Realism and the New Testament* (1989).

James Alvin Sanders (1927–). He has published studies on the Dead Sea Scrolls (1965) and a number of important works on the canon, including *Torah and Canon* (1970), *Canon and Community* (1984) and *From Sacred Story to Sacred Text* (1987). His research has contributed substantially to a renewal of interest in canonical study.

Raymond Edward Brown (1928–). He studied under W. F. Albright and became Professor of New Testament at Union Theological Seminary in New York (1971). He is the leading American Roman Catholic scholar in New Testament studies, and a pioneer of biblical criticism in those circles. His main work has been on the Johannine literature. His two-volume commentary on the gospel (1966, 1970) and his commentary on the epistles (1982) are classics. He has also written *The Critical Meaning of the Bible* (1981), as well as important studies of both the infancy and the passion narratives in the gospels.

Leander Keck (1928–). He was Professsor of New Testament at Vanderbilt (1959) and Emory (1972) Universities, before going to Yale (1980). His main work is *A Future for the Historical Jesus* (1971). His approach is close to the liberal, socio-anthropological position associated with the 'new Yale theology'.

John Adney Emerton (1928–). Regius Professor of Hebrew at Cambridge (1968), he has worked on Syriac texts relating to the Bible, and edited numerous collections of papers on philological subjects.

Dan Otto Via (1928–). An important representative of structuralist hermeneutics, he has written on the *Parables* (1967) and on *Kerygma and Comedy in the New Testament* (1975).

James Leslie Houlden (1929–). He taught New Testament at Oxford (1960) and at King's College, London (1977). His main books are *Ethics and the New Testament* (1973), *Patterns of Faith* (1977) and *Explorations in Theology* (1978). He has also written commentaries on Paul's 'captivity' epistles (1970), the Johannine epistles (1973) and the pastorals (1975). His approach is extremely liberal, and hostile to conservative positions generally.

Anthony Ernest Harvey (1930–). This liberal English scholar is closely associated with the attempted demythologizing of Christian doctrine. He gave the Bampton Lectures in 1980, published as *Jesus and the Constraints of History* (1982), in which he attempts to establish a historically reliable base of knowledge about Jesus.

Hans-Dieter Betz (1931–). Professor at Chicago (1978), he is a leading authority on ancient rhetoric and its application to the New

Testament. His commentaries on Galatians (1979) and 2 Corinthians 8 – 9 (1985) reflect this so-called 'rhetorical criticism'.

James Michael Efird (1931–). He taught for many years at Duke University, and has written a number of widely used books dealing with both Old and New Testament interpretation. His particular interest is prophecy and its fulfilment. Among the best known are *New Testament Writings* (1980), *Old Testament Writings* (1982), *Old Testament Prophets Then and Now* (1982), and *How to Interpret the Bible* (1984). He has also written commentaries on Daniel and Revelation (1978), Jeremiah (1979) and a study entitled *Revelation for Today* (1989).

Peter Stuhlmacher (1932–). Lecturer and Professor of New Testament at Tübingen since 1959, except for a short period at Erlangen (1968–72), he is the author of numerous articles on the subjects of biblical theology and interpretation. Many of these were collected together as *Schriftauslegung auf dem Wege zur biblischen Theologie* (*Scripture Exposition on the Way to Biblical Theology*) (1975). He has also written *Vom Verstehen des Neuen Testaments: Eine Hermeneutik* (*Understanding the New Testament: A Hermeneutic*) (1979). His other works include *Gerechtigkeit Gottes bei Paulus* (*The Righteousness of God in Paul*) (1962) and *Das Paulinische Evangelium* (*The Pauline Gospel*) (1967). His outlook is generally conservative, though still within the mainstream tradition of German historical criticism.

Eberhard Jüngel (1932–). A pupil of Fuchs, he was Professor of Systematic Theology at Zürich (1967) and then at Tübingen (1969). Though mainly a systematic theologian, he has written on New Testament themes, notably in *Jesus und Paulus* (1962).

John Dominic Crossan (1934–). A major exponent of hermeneutical theories relating to literary criticism of the Bible, he has worked on the *Parables of Jesus* (1973) and has published extensively on structuralism.

Robert Tannehill (1934–). He is a pioneer of the literary approach to biblical interpretation, and his works develop this theory. Among them are *Dying and Rising with Christ* (1967), *The Sword of his Mouth* (1975) and *The Narrative Unity of Luke-Acts: A Literary Interpretation* (1987).

Robert Alter (1935–). Professor of Hebrew and Comparative Literature at the University of California, Berkeley (1969), he is a leading exponent of literary approaches to the Bible. His main books are *The Art of Biblical Narrative* (1981) and *The Art of Biblical Poetry* (1985).

Edwin Parrish Sanders (1937–). He was responsible for a major reorientation in Pauline studies in *Paul and Palestinian Judaism* (1977), and *Paul, the Law and the Jewish People* (1983). In common with K. Stendahl, he is convinced that Luther misunderstood Paul, and that Protestant interpretation of the New Testament has been fundamentally flawed as a result. His study of *Jesus and Judaism* (1985) was similarly iconoclastic in its radical reassessment of the relationship of Jesus to the religion of his time.

Anthony Charles Thiselton (1937–). He is Professor of Theology at Nottingham University and a leading authority on hermeneutical theory. His main books are *The Two Horizons: New Testament Hermeneutics and Philosophical Description* (1980) and *New Horizons in Hermeneutics: The Theory and Practice of Transforming Biblical Reading* (1992). He is a conservative evangelical, and his work offers an outstanding example of how a scholar of that persuasion can penetrate the abstruse world of German philosophy at the deepest level.

Ernest Wilson Nicholson (1938–). Oriel Professor at Oxford (1979–90) and now Provost of Oriel College, his many works include *Deuteronomy and Tradition* (1967), *Preaching to the Exiles* (1971), *Exodus and Sinai in History and Tradition* (1973), and *God and his People* (1986), as well as a two-volume commentary on Jeremiah (1973, 1975).

James Douglas Grant Dunn (1939–). Professor of New Testament at Durham, his theological position is on the liberal edge of modern evangelicalism. His has written a number of works from a critical perspective, including *Jesus and the Spirit* (1975), *Unity and Diversity in the New Testament* (1977), *Christology in the Making* (1980), *Jesus, Paul and the Law* (1990) and *The Partings of the Ways between Christianity and Judaism* (1991). He has also written a two-volume commentary on Romans (1988).

Gerd Theissen (1944–). Professor of New Testament at Heidelberg (1980), he has pioneered modern sociological and psychological interpretation of the Bible. His works include *The Miracle Stories of the Gospels* (1974), *The First Followers of Jesus* (1977), *On Having a Critical Faith* (1978), *Psychological Aspects of Pauline Theology* (1983), and an ambitious attempt to reconstruct a life of Jesus, *The Shadow of the Galilean* (1986).

Richard John Bauckham (1947–). Professor of New Testament at St Andrews (1991), he has written extensively on many subjects, and has specialized in apocalyptic literature. His major New Testament writings have been *The Bible and Politics* (1989), *Jude and the Relations of Jesus* (1990), *The Theology of Revelation* (1993) and a highly regarded commentary on 2 Peter and Jude (1983). A conservative evangelical scholar, he is doing much to put theological concerns at the forefront of mainstream biblical scholarship today.

Hugh Godfrey Maturin Williamson (1947–). Regius Professor of Hebrew at Oxford (1992), he has published *The Book Called Isaiah* (1994) in which he defends the unity of the book as a post-exilic composition, as well as commentaries on 1 and 2 Chronicles (1982) and on Ezra and Nehemiah (1985, 1987). He too is a conservative evangelical scholar, whose work is a blend of traditional evangelical concerns (*e.g.* for the unity of Isaiah) and a responsible use of the best critical methods, which he has employed to challenge many of the received assumptions of contemporary scholarship.

The issues

The main issues in contemporary academic interpretation can be outlined as follows.

1. *Is it possible to study the Bible in a way which leaves theology to one side?* This has certainly been attempted in the past generation, with varying degrees of success. Granted that technical studies of one kind or another can be written without theological intrusions, is it possible or desirable to stop at that? Can we assume that people will be interested in the ultimate purpose of the material they are studying, or should this question be left for individuals to decide as they see fit?

2. *Is it possible or desirable to integrate traditional critical studies with other disciplines?* This question has become one of the utmost importance, and has caused considerable controversy. Often, traditional links with classical philology, history and philosophy have been weakened, to be replaced by anthropology, sociology, linguistics and literary criticism. Is this valid, or should critical scholarship stick to its traditional paths? There is an important issue of quality control here; given that no one scholar can hope to master every discipline, is it better to pursue a narrow area in depth or cover a broad range at the risk of being superficial? Dividing up the field into different specialities is only a partial answer to this problem. It is easy to make mistakes in a specialized area, and scholars who rely on others for their data and conclusions may be seriously misled. This has already happened when biblical scholars have misappropriated certain archaeological discoveries, and problems of that kind are liable to multiply rather than diminish as interdisciplinary links increase.

3. *Is it possible to maintain the unity and integrity of biblical studies as a*

discipline in its own right? This has become a major issue in recent years, as scholars have increasingly regarded the Old and New Testaments as anthologies of ancient Hebrew and early Christian literature. The Old Testament will retain its central place in ancient Hebrew literature since almost everything else has been lost, but the New Testament is in a different position. Placed within the context of first-century Judaism, it now appears as only one option among many. Even within Christian circles, it is by no means a full record of the early church, as the rediscovery of large quantities of Gnostic material has revealed. The fact that this literature was lost or ignored for more than eighteen centuries does not deter historical critics, who may regard it as even more valuable evidence, since it has obviously not been tampered with during that time.

At a different level, the increasing specialization of recent scholarship has made it difficult for most researchers to have a full grasp of even one of the Testaments, let alone both. The separation which was made at the beginning of the nineteenth century on theological grounds is now a practical necessity, because of the vast amount of material involved. We may not have reached the stage where each book of the Bible has its own specialist department, but that day is nearer now than it ever was in the past. A sense of the unity of the Bible is getting ever harder to achieve, and the grounds on which such unity must be based are elusive, in spite of the attention which has recently been paid to the hermeneutical significance of the canon.

The methods of interpretation

The contemporary academic scene is characterized by a wealth of different approaches to the biblical text. In this section we shall examine the most significant of these, apart from those which have a special social or political significance, which we shall leave until the next chapter. Here we shall look at the following hermeneutical theories and methods: historical criticism as it has developed since about 1975; attacks on the historical-critical method; canonical criticism; the new literary criticism; the new hermeneutic; and structuralism.

Historical criticism since about 1975

The survival of the historical-critical method as the dominant form of academic biblical interpretation can no longer be taken for granted, but it is still the most important one in university departments of biblical studies. At the present time it is evolving rapidly, and there have been a number of significant new developments which have overturned some of the accepted results of earlier criticism.

In the Old Testament, the assumption that archaeology provides a secure basis for dating the patriarchal period in Israel's prehistory has been increasingly questioned. It can no longer be confidently claimed that the figures of Abraham, Isaac and Jacob are historical in the same sense as later figures in Israel's history are, and the formerly positive and conservative relationship between archaeology and the Bible has come under increasing attack. A landmark in this respect was the publication of T. L. Thompson's thesis *The Historicity of the Patriarchal Narratives: The Quest for the Historical Abraham* (1974). This was a thoroughgoing critique of the Albright school of archaeology, and made the following salient points.

1. Albright emphasized the similarities between the tablets found at Mari and Nuzi and the biblical record, and totally ignored the many dissimilarities. This resulted in a one-sided case in favour of the historicity of the biblical data, which could not be properly supported by the evidence.

2. Albright linked his assertion that there had been an invasion of Mesopotamian nomads into Palestine about 2000 BC (which was based on the Genesis record) with his assertion that contemporary Palestinian culture was that of an intrusive, non-urban nomadic group (which was based on archaeological discovery). This linkage was dubious in the extreme, since there was no evidence that the culture of Palestine in the period under consideration was the product of a nomadic invasion from Mesopotamia.

3. Albright's principle of harmonization between the biblical texts and the archaeological evidence distorted the significance of each in its own right; everything was made to fit, whether it really did so or not.

Albright's arguments in favour of a thirteenth-century exodus and conquest of Canaan also came under close scrutiny. In an article published in 1977, P. M. Miller pointed out that the archaeological evidence fell far short of what would be required to prove the accuracy of the biblical texts, and that Albright had had to rely on silence to fill in gaps in the evidence. Working from the opposite end of the spectrum, J. Bimson, a conservative evangelical scholar, tried to prove (1978) that the exodus and conquest had taken place in the fifteenth century, and in the process exposed a number of weaknesses in the methods used by Albright and his school.

It is still too early to say which of these arguments will carry the day, but enough has now been written to make it plain that Albright's harmonization of the Bible with the archaeological data cannot be sustained. No doubt there are weaknesses in the approaches offered by his critics, and as yet no-one has succeeded in imposing an alternative synthesis, but the issue is once again wide open. Suffice it to say that early dating can still be defended on scholarly grounds, and there can be no going back to the scepticism of the nineteenth century on this score. At the same time, the intensive archaeological surveys which have been carried out since 1967 by Israeli scholars have yielded results closer to the theories of Alt than to those of Albright, leaving the impression that the Israelite penetration of Palestine was a gradual process, rather than a sudden invasion from east of the Jordan.

In other areas, critical study of the Old Testament has developed only marginally since 1975. Most attention has been devoted to literary analyses of the data, and historical questions have played a minor part in research. Different theories continue to be put forward about particular books, but without affecting the overall picture which had previously been established.

New Testament study has undergone much greater changes since 1975, mainly because of the impact of the theories of E. P. Sanders and B. F. Meyer. Sanders set the ball rolling in 1977, when he published his major study on Paul. In this he attempted to show that the entire post-Reformation tradition of interpretation was fundamentally flawed, because it portrayed rabbinical Judaism as a legalistic religion not unlike sixteenth-century Roman Catholicism. Sanders argued that this was quite untrue, and that the rabbis believed that keeping the law was not a matter of earning favour with God, but of expressing the reality of membership in the covenant of grace. By drawing extensively on the literature of the period, he was able to show that the traditional picture of the rabbis (and of the Pharisees) had emphasized their undoubted pettiness in some areas, and ignored the fact that they were equally capable of profound spiritual insight in others. Whether this change in perception will have much impact on scholarly estimation of Paul's teaching remains uncertain, but it is undoubtedly leading to a thorough re-evaluation of the nature of the opposition he faced.

B. F. Meyer's work (1979) is significant for launching what is now called the 'third quest' for the historical Jesus. The 'third quest' prides itself on its historical method, and Meyer's work is solidly grounded in philosophical theory. He asks what it was that Jesus aimed to do, and answers that his chief purpose was to 'restore Israel' in line with the general eschatological hope of the period. He makes a radical distinction between what Jesus said and did in public, and what he revealed about himself in private. In the former domain he contented himself with an appeal to reform, but in the latter he embarked on a spiritual revolution. Eventually, his disciples began to realize that Jesus' private revelations were programmatic for his public behaviour, and that he wanted to see a far-reaching spiritual transformation of the nation.

Meyer's ideas have been picked up and developed by M. J. Borg (1984). Borg has situated Jesus clearly in the midst of the political and religious life of his time, though not in the way in which Reimarus had done. Rather than portray him as a political revolutionary, Borg sees him as the latest in the traditional line of Israel's prophets, pointing the people away from a false political hope, and urging them to imitate the merciful nature of God. In particular, Borg seeks to transform the eschatological language used by Jesus and to explain it, not as the preaching of a future kingdom, but as the application of transcendent categories of thought to present realities. In favour of this hypothesis, he points out that Jesus commanded his followers to flee Jerusalem (Mt. 24:15–22), which does not suggest that he imagined its destruction to be the end of the world. What Jesus believed was that the Jewish order in which he lived would soon come to an end – a prophecy which was fulfilled in the events of AD 66–73.

Another major contribution to the 'third quest' was made by E. P. Sanders (1985), who criticized some of its assumptions and tried to focus its attention more closely on certain historical facts that it was in danger of overlooking. Sanders' main point was that Jesus died not for an idea, but for what he actually did. Scholarship which began with the sayings of Jesus, rather than with his deeds, was fundamentally misguided. The centre of Jewish religion was the temple worship, and when Jesus started to attack that, he was doomed. The Jewish establishment could tolerate any number of infringements of the dietary and sabbatarian laws, but not a frontal attack on its sacrificial system. There are many weaknesses in points of detail in Sanders' reconstruction of events, but his main thesis continues to stimulate further research.

The 'third quest' for the historical Jesus is both more secular and more Jewish in tone than the 'new quest' of the 1950s and 1960s, but there are two fundamental issues which both have had to address. The first of these is the relationship between Jesus and Judaism. This is not merely a question of explaining the content of his teaching, but of deciding why it was that he was crucified. It is also a matter of trying to work out how an advanced theological interpretation of his life and death came into existence so soon after the actual events, if Jesus himself was not responsible for this. The second big issue is the relationship of Jesus to the early church. It is now increasingly recognized that the elements of continuity are more significant than those of discontinuity, and that the idea that Paul or the early Christians completely corrupted Jesus' teaching is unlikely to be correct. But what the links were is harder to say, especially if the 'third quest' continues to exclude theological issues from consideration.

In the end, it is impossible to give an adequate picture of Jesus if theology is put to one side; the problem of the resurrection, and of the worship accorded to Jesus by the early church, will always rear its head in discussion. It is here that the 'third quest' is weakest, and that the world of New Testament scholarship awaits a new synthesis. Nevertheless, the fact that it has a much more positive approach to the historical reliability of the documents we do have, and that it is prepared to grant considerable credence to the deeds attributed to Jesus in the gospels, is a promising start towards the eventual development of a picture of his life and work which will command general assent.

Alternatives to historical criticism

The conservative attack

At the same time as historical criticism has been undergoing a series of facelifts, it has also come under increasing attack as a method. In 1977 the German scholar Gerhard Maier published his programmatic work, *The End of the Historical-Critical Method*, in which he pointed out the many defects of historical criticism. In particular, Maier offered the following arguments.

1. Historical criticism is analytical rather than synthetic. It is good at breaking things down into little pieces, but not at putting them together again. Yet the New Testament has been put together into what the early Christians regarded as a coherent whole, and it is essential to know how and why this was done. If analysis of the texts leads only to fragmentation, it gets us nowhere.

2. Historical criticism has failed to develop a coherent system of thought. It uses different criteria to evaluate different pieces of evidence, with little thought for the whole. Again, this is a problem of

analysis over synthesis, compounded by the fact that not all the analysis proceeds from the same basic assumptions.

3. Historical criticism relies on inadequate data. It is impossible to reconstruct the ancient world in a way which would be universally accepted as a proper basis for historical analysis; even when this or that event turns out to be 'true', it cannot be fitted into a coherent whole where each element is adequately supported by relevant evidence. Its conclusions are therefore never more than hypothetical, however plausible they may be.

4. Historical criticism concentrates on the accuracy of the biblical text as a factual record, and tends to ignore the applicability of the text for today. It may be very interesting to know whether the walls of Jericho actually fell or not, but what difference does it make to our spiritual life now? Historical criticism investigates questions like this one without giving the slightest thought to the spiritual dimension of the text. It is reductionist in its approach to the Scriptures, and therefore inadequate as a hermeneutical method.

Maier, who is a conservative evangelical, went on to argue that only a thoroughgoing theological approach to the data, taking their historicity into account but not being mesmerized by it, could restore biblical hermeneutics to life. He has developed this perspective in his *Biblical Hermeneutics* (1990; Eng. trans. 1994), which argues for a recovery of the doctrine of revelation. For Maier, this is linked to the voice of the Holy Spirit bearing witness in our hearts by faith. Those who expound the biblical text from this perspective will find that their exposition also becomes a witness to the revelation which they are seeking to proclaim. Here we are moving among concepts familiar in traditional Protestantism, but all but forgotten in the world of critical biblical study. Whether Maier will succeed in his aim of restoring theology to the centre of biblical study remains to be seen, but it is significant that he has been supported to some extent from within the critical fraternity, notably by Peter Stuhlmacher (1979). Mention might also be made of the remarkable case of Eta Linnemann, who after being trained in the standard liberalism of the German universities was converted to a conservative evangelical faith, and has subsequently devoted her life to a root-and-branch critique of her earlier views.

Canonical criticism

Another form of attack on historical criticism is that which focuses its attention on the phenomenon of the canon. Canonical criticism must not be confused with the study of how the canon originated. It accepts the existence of the canon in its present 'shape', and tries to explain its development by investigating the principles which underlie it. As the phrase was first used by J. A. Sanders (1972), it referred to the hermeneutical presuppositions of the redactors who originally produced the canon. According to Sanders, although later generations have appropriated the canon to their own religious needs, the starting-point for all interpretation remains the text as it was put together by the original redactors, and so their interpretation of the material plays a foundational role in all subsequent study of the Bible.

However, canonical criticism has subsequently been taken over and revamped by B. S. Childs, with whom the term is now indelibly associated. Childs has gone further than Sanders and maintains that the canonical study of the Bible is opposed to the historical-critical method. For him, a theologically based interpretation of the Bible must begin with the final form of the text and relate its findings to the entire canon. Childs is mainly concerned with how a passage functions within its canonical context, though it is not altogether clear how he defines that. Which came first, the passage or its context? There would appear to be a circular argument here from which it is impossible to escape.

In some ways Childs's approach is a return to the Reformation idea that each passage of Scripture must be read and interpreted as part of 'the whole counsel of God', but he fully accepts the results of critical scholarship and evaluates his material accordingly. He is also unwilling to attach his theories to any theological principle beyond that of canonization itself, so that he does not rely on anything like the Reformation concept of 'covenant theology' to give coherence to his theories. His approach has been severely criticized on the grounds that it is self-contradictory (because at one level he accepts historical criticism while at another level he rejects it) and anti-historical (because he refuses to consider the *Sitz im Leben* of the canonical redactors). Nevertheless, there can be no doubt that the fundamental question asked by canonical criticism remains an essential item on the agenda of current critical scholarship.

The new literary criticism

Before the rise of historical criticism in the early nineteenth century, literary issues formed a substantial part of biblical scholarship. This was true even of the early Enlightenment theologians, who were interested in historical details only when they could be used as evidence to attack the 'infallibility' of the biblical text. Even in the nineteenth century there were scholars who valued John's gospel more highly than the synoptics because it was more literary in style. Form criticism represented a return to literary interests, but it took some time for this to become apparent. Gunkel's ideas were adapted to the needs of the kerygmatic theology of the 1920s, and it was not for another generation that the purely literary element surfaced once more.

In the meantime, of course, there had been considerable developments in literary theory outside the field of biblical studies. Even in the 1920s, I. A. Richards and T. S. Eliot were developing a type of criticism which abandoned history as a model and insisted that works of art be judged primarily on aesthetic grounds. Literary criticism of this type developed three distinct methods of enquiry. First there was author-centred criticism, which sought to examine the original intention of the author in writing. This made some sense, but it was ultimately untenable, for several reasons. First, it could not be known what the author's intention was, unless he spelt it out, which he rarely did. Deciding what his intention might be on the basis of the finished product was a largely subjective exercise, more likely to reflect the concerns of the interpreter than those of the writer. Second, it occasionally happened that the author's intention was quite different from the general perception of readers. The classic case of this is the work of Nikolai Gogol, whose satirical pieces condemning Tsarist misrule were intended to buttress the régime, not destroy it. But public perception of his work was exactly the opposite, much to Gogol's distress. Even during his lifetime, the famous Russian literary critic, V. Belinsky, praised his work to the height, while at the same time condemning Gogol himself as a hopeless reactionary who did not understand the true significance of his own work.

Author-centred criticism clearly had its limits, and it was soon supplemented by text-centred criticism. This form of literary analysis could trace its origins back to Aristotle, and concentrated on the inner composition of the work being studied. There were certain criteria of harmony and appropriateness that could be used to judge the aesthetic value of a piece of literature, and they would be valid regardless of the author's intentions. However, the difficulties with text-centred criticism were just as serious as those encountered by author-centred criticism. First, it was based entirely on form, not on content. At one extreme, it could be argued that the telephone directory is a beautiful piece of work, perfect in its simplicity, but it would be hard to claim that it is a work of great literature. Text-centred criticism also ignored the problem of a text's function, which was further related to its accessibility. Certain beautiful texts have died (or have never come alive) in western culture because the principles on which they were written have not been understood or appreciated by most educated westerners. A classic example of this is the Qur'an, which is universally recognized as the masterpiece of Arabic literature, but which leaves most westerners cold, because we are unable to understand (or sympathize with) the principles which lie behind it.

Lastly, there is reader-centred criticism, which has proved to be the most popular option in recent years. This type of criticism emphasized the importance of the reader and his or her perception of the text, which could live only to the extent that he or she was able to absorb and appreciate it. It did not matter if the reader distorted the original intention of the writer, so long as the greatness of the text continued to be appreciated. The advantage of reader-centred criticism is that it is the most easily ascertained; all critics are themselves readers. But the subjectivism of this approach is also obvious. Not every reader is a skilled critic, yet reader-centred criticism cannot easily distinguish between readers who know what they are talking about and readers who do not. Nevertheless, it is this type of literary criticism which has become dominant in modern research generally, and it has been readily applied to the Bible.

Another important feature of literary criticism is its relative indifference to historical questions. Source, form and redaction criticism, as these had been adapted to biblical studies, were of little interest to the literary critics. They were concerned with the final state of the text, and the literary effect which it had on readers. In this sense, it was closer to canonical criticism. However, the logic of literary criticism went deeper than that. For great literature is not written by committees, or by groups of redactors working over a period of centuries. Great literature is the product of individual geniuses, and in this respect literary criticism of the Bible tended to support the idea that its main texts were composed by single authors, rather than pieced together by groups of one kind or another.

This in turn raised the question of whether the Bible could really be considered 'literature' in the aesthetic sense. It did not fit into the codification by 'genres' which form criticism had tried to impose on it, with the result that the critics found themselves inventing new 'genres' to cope with the biblical phenomena. Nor could the Bible be divorced from history. Even if its details were 'wrong' to some degree, it was still very much a historical document, concerned to record events which had actually happened. Parts of the text were of a different character, and could legitimately be considered 'non-historical', and literary criticism was more successful with these, but the (claimed) historicity of the main text was beyond dispute. Literary criticism also had trouble dealing with the religious dimension of Scripture, which was not easily susceptible to literary analysis.

Having said that, literary criticism has concentrated on certain types of literature which are thought to be widely represented in the Bible. The first of these is *narrative.* Much of the Bible is a story, and how it is told is one of the great glories of the text. Whatever else the writers of Scripture were, they were good story-tellers, with a particular gift for making their story as realistic as possible. This is a particularly important point, because much nineteenth-century criticism of Scripture was rooted in what appeared to be the fantastic improbability (and therefore lack of historical realism) of the textual narrative. By re-establishing the text's 'realism' on a literary basis, modern critics have helped to give it greater credibility; the story is 'true to life', even if it never actually happened.

This was the line pursued by Erich Auerbach and adopted by C. S. Lewis, who went one stage further and claimed that biblical narrative was realistic because it was real; it had actually happened in just the way it is told. This view has, however, been challenged, notably by R. Alter, who regards biblical narrative as essentially fiction with a history-like quality. Most exponents of a narrative reading of Scripture appear to find themselves somewhere in the middle of this debate. They are prepared to accept that large parts of Scripture may well be 'true' in a scientific, historical sense, but are not willing to affirm that all of it (or at least as much of it as claims to be) is historical fact. For them, historicity is a secondary issue, which does not affect the truth of the narrative as such. What is important, though, as Hans Frei maintained, is that the modern interpreter be willing to start with the biblical world and let its narratives define what is 'real', so that our lives today have meaning to the extent that they fit themselves into that framework. In other words, the Bible must be read within its own self-understanding, and not through the distorting lens of a modern, essentially alien hermeneutic.

Another branch of literary criticism is *rhetoric.* This has been adapted from an ancient Greek category and applied with greatest success to the Pauline epistles. The gist of rhetorical criticism is that the text is concerned to propagate an argument, which it does by using certain rhetorical devices. There is no particular reason why this should not be so, of course, but apart from elucidating a few phrases here and there, it is hard to see that this type of criticism will have a major effect on biblical interpretation. Most people have known for a long time that Paul was arguing against opponents of one kind or another; pointing this out once more seems somehow unnecessary.

Attempts to explore other types of literary effect have been less successful. Edwin Good has written about *Irony in the Old Testament* (1965), but although irony may be present in the text, it seems to be of secondary importance for interpretation. Much the same must be said of D. O. Via's attempts to find 'comedy' in the gospels. Via has also written extensively on the literary 'genre' of parable, though in this case with more justification for his theories.

The main weakness of the literary approach, interesting and important though it is, is that it too often puts form before content. Beautiful meaninglessness is preferred above ugly significance – an aesthetic aberration which cannot do justice to the gospel of him who was 'without form or comeliness'. In the Bible, literature is a means to an end, not an end in itself, and literary critics must therefore accept that they can never play more than a secondary role in its interpretation.

Structuralism

Closely linked to literary criticism is 'structuralism', which originated in the linguistic theories of Ferdinand de Saussure, which distinguished sharply between what he called *langue* and *parole*. According to Saussure, *langue* was the underlying structure of a language, which found expression in conventional words (*parole*). These words were arbitrary, and might change from time to time, just as they differ from one language to another. But the underlying meaning of a word stays the same. Translation is therefore basically an affair of *parole*, not of *langue*. Saussure realized, of course, that words were not the only means by which things could be signified. Gestures were often equally important, as was intonation. Anything which might convey a meaning in this way could be called a 'sign', which for him was an essential component of language. Out of this theory has grown the concept of 'semeiology' (from the Greek work *sēmeion*, meaning 'sign'). Every language possesses its own semeiology, or 'code language', which must be cracked before it can be understood. Translation is therefore the business of exchanging one code for another in order to express the same *langue* using a different *parole*.

From his purely linguistic observations there quickly developed a complex theory of sign relationships underlying the whole of human culture. The anthropologist Claude Lévi-Strauss took it up and applied it to the study of myth. He claimed that myths often display a structure in which two opposites appear to be working together. This kind of dualism may in fact be essential to the myth, and thus form part of a deeper structural reality. Structuralism made a great appeal to Marxists, because it offered the possibility of applying their deterministic theories to literature. Not surprisingly, therefore, it was the Russian critic, V. Propp, who first developed it in this direction by isolating thirty-one different categories of folk-tale, into which all existing folk-tales could be fitted.

In one important sense however, structuralism is the very opposite of Marxism; it has no interest in the concept of history. Structuralist literary interpretation is concerned exclusively with texts as they exist, and seeks to understand them. It has no interest in trying to determine what has made them what they are. For this reason, it has been embraced by some biblical scholars as a way of escaping from the historical-critical method, but it has not been very successful. Even its supporters admit that structuralism does not aim to teach us anything we did not know before; its purpose is rather to explain what we know already. In biblical studies it has turned out to be much the same as form criticism, with only a few additional details. For example, in the story of the healing of the man with the withered hand (Mk. 3:1–6), structuralism claims that there is a deep-seated opposition between Jesus and the Pharisees, which reveals the fact that the story has more to do with Jesus' relationship to the law than with his power of healing. But any reasonably attentive reader would have gathered that already. Structuralists happily admit this, saying that that merely demonstrates the accuracy of their method. That it may also indicate its superfluity is less easily admitted, but seems to many biblical scholars to be the obvious conclusion.

Structuralist presuppositions have come under attack from Jacques Derrida (1930–), whose method is called 'deconstructionism'. Derrida has pointed out that there are often inconsistencies in texts which make a structuralist approach difficult, if not impossible. He is less confident than most structuralists that there is any meaningful link between signs and the things they signify; it all seems to be in the mind. Critics of Derrida deplore what they regard as his extreme scepticism, but he has at least demonstrated that the structuralist approach is not free from some quite serious criticism.

His views have not penetrated very deeply into the world of biblical studies, though they have been used to some extent by J. D. Crossan and others. For most interpreters of the Bible, deconstructionism, like structuralism, is simply too obscure and esoteric to make much sense.

The new hermeneutic

Quite as complex and as confusing as structuralism, and in some ways not unlike it, is the so-called 'new hermeneutic'. This is a philosophically based way of reading literary texts, rooted in the work of Martin Heidegger and the hermeneutical trio of Gadamer, Fuchs and Ebeling. Its greatest exponent in the English-speaking world is A. C. Thiselton, who continues to write extensively on the subject. The new hermeneutic is basically an existentialist way of reading a text. It begins with the presupposition that both the text and the reader dwell in a 'horizon' which governs the way in which they understand and appropriate meaning. If a text is contemporary with us, its horizon is probably (though not necessarily) the same as ours, and we should have relatively little difficulty in understanding it. But if a text comes from a different time or culture or both, its horizon will be different from ours, and we shall not understand it as readily.

In terms of Bible reading, the problem of horizons first became acute when translators started trying to put the biblical texts into tribal languages which lacked the concepts necessary to produce a literal rendering of it. How could one explain trees to an Eskimo, or snow to an Amazonian Indian? From this simple level, more complex problems began to emerge. The sacrificial system of the Old Testament was not paralleled in every culture. Tribal relationships could be very different, and lead to serious misunderstanding. Western urbanized people also felt alienated from the world of the Bible, which spoke of a way of life long since abandoned. Even when the words existed to translate the texts, their associations might be very different. A classic example of this is the word 'Pharisee', which had a different connotation in Jesus' day from what it has now. To the disciples of Jesus, Pharisees were models of religious observance, to be admired and respected, but to us, they are religious hypocrites. We expect the Pharisees to be the 'bad guys', but Jesus' hearers would have been shocked by this suggestion.

Considerations of this kind have produced an entirely new way of translating the Bible, in which 'dynamic equivalence' has replaced literal translation. This can be seen most obviously in the way in which psychosomatic imagery in the Bible is treated. Where Paul often refers to the bowels as the seat of compassion, this usage is both unfamiliar and vulgar-sounding in modern English, and so tends to be replaced by abstract words like 'concern'. This may convey something of the meaning, but it ignores the psychosomatic dimension, which is an important part of biblical anthropology and cannot simply be written out of the text. In that respect, there is no 'dynamic equivalence' at all in this translation.

Another result of the new hermeneutic which is equally debatable is the development of the concept of 'cultural conditioning'. In this case the horizon is created by the 'culture', which stands outside the text and judges it. 'Culture' as a concept is notoriously difficult to define at the best of times, and almost impossible when it comes to something like the Bible. Is there only one culture in the Scriptures, or are there several? Did Jesus live in a Mediterranean culture, a middle-eastern culture, a Jewish culture or a Galilean culture? Where are the boundaries, and what are the features which determine who belongs and who does not belong to a specific cultural area? Yet in spite of these difficulties, it is widely assumed today that everything in the Bible is conditioned by its 'culture', and that because we live in a different 'culture' (which is taken for granted) we have a right to adapt its teaching to suit the circumstances. This is felt to be obvious enough when it comes to the question of women covering their heads in church, but it has been taken much farther than this. Even the fact that the apostle Paul appeals to the order of creation and the fall to justify male headship (1 Tim. 2:11–15) is dismissed on the ground that that is what one must expect from somebody trained in the culture of a first-century Pharisee; it has no significance today.

The use of the word 'Pharisee' as an example of how one horizon differs from another demonstrates the main weaknesses of the new hermeneutic as a method of biblical interpretation. First, it is not certain to what extent the Pharisees were highly respected – they may equally well have been secretly resented by the average Jew of Jesus' day. Second, if it is true that for us a Pharisee is a religious hypocrite, the reason is that Jesus taught this to his disciples, who have passed it on to us. It is not just a question of living in a different horizon; the word 'Pharisee' would never have entered our vocabulary at all if Jesus had not used it in the way he did. There is therefore an essential historical link between Jesus and us, which must be respected when a word such as this is being interpreted. Unfortunately, the new hermeneutic finds it hard to cope with historical evolution; it tends to leap from one horizon to another, without paying much attention to links in between. Perhaps it is for this reason that it has been used most frequently to interpret the parables, which are basically non-historical.

Conclusion

It is still too early to say whether the historical-critical method will ever lose its central role in biblical interpretation. Of the other methods surveyed here, it is probable that most will make only a modest contribution to biblical studies, and some will no doubt disappear without trace. Neither structuralism nor the new hermeneutic seems likely to catch on for long, because they are both tied to philosophical concepts which are now going out of fashion. Literary criticism will doubtless have a more lasting impact, because the Bible is clearly 'literary' in some sense or other, but literary theories change fairly frequently and therefore this type of criticism is unstable. Canonical criticism is also likely to stay around, though probably in a considerably modified form. For the present, therefore, it seems best to conclude that although historical criticism has been challenged by these alternative methods, it has not yet been overthrown. Whether it will ever regain the unquestioned supremacy of the past, however, remains to be seen.

BIBLIOGRAPHY

J. Barr, *The Semantics of Biblical Language* (Oxford: Oxford University Press, 1961).

R. Barthes, F. Bovon, F.-J. Leenhardt, R. Martin-Achard and J. Starobinski, *Structural Analysis and Biblical Exegesis* (Pittsburgh: Pickwick, 1974).

J.-M. Benoist, *The Structural Revolution* (London: Weidenfeld and Nicolson, 1979).

E. W. Bullinger, *Figures of Speech used in the Bible* (London: Eyre and Spottiswoode, 1988).

G. B. Caird, *Language and Imagery of the Bible* (London: Duckworth, 1980).

J. Calloud, *Structural Analysis of Narrative* (Philadelphia: Scholars Press, 1976).

M. J. Christensen, *C. S. Lewis on Scripture* (London: Hodder and Stoughton, 1980).

P. Cotterell and M. Turner, *Linguistics and Biblical Interpretation* (London: SPCK, 1989).
J. C. Croatto, *Biblical Hermeneutics: Towards a Theory of Reading as the Production of Meaning* (Maryknoll: Orbis, 1987).
A. R. Crollius (ed.), *Bible and Inculturation* (Rome: Gregorian University Press, 1983).
R. Detwiler, *Story, Sign and Self* (Missoula: Scholars Press, 1977).
R. J. Erickson, *James Barr and the Beginnings of Biblical Semantics* (Notre Dame: Foundations, 1984).
H. Frei, *The Eclipse of Biblical Narrative* (New Haven: Yale, 1974).
A. Gibson, *Biblical Semantic Logic* (Oxford: Blackwell, 1981).
G. Green (ed.), *Scriptural Authority and Narrative Interpretation* (Philadelphia: Fortress, 1987).
R. J. Howard, *Three Facets of Hermeneutics: An Introduction to Current Theories of Understanding* (Berkeley: University of California Press, 1982).
D. Jobling, *The Sense of Biblical Narrative* (Sheffield: JSOT Press, 1978).
A. M. Johnson (ed.), *Structuralism and Biblical Hermeneutics,* (Pittsburgh: Pickwick, 1977).
G. A. Kelly, *The New Biblical Theorists: Raymond E. Brown and Beyond* (Ann Arbor: Servant, 1983).
B. C. Lategan and W. S. Vorster, *Text and Reality: Aspects of Reference in Biblical Texts* (Atlanta: Scholars Press, 1985).
T. Longman III, *Literary Approaches to Biblical Interpretation* (Grand Rapids: Zondervan; Leicester: Apollos, 1987).
E. V. McKnight, *Post-Modern Use of the Bible: The Emergence of Reader-Oriented Criticism* (Nashville: Abingdon, 1988).
G. Maier, *The End of the Historical-Critical Method* (St Louis: Concordia, 1977).
———*Biblical Hermeneutics* (Wheaton, IL: Crossway, 1994).
R. Moorey, *A Century of Biblical Archaeology* (Cambridge: Lutterworth, 1991).
R. Morgan and J. Barton, *Biblical Interpretation* (Oxford: Oxford University Press, 1988).
S. Neill and N. T. Wright, *The Interpretation of the New Testament 1861–1986* (Oxford: Oxford University Press, 1988).
D. Patrick and A. Scult, *Rhetoric and Biblical Interpretation* (Sheffield: Almond, 1990).
D. Patte, *The Religious Dimensions of Biblical Texts* (Atlanta: Scholars Press, 1990).
———*What is Structural Exegesis?* (Philadelphia: Fortress, 1976).

D. and A. Patte, *Structural Exegesis: From Theory to Practice* (Philadelphia: Fortress, 1978).
N. R. Petersen, *Literary Criticism for New Testament Critics* (Philadelphia: Fortress, 1978).
R. M. Polzin, *Biblical Structuralism: Method and Subjectivity in the Study of Ancient Texts* (Missoula: Scholars Press, 1977).
P. Ricoeur, *The Conflict of Interpretations: Essays in Hermeneutics* (Evanston: Northwestern University Press, 1974).
———*Essays on Biblical Interpretation* (Philadelphia: Fortress, 1980).
———*Interpretation Theory: Discourse and the Surplus of Meaning* (Fort Worth: Texas Christian University Press, 1976).
R. B. Robinson, *Roman Catholic Exegesis since* Divino afflante Spiritu: *Hermeneutical Implications* (Atlanta: Scholars Press, 1988).
R. L. Rohrbaugh, *The Biblical Interpreter: An Agrarian Bible in an Industrial Age* (Philadelphia: Fortress, 1978).
J. F. A. Sawyer, *Semantics in Biblical Research* (London: SCM, 1972).
M. Silva, *God, Language and Scripture: Reading the Bible in the Light of General Linguistics* (Grand Rapids: Zondervan; Leicester: Apollos, 1990).
P. Stuhlmacher, *Historical Criticism and Theological Interpretation of Scripture* (Philadelphia: Fortress, 1977).
A. C. Thiselton, *New Horizons in Hermeneutics* (London: HarperCollins, 1992).
A. C. Thiselton, *The Two Horizons* (Exeter: Paternoster, 1979).
C. Tuckett, *Reading the New Testament: Methods of Interpretation* (London: SPCK, 1987).
S. Ullman, *Semantics: An Introduction to the Science of Meaning* (Oxford: Blackwell, 1962).
K. J. Vanhoozer, *Biblical Narrative in the Philosophy of Paul Ricoeur: A Study in Hermeneutics and Theology* (Cambridge: Cambridge University Press, 1990).
H. Westman, *The Structure of Biblical Myths: The Ontogenesis of the Psyche* (Dallas: Spring Publications, 1983).
W. Wink, *The Bible in Human Transformation* (Philadelphia: Fortress, 1973).
S. Wittig (ed.), *Structuralism* (Pittsburg: Pickwick, 1977).

A case study: the parables of Jesus

In the twentieth century few areas of New Testament study have been as widely discussed as the parables of Jesus. They are not 'historical' records in the strict sense; nobody supposes, for example, that there was once a good Samaritan on the road to Jericho. Whatever we think about the historicity of the rest of the gospels, it is obvious that Jesus invented stories of this kind to make moral and spiritual points. But how should these stories be interpreted? For many centuries it was customary to treat them as allegories, on the principle that the clearer parts of Scripture must be used to interpret the more obscure parts. This meant that the teaching of Jesus and the apostles about his life and death could be applied to the parables, which on the surface seemed to have little spiritual value. Here we must distinguish spiritual from merely moral value, which a parable might have in its literal meaning. This did not impress the fathers of the church, because similar stories could easily be found in Plato and other pagan philosophers. What they were looking for in the gospels was something unique and superior to that. The classic example of a spiritual interpretation of the parables is the account of the good Samaritan given by Augustine (*Quaestiones Evangeliorum* 2.19). As abridged by C. H. Dodd, it reads:

> *A certain man went down from Jerusalem to Jericho:* Adam himself is meant; Jerusalem is the heavenly city of peace, from whose blessedness Adam fell; Jericho means the moon, and signifies our mortality, because it is born, waxes, wanes and dies. Thieves are the devil and his angels, who stripped him, namely of his immortality; and beat him, by persuading him to sin; and left him half-dead, because in so far as man can understand and know God, he lives, but in so far as he is wasted and oppressed by sin, he is dead; he is therefore called half-dead. The priest and Levite who saw him and passed by, signify the priesthood and ministry of the Old Testament, who could profit nothing by salvation. Samaritan means Guardian, and therefore the Lord Himself is signified by this name. The binding of the wounds is the restraint of sin. Oil is the comfort of good hope; wine the exhortation to work with fervent spirit. The beast is the flesh in which He deigned to come to us. The being set upon the beast is belief in the incarnation of Christ. The inn is the Church, where travellers are refreshed on their return from pilgrimage to their heavenly country. The morrow is after the Resurrection of the

> Lord. The two pence are either the two precepts of love, or the promise of this life and of that which is to come. The innkeeper is the Apostle Paul. The supererogatory payment is either his counsel of celibacy, or the fact that he worked with his own hands lest he should be a burden to any of the weaker brethren when the Gospel was new, though it was lawful for him 'to live by the Gospel'.

There were many variations on this theme in later centuries; in particular, the two pence were frequently understood as either the two Testaments or the two principal sacraments, or even as the bread and wine of the Eucharist. The innkeeper also varied somewhat; to many, he was the pope. In assessing Augustine's interpretation, it is easy to see that the points he makes are often reasonable enough, though admittedly some are far-fetched. The real difficulty is the incongruity between the setting of the parable and the theological framework Augustine is trying to impose on it. For example, the relationship between Jews and Samaritans would have been understood very differently by Jesus' disciples; one would hardly imagine them identifying the Lord with a Samaritan.

The Reformers did not accept this allegorizing of the parables, as can be seen from Calvin's remarks. On the subject of the good Samaritan he wrote:

> The allegory which is here contrived by the advocates of free will is too absurd to deserve refutation. According to them, under the figure of a wounded man is described the condition of Adam after the fall; from which they infer that the power of acting well was not wholly extinguished in him; because he is said to be only half-dead. As if it had been the design of Christ, in this passage, to speak of the corruption of human nature, and to inquire whether the wound which Satan inflicted on Adam were deadly or curable; nay, as if he had not plainly, and without a figure, declared in another passage, that all are dead, but those whom he quickens by his voice (Jn. 5:25). As little plausibility belongs to another allegory, which, however, has been so highly satisfactory, that it has been admitted by almost universal consent, as if it had been a revelation from heaven. This Samaritan they imagine to be Christ, because he is our guardian; and they tell us that wine was poured, along with oil, into the wound, because Christ cures us by repentance and by a promise of grace. They have contrived a third subtlety, that Christ does

> not immediately restore health, but sends us to the Church, as an innkeeper, to be gradually cured. I acknowledge that I have no liking for any of these interpretations; but we ought to have a deeper reverence for Scripture than to reckon ourselves at liberty to disguise its natural meaning. And, indeed, anyone may see that the curiosity of certain men has led them to contrive these speculations, contrary to the intention of Christ.

As for his own interpretation of the parable, Calvin has relatively little to say. His reading was strictly literal, and he brought the traditional enmity of Jew and Samaritan to bear on his exposition. But he said nothing about 'parable' as a literary device; for him, it was a straightforward story telling an obvious, and universal moral tale. As he put it:

> Here, as in a mirror, we behold that common relationship of men, which the scribes endeavoured to blot out by their wicked sophistry; and the compassion, which an enemy showed to a Jew, demonstrates that the guidance and teaching of nature are sufficient to show that man was created for the sake of man. Hence it is inferred that there is a mutual obligation between all men.

In our own time, C. H. Dodd has pointed out that the gospels lend encouragement to allegorical interpretation, as in the example of the parable of the sower, which Mark supposedly interprets in an allegorical way. Dodd quoted A. Jülicher, whose epoch-making book *Die Gleichnisreden Jesu (The Parables of Jesus)* appeared between 1899 and 1910. Jülicher took Mark 4:11–20 as the key text in support of this view. In response to a question from one of his disciples, Jesus is portrayed as saying: 'To you is granted the mystery of the kingdom of God, but to those outside everything comes in parables, in order that they may look and look but never see, listen and listen but never understand, lest they should be converted and forgiven.'

In examining what then follows, Dodd makes the following points.

1. The explanation of the parable contains seven words which are not used elsewhere in the synoptic gospels, but which are frequently found in Paul and in other apostolic writings. This strongly suggests that we are dealing here with a piece of apostolic tradition, not with the authentic record of what Jesus taught.

2. The explanation of the parable is confused. The seed is the Word, but the crop which emerges is composed of different classes of

people. This goes against the Greek conception of the 'seminal Word' (*logos spermatikos*) which Dodd assumed lies behind the passage. The 'seminal Word' would produce fruit like itself, not something different.

3. Parables are explained as mysteries contrived to prevent those who were not predestined to salvation from understanding the teaching of Jesus. This, said Dodd, reflects the theology of the early church, not the teaching of the Saviour, and was designed to explain why the chosen people did not accept his message. Dodd could not accept the notion that Jesus ever wanted people not to understand him.

4. Parables were frequently used by the rabbis, and would not have been understood allegorically by the Jews. Therefore, Dodd argued, Mark's interpretation must reflect Gentile influence at this point. In the Hellenistic world, myths were frequently interpreted allegorically, so this would have been thought perfectly natural from a Christian teacher.

Dodd then gave his own definition of a parable:

> At its simplest, the parable is a metaphor or simile drawn from nature or common life, arresting the hearer by its vividness or strangeness, and leaving the mind in sufficient doubt about its precise application to tease it into active thought.

According to him there were different types of parable, which might elaborate the simple metaphor in different ways. However, he was quite clear about how a parable differed from allegory. He said:

> The typical parable, whether it be a simple metaphor, or a more elaborate similitude, or a full-length story, presents one single point of comparison. The details are not intended to have independent significance. In an allegory, on the other hand, each detail is a separate metaphor, with a significance of its own.

What was crucial was the inner coherence and simplicity of the parable; only one message was intended, and only one line of thought was being pursued. The hearer was meant to apply the story as a whole, without seeking to find hidden meanings behind every word. Parables were true to nature, and to life experience – which is precisely what Calvin had said. Everything was natural, as far as it goes; if there was a surprise (as for example, the fact that a Samaritan was prepared to help a Jew), this was intended and gives the story its point. Any secondary meanings, or extensions of meaning to other situations must be held firmly in check. They might be valid enough in themselves, but they were not part of the interpretation of the parable.

Dodd justified this assertion on theological grounds. The realism of the parables reflected the fact that the kingdom of God which Jesus proclaimed was deeply natural; it was the way things were meant to be. That reality it often out of step with this was the problem with which Jesus and his followers had to deal, but the parables set out the norm, and they did so in a natural way. Dodd also maintained that allegory was essentially a decorative explanation of teaching which was already accepted as true, whereas a parable was essentially an argument. Jesus was tackling the deep-seated prejudices of his hearers, and using the story form as a vehicle for changing their perception of their own behaviour.

Up to this point, Dodd followed Jülicher, but here he began to differ from his model. Jülicher had preferred to make the 'true' interpretation of parables as broad as possible, and in so doing had removed any possibility of allegory. The result, however, was so banal as to make one wonder whether a parable was really worth telling. Dodd could not accept the idea that Jesus was just another moral teacher; his teaching was the sign and spark of a great spiritual crisis which his presence provoked. For this reason, argued Dodd, the interpretation of the parables must be sought in the situation in which they were delivered.

Unfortunately, the evangelists frequently related a parable in different settings, and sometimes attached different interpretations to the same story (or conversely, did not give any interpretation at all). We therefore have to work out what we think is most likely, and that is by no means easy. At this point, Dodd recognized the importance of form criticism, which insisted on the *Sitz im Leben* of the parables as the main key to their interpretation. But Dodd was a long way from being a convinced form critic. To his mind, discounting the evangelists' interpretation(s) entirely, as both Jülicher and the form critics were inclined to do, would have been going too far. Some of the parables probably contained the teaching of Jesus himself, and even if Jeremias might have gone too far in saying that we could recover his actual words, there was no doubt that the flavour of the narrative reflected what we would expect from Jesus. Dodd did not say this on purely subjective grounds, but tried his best to substantiate his views from the general tenor of the gospels.

At the heart of Dodd's understanding of the parables was Jesus' teaching about the 'kingdom of God'. Whether this was mentioned explicitly or not, it seemed to underlie all the parables in one way or another, and it was there that the interpreter must begin. By examining contemporary Jewish usage, Dodd discovered that the term 'kingdom of God' could have two distinct meanings.

1. The kingdom of God might refer to the rule of God over his people Israel. This rule was effective in so far as Israel was obedient to the Torah, the law in which God's will was revealed. In this sense, the kingdom of God was a present reality.

2. The kingdom of God might also be a universal divine rule, to which the whole world would one day submit. In this sense, it was not a present reality, but a future hope, a sign of what would be in the last days (*eschaton*). The realization of this eschatological rule would be accompanied by divine judgment on those who had rejected him, and deliverance for those who had accepted his sovereignty.

Dodd accepted that the teaching of Jesus was similar to that of the rabbis in many ways. The rabbis spoke of taking the kingdom of God upon oneself, and Jesus reflected something of this when he talked of receiving the kingdom of God as a little child (Mk. 10:15). But whereas the rabbis understood this to mean scrupulous observance of the Torah, Jesus did not. For him, the way of the little child stood in contrast to that of the 'wise and the intelligent' (Mt. 11:25). To some extent this could be explained by saying that for Jesus, the kingdom of God was portrayed as both a present and a future hope, so that the 'extra' ingredient in his teaching could be interpreted as eschatological.

But Dodd was forced to recognize that there is another sense in which this 'eschatological' kingdom also comes in the here and now. When Jesus said that 'the kingdom of God has come to you' (Mt. 12:28), it was a fact of present experience in a way which was not like rabbinic teaching. Eschatology had broken into the present in a new and radical way. And at the centre of this eschatological breakthrough stood the parables of Jesus. This is why they are so important for our understanding of his life and teaching.

One important aspect of that teaching, which caused enormous scandal at the time, was Jesus' apparent friendship with 'publicans and sinners'. Jesus' own reply was that it is the sick who need a doctor. Three parables, all of them in Luke 15, bring out this message in different ways: the parables of the lost sheep, the lost coin and the prodigal son. Parables that occur in both Luke and Matthew are set in different contexts. Dodd concluded that Luke's version was the more historically accurate, because the *Sitz im Leben* was 'right', and this was his approach generally. For example, in the parable of the great feast (Lk. 14:16–24 and Mt. 22:1–13), Luke has two sets of last-minute invitations to those who were not originally invited, whereas Matthew has only one, and, in addition, includes the example of the man without a wedding garment. Dodd interpreted this to refer to the struggle over the admission of Gentiles into the church. Luke was in favour, and so stressed this point in his account. Matthew was cautious, and so pointed out the dangers of letting Gentiles into the church too easily. Jesus, of course, would not have been so restrictive – although that may say more about Dodd's own desires than about the actual teaching of Jesus himself.

The most difficult of all these parables is that of the wicked husbandmen (Mk. 12:1–8). Jülicher regarded it as an allegory constructed by the early church, and referred to the death of Jesus. Dodd rejected this interpretation, arguing that the wicked husbandmen are far too realistically portrayed to be regarded as allegorical. Greed and murder were sufficiently common not to have to be written off in this way. For good measure Dodd added that the unsettled conditions of Palestine before the Jewish revolt were an ideal *Sitz im Leben* for just this kind of thing. He interpreted the parable as a direct reference to the injustices being perpetrated by landlords in contemporary Palestine, and said that Jesus meant that God's justice would eventually uproot the entire society – as indeed happened in AD 70. The unjust murder of the beloved son merely demonstrated that both sides were guilty in this unsatisfactory social situation, and that both would suffer accordingly. To relate it to the death of Christ, argued Dodd, is understandable but unnecessary; the *Sitz im Leben* suggested above explains it well enough.

Dodd then went on to distinguish a second group of parables, those which portray an impending crisis. He recognized that these parables (the faithful and unfaithful servant; the ten virgins, *etc.*) have frequently been read as meaning that Jesus foresaw a period of waiting between his death and his second coming. Dodd denied this, and claimed that Jesus never went beyond the immediate situation in which the parables were spoken. His first coming was the event which provoked the crisis, and it was by their response to him in the here and now that his hearers would be judged. The introduction of the second-coming motif came later; it was an adaptation of these parables made by the early church, to reflect a situation which Jesus had not envisaged.

Dodd also distinguished a third group of parables, which he

defined as parables of 'growth'. These included such well-known stories as that of the sower, the tares and the mustard seed. As we have already seen, Dodd believed that the parable of the sower comes complete with an allegorical interpretation in the gospels as we now have them, but he rejected this, except as an interpretation imposed on the original parable by the early church. The parables of growth were clearly eschatological, in Dodd's view, because they point in some sense to the future fulfilment of what is present now only in part, but he did not accept that this is their main function. As he said,

> The parables of growth, then, are susceptible of a natural interpretation which makes them into a commentary on the actual situation during the ministry of Jesus, in its character as the coming of the Kingdom of God in history. They are not to be taken as implying a long process of development introduced by the ministry of Jesus and to be consummated by His second advent, though the Church later understood them in that sense. As in the teaching of Jesus as a whole, so here, there is no long historical perspective: the *eschaton*, the divinely ordained climax of history, is here. It has come by no human effort, but by an act of God; and yet not by an arbitrary, catastrophic intervention, for it is the harvest following upon a long process of growth. This is the new element which these parables introduce. The coming of the Kingdom is indeed a crisis brought by divine intervention; but it is not an unprepared crisis, unrelated to the previous course of history. An obscure process of growth has gone before it, and the fresh act of God which calls the crisis into being is an answer to the work of God in history which has gone before.

In the final analysis, the proclamation of the kingdom of God was a crisis calling for decision and bringing judgment with it, and the parables were a key element in challenging people to face up to this. So central a role for them had scarcely been imagined before, but thanks to Dodd's researches it has become a major theme of modern scholarship.

Another follower of Jülicher, who moved off in a slightly different direction, was J. Jeremias. Jeremias believed that it was possible to go behind the layers of church interpretation and discover the very words (*ipsissima verba*) of Jesus himself in the parables. In a manner which parallels Dodd's approach, while going beyond it in thoroughness, Jeremias developed the crisis theme in great detail, pointing out that it might already have been too late for a decision to be made, so imminent was the impending judgment. Like Dodd, he was forced to consider that the early church modified this teaching considerably, projecting the immediacy of the original challenge into a more distant future.

The historicist interpretation of the parables, which Jeremias so eloquently propounded, was commended by much of the scholarly world for laying an indispensable foundation for further interpretation. It can even be said that a scholarly consensus emerged, which Craig Blomberg (1990) has helpfully summarized as follows:

1. Throughout the history of the church, most Christians interpreted the parables as allegories.

2. Modern scholarship has rightly rejected allegorical interpretation in favour of an approach which sees each parable as making only one main point.

3. Nevertheless, the parables as they appear in the gospels do have a few undeniably allegorical elements, but these are the exception and not the rule.

4. Thus the occasional explicit interpretations of parables in the gospels are additional exceptions to Jesus' usual practice, and they too are not to be taken as normative.

5. Apart from this small amount of allegory, most of the parables and most parts of each parable are among the most indisputably authentic sayings of Jesus in the gospels.

But it was not long before this consensus was criticized, because the more the various layers were peeled off, the less there was to interpret, and the more banal the ultimate conclusions seemed. The continuing development of literary methods of biblical interpretation threw the doors open once more, and another picture began to emerge. One well-known example of this can be found in the work of E. Fuchs and the so-called 'new hermeneutic'.

The new hermeneutic encouraged a fresh departure in parable interpretation by focusing on the phenomenon of language. Its supporters claimed that parables must be understood in a completely different way from the one in which ordinary human conversation was analysed. In their view, parables constituted a 'language event' which opened up a new world and impelled the hearer to a decision. The crisis approach of Dodd and Jeremias was therefore retained, but the *Sitz im Leben* which they outlined was abandoned. The decision-making process was not one which could be tied to a particular moment in history; it applied to all time. As such, parables acquired yet another, and equally deep, significance. In literary terms they were something of a cross between proverb and prophecy; they taught wisdom in everyday life, as did the proverbs, but at the same time they challenged the inadequacies of normal human behaviour and rebuked them with the threat of judgment, in the manner of prophecies. This dual function came to be seen as their special genius, and was cited as yet another reason for their central, linking role in the gospel texts.

Post-critical literary analysis has usually discovered forty-one parables or parabolic sayings in the gospels, which may be subdivided into the following types.

1. *Parables derived from proverbs.* There are twelve of these in all, of which four are 'simple' parables and the remainder have been expanded to include a narrative section. Of these, four deal with matters of everyday experience and four are warnings of the coming judgment. The lamp (Mk. 4:21) and the salt (Mk. 9:50) are examples of the simple type, the story of the two debtors (Lk. 7:41) reflects everyday experience and the story of the man with the two sons (Mt. 21:28–32) points to a future judgment.

2. *Parables of discovery and response.* There are fourteen of these in all, of which ten focus on the kingdom (rule) of God which will reshape the future, and four on action in crucial situations. Of the first type, four focus on the theme of the hiddenness and mystery of the kingdom, including the parables of the fig tree (Mk. 13:28) and of the wheat and the tares (Mt. 13:24–30). Four more emphasize the theme of God's gift and the surprise associated with that; these include the parable of the sower (Mk. 4:3–8) and of the pearl of great price (Mt. 13:45). A third group, consisting of the parables of the lost sheep (Mt. 18:12) and of the lost coin (Lk. 15:8) emphasizes the theme of discovery, and the joy which that brings. Of the second type, two parables commend adequate action in a given situation; these are the parables of the friend at midnight (Lk. 11:5–8) and of the unjust judge (Lk. 18:2–5), and two more deal with action which was a failure: that of the rich fool (Lk. 12:16–20) and that of the wedding garment (Mt. 22:11–14).

3. *Narrative parables.* These are divided into two main types. The first type are those in which there is a reversal of status. There are six of these and they all occur in Luke, who uses them as ethical examples. Parables of this type are the good Samaritan (Lk. 10:30–37), the rich man and Lazarus (Lk. 16:19–31) and the prodigal son (Lk. 15:11–32). The second major type is that of the so-called 'servant parables', which subdivide according to whether the result is expected or unexpected. Of the first of these groups there are five

examples in the gospels, of which the parable of the talents (Mt. 25:14–30) and of the ten virgins (Mt. 25:1–13) may be regarded as typical. To the second group belong the four parables where the result is unexpected, *e.g.* the parable of the unmerciful servant (Mt. 18:28–38) and of the unjust steward (Lk. 16:1–8).

Parables may be categorized in this way, but they cannot be fully explained by an exegete. Reader (or hearer) participation is an essential ingredient in parable-telling, as Pheme Perkins makes clear:

> . . . we cannot enter into the dynamics of the parable if we simply ask informational questions. We need to appreciate the special vision and creativity in the parables of Jesus. We need to explore the wide range of human experiences presented in the parables. Perhaps we need to look at our own experience to see how the experiences in the parables address us. These dimensions of the parable draw upon our resources of imagination and sensitivity. Many of the parables even challenge us to create our own conclusions about the story which is half finished . . . In short, we have to participate in the process of parable telling.

Here the literary approach which starts with a reader-centred criticism reaches its ultimate climax. Not only is the reader invited to view himself against the parable, but he is also asked to share in formulating its meaning – the ultimate step towards independent literary creation!

With this in mind, let us take another look at the parable of the good Samaritan (Lk. 10:29–37). The occasion for this parable is a legal question: how far does the concept of 'neighbour' extend? This was doubtless a real question in first-century Palestine, where many different groups lived side by side in mutual indifference or hostility. Most people would have assumed, however, that members of one's own group would come into this category. But as Jesus tells the story, it becomes apparent that neither the priest nor the Levite is able to help the unfortunate victim. Why is this? Modern readers instinctively turn to anticlerical feelings to explain what to us is outright hypocrisy. We think of the priest and the Levite as representatives of a certain moral standard, which they proceed to ignore when it is inconvenient, or when nobody else is looking. By doing this, of course, we are expressing something about the way in which we regard the clergy today, and not necessarily saying anything about ancient views of the matter.

It is at least possible that most ancient readers, especially Jews, would have appreciated that the reason why the priest and the Levite could not help was that the demands of ritual purity forbade them from coming into contact with a man in such a condition. In essence, it was the same problem that Jesus faced when he healed on the Sabbath day – humanitarian compassion conflicted with ritual duty, and the Jews had been taught to prefer the latter. A 'heretical' Samaritan, on the other hand, may not have been bound by this constraint, and could therefore give assistance when required. It seems quite possible that the hatred between Jews and Samaritans was largely on the Jewish side; if this was indeed the case, the parable was a rebuke to Jewish self-righteousness in a way which affected the entire nation, and not just its clerical representatives.

There seems to be little doubt that Jesus intended to teach us to love our enemies in this parable, but it is not immediately obvious who is expected to love whom. On the surface, it is the Samaritan who shows love for the unfortunate Jew, but it is quite likely that Jesus' real intention was to teach the opposite: by putting themselves in the place of the unfortunate victim, Jews should have realized that they were not a superior race, and that they also depended on the good will of others. It was therefore incumbent upon Jews to love other races, and not to look down on them. Perkins supports this 'deeper' meaning of the parable by appealing to the principle of 'opposites' which attract each other in the course of the story, and ultimately turn it on its head.

The wider application of the parable's message is more complicated. Many interpreters are inclined to look for 'parallel' situations in the modern world, *e.g.* Protestant and Catholic in Northern Ireland, black and white in South Africa, or best of all Jew and Arab in modern Palestine. These analogies may have a certain validity within their own context, but as general interpretations of the parable they are too restrictive. Most of us find ourselves outside these situations, and can therefore adopt a position of comfortable self-righteousness with regard to them, which is the very opposite of what Jesus was trying to teach. The true message of the parable is that compassion cannot be limited to certain situations or classes of people. Where there is a need it must be met, without regard to human distinctions, which become barriers to love. This is not to say that there are not situations in which those barriers need to be maintained – Jesus would not have accepted the Samaritan as a religious equal – but that they should not become excuses which prevent us from carrying out the weightier demands of the law. In putting this message into a parable, Jesus was dressing up a conventional Old Testament theme in a way which would challenge the complacency of those who heard him. In theory, they should have been able to work it out for themselves, but over-familiarity with the text of the law, and a certain blinkered way of interpreting it, had dulled their receptivity to God's commands.

The use of literary theories to elucidate the meaning of a parable is of great service, provided that they are kept within their proper bounds. In the above example, there are two areas in which modern interpreters are liable to be guided by their prejudices rather than by the story itself. The first of these, as we have already mentioned, is the tendency to connect the Jew–Samaritan opposition with a similar situation in the world today, thereby distancing it from most of us. The second is the tendency to confuse moral and religious issues, as if the former automatically embrace the latter. This can be seen most clearly in the urge to 'love' the Samaritan by deciding that in the end, our common humanity is more significant than the differences which separate us. Applied to modern life, this might easily suggest that doctrinal and other 'religious' differences do not matter and that the human race should unite on the basis of brotherly love. This was not at all what Jesus was saying, and such an interpretation extends his meaning beyond what can be drawn out from the text – and is in direct contradiction to what is stated elsewhere (*e.g.* Jn. 4:24).

Other modern interpretations of the parables make few advances beyond this, though the canonical criticism of B. S. Childs insists that the literary approach is theologically inadequate. However true it may be that we can find a moral to the story and apply it in our own life situations, it must always be remembered that the 'canonical shape' of the gospels excludes the possibility that moral teaching is their main purpose. The parables, along with every other part of the gospels, have another function altogether: to bear witness to the supreme saving act of God in Christ. An interpretation of the parables which does not take this into account has missed the major point. In the case of the good Samaritan, this must involve a particular interpretation of God's love, which comes to sacrifice itself in order to overturn our self-righteousness and bring healing to the nations. Yet it is curious to note how, once this theological approach starts to take root, ancient allegory is only a short step away. If God is at work in the world, why should it be impossible to interpret the good Samaritan as Jesus, and the poor victim by the wayside as sinful humankind? At the end of the day we are nearer the point of departure than we could ever have imagined, and the ancient interpretation comes to seem less improbable after all. Blomberg sums it up well: according to his analysis, modern criticism claims to have demonstrated that the parables are much more allegorical than the traditional scholarly consensus has thought, and that many parables make more than one point. Whether these features make them more authentic or less so is a matter of dispute, but in purely literary terms it hardly matters. For the historian of biblical interpretation, however, the message is clear: the contemporary reaffirmation of allegory, whether correct or not, at least demonstrates that the 'communion of the saints in every age' is more of a reality than we might at one time have thought possible.

BIBLIOGRAPHY

C. Blomberg, *Interpreting the Parables* (Downers Grove, IL: IVP; Leicester: Apollos, 1990).

B. S. Childs, *The New Testament as Canon: An Introduction* (London: SCM, 1984), pp. 531–540.

J. D. Crossan, 'A Basic Bibliography for Parables Research', *Semeia* 1 (1974), pp. 236–274.

C. H. Dodd, *The Parables of the Kingdom* (London: Nisbet, 1935).

J. Drury, *The Parables in the Gospels* (London: SPCK, 1985).

J. Jeremias, *The Parables of Jesus* (London: SCM, 1963).

P. R. Jones, *The Teaching of the Parables* (Nashville: Broadman, 1982).

S. Kistemaker, *The Parables of Jesus* (Grand Rapids: Baker, 1980).

D. Patte (ed.), *Semiology and Parables: An Exploration of the Possibilities offered by Structuralism for Exegesis* (Pittsburgh: Pickwick, 1976).

P. Perkins, *Hearing the Parables of Jesus* (Ramsey, NJ: Paulist Press, 1981).

D. O. Via, *The Parables* (Philadelphia: Fortress, 1967).

12

Social trends in interpretation

Introduction

The second world of discourse in contemporary biblical interpretation is that of current social and political issues. Those concerned about them may be critical scholars who fully accept the conclusions of the first group, but they may also have come to regard them as 'irrelevant'. To them the most important thing is 'orthorpraxis' as opposed to 'orthodoxy'. 'Orthopraxis' means putting theology to work in a practical way in order to manifest the kingdom of God in deeds, not merely in words. The traditional churches are frequently condemned for being content to pray and preach while flagrant social injustices go uncorrected. Putting this right means shaking these churches out of their complacency, and developing a political stance which pits the Bible against the oppressive ideologies of our time. Theologians of this type are frequently criticized for their one-sided agenda; all too often, oppression is the exclusive preserve of western capitalism, white supremacy and male chauvinism. But it is possible that these theologians may one day turn on the causes they now support with the same critical spirit which they display towards their current targets.

In recent years many theologians in the Third World have expressed their deep dissatisfaction with an academic approach to Bible study which has little relevance to the practical problems they have to face. To these theologians the fact that the Scriptures have a good deal to say about political and social justice, especially in the Old Testament, is of the utmost importance in addressing the basic needs of their own societies.

From the Third World, concerns of this kind have gradually spread more widely. Theologians and biblical scholars in the western world are now far more likely to be challenged to think through the practical implications of their ideas than at any time in the past 300 years. Political statements are being made by the churches to an extent which would have been unthinkable a generation ago, and faithfulness to the biblical message is cited as the main reason for this. Under the banner of justice, the search for 'orthopraxis' has broadened to include social issues which have long been ignored or sidestepped by the church's leaders. The place of women in the church and in society is a major example of this, and a 'women's hermeneutic' of the Bible is currently being developed. Whether this will become an important aspect of biblical studies in the future is hard to say, but for the moment at least it is a serious challenge to traditional ways of thinking.

Common to the hermeneutic of 'orthopraxis' is the belief that the interpreter of Scripture must begin with the real problems which people in the world are facing, and look for answers to them in the Bible. This is in sharp contrast to the traditional, 'orthodox' model of interpretation, which starts with the Bible and seeks to apply its teaching to contemporary reality. According to most proponents of 'orthopraxis', the traditional approach runs the risk of being irrelevant, because it asks questions which nobody else is asking, and proposes solutions which nobody else understands. Opponents of the 'orthopraxis' model reply that it is far too subjective, and is liable to take the Bible out of context, thereby misinterpreting it, even in places which may seem on the surface to lend support to the 'orthopraxis' argument. As always, there is an element of truth on both sides of this debate which must be taken into account. The call for 'relevance' is a necessary one, especially when academic scholarship has become so obviously divorced from the practicalities of church life. At the same time, 'relevance' can never be the only criterion for interpretation, since the Bible speaks to our situation from the outside, as well as from within. A balance must be struck between subjective and objective considerations if this kind of hermeneutic is to last beyond the present generation.

The interpreters and their work

Jacques Ellul (1912–94). A French Protestant lay theologian who taught law and sociology at Bordeaux from 1946, he was a strong critic of leftist ideology, and of theologians who tried to adapt

Christianity to it. Most of his writings deal with various aspects of modern sociological reality, but a number are specifically theological and biblical in orientation. Among the latter are *The Presence of the Kingdom* (1948; Eng. trans. 1951), which is a study of the teaching of Jesus on the kingdom of God; *The Judgment of Jonah* (1951; Eng. trans. 1971); *The Politics of God and the Politics of Man* (1966; Eng. trans. 1972), which is a study of 2 Kings; *The Meaning of the City* (1970), which examines urban civilization in the light of the biblical teaching about the city; and *Apocalypse: the Book of Revelation* (1975; Eng. trans. 1977), which he interprets as the consummation of human life outside the domain of Satan's rule. Ellul enjoyed a certain vogue in the USA in the 1970s, but his influence has since waned. Generally speaking, his approach is too idiosyncratic to have made much impact on biblical scholars, though he has been more appreciated by social scientists.

José Miguez Bonino (1924–). He is a Protestant liberation theologian who teaches in Buenos Aires. His most prominent work is *Doing Theology in a Revolutionary Situation* (1975).

Juan Luís Segundo (1925–). A Jesuit liberation theologian from Uruguay, he has written on *The Historical Jesus* (1986) and *Paul* (1986).

Norman Karol Gottwald (1926–). He has taught at the New York Theological Seminary since 1980, and is a leading Marxist interpreter of the Old Testament. His main book is *The Tribes of Yahweh* (1979), in which he portrays the Israelite 'conquest' of Canaan as a peasants' revolt within the society of the time.

Gustavo Gutiérrez (1928–). This South American liberation theologian sees the exodus as the archetype of social and political liberation, and interprets Jesus in political terms. His main work is *A Theology of Liberation* (1971).

Peter Berger (1929–). A sociologist of religion, he has written widely on theological subjects from outside the discipline. His most important works are *The Social Construction of Reality* (1966), *The Sacred Canopy: Elements of a Social Theory of Religion* (1967), *A Rumour of Angels* (1969), and *The Heretical Imperative* (1979).

Abraham Johannes Malherbe (1930–). This South African biblical scholar has taught in the USA since 1969. His books, *Social Aspects of Early Christianity* (1975) and *The Cynic Epistles* (1977), have furthered sociological research in New Testament studies.

Wayne Atherton Meeks (1932–). Professor at Yale from 1973, he is a leading social historian of the early church. His many books include *The Writings of St Paul* (1972), *The Prophet-King: Moses*

Traditions and the Johannine Christology (1967), *The First Urban Christians* (1983) and *The Moral World of the First Christians* (1986).

Phyllis Trible (1932–). She has taught at several American seminaries, most recently at Union Theological Seminary in New York (1979). She is a leading feminist theologian and biblical interpreter, and has written *God and the Rhetoric of Sexuality* (1978).

John Hall Elliott (1935–). He is Professor of Theology at San Francisco (1975), his most important work to date being a sociological commentary on 1 and 2 Peter and Jude (1986).

Leonardo Boff (1938–). He is a Brazilian Roman Catholic liberation theologian, whose views have been suspect at the Vatican. His most important book is *Jesus Christ Liberator* (1972).

Elisabeth Schüssler Fiorenza (1938–). Professor of New Testament at Notre Dame (1970) and at the Episcopal Divinity School in Cambridge, Massachusetts (1984), she is a leading feminist interpreter of the New Testament. She has written extensively on the book of Revelation (1972, 1981) and has published controversial works such as *In Memory of Her* (1982) and *Bread not Stone* (1984).

The issues

The issues which confront modern social interpreters of the Bible can be summed up as follows.

1. *Is it possible to use an ancient text to solve current social, economic and political problems?* In what way can theologians use examples of teaching and behaviour taken from a different context when trying to address the issues of today?

2. *Is it possible to find a single hermeneutical principle by which Scripture may be applied in the present situation?* Can 'justice' play this role, and if so, what does it mean in practice? How can such a term be interpreted in concrete situations?

3. *Is it possible to relate a hermeneutic of this kind to a tradition which transcends the concern of the moment?* Is there a link between what proponents of 'orthopraxis' are saying and the age-old witness of the church to the gospel, or is 'orthopraxis' a kind of rebellion against tradition? Has the 'church' become so much a part of the establishment that it is effectively an enemy to be combated in the name of Christ? And if this is so, can the church be turned inside out in the name of faithfulness to a message which the majority of Christians have never heard or understood? To what extent is it possible or legitimate to let the world set the agenda for the church?

The methods of interpretation

Sociological theory

The influence of sociological theory on biblical interpretation has grown dramatically in the past generation, with results which have been highly controversial. One of the main reasons for this is that biblical scholars have traditionally been trained to think in historical terms, which may be quite different from what is normal for social scientists. History is concerned with human development through time, and looks for particular events which have shaped that process. No historian would assume that what has happened in one time and place will be paralleled elsewhere; each situation and event is unique in itself, and he or she will be suspicious of any assumed 'parallels'. Sociology, on the other hand, looks for what is general or typical in any given society, and seeks to find similar models elsewhere. It is much less concerned with development through time, and prefers to deal in theoretical concepts which can be applied across temporal and spatial barriers. For a sociologist, 'history' may be little more than the source of the social traditions which are imposed on people without their consent. This may be accepted as inevitable, but in certain types of sociological theory it may also be resented, so that 'history' can come to be seen as a great enemy of freedom.

In looking at the Bible, the sociologist is primarily concerned to discover types of social structures. Defining what is meant by a 'society' is the first problem. It might be fairly clear that Israel under the monarchy constituted a 'society', since there was a state organization which gave some kind of structure to the nation's life. But things are much less clear for the patriarchal period, and they become more complicated still after the exile. To what 'society' did Jesus belong, for example? At one level, he was a Galilean, at another he was a Jew and at another he was a subject of the Roman Empire. As the events of his trial make only too clear, these 'societies' competed for influence, and each had a role to play in his life. Which one, if any, was determinative? The same problem recurs when dealing with the early church, which lived in the Jewish and the Graeco-Roman worlds simultaneously.

Sociologists like to interpret the religious life of a nation in terms of 'institutions' and of 'roles' which individuals within the nation occupy. These institutions and roles may not all be found in every society, but they are types which are widespread. In particular, there are often counterparts in our own time to religious institutions in ancient Israel. Because of this, analysis done on modern phenomena can be read back into the ancient world on the assumption that all societies function in more or less similar ways. It will be obvious that supporters of this method are put off by the historian's insistence on the uniqueness of any given society's development, and may retort that if Israel was unique in that way, it is hard to see how or why it should serve as a model for Christians now. On the other hand, there is always a danger that 'typical' phenomena will turn out to be imperfect analogies, and produce only highly misleading interpretations. It is also questionable how far past civilizations can be explained in terms of modern sociological theory. A very serious problem in dealing with the ancient world is the lack of data; it is simply not possible to reconstruct the economic life of the Israelites with any degree of precision, so that a good deal of modern social analysis cannot be applied to the Bible.

In spite of these drawbacks, however, sociologists have used their theories to interpret the biblical data, and have come up with a number of interesting suggestions. First of all, they have identified role models in society, of which 'prophet' and 'priest' are the most typical. A prophet is a charismatic figure, emerging out of nowhere to challenge the basic social structures in the name of deeper principles which have been forgotten or corrupted. A priest, on the other hand, is identified as a guardian of the established order who has to pick up the pieces and carry on when the wave of prophetic indignation has spent itself. Similar role models can be seen in modern religious life: the priests of the Christian religion are the guardians of tradition, whose life is periodically disturbed by charismatic prophets who challenge their authority and question the basis of the institution which they serve – the church.

Sociological thinking has enabled a number of interpreters of the Bible to bring the prophets of Israel back to life in a way which critical scholarship has failed to do. It is hard not to notice that the prophetic voice has been preserved in Scripture more than the priestly, though it must be admitted that priests probably did most of the actual preserving. The conclusion from this is that it is the prophetic witness which needs to be constantly re-emphasized, and so many modern theologians have become 'prophets', speaking to the problems of our society in the way that their ancestors did to the problems of theirs.

Another very important distinction is the one between 'church' and 'sect'. A 'church' is a religious institution which embraces, or seeks to embrace, the society as a whole. Its norms are those which are publicly accepted, and probably imposed by the law. A 'sect', by contrast, is a religious group which exists within the larger society but is distinct from it. The reasons for this may vary from case to case, but usually members of a sect are more deeply committed to the religious values which they profess, and they are certainly more aware of the fact that the majority in society does not think the way they do. In modern times, this distinction is fairly plain, at least in general terms. We are all used to the difference between the 'mainline' churches which seek to live a fully public life, and smaller groups which have separated themselves to varying degrees from wider society.

Problems arise when this distinction is read back into ancient Israel, or into the early church. If we accept that the temple worship was the 'church' of Israel, where do we find the 'sects'? Can we say that the Qumran community, for example, was a sect? What about the Samaritans, or the first Christians? If Christianity began life as a 'sect', when did it become a 'church'? To a theologian, the church has always been the church, even when it has been a 'sect' in sociological terms, and the norms which ought to govern its life are the same now as they were then. The problem here is largely one of technical language and definition. Sociologists use words which theologians understand differently, and *vice versa*. 'Church' is an excellent example of this; for the theologian, the church is a unique institution, which is basically spiritual in nature. For the sociologist, on the other hand, it is a typical institution, with many parallels in other societies. Its spiritual character may be admitted up to a point, but not its uniqueness.

Moving on from this, anthropological insights have also been brought to bear on biblical interpretation, sometimes with curious results. For example, it has been noted that in many primitive societies there is a collective resistance to empirical reality if it is incompatible with a tribe's beliefs. In order to compensate for this incompatibility, many tribes invent explanations to cover what anthropologists call 'cognitive dissonance'. Applying this theory to early Christianity, some theorists have explained the doctrine of the resurrection of Christ in this way. The disciples of Jesus, unable to accept the reality that he had been crucified, banded together and created a psychological compensation for this unacceptable fact: Jesus was not really dead; he was alive. This suggestion can be found in John Gager's *Kingdom and Community* (1975), though Gager is careful to state that 'cognitive dissonance' was not the only factor motivating the early disciples.

Sociological theory has proved to be most attractive in the interpretation of the early church. This is because the Pauline epistles provide evidence of a kind which is lacking elsewhere in the Bible, which can be supplemented from archaeology and contemporary literature in a way that is impossible for the Old Testament. Daily life in the Roman Empire can be reconstructed to a reasonable degree, and it is therefore possible to suggest some theoretical reconstructions of the social composition of the first Christian communities. This has been the special concern of Wayne Meeks, who has sought to explain the beliefs of the Pauline communities in the context of the social structures of the time. Meeks relates Paul's theological and ethical pronouncements to the type of people whom he was addressing, and tries to suggest reasons why particular beliefs may have been more attractive to certain types of people. Meeks also analyses the Pauline language of 'belonging' and of 'separation', to try to determine who was part of the Christian in-group and who was not.

In studies of this kind, it is very important to distinguish carefully between two rather different things. It has long been understood that the early Christian communities were largely made up of trading communities which spread across the Mediterranean world; that much is evident from Acts and the Pauline epistles. Paul moved in a world of tentmakers and ship-owners, and many of the churches he founded were in prominent trading centres. But what Meeks is trying to show is that Paul's gospel was designed to appeal to that class of person more than to any other, so that an aristocrat or a peasant would have found the atmosphere in one of Paul's congregations somewhat uncongenial. We have no real way of knowing this, of course, because of our limited data. We do know that there were not many rich, wise or famous people in the churches (1 Cor. 1:26), and it seems that there was a certain tendency to prefer those who were well off to those who were poor (Jas. 2:1–4). But statements of this kind are too general, and too easily understandable as common human traits, to be of much use in constructing a viable social theory. Likewise, although it is possible that social tensions underlay the strained relationships evident in the Corinthian church, we know too little about them to be sure. In all probability, they were one of a number of factors involved, and were not perceived by Paul to be the most important issue.

When all is said and done, it must be confessed that most biblical interpreters find sociology difficult to come to terms with. Their main reservations about it may be expressed as follows.

1. Sociology is 'reductionist' because it prefers to speak in generalities and ignore specific details. This means that what it ends up with is often a kind of lowest common denominator, which might tell us something about patterns of human behaviour in general without saying much about the particular instance(s) in question. Sociologists retort that reading the Bible from any one point of view is 'reductionist'; what is needed is an interdisciplinary effort embracing as broad a field of knowledge as possible.

2. Sociology requires data which are not available for the ancient world. Whatever usefulness it might have nowadays, it is simply not applicable to biblical studies. Sociologists retort that this is to misunderstand the use of sociology when dealing with models in the historical past. Their purpose is to explain the available data by analogy with developments elsewhere, not to conduct an in-depth analysis of ancient society. Nice as it would undoubtedly be to have more information, this is not as necessary as some theologians assume.

3. Sociology is essentially deterministic in its approach, and cannot adequately explain the individual and personal elements working for change in actual situations. This is particularly serious in the study of the Bible, where the role of specific individuals, especially Jesus, is so central. Sociologists retort that determinism is only part of the story. If we are to appreciate what is unique about Jesus, we must first understand what is common to him and to other prophets *etc.* If we fail to do this properly, we may end up worshipping Jesus for entirely the wrong reasons.

Perhaps the fairest thing to say at the present time is that debate is still going on among theologians as to how far sociological theories and insights can be integrated into biblical studies. Some tension between the two disciplines will probably always exist, though there are signs that a *modus vivendi* may eventually be attained. As C. Tuckett (1987) has written:

> In terms of results obtained, much that is new and original has been achieved by approaches to the New Testament texts from a sociological point of view. In terms of basic method, however, it must be said that there is little here which differs fundamentally from the traditional approaches to the text associated with the historical-critical method. Sociological approaches have taught us to broaden our vision when interpreting the New Testament; but they do so by encouraging us to use many of the same basic methods as we have in the past.

Liberation theology

Based on a largely sociological approach, but applying it to a particular situation, is the phenomenon of liberation theology, which was first developed in Latin America as a response to the extremes of social injustice in that part of the world. Liberation theology has been strongly influenced by Marxism, though it is not necessarily tied to it. Among biblical scholars, its most consistent advocate has been Norman Gottwald, whose great book *The Tribes of Yahweh* (1979) stands as a monument to this approach. Gottwald derives his basic categories from Karl Marx, and interprets social change in purely material terms, *e.g.* the need of the tribes to feed themselves. As far as Gottwald is concerned, the Israelite 'conquest' of Canaan was not an invasion from without but a class revolt from within. We have already seen how the first part of this thesis has been supported from some archaeological evidence, which points to a slow drift of Israelite tribes into Canaan, rather than to a full-scale invasion on a single occasion; but the connection between this and the concept of a 'class struggle' is Gottwald's own.

Biblical scholars are (rightly) suspicious of Gottwald's reasoning, and it seems probable that his hypothesis will eventually be rejected on the ground that the historical and linguistic evidence does not support it. What may be more difficult to counter, however, is his assertion that Israelite 'Yahwism' was originally an egalitarian movement, with revolutionary implications for all societies, ancient and modern. As one who stands in this tradition, Gottwald claims that it is imperative for the modern Christian to become a 'participant' – though it is not always clear what it is that the Christian is supposed to participate in. In Gottwald's interpretation, 'orthopraxis' has become an end in itself; the object in view is less easily discernible.

This is not true, of course, for the liberation theology of Latin America, whose social and political goals are extremely clear. Most of the theologians involved in it derive their main inspiration from the book of Exodus, complemented by prophets such as Amos and Hosea. The exodus is interpreted as the archetype of a people's struggle for liberation from an oppressive economic and political tyranny. God is seen to be on the side of the poor and downtrodden, choosing charismatic leaders as his instruments for setting his people free. Violence is by no means excluded from the picture; on the contrary, it is seen as a way of meting out justice on the oppressors. Jesus is portrayed in liberation theology as one who preached the 'kingdom of God', by which he meant an age of happiness and freedom when the bondage of the past would be forgotten. The kingdom of God would involve the transformation of an intolerable situation. This in turn would mean overcoming sin in its social and collective dimensions – in structures and in groups. In Latin America the problem of the poor is their 'alienation' from society, and it is this which a church which truly follows Jesus must seek to overcome.

Liberation theologians emphasize the political dimension of Jesus' teaching, pointing out that it is impossible to spiritualize away his attacks on the rulers of the day. Gustavo Gutiérrez believes that the Latin American situation will inevitably lead to a violent confrontation, though he does not press this point. Other liberation theologians, such as Leonardo Boff, stress the absolute necessity of a non-violent approach, which to them is the only one fully in keeping with Christ's teaching. Still others, such as Juan Luís Segundo, take a mediating position. Non-violence may be the ideal, and it is certainly what Jesus practised in his own situation, but we cannot rule out the possibility that he would have adopted a different approach in other circumstances. The real task in Latin America is to decide whether the aims of Jesus can be accomplished peacefully or not. If not, then violence may be the lesser of two evils.

As with sociological perspectives in general, liberation theology has come under widespread suspicion from biblical interpreters, who see it as a distortion of the Bible's meaning. In particular, the following points are made against it.

1. Liberation theology reduces faith to politics. An essentially spiritual, otherworldly message is distorted in favour of short-term political aims in particular countries. This is not to deny the seriousness of the social situation being addressed, or the need for Christians to do something about it. Rather it is to question whether the circumstances of the moment ought to be allowed to govern the church's interpretation of the Bible. Conservative sympathizers with liberation theology believe that it is too dogmatic in this respect, and not sufficiently able to appreciate that theology must embrace a wider perspective. Defenders of liberation theology reply that few if any liberation theologians make such extravagant claims; it is largely because they do not discuss the wider implications of their beliefs that this impression has been given.

2. Liberation theology gives a one-sided interpretation of the Bible, by stressing its political element, and it overstresses human activity in the process of liberation. Undoubtedly there is some substance in this argument, particularly in the more extreme forms of liberation theology. The view that justice must be done regardless

of the cost is certainly not the only way in which the Scriptures can be read, especially if 'doing justice' means resorting to violence. The Bible stresses that God acts in human history to help the helpless, not that the oppressed must band together to help themselves. This is an important point, which is easily missed in liberation theology.

3. Liberation theology uses the Bible to support its own political ends, a charge which is particularly justified in the writings of some of its more extreme Latin American exponents. But its defenders argue that these extremists are not typical of liberation theology as a whole. In particular, it is inaccurate to say that liberation theology is the prisoner of Marxist determinism. There are some individuals who read the situation through Marxist eyes, but the problems of Latin America are real, and will not change if Marxist ideology is abandoned. Many liberation theologians would claim that they are offering a Christian alternative to Marxism, and see the justification for their activities in their reading of the Bible. As A. F. McGovern (1983) has expressed it, liberation theology challenges the church to consider these theological propositions: (a) God reveals himself in history. (b) God desires the full human freedom of his people, at every level of their life. (c) God reveals a very special concern for the poor and is angered by injustice done against them. (d) Jesus sought to bring God's liberating power and justice to all. (e) Jesus identified in a very special way with the marginal people of society, the outcasts, the poor. (f) Jesus denounced those who placed burdens upon the poor and who placed legalism (law and order) over human need. (g) Jesus sought to 'break the power of evil and sin' in the world. (h) Jesus' actions were seen as a threat to those in positions of power.

These propositions are not above criticism, and some of them are tendentious, to say the least. But most liberation theologians insist that they cannot simply be ascribed to a Marxist analysis of the Bible, so that the charge that they are using the text merely for political ends does not stick.

As with other types of theology based on social theories, liberation theology is rooted in a particular situation which calls for action on the church's part. Christians cannot simply sit back or proclaim an otherworldly gospel when corrigible injustices are staring them in the face. At the same time, theologians have a duty to see beyond their circumstances, as well as to apply God's truth to them. It is this aspect of the matter which has caused the greatest disquiet, and where liberation theology will have to come to maturity if it is to last beyond the time and place which created it. For the moment, it can be said that it has influenced protest movements in different parts of the world, especially in southern Africa, and has played an important part in the 'bias to the poor' which is evident in the social concerns of many churches in the First World. But is has done little to shape the way the Bible is interpreted in academic circles, and it must be seriously questioned whether it has much of a future in this respect.

Feminist theology

Another branch of sociological interpretation with considerably greater potential for influencing the church's interpretation of the Bible is feminism. This was not originally a very significant part of either sociological theory or of liberation theology, but it has emerged in recent years as women have advanced into positions of leadership in the church. The language of 'oppression' used by South American theologians has been taken over and adapted to feminist concerns, sometimes in a way which is rather incongruous. As with liberation theology, feminist theology starts with a concrete situation. Most people agree that the role of women in church life has been undervalued over the years, and that women have been discriminated against by men to some extent. In this case, however, the tendency to exaggerate is much greater than it is with liberation theology.

The problem of male–female relationships is a universal one, as far as feminists are concerned, and women suffer as much discrimination in the West as they do in the Third World. Furthermore, this discrimination is often the result of a certain reading of the Bible which on the surface appears to be quite justified. Feminist theology differs from most other models of this kind in that it attacks the Bible as well as the church, and insists that both must be changed. The position is stated with great clarity by J. L. Hardegree Jr (1983), a male theologian:

> . . . we must be prepared to accept the reality of aspects of the Bible with which we disagree. An example is the masculo-centric language and general male-chauvinist attitudes we find in the Bible. The Bible must not be forgiven at this point; it must be defeated. How this is to be done is not yet entirely clear. For the present we must be firm in our argument against such evils or limitations as they are found in the Bible, for example, refusing to use any such offending passages in liturgical expressions without rewording them into language that shows full appreciation for women as well as men.

This approach has led to widespread doctoring of the English language, because of the double use to which the word 'man' can be put. At bottom is a misunderstanding about the meaning of language which has caused a great deal of confusion. In the Bible, masculine nouns and pronouns are used to include both sexes – a practice which is very widespread in the world's languages and has never been thought of as 'sexist'. On a more serious level, one of the reasons sometimes advanced for continuing this practice in the church is that the use of feminine imagery, apart from being just as restrictive, has the connotation of a fertility cult. There is also the practical problem that the Saviour of the world was a male and that Christology as we know it could not function otherwise. If God were female and her daughter were the promised Messiah, how would she have acquired a human nature? One could not imagine sexual intercourse between Joseph and the divine Mother unless she also became incarnate first, but that would destroy the Daughter's unique character. It is thus impossible to press feminism to its logical conclusion and still remain within the bounds of traditional Christian faith – a point which is readily appreciated by those concerned to defend the latter.

From the feminist perspective, biblical history should be read as two great moments – creation and redemption – at which women and men were fully equal. Following each of these, however, women lost their equality with men and declined in status. In the Old Testament, this was enshrined in the law of Moses, and in the everyday life of the people. Religious observances were a male preserve, and only males bore the sign of the covenant, circumcision. To the extent that this was ever explained, it was said that Eve had sinned first and led Adam astray in the Garden of Eden. Subordination to the male was therefore the woman's punishment (*cf.* 1 Tim. 2:11–15).

In the New Testament, Jesus re-established the equality of male and female (*cf.* Gal. 3:28), but this was soon pushed into the background by a male-dominated church which was deeply affected by something called 'patriarchy', a sociological term meaning 'male domination'. (Note how different is the sociological from the theological use of this term; to a theologian, 'patriarch' is a term of honour applied either to Abraham, Isaac and Jacob, or to the heads of the most important eastern churches.) This problem and the way to confront it are both spelled out by Elisabeth Schüssler Fiorenza (1983):

> The patriarchalizing and institutionalizing process in the early church is not a mere *fait accompli* but an early move in a

> continuing 'power play' that requires a critical sociological and theological analysis to recover Biblical and theological ground for woman's full place in today's Church. The sexual equality of the Jesus movement and of the first Christian missioners must be reaffirmed by an egalitarian interpretive model that fully recognizes the conflict between equality and hierarchy within the early Church – a battle that has been re-opened in our time.

Criticism of feminist theology is usually made along the following lines.

1. It is contrary to what the Bible says and teaches. This is sometimes admitted by defenders of feminism, who argue that the Bible is wrong in this respect. Some feminists will admit that biblical teaching was progressive in the context of the time (this is especially true of Jesus), but that it is no longer adequate. The Bible must be updated, and where necessary, replaced. Upholders of biblical authority, however much they may sympathize with some of the points made by feminists, cannot follow them in this. The historical record remains what it is, whatever the feelings of modern interpreters may be. To alter it arbitrarily, even in the best of causes, is to go against the plain meaning of the text and to produce other distortions (such as the Christological problem mentioned above).

2. It fails to recognize that the Bible's use of masculine language is not sexist, but inclusive. This may be difficult for some women to understand or accept, but it is a fact nevertheless, and one which makes sense in its context. To argue that Scripture has a male-chauvinist bias, or that it is full of 'patriarchy', is to impose a false model on it. What the Bible really teaches is that men and women are complementary to one another. As human beings, they are both equal and different. The modern feminist idea of 'equality' is a unisex concept, which is not biblical at all. By maintaining that there are no significant differences between the sexes, feminism runs the risk of destroying human society by reducing everyone to the androgynous concept of 'human being' or 'person'.

3. It has completely subordinated the Bible to its own agenda. The charge often laid against liberation theology is probably even more appropriate in this case. An example may be taken from the comment of E. A. Judge (not a feminist) who has written (1972) of the women in the Pauline churches:

> The status of women who patronized St Paul would particularly repay attention. They are clearly persons of some independence

> and eminence in their own circles, used to entertaining and running their own salons, if that is what Paul's meetings were, as they saw best.

The unprejudiced observer might think that Judge was expressing a high view of women's role in Paul's day, but this is not what E. S. Fiorenza thinks. Her comment (in Gottwald, 1983) on Judge's remark is as follows:

> This misinterpretation reduces the influential role of women in the early Christian movement to that of housewives permitted to serve coffee after Paul's lectures! Since exegetes of the New Testament take it for granted that the leadership of the early Christian communities was in the hands of men, they assume that those women mentioned in the Pauline letters were the helpmates and assistants of the apostles, especially of Paul.

It is hard not to think that Fiorenza's reading of Judge is perverse, and dictated by an agenda which neither he nor the New Testament was aware of.

Closely tied to this is the question of women's part in the leadership of the early church, and here again feminist theology can display a perversity which is almost breathtaking. The paucity of references to women in leadership roles in the New Testament may be explained not as a fact of life at the time, but as a reflection of the polemical purposes of the Pauline epistles. The reason Paul apparently did not mention women leaders more often was because there was no need to; they were not causing the trouble he was trying to deal with. The restriction of terms such as *episkopos* (bishop) and *presbyteros* (elder) to males is a result of later prejudice; as the use of *diakonos* (deacon) demonstrates, these terms could apply to women as well as men. Again, the lack of examples to substantiate this argument is held to be fortuitous and means nothing.

Equally peculiar are the attempts to make the Greek word *kephalē* (1 Cor. 11:3) mean 'source' instead of 'head', when the former meaning is scarcely attested in ancient Greek literature and does not fit the context. Even the effort to make the Greek word *authentein* mean 'dominate' instead of 'have authority over' (1 Tim. 2:12), though more plausible, smacks of special pleading. Whatever evidence can be produced in support of this idea, the fact remains that *authentein* has never been read this way, nor would such a meaning be likely to occur to anyone not aware of the feminist position. It is instructive to note that *The Women's Bible Commentary* (1992) is cautious about the 'source' idea, though basically favourable to it, and knows nothing about the alternative meaning of *authentein.* It is well known that the main theological objection to the leadership of women in the church is based on the teaching of the pastoral epistles, and so it is extremely important for feminist interpreters to insist on their non-Pauline origin. It is worth quoting *The Women's Bible Commentary* at length on this point:

> The author appeals to the creation stories as justification for women's subordination. Adam was created first, then Eve; furthermore, it was Eve, not Adam, who 'was deceived and became a transgressor'. The Greek wording suggests that the author may be appealing to a Jewish tradition in which the serpent seduces (not simply 'deceives') Eve. If so, her sin is sexual. Paul also uses Adam's prior creation to argue for women's subordination (1 Cor. 11:8–9). However, according to Paul, Adam, the first human, committed the first sin – disobedience (Rom. 5:12–21). Furthermore, Christians are a new creation in which sin is overcome and there is no 'male or female' (Gal. 3:28). For Paul, the subordination of woman to man was part of the old order of creation but not part of the new creation in Christ. Thus, the author of the Pastorals contradicts Paul and other early Christian understandings.

It is not difficult to demonstrate the role of special pleading in the above quotation. It may be that the author is appealing to a Jewish tradition, but this is not at all certain, and no evidence is supplied to support such an assertion. The reference to Romans 5 is quite perversely applied here; it is true that Adam is held responsible for the first sin, but that certainly does not remove the role of Eve, and in no way contradicts what is being stated in 1 Timothy. Lastly, the interpretation of Galatians 3:28 is simply wrong. Paul did not say that sin had been overcome in such a way as to abolish any distinction between male and female; that is not what Galatains 3:28 is about. All he said was that in Christ, the entire human race has a common Saviour, so that at that level distinctions of the male–female kind do not matter.

Perhaps the biggest problem with feminist biblical interpretation is that so many women take criticism of it personally. To deny the kind of thing which *The Women's Bible Commentary* is asserting often comes across as an attack on women as such, which it is not. Sadly, there is no denying that feminist theology frequently involves an emotional commitment on the part of those who practise it, which is absent from other types of theology. This is a pity, because it makes any kind of critique very difficult, and exposes the church to the danger that a false theological position will be accepted simply because to do otherwise would give offence to half its membership. Perhaps never before in church history has the interpretation of the Bible been exposed to a danger quite as subtle and as all-pervasive as this one.

Conclusion

It must be stressed that the methods of interpreting the Bible outlined above are still tentative and only partially accepted in academic circles. In the churches there is usually even greater suspicion of them, though the feminist hermeneutic may be making greater headway at the moment. It is quite likely that other types of interpretation will emerge within this broad social category, as new issues arise. Already there are signs that we may soon be faced with an ecologist theology, for example, which in certain aspects may not be very far removed from pantheism. By the same token, issues which have been prominent in recent years may fade away. Liberation theology may not long survive the demise of Marxism as a political ideology, and feminist theology may turn out to be equally unstable in the longer term. At the moment, we simply do not know what will happen. We can only record what has been said and done in the past few years, and wait to see what the future will bring.

BIBLIOGRAPHY

M. Bal, *Lethal Love: Feminist Literary Readings of Biblical Love Stories* (Bloomington and Indianapolis: Indiana University Press, 1987).
D. G. Bloesch, *Is the Bible Sexist?* (Westchester: Crossway, 1982).
R. and J. Boldrey, *Chauvinist or Feminist? Paul's View of Women* (Grand Rapids: Baker, 1976).
M. L. Branson and C. R. Padilla (eds.), *Conflict and Context: Hermeneutics in the Americas* (Grand Rapids: Eerdmans, 1986).
M. Evans, *Woman in the Bible* (Exeter: Paternoster, 1983).
C. H. Felder (ed.), *Stony the Road We Trod: African American Biblical Interpretation* (Minneapolis: Fortress, 1991).
E. S. Fiorenza, *In Memory of Her: A Feminist Theological Reconstruction of Christian Origins* (London: SCM, 1983).

———' "You are not to be called Father." Early Christian History in a Feminist Perspective', in N. Gottwald (ed.), *The Bible and Liberation* (see below), pp. 394–417.

J. A. Fischer, *God Said: Let There be Woman. A Study of Biblical Women* (New York: Alba House, 1979).

N. Gottwald, *The Hebrew Bible: A Socio-Literary Introduction* (Philadelphia: Fortress, 1985).

———*The Tribes of Yahweh* (Maryknoll: Orbis, 1979).

———(ed.), *The Bible and Liberation: Political and Social Hermeneutics* (Maryknoll: Orbis, 1983).

J. L. Hardegree Jr, 'Bible Study For Marxist Christians', in N. Gottwald (ed.), *The Bible and Liberation*, pp. 94–107.

J. B. Hurley, *Man and Woman in Biblical Perspective* (Leicester: IVP, 1981).

G. W. Knight III, *The New Testament Teaching on the Role Relationship of Men and Women* (Grand Rapids: Baker, 1977).

G. G. Koontz and W. Swartley (eds.), *Perspectives on Feminist Hermeneutics* (Elkhart: Institute of Mennonite Studies, 1987).

A. F. McGovern, 'The Bible In Latin American Liberation Theology', in N. Gottwald (ed.), *The Bible and Liberation*, pp. 461–472.

I. J. Mosala, *Biblical Hermeneutics and Black Theology in South Africa* (Grand Rapids: Eerdmans, 1989).

C. A. Newsom and S. H. Ringe (eds.), *The Women's Bible Commentary* (Louisville, KY: Westminster/John Knox; London: SPCK, 1992).

C. Rowland and M. Corner, *Liberating Exegesis: The Challenge of Liberation Theology to Biblical Studies* (London: SPCK, 1990).

W. Swartley, *Slavery, Sabbath, War and Women: Case Issues in Biblical Interpretation* (Kitchener and Scottdale: Herald, 1983).

C. Tuckett, *Reading the New Testament: Methods of Interpretation* (London: SPCK, 1987).

A case study: Exodus

The book of Exodus has long been recognized as being of central importance for Old Testament theology. It contains God's revelation of his holy Name, YHWH (Yahweh), in the third chapter, and the Ten Commandments in the twentieth. There is also the detailed account of how God sent plagues on Egypt to persuade Pharaoh to let the Israelites go, and then the dramatic exodus itself. In many ways, it is the key book of the Pentateuch, because it explains the seminal events which led to the emergence of Israel as a nation. Yet in spite of its importance, it is probably only in the liberation theology of the late twentieth century that Exodus has been given a primary role in determining the shape of Christian theology. We must bear this in mind, as we look at the way in which the book has been interpreted over the centuries.

To make matters simpler, we shall concentrate here on three main passages in the book. The first of these is the call to Moses (3:1–14). The second is the exodus itself (13:17–14:31) and the third is the Ten Commandments (20:1–17).

The call to Moses

Although ancient Jewish exegetes said relatively little about the call to Moses, it is frequently referred to in the New Testament. This is remarkable when we remember that Jesus and his followers emphasized the role of Abraham in the founding of Israel's faith, and somewhat downplayed that of Moses. For example, in Matthew 22:32 (Mk. 12:26; Lk. 20:37) Jesus cited Exodus 3:6 as proof of the resurrection of the dead, against the Sadducees who denied it. Many modern commentators have claimed that Jesus' use of the Exodus passage is midrashic and abuses the original meaning of the Old Testament text. Their argument is that Exodus was referring to what God had done in the past, through Abraham, Isaac and Jacob, whereas Jesus used the same text to prove that the patriarchs were still alive.

However, recent study of rabbinical exegesis has shown that Jesus' argument would have been completely familiar and acceptable in those circles, because passages from the Torah were frequently used to prove that there was a resurrection of the dead. More to the point for the modern exegete, it is clear that Exodus 3 is not simply referring to a distant past; it is bringing that past to bear on the present. It is precisely because the God of the patriarchs has revealed himself once more that Moses can know that the power at work in them will once more be displayed in the liberation of Israel. The patriarchs belonged to this ongoing history, and gave shape to it; therefore, they were still alive in the thinking of the writer of Exodus, and Jesus' interpretation brings out this deeper meaning.

Exodus 3 is mentioned again in Stephen's speech (Acts 7:30), where Moses' resistance to the call of God is played down – as it is also in Philo and Josephus. The New Testament's use of the name YHWH (Ex. 3:14) is a complex issue, but it should be noted that it occurs in Revelation 1:8, where John picks up the Septuagint's rendering of the Hebrew and uses it to describe the God who is.

In the early church, Exodus 3 was a favourite theme, and nearly every commentator of Scripture left a treatise on it. The angel who revealed himself to Moses at the burning bush was almost universally identified with Christ, though Augustine modified this somewhat, and thought of the angel as representing Christ. The reason for this was his anti-Arian stance; for him, to identify the angel with Christ was to run the risk of seeing the Son of God as a created being. The main concentration, however, was on the revelation of the divine name, which the church fathers identified with the Platonic concept of Being (*ousia*). This interpretation continued to dominate discussion throughout the Middle Ages, and it provided Christian philosophers and theologians with their point of departure. As Etienne Gilson (1936) wrote:

> Exodus lays down the principle from which henceforth the whole of Christian philosophy will be suspended. From this moment it is understood once and for all that the proper name of God is being, and that . . . this name denotes his very essence.

The burning bush was frequently used as an allegory of the virgin Mary, on the ground that Mary, like the bush, was on fire with the presence of God in her womb, yet she was not destroyed by it.

The Reformers inherited this philosophical tradition with its Christological overtones, but they interpreted it in their own way. Luther plumped for an allegorical interpretation, claiming that allegory was fine if it was rooted in Christ. Calvin's interpretation was more sophisticated, though he too opted for a Christological meaning, on the ground that the Old Testament saints never had any contact with God except through Christ the mediator. The voice which spoke from the burning bush was therefore that of Christ, though he remained concealed until his incarnation. In later Reformed thought, the bush was frequently identified with the persecuted church, and as such it remains the symbol of the Church of Scotland and its Presbyterian daughter churches around the world.

Calvin rejected the idea that Exodus 3:14 could be interpreted in a Platonic manner, on the ground that Plato failed to do justice to God's power and his providential ordering of all things. This was taken up in later Reformed theology, and is now a commonplace of interpretation. As J. Plastaras (1966) has written:

> It is difficult to translate Exodus 3:14 into western language because in the process we inevitably impose upon the Hebrew text categories of being and essence which were quite foreign to the Hebrew mind. The ancient Greek and Latin translations of the Old Testament unconsciously but radically changed the meaning of the Hebrew text . . . in terms of essential being . . . In fact the name Yahweh defines God in terms of active presence.

This view may be regarded as typical among most modern exegetes, but it is by no means above criticism, as J. Barr (1961) has shown. The Hebrews had a concept of being, as well as one of action, and it is much too simplistic to interpret Hebrew thought in such a one-sided way. This does not mean that the Hebrew writer was a forerunner of Plato, as most ancient commentators supposed, but it suggests that they were closer to one another than is often thought nowadays.

Perhaps the fairest comment is that of B. S. Childs (1974):

> The being and activity of God are not played against each other, but included within the whole reality of the divine revelation. God's nature is neither static being, nor eternal presence, nor simply dynamic activity. Rather, the God of Israel makes known his being in specific historical moments and confirms in his works his ultimate being by redeeming a covenant people.

Modern exegetes have devoted a great deal of attention to what they see as the origin of the cult of Yahweh in these verses, but without significant results. Norman Gottwald (1985) has summed this up as follows:

> It is contended that Moses derived his belief in Yahweh, along with many cultic and legal practices, from his Midianite father-in-law. Jethro is called 'priest of Midian' and joins (presides at?) a feast with the Israelites as they celebrate the deliverance from Egypt (Ex. 18). Kenites/Rechabites, who appear to have been a subgroup of Midianites, lived among the Israelites in Canaan and were ardent devotees of Yahweh (Jdg. 1:16; 4:11; 1 Sa. 15:6–7; 2 Ki. 10:15–27; Je. 35:1–11). Some of the advocates of the so-called Kenite hypothesis of Yahwistic origins have contended that the voluntary adoption of a new deity by Moses and Israel contributed the element of a radical ethical choice to Israelite religion, but, judging by other known group conversions to a new faith, this seems to be an arbitrary and excessive claim.

Gottwald goes on to discuss the archaeological evidence, which is equally inconclusive, and in the end he maintains that it is just as likely that Moses introduced Yahwism to the Midianites as the other way round.

In the context of liberation theology, the call to Moses must be regarded as ambiguous. If it is true that Moses was raised up as a charismatic leader of his people, it is equally true that the text emphasizes that only God can bring justice (Ex. 3:7–9) and implies that Moses will get nowhere by his own efforts. For a rather different angle, the feminist views of D. O'D. Setel (1992) deserve to be quoted:

> According to Exodus, the name Yahweh is established in contrast to the name El Shaddai (6:3). Both are uncertain in their meaning . . . The origins of the term 'Shaddai' are unclear. It has been traced to a term for mountain, and the name El Shaddai would thus mean 'the mighty one of the mountain', more commonly, 'God Almighty'. However, a primary meaning of the same root word is 'breast', raising the possibility that the early Israelites may have had an understanding of the deity as motherlike as well as fatherlike . . .

The exodus and deliverance of Israel

This is another high point in the Exodus account, which has received a lot of attention from exegetes. Josephus tried to rationalize it as far as he could, regarding Israel's deliverance as a matter of luck with the wind and weather, as much as a special divine intervention. Philo, on the other hand, allegorized the story completely, regarding it as a picture of how God casts harmful passions into the abyss and destroys them. In the New Testament the traditional Jewish view that God liberated his people because of his promise to the patriarchs was taken over and transformed in the light of Christ. This is especially prominent in Matthew's interpretation of Hosea 11:1 ('out of Egypt have I called my son') as a reference to the fulfilment of the exodus in the life of Jesus. In this way, Jesus is not merely a participant in the ongoing life of Israel, but the one who ushers in the messianic age which the original exodus only foreshadowed.

As far as the theme of liberation from oppression is concerned, the New Testament is sceptical. In Acts 13, Paul refers to this great event, but concludes that Israel did not gain its freedom as a result. True freedom is possible only in Christ. Similarly, in 1 Corinthians 10, Paul started out with a favourable reference to the exodus, and the importance of passing 'under the cloud and through the sea', but his major point was that in spite of God's wonderful acts of mercy, the majority of the nation failed to live up to the promises and did not attain salvation. He reinforces this by emphasizing that the exodus did not achieve its intended goal, and that the covenant made at Sinai was but the shadow of a better covenant to come.

The early church took its cue from 1 Corinthians 10 and interpreted the exodus story in terms of baptism. The drowning of the enemy in the sea became the prototype of the burying of our sins in baptism. The exodus itself represented a passing from earthly things to heavenly ones, and the freedom won by the people was portrayed above all as freedom from sin. Medieval exegesis continued this tradition, embellishing it here and there, though among Jewish exegetes there was a return to rationalistic explanations of the crossing of the sea. Ibn Ezra, for example, thought that Israel did not really cross the sea at all, but merely went some way into it and returned to the same side from which it had left.

The Reformers broke with earlier tradition much more clearly here than in Exodus 3. Luther interpreted the rescue of the Israelites as an example of how Christian faith functions. Human reason can see no way out of the situation, but, by faith, God accomplishes the impossible. In doing so, he may use human agents (such as Moses), but these are strictly unnecessary. Calvin goes one step further in insisting that God prepared the situation in order to demonstrate to the people that it was only by his power that they could survive and eventually obtain salvation.

Rationalistic interpretations of the miracle re-entered the field in the seventeenth century, as in J. Le Clerc's discussion of the subject (1693). Archaeologists and explorers then tried to find the spot where the Israelites might have crossed, and to calculate how it could have happened. Among critical scholars the need for this kind of interpretation was removed by the development of the documentary hypothesis. By dividing the narrative between J and P it became possible to emphasize theological factors in the different accounts which bore little relation to historical facts. In this reconstruction, J was more 'realistic' and P was more 'fantastic', but both were writing to make a number of theological points which have little to do with history.

Norman Gottwald discusses the different possibilities regarding the exodus, and concludes by saying that our evidence is too scanty to enable us to do more than guess at what actually happened. However, he lays considerable stress on the passages elsewhere in

Exodus (3:21–22; 11:2–3a; 12:35–36) which suggest that Israel plundered the Egyptians before leaving. He explains:

> There may once have existed an independent alternative version of the means of exodus: not a sea crossing but a clandestine flight with stolen goods. Interpreters who insist that the sea crossing must rest on some actual experience, however irrecoverable to our view, not only overlook the option of a secret flight but also take little account of the possibility that the theme of the sea as a cosmic force of chaos and death may have been used to heighten the significance of the exodus. It has also been proposed that the experiences of more than one group of escapees from Egypt have been combined in the Biblical traditions, in which case the secret flight and the crossing of the sea should be associated with two separate exoduses.

Gottwald does not elaborate on the significance of the exodus for the people's freedom, partly because he sees the Israelite occupation of Canaan as a peasants' revolt from within the society, not as an invasion from without. Latin American liberation theologians go much farther than this. For them, the exodus is the basis of the new community of believers, and must therefore be allowed to determine its character. A church based on exodus theology is one which cannot be assimilated or conquered by surrounding forces, and which is constantly trying to escape from the social roles imposed upon it by the surrounding society. The Christian life is a constant struggle for self-realization, a fight against the pressures which weigh down on us from the world around. The exodus becomes the only way in which a believer can fully understand the meaning and potential of creation, which depends on a sense of freedom for its realization. J. Cardonnel (1968) has expressed this as follows:

> Sacred history, the conscious history of a people, does not begin in Genesis but in Exodus. The concrete experience of liberation is the only way to discover the fact of creation. It is only the deeply lived experience of oppression that prompts man to work towards his radical liberation, in which process he can come to discover that the world is a creation.

In an earlier work (1964) he had already tied this to the political 'option for the poor' which is so characteristic of liberation theology in general. As he says,

It is first and foremost in making the cause of the oppressed his own that God does his work and manifests the fact that he is God. He reveals himself as the one who rouses and creates a people who had not existed as such before. Whereas other deities simply endorse the victories of their people, the specific character of the one and only God is the fact that he intervenes in the very midst of abandonment and dereliction. His divine revelation begins with the liberation of the most oppressed and tortured people, who thereby move prophetically from oppression to liberation.

Cardonnel sums up his exodus theology as follows:

The revealed God to whom I offer my faith is infinitely different from the deity of deism. He is not a 'supreme being' whose loveless benevolence derives from his arbitrary power. Rather, he it is who intervenes in the history of human beings. The originality of revelation lies in the fact that God makes himself known by quickening the spirit of a people threatened with total defeat. That is the real meaning of Israel's destiny, which anticipates the passover of all peoples from a fatalistic order to an order of freedom. There is some undeniable affinity between God and weakness. The eternal one is revealed in the despised and oppressed in order to confound the powerful.

Feminist interpretation follows that of liberation theology and applies it particularly to the case of women, though not exclusively. To quote D. O'D. Setel:

In the United States the story of the exodus holds special significance for African Americans, who have identified their own experience of slavery with that of the Israelites. This emphasis on identification with and preference for the disempowered is an explicit and central aspect of many feminist theologies. Such a perspective has encouraged the development of a feminist approach to understanding Biblical materials that evaluates the authority of texts on the basis of their affirmation of the full humanity of women. Liberation Theology's understanding of the centrality of divine concern for the oppressed has also influenced feminist theologians who believe that the liberation of women is inextricably tied to the elimination of racism, classism, anti-Semitism, homophobia and other forms of oppression.

This is powerful rhetoric, but it is hard to see how it is applied to the actual text of Exodus. When we turn to the story of the deliverance of the people, we discover that all the attention is focused on Miriam, and the song she sang to celebrate the victory over the Egyptians. Here the main concern is quite different from anything suggested by the last quotation. Setel writes:

> Miriam's association with the Song at the Sea challenges several stereotypes about women in ancient Israel. It conveys an image of women as singers of war songs, which is supported by other biblical texts (Jdg. 5; 1 Sa. 2:1–10). These militaristic hymns are among the oldest examples of Hebrew poetry. Although scholars have generally assumed that poetry, like other cultural creations, was exclusively the work of men, these examples raise the question of women's role in originating and developing poetic forms.

Liberation of the oppressed has given way to literary criticism and the origin of poetry, but only because a woman is mentioned as the singer.

For B. S. Childs, the exodus contains within itself a statement of its own limits, and a promise of a future and more glorious deliverance. He writes:

> Already within the Old Testament the inability of Israel to maintain itself as the new Israel was clearly recognised by the prophets. God must provide a new covenant, not like the one made with the fathers when he brought them from Egypt. Because there can be no full redemption from bondage until one is freed from sin and death, the people of God await with eager expectancy the final redemption from the world of evil. The exodus then becomes only a hint of what will come in full power at the end. The exodus from the bondage of Egypt serves as a foretaste of the final joys of life in the presence of God.

Here the temporal intersects with the transcendent, and the authentic Christian message of eschatological hope is sounded. It is just this dimension which is lacking in modern liberation theories, and which must call into question their connection with the gospel message.

The Ten Commandments

There can be few Old Testament texts which have been more familiar to generations of worshippers than the Ten Commandments. They play a central role in the teaching of Jesus, where the Jews of his day are frequently castigated for their literalistic and reductionistic interpretation of them. Jesus did not hesitate to quote these commandments, either collectively or individually, as archetypal of the obedience which God requires from his people, and which Israel so signally failed to give. The Pharisees showed great dexterity in interpreting different commandments in ways which perverted their original intention. Their law of Corban, for example, was intended to circumvent the fifth commandment, and the need to provide for their aged parents (Mt. 15:4). They were also famous for their rigid and hypocritical observance of the Sabbath (Mk. 2:27). In the Sermon on the Mount (Mt. 5), Jesus went into the commandments in detail, to point out how the spirit of the law must be observed, and not merely the letter. The apostle Paul also upheld the authority of the commandments within the framework of the gospel (Rom. 13:8; Eph. 6:2), and there is no indication that he thought that they had been abrogated or superseded by the coming of Christ. This is important for our understanding of Paul's attitude towards the law of Moses, because the Ten Commandments were the climax of its teaching. If they were still valid in his eyes, there is little ground for claiming that his theology was 'antinomian'.

In the early church, various lines of interpretation soon emerged. Some (*e.g.* the *Didache*) treated the commandments as the basis for a code of ethics, giving a legalistic twist to the proclamation of the gospel. Others (Justin Martyr, Irenaeus, Tertullian) rejected their authority on the ground that Jewish laws had been superseded by Christ, but were prepared to accept those elements in them which accorded with natural law. Jewish law was reduced to the common elements which it shared with pre-Christian paganism, and thus the unique claims of the Jews to be the people of God were dismissed. Augustine rejected such a crude approach, and argued that the Ten Commandments were just as spiritual as any part of the New Testament. The Christian filled with the Spirit is set free to obey the law, and to show forth its fruits in his life. According to him, the Ten Commandments were the Christian's charter of freedom, and had a wholly new spiritual function as a result.

Thomas Aquinas was the first to elaborate a distinction between the moral, ceremonial and judicial aspects of the law, which he worked out with great precision. According to him, the moral law was still in force, whereas the other two aspects of the Mosaic law had been abrogated to varying degrees by Christ. The Ten Commandments naturally belonged to the moral law, and were therefore still in operation. Aquinas's division of the law into these constituent parts has proved remarkably durable, and is still frequently found today, although the theoretical basis for it has largely been discounted by modern research.

The Reformers made the Ten Commandments a major element in their catechisms, which is how they entered the deepest consciousness of the Protestant churches. Luther's approach combined that of Tertullian with that of Augustine; the Jewish law is dead and has no relevance as such, except in so far as it reflects the natural law common to all. However, when viewed in the light of the cross of Christ, the commandments take on a new life, and become the clearest form of Christian instruction we could ask for. Calvin emphasized this last point, and stressed that the Christian must use the Old Testament law for the purpose for which it was given. This purpose may be defined as the opposite of whatever it is that is prohibited. It is not enough, for example, to avoid committing adultery; the Christian must actively promote a life of chastity and purity within the bonds of marriage.

The rise of critical scholarship naturally led to a number of questions being asked about the form and purpose of the Ten Commandments, but their prestige was such that their Mosaic origin was generally upheld until the time of H. Ewald and even later. Wellhausen was almost the first to assert that the Ten Commandments must be late, because they reflect a universal moral code. He insisted, for example, that a general prohibition of images would have been impossible in early Israel, and this view carried the day, in spite of intense opposition from conservatives.

A different perspective was opened up in 1934 by A. Alt, whose form-critical approach demonstrated that Wellhausen was wrong about the late dating, although Alt continued to believe that the Ten Commandments were a secondary legal code about which it was impossible to say very much. This appears to be the generally accepted critical view nowadays, on which B. S. Childs has this to say:

> Certainly, the modern critical period has brought a new dimension of philological and historical precision to bear. Yet to the extent to which the scholar now finds himself increasingly estranged from the very substance which he studies, one

wonders how far the lack of content which he discovers stems from a condition in the text or in himself.

N. Gottwald accepts a relatively early dating for the commandments, but approaches them from the standpoint of their relative vagueness, which he takes to be a sign of their primitive character. He writes:

> It is evident that these pithy prohibitions are far from clear in specifying the exact conduct they exclude from the community. It is reasonably certain that many modern interpretations of the jurisdictional force of the Decalogue did not apply in ancient Israel. The prohibitions did not treat swearing in common speech, did not regard a married man who had sex with an unmarried woman as adulterous, did not forbid capital punishment, killing in war, or abortion, and did not validate the right to hold unlimited amounts of property. All these are 'revisionist' interpretations which can only be argued for as extensions of the 'principles' or 'spirit' of the Decalogue instead of mandates laid down in the Decalogue.

Liberation theology, intriguingly, seems to have little to say about the Ten Commandments. This may well reflect a certain predilection for a 'situation ethic' according to which the circumstances of the moment may dictate what response is appropriate on the part of the Christian. The prohibition of murder, or of stealing, might not be applicable in a context where revolutionary violence and the forcible redistribution of wealth was the only option available to those seeking to bear faithful witness to the gospel. Feminist interpretation tends to be equally vague. As Setel writes:

> The commandments in Ex. 20:1–17, considered to be at the very heart of both Jewish and Christian belief, state explicitly that it is a male community to whom they are addressed. In Hebrew, the pronoun 'you' is in a masculine singular form. In translation, the subject is also clear in v. 17, which refers to 'your neighbour's wife' (literally 'woman'). Like so many other Biblical texts, however, this passage contains what appears to be a contradictory perspective when in v. 12 it instructs members of the community to honour mother as well as father. These passages serve as reminders that patriarchy, as the rule of the father, is a system of domination based not only on sex and gender but also

> on age. Within patriarchy, therefore, women as parents have authority over children. Elsewhere it is evident that through this authority they can serve as agents, as well as being victims, of oppression.

It is refreshing to find a feminist theologian who is prepared to admit that women can occasionally be agents of oppression, as well as victims of it, though a little alarming to discover that this occurs in the context of exercising legitimate parental authority. But given the overall tenor of the remarks made above, we should perhaps be grateful that Setel has not said that women are free to disobey the commandments on the ground that the commandments were not addressed to them, and that it is therefore quite all right for them to covet their neighbour's husband!

The final word on the contemporary relevance of the Ten Commandments ought probably to go to B. S. Childs, who writes:

> The theological challenge for the church today is to give to the divine commandments a form of 'flesh and blood' which not only strives to be obedient in the hearing of his word, but is equally serious in addressing its imperatives with boldness to the contemporary world. The church must speak to a thoroughly secular age which no longer understands the meaning of a divine word.

Childs and the liberationists agree that we must speak to a secular world, but where the latter seek to accommodate themselves to secularism, he maintains the transcendence and 'strangeness' of the divine Word in our society today, as in every age. This 'strangeness' is of the essence of the gospel, and calls us to a deliverance, and to the inheritance of a kingdom which is not of this world.

BIBLIOGRAPHY

B. S. Childs, *Exodus* (London: SCM, 1974).

J. S. Croatto, *Exodus: A Hermeneutics of Freedom* (Maryknoll, NY: Orbis, 1981).

J. I. Durham, *Exodus* (Waco, TX: Word, 1987)

A. Fierro, 'Exodus Event and Interpretation in Political Theologies', in N. Gottwald (ed.), *The Bible and Liberation* (Maryknoll: Orbis,1983), pp. 473–481.

G. North, *Moses and Pharaoh: Dominion Religion versus Power Religion*

(Tyler, TX: Institute for Christian Economics, 1985).

D. O'D. Setel, 'Exodus', in C. A. Newsom and S. H. Ringe (eds.), *The Women's Bible Commentary* (Louisville: Westminster/John Knox; London: SPCK, 1992).

13

Evangelical trends in interpretation

Historical introduction

The third world of discourse in contemporary biblical interpretation is that of conservative evangelicalism. This is a movement within the Protestant churches whose adherents have rejected the critical assumptions of Enlightenment thought to a greater or lesser degree. They seek to maintain the theology of the Reformation, though in practice this has frequently been modified. Conservative evangelicals continue to manifest all the traditional divisions of Protestantism – between Lutherans and Reformed, Calvinists and Arminians, Baptists and paedobaptists (i.e. those who accept infant baptism), Episcopalians and Presbyterians. But when set alongside the other two groups, it is clear that they belong together, and they have often formed alliances to protect the values which they hold in common. Conservative evangelicals tend to regard the first world of discourse as their mission field, and are ambivalent towards the second one. They frequently sympathize with the cause of fighting injustice, but doubt whether the way it is defined, or the methods adopted to combat it, are really consonant with scholarly standards or traditional theological positions.

At the present time, evangelicals (who have largely dropped the adjective 'conservative', because they regard it as self-evident theologically, but potentially misleading politically) are most numerous and influential in the English-speaking world, though they are experiencing rapid growth in Latin America and in China, among other places. They are relatively weak in continental Europe, where it is often difficult for them to exist as a distinct group within a Protestant state church. In Roman Catholic and Eastern Orthodox countries they appear as a sectarian fringe and are frequently confused with Jehovah's Witnesses and the like, however unfair that may be. The main reasons for this are their small size and the fact that they engage in proselytism within the wider, nominally Christian community.

Defining evangelicals precisely is difficult, but they have a strong sense of group identity and of inner cohesion, which is a result of what happened to Protestantism in the late nineteenth century. Up until about 1880, a conservative reading of the Bible was taken for granted in most parts of the English-speaking world, and in this respect evangelicals were no different from others. Liberalism of the German type was not unknown, but it was rare. However, in a very short space of time, the new liberalism from Germany took over almost everywhere, sometimes after having been introduced by evangelicals. For many evangelicals in the nineteenth century, the principle of *sola Scriptura* meant that traditional doctrinal formulae could be ignored or dismissed as 'Catholic'. To their way of thinking, biblical interpretation was set free to adopt historical-critical methods without prejudice to personal faith, which did not depend on 'dogma'.

By the 1920s, the evangelical movement, which had been distinguished as the missionary and crusading wing of Protestantism, had split in two, leaving the conservatives, who continued to maintain the classical doctrine of Scripture, a discouraged and alienated rump. In Britain it was a small minority within the Church of England, and a declining force outside it. In the USA it unfortunately became associated with a mentality which exalted ignorance in the place of science. This debased type of evangelicalism came to be called 'fundamentalism', after a series of twelve booklets known as *The Fundamentals*, which had been published between 1910 and 1915. In fairness, it should be pointed out that these booklets, far from being obscurantist, had been written by the best conservative scholars of the day. It was their misfortune that the name was later adopted to describe a theological position with which they were only partly in sympathy. A series of damaging court trials brought 'fundamentalism' into disrepute, and this rubbed off on more respectable conservatives, some of whom were actively opposed to the behaviour of the 'fundamentalists'. When the conservative Princeton Theological Seminary was reorganized along more liberal lines in 1929, it seemed as if conservative evangelicals had no future in academic life.

In this situation, the few remaining intellectuals among the evangelicals banded together to fight back. In Britain, the Tyndale Fellowship for Biblical (and later also for Theological) Research was founded in 1944. Operating out of Tyndale House in Cambridge, its aim was to restore an academically respectable conservative evangelicalism. In the United States new seminaries were founded to carry on the old traditions. Most prominent of these was Westminster Theological Seminary in Philadelphia, which was started by those professors who felt obliged to leave Princeton in 1929. Others soon followed, and by the 1950s there was a new network of seminaries which were staffed and funded by conservative evangelicals.

The process of recovery was slow, and it was not until the 1970s that evangelicals could again speak with a confident voice to the scholarly community. There, it must be said, they were often greeted with a mixture of suspicion and derision. They were suspected because of their supposed links with 'fundamentalism', and because it was widely felt that they had their own agenda which they were seeking to impose on others. They were derided because of their conservative views, which were not fashionable in academic circles at the time. Nevertheless, they made steady progress. Before long, a large proportion, and sometimes even the majority, of ministerial candidates in most of the main churches were from an evangelical background. Most Sunday School work and most evangelistic activity was conducted by them, so their churches grew at a much faster rate than others. Networks of 'fellowships' in universities and in the professions created bonds which supported a vast array of para-church organizations.

With growth, however, came diversity, and the closely knit world of evangelicalism was less prepared to face the consequences of this. In 1945 it could be assumed that an evangelical had a fairly well-worked-out theology, and that he was well aware of why he could not accept the prevailing liberalism of the universities and the church establishments. By the 1970s, however, a new generation had emerged, among whom that awareness had largely faded. Although there was continuing, and even impressive growth in the churches, there was little sign of the leadership which had inspired earlier generations. A few still continued to promote the traditional theological concerns, but, for many, evangelicalism had become a form of spirituality with a vaguely defined theological content. Serious theology, always the preserve of a minority, was virtually banished from the scene. Preaching, on which an earlier generation had prided itself, and which underwent a revival in the 1950s, went out of fashion once more. In their efforts to become academically respectable, many younger scholars got bogged down in PhD research and lost contact with the churches from which they had come, so that when they went back into the ministry they could not communicate to their flocks. Bible study all too often became either an esoteric pursuit among academics or a free-for-all of ignorance in the churches. The lack of theological input showed up most painfully when it came to issues on which the Bible was unclear, but which had to be discussed and sorted out in the churches – the role of women being perhaps foremost among them. Faced with challenges like these, evangelicals soon discovered that they had no common mind on most issues – not even on the infallibility of the Bible.

This was the most serious problem of all, and a number of evangelical scholars determined that they had to fight for a view of Scripture which could be established as 'evangelical' to the exclusion of alternatives. An International Council on Biblical Inerrancy was formed, which produced two important declarations: one on the 'inerrancy' of Scripture (1978) and one on hermeneutics (1982). The purpose of these declarations was clearly exclusive; their framers wanted to draw the line beyond which no scholar could go and still call himself an evangelical. They are useful to the extent that their clarity enables everyone to see what a classical 'inerrantist' is expected to look like today. But when they are applied to the existing world of evangelical scholarship, it soon becomes clear that things are not so simple.

In actual fact, very few evangelical biblical scholars would subscribe to everything in the declarations, and although a number of evangelical institutions in the USA use them as benchmarks when hiring faculty, in practice most of them have to adopt a certain tolerance on particular points (which vary, of course, from scholar to scholar). The (American) Evangelical Theological Society still expects its members to subscribe to a doctrine of scriptural 'inerrancy' more or less along ICBI lines, but in practice it tends to avoid serious discussion of the issue. On the other hand, neither the Tyndale Fellowship in Britain, nor its younger American cousin, the Institute for Biblical Research (founded in 1970), has such a requirement. Without conducting a survey of their members, it is impossible to say for sure how many would subscribe to the ICBI declarations, either in full or in large part, but the very fact that neither professional organization has been willing to adopt a statement on the issue suggests that support for 'inerrancy' as a defining exegetical or hermeneutical principle is not great among evangelical biblical scholars.

Nevertheless, despite its internal problems, evangelicalism remains a visible force within the Protestant churches which is quickly recognized by those outside it, as well as by those within it. There are differences of culture and emphasis between evangelicals in Great Britain and the USA, but these are not sufficient to prevent a high degree of interaction. Anglo-Saxon evangelicalism has managed to attract a certain following among Lutheran and Reformed Protestants in continental Europe, whose church traditions are very different, and there are even signs of outreach to conservative Roman Catholic and Eastern Orthodox groups, in spite of historical antagonism. The main evangelical organizations, such as the Tyndale Fellowship in Great Britain and the Evangelical Theological Society in the USA, retain their distinctive identity and their witness. Whether this will continue once the older generation of evangelicals, who knew why these organizations were formed and who fought for their principles, leaves the scene remains in some doubt, but for the moment it can still be said that there is such a thing as a distinctively evangelical approach to the Bible and its interpretation. It is that which this chapter seeks to examine.

The interpreters and their work

In line with the evolution of conservative evangelicalism in the twentieth century, the exponents of this position may be divided into three fairly distinct groups. The first of these consists of those scholars who fought against the rise of liberalism in the early years of the century, and who, on the whole, lost the battle at that time. Today they are regarded as the forerunners of modern evangelicalism, and some of their works have become evangelical classics. The second group consists of those scholars who consciously sought to revive a conservative tradition of scholarship among evangelicals. They came of age in the years after 1945 and are now mostly retired or, in some cases, no longer alive. The third group consists of the younger generation, brought up since 1945, which is coming to prominence at the present time. They are by far the most numerous, and it is difficult to say at this stage who among them will leave a lasting impression. In this survey, it has not been possible to list more than a small number of them, though it is hoped that they provide a representative sample of the movement as a whole.

The forerunners

James Orr (1844–1913). A leading Scottish Old Testament scholar and one of the authors of *The Fundamentals*, he argued in *The Problem of the Old Testament* (1906) that a criticism based on evolutionism and anti-supernaturalism was not persuasive. For him, traditional arguments retained a great deal of their force, and were to be preferred unless serious evidence to the contrary could be produced. Orr was conservative in his exegesis, but less dogmatic than his American contemporaries.

James Denney (1856–1917). A Scottish New Testament scholar, he defended the traditional evangelical doctrine of Christ's substitutionary atonement against the views of liberal German scholars such as A. Ritschl. However, he was more accommodating to biblical criticism, and disliked the dogmatic conservatism of contemporary American scholarship even more than Orr did.

John Davis (1854–1926). Professor of Old Testament at Princeton, and author of a well-known Bible dictionary (1898), Davis defended a conservative theology against those liberals whose work showed a bias against the supernatural and a preference for evolutionary modes of thought, but he argued that there was no reason why conservatives should not be fully engaged in critical literary and archaeological studies.

Robert Dick Wilson (1856–1930). Professor of Old Testament at Princeton and a leading founder of Westminster Seminary in 1929, his main interest was in defending the historical character of the book of Daniel. In 1926 he published his *Scientific Investigation of the Old Testament*, in which he concluded, on the basis of comparative literature from other middle-eastern sources, that the traditional dates and authors of the main Old Testament books were correct, though the Pentateuch may have been touched up slightly by later redactors.

John Gresham Machen (1881–1937). Professor of New Testament at Princeton and later at Westminster, his scholarship was the outstanding monument of evangelicalism in the 1920s. He was a leading campaigner in the struggle against liberalism, and led the departure of the conservatives from Princeton in 1929. In 1921 he published *The Origin of Paul's Religion*, which was a careful restatement of a conservative position over against the radical theories of Weiss and Bousset. Machen tried to show that Paul's teaching was in line with that of Jesus, and that only the supernatural character of Jesus' life and ministry could fully explain it. His attack on liberal theology, *Liberalism and Christianity* (1923), remains a classic of its kind. In 1930 he produced *The Virgin Birth of Christ*, which was another scholarly defence of traditional views, closely tied to his own personal faith in Jesus.

Geerhardus Vos (1862–1949). Professor of Biblical Theology at Princeton (1893–1932) and afterwards a strong supporter of Westminster Seminary, Vos developed a specifically evangelical version of biblical theology. He accepted that the Bible was the product of historical development, but regarded this as the work of divine revelation, not of religious evolution. He was a strong defender of the traditional authorship and dating of the major books of the Old Testament, and wrote extensively on these questions.

Oswald Thompson Allis (1880–1973). Professor of Old Testament at Princeton (1914) and then at Westminster, he contended for the Mosaic authorship of the Pentateuch and the unity of the book of Isaiah. His general approach was similar to that of R. D. Wilson.

Herman Sasse (1895–1976). A late representative of the Lutheran confessional traditional of Hengstengberg, Keil and Delitzsch, he exercised considerable influence among conservative German pastors and theologians, as well as among Lutherans in Australia and in the USA. His most important hermeneutical statement appeared in his *Briefe an lutherische Pastoren* (*Letters to Lutheran Pastors*) (1950).

The new generation

Ned Bernard Stonehouse (1902–62). Professor of New Testament at Westminster Seminary from 1937, he embarked on a careful critical study of the gospels which did much to reconcile modern discoveries with traditional views of the authenticity of the texts. His major works were *The Witness of Matthew and Mark to Christ* (1944) and *The Witness of Luke to Christ* (1951). In 1946 he edited *The Infallible Word*, a symposium of scholars on the subject of biblical inspiration and authority which set the tone for the next generation. A posthumous work, *Origins of the Synoptic Gospels: Some Basic Questions* (1963), indicated an acceptance of the literary freedom and personality of the different gospel writers.

Edward John Young (1907–68). He taught at Westminster Theological Seminary, Philadelphia (1936), and wrote a number of works on the Old Testament from a classically conservative standpoint. Of particular note are his *Introduction to the Old Testament* (1949), his commentary on Daniel (1949) and his three-volume commentary on Isaiah (1965–71), in which he mounted the most detailed defence to date of the unity of the book as the work of the eighth-century BC prophet.

David Martyn Lloyd-Jones (1899–1980). A prominent Welsh preacher, and minister of Westminster Chapel in London from 1938 to 1968, he is chiefly remembered for his attempt to revive the Puritan tradition of expository preaching. He has left extensive sermons on Romans and Ephesians, as well as a number of other works, including a magisterial study of *The Sermon on the Mount* (1959–60).

George Eldon Ladd (1911–82). He taught at Fuller Theological Seminary in California from 1950. His work was characterized by theological conservatism, intellectual integrity and critical freedom. In his first major work, *Crucial Questions about the Kingdom of God* (1952), he sought to address some of the issues raised by C. H. Dodd. Although at first a dispensationalist, he later moved away from that position and adopted one of 'historic premillenarianism'. His other major works include *The New Testament and Criticism* (1967) in which he argued for a high view of scriptural authority combined with a frank acceptance of the need for responsible critical scholarship, and his magisterial *Theology of the New Testament* (1974), which attempted to offer evangelical students a coherent and comprehensive picture of the New Testament as a whole.

Frederick Fyvie Bruce (1910–91). Rylands Professor of Biblical Exegesis at Manchester from 1959 to 1978, he was the author of many monographs on different aspects of biblical studies. He also wrote commentaries on Acts (1953; revised 1990), Hebrews (1964), Romans (1969), 1 and 2 Corinthians (1971) and Colossians, Philemon and Ephesians (1984). He was one of the principal founders of the Tyndale Fellowship for Biblical Research (1944), and he played a major role in the training of a whole generation of researchers, both in Britain and in the USA. His work set a very high standard of philological study in the classical British tradition of Lightfoot and Ramsay.

Donald Guthrie (1915–92). He taught for many years at London Bible College and wrote an important *New Testament Introduction* (1970) as well as a *New Testament Theology* (1981). Other works of his included commentaries on the pastoral epistles (1957), Galatians (1969) and Hebrews (1983), in addition to a study of Revelation (1987). His work is characterized by careful, conservative analysis of the relevant philological and archaeological data, and concern for theological integration of scholarly research was a hallmark of his teaching and writing.

Otto Michel (1903–93). Professor of New Testament at Tübingen and the leading representative of the so-called 'Hallenser Theologie' after 1945, Michel was one of the main links between the conservative tradition of eighteenth- and nineteenth-century Swabian pietism and the post-1945 generation of German evangelicals. His works include *Das Zeugnis des Neuen Testaments von der Gemeinde (The Witness of the New Testament concerning the Local Church)* (1986) and a collection of articles and essays entitled *Dienst am Wort* (*Ministry of the Word*) (1986).

Roland Kenneth Harrison (1920–93). He taught at Wycliffe College, Toronto, from 1960 until his retirement. He wrote commentaries on Jeremiah with Lamentations (1973) and Leviticus (1980), and was the first general editor of the New International Commentary on the Old Testament. He also wrote a *History of Old Testament Times* (1957), *The Dead Sea Scrolls* (1961), a widely used *Introduction to the Old Testament* (1969) and *Teach Yourself* (Biblical) *Hebrew* (1955). He was a staunch, if sometimes acerbic, defender of classical conservative opinions in Old Testament criticism.

Everett Harrison (1902–). A graduate of Princeton, he taught for a few years at Dallas Theological Seminary before becoming one of the founders of Fuller Seminary in 1947. His main work has popularized traditional evangelical views for a wider audience, and thus been more influential than that of some scholars. He was editor of the Wycliffe Bible Commentary and made several important contributions to the *International Standard Bible Encyclopedia.* His *Introduction to the New Testament* (1964) was widely used for a generation. He accepted both the infallibility and the inerrancy of Scripture, but was uneasy about some of the rather wooden and insensitive ways in which these doctrines were being applied by evangelical dogmaticians.

John William Wenham (1913–96). Warden of Latimer House, Oxford, from 1970 to 1973, he was well known for his *Elements of New Testament Greek* (1965). He also published important chronological studies on the dating of Easter (1984) and on the synoptic gospels (1991), as well as a number of other works, including *Christ and the Bible* (1972).

Frank Derek Kidner (1913–). He taught at Oak Hill College, London (1951), and was then Warden of Tyndale House, Cambridge (1964–1978). He has written a number of books on the Old Testament, and in particular commentaries on Proverbs (1964), Psalms (1973–5), Ecclesiastes (1976) and Ezra-Nehemiah (1979). His work is noted for its clarity of presentation and for its sturdy defence of conservative positions on critical matters.

Leon Lamb Morris (1914–). He taught at Ridley Hall, Melbourne, from 1945, except for a two-year stint as Warden of Tyndale House, Cambridge (1961–3). He is a prolific author and is noted for a number of extremely thorough and useful commentaries on different parts of the New Testament, including 1 Corinthians (1958), 1 and 2 Thessalonians (1959), Revelation (1969), John (1971), Luke (1974), Hebrews (1981), Romans (1988), Matthew (1992) and Galatians (1996). He has also written *New Testament Theology* (1986) and has collaborated on an *Introduction to the New Testament* (1992). He is well known for his defence of the penal substitutionary doctrine of the atonement, especially in controversy with the more liberal views of C. H. Dodd.

Gleason Leonard Archer (1916–). A Presbyterian minister, he taught at Fuller Theological Seminary (1948) before going to Trinity Evangelical Divinity School (1965). He is the author of many books on Old Testament themes, including an important *Survey of the Old Testament* (1964, 1974), a *Theological Wordbook of the Old Testament* (1980) and *Old Testament Quotations in the New Testament* (1983). He has also written study manuals on Hebrews (1957) and Romans (1959), and an *Encyclopedia of Bible Difficulties* (1982). His approach to critical questions is thoroughly conservative in the classical mould.

John Alexander Motyer (1924–). Principal of Trinity College, Bristol, from 1971 to 1981, he has written many commentaries and studies on various books of the Bible, which are noted for their combination of scholarship with pastoral concern. Among them are commentaries on Amos (1984), Philippians (1984), James (1987) and Isaiah (1993).

Ralph Philip Martin (1925–). He taught at London Bible College (1959) and Manchester (1965) before going to Fuller Seminary in Pasadena, California (1969). He is now Professor of Biblical Studies at the University of Sheffield. He has written a number of important exegetical studies on Philippians, including at least two commentaries on that epistle (1959, 1980). He has also written commentaries on 1 and 2 Corinthians (1968), Ephesians (1971), Colossians (1972) and Mark (1972). His *magnum opus* is a commentary on 2 Corinthians, in the Word Commentary series (1986).

Edward Earle Ellis (1926–). A scholar's scholar, his work has been largely confined to academic publications. His approach to critical issues of New Testament scholarship is cautious, though he has generally stayed out of the recent controversies over biblical inspiration. His many works include *Paul's Use of the Old Testament* (1957), *Paul and his Recent Interpreters* (1967), *The World of St John* (1984), *Pauline Theology* (1989) and *The Old Testament in Early Christianity* (1991). He has also written a commentary on Luke (1966), and was the founder and first president of the Institute for Biblical Research (IBR).

Roger Thomas Beckwith (1929–). Librarian (1963) and then Warden (1973) of Latimer House, Oxford, he has written widely on various theological subjects. His main contribution to biblical studies is his magisterial study, *The Old Testament Canon of the New Testament Church* (1985), in which he demonstrates that there are excellent reasons for maintaining that the canon of the Old Testament was fixed by 150 BC at the latest.

Richard Norman Longenecker (1930–). He taught at Wheaton College (1956) and Trinity Evangelical Divinity School (1963), before going to Wycliffe College, Toronto (1973). He has written *Paul, Apostle of Liberty* (1964), *The Christology of Early Jewish Christianity* (1970), *The Ministry and Message of Paul* (1971), and a much acclaimed *Biblical Exegesis in the Apostolic Period* (1974). His recent commentary on Galatians (1990) has also carved out an important niche.

Elmer Arthur Martens (1930–). He teaches at the Mennonite Brethren Biblical Seminary in Fresno, California (1970). He is an accomplished Old Testament scholar and has written widely on a number of Old Testament themes. His major books are *God's Design: A Focus on Old Testament Theology* (1981; 2nd edn 1994) and a commentary on Jeremiah (1986).

Bruce Kenneth Waltke (1930–). He has taught at Dallas Theological Seminary (1958), Regent College, Vancouver (1976), and Westminster Theological Seminary, Philadelphia (1985). Since 1991 he has been Professor of Old Testament at Regent College. His approach to critical issues is classically conservative, as can be seen especially in *Creation and Chaos* (1974). He has also written a commentary on Micah (1988) and a number of important articles on various Old Testament themes and Hebrew grammar.

Robert Horton Gundry (1932–). He has taught at Westmont College, Santa Barbara, California, since 1962, and is the author of a widely used *Survey of the New Testament* (1970). Among his many other writings, special mention may be made of *The Use of the Old Testament in St Matthew's Gospel* (1967), and *Soma in Biblical Theology* (1976). Within evangelical circles, he has been a pioneer in the introduction of critical methods and conclusions in New Testament study, and this has led him into controversy over inerrancy, which he rejects. After the publication of his controversial commentary on Matthew, he was forced to resign from the IBR.

Walter Christian Kaiser Jr (1933–). He taught at Wheaton College (1958) and Trinity Evangelical Divinity School (1966), before going to Gordon-Conwell Theological Seminary in Boston (1993). His writing reflects a conservative approach to the Old Testament and is marked by a special concern for practical, pastoral application. Among his many books, special mention may be made of *The Old Testament in Contemporary Preaching* (1973), *Towards an Old Testament Theology* (1977), *Toward an Exegetical Theology* (1981), *The Uses of the Old Testament in the New* (1985) and *Back to the Future: Hints for Interpreting Biblical Prophecy* (1989). He has also written a commentary on Ecclesiastes (1979).

Ian Howard Marshall (1934–). Professor of New Testament at Aberdeen, he is author of an important commentary on Luke (1978). He has also written commentaries on Acts (1980), the Epistles of John (1978), 1 and 2 Thessalonians (1983) and 1 Peter (1991). Other works include *The Origins of New Testament Christology* (1976), *Biblical Inspiration* (1982), and *Jesus the Saviour* (1990). A pupil of F. F. Bruce, he has also supervised a number of research scholars in New Testament studies.

Gordon Donald Fee (1934–). He taught at Southern California College (1966), Wheaton College (1969) and Gordon-Conwell Theological Seminary in Boston (1974) before going to Regent College, Vancouver (1986). His Assemblies of God (Pentecostal) background has given him a particular interest in relating the work of the Holy Spirit to the biblical text, and he has written a number of books and articles on this subject. Among his more important works are *New Testament Textual Criticism* (1981), *How to Read the Bible for All its Worth* (1982), *New Testament Exegesis* (1982, 1993), *Gospel and Spirit: Issues in New Testament Hermeneutics* (1991), and *God's Empowering Presence: The Holy Spirit in the Pauline Epistles* (1994). He has also written commentaries on 1 and 2 Timothy (1984), 1 Corinthians (1987), and Philippians (1995).

The inheritors

Peter Craigie (1938–85). He taught at Calgary until his death and wrote a number of important Old Testament studies, including commentaries on Deuteronomy (1976), Ezekiel (1983), Psalms 1 – 50 (1983) and the minor prophets (1984–5). His posthumous work,

The Old Testament: Background, Growth and Content (1986), is a general introduction to the subject.

Gerhard Maier (1937–). Tutor since 1970 and now Rector of the Albrecht-Bengel-Haus, an evangelical study centre in Tübingen, he is probably the leading conservative biblical scholar in Germany today. His book *Das Ende der historisch-kritischen Methode* (*The End of the Historical-Critical Method*) (1974) caused a sensation and led to a public debate with Peter Stuhlmacher. He has also published *Die Johannesoffenbarung und die Kirche* (*The Revelation of John and the Church*) (1981) and more recently *Biblische Hermeneutik* (*Biblical Hermeneutics*) (1990; Eng. trans. 1994), in which he develops a systematic method of biblical exegesis and theological exposition.

Edwin Masao Yamauchi (1937–). He has taught at Rutgers University (1964) and at Miami University in Oxford, Ohio, since 1969. He is a major authority on Gnosticism and other fringe cults surrounding the growth of early Christianity. Among his many publications in the field are *Pre-Christian Gnosticism* (1973), *The Scriptures and Archaeology* (1980), *New Testament Cities in Western Asia Minor* (1987) and *Persia and the Bible* (1990).

Richard Thomas France (1938–). Warden of Tyndale House (1978–1981) and Principal of Wycliffe Hall, Oxford, from 1989 to 1995, he has written widely in the field of New Testament studies. His first major work was a detailed study of *Jesus and the Old Testament* (1971), and he has also produced *The Evidence for Jesus* (1986) and a commentary on Matthew (1986). His most recent work is *Women in the Church's Ministry: A Test Case for Biblical Hermeneutics* (1995), in which he defends the ordination of women to the church's ministry.

Klaus Haacker (1942–). He was a researcher at the Institutum Iudaicum, Tübingen (1970–74), and subsequently Lecturer and Professor (1975) of New Testament at the Kirchliche Hochschule, Wuppertal. He is closely linked with Otto Michel and Martin Hengel, and is among the most articulate evangelical scholars in Germany today. His many works include *Die Stiftung des Heils: Untersuchungen zur Struktur der johanneischen Theologie* (*The Conception of the Holy: Researches on the Structure of Johannine Theology*) (1972), *Die Autorität der Heiligen Schrift* (*The Authority of Holy Scripture*) (1972), *Neutestamentliche Wissenschaft: Eine Einführung in Fragestellungen und Methoden* (*New Testament Science: An Introduction to Issues and Methods*) (1981) and *Biblische Theologie als engagierte Exegese* (*Biblical Theology as Applied Exegesis*) (1993), a collection of articles and lectures originally written between 1970 and 1992.

John Edgar Goldingay (1942–). He has taught at St John's College,

Nottingham, since 1970, and is now Principal there. He has written widely in the field of Old Testament interpretation, and has sought to combine the responsible use of critical methods with a commitment to orthodox biblical theology. His writings include *Theological Diversity and the Authority of the Old Testament* (1987), *Approaches to Old Testament Interpretation* (1990), *and Models for Scripture* (1994). He has also written the Word commentary on Daniel (1989).

Gordon John Wenham (1943–). Son of John Wenham and a distinguished Old Testament scholar in his own right, he taught at Belfast (1970) before moving to Cheltenham in 1981. He has published a two-volume commentary on Genesis (1987, 1994), as well as commentaries on Leviticus (1979) and Numbers (1981). He was also one of the editors of the fourth edition of the *New Bible Commentary,* published by IVP. His commentaries are noted for their exacting standards of philological research and their commitment to conservative theological positions on some of the more sensitive issues in Old Testament study.

Moisés Silva (1945–). Of Cuban origin, he taught at Westmont College in Santa Barbara, California (1972), before going to Westminster Theological Seminary in Philadelphia (1981). He has written extensively on hermeneutical issues, and is one of the leading representatives of the classical Warfield position today. Among his books are *Biblical Words and their Meaning: An Introduction to Lexical Semantics* (1983, 1994), *Has the Church Misread the Bible? The History of Interpretation in the Light of Current Issues* (1987), *God, Language and Scripture: Reading the Bible in the Light of General Linguistics* (1990), *An Introduction to Biblical Hermeneutics: The Search for Meaning* (1994, co-authored with W. C. Kaiser) and *Pauline Exegesis: Galatians as a Test Case* (1995). He has also written a commentary on Philippians (1988).

Donald Arthur Carson (1946–). He teaches at Trinity Evangelical Divinity School near Chicago, and has written a number of important studies of the New Testament, including a magisterial commentary on John (1991). He has also been active on the conservative side in the debates among American evangelicals on inerrancy and the problem of biblical hermeneutics.

Christopher Joseph Herbert Wright (1947–). He teaches Old Testament at All Nations Christian College near London, where he has been Principal since 1993. He has written a number of important studies in Old Testament theology, including *Living as the People of God* (UK) = *An Eye for an Eye* (US) (1983) and *God's People in God's Land* (1990). He has a great ability to bring sound scholarship within the reach of non-specialists, and many of his works are oriented in that direction.

Nicholas Thomas Wright (1948–). Dean of Lichfield Cathedral (1993), he edited the second edition of S. Neill's *Interpretation of the New Testament* (1988). He has written works of New Testament theology, including *Climax of the Covenant: Christ and the Law in Pauline Theology* (1991) and *The New Testament and the People of God* (1992). He has also written a commentary on Colossians and Philemon (1986), and is currently working on a five-volume work entitled *The New Testament and the Question of God*, of which the first two volumes had appeared by 1995.

Douglas John Moo (1950–). He has taught at Trinity Evangelical Divinity School since 1974, and writes mainly on New Testament themes, where he is noted for his careful and exacting scholarship. His chief works so far are *The Old Testament in the Gospel Passion Narrative* (1983) and *The Rapture: Pre-, Mid- or Post-Tribulational?* (1984), as well as commentaries on James (1985) and Romans 1 – 8 (1991). A fuller commentary on Romans is in preparation.

Ben Witherington III (1951–). Currently teaching at Asbury Seminary in Kentucky (1995), he has published a number of studies in the New Testament, including several in which he has reassessed the role of women. His main works include *The Christology of Jesus* (1980), *Women in the Ministry of Jesus* (1984), *Women in the Earliest Churches* (1988), *Women in the Genesis of Christianity* (1990), *Jesus, Paul and the End of the World* (1992), and *Conflict and Community in Corinth: A Socio-Rhetorical Commentary* (1994).

Craig Leonard Blomberg (1955–). He has taught at Denver Theological Seminary since 1986 and is the author of a number of important New Testament studies. Particularly noteworthy is *Interpreting the Parables* (1990) in which he re-examines the parables of Jesus and questions some of the main assumptions of modern criticism.

The issues

The main issues which the evangelical movement since 1945 has sought to address may be expressed as follows.

1. *Is it possible to maintain an academically respectable scholarship and a conservative theological position of the orthodox evangelical type?* To some extent this question had been answered in the affirmative by the neo-orthodox school of Karl Barth before the war, but Barth's approach was unacceptable to evangelicals because of his weak doctrine of Scripture. By 'orthodox', evangelicals meant the doctrine of

Scripture which had been elaborated by the Protestant scholastics of the seventeenth century, and which had been passed down through bodies such as Princeton Theological Seminary, whose greatest theologian, Benjamin Breckenridge Warfield (1851–1921), had worked out the doctrine of the infallibility and inerrancy of Scripture in a way designed to meet the needs of a post-critical generation. The Warfield line was later expanded and updated by evangelical theologians such as Bernard Ramm (1916–93) and James Innell Packer (1926–), but it has not been fundamentally altered. It remains the basic ingredient in all current doctrinal discussion of the nature and authority of Scripture among evangelicals today.

2. *Is it possible to elaborate a kind of basic orthodoxy which can embrace a wide range of conservative Christians without losing its coherence?* Modern evangelicalism is thoroughly ecumenical – much more so, in fact, than any other branch of the church. Old denominational distinctives still exist, but they are no longer felt to be barriers in the way they once were. Even such delicate matters as baptism are increasingly being pushed to one side and they now scarcely surface as practical problems in academic circles (though they may often be discussed as academic issues). But although there is a practical ecumenism among evangelicals at the popular level, there is as yet no systematic theology to go with it, so it is difficult to know on what principles this new-found fellowship is supposed to be based.

3. *Is it possible to be a genuine part of a wider church and academic world, and yet still maintain a distinctive identity?* This is perhaps the greatest problem of all for evangelicals at the present time. An evangelical Anglican will probably feel closer to an evangelical Baptist than to another Anglican, but if this is the case, what does the denominational label actually mean? In academic circles, is it possible for evangelicals to operate in a neutral way, without favouring their own position? Others have the same problem, of course, to varying degrees, but it is more acute for evangelicals because of the missionary nature of their convictions. They are not a church, as Roman Catholics are, and therefore have no identity other than the one which they have created for themselves. This involves a rejection of theological pluralism, and evangelicals cannot feel entirely comfortable in an atmosphere where such pluralism is encouraged. Recently there have been signs that evangelicals are prepared to reach out to theological conservatives in the Roman Catholic and Eastern Orthodox communions, and this may prove to be easier than engaging in dialogue with liberals in their own churches. But theological conservatives also tend to hold firmly to those distinctive

doctrines which caused church division in the first place, and this impedes whatever movement towards unity there is.

4. *Is it possible to be academically respectable and evangelistically committed at the same time?* Evangelicalism is a missionary movement, and although many would see no difficulty in maintaining a scholarly stance in the classroom and an evangelistic one in the pulpit, it may be a different story when it comes to proselytizing among the academic community. Are evangelicals concerned to convert other scholars to their theological standpoint, or are they content to feed enough of their own people into the system to take it over in the end? There is no doubt that the fear of proselytizing has been a major barrier to the acceptance of evangelicals by the scholarly community in general; but can evangelicals abandon this without losing an essential component of their identity? Experience has shown that the more 'respectable' the church is, the less it will preach the gospel; how great a danger is this for evangelicals now?

5. *Is it possible for evangelicals to enter fully into modern theological and hermeneutical debates?* Can an evangelical be a liberation theologian or a feminist? Is it possible to adopt the new hermeneutic as a method for interpreting the Bible? To what extent are evangelicals obliged to defend the theology of past generations? Are there pre-programmed answers to every question, or is there freedom to discover new truths in the Scriptures? If so, how can these truths be tested in the churches without evoking the charge of heresy? Conservatism and innovation do not naturally go together, and the human temperament is such that clashes are inevitable at this point. Evangelicalism is by definition a conservative movement, so it is the innovators who are invariably suspect. Does this mean that it is condemned to irrelevance and death in the next generation? Or will the innovators take over, and in the process uproot evangelicalism from its moorings?

The methods of interpretation

The Warfield (Old Princeton) approach

Any discussion of modern evangelicalism and its interpretation of the Bible must begin with the approach laid down by B. B. Warfield in a series of articles published from 1880 until his death in 1921, and subsequently collected in *The Inspiration and Authority of the Bible* (1948). Warfield's position is recognized as classical both by evangelicals themselves, who generally continue to profess their allegiance to it, and also by those who attack the evangelical position, which they normally identify with his.

In essence, Warfield followed the scholasticized Calvinist tradition which he had inherited from the seventeenth-century Swiss theologian, François Turretin. To this might be added the fruits of Scottish 'common-sense' philosophy, as this had been developed in the eighteenth century. He believed in the fundamental complementarity of general and special revelation, 'general revelation' being the standard Protestant term for what Thomas Aquinas and the Catholic tradition called 'natural theology'. This meant that the special revelation given by God in Scripture would tie in with what could be known by the human mind independently. In other words, the truth claims of the Bible could be tested by the normal criteria of history, archaeology and the relevant sciences.

This meant that the theologian's first task must be to establish a method of enquiry which would be universally valid and persuasive. As he put it,

> [Christianity] has come into the world clothed with the mission to reason its way to its dominion. Other religions may appeal to the sword, or seek some other way to propagate themselves. Christianity makes its appeal to right reason, and stands out among all religions, therefore, as distinctively 'the Apologetic religion'.

The Scottish influence convinced Warfield that the knowledge of God was acquired in the same way as any other form of knowledge – through the senses. He believed that it was possible to profess belief in God on the basis of natural proofs, without the intervention of the Holy Spirit. On the other hand, he also maintained the work of the Spirit was essential if the faith obtained by reason was to become a means of salvation. As he said, 'The action of the Holy Spirit in giving faith is not apart from evidence, but along with evidence; and in the first instance consists in preparing the soul for the reception of the evidence.' Applying his theory to the Bible, Warfield maintained that Scripture contained marks (*indicia*) of its perfection which could be perceived by the human mind but not fully appreciated until that mind was renewed by the Spirit. In his own words: 'When the soul is renewed by the Holy Spirit to a sense for the divinity of Scripture, it is through the *indicia* of that divinity that it is brought into its proper confidence in the divinity of Scripture.' Thus science could demonstrate that Scripture was factually inerrant, but this would have no significance unless and until the mind was transformed by the saving power of God. At that point, the inerrancy of the Bible would become one of the basic foundations of the Christian life, since it would be by the light of the inerrant Word of God that the Christian would know how to live.

In assessing Warfield's doctrine, it is essential to remember that he started with a general principle and moved from that to discussion of particular cases. In this his method was the exact opposite of that which is usually pursued by critical scholars. The modern critic normally prefers to examine each piece of evidence independently, and then piece it together into a wider whole. If the evidence can be shown to be accurate, then the critic will have no objection to the notion of 'inerrancy' because it is a fact which has been demonstrated to be true. Warfield, on the other hand, began with the prior assumption of inerrancy on the ground that the Bible was the Word of a God who could not err, and dealt with objections to this view as they arose in the course of study. This fundamental difference of approach, as much as anything else, accounts for the difficulties which many critical scholars have had with his doctrine.

Warfield explained his concept of scriptural authority as follows:

> The authority of the Scriptures thus rests on the simple fact that God's authoritative agents in founding the Church gave them as authoritative to the Church which they founded. All the authority of the apostles stands behind the Scriptures, and all the authority of Christ behind the apostles. The Scriptures are simply the law-code which the law-givers of the Church gave it.

This assertion enabled Warfield to make an important distinction between the canon of Scripture and other apostolic writings which did not belong to it. According to him, it was not those books which the apostles wrote, but those which they gave to the church as law, which constitute the authoritative body of scriptural writings.

In his understanding of biblical inspiration, Warfield claimed to be following the ancient tradition of the church, according to which the Spirit had superintended the authors' choice of words. This meant that the Bible was 'verbally inspired', though in a less mechanical way than had normally been asserted in earlier times. Warfield wanted to give the human authors of Scripture as much intellectual autonomy as possible, which is why he rejected the Christological model as the basis for his doctrine of inspiration. To his mind, the Bible was not the fruit of hypostatic union between God and humanity, in which the only voice speaking would have been the voice of God. Instead, it was the fruit of a co-operative effort between God and humanity, in which both played their part in producing a divine-human work.

The end result of all this was that the Bible's claim to divine inspiration and authority could be tested by the normal scientific criteria. Warfield wrote:

> By all means let the doctrine of the Bible be tested by the facts and let the test be made all the more, not the less, stringent and penetrating because of the great issues that hang upon it. If the facts are inconsistent with the doctrine, let us all know it, and know it so clearly that the matter is put beyond doubt.

Warfield believed that the 'facts' included everything the Bible mentioned, whether these had to do with matters of faith or not. For him, what the Scriptures said about history and natural science was just as authoritative as anything else they might contain. This is a point which opponents of the Warfield theory frequently regard as its main weakness, but Warfield felt that he was safe in making this assertion, because he believed that the Bible would stand up to any serious criticism levelled against it. Discrepancies which the critics had noticed could be explained in one of several ways. First, the text may have been corrupted in transmission. Warfield did not exclude this possibility, but admitted it quite freely. To his mind, only the original texts (the so-called 'autographs') were inspired, but although these have been lost, what we now possess is sufficiently close to them as to make little practical difference.

The second possibility was that our present knowledge is inadequate; when there is a discrepancy between what we believe to have been the case and what the Bible actually says, it is better to trust the evidence of the text until such time as it can be shown to be wrong.

A third possibility is that we may not have understood the author's intention. For example, the authority of a book such as Job may not depend on being able to show that there was once such a person in the land of Uz; it may well be that the author intended Job to be a fictional character from the start. This theory of 'authorial intention' can be stretched a long way; later followers of Warfield would occasionally go so far as to suggest, for example, that the attribution of the Song of Songs to Solomon was part of the author's intention to associate it with the wisdom tradition, and had nothing to do with the historical Solomon. Likewise, R. H. Gundry felt free to suggest, in his commentary on Matthew, that the visit of the magi to the holy family was fictional midrash.

Because of this, it is now possible to find defenders of 'inerrancy' whose critical conclusions scarcely differ from those of scholars not committed to the Warfield position. Nevertheless, although some theologians have pointed this out, and have tried to abandon the Warfield model as a working hypothesis in biblical interpretation, resistance to such a move has been strong. It seems that most evangelicals remain committed to a theological position similar to that which Warfield laid down, even if they are not always consistent, or do not always know how they should apply it in a given situation. This apparent contradiction is possible because of the difference in method between Warfield and critical research; the former, as we have already stated, begins with a general principle, the latter with specific examples. It is where these two approaches clash that trouble arises, and different evangelical scholars go their separate ways.

In the late 1960s and early 1970s, the question of the inerrancy of Scripture once more became a burning issue in the United States. Evangelicals elsewhere were also affected by this, though to a much lesser extent. The International Council on Biblical Inerrancy was created in 1977 with the express purpose of expounding Warfield's teaching in modern dress. It held a consultation in Chicago on 26–28 October 1978 and produced a declaration on the subject which they hoped would become standard in evangelical circles. This declaration consists of the following five statements:

> 1. God who is Himself Truth and speaks truth only, has inspired Holy Scripture in order thereby to reveal Himself to lost mankind through Jesus Christ as Creator and Lord, Redeemer and Judge. Holy Scripture is God's witness to Himself.
>
> 2. Holy Scripture, being God's own Word, written by men prepared and superintended by His Spirit, is of infallible divine authority in all matters upon which it touches: It is to be believed as God's instruction, in all that it affirms; obeyed as God's command, in all that it requires; embraced, as God's pledge, in all that it promises.
>
> 3. The Holy Spirit, Scripture's divine Author, both authenticates it to us by His inward witness and opens our minds to understand its meaning.
>
> 4. Being wholly and verbally God-given, Scripture is without error or fault in all its teaching, no less in what it states about

God's acts in Creation, about the events of world history, and about its own literary origin under God, than in its witness to God's saving grace in individual lives.

5. The authority of Scripture is inescapably impaired if this total divine inerrancy is in any way limited or disregarded, or made relative to a view of truth contrary to the Bible's own; and such lapses bring serious loss to both the individual and the Church.

To these statements were appended nineteen additional articles, which attempted to elucidate their meaning. The International Council on Biblical Inerrancy soon realized that it was not enough to restate the case for biblical inerrancy by itself. Equally important was the question of how the inerrant text was to be interpreted, and this raised serious hermeneutical questions which the Princeton approach had not had to face. At a second consultation in Chicago, held on 10–13 November 1982, a set of twenty-five more articles was issued, dealing especially with hermeneutical problems. These articles, like their predecessors, were intended to become a touchstone of modern evangelical interpretation.

To what extent can the two Chicago declarations be regarded as representative of current evangelical thinking about biblical interpretation? Many evangelical biblical scholars, and probably almost all those outside the USA, would hesitate to accept them *in toto*, either because they disagree with specific points, or because they do not believe that statements of this kind are necessary or even helpful. Certainly a body such as the Tyndale Fellowship would never adopt them, nor would its American equivalent, the Institute for Biblical Research. This is because few evangelical exegetes have shown much sign of applying the Chicago principles to their work with any consistency, and many see them as theologically unnecessary and hermeneutically dubious. In addition, however conservative they may be, exegetes are highly resistant to any dogmatic formulation which might restrict their freedom of enquiry.

On the other hand, inerrancy continues to be defended by evangelical systematic theologians, mainly on the ground that it is the only view which is fully consistent with a biblical doctrine of God. If the Bible contains errors, this argument goes, then it can hardly claim to be the Word of the omniscient and omnipotent God. It is difficult not to conclude that there is a great difference in approach between many evangelical exegetes, on the one hand, and the leading evangelical theologians on the other. Whether this tension can be resolved to everyone's satisfaction may be doubted; it seems more likely that evangelicals will continue to live with differences of opinion on this matter for the foreseeable future.

Conclusion: evangelical strengths and weaknesses

The main strengths of evangelical biblical interpretation can be summarized as follows.

1. Its quality is universally recognized in the field of textual criticism. Thanks to the careful and patient work of generations of scholars, we now have biblical texts which are as close to the 'autographs' as we are likely to get. Evangelicals have played an important part in bringing this about, and they continue to cultivate linguistic and textual skills to a degree scarcely paralleled elsewhere.

2. It is coming increasingly to the fore in the production of biblical commentaries. There are now several series which bear an evangelical label. These range from the Communicator's Commentary, which is primarily designed for preachers, to the Tyndale Commentaries, which are similarly introductory, though with more critical comment, through to full commentaries on the Greek and Hebrew texts, of which the most notable are the New International Commentaries, the Word Commentaries, and the New International Greek Text Commentary. Several more series are available or planned, and no doubt others will appear in the future.

3. It leads the field in Bible translation. The missionary zeal of evangelicals has kept alive the desire to translate the Bible into as many of the world's languages as possible. At the same time, there is a similar desire to produce new and better versions in the major languages of the world, and notably in English. Evangelicals do not always produce the best translations, but they have the greatest number and the greatest variety of them. At the present time, the main monument to their translation techniques and qualities in English is the New International Version (1979) which has largely replaced earlier versions in popularity among evangelicals.

Its main weaknesses, on the other hand, can be summarized as follows:

1. There is a noticeable gap between theory and practice. Evangelical theologians have worked out a detailed understanding of biblical inerrancy, and of the principles of hermeneutics, but these are not always brought to bear on the actual production of

commentaries. There is no generally agreed theological structure in which the application of these stated principles can take place. Doctrine plays a rather limited role in many evangelical circles, which at the popular level are often highly experiential and individualistic. The recent rapid spread of charismatic tendencies, unchecked by theological principles, is symptomatic of this.

2. It tends to be unable to come to a common mind in areas where the Bible is unclear. This had traditionally been the problem with church order, and it resurfaces today in discussions about the proper role of women, the exercise of spiritual gifts, and so on. A certain unwillingness to take church tradition seriously may contribute to this disarray, and evangelicals often find it hard to come to terms with church history. The concept of *sola Scriptura* and the belief in the indwelling presence of the Holy Spirit today are often too strong for the claims of tradition to be highly valued. But it must also be said that those evangelicals who do recognize the importance of tradition tend to be most concerned to defend the practices of their own denominations, consciously or subconsciously turning the apostles into Presbyterians or Baptists.

3. It tends to be reactive rather than pro-active. Evangelicals do not set the agenda for the life of the wider church, and there is little in their training which would equip them for such a role. For over a century now they have been chiefly concerned to defend entrenched positions, not to blaze new trails, with the result that novelty is too often equated with heresy, and the evangelical world goes nowhere. When they were fewer in number, evangelicals usually let the world pass them by, but now that they are so much more influential, they can no longer do that. The danger is that, without a viable theology to cover matters not expressly stated in Scripture, evangelicals will either be persuaded to accept what more liberal elements in the church want, or they will split yet again, along somewhat different lines than in the 1920s, but with a similar loss in strength and influence for another generation.

4. It tends to be more interested in gaining scholarly respectability than in feeding its own spiritual flock. This is a major problem which evangelical scholars have to face. To what extent is it proper to adopt the language and concepts of the scholarly world, if this means distancing oneself from the ordinary congregation? A simple example will suffice: should an evangelical be prepared to speak of the 'Easter-event' instead of the resurrection of Christ? What does the former term convey, except perhaps the suspicion that it is a way around belief in the bodily resurrection of Jesus? A traditional

strength of evangelicals has been their close links to the ordinary Christian, but at the present time this is in danger of being lost in favour of the exclusive pursuit of scholarly goals and interests.

What does the future hold for conservative evangelicalism? As far as the work of individual scholars is concerned, there is no doubt that evangelicals are now participating in mainstream academic debates to a degree which would have astonished the generation which remembered the 'fundamentalist' controversies of the 1920s. In both quality and quantity, their work ranks with the best which is currently being produced, and when attacks have been made, as for example by J. Barr (1977), scholars who would in no sense identify themselves with the evangelical camp have come to their defence. But as this has happened, it has also become more difficult to defend the continuing existence of distinctively evangelical organizations.

Why is the Tyndale Fellowship needed, if its members can move freely in academic circles? Conversely, why should such a body want to exclude scholars simply because they do not share a certain conservative theology? The only justification for the continued existence of such bodies is that their theological position is both different from that of most mainstream scholars and too important to be discarded. For evangelicals, the Bible is the divinely inspired Word of God, even if many of them find it hard to accept 'inerrancy' as the right way to express this, and it is the power of eternal life for those who hear and obey its message. As long as evangelicals continue to believe that, they will maintain a distinct existence, even if it is less separate than it has been in the past. Ultimately, it is their doctrine, not their exegetical methods or conclusions, which distinguish evangelical scholars from others in the field, and it is precisely this factor which is liable to continue to provoke a certain unease in the wider academic community. Whether, and to what extent, this abiding sense of 'otherness' can be overcome, is a question which only the future can answer.

BIBLIOGRAPHY

J. Barr, *Fundamentalism* (London: SCM, 1977).

L. Berkof, *Principles of Biblical Interpretation* (Grand Rapids: Baker, 1952).

C. Brown, *History and Faith: A Personal Exploration* (Leicester: IVP, 1987).

———(ed.), *History, Criticism and Faith* (Leicester: IVP, 1976).

D. A. Carson and J. D. Woodbridge (eds.), *Hermeneutics, Authority*

and Canon (Grand Rapids: Zondervan, 1986).
R. T. France, 'Evangelical Disagreements about the Bible', *Churchman* 96 (1982), pp. 226–240.
S. Kistemaker (ed.), *Interpreting God's Word Today* (Nutley: Presbyterian and Reformed, 1970).
G. M. Marsden, 'Fundamentalism as an American Phenomenon: A Comparison with English Evangelicalism', *Church History* 46 (1977), pp. 215–232.
I. H. Marshall, 'F. F. Bruce as a Biblical Scholar', *Journal of the Christian Brethren Research Fellowship* 22 (1971), pp. 5–12.
M. A. Noll, *Between Faith and Criticism: Evangelicals, Scholarship and the Bible in America* (Grand Rapids: Baker, 2nd edn, 1991).
——— (ed.), *The Princeton Defense of Plenary Biblical Inspiration* (New York: Garland, 1988).
V. Poythress, *Science and Hermeneutics* (Leicester: Apollos, 1988).
E. D. Radmacher and R. D. Preuss (eds.), *Hermeneutics, Inerrancy and the Bible* (Grand Rapids: Zondervan, 1984).
B. Ramm, *Protestant Biblical Interpretation: A Textbook of Hermeneutics* (Grand Rapids: Baker, 1973).
J. B. Rogers and D. K. McKim, *The Authority and Interpretation of the Bible* (San Francisco: Harper and Row, 1982).
M. Silva, 'Ned B. Stonehouse and Redaction Criticism', *Westminster Theological Journal* 40 (1977–8), pp. 77–88; 281–303.
A. M. Stibbs, *Understanding God's Word* (London: IVP, 1961).
M. S. Terry, *Biblical Hermeneutics: A Treatise on the Interpretation of the Old and New Testaments* (Grand Rapids: Zondervan, 1961).
J. D. Woodbridge and D. A. Carson (eds.), *Scripture and Truth* (Grand Rapids: Zondervan, 1983).
D. F. Wright, 'Soundings in the Doctrine of Scripture in British Evangelicalism in the First Half of the Twentieth Century', *Tyndale Bulletin* 31 (1980), pp. 87–106.

A case study: Acts

The interpretation of the Acts of the Apostles has occupied a central place in the discussion of early Christian origins since the time of F. C. Baur and the Tübingen school, and it has been of major importance in the struggle of evangelicals against liberal trends in biblical criticism. Baur believed that Acts was a synthesis between Jewish and Gentile forms of Christianity, and that it came from a much later time than that of Paul or Luke. As far as he was concerned, its historical value was virtually nil. Since Baur's day battle has raged over Luke's reliability as a historian and, as a consequence, over the nature of primitive Christianity. In this survey, we shall look briefly at traditional views of the book, then at the Tübingen thesis and answers to it, and finally at two modern commentators who best represent the opposing traditions in modern scholarship.

Pre-critical study

Acts was surprisingly little studied in the age before critical scholarship made its appearance. For the pre-Reformation period, there are only nineteen surviving books or fragments dealing with it. Of these, the oldest are by Origen and his contemporary, Pamphilus of Caesarea. From the fourth century there are commentaries by Ephrem Syrus, Didymus the Blind, Eusebius of Emesa and Euthalius the Deacon. The fifth century has bequeathed us works by John Chrysostom, Cyril of Alexandria, Ammonius of Alexandria, Hesychius of Jerusalem and Arator. Later centuries produced one commentary each up to the twelfth, with the exception of the tenth century for which there are two. Listing them by centuries we have the following:

Century	**Syriac**	**Greek**	**Latin**
6th		Oecumenius	Cassiodorus
7th		Andrew of Caesarea	
8th			Bede
9th	Isho'dad of Merv		
10th			Leo Magister
11th		Theophylact of Ochrid	
12th	Dionysius bar Salibi		

The wide range in language and place of origin indicates that there was no common tradition; apart from Theophylact, who must have known Oecumenius, there was probably no contact between these different writers at all.

The first modern commentary on Acts was written by Calvin (1552, 1554), who showed no interest in problems of authorship, date or historical background. His understanding of Acts was that it is a sacred history designed to show that God has always cared for his church, and has always stood ready to protect it. He placed great emphasis on the important role assigned to the Holy Spirit in the text, a point which has since been universally recognized. Calvin also demonstrated an awareness of the importance of the speeches for the narrative, and knew, too, that the canonical Acts was very different in character from the fanciful tales recorded in the various apocryphal Acts. Calvin never doubted the essential historicity of the text, and when occasion demanded he went into historical and geographical details relevant to his exposition. He was, however, prepared to recognize that Luke may not have been entirely accurate in his reporting, as, for example, when he said that Paul spoke 'Hebrew' (Acts 22:2) rather than 'Aramaic'. However, these are minor points which almost always have a satisfactory explanation which does not detract from the overall historicity of the text.

The next major advance in the study of Acts was made by J. A. Bengel (1734), who pointed out that the book is an account of the Acts of the risen Lord dwelling in his church through his Holy Spirit, and also that it places special emphasis on the triumphant progress of the gospel from its origin in Jerusalem to the centre of the known world – Rome. Another significant early commentator was W. Paley (1790), who was the first to discuss the relationship between the Paul of the epistles and the Paul of Acts in any detail. His method was to go through the epistles and look for 'undesigned coincidences' which would dovetail with the record of Acts. His basic assumption was that neither writer knew the other's work, and that therefore such 'coincidences' would demonstrate the truth of the underlying story. Given the primitive nature of Paley's research, it is remarkable how often he got it right. Today, most commentators are agreed that Luke wrote Acts without consulting Paul's epistles, and many of the 'coincidences' have stood the test of time.

Paley emphasized the agreements between the epistles and Acts, and believed that these were sufficient to guarantee the substantial historicity of the latter. But only a few years later, F. C. Baur would take a very different approach. For him, it was to be the differences between these two primary sources which were significant, and the epistles which were to be trusted in case of divergence. Already in Paley's time, J. D. Michaelis had been asking why Acts had been written. It was clear to him that Luke was not writing a general history of the church, or even the life of Paul, since, if either of those things had been his main purpose, he would have included far more material. Michaelis concluded that the purpose of Acts was twofold. First, it was intended to show that the truth of the Christian religion was demonstrated by an outpouring of the Holy Spirit in wonder-working power on the day of Pentecost – a fact which every believer in Christ was obliged to acknowledge. Second, Luke wanted to show that the gospel was intended for Gentiles as well as Jews, and that while the Gentiles received it warmly, the Jews persecuted Paul for admitting them into the church.

Historical criticism and the development of the Tübingen hypothesis

The first person to question the basic historicity of Acts was W. M. L. De Wette (1826). He believed that Luke intended to write a history of early Christianity, and that the special features mentioned by Michaelis were accidental. The defects in the history were the result of the author's incompetence, not part of a deliberate plan. In particular, he rejected any suggestion that Luke may have known Paul personally, or travelled with him; the so-called 'we' passages in the text (16:10–17; 20:5–15; 21:1–17; 27:1 – 28:19) are ultimately literary fictions. De Wette believed that the book had been written sometime after AD 70, and that the narrative had been broken off about AD 62 because Luke lacked either the time or the ability to carry the story further.

This was the point which critical study of Acts had reached before Baur got to work. He first put forward his thesis that the early church was a disparate body, split among various factions, in an essay written on 1 Corinthians (1831). In fact there were only two main tendencies at work, in spite of the multiplicity of factional parties. One was Jewish and focused on Peter, and the other was Gentile, focusing on Paul. Paul had made a complete break with the apostles in the Jerusalem church, and was effectively preaching another gospel, that of salvation by faith without works. The other apostles, by contrast, had not fully emerged from Judaism and remained tied to a works-righteousness which would eventually feed into the construction of 'early Catholicism'. Baur did not apply his thesis to Acts at that stage, but of course it was fundamental to his whole approach. In 1838 he suggested for the first time that Acts was the work of a Paulinist who was trying to bring the two sides together by showing that Paul was more Petrine than most people imagined, and, conversely, that Peter was more Pauline. Among other things, this naturally led to a minimizing of the differences between the two apostles, which had been clearly stated in Galatians.

Baur's ideas were developed further by his disciples. A. Schwegler

(1846) believed that Acts was an attempt to reconcile the opposing parties in the church and that its author played fast and loose with history in order to achieve that aim. According to him, the book reflects the situation in the church in the first half of the second century, when the Jewish party was supposedly still dominant. E. Zeller (1854) believed that the Peter–Paul dualism was an invention of the author, who was more concerned to explain and resolve the conflicts of his own time (early second century) than to describe the true apostolic origins of Christianity. The fact that Acts does not stress the faith–works dichotomy in the same way as Galatians or Romans was proof enough to them that the book must be of relatively late date, when that particular controversy was already fading into the background.

The Tübingen picture of Acts had by now taken shape, but the clearer it became in its general outline the more vulnerable it was to attack on details. In 1851 G. Lechler accused the Tübingen theologians of having invented a most improbable scenario for the development of primitive Christianity. The idea that Paul had made a complete break with the other apostles and had started preaching a different gospel struck him as totally implausible. Lechler claimed that Paul observed the Mosaic law when appropriate, and had not broken with Judaism as much as Baur and others claimed. More important still, he argued that Jewish Christianity lost its influence after AD 70, and could not have played the role the Tübingen school assigned to it after AD 100. The Catholic church therefore did not arise as a synthesis of Jewish and Gentile Christianities, but emerged from an exclusively Gentile milieu. Its legalistic and 'Judaizing' features were the product of its own internal evolution, and not the result of Jewish influence.

The Tübingen thesis was further modified by a number of scholars in Germany, but in spite of all the changes which were suggested, one main point remained dominant throughout. This was that the Paul of Acts was a different person from the Paul of the epistles. Generally speaking, the latter was regarded as authentic, and the former as a fictitious reconstruction by a hero-worshipping Paulinist, though not everyone agreed with this. There was a small reaction in the other direction, spearheaded by A. Loman (1882) and R. Steck (1888), both of whom believed that it was the Paul of the epistles who was a fictitious character, re-created by a school of disciples who actually wrote the letters, and that Acts offered a more reliable historical account.

After Tübingen

By the latter half of the nineteenth century it was becoming clear that Baur's thesis was not winning general acceptance. Outside Germany it was almost universally rejected, especially in England, where the researches of J. B. Lightfoot were directed against it. Even in Germany attention shifted away from Baur's concerns to the question of sources used by the author, and there were a great many attempts made to show that Luke had used a number of earlier writings, including a travel journal written by one of Paul's companions. But this source criticism proved fairly barren in the end, since everyone came to realize that Luke had made the story his own, whatever sources he may have relied on. The most extreme form of this view was put forward by A. Loisy (1920), who suggested that an originally historical account of the early church had been drastically revised by a Paulinist concerned to write a propaganda document in praise of his hero.

The next stage was marked by the work of M. Dibelius (1923), who brought form-critical techniques to bear on the study of Acts. Dibelius demonstrated that Acts could not be broken down into smaller units in the same way that Luke's gospel could, and he therefore concluded that he did not have the same abundance of source material to draw on. Acts was basically an original composition, put together from an original travel book and supplemented by a great deal of Luke's own work, especially the speeches. Dibelius discovered no fewer than twenty-four of these, making up nearly a third of the text. It was in these speeches that the meat of Luke's message was to be found, for they contained his understanding both of the gospel and of Paul.

Dibelius went on developing his views for the rest of his life, and a final collection of his ideas on the subject of Acts was published in 1951, four years after his death. His conclusions may be summed up as follows.

1. Luke was the author of Acts, and not merely the compiler of existing traditions about Paul.

2. Luke was a genuine historian, but in the ancient, not in the modern, sense. This means that he frequently modified events in order to present them as 'typical'. He exaggerated the communal aspects of the first church's life in order to emphasize the phenomenon of communism, just as he minimized the conflicts between the apostles in order to stress the reality of an apostolic ideal which the church ought to follow.

3. Luke was a preacher with a definite message to tell of God's providential ordering of events. What he provides in Acts is not merely an account of events, but a description of how God worked out his plan of salvation in and through the events in question.

Dibelius without a doubt set the main trend in German critical research concerning the Acts of the Apostles as these are read today. By bringing out the identity of the author, he was able to turn attention away from historical details and concentrate instead on the theological message which Luke was trying to convey. History now took a back seat to theology, which Dibelius regarded as the chief purpose behind the composition of the book. This led H. Conzelmann (1954) to propose that Luke replaced the eschatological emphasis of the primitive church with a theology of history according to which the present age, from the death of Christ until the parousia, is the age of the church, intended as such by God. In Lutheran terms, Luke replaced the *theologia crucis* ('theology of the cross') with a *theologia gloriae* ('theology of glory'), or, as we might say, he turned a moment of crisis into a period of triumph.

As a final synthesis of this development, we may cite E. Haenchen's introduction to his massive commentary on Acts (Eng. trans. 1971, from the fourteenth German edition of 1965):

> The real subject of Acts is the *logos tou Theou* (Word of God) and its growth. It is certainly proclaimed by men and authenticated by God through signs and miracles. This theology is no steep tumble from the Pauline heights – for on those heights Luke never stood. His teaching is one of the many variants of Gentile Christian theology which – more or less independent of the great Apostle to the Gentiles – grew up alongside and after the theology of Paul. The germs of what then evolved into early Catholicism may well have lain, even before Luke's time, in this Gentile theology, which bore in itself a tendency to law and observances even where it was not influenced by Jerusalem.

The conservative approach

Far removed from the speculations of German theologians about the theological purpose of Acts is the pragmatic approach of the majority of English-speaking scholars. Always much more conservative in these matters than their German colleagues, the majority of English-speakers were very reluctant to abandon the claims of historicity which Acts made for itself. The reasons for this were deeply rooted in the education of most British scholars, which concentrated heavily on the minute philological study of the classics and left philosophy to one side. The Germans, on the other hand, were predominately philosophical in outlook, and much less sympathetic to the disciplines of historical research, such as archaeology.

It is entirely characteristic of the British mentality that the first major contribution to the study of Acts should have been made by an amateur layman, J. Smith. He wintered in Malta in 1844–5, and used his expert training as a yachtsman to chart the course of Paul's famous sea voyage. In his book, *The Voyage and Shipwreck of St Paul* (1848), he produced a firsthand study of nautical conditions in the region, which remains a classic. In this study he demonstrated that Luke's narrative was an eye-witness account of a real event. In his own words:

> No sailor would have written in a style so little like that of a sailor; no man not a sailor could have written a narrative of a sea voyage so consistent in all its parts, unless from observation. This peculiarity of style is to me, in itself, a demonstration that the narrative of the voyage is an account of real events, written by an eyewitness.

Smith's work was followed in 1852 by H. Alford's Greek Testament, which was the first English commentary to take contemporary German scholarship seriously. Alford was sympathetic to historical criticism, but well aware of the bias which affected the work of many of the critics. In particular, he was greatly disturbed by the anti-supernatural bias which seemed to dominate so much of their work. As he wrote,

> The prevalent opinion of recent critics in Germany has been that the book was written much later than this (*i.e.* AD 63). But this opinion is for the most part traced to their subjective leanings on the prophetic announcement of Lk. 21:24. For those who hold that there is no such thing as prophecy (and this is unhappily the case with many of the modern German critics), it becomes necessary to maintain that the verse was written after the destruction of Jerusalem. Hence, as the Acts is the sequel to the Gospel, much more must the Acts have been written after that event. To us in England, who receive the verse in question as a truthful account of the words spoken by our Lord, and see in them a weighty prophetic declaration which is

> even now not wholly fulfilled, this argument at least has no weight.

Alford had put his finger on what was to become the chief point of difference between the critical scholarship of Germany and that of the English-speaking world. At a later date, when German ideas had penetrated more deeply, and Alford's statement about England's faithfulness to the teaching of Christ could no longer be made with the same assurance, the conservative wings of the English-speaking churches would go on reflecting his views. Neither Smith nor Alford was an evangelical, but it was they, with their high doctrine of Scripture, who would continue to maintain the position which in Alford's day had been shared by the churches as a whole, and make it a hallmark of their own approach. It is therefore historically inaccurate to regard the conservative evangelical approach to biblical criticism as sectarian, reactionary or 'fundamentalist'. In essence, it is a continuation of a type of scholarship which was not specifically evangelical in origin, but which regarded the close link between New Testament criticism and historical research as basic to all serious study, and which presumed that an ancient text must be taken at face value and examined accordingly.

It would be wrong to say that the Tübingen school had no followers in England; there were in fact at least two who ventured into print. The first of these was S. Davidson, whose *Introduction to the Study of the New Testament* (1868) is little more than a compendium of Tübingen views, with little critical appreciation of their strengths and weaknesses. Somewhat later came *Supernatural Religion: An Inquiry into the Reality of Divine Revelation* (1874), which was the work of W. R. Cassels (1826–1907), though published anonymously. Cassels was not a bright or original scholar, but he was aware of the Tübingen school's approach and believed that it was by and large correct. In particular, he rejected the supernatural claims of Christianity, and on that basis refused to accept the authenticity of the Acts of the Apostles. His conclusion is worth quoting:

> Written by an author who was not an eye-witness of the miracles related; who describes events not as they really occurred, but as his pious imagination supposed they ought to have occurred; who seldom touches history without distorting it by legend, until the original elements can scarcely be distinguished; who puts his own words and sentiments into the mouths of the Apostles and other persons of his narrative; and who represents almost every

> phase of the Church in the Apostolic age as influenced, or directly produced, by supernatural agency – such a work is of no value as evidence for occurrences which are in contradiction to all experience. The Acts of the Apostles, therefore, is not only an anonymous work, but upon due examination its claims to be considered sober and veracious history must be emphatically rejected. It cannot strengthen the foundations of super-natural religion, but, on the contrary, by its profuse and indiscriminate use of the miraculous, it discredits miracles, and affords a clearer insight into their origin and fictitious character.

Here the Tübingen influence is clear, and it elicited a reply from the greatest textual scholar of the age, J. B. Lightfoot. In a devastating critique of Cassels, Lightfoot exposed the author's lack of classical learning, and his habit of quoting from other works in such a way as to prove the exact opposite of what those works were really trying to say. However, Lightfoot's major contribution to the debate about Acts lay elsewhere. His commentaries on the Pauline epistles and his study of the apostolic fathers (1885–90) demonstrated beyond doubt that there was not the slightest trace of a conflict between Peter and Paul at the end of the first century. The Tübingen critics had ignored or discounted the mass of evidence which told against their hypothesis, and had simply imposed that hypothesis on the data.

In his few remarks on Acts, Lightfoot drew attention to the fact that it was extremely difficult for a writer to get the titles of Roman government officials right. There was such a variety of them, and they changed so frequently, that unless a historian had a very good knowledge of his subject, confusion was almost inevitable. Yet on this point, Acts displays an accuracy which is truly astonishing, and very difficult to imagine in a non-contemporary writer. A good example of this is the fact that the province of Achaea (Corinth) was normally governed by a propraetor, but for a few years he was replaced by a proconsul. It was during that short time that Paul visited the city, and his meeting with the proconsul Gallio is faithfully recorded by Luke (Acts 18:12-17). This was dramatically confirmed in 1905, when an inscription was discovered at Delphi which mentioned the proconsul by name and dated his sojourn in Corinth to AD 51.

Lightfoot did not delve deeply into archaeology, but he recognized its importance for the study of Acts. In his own words:

> No other work affords so many tests of veracity; for no other has such numerous points of contact in all directions with con-

temporary history, politics and topography, whether Jewish or Greek or Roman.

The course which the study of Acts was henceforth to take in the English-speaking world was now firmly established. That Luke would come out of the test with flying colours, Lightfoot had no doubt. He wrote:

> If, for instance, we confine ourselves to geography, we accompany the Apostle by land and by sea; we follow him about in Jerusalem, in Palestine and Syria, in Asia Minor, in Greece, in Italy. The topographical details are scattered over this wide expanse of continent, island and ocean; and they are both minute and incidental. Yet the writer is never betrayed into an error. When we turn from geography to history, the tests are still more numerous, and lead to still more decisive results. The laws, the institutions, the manners, the religious rites, the magisterial records, of Syria and Palestine, of Asia Minor, of Macedonia and Greece, all live in the pages of this narrative.

As for the supposed theological purpose of Acts, Lightfoot remarks that it is 'the continued working and presence of Jesus, no longer in the flesh, but in the Church'. As far as he was concerned, there was no evidence to support the contention that Luke was trying to reconcile opposing factions in the church, or that he was out to promote what later became 'early Catholicism'.

Lightfoot's work was programmatic for what was to follow. Though not himself a member of the evangelical party in the Church of England, his views on the text were sufficiently close to theirs to be widely accepted. In particular, it was his double affirmation that Acts was the ideal book to use when testing the New Testament against contemporary records, because of its many points of contact with them, and that when tested in this way, Acts was found to be without error, which conservative evangelicals were later to rely on. But it is important to stress once again, that at the end of the nineteenth century, views which are now associated with conservative evangelicals were widely shared in British scholarly circles. As far as most British scholars were concerned, Luke was a careful historian who wanted to describe the origins of the Christian church, and who did so on the basis of his own eye-witness investigations, as well as on the reports of others whose testimony was equally reliable. His selection and arrangement of the material demonstrated that he had a clear theological purpose in writing, but this was not an attempt to cover up or to reinterpret the facts.

Lightfoot's hunches and suggestions about the value of archaeology were put to the test by Sir William Ramsay, whose important book on Paul appeared in 1895. Ramsay's importance does not lie merely in the fact that he was able to demonstrate the truth of Lightfoot's remarks about Acts. Even more important, from the standpoint of conservative evangelicalism, was the fact that he had begun his research as a follower of the Tübingen hypothesis, but the more he looked into the question, the less he was persuaded by it. In the end, Ramsay was converted – the word has a special significance in this context – to the view that Luke was one of the most accurate historians who ever lived, and that his account of events in Acts was entirely trustworthy.

Of special importance was his contribution towards resolving the apparent discrepancies between Acts and Galatians. Ramsay proposed, first of all, that the Galatians to whom Paul wrote were not the ethnic Celts who inhabited the northern part of the Roman province of Galatia, but the Hellenized inhabitants of its southern cities – Antioch, Iconium, Lystra and Derbe. Following on that, Ramsay proposed an entirely new chronology for the visits which Paul made to Jerusalem (Gal. 1 and 2). This can best be appreciated by setting the two main views side by side as in the table below.

	Traditional view	**Ramsay**
Gal. 1:18	Acts 9:26	Acts 9:26
Gal. 2:1	Acts 15	Acts 11:30
Galatians written at this point		
		Acts 15

On Ramsay's calculation, therefore, Paul went to Jerusalem three times, and only on the third occasion did he discuss the question of the Galatian converts with the other apostles in the way described in Acts 15. The discrepancies between that chapter and what is written in Galatians disappear if we accept that the council recorded in Acts 15 had not taken place when the epistle was composed. This in turn would make Galatians the earliest of Paul's letters (*c.* AD 48 or 49), and probably the oldest document in the New Testament. Ramsay's views have not gained universal acceptance, but it is generally admitted that those with the greatest knowledge of the archaeological evidence and the geography of the region in question are also the most likely to accept them.

Perhaps the greatest compliment paid to Ramsay was the fact that at least one major German scholar, T. Zahn, accepted his views and made them widely known in Germany through his two-volume commentary on the book (1918, 1921). But even before that time, no less an authority than the great liberal New Testament scholar, Adolf von Harnack, had made two extensive defences of the Lucan authorship of Acts (1906, 1908). It took him longer to come round to the opinion that it had been composed about AD 62, but by 1911 he had espoused that as well. A positive view of 'Luke the historian' had at last made its way into the citadel of German liberal criticism.

By the 1920s, it was possible to speak of two opposing schools of thought regarding Acts, which have continued to go their separate ways since that time. As W. W. Gasque, who has written the history of this development, says:

> . . . the division of opinion in regard to the historical value of Acts . . . continued into the twentieth century with little likelihood of the issues being resolved. The two points of view were restated, modified to some degree, with a vast amount of additional evidence in favour of the historical approach. Unable to convert the representatives of the opposing viewpoints, both seemed to give up in their attempts to convince the opposition and went on their own separate ways . . . Without wishing to be unduly pessimistic one must confess that it seems quite unlikely that there will be a rapprochement of the two viewpoints at any time in the near future.

An attempt to achieve something of this kind was made by K. Lake and H. J. Cadbury, who published their joint commentary on Acts in 1933. This work is a masterly study of the philological evidence, and demonstrates a grasp of the problems raised by the book of Acts which is scarcely paralleled elsewhere. Where it falls down badly is in the area of theology; Lake and Cadbury were both liberals of the pre-1914 variety, and had little appreciation of theological issues. Considering that they were writing at a time when Barthian neo-orthodoxy was increasingly widespread, this must be regarded as a major failing of their work. Nevertheless, their overall approach to the material was far more conservative than might have been expected. Though they were cautious about the support which they were prepared to give to Ramsay, there were generally far more critical of the German sceptics, whose criticism they regarded as unduly negative in tone.

It is important at this juncture to realize that Lake and Cadbury represented the liberal wing of English-speaking scholarship; the fact that they were as conservative as we have indicated here merely demonstrates how ultra-conservative most other Anglo-Saxon scholars were. In Britain especially, the tradition of Lightfoot continued to exert the strongest influence on many different schools of theological thought. This is evident from the work of the Anglo-Catholic scholar W. L. Knox, who accepted the historical reliability of Acts (1948), and even argued that Luke faithfully represented Paul's theology. No doubt this owed something to his Anglo-Catholic approach, in that he was concerned to demonstrate that even Paul did not say much about 'justification by faith' outside Galatians and Romans. As far as Knox was concerned, it was precisely because Luke did not emphasize this point, so dear to the Lutherans, that he gave a good exposition of Paul's true doctrinal position.

However, the most significant work on Acts which has been undertaken in English in recent years is that by F. F. Bruce. Bruce wrote two distinct commentaries, one on the Greek text (1951; revised third edition, 1990) and another on the English text of the American Standard Version of 1901 (1952; revised in 1988). The first is a careful historical and linguistic study along the lines laid down by Lightfoot; the second is considerably expanded and much more theological in style and content. The special importance of these commentaries is that they have set a standard for conservative evangelical exposition, not merely of Acts, but of the entire Bible.

Bruce began his study of Acts where Ramsay left off. He was critical of those scholars who failed to take Ramsay seriously, though he was also aware that Ramsay sometimes stretched the evidence in ways which are unhelpful. However, on the main points the two scholars were agreed. Both believed that archaeological research confirmed what Lightfoot and others had stated on other grounds: Luke is a historian without peer in the first century AD, and his work is a substantially accurate account, as far as it goes, of what transpired in the early Christian communities.

Bruce insisted that the 'conflict' between the Pauline epistles and the data of Acts is apparent rather than real. He emphasized that Paul himself respected the other apostles, and mentioned that he was in fellowship with them (Gal. 2:9). Peter's concessions to the Judaizers he regarded as an act of hypocrisy, since this action did not correspond to Peter's own convictions (Gal. 2:13). On the wider question of agreement between the portrait of Paul in the epistles and that in Acts, Bruce had this to say:

> It is the Paul who repeats in Romans: 'To the Jew first, and also to the Greek', who in Acts visits the synagogues first in city after city, and who in Pisidian Antioch declares to the envious Jews: 'It was necessary that the Word of God should be spoken to you first.' It is the Paul who suffers so much from Jewish hostility in Acts who can speak of the Jews in 1 Thessalonians 2.15ff. as those 'who killed both the Lord Jesus and the prophets, and have persecuted us, and do not please God, and are contrary to all men, forbidding us to speak to the Gentiles, that they should be saved'. It is also the Paul who in Acts refuses to stop offering the Gospel to his brethren according to the flesh in spite of all his bitter experiences from their hands, who in Romans 9:2f. tells of his great sorrow and unceasing anguish of heart at their refusal to receive the Gospel, and is willing himself to be accursed, if only his heart's desire and prayer to God for their salvation be accomplished.

As far as Luke's own theological purpose in writing is concerned, Bruce followed the Lightfoot line, though in a somewhat expanded form. He argued that Luke's aim was to show that the gospel spread without hindrance to the Gentiles, and that Paul was able to proclaim his message freely in the imperial capital itself. The essentially positive note on which Acts ends is evidence that it must have been written before the Neronian persecution of AD 64. Other factors also contribute to this view, such as the fact that Luke does not make use of the Pauline epistles, nor is there any indication that the apostle was not still alive at the time of writing. Above all, there is no indication of the Jewish revolt of AD 66–73 or of the fall of Jerusalem in AD 70, some mention of which would seem to have been inevitable if the book was written after those events.

Bruce's commentary is thus cautious and conservative in a way which is typical of the best evangelical scholarship at the present time, but it is in no sense sectarian. At every point, he relied firmly on the research of those who preceded him, and never made theological assertions which cannot be adequately supported by the text. If there is a charge of theological bias to be made, it is surely against those who have followed the dictates of the Tübingen critics, and the more recent views of Dibelius.

Bruce and Haenchen compared

To get a clearer idea of how the two main traditions in contemporary Acts research differ from one another, it is perhaps easiest to look at their two most prominent modern representatives: F. F. Bruce for the conservative evangelical side, and E. Haenchen for the liberal point of view. A brief examination of some of the key passages in Acts will bring out the similarities and differences between the two scholars. Significant points in each commentary are highlighted.

> 1:8: *But you will receive power when the Holy Spirit has come upon you, and you will be my witnesses in Jerusalem, in all Judea and Samaria, and to the ends of the earth.*
>
> *Haenchen:* After it has been made clear what the Christians must renounce, they learn what they are to be given: the disciples will receive the Holy Spirit and then be Jesus' witnesses to the ends of the earth. This utterance is command and promise in one. It defines for the Church the terms of its commission (the apostles are only the Church's representatives, hence they may stay quietly in Jerusalem and allow Paul to carry on the main mission). As Acts presents it, the Christian Church is a missionary Church. Hence the other problem posed by the disciples' question of verse 6 is also resolved: the world-mission here decreed presupposes that salvation is not restricted to Israel.
>
> The words of Jesus however have yet another implication. In laying down the course of the Christian mission from Jerusalem to the 'end of the earth', they also prescribe the content of Acts: the progress of the Gospel from Jerusalem to Rome. Thus what any normal statement of contents would have mentioned in verse 3 is here brought home to the community by the Lord himself as a God-willed sequence of events.
>
> *Bruce:* Instead of the political power which had once been the object of their ambitions, a power far greater and nobler would be theirs. When the Holy Spirit came upon them, Jesus assured them, they would be vested with heavenly power – that power by which, in the event, their mighty works were accomplished and their preaching made effective. As Jesus had been anointed at his baptism with the Holy Spirit and power, so his followers were now to be similarly anointed and enabled to carry on his work.

This work would be a work of witness-bearing – a theme which is prominent in the apostolic preaching throughout Acts.

Immediately we can perceive, from these two treatments of the same verse, how different is the feel of one commentary from the other. Haenchen sees everything in the light of Luke's Paulinist bias; Bruce never mentions this. Bruce concentrates on the experience of the believer (for here the apostles are merely the first of a company which would eventually embrace us as well); Haenchen almost regards the early church as being manipulated by an appeal to some divine decree which is over and above it. His whole approach is completely different from Bruce's, and much further removed in feel from the needs and aspirations of a modern church community.

9:26: *When [Paul] had come to Jerusalem, he attempted to join the disciples; and they were all afraid of him, for they did not believe that he was a disciple.*

Haenchen: According to Luke, Paul wanted to join the Jerusalem congregation, but was mistrusted until Barnabas introduced him to the apostles. At first sight this all seems very plausible. But the story only makes sense if, as Luke of course erroneously assumes, Paul went to Jerusalem very shortly after his call. Only with such a brief interval could people there still not be informed of his conversion. In fact, however, Paul did not get to Jerusalem until three years later, by which time everybody there knew what had happened in Damascus. Apart from that, it is inconceivable that the truth about Paul should be known to Barnabas, but not to the apostles. In other words, the ground on which this entire Lucan edifice is erected will bear no weight, and all must come toppling down.

Bruce: Luke says that this incident took place 'when many days had elapsed'; Paul, more definitely, says in Gal. 1:18 that it was three years after his conversion (by inclusive reckoning, no doubt) that he went up to Jerusalem – and from the narrative of Acts he seems to have gone to Jerusalem immediately after his escape from Damascus.

It is not so easy to reconcile Luke's description of Saul's public activity at Jerusalem in association with the apostles with the statement in Gal. 1:22 that, until the time of his departure for Syria and Cilicia (and after that), he remained unknown by face

> to the churches of Judaea, which knew of him only by hearsay. One commentator removes the phrase 'in Jerusalem' from v. 28 . . . Thus, we are assured, the whole difficulty vanishes. It does not, and even if it did vanish, one must have reservations about an emendation, however ingenious it may be, which is proposed not because it has any textual attestation but because its adoption will help to remove a discrepancy.

This passage is one of the most difficult in Acts, because it appears to contradict Paul's own statement in Galatians, which every commentator accepts as primary. Did Luke not know of Paul's sojourn in Arabia? How was it possible for the Jerusalem church to remain in ignorance of him, if he had gone to Jerusalem straight after his conversion, in the way that Luke seems to suggest? There are various possible ways of reconciling the two accounts, but neither Haenchen nor Bruce tries to do so. Haenchen's solution is simple: Luke was in error. Bruce cannot bring himself to say that, so he skirts round the issue with various important but secondary observations. It is hard not to feel that neither commentator has really grappled with the problem; Haenchen's solution is too simple, Bruce avoids a solution altogether. At this point more work needs to be done to try to resolve the apparent difficulty which Luke's description of events presents.

> 28:24: *Some [of the Jews] were convinced by what [Paul] had said, while others refused to believe.*

> *Haenchen:* It is first of all noteworthy that Paul describes all Jews as obdurate, even though some – as is expressly said – 'were convinced'. This difficulty arises from the fact that Luke here of necessity has to unite two conflicting ideas. For one thing the Christian message, according to his account, is essentially in agreement with Judaism. Luke had illustrated this in the fictitious scene before the Sanhedrin in 23:7ff., through the assent which the Pharisees accord to Paul. Here Luke has not taken the trouble to introduce again the opposition between the Pharisees and the Sadducees; it is also out of place for Rome. Then the only possibility left to him was simply to make one group of Jews agree with Paul. On the other hand, however, it was by no means his intention to portray a Jewish conversion here; on the contrary, he wanted to present the Jewish reserve against the Christian message, that obduracy which compelled the

mission to the Gentiles. The two together necessarily produced the tension in our text, that many Jews 'were convinced' and yet all are treated as obdurate.

Bruce: Some of Paul's visitors were impressed by what he said, but the majority remained unconvinced. The bulk of the Jewish community in Rome, leaders and led alike, declined to acknowledge Jesus as Messiah. This fulfilled the pattern that had been set in one city after another to which Paul had brought the Gospel. Since the Jewish people, who had the prescriptive right to hear it first, would not accept it, it had to be offered direct to Gentiles . . . As before in Pisidian Antioch (13:46), Corinth (18:6) and Ephesus (19:8–10), so here again in Rome he announces – and this time with a note of solemn finality – that henceforth the Gentiles will have priority in hearing the word of life and that, unlike the Jews as a whole, they will accept it.

Both Bruce and Haenchen, in their different ways, state that the gospel was rejected by the Jews and that Paul turned to the Gentiles instead. However, the context of this and the motives for Paul's change of direction are put very differently by the two commentators. Haenchen portrays Luke as obsessed with finding disagreements among the Jews themselves. According to him, there was always a group of Jews ready to follow the new teaching, though this group could not be defined in terms of existing Jewish sects. At the same time, says Haenchen, Luke was concerned to portray the Jews in the worst possible light, so as to justify the main purpose of the book – the mission to the Gentiles, and the virtual abandonment of the Jews which was to take place after AD 70. Hence he finds a 'contradiction' in the text; Luke recognizes that some Jews believed Paul's message, but in the same breath he condemns them all as obdurate.

Bruce, on the other hand, does not say anything about internal divisions among the Jews. Nor does he think that Paul condemns all Jews as obdurate; this description properly applies only to those who refused to believe in Christ. They were the majority, but the fact that they refused to believe was regarded by Paul as a serious misfortune and setback to the Gentile mission, which he originally hoped would be accomplished through the conversion of the Jews. It was only when this had obviously failed that Paul turned elsewhere, with some regret. Acts is therefore not to be seen primarily as almost anti-Semitic propaganda for a Gentile mission, but as a reluctant description of a sad fact of early church life, that those to whom Jesus had come refused to believe in him.

Comparing these two commentaries, it is obvious that Bruce tended to give Luke the benefit of the doubt, even when he could not solve every problem, whereas Haenchen was ready to judge that Luke was mistaken or misled at various points – also that he was theologically biased in a historically inaccurate way. As a conservative evangelical, committed to the supreme authority and infallibility of Scripture, Bruce could never say anything like that. But at the same time, it is noteworthy that he was not afraid to acknowledge difficulties, and to leave them unresolved when there is insufficient evidence. Certainly he was against any emendation of the text simply for the purpose of harmonization, and in this his integrity as a critic shines through. At the end of the day both commentators left plenty of issues open for future scholars to ponder, but neither was unfaithful to his basic convictions. In their writings we get a good idea of how the academic world is currently divided between liberal and conservative tendencies, and learn something of what is involved in trying to express and defend each of these positions.

As a footnote to this survey, it may be added that evangelicals continue to produce a great deal of first-class historical work on Acts. Of particular note is the extremely detailed study by Colin Hemer (1940–87), entitled *The Book of Acts in the Setting of Hellenistic History* (1989), and the six-volume Tyndale House project, *The Book of Acts in its First-Century Setting* (1993–6). Each of these works presents, in minute detail, the evidence for the historicity of this New Testament book, and thus continues the tradition which has come to be so closely associated with modern conservative evangelicalism.

BIBLIOGRAPHY

F. F. Bruce, *The Book of Acts* (Grand Rapids: Eerdmans, 1988). (Revision of 1952 edition.)

W. W. Gasque, *A History of the Criticism of the Acts of the Apostles* (Tübingen: Mohr, 1975).

E. Haenchen, *The Acts of the Apostles: A Commentary* (Oxford: Blackwell, 1971).

I. H. Marshall, *Acts* (Leicester: IVP, 1980).

Conclusion

The history of biblical interpretation is a complex and difficult subject. Examining the past always involves a controversial process of selection, and it is not easy to know which aspects of it will speak most clearly in the future. The current scene is particularly complicated; never before has there been so much effort devoted to the study of the Bible, with so many different ends in view. Modern scholarship is less united in its aims now than it has ever been, and the interpretation of the Bible has diversified to the point where no one person can master it all.

In such a situation, predicting the future course of events is almost impossible. It may be that a new synthesis will be found, which will draw scholars back together. If so, that synthesis will have to embrace the fruits of critical research, but not in such a way as to deny the legitimate use of the Bible in the devotional life of the church. The split between these two things is one of the great tragedies of the past two centuries, and unless it can be overcome there is little future for academic Bible study. For whatever we think about it, the Bible lives as the book of the church, and it is from the bosom of the believing community that scholars arise to study and expound it. If that link is severed it is not the church which will die but the academic study of the Bible. The church would be the poorer without it, no doubt, though not fatally crippled. As has happened in the past, new forms of biblical interpretation would arise to take the place of the ones which have been rejected, and the spiritual life of the Christian community would continue along its historic path.

It is becoming increasingly clear in all branches of biblical study that any new synthesis will have to be theological, as well as purely academic. It is quite possible for scholars to agree about critical methods, and yet be very far apart in matters of interpretation. Ultimately this is due to theological factors which are often not properly appreciated by biblical scholars themselves. The basic issue is whether the supernatural can be taken into account as a contributory factor in human history. To put it more simply: is there a God in control of events? The practical denial of that idea, more than anything else, has determined the course taken by so much critical scholarship in modern times, and if it is followed to its logical conclusion, the Bible ceases to be a historical record of events. For the claims of Christianity are unashamedly supernatural in character; what really matters about Jesus is not his moral teaching, but his extraordinary acts of saving power and significance. The Sermon on the Mount might conceivably have been delivered by another great teacher; the resurrection from the dead remains unique. At the end of the day, what we think of the Bible will depend on what we think of Christ; the two belong inseparably together.

When we turn from matters of general principle to questions of detail, we can say with some confidence that the textual and linguistic study of the Scriptures will continue to develop even more refined techniques than it has had in the past. Already there are lexical and grammatical aids available which earlier generations scarcely dreamed of, and the invention of the computer has made it possible to recover in seconds the entire corpus of ancient Greek or Hebrew vocabulary and usage. But whether this is really an aid to understanding these languages is another question. Languages are not simply word-puzzles; they have a life and an integrity of their own which cannot be reduced to computer analysis. This has become painfully apparent in the recent abuse of word study in the Bible, which involved drawing out meanings which the context and the general 'feel' of the language indicate are quite impossible. The most notorious example of this is the interpretation of *kephalē* 'head', as 'source' in 1 Corinthians 11:3, but there are other examples, and an uncontrolled use of this method is liable to produce disastrous results.

In terms of the biblical text, it is now unlikely that any dramatic new discoveries will be made which will substantially alter it. There may be a few improvements here and there, but the agreed Greek text of the New Testament is too widely attested to allow of serious challenge from new source material. This is equally true of the Hebrew and Aramaic texts of the Old Testament, which in any case have never displayed the same variety. Questions of authorship and dating will no doubt continue to form the substance of doctoral dissertations, and there is still a good deal of work to be done here, especially in the Old Testament. But scholars are increasingly accepting that there are limits to our knowledge which are unlikely to be overcome. The assertion that the present state of a text is 'late' (*c.* 200 BC) says little about its ultimate origin; the process of redaction may have extended over a long period of time, and is in any case largely hidden from our eyes.

As far as the New Testament is concerned, few would now seriously dispute that it was almost all in existence by AD 100 at the very latest; the one possible exception to this is 2 Peter, and even that is debatable. The Tübingen hypothesis of a primitive conflict between Judaizers and Hellenists is not dead, but it is now understood that matters are less simple than Baur supposed, and recent research is broadening the picture considerably. It seems safe to suppose that the Jewish background to early Christianity will be even more important in the future, and that rabbinic studies will become an essential ingredient in New Testament research. The great task here will be to avoid going to the extreme of denying the special nature of Christianity altogether. There will also be the challenge of integrating Jewish studies in the New Testament period with the interpretation of the Old Testament. This has always been one of the greatest problems for Christian biblical exegetes, and there is no sign that it will be any less so in the days ahead.

The question of historicity will continue to be important, though it seems likely that it will take a new twist in the future. Recent investigations into the background of the Bible have anchored it in the contemporary culture to a degree which would have been undreamed of 200 years ago, but this has also made it more difficult to decide how the Scriptures can be used in our situation today. Historical study is a relativizing discipline, which runs the risk of destroying the practical significance of a text even as it illuminates its 'true' meaning. It may be very interesting to know that a particular book of the Bible was composed for such and such a reason, but what difference does that make to the average Christian nowadays? If preachers, faced with the need to be relevant to their congregations, have to impose their own agenda on the text in order to satisfy people's spiritual needs, the historicity of Scripture will be fatally compromised; that is the lesson of allegorical interpretation. But if scholars cannot relate their historical studies to contemporary needs, then they are denying another important aspect of the historicity of Scripture: its ability to speak to people of different times and places, and to relate to their particular situation.

All the signs are that it is this need which will become ever more pressing in the years ahead. The modern world has little patience with antiquity for its own sake; if an ancient book is going to continue to occupy a major part of academic life, it will have to demonstrate its continuing relevance in today's society. This will be even more true as Christianity spreads beyond its historic homelands and becomes indigenous to large parts of Africa and Asia. Some people believe there will be a growing interaction of the native cultures and religions of these countries with Christianity, and this may have a considerable impact on the way the Bible is studied there. But it is also true that the whole world is becoming increasingly westernized, and the issues which affect people in China, Korea or Japan are now scarcely different from those which touch Christians in Europe, North America and Australasia.

It is quite likely that the greatest effect of the spread of Christianity around the world will be to concentrate academic study of the Scriptures into one single language, English. Western scholars will not learn oriental languages in large numbers, nor do Asians find it convenient to master more than one European tongue. English is already the universal language in most sciences, and biblical interpretation seems destined to follow suit. The result will be a rapid and automatic transfer of information in the global village, which will ensure considerable cohesion of thought even as there is increasing ethnic diversity in the universal church.

In the search for a way forward in biblical studies, the role of conservative evangelicals may well prove to be crucial. They have retained a deep interest in textual matters, and links with the grassroots of the church, where the fruits of scholarship can be tested in the preaching and in the spiritual life of ordinary Christians. Recently they have begun to reach out to conservative Roman Catholic and Eastern Orthodox Christians as well, and it is quite possible that both of these will be just as influenced by them as more liberal Catholics have been by so-called 'mainstream' Protestants. Their theological commitment is such that they cannot be content with irrelevant knowledge; they are forced by their convictions to sift through the mass of information in a way which will produce a message of spiritual power for the church today.

In the world of 'pure' scholarship, such a commitment is bound to be suspect, because it suggests that knowledge is being used for ends other than itself, and therefore it is somehow being corrupted. A little reflection ought to be enough to dispel this fear, however. 'Pure' knowledge does not exist; even the scholar who keeps his information to himself, or who dresses it up in hieroglyphics which only the initiated can hope to understand, is using his knowledge for a purpose – which might well be no more noble than an attempt to justify his own existence. Orthodox conservatives should not be afraid to proclaim what their religious commitment is, nor should they hesitate to remain faithful to it in the days ahead. The liberal consensus is not what it was; the old confidence has been lost, and an unprecedented pluralism is taking its place. Now may be just the time when a new generation, fired with the desire to see the Bible live once again as the motivating force in the church's spiritual life, can make its mark.

Whatever happens, though, and however the future course of events may be worked out, the Christian cannot doubt that the interpretation of the Bible is in the hands of God, who by his Holy Spirit enlightens and strengthens the church. It is this confidence which guided the great expositors of the past, and which will raise up and nourish the great interpreters of the future. Let us pray that in our time we may see a work of God in the sphere of biblical interpretation which will be of lasting significance for the life of his people here on earth.

General bibliography

B. W. Anderson, *The Living Word of the Bible* (London: SCM, 1979).

Annali di Storia dell' Esegesi (Bologna: Edizione Dehoniane, 1984).

P. Beauchamp, *Le Récit, la lettre et le corps: Essais bibliques* (Paris: Cerf, 1982).

E. C. Blackman, *Biblical Interpretation: The Old Difficulties and the New Opportunity* (London: Independent Press, 1957).

J. Blank, *Schriftauslegung in Theorie und Praxis* (München: Kösel, 1969).

F. Bovon, *Exegesis (Genesis 22 and Luke 15)* (Pittsburgh: Pickwick, 1977).

C. Braaten, *History and Hermeneutics: New Directions in Theology Today* (London: Lutterworth, 1968).

S. Brams, *Biblical Games: A Strategic Analysis of Stories in the Old Testament* (London: MIT Press, 1980).

R. E. Brown, *The Critical Meaning of the Bible* (London: Geoffrey Chapman, 1981).

W. Bühlmann, *Stilfiguren der Bibel* (Fribourg: Schweizerisches Katholisches Bibelwerk, 1973).

E. J. Carnell, *The Case for Orthodox Theology* (London: Marshall, 1961).

D. A. Carson, *Exegetical Fallacies* (Grand Rapids: Baker, 1984).

F. W. Danker, *Multipurpose Tools for Bible Study* (St Louis: Concordia, 1970).

R. M. Davidson, *Typology in Scripture: A Study of Hermeneutical Typos Structures* (Berrien Springs, MI: Andrews University Press, 1981).

B. Demarest, *A History of Interpretation of Hebrews 7:1–10 from the Reformation to the Present* (Tübingen: Mohr, 1976).

E. Drewermann, *Tiefenpsychologie und Exegese* (Olten: Walter, 1984–5).

P. Eicher, *Offenbarung: Prinzip neuzeitlicher Theologie* (München: Kösel, 1977).

P. Fairbairn, *The Typology of Scripture Viewed in Connection with the Whole Series of the Divine Dispensations* (Edinburgh: T. and T. Clark, 1870).

F. W. Farrar, *History of Interpretation* (London: Macmillan, 1886).

D. S. Ferguson, *Biblical Hermeneutics: An Introduction* (London: SCM, 1987).

K. Frör, *Biblische Hermeneutik* (München: Kösel, 1964).

P. Fruchon, *Existence humaine et révélation: Essais d'herméneutique* (Paris: Cerf, 1976).

D. P. Fuller, *Gospel and Law: Contrast or Continuum?* (Grand Rapids: Eerdmans, 1980).

L. Goppelt, *Typos: The Typological Interpretation of the Old Testament in the New* (Grand Rapids: Eerdmans, 1982).

R. M. Grant and D. Tracy, *A Short History of the Interpretation of the Bible* (London: SCM, 1984).

J. Greisch, K. Neufeld and C. Theobald, *La Crise contemporaine: Du modernisme à la crise des herméneutiques* (Paris: Beauchesne, 1978).

P. Grelot, *La Vie de la Parole de l'Ancien au Nouveau Testament: Etudes offertes à Pierre Grelot* (Paris: Desclée, 1987).

L. Grollenberg, *A Bible for our Time* (London: SCM, 1979).

A. H. J. Gunneweg, *Understanding the Old Testament* (London: SCM, 1978).

E. Güttgemanns, *Fragmenta semiotico-hermeneutica: Eine Texthermeneutik für den Umgang mit der Heiligen Schrift* (Bonn: Linguistica Biblica, 1983).

R. L. Harris, S.-H. Quek and J. R. Vannoy (eds.), *Interpretation and History* (Singapore: Christian Life, 1986).

J. H. Hayes and C. Holladay, *Biblical Exegesis: A Beginner's Handbook* (Atlanta: Eisenbrauns, 1982; London: SCM, 1988).

G. M. Hyde (ed.), *A Symposium on Biblical Hermeneutics* (Washington: Seventh Day Adventists, 1974).

M. A. Inch (ed.), *The Literature and Meaning of Scripture* (Grand Rapids: Baker, 1981).

C. B. Johnson, *The Psychology of Biblical Interpretation* (Grand Rapids: Zondervan, 1983).

R. K. Johnston (ed.), *The Use of the Bible in Theology: Evangelical Options* (Atlanta: John Knox, 1985).

O. Kaiser, W. G. Kümmel and G. Adam, *Einführung in die exegetischen Methoden* (München: Kaiser, 1969).

O. Kaiser and W. G. Kümmel, *Exegetical Method: A Student's Handbook*

(New York: Seabury, 1963).
F. F. Kearley, E. P. Myers and T. D. Hadley (eds.), *Biblical Interpretation: Principles and Practices. Studies in Honor of J. P. Lewis* (Grand Rapids: Baker, 1986).
R. Kieffer, *Essais de méthodologie néo-testamentaire* (Lund: Gleerup, 1972).
A. G. Knevel, M. J. Paul and J. Broekhuis, *Bijbel en Exegese: Het gezag van de Bijbel* (Kampen: Kok, 1987).
E. G. Kraeling, *The Old Testament since the Reformation* (London: Lutterworth, 1955).
E. Krentz, *The Historical Critical Method* (Philadelphia: Fortress, 1975).
J. L. Kugel and R. A. Greer, *Early Biblical Interpretation* (Philadelphia: Westminster, 1986).
W. G. Kümmel, *The New Testament: The History of the Investigation of its Problems* (London: SCM, 1973).
G. W. H. Lampe and K. J. Woollcombe, *Essays on Typology* (London: SCM, 1957).
G. Lohfink and R. Pesch, *Tiefenpsychologie und keine Exegese* (Stuttgart: Katholisches Bibelwerk, 1987).
S. B. Marrow, *Basic Tools of Biblical Exegesis* (Rome: Biblical Institute Press, 1976).
K.-H. Michel, *Sehen und Glauben* (Wuppertal: Brockhaus, 1982).
A. Mickelsen, *Interpreting the Bible* (Grand Rapids: Eerdmans, 1972).
K. H. Miskotte, *Zur biblischen Hermeneutik* (Zollikon: Evangelischer Verlag, 1959).
R. Morgan and J. Barton, *Biblical Interpretation* (Oxford: Oxford University Press, 1988).
G. R. Osborne, *The Hermeneutical Spiral: A Comprehensive Introduction to Biblical Interpretation* (Downers Grove, IL: IVP, 1991).
A. G. Pope, *A Directory of Exegetical Aids for Bible Translators* (Dallas: Summer Institute of Linguistics, 1989).
G. Prickett, *Words and the Word: Language, Poetics and Biblical Interpretation* (Cambridge: Cambridge University Press, 1988).
The Proceedings of the Conference on Biblical Interpretation 1988 (Nashville: Broadman, 1988).
M. N. Ralph, *Plain Words about Biblical Images: Growing in our Faith through the Scriptures* (New York: Paulist Press, 1989).
W. Richter, *Exegese als Literaturwissenschaft: Entwurf einer alttestamentlichen Literaturtheorie und Methodologie* (Göttingen: Vandenhoeck und Ruprecht, 1971).
P. Ricoeur and E. Jüngel, *Metapher: Zur Hermeneutik religiöser Sprache,*

Evangelische Theologie Sonderheft (München: Kaiser, 1974).
L. A. Schökel, *Hermenéutica de la Palabra* (Madrid: Ediciones Cristiandad, 1986).
S. J. Schultz and M. A. Inch, *Interpreting the Word of God: Festschrift in Honor of Steven Barabas* (Chicago: Moody, 1976).
M. Silva, *Biblical Words and their Meaning* (Grand Rapids: Zondervan, 1983).
———*Has the Church Misread the Bible? The History of Interpretation in the Light of Current Issues* (Leicester: Apollos, 1987).
J. D. Smart, *The Interpretation of Scripture* (London: SCM, 1961).
Y. Spiegel, *Doppeldeutlich: Tiefendimensionen biblischer Texte* (München: Kaiser, 1978).
D. Stacey, *Interpreting the Bible* (London: Sheldon, 1977).
H. Stadelmann, *Grundlinien eines bibeltreuen Schriftverständnisses* (Wuppertal: Brockhaus, 1985).
J. Steinmann, *Biblical Criticism* (London: Burns and Oates, 1959).
K. Stendahl, *Meanings: The Bible as Document and as Guide* (Philadelphia: Fortress, 1984).
P. A. Stücki, *Herméneutique et dialectique* (Geneva: Labor et Fides, 1970).
W. Swartley, *Essays on Biblical Interpretation: Anabaptist-Mennonite Perspectives* (Indiana: Institute of Mennonite Studies, 1984).
M. Tardieu, *Les règles de l'interprétation* (Paris: Cerf, 1987).
P. Toinet, *Pour une théologie de l'exégèse* (Paris: FAC-Editions, 1983).
R. A. Traina, *Methodical Bible Study: A New Approach to Hermeneutics* (Wilmore, KY: Asbury Theological Seminary, 1952).
B. Uffenheimer and H. G. Reventlow (eds.), *Creative Biblical Exegesis: Christian and Jewish Hermeneutics through the Centuries* (Sheffield: JSOT Press, 1988).
M. Wadsworth (ed.), *Ways of Reading the Bible* (Brighton: Harvester, 1981).
C. M. Wood, *The Formation of Christian Understanding* (Philadelphia: Westminster, 1981).

Index of names

Index of subjects

Index of Scripture passages